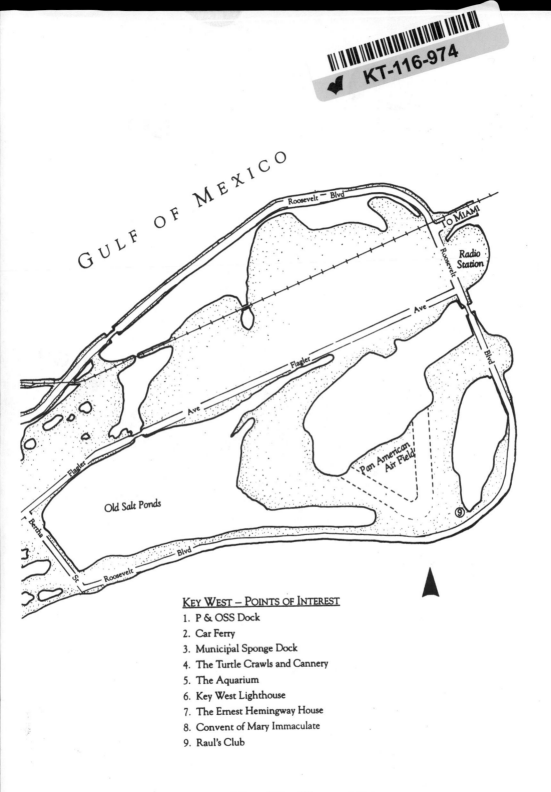

GULF OF MEXICO

Roosevelt – Blvd

TO MIAMI

Roosevelt

Radio
Station

Ave

Flagler

Blvd

Ave

Flagler

Pan American
Air Field

Old Salt Ponds

⑨

Bertha

Blvd

St.

Roosevelt

KEY WEST – POINTS OF INTEREST

1. P & OSS Dock
2. Car Ferry
3. Municipal Sponge Dock
4. The Turtle Crawls and Cannery
5. The Aquarium
6. Key West Lighthouse
7. The Ernest Hemingway House
8. Convent of Mary Immaculate
9. Raul's Club

Map of Key West, c. 1936.

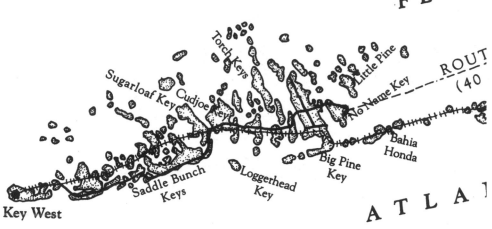

FLOR

Torch Keys

Little Pine

ROUT
(40

Sugarloaf Key

Cudjoe Key

No Name Key

Bahia
Honda

Big Pine
Key

Saddle Bunch
Keys

Loggerhead
Key

Key West

ATLA

"Of all Hemingway biographers, Reynolds is by far the most indefatigable."   —Brenda Wineapple, *The Nation*

"Michael Reynolds is a worthy successor to Carlos Baker as the definitive biographer of Ernest Hemingway."
—Bernice Kert, author of *Hemingway's Women*

"Despite the temptations presented by the subject's complex nature—his deep depressions, manic elations, tough, swaggering virility combined with a child-like dependence on his various wives—Reynolds manages to eschew the psychobabble fashionable in literary biographies today. He allows the reader to interpret the effect of Hemingway's neuroses upon his novels, and one follows, almost breathlessly, the story of the life."   —Dorothea Strauss, *Baltimore Sun*

"[Reynolds] has unearthed an amazing collection of details from documents undiscovered or neglected by others . . . All of that background and fresh detail give Reynolds' biography an authority no other has equaled."   —Scott Donaldson, *Minneapolis Star Tribune*

"The bona fide expert who has ensured his own place in American literary history."   —Raleigh *News & Observer*

"Reynolds's penetrating analysis and meticulous scholarship reveal Hemingway in all his complexity as man and artist, with no flaw glossed over. The hypocrisy, selfishness, paranoia, the discipline, genius, and ruthlessly self-promoting ambition—all are illuminated and woven into a narrative as compelling as a novel."   —*Choice*

HEMINGWAY

THE 1930s THROUGH THE FINAL YEARS

MICHAEL REYNOLDS

W. W. NORTON & COMPANY

NEW YORK   LONDON

For information about permission to reproduce selections from this book,
write to Permissions, W. W. Norton & Company, Inc.,
500 Fifth Avenue, New York, NY 10110

For information about special discounts for bulk purchases, please contact
W. W. Norton Special Sales at specialsales@wwnorton.com or 800-233-4830

Manufacturing by RR Donnelley
Production manager: Louise Mattarelliano

Library of Congress Cataloging-in-Publication Data

Reynolds, Michael S., 1937–
Hemingway : the 1930s through the final years / Michael Reynolds. — 1st ed.
p. cm.
"Book 1 previously published as Hemingway: the 1930's ;
Book 2 previously published as Hemingway: the final years"—T.p. verso.
Includes bibliographical references and index.
ISBN 978-0-393-34320-5 (pbk.)
1. Hemingway, Ernest, 1899–1961. 2. Hemingway, Ernest,
1899–1961—Last years. 3. Spain—History—Civil War, 1936–1939—
Literature and the war. 4. Authors, American—20th century—Biography.
5. Journalists—United States—Biography. 6. Depressions—United States.
I. Reynolds, Michael S., 1937– Hemingway. II. Title.
PS3515.E37Z754665 2012
813'.52—dc23
[B]
2011051995

W. W. Norton & Company, Inc.
500 Fifth Avenue, New York, N.Y. 10110
www.wwnorton.com

W. W. Norton & Company Ltd.
Castle House, 75/76 Wells Street, London W1T 3QT

1 2 3 4 5 6 7 8 9 0

Dialectic and bizarre, we traveled on
To Roncesvalles and Blois, to Krasnador,
Caux and Hurtgenwald, Avila and Gijon.
For sharing everything he knew,
For all the meals with wine and laughter,
This is his book, and I, his debtor,
Hold him ever as my standard measure.

and for Ann,

who shared the research on all five volumes,
    who came across the pass at Roncevaux,
    who remembered the names,
    who read between the lines,
    who made the difference.

ye ben verrayly
The maistresse of my wit, and nothing I.
My word, my werk, is knit so in your bonde,
That, as an harpe obeyeth to the honde
And maketh hit soune after his fingeringe,
Right so mowe ye out of myn herte bringe
Swich vois, right as yow list, to laughte or pleyne.
Be ye my gyde and lady sovereyne;
As to myn erthly god, to yow I calle,
Bothe in this werke and in my sorwes alle.

GEOFFREY CHAUCER

CONTENTS

Book I

CONTENTS

Book II

CONTENTS

BOOK I

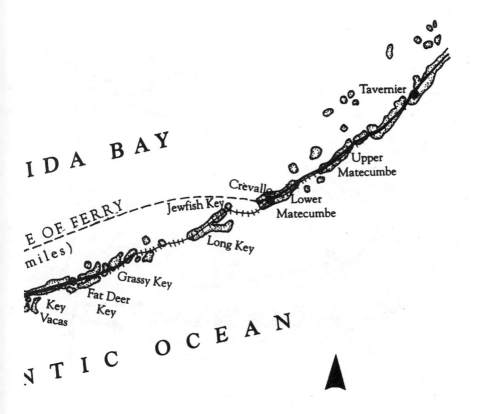

Map of the Florida Keys before the 1935 hurricane destroyed
the rail line.

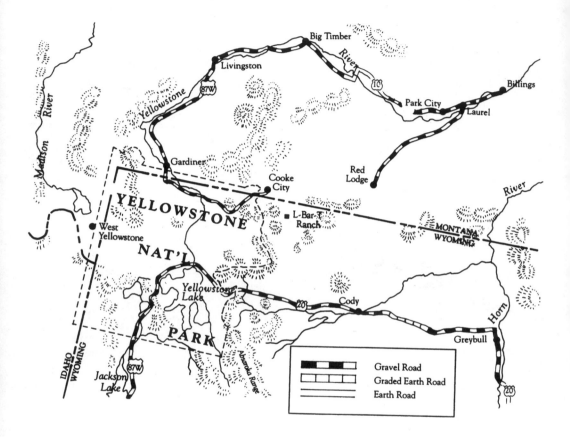

The isolated L-Bar-T Ranch area east of Yellowstone National Park, where the Hemingways fished and hunted throughout the 1930s.

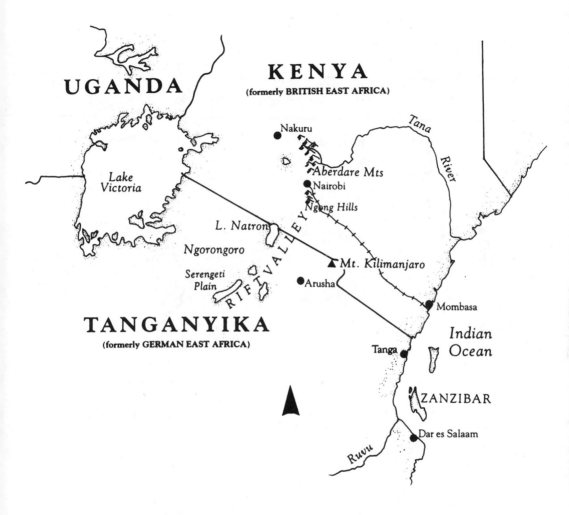

Area of East Africa where the Hemingways were on safari in 1933–34.

The 1937 division of Spain during the Civil War before Franco's Nationalist forces broke through to the Mediterranean.

PROLOGUE

I N 1 9 1 8 , W H E N young Hemingway passed through New
York on his way to the Great War, no one took notice. Nor was
anyone interested when he and his bride sailed from New York
for France in 1921. Four years later, when he returned to break his
contract with Horace Liveright and sign with Scribner's, he attracted
little attention outside of the Left Bank. By the time of his first
divorce, he had published *The Sun Also Rises* (1926), and there was
a small blurb in the *New York Times*. When he came through New
York in December of 1928 to deliver the typescript of his new novel,
a New York gossip columnist interviewed him but, with no pressing
need to run the story, did not use it until three months later:

> *New York, March 8–New York had a visiting novelist this winter who*
> *made no effort to be a bright boy at the tea table, spurt epigrams or*
> *comment on crude American manners. He was Ernest Hemingway,*
> *who has a cherubic moon of a face and a cocoonish mustache and*
> *although a product of Chicago, lives in Paris and made his reputation*
> *there. . . . Hemingway is one of the fabled writing geniuses in real life*
> *who cares nothing about financial rewards of his trade. . . . [He] has*
> *just finished a novel promised to a magazine at a big price, but at the*
> *last moment was touched by a sentimentality and begged off. He gave it*
> *for a very small price to a magazine that bought his first story.*[1]

The gossiper got the story about half right: a draft was typed, but *A Farewell to Arms* was three months from being finished, and the $16,000 *Scribner's Magazine* was paying Hemingway for serial rights was hardly a "small price." Nor had *Scribner's* published his first short story. Nor did Ernest usually make sentimental decisions about money. But who would care or long remember if the story was right or wrong? Its fleeting importance was that it kept Ernest's name before the public, whose appetite for inside information about the famous and the infamous was awakening. Before the approaching decade was out, newsstands would offer *Time, Life,* and uncounted fan magazines to feed that appetite. As the real and fictional lives of cultural figures were becoming public domain, Ernest Hemingway was coming home in time to catch the wave that would carry a few from his generation into the next decade.

As the Twenties drew to a close, many a familiar name was fading from view. Scott Fitzgerald, who claimed to have invented the Twenties "flapper," would be forgotten within ten years, along with others who stayed too long abroad or failed to read right the signs of the time. Literary magazines once the heartbeat of the period were disappearing: gone were the *transatlantic review, Ex Libris, Liberator, Der Querschnitt, The Egoist,* and *Exile. This Quarter* and *Little Review* were fading. Within a year, talking pictures will replace silent stars with fresh faces speaking intelligible English. Within four years, the nation, mired in a economic depression beyond comprehension, will repeal prohibition along with the Republican Party as it embraces Franklin Roosevelt's New Deal. By the end of the Thirties, Ernest Hemingway will be as well known as many sportsmen, movie stars, gangsters, and politicians. In his first eight Paris years, he became a literary cult figure. During the next ten years, he will become an American icon. It is an old American story of promise fulfilled through fortitude and good fortune, a tale of rewards beyond all expectation, a cautionary tale of the Dream and its dark side.

Chapter One

1929

THE MUSIC CHANGES

Paris and Spain

MAY 5, HENDAYE, on the Atlantic coast of France at the Spanish border: the spring season, declared open, brings moneyed Parisians and American tourists to nearby Biarritz but few yet to Hendaye. Where the Bidassoa River edges the town and empties into the Bay of Biscay, there stretches out a gentle, cupped white beach, backed by several small hotels. There are people on the beach, walking or sitting in the morning sun. No one is swimming.

In the breakfast room of the Hotel Barron where he finishes his coffee and brioche, Ernest Hemingway reads the Paris letter from Pauline. Their young son, Patrick, is recovering nicely from the flu, and at the American Hospital, Pauline is having something painful done to her infected sinus cavities which makes everything better. Very soon, she is sure, he should be able to rejoin them. Ever since the influenza epidemic of 1917 drowned soldiers in their own phlegm, Ernest has been mortally afraid of the flu. Pauline said she understood when he left her sick in Paris with their sick son and his insolent sister and his former wife and all the problems of returning to Paris. She is going to get well, she says, and then he will come home.[1] As soon as he can get his head working, he promised her, as soon as the words are right. Four years earlier in Hendaye, alone at the Barron, he finished *The Sun Also Rises*; he has come back to a good writing place, trusting that the luck will return.

Each morning, just as he had done on the *Yorck* crossing from New York, he reopens the typescript for his new novel and rereads the final chapter, at the end of which his narrator, Frederic Henry, tries to explain what happened to himself and several other characters after the Great War. Lamely Frederic concludes, "I would tell what has happened since then but that is the end of the story." In mid-February when Hemingway accepted *Scribner's Magazine's* offer of $16,000 to serialize the novel, he knew he must revise the ending. For three months now, he has tried again and again to get it right. He has tried it complicated, and has tried it plain. Nothing satisfies him.

On July 8, 1918, beside the muddy Piave River on the Venetian plain, a night mortar shell ruined his right knee, filled his legs with shrapnel, and left him with a concussion; after less than a month at the front lines, Hemingway spent the remainder of the war recuperating in a Milan hospital, where he fell in love with a nurse eight years his senior. Ten years after the experience, he has created a war more real than any he had known. He gives his war wound and his nurse to Frederic Henry; to his fictional nurse, he gives his second wife's pregnancy. From his first marriage with Hadley Richardson, he takes their good times at Chamby when the roads were iron-hard and they deeply in love. From maps, books, and close listening, he has made up a war he never saw, described terrain he never walked, and re-created the retreat from Caporetto so accurately that his Italian readers will later say he was present at that national embarrassment.

Begun in Paris and continued on his transatlantic voyage to Key West, the novel moved with Hemingway through the summer of

1928. From Key West to Pauline's home in Piggott, Arkansas, and on to the best hospital in Kansas City, he wrote steadily while Pauline prepared to deliver their son. In the Kansas City hospital, Ernest watched the surgeon perform the cesarean section. At the end of July he left Pauline to recover in Piggott while he drove to Sheridan, Wyoming, where, on August 22, he finished his first draft, 650 handwritten pages.

Over the next four months, Hemingway was steadily on the road: Piggott, Chicago, New York, Chicago, Piggott, Key West, and back to New York to meet his first son, John, arriving from Paris. On December 6, 1928, father and son boarded the train for Key West; outside of Philadelphia, Hemingway received the Oak Park telegram telling him his father was dead. Clarence Hemingway, depressed and ill, had committed suicide. During the week after his father's funeral, Hemingway sorted out his mother's financial problems and revised the first half of his war novel. Returning to Key West, he quickly completed his revisions, and on January 22, 1929, the typed draft was finished except for the ending.

When Ernest and his family sailed for France, the telegram waiting for them at the boat was from Max Perkins wishing them luck and asking Ernest, "If you see Scott in Paris write me soon how he is."[2] Max was worried about his friend's drinking and his marriage, and worried about his publishing company's continuing advances against the Fitzgerald novel that remained only promises. The last letter Hemingway mailed before sailing asked Max not to give Fitzgerald the Hemingways' Paris address: "Last time he was in Paris he got us kicked out of one apartment and in trouble all the time (insulted the landlord, peed on the front porch—tried to break down the door 3-4 and 5 A.M. etc.)."[3] But the Hemingways were too well placed to go unnoticed in St. Germain, and Fitzgerald knew their apartment on rue Férou quite well from 1927. In April, when Scott, Zelda, and their daughter, Scotty, arrived in Paris, they took an apartment on rue Palatine, less than a block around the corner from the Hemingways, whose church, St. Sulpice, was also the parish church where Scotty Fitzgerald was taken to Mass.

Arriving in Paris with too many endings for his novel and none of them right, Hemingway went alone to Hendaye to close the book. Because he had lived in the novel, inventing it day by day, he did not know from the beginning that Frederic, his American ambulance driver on the Italian front, would end up in Switzerland standing over the lifeless body of Catherine, who died giving birth to their stillborn child. Significant characters developed early in the story—the surgeon and the priest—disappear during the retreat from Caporetto, and try as he did to bring them back in the conclusion, every effort is off-key and forced.[4] In his modest room at the Hotel Barron, galleys for the novel's last installment with the still flawed ending wait his attention while in Paris the first installment has appeared in the May issue of *Scribner's Magazine*.

As Hemingway is correcting those last galleys in Hendaye, Owen Wister—author of *The Virginian*, close friend of Hemingway's boyhood hero Teddy Roosevelt, and fellow Scribner's author with whom Hemingway visited the previous summer—has, in Philadelphia, finished reading at Hemingway's request a complete set of the magazine galleys.[5] To the delight of Max Perkins, Hemingway's editor, Wister then writes a wonderful publicity blurb:

> *In Mr. Ernest Hemingway's new novel,* A Farewell to Arms, *landscape, persons, and events are brought to such vividness as to make the reader become a participating witness. This astonishing book is in places so poignant and moving as to touch the limit that human nature can stand, when love and parting are the point. . . . And he, like Defoe, is lucky to be writing in an age that will not stop its ears at the unmuted resonance of a masculine voice.*[6]

In a separate statement to Perkins, Wister voiced his concerns about Hemingway's use of the first-person narrator and the novel's conclusion, suggesting that the nurse's death be softened and that the ending bring together the two themes of love and war. Perkins agrees completely. The book's flaw, he tells Wister, is that the war story and the love do not combine. "It begins as one thing wholly, and ends wholly as the other thing." If only the war were in some way responsible for the nurse's death in childbirth. "As to the third person," Perkins says, "I believe he did intend to attempt it in this book, but abandoned it. I do hope that he may adopt it in the next."[7]

The first letter Ernest received when he returned from Hendaye was a dinner invitation from Scott for Pentecost Sunday or the following Monday holiday.[8] In honor perhaps of the impending Pentecost when fiery tongues once descended upon those huddled in an upstairs room, Scott signed the letter:

> *God Save us, Preserve us, Bless us*
>
> *Yrs. in Xt.*
>
> *Fitzg—*

Beneath his signature he drew three crosses upon a hill with a smiling sun above and below a sign: "To Jerusalem, Your Opportunity, 1 Mile." Writing in his slightly paternal, joking voice of 1925, Fitzgerald masked the anxiety he felt about their relationship, which his wife, Zelda, resented, and about his own failed but never forgotten Catholicism.

The day after receiving Fitzgerald's dinner invitation, Hemingway put the final magazine galleys, with the exception of its last page, into the mail, telling Robert Bridges, *Scribner's Magazine* editor, that for ten days he had been revising the last three paragraphs and they were "almost right." He promised to get them on the fast mail boat leaving May 23 and due in New York on May 31.[9] The following day in New York, Max was assuring Ernest by mail that he could continue working on any parts of the story that bothered him, meaning the part that bothered Max: the end of story. If only the physical details of Catherine's pain were reduced, the reader (Max) might not squirm so, losing the thread of the story. Then there is the nagging question: where did the war disappear to? "Love and War," Max said, "combine, to my mind, perfectly to the point where Catherine and Lieutenant Henry get to Switzerland; thereafter the war is almost forgotten by them and by the reader. . . . I can't shake off the feeling that war, which has deeply conditioned this love story—and does so still passively—should still do so actively and decisively."[10]

By that time the Hemingways and Fitzgeralds have exchanged dinners somewhat less than successfully: Zelda cold and distant; Pauline too obviously tolerant; Scott trying too hard; Ernest not hard enough; all uncomfortable. Scott said: "It worked out beautifully didn't it. . . . it was a more irritable Ernest, apprehensively telling me his whereabouts lest I come in on them tight and endanger his lease. The discovery that half a dozen people were familiars there didn't help my self esteem."[11] And Zelda said: "We came back to rue Palatine and you, in a drunken stupor told me a lot of things that I only half understood: but I understood the dinner we had at Ernest's. Only I did not understand that it mattered."[12]

No matter how badly their reunion had gone, Ernest could not refuse Scott when he asked to read the new novel, the typescript of which Fitzgerald took with him to make extensive suggestions for more changes:

Eliminate the opera singers in Milan: "just rather gassy."

Take out the entire chapter where Frederic and Catherine spend the afternoon at the fixed horse races: "dull and slow."

Tighten the overwritten scenes in Switzerland.

Don't let Catherine go on and on about her pregnancy: "This could stand a good cutting. . . . the brave expectant illegitimate mother is an *old situation*."

Catherine's glib speeches could be cut: "Don't try to make her make sense."

"Our poor old friendship," Scott said, "probably won't survive this but there you are—better me than some nobody in the Literary Review that doesn't care about you & your future."[13]

With the novel's first installment published in the May issue of *Scribner's Magazine* and with final magazine galleys corrected and returned, Scott's suggestions served no useful purpose, saying more about his own writing than about Ernest's. After four years of work and continuous promises of finishing, Fitzgerald had barely two chapters to show for his continuous revisions of what would, in

another five years, become *Tender Is the Night*. He completely misunderstood Ernest's use of the fixed horse race as a deterministic
metaphor for man's condition, and Scott's unsympathetic reading of
the nurse, Catherine, said more about his relationship with Zelda
than it did about Ernest's text. At the bottom of the ninth and final
page, Hemingway wrote: "Kiss my ass."

But Hemingway found enough merit in Scott's suggestion that
an early rhetorical passage be moved to the end to test it: "If people bring so much courage to this world the world has to kill them
to break them, so of course it kills them. . . . It kills the very good
and the very gentle and the very brave impartially. If you are none
of these you can be sure it will kill you too but there is no special
hurry." Hemingway typed the passage but rejected the solution, perhaps because he did not want to increase his debt to Fitzgerald, on
whose advice three years earlier he had cut the opening eight pages
of *The Sun Also Rises*.[14]

———

June 23, Paris, Place St. Sulpice. The three-tiered fountain, with
its carved cardinals, mewling stone lions and circling pigeons,
dominates the square where a Sunday morning of parents, grand-
mothers, and small children are entering between hulking gray
stone church towers to attend ten-o'clock Mass. All ivory and gold
the altar, Christ crucified on the left and risen on the right, side
altars cusping the congregation. Church bells are ringing.

———

Dressed for Mass, Ernest, Pauline, her sister, Jinny, and their uncle,
Augustus Pfeiffer come out the barred door and into the courtyard of
6 rue Férou. As they pass through the iron gate, they are framed by
two white sphinxes that are elevated on either side of the entry. At one
end of the narrow, cobblestoned street stands their parish church; at
the other end, the Musée du Luxembourg: both within a stone's throw
and both reassuring in their complementary ways.

Uncle Gus, thin and grayed, walks younger than he looks, a
pinched-faced man whose smile offsets his sharp eyes. He has been

in Europe for some weeks acquiring new holdings for the Richard Hudnut Corporation, which is to say for himself, majority owner of the company's stock. He has also found one or two interesting chess sets to add to his rather fine collection. Uncle Gus is married but has no children, a condition which makes his two nieces that much more valuable to him.

On his arm, Jinny listens intently to the old gentleman. When she speaks and he smiles, the family resemblance is strong. Having lived in Paris for more than five years on her trust fund, Virginia Pfeiffer is fluent in French and in the ways of the city. She is a pleasant companion, always ready to do a good turn: take care of Patrick, house-sit the apartment, find someone to fix the furnace. Witty, well-dressed but not flashy, she and Pauline have come a long way from Piggott, Arkansas, where their father moved the family from St. Louis to become a gentleman farmer and village patron. In Piggott, only one or two close friends understood how strange Jinny was in that cotton-field town, but in Paris, where nothing is strange, Jinny is very much at ease. If she prefers the company of women to men, she is far from alone in the city of lights.

Behind uncle and niece walk Ernest and Pauline. Smartly dressed but pale from her illness and the wet spring, Pauline seems fragile beside her husband, who stands almost a foot taller than she. After the pain of her sinus drainage and the lost sleep with fever-ridden Patrick, after all the small but demanding duties that fell to her upon their return to Paris (find a maid, balance accounts, replace lost linen, greet old friends), and after the anxiety of Ernest's inability to finish his novel, she, too, is smiling, for those stresses are behind them. Before them is the promise of another Spanish summer. She is thirty-three years old, wife and mother, securely funded, and married to one of the most interesting men of her generation. Pauline Hemingway has every reason to smile.

Taller and younger than the Pfeiffers around him, Ernest is aging more quickly than some of his peers. At twenty-eight, his receding hairline making prominent his widow's peak, his face looks heavy behind his black mustache, and his bulk fills his dark suit completely. Twice married, twice a father, once divorced, he is becoming the authority figure he imagined himself to be a few years earlier. Soon Pauline will be calling him "Papa." This morning he, too, is smiling, for he has found his novel's conclusion: no explanations, no maundering about lost characters, Catherine and the baby dead in Lausanne, and Frederic alone, walking back to his hotel in the rain. The previous evening, Owen Wister, who was passing through Paris and whose concerns about the ending Ernest knew, was with him for supper. After reading the new ending, Wister said, "Don't touch a thing!"[15] Having exhausted himself in the book for fifteen months, Hemingway's storehouse is empty, his mind briefly at rest.

There is now a misty rain falling lightly in rue Férou: a damper for the first day of the Grande Semaine and the steeplechase at Auteuil perhaps, but a fair Sunday nevertheless as Ernest enjoys that brief moment of well being that comes with a finished book. Soon enough he will face again the certainty that only two conditions exist for a man of letters: either he is writing, or he is not. He might ease his driven need by answering letters, taking notes, or keeping a journal, but no matter what he tells himself, he feels slightly fraudulent until the next book begins. Later Ernest said that the writing of the book should destroy the writer. If there is anything left, he has not worked hard enough. The writer himself does not matter: the book is everything. Others will tell him how much they like the new novel, but their praise will not bring back the wonder of writing it, nor can praise fill up the emptiness left by its departure, nor dull the anxiety of searching for the next book.

Having no other way to put it forcefully, Hemingway said that within the writer there was his death, and that death was the book. Physically, he might survive any number of books, but each one would kill off a part of him, a piece of what he knew, leaving the book with a life of its own.[16] The last five years of steady writing have killed off more of him than he can admit: two novels, one satire (*Torrents of Spring*), and two volumes of short stories. Writing only about what he knew best from his own life and the lives of friends, he has used up the experiences that life had given him as a gift. It was like closing out a bank account in which nothing remains but small change.

As soon as the May issue of *Scribner's Magazine* appeared, his new life solidified, irrevocably, leaving behind certain pleasures, while opening possibilities and expectations only dreamed of earlier. Never again will he lack an audience; never again will he read a rejection letter. *The Sun Also Rises* plucked him out of the bush leagues of the small literary magazines and made him a talent worth watching. *A Farewell to Arms* will take him into the major league of best-selling authors, where soon an entourage—lawyer, agent, editor, and publisher—will be continually looking after his and their professional best interests. Soon enough he will need dollar, pound, franc, mark, and peseta accounts at the Morgan Guaranty Bank to accommodate his various royalties. In ten years of continuous work, he has transformed himself from the precocious, war-wounded teenager writing clichéd imitations into one of the best young writers of his generation. At twenty-four he had little to show for all his ambition; at twenty-nine he has written two of his century's best novels.

Possibilities, which he once sought so ardently, now come uninvited for his consideration. Before he could leave Paris for the drunken feria of San Fermin, Janet Flanner insisted on an interview for a *Ladies' Home Journal* article she is writing on expatriates, which he will be in, she says jokingly, whether he cooperates or not.[17] Nino Frank, the editor of *Bifur*, a new literary journal, says that James Joyce told him that Ernest might give him one of his short stories for the premier edition of the journal.[18] *The Forum* wants Ernest to send them a short story: "Two thousand words is the desired length and in any case the stories must not exceed three thousand words. . . . the story must contain narrative or at least plot. . . . not be merely a sketch. . . . We will pay five hundred dollars for the first serial rights."[19] George Antheil wants Ernest to collaborate on a play similar to what young Bert Brecht has done in Berlin with *The Threepenny Opera*. "The composer [Kurt] Weil, who wrote the music, has been begging me to find an American writer who would work out something with us (Weil and I) for Berlin. . . . You are the only boy who could do this thing if you would."[20] Victor Llona wants to translate and publish "Ten Indians" in an anthology of American writers. The pay is only two hundred francs ($8) but it will be "excellent publicity." Four days later, he says André Maurois has agreed to write the introduction for the story. "Being by Maurois, your introduction will be the most arresting in the Anthology."[21] Paul Johnson wants Ernest to contribute to a "series of six prose pamphlets, each containing an essay or short story . . . boxed together . . . to sell at $10.00 the set. . . . The only rules [are] . . . that the contribution be a short story or literary essay, and that the minimum length be 2000 words. . . . Random House is prepared to pay $200.00 on acceptance." Those invited to compete for the six slots are Sherwood Anderson, Thomas Beer, James Branch Cabell, Willa Cather, Joseph Hergesheimer, Conrad Aiken, Theodore Dreiser, Ellen Glasgow, Ernest Hemingway, and Thornton Wilder.[22]

In early August, *Collier's Weekly* offered $750 for a thousand-word sketch and more for a five-thousand-word story. "If they like that," Paul Reynolds, Hemingway's would-be agent, told his editor, "they would order more."[23] When Ernest did not respond to the offer, *Collier's* came back with an offer of $30,000 for the serial rights to his next novel, with a $1,000 down payment for the right of first refusal. "They will pay you twenty-five hundred dollars ($2500) for any short stories of yours that they buy," he was told.[24] Every bait went untouched.

In Conway, Massachusetts, Archibald MacLeish finishes reading the May installment of *A Farewell to Arms* and writes Ernest that it is so good that it frightens him. "Your book," he says, "starts like Tolstoy—it starts slow and deep & real the way Tolstoy starts—it is like the beginning of a year not the beginning of a book—(& the first chapter is a magnificent poem)—& I am afraid you are not only a fine writer which I have always known but something a lot more than that & it scares me. I can't go on with this. It is murder to talk about it this way."[25] Three days earlier in Boston: "The June issue of *Scribner's Magazine* was barred from the book stands here yesterday by Michael

H. Crowley, superintendent of police, because of objections to an installment of Ernest Hemingway's serial, *A Farewell to Arms*. It is said that some persons deem part of the installment salacious."[26]

In Paris, while Ernest, Jinny Pfeiffer, and Guy Hickok ready themselves for the two-day drive to the feria of San Fermin, the Grande Semaine finishes its course of fashion displays and featured handicaps at the several racetracks. As the city fills with noisy tourists and its permanent residents leave for country places, the summer seems no different from any other in the Twenties. Some notice that fewer Americans are in Paris, but at the several European entry ports, great ocean liners—*Aquitania, Lancastria, Gripsholm, Ile-de-France, Majestic, President Harding, Deutschland, Mauretania*—continue to disgorge their traffic. Action on the Paris Bourse slows to a crawl. "Midsummer drowsiness is drugging business on the London stock exchange," the *Tribune* reports. "Public apathy is becoming increasingly apparent." On Wall Street, "Indications are for a peaceful summer . . . and a gradual accumulation of strength which should express itself in a rising stock market with the approach of autumn." On Monday morning, a share of U.S. Steel is selling at 179.[27]

The summer *transition* manifesto—signed by Kay Boyle, Harry and Caresse Crosby, and Hart Crane among others—insists that the Left Bank coterie writers are alive and well. Its eleventh article states flatly: "The plain reader be damned."[28] Ernest's name, which two years earlier the revolutionary journal gladly featured, is nowhere in sight. That part of his life—the Left Bank literary life; the *transatlantic, This Quarter, transition* life—is finished. As the *New York Evening Post* reported: "The Hemingway who sat nightly in the Latin Quarter is no more. . . . [*The Sun Also Rises*] marked his permanent exodus from the Dome, the Rotonde, and the rest of the Bohemian resorts in Montparnasse."[29] That summer and fall all appeals for his fiction, all promises of money large and small, go unattended. He and his world are in flux. The plain reader, so roundly damned by *transition*'s elitists, is waiting for a new fiction to be written by plain authors; very soon plain characters will step onto a proletariat stage waiting to be built.

Late that week, the U.S. Secretary of the Treasury announces that the government is ending the fiscal year with a $170 million surplus, and President Hoover predicts that eighteen more years of prosperity will retire the national debt completely. The Democrats are

> *expected to seize upon these figures to support their demands for further tax cuts at the bottom of the scale. They contend that the last tax reduction voted by Congress benefited big corporations and wealthy persons far more than it did the small-salaried class. The Republicans contend that by reducing the tax burdens of wealth and big business, the Government increased the general prosperity of the country through development of industry and commerce.*[30]

On the big board, U.S. Steel closes the week at 188.

At Pamplona on July 6 precisely at noon, the feast of San Fermin begins with a ceremonial rocket, cannon fire, and music. This summer so many cars arrive that the Plaza de la Constitución and all its side streets are gridlocked. The following morning, the dead awake to a brassy band in the plaza calling them to watch the 7:00 a.m. *encierro*, the running of that day's bulls from their holding pens down barricaded streets to Plaza de Toros. The Hemingway party, arriving early to acclimatize, are strategically housed at Hotel Quintana. From their small balcony, they have an excellent view of the narrow Calle de la Estafeta, down which come young runners wearing red *boinas* and sashes followed closely by bulls clattering on the cobblestones. This year no one is grievously hurt; two are wounded, but walk away. By midmorning the bulls and runners are replaced by the solemn procession of San Fermin led by the Bishop of Navarra followed by mounted Guardia Civil, choirs of children, parish church councils both local and visiting, church and municipal dignitaries, various guilds, and assorted bands of singers and dancers. The spiritual soon gives way to the carnal: flute, drum, and bagpipers leading rowdy street dancers before the procession of gigantic papier-mâché royal couples—Ferdinand and Isabella—and strange *cabezudos*, little people with big heads. And everywhere the Riau Riau clubs were dancing, pulling even overweight newsmen like Guy Hickok into their ritual:

> We stood four feet apart, arms up, on tiptoe, waiting for a place in the music to start. It came and we began. Tum, tum, tum to the left. Tum, tum, tum to the right. Both of them over again. Then at a shrill tumult in the music we whirled (that is he whirled and I did my best) and began again. It became very involved and it was only by watching his feet and forgetting everything else in the world that I kept in the same dance with him. Sometimes we whirled one way, sometimes another. Twice he leaped in the air, with me in on only the second leap. Once the whirl was preceded by a quick drop to one knee. Then it stopped.[31]

At four-thirty, as the day cools somewhat, bullfights begin, lasting well into evening. Blood stains the sand arena, flowers and full *botas* fall on the heroic, cushions on those who fail. This day a careless banderillero's arm is ripped open by a horn of an Encinas bull. That night on the plaza, Japanese fireworks and illuminated balloons alternate with music, dancing, and always drinking.[32] Guy Hickok described it all for his newspaper:

> The whole square is a confusion of unorganized noises for hours before the fireworks begin. An uncountable moving mob mills about the square, plunging into and out of the wine shops under the arcades around it, singing and dancing in groups in the square itself, trying to climb the two greased poles, and never succeeding, trying to ride the two big barrels swung between poles, barrels apparently on ball bearings, so quickly do they turn and throw would-be riders to the ground.[33]

While Guy was sitting with Ernest under the arcade at the Iruña, a magazine writer spotted them

> at a table against one of the pillars, with a bottle of beer in front of him, and a newspaper folded to the criticism of yesterday's bull-fight,

exchanging idle comments with two friends, heedless of the racket
that encompasses him, surveying the crowd with the friendly eye of a
man who reads a familiar story, . . . Ernest Hemingway, the author
who discovered Pamplona.

He is dressed in loose tweeds, his collar is low and soft and his
necktie is pulled awry; he is hatless and one foot is thrust into a
clumsy woolen carpet slipper. Somehow he cut his foot a day or so
ago. With his dark hair and his dark mustache, his coloring is incon-
spicuous in the crowd of dark-haired Spaniards; but his poise and
his strength are not. The vitality of the man is apparent even when
he is motionless; it is an unobtrusive force which manifests itself by
no overt gesture, yet it is pervasive and inescapable. . . . Hemingway
is real; he is content to be only himself: Pamplona is real, unlike any
city but itself. And in Pamplona Hemingway seems at home.[34]

"Discovered Pamplona" was shorthand for saying, "He gave us
the drinker's dream, the prohibitionist's nightmare." No matter how
experienced a drinker one thought himself, he was likely a novice at
the week of San Fermin, where drinking was not an occasion but a
steady state, a condition as pervasive as sunlight. By week's end the
Pamplona air itself is rich with fumes of rioja consumed from goat-
skin *botas* worn loosely slung from the neck.

There was plenty of drinking that year at Pamplona, but not so
much that they did not see what was happening in the bullring.
With Hemingway beside him, Guy was able to write with shrewd,
inside knowledge while seeing his first bullfights. During the first
five corridas, two matadors were gored and three picadors were
seriously hurt when their bulls gored their horses, lifting them up
and over on top of the horsemen. There were stunning moments
in the ring when Felix Rodríguez danced too close with his bull as
he slipped the sword into the killing spot, and with Ernest's help,
Hickok saw it:

While he still gripped the sword, the horns caught him under one
arm, lifted him and flung him down. The bull lunged at him in a

last second of fury, scattering sand as he hooked viciously with right horn and left, bearing down his weight. Others flicked their capes to draw the bull away. Felix Rodríguez was carried to the infirmary. In a quarter of an hour he was back, his neck bandaged and blood showing on his white pleated shirt, but smiling that debonair super-Hollywood smile. He stood ten minutes, then fainted and was carried out again.[35]

Ten days after the feria and safely returned to Paris, Hickok, a happily married expatriate newsman, wrote Hemingway about seeing Jinny Pfeiffer in Paris:

I didn't expect Jinny to look so good without Pernod glasses. I thought . . . I could look at her with indifference. But she came along looking so cool and calm and her eyes so shiny black and everything so nice that . . . it was a God Damned awful experiment in chemistry that you performed down there professor Hemingway. You take a fat forty-one year old innocent and pour him full of everybody's absinthe and bulls blood [Sangre de Torres wine] and trout water and a week of sparks and riau-riau and bombs and keep something like Jin . . . around all the time and what the Hell could you expect to happen. I'll bet a bull I don't get her out of my head inside a year.[36]

———

Paris, August 1. At the sign of the Black Manikin, where Edward Titus makes his living, his latest publishing venture is in the window—*Kiki's Memoirs*. Everyone on the Left Bank knows Kiki, the most famous model of Montparnasse and wife of enigmatic photographer Man Ray, whose lush nude displays of her body are not the least attraction of the book. "Did you know Kiki?" Ernest asks. "Did you ever see her bare? Did you once see Shelley plain and did he stop and speak to you? I'd rather have seen Kiki than Shelley."[37]

———

In Santiago de Compostela, the Hotel Suizo is not the ancient town's most resplendent hotel nor its most favored. Stuck into a side street without redeeming qualities, it has no elegant foyer, nor spacious dining room to attract the wealthy. The Suizo's dining room, barely two tables wide, is plain but adequate with starched white tablecloths and a standing array of waiters.[38] It is the class of hotel that Hemingway habitually chooses, neither shabby nor elegant, family-owned and giving good value for its price: "good pension for 10 pesetas, good rooms, wonderful god damned town and fine hilly country, Galicia."[39] The Hemingways have not come to Santiago for the bullfights, which are "all shot to hell," he tells Waldo Peirce. After the Pamplona feria, Guy Hickok, Pat Morgan, and Jinny Pfeiffer returned by train to Paris, and Pauline joined Ernest at Hendaye to drive to the Valencia feria, where the bullfights were much better than in Pamplona. Now, after a warm month on the road, they are in cooler Santiago, its pilgrims departed, its hotels half empty, and where afternoon showers wash the stone city to a glistening shimmer. Most come, by whatever route, to this sanctuary either to pray or to fish. Ernest has come for both reasons, and another of his own.

Watching him bring a novel to completion is not a new experience for Pauline, for she, as the other woman, was intimately involved with Ernest when he finished *The Sun Also Rises*. She remembers the strain to the breaking point that novel put on his marriage with Hadley. She remembers that he left a wife and son in Paris to finish his fiction alone in Hendaye, and afterward became a stranger to Hadley, arguing about little things and anything. This summer in Spain, without another woman's presence to explain his erratic behavior, Pauline sees the pattern repeat itself in smaller ways. The sexual rush of her dyed blond hair with which she surprised him at Hendaye has worn off, and she is worried. In the cathedral of St. James, she lights her several candles, each for its separate problem.

When they arrived at the Suizo, their baggage contained unfinished stories which Pauline brought with her from Paris,[40] stories to which Ernest now returns but in a mood ill suited to finishing them.

Smarting from the avuncular advice of Fitzgerald and Owen Wister, he continues to fret over Max Perkins's failure to support his full usage of the English language. Max restored some of the words deleted by *Scribner's Magazine*—"Jesus Christ," "son of a bitch," "whore," and "whorehound"—but others, like "cocksucker," were impossible to print in 1929 America. No matter that their competition, Remarque's *All Quiet on the Western Front*, was using "the word shit and fart etc. never dragged in for coloring but only used a few times for the thousands of times they are omitted."[41] With the argument settled by blank spaces in his text, Ernest cannot let loose of the issue, for he feels that he has betrayed his dedication to honest writing.

When not writing, he frequently takes their 1929 Ford off by himself to fish one of the several local streams famous for trout. On August 12, with new sunglasses, newspapers, and a sack full of tomatoes and onions for lunch, he spends the day fishing the Río Ulla as far as the upper dam. On the way home along the new railroad bed, he stops to cook the trout with salty country ham. Then, one after the other, two tires go flat. After patching the inner tubes by flashlight, he finally arrives back at the hotel at 11:15 p.m. With Pauline beside him in bed and his beer bottle on the side table, he adds, "No fights for two days."[42] Waking the next morning tired from his excursion, he spends the day quietly in Santiago. While reading of yesterday's bullfights in the newspapers, as he customarily begins his day, he also scans the pages for information on the new Spanish constitution and how the various revolutionary movements fare.

All that August there are signs to be read by the close observer. In Nuremberg, where it eventually would come full circle, the reporter saw what was happening, but misread the equation:

Rival militant Nationalists of all shades buried the axe today when 120,000 uniformed Hitlerites marched past their leader, Adolph Hitler, beside whom stood Prince August Wilhelm, one of the Kaiser's sons, . . . evidence that a united monarchist bloc is coming into existence in Germany.[43]

U.S. Steel rises to 215, approximately the weight of Florence Martin, better known as Flossie, the "Dowager of the Dôme," the "Duchess of Montparnasse," who was giving up her domain to return to the United States.[44] The financial page might say, "No Midsummer Recession of Business Is Feared in U.S.,"[45] but beneath the surface of the Twenties, tectonic plates are shifting.

Midmorning in Santiago, Ernest gets his hair cut, purchases supplies, and checks with the *patrón* for mail forwarded from Paris. On $5 a day, he claims they are living cheaper than in Key West.[46] After their late lunch, Pauline works on unanswered letters, writing to Katy Smith that they hope she is soon to be Mrs. Dos Passos. (Ernest underlined that entry in his daybook, thinking perhaps of how much he once wanted Katy and later wrote the story of having her, a story he could never print.)[47] It was a day for marriages: a redirected telegram arrives announcing that Ernest's ambulance-driving friend from the war Bill Horne has married someone called "Bunny."

With the shutters drawn against the afternoon heat and with Pauline writing letters at the desk, Ernest stretches out to read from the pile of books with which he always travels. Today he chooses the Dumas historical novel *Les Quarante-cinq* and D. H. Lawrence's novella *St. Mawr*. Five years later, Dumas will contribute a single line to the text of *Green Hills of Africa*.[48] That evening, he notes in his daybook that at lunch he drank "*1 bottle beer*" costing sixty-five centavos. The underlining is for Pauline's benefit in their continuing disagreements about his drinking, which is causing his fingers to swell. Before turning out the light that night, he adds and underlines: "*3 days without any fights.*"[49] Between books, between countries, he is at odds with himself.

———

September 2, Palencia, Spain. A hotel room with a double bed; on a night table, bullfight tickets, glasses, a bottle of mineral water, a newspaper, and several books. Shutters are closed against the midday heat, but they do not prevent the temperature from rising in this room on the unshaded side of the hotel. On the bed, Ernest is stretched out, reading. Pauline is not in the room. Whenever he shifts position, he winces from a pulled groin muscle. Street noise of a feria and a faint haze of dust hang in the air that seeps into the room.[50]

———

He is always reading current fiction in the way that painters visit galleries or musicians listen to the Victrola, but he also reads to accumulate information in specific areas: military history, biography, travel, and natural history. Like his boyhood idol Theodore Roosevelt, he travels with his own library carefully chosen for divergent moods as a man might lay in specific wines in anticipation of certain meals. In Palencia he is reading to pass the time until the afternoon corrida begins. Yesterday the fights were excellent, and he anticipates another good day. He studies the corrida and its attendant drama with the detachment of a natural historian who, four years earlier, said that he wanted to write "a sort of Doughty's Arabia Deserta of the Bull Ring, a very big book with some wonderful pictures."[51]

From Santiago, he wrote Max Perkins that he had a vague idea about his next book—a collection of sketches of "things and places— not so much about people"—bullfight and fishing sketches; places like Key West, Santiago, Paris, Constantinople: something between essays and reminiscences. He could see three kinds: quiet ones, funny ones, and immoral ones. Maybe the magazine would take the quiet ones. The book itself would be something like W. H. Hudson's *Long Ago and Far Away*. Better to be writing something rather than trying like Scott to write a masterpiece; the next novel would have to wait until his "Goddamned imagination" began to function once again.[52]

Now in his fifth Spanish summer, he is gathering field notes for a book he does not yet understand, a book which will take another two years to complete. When it is finished, it will be a history of the bullfight, a guide to its present performance, a collection of morality tales, a book about writing, a book of natural history with a touch of *Don Quixote*, a book more complex than anything he has yet attempted. To that end he has registered the deaths of several hundred fighting bulls in his well-trained memory, bulls whose color, size, and speed he can remember. What is not in memory is there in the bullfight newspapers and magazines he has collected. For the history, he has recently acquired *Paginas Tauromacas* to add to his growing library.[53]

He is also reading medieval history, a subject in some ways not that far removed from the bullfight.[54] Hemingway is not looking for subject matter; he has plenty of that closer to home. Nor does he have any desire to resuscitate the long ago and far away. Like so many of his generation—the men who went to the Great War to make the world safe for democracy—he is looking for values that remain valid no matter how the stock market fluctuates or which way the political climate turns. One obvious source of stability is the Catholic Church, which has come through almost two millennia with its tenets intact. Having first satirized authors of his generation turning to the church ("The Lord is my shepherd, I shall not want him for long"),[55] Hemingway, too, embraced Catholicism, partially as the price for embracing Pauline Pfeiffer, a dedicated Catholic. If he sometimes seems less concerned about his soul's fate in the *hereafter* and more worried about sustaining himself in the *here and now*, his religious need is no less genuine or deeply seated.

With his conversion to Catholicism, Hemingway was remolding himself and eventually the characters he created. Leaving behind the passive young men of his early period, vulnerable men to whom unfortunate things happened, he was searching in no organized fashion for that man's *other*, the active man who chooses his fate rather than letting it choose him. Outlaws, spies, and revolutionaries are part of his reading, men operating outside the social contract but not without access to its comforts. The bullfighter and the boxer continue to interest him, both as men isolated by their art and as metaphors for the artist. In the background of this search, standing tall, is Chaucer's medieval Knight, his armor stained with usage, his list of battles writ large across his face. The warrior who "loved chivalrie, Trouthe and honour, fredom and curteisie." This knight was God's mercenary, going to all the wars of his time, choosing the side he thought most just. At the end of his tale, Chaucer's Knight laid down two guiding principles which would become central to Hemingway both man and author: to make "virtu of necessitee" and "for a worthy fame, to dyen when that he is best of name."

In his first Paris period, Hemingway sometimes pretended to more extensive war experience than his one month as a Red Cross ambulance driver had actually provided. In fact, he did not speak of the Red Cross, and friends accumulated tall tales of his fictional experience with Italian Arditi who plugged their bullet wounds with cigarette butts and who preferred the knife to the gun.[56] But he had experienced the big wound: the night mortar shell that killed the man standing next to him nearly crippled Ernest for life. Maybe he had not walked "eye deep in hell," but he had come home to the "old men's lies" that Pound described. Raised Republican in Republican Oak Park, he could not support the party that rejected the war and its veterans, nor could he support the Democrats who sent him off to it wearing a blindfold. At postwar conferences at Genoa and Lausanne, he witnessed the old order doing business as usual, protecting business. He listened to their promises and observed the consequences without taking sides. In 1924, his "Earnest Liberal" lamented:

> *I know that monks masturbate at night*
> *That pet cats screw*
> *That some girls bite*
> *And yet*
> *What can I do*
> *To set things right?*[57]

What, in fact, could anyone do in the face of the tourist trade, the Post-Toasties and Lucky Strike marketplace. Europe was more Americanized than ever, he told his mother-in-law. "Coca Cola sold all over Spain. Chewing gum too."[58]

What could a citizen do but place his faith in the market, where U. S. Steel rose fifty points to 257? Who could argue with a 300 percent return on his money in thirty-two days? Brother, take a ride on the Reading. Take a flier on futures. Have confidence in the confidence men running the pools. As the *Tribune* reported,

> *Scare after scare in speculative circles has been followed, after a brief recession, by the resumption of an upward movement in the New York stock market that has shattered hopes that the advance had finally been checked. . . . stocks soaring to new heights is regarded as evidence that the Federal Reserve . . . authorities have lost control of the credit situation. While there is considerable unemployment in the big cities, the confidence in business is unimpaired.*[59]

Elsewhere, confidence in various cultural establishments waned:

BOMB SET OFF IN BASEMENT OF REICHSTAG
National Social Group Blamed

"The national Socialist gang which has been terrorizing small towns in northern Germany for the past six months" was blamed for the explosion. Chalked on a lamppost they found "the Fascist swastika with the words 'Greater Germany Wake Up.' "[60] In Palestine, disagreement on who could do what at the Western Wall set loose an Arab effort to exterminate the Jews, who, they said, were trying to usurp a homeland in Palestine. The Grand Mufti of Jerusalem incited the bloodletting, which in two days killed thirty Jews and brought British bayonets to town restoring order.[61]

Meanwhile at various bookstores in Paris, London, and New York, the final issue of *Little Review* carried Hemingway's sarcastic "Valentine for Mr. Lee Wilson Dodd and Any of His Friends Who Want It," which concluded with some painful advice for those critics who found his characters too sordid:

> *If you do not like them lads*
> *One thing you can do*
> *Stick them up your —— lads*
> *My Valentine to you.*

In their opening remarks, editors Margaret Anderson and Jane Heap explained why they were closing down *Little Review*, where they first serialized Joyce's *Ulysses* when no one would publish it, closing the review whose contributors included almost every important author of the era. Anderson said, "Even the artist doesn't know what he is talking about. And I can no longer go on publishing a magazine in which no one really knows what he is talking about."[62] That Monday morning, September 2, 1929, the bull market peaked at prices not to be seen again for a quarter of a century. The *Titanic* is sinking, but no one has yet informed the passengers.

In early September, Ernest and Pauline grow weary following the cartels, two days with Sidney Franklin, the Jewish bullfighter from Brooklyn, just then a curiosity in Spain. More arena afternoons, more blood and sand, and afterward a warm hotel room with too much noise outside in the street, and, later, a meal of several courses not ending before midnight. A Madrid street thief picks Hemingway's pocket: passport, *carte d'identité*, *cartes gris* and *verte*, everything but his money. Then, discovering the name of his victim, the thief returns it all to him at his hotel. The summer is finished: time to leave.

On September 12, Ernest and Pauline drive into Hendaye, checking into the Ondarraitz Hotel, with, as advertised, a "splendid view of the sea and the mountains." Six days later, refreshed with late mornings and beach afternoons, they leave Spain to return to Paris. For two months he and Pauline have been each other's best and worst company: no Fitzgerald in their nights; no child in their days, little Patrick summering with his nursemaid in Compiègne. They've had fine afternoons at the bullring and lazy strolls on the Hendaye beach, but many tense, awkward moments as well, with apologies afterward. Unable to touch her husband in his dark times, Pauline has studied the rise and fall of his irregular moodiness, his quick-trigger anger. She and those who know him worry about these unexpected emotional explosions. At the end of the year, Paul Nelson advises him: "I want you to go see Dr. Fortier or Dr. Vannier before leaving. You need to stop burning up what you don't replace. Go ahead. Don't be a thick head. You owe it to us all. It's fine to be down low but you have to go up to go down."[63] This summer, for all its pleasures, has taken its toll: too many road miles, too much dust, too many bottles of red wine, too many heavy Spanish meals too late at night.

Waiting for the publication of his novel has also taken its toll. From Madrid, he sent nagging telegrams to Max Perkins, worrying about getting the text right and worrying about libel. "What did you do about the note in the front?" he asked. "That in the English edition reads—None of the characters in this book is a living person, nor are the units or military organizations mentioned actual units or organizations."[64] When he cannot lose himself in the moment, whenever he starts thinking about the book, he turns edgy, prickly, tense. By mail, Fitzgerald kids him about his "nervous bitterness," and Ernest tries to roll with the joke: "On re-reading your letter I find it *Is Not Snooty at all*. And old Hem wrong again. Evidently a prey to his nervous bitterness!"[65] But words cannot mask the fact that he is anxious about the worth of his new fiction. "That terrible mood of depression," he tells Fitzgerald, ". . . is known as The Artist's Reward. . . . Summer is a discouraging time to work—You don't feel death coming on the way it does in the fall when the boys really put pen to paper."[66] Whether or not this cheers Fitzgerald is unrecorded, but it describes only too well Hemingway's summer. Packed in their backseat suitcases, along with ticket stubs, hotel bills, and *The History of the Crusades*, are fragments of fiction, stories ragged and unfinished. A year has passed since he completed the first draft of *A Farewell to Arms*, a year of revisions, letters, telegrams, and these unfinished stories. With little patience, the writer is waiting once again on his muse, who is somewhere else this summer.

When he is not writing well, he is liable to all manner of physical problems from a chronic strep throat to minor injuries. As this summer closes, his fingers are swollen from too much wine, he thinks; his pulled groin muscle still pains him; his injured foot, barely healed. When he was the Doctor's son, young Hemingway learned that injuries and sickness brought him attention; at twenty-nine, he buried his father, who from worry, fear, and deep melancholy put a bullet through his brain. Now, the Doctor's son does not seek injury out, but it finds him as if it were his brother. When he hurts, those about him are the first to know. Wife and mother, nurse and lover, Pauline answers his needs with an intensity he seldom experienced from Hadley. She ministers unto his pains and responds to his fantasies. On this day along the river, the wind ruffling her now blond, short-cropped hair, Pauline Hemingway is a woman accomplished: she has wed and bred with a man much desired, giving him a son and taking him to new levels of financial ease and sexual excitement. She shares his anxiety about *A Farewell to Arms*'s incipient reception: *The Sun Also Rises* was Hadley's book; this one, while dedicated to Uncle Gus for all his gifts, is, nonetheless, her book.

––––––

October, Paris in the fall. Rain with a little weak sunlight in the late afternoons. Rain sometimes hard enough to short out the circuits and stall the evening metro. Rain to dull the donkey races and dampen the opium pipes at Harry Crosby's country place, Moulin d'Ermenonville. Rain to take the edge off of the Prix de l'Arc-de-Triomphe, where Peter Pickem (né Harold Stearns) picked Kantar to win. While Paris listened to it on the radio, Ernest and Pauline catch the beauty of the green track from Crosby's box; Harry and Caresse with their two whippets, Narcisse and Clytoris, watch Harry's money on Kantar to win disappear as did so many of his whims. Rain is not the friend of Harry Crosby, worshiper of the sun, whose black tattoo he wears etched between his shoulder blades. Harry, on his way to death, takes Kantar's loss quite well.[67]

––––––

On Saturday, October 19, panic swept through the American stock market like a cholera plague. Smart ones, like Bernard Baruch, had been quietly reducing their holdings for some time now, but the shoe salesman in Detroit and the cotton broker in Memphis held on as long they could. When the market closed, those on the margin were out of the game and with them ten to fifteen billion dollars of paper profits disappeared as easily as smoke. U.S. Steel closed at 209. That same Saturday, in the street window of Sylvia Beach's Shakespeare and Company, the newly minted *A Farewell to Arms* was on display. Published in New York on September 27, a copy of the book reached Hemingway on October 3. His reaction was immediate: Scribner's was trying to sabotage the book. The reclining woman on the dust jacket was "lousy and completely unattractive decadence, i.e. large misplaced breasts" which would only inflame a censor. His name was so small it could not easily be read, and the title was obscured. He, himself, could not find the book until a clerk pointed it out to him. "All I get out of this book," he said, "is disappointment." He never should have compromised on the language. "The fact that I do it on account of my family is no excuse and I know it. I'm a Professional Writer now—than which there isn't anything lower—I never thought I'd be it and I'm damned if I'm going to do it anymore." All he wants is one copy of the book, even bound, uncorrected galleys, with all the words exactly as he wrote them. That will take "some of the curse off it."

The letter rambles on in convoluted sentences that increasingly slope downhill to the right. Maybe the dust jacket wasn't all that bad. When he first saw *The Sun Also Rises*, his reaction was similar; that novel "looks very fine now—so maybe this one is fine too." There remains the question of "the alibi note." Since his contract holds him responsible for libel suits, the disclaimer, which Scribner's finally put in the second printing, was an insurance policy. Not that anyone could possibly sue, but maybe the Italians would. "Using so many Italian names there must be people with those names." No one in the book was real, and in 1917, the Red Cross hospital "did not exist—there is no possibility of any libel there."[68]

What finally eased the pain of parturition were the book sales. On October 15, Perkins, in answer to Hemingway's letter and telegram asking about sales, wired his worried author that the first printing of thirty thousand copies was sold out and two more printings of ten thousand copies each had been run. "Prospects excellent."[69] On the heels of the telegram, Max wrote Ernest, telling him there were two $3,000 checks in the mail as well as good reviews. He tried to explain "the line of thought that led to the present design" of the dust jacket: the designer was the best in the business; the office was nervous about too much War on the cover. "We wanted no helmets or artillery." What Max was really worried about were the literary wolves ready to snap up a young, hot commodity like Ernest. He was sure, he said, that Ernest would come to him before making a publishing change. Scribner's would go to any length to keep its prize author happy, but Max "did not want anything personal ever to hold you back from it. . . . if you get to feel dissatisfied and thought we could not rectify the trouble, I wouldn't want you to be held back just because I was such a wonder as a Tarpon Fisherman."[70]

On Sunday the Paris *Tribune* review calls *A Farewell to Arms* "technically and stylistically the most interesting novel of the year . . . a blossoming of a most unusual genius." The story was "brutal . . . awesome . . . terrific . . . vulgar . . . beautiful."[71] The Paris reviewer's enthusiasm was redoubled by the New York critics. The day after its publication, the *New York Sun* said parts of the novel were "magnificently done . . . the finest thing Hemingway has yet done."[72] Malcolm Cowley found "a new tenderness" in the story which he called "the most important book" Hemingway had written.[73] *The New Yorker* loved it; *Saturday Review* gushed; *The Nation* said, "It is a real occasion for Patriotic rejoicing."[74] Of course, each reviewer found some flaw, something overdone, underwritten, or undeveloped. For one it was too much dialogue and not enough scenery; for another it was too much detachment and not enough emotion. Some thought it less than *The Sun Also Rises*; others thought it brighter, as if the two books were comparable.

The *Tribune* review, which started so well, could not let the novel go without saying:

> *Ernest Hemingway is the direct blossoming of Gertrude Stein's art. Whether he consciously was influenced by her no one, of course, can say. But he does in "A Farewell to Arms," what Gertrude Stein did in "Three Lives," except that he does it in a longer, more complicated medium and with more certain power. There are whole pages in the new book which might have been written by Gertrude Stein herself,*

except that, even in their most tortuous intricacies, the reader is perfectly clear about what Mr. Hemingway is saying and why he is saying it that way.[75]

Who invented young Hemingway? I did, said Ezra, with my blue pencil. Oh, but someone was following me who was always following, said Gertrude, and it certainly looked like Ernest. No, no, wheezed Ford, it was I who set him the proper example, gave him the lesson of the word exact. There would be no end to the question of influence; he could see that now, but the Gertrude Stein attributions were irksome. Yes, he had gone to her early for writing lessons, studied her technique, written his imitations and his parodies. And, yes, some of what he learned was still apparent, but he knew this book was so far beyond Gertrude's range that comparisons were almost funny.

The next evening, it was Gertrude herself whom he literally bumped into at close, public quarters, where both were polite. His divorce from Hadley two years earlier also marked the end of his regular afternoons at the Stein-Toklas apartment on rue de Fleurus. Gertrude and Alice, godmothers to Hemingway's first son, were hurt by his changing partners; Alice, who never approved of Hemingway, used the occasion to drive the wedge between the two writers. From the beginning, Alice told Lovey, as she called Gertrude, that Ernest was crude, vulgar, and less than virile, a rotten pupil "who never got past the second lesson." And Gertrude would tell Pussy, as she called Alice, that it did not matter.[76] That was when he was so attentive, almost like a courting lover. When those flowers faded, so did Gertrude's enthusiasm, and Alice ruled. Alice almost always ruled.

On Tuesday morning, Gertrude's note arrived at rue Férou, asking Hemingway to bring Scott Fitzgerald and Allen Tate to an evening at her apartment, an invitation which implicitly invited Ernest without having to say it. He rattled off a note to Fitzgerald, explaining the invitation. "She claims you are the one of all us guys with the most talent, etc. and wants to see you again."[77] Of course, Gertrude was perfectly capable of inviting Fitzgerald without benefit of Ernest's help. Scott, who was Alice's delight, was no stranger to rue du Fleurus, having visited there with and without Ernest several times. Figuring that it was better to enter the Gorgon's lair with plenty of support, he rounded up the Fitzgeralds, Ford Madox Ford, John Bishop and his wife, Allen Tate, and Caroline Gordon to accompany himself and Pauline.[78] If Hemingway suspected that he was being set up for a public embarrassment, he was not worried. In his pocket he had an invitation from *The Bookman* to write, for $200, a "tribute" to Gertrude.[79]

On Wednesday evening, the Hemingways and their accompaniment are met at the door by Alice, the tiny gatekeeper who looks like a gypsy, questions everyone, and forgets nothing. Ushered past mirror and umbrella stand, they move through the studio salon filled with heavy Spanish furniture to the small dais where Gertrude Stein is speaking to other guests. Chinese tea and American cake wait in the back room beside cups and plates as if the century has not yet turned. Then walls of paintings appear, slowly in the lamplight, slower in the candlelight—Braque, Gris, Matisse, Picasso—as closely packed as family photographs. The focal point is a nude girl holding a basket of red flowers, her hair black as pitch, her body dead white, beneath her feet Picasso's signature. Gertrude, seated beneath Picasso's portrait of her that she has come to resemble, her hair now more shortly cropped than Ernest's, begins to laugh infectiously at someone's remark, laughter rolling down the scale until it seems to shake the room.[80]

Ernest, on his best behavior, joins the men circled around Gertrude, who is lecturing on American literature. Emerson, she says, was the first American genius moving toward the elimination of subject matter. Subject matter is European and passé. Hawthorne was impossible, too European. Whitman and Dickinson had their moments, but Henry James, even if he was too European, was the next step forward after Emerson, moving away from experience and toward abstraction. Ford, she says, looking him straight in the eye, will never count at all. This literary genealogy, of course, led straight to Gertrude Stein, who is the climax of American genius.[81]

During the tea and cakes, Hemingway does not take exception when Gertrude chooses to praise Scott to him, does not point out that

Scott's long-awaited novel looks to be even longer in its awaiting. She says she likes *A Farewell to Arms*, but whenever he begins to remember rather than invent, the book is flawed. He does not ask her which parts she thinks he was remembering. Scott, walking up in the middle of their conversation, misunderstands when Stein tells him that he and Ernest burn with unequal flames. Fitzgerald, who is overly sensitive to the two novels Hemingway has written while he has not finished one, is hurt by what he takes to be a slight to his talent. Nothing Hemingway can tell him as they walk homeward can wash the bad taste away. Outside it is a warm October evening. A passing rain has left the air clear and fresh. As the young visitors walk in small groups back toward the Luxembourg, Fitzgerald is somewhat ahead of Allen Tate, who hears Scott repeating to himself, "I have seen Shelley plain."[82]

The next morning Scott's note arrives quite early, asking if Ernest was annoyed by his, Scott's, remarks. (He wants reassurance; he wants Ernest to like him truly, but somehow he always manages to create a scene.) Gertrude, he says, thinks that Hemingway is the superior writer. In what has become an emotionally expensive friendship, Ernest once more plays the older brother. What Scott took for a slight, Ernest tells him, was a Stein compliment; she has never had anything but praise for Scott. She was trying to say that he, Ernest, had the smaller talent, had to work harder for his results. Comparisons and talk of superiority are all "horseshit." Scott is "touchy" because his novel is not finished. Ernest understands and does not mind. Writers, he tells Scott, "are all in the same boat. Competition within that boat—which is headed toward death—is as silly as deck sports are."[83]

Six hours later in New York City, someone noticed that water was pouring into the hold of the good ship Wall Street:

GREATEST OF ALL STOCK

MARKET CRASHES WIPES OUT

BILLIONS IN SELLING HYSTERIA

It came today—the supreme crash in the stock market that the financial Jeremiahs predicted last year when the Babylon of paper prosperity was soaring to undreamed heights.

It came with a vengeance, the long delayed reckoning, and it surpassed anything that the most gloomy had predicted.[84]

New York bankers, pooling their money to shore up the damage, were barely able to stop the ship from going down. President Hoover announced that the business of the nation was sound, that conspicuous consumption was a healthy sign. U.S. Steel rode out that day's panic, closing at 204.[85] On Friday the market rallied as professionals picked over the remains, looking for bargains. Bernard Baruch bought 5,500 shares of American Smelting. The following Tuesday even Baruch abandoned ship, selling when he could find a buyer as the market dropped into an abyss without apparent bottom. In Paris, Americans, who arrived secure in their paper profits, were jamming the steamship lines seeking cheap passage home. U.S. Steel closed that day at 174, an offer with no takers. "I hope to Christ you weren't caught in the market," Hemingway wrote to Max Perkins on the last day of the month. Like most Americans, Ernest thought the "slump" momentary; by election time in 1932, Hoover would have brought the economy back. Meanwhile, in New York at the Hotel Pennsylvania, George Olsen was singing a new lyric, "Happy Days Are Here Again," to a less than enthusiastic audience.[86]

———

Berlin, November 15. After the six-day bike races and negotiations with Rowohlt for serializing *A Farewell to Arms* in German, he stops at Alfred Flechtheim's gallery on Konigsallee, where he is stunned once more by a small Klee watercolor, its disturbing face and its outrageous price. He makes a down payment in marks, the remainder to be paid at Flechtheim's Galerie Simon in Paris. The Mussolini-like face, under construction, two tiny men with baskets climbing ladders across its surface, is an unlovely but accurate metaphor: all across Europe tyrants are rising.[87]

———

On the stuffy night train to Berlin, Ernest could not let go of his letter to Max without scrawling across the back of the last page: "Remember O[wen] W[ister] et al wanting me to tone down or cut out some of the last chapter? That's why they're reading the damn book. It's no fun for me on acct. of the blanks. Now I can never say shit in a book. Precedent. When you make your own precedent once you make the wrong precedent you're just as badly stuck with it. It takes away from the interest in writing fiction."[88]

By the end of the summer he began signing his letters "E. Cantwork Hemingstein," which was not entirely true. He finished a made-to-order essay on bullfighting for the newly formed *Fortune* magazine, where Archie MacLeish was now working. Picking up $2,000 while practicing for his book on Spain was a safe thing to do, offending nobody. He was working now on an introduction that Edward Titus, a Left Bank bookseller and sometime publisher, asked for the English translation of *Kiki's Memoirs*. Hemingway wrote that the era of Montparnasse was "definitely marked as closed when she, Kiki, published this book. . . . although nobody knows when they start everybody is pretty sure when they are over and when, in one year, Kiki became monumental and Montparnasse became rich, prosperous, brightly lighted, dancinged, shredded-wheated, grape-nuts-ed or grapenutted . . . and they sold caviar at the Dôme, well, the Era for what it was worth, and personally I don't think it was worth much, was over."[89] He never thought much of the Montparnasse crowd of talkers who never got around to writing or painting what they talked about so well, so late, so long. As for "rich, prosperous, brightly lighted," who but Ernest and Pauline fit that farewell.

Edward Titus was also responsible for a story that Ernest was writing, a story *Scribner's Magazine* would never publish. Earlier in the fall, Titus, who had resuscitated Ernest Walsh's defunct periodical, *This Quarter*, challenged bisexual and infamous gossip Robert McAlmon and recently arrived Canadian writer Morley Callaghan to a literary contest: each was to write a story about two homosexuals. McAlmon, married to a lesbian, defaulted; Callaghan, a protégé of Hemingway's, wrote "Now That April's Here," in which a male homosexual leaves his lover for a woman. Without formally becoming part of the challenge match, Hemingway was working on a story in which a writer's female lover leaves him for another woman, a story he called "The Sea Change."[90] It was a very quiet story without offending words and almost no action, a strange story rich in understatement.

––––

Christmas Eve, Montana-Vermala, Switzerland. The Palace Hotel for consumptives—a pale stone building with many balconies facing east to catch the morning sun. Inside the Murphys' parlor there are white fur rugs on the floor, several chairs, a spirit lamp heating wine seasoned with cinnamon and lemons. On a low table sits a wind-up phonograph, but there is no music playing.

––––

From the balcony, looking out over the frozen valley of the Rhône fifteen hundred feet below them, the guests can see snowfields glowing blue-white in the moonlight. Wrapped in heavy coats and muffled against the constant chill, those in the room speak in whispers. Ernest and Pauline Hemingway, Pauline's sister, Virginia Pfeiffer, Scott and Zelda Fitzgerald, John and Katy Dos Passos, Dorothy Parker, and Donald Ogden Stewart have gathered to support Gerald and Sara Murphy in the attempt to save their oldest son, Patrick, who has contracted the frequently incurable tuberculosis. These are the Murphys whose Villa America at Antibes summered so many of the beautiful people during the Twenties: Cole Porter, Pablo Picasso, the Fitzgeralds, and the Hemingways. Gerald collaborated with Porter on a comic opera, studied with Fernand Leger, and in his own Paris studio painted beautifully flattened consumer products on large canvases. Sara organized and cared for her brood and all who visited, providing meals for the hungry and a shoulder for the weepers. These two have never before encountered an obstacle their money or their intelligence could not overcome. Now they face their son's illness with the same diligence and good humor with which they earlier planned beach parties.

The Murphys occupy six rooms, having brought themselves to the mountain with their three children, maid and chauffeur, an automobile, three dogs, eleven trunks, and seventeen suitcases, not to mention accouterments purchased locally. Each evening they and their old friends assemble to drink quiet gluhwein toasts while Patrick sleeps in the adjoining room, his infected lung collapsed by gas injections.[91] Turning to Sara, Scott says, "I don't suppose you have ever known despair?" Sara turns away, too angry to answer and too polite to show it.[92] No matter how charming Gerald and Sara appear, they cannot completely mask their distracted hearts, nor can their chilled guests evade the pall that fills the room. Of the four novelists and two humorists in the room, not one of them will ever write publicly about that evening or any other in the Palace Hotel, not even Fitzgerald, who has appropriated Sara and Gerald as characters for his novel in progress.

Two weeks earlier, in a borrowed New York City studio, the compulsive Harry Crosby lay down with a small pistol beside a consenting lover, whom he shot before putting a bullet into his own brain. Two days later, Archie MacLeish, after standing night vigil over Harry's body, wrote, "Recklessness and freedom of soul are dangerous things and those who condemn them condemn them with reason. As those who love them suffer for them. But without those fires lighted sometimes in the world it would be a dark and hopeless place."[93]

Chapter Two

1930

THE ARTIST'S REWARD

Key West, Cooke City, and Billings

SEVENTEEN UNPLEASANT DAYS at sea in a small ship, heaving and rolling through heavy swells, bring the Hemingways finally to freezing New York long enough to visit Ada MacLeish in the hospital, Max Perkins in his office, Henry Strater in his painter's studio, and one or two lawyers for good measure.[1] New York was full of literary gossip, which Ernest loved, and Max, laconic as ever, tried to ignore. With the pale blue eyes of a dreamer, his hat ever present indoors and out, its brim set back to amplify conversation for his poor hearing, Max Perkins was an unlikely man to edit Ernest Hemingway. In fact, he did little editing, which is why they got along as well as they did. Instead he was Ernest's corporate protector, confidant, banker, and private book buyer. When an advance was needed, Max signed the deposit slip; when Ernest raged against the realities of commerce, Max always responded in a lower register. With his inability to spell or punctuate correctly, Max seemed ill suited to his trade, but his passion for literature and his uncanny ability to bond with his authors made him the perfect editor for Hemingway. During this New York visit, Hemingway needed Max's help, but not with literary matters. With a loan from Uncle Gus and royalties from the first sixty thousand copies of *A Farewell to Arms*, Ernest established a trust fund for his mother, who once berated him for having overdrawn his emotional bank account with her.

At every turn in the city, someone wants a piece of him, for Ernest Hemingway is now a considerable property. The *New York Times Book Review* carried Scribner's block advertisement featuring *A Farewell to Arms* and Tom Wolfe's *Look Homeward, Angel*. Hemingway's novel, the ad said, "should have had a publishing season to itself. . . . It is so great a book that praise of it sounds like empty babbling." Despite the Wall Street panic, sales of the novel passed eighty thousand copies before Hemingway arrived.[2] Ernest's sometime literary agent, Paul Reynolds, is negotiating the theater version of the novel with the lawyer of playwright Lawrence Stallings and the lawyer of the producer Al Woods. This is the new country, the artist's reward, all quite flattering but not without its potential loss of freedom. With editor, publisher, lawyer, agent, wives and children, mother and siblings dependent upon his writing, he can feel the trap of responsibility beginning to close around him. Part of him still admires the fine homes and families of Oak Park, seeks the responsibility, wants to be called "Papa," the provider of largess, the giver of names, the man in the house. The other side of him is never easy in any place called home.

Two days in and out of New York with the *Bourdannais*, stopping only a day in Havana, they arrive finally in Key West on February 2.[3] While they and Henrietta Lechuer, Patrick's French nanny, move luggage into a rented frame house on Pearl Street, the sun is setting, and lights are coming on in kitchen windows. At Joe Russell's place near the waterfront, sailors are lining up at the bar; on Division Street, a Jesuit priest is patiently holding his fast in order to say evening Mass; on Amelia Street, the last cockfight is over and bets are being paid off. Black washerwomen leaving the Casa Marina Hotel, grizzled fishermen drinking cold beer at the Thompson Icehouse, children playing capture-the-flag in the Bayview park, grandfathers gathering at the Cuban consulate for dominoes, and sailors from the battleship *Maine* resting in the graveyard at the foot of Pauline Street: it is an ordinary evening, warm and without incident, in Key West. On Pearl Street, Ernest and Pauline sort out their scant belongings stored with the Thompsons a year earlier. Paris, Key West, Piggott, Kansas City, Sheridan, Chicago, Key West, Paris, Spain, Paris, Switzerland, Paris, Key West: for two years, they have not lived under one roof longer than a month or two at a time. Without knowing it, they have come to their *querencia*, that part of the ring where the bull feels secure. It is not home, but it feels like it.

Ernest has come to Key West to write and fish, in that order, but somehow it does not work out as imagined. Despite her new trust fund, his mother in Oak Park is not without needs: car insurance, new gutters, and taxes; his sister, Carol, needs tuition help at Rollins College. And when, his mother wants to know, when would she be told if her oil paintings would be in the Paris Spring Salon? Did he plan to have anyone let him know? "Drat her," said Hadley, his first wife, who was left with the paintings. "Not for me and the pictures but for you and everything. Thank God you are removed from her these days."[4] Easier to say than do: his mother, he found, was always with him. Call her a bitch as he might, Grace Hall Hemingway, former voice teacher, contralto, and now self-taught painter, was a force always in his life, and he was his mother's son.

At the same time, New England painter and old friend Waldo Peirce, in Paris settling a divorce from his wife Ivy, sent his very young, maybe too young, wife-to-be, Alzira, to Key West with money (but not enough money) to await his now delayed appearance. In a village so small, her unwed pregnancy became public information as soon as she went to the local doctor. Having lent her a little money and then more money, Ernest was trying to be helpful, but if Waldo was thinking of living with his Alzira out of wedlock in Key West, Ernest had to say,

> *What's simple as hell in Paris is complicated as same in U.S.A. or*
> *K.K.K. . . . if you're planning to stay somewhere and have a baby*
> *K.W. is too small a place now that you . . . are known by so many*
> *local merchants. . . . Guys like you and me that live and have lived*
> *around and don't give a damn what people say about anything so long*
> *as the law aint invoked are one thing and merchants that have to live*
> *on in a town and have people say to them "so your swell friends just*
> *turned out to be a bunch of scandalous bastards" are another.*[5]

The "merchants" referred to were Charles and Lorine Thompson, but
the voice speaking was from Oak Park; without yet admitting it to himself, Hemingway, too, was about to become a "local merchant."

To Peirce, he claimed Key West was no longer a place to work,
but it was largely because of his own invitations to friends that his
writing was disrupted. Mike Strater, Max Perkins, Pat Morgan,
John Herrmann and Josephine Herbst, John and Katy Dos Passos,
Archibald and Ada MacLeish all came down from New York. John
and Josie were there on their own initiative, but the others came at
Hemingway's calling: it is never enough to be in a good place without a gang of admirers to instruct. The Over Sea Hotel, at a dollar a
night, housed a steady flow of Hemingway customers, who are like
his summer people at Walloon Lake, like his Paris people at Pamplona, like the winter people on Swiss ski slopes. To Charles and
Lorine Thompson, trapped in Key West by the Thompson name and
its attendant responsibilities—icehouse, hardware and chandlery,
fish—the Hemingways are liberators who open doors to the wide
world. Charles plays younger brother to Ernest while Lorine becomes
Pauline's closest friend. The Hemingways need only ask, for no task
is inconvenient for the Thompsons, and the Hemingways do regularly ask. In Key West, whose population has dwindled almost by
half in a ten-year period and where the twelve thousand who remain
are largely down on their luck, the Hemingways and their entourage
are an unexpected windfall.

As usual, Hemingway does nothing by halves. While making enormous emotional demands upon those around him, he brings to them

his intensity. Waldo Peirce said that Hemingway "could make a fisherman for a day out of anyone." He was "the best host and sportsman and the most generous, always giving first chance to the visiting firemen and a more than even cut of Fundador [brandy]."[6] No visitor is left untouched. Archie MacLeish, referring to Ernest's impact on his poetry, said:

> *Every time I see you . . . I get a new revelation from god about the whole business—about why it's worth while to play as well as you can play to an empty house and an old gentleman in the last row. . . . somehow you make it all right for me to go on no matter how empty they make it on my side of the street. Also, goddam it, I like being with you. . . . As you saw I am no fisherman. But I got more out of those days on the water and my clumsy efforts at trolling than I've gotten out of anything in years. I can't get that day on the Gulf Stream out of my eyes.*[7]

Having hired Burge, a local fisherman, by the month for $130 to be his guide and paid another $125 a month for Burge's fishing boat, Ernest considers any day without fishing a day wasted. Add on the cost of liquor and gasoline, of food and rent, of loans to friends and family bills, and Hemingway's monthly expenditures, the jot and tittle of which he keeps exactly, mount up. In April he spent $1,200, which was only $100 less than the average 1930 income for full-time employees.[8] Given that his total earnings for 1929 were $18,416 with another $6,000 from Pauline's trust, the Hemingways were living and spending at a level far removed from his early Paris days or his earlier days in Oak Park.[9] He was, in fact, living even more intensely the life he once admired and sometimes envied of wealthier Oak Park families. In Key West—a village of peeling paint and outrageous flowering plants—with their small child, his French maid, and their seemingly endless flow of visitors, Ernest and Pauline were conspicuous among the usual winter visitors.

When the morning breeze picked up at sunrise, clearing out the night mosquitoes, Ernest began his Key West day at his writing tablet with pencil in hand. In May he finished the ending to "Wine of Wyoming," a curious marriage tale three-quarters written two years earlier. Low-key and oblique, the story contrasts husbands and wives, America and France, past and present against the background of prohibition. The Fontans are displaced French Catholics trying to live in Wyoming as if it were France. The narrator and his wife are summer people passing through a country that looks to them like Spain. It is a story of lost amenities, displaced customs, echoing Villon's rhetorical question "Where are the snows of yesteryear?" "The summer was ending," the narrator tells us, "but the new snow had not yet come to stay on the high mountains; there was only the old sun-melted snow and the ice, and from a long way away it shone very brightly."[10] American promises were always brightest from a distance. As Hemingway writes these words, morning heat is rising in the room. Soon he will begin to sweat.

To Waldo Peirce he writes, "My simple idea of coming to Key West to write and see no one and fish when through writing appeals to no one."[11] By May 20, despite complaints about Paris intruders, despite the wonderful time-consuming run of high-leaping tarpon and a six-stitch cut on his writing hand from the Thompson punching bag, Ernest has completed seventy-four pages[12] on a book like no other he knew, a book without models or comparisons, a book in several voices, many tenses, and doubling points of view. About many things—the rearing, fighting, and demise of bulls, a history of bullfighters, an explanation of their art, a guidebook to Spain, a discussion of writers and their craft, of critics and their shortcomings, a book of landscapes with and without figures, a philosophy of life in the lap of death, a Spanish food and wine digest—it is a discursive book of huge risks which no publisher would have encouraged had the author not been Ernest Hemingway. But he is Ernest Hemingway, and it is a book of natural and unnatural history which he must write to redeem himself from his self-phrased epithet: *Professional Writer, of which there is nothing lower*. Refusing to be merely a fiction writer, he insists here and later that he is a man of letters. Eventually he will call this book *Death in the Afternoon*.

As the Hemingways made plans to escape from the tropical heat to the high country of the west, Ernest wrote Uncle Gus the bene-factor, explaining what sort of a book he was writing and what he needed for reference. Gus immediately sent a shopping list to his Hudnut man in Barcelona, advising him that "Mr. Hemingway is very anxious to get the books." All he needed were subscriptions to four bullfight periodicals, bound back issues of four other periodi-cals, and a few crucial histories of tauromachia. The next day, wor-ried that the mail would take too long, Uncle Gus telegraphed his Barcelona man the list of books.[13] On June 7, Ernest put Pauline, Patrick, and Henrietta on the train to Jacksonville to connect for Pig-gott, and a week later, he stepped onto the Havana Special return-ing to New York to meet his five-year-old son, John Hadley Nicanor Hemingway, arriving from France.[14]

After checking into the Brevoort Hotel off Washington Square, Ernest has four days to take care of business. At the Scribner's offices on Fifth Avenue, Hemingway convinces Max Perkins that they should reissue his 1925 book, *In Our Time*, as it was written and meant to be read. To avoid having the book banned, Boni & Liveright, the original publishers, made Ernest take out the open-ing story, "Up in Michigan," and forced him to make changes to "Mr. and Mrs. Elliot." If they can strike a deal with Horace Liver-ight about the publishing rights, Ernest will provide revised copy for those two stories and perhaps write an introduction. Despite the depressed state of publishing and stiff competition from Doubleday with its "Dollar Books," reissuing was a sound idea, for fewer than fifteen hundred copies of the book were printed earlier. Max agrees without having seen either of the two censored stories; a hotter ver-sion of *In Our Time* would be good business, keeping the Heming-way market primed for his new book, which Max hopes to publish within a year, a book he has not seen and about which Hemingway is not forthcoming. Max may think it is a novel.

Hemingway also does some quick business with Louis Cohn, book dealer and sometime publisher, who wants to compile a bib-liography of Ernest's work to date. It will be a limited edition (five hundred copies) with a stiff price tag ($6). In April, Ernest said he might write an introduction for $350 "so long as I get it in cash and whenever I want it."[15] Now in June, he is having second thoughts. To become involved with limited editions or bibliographies of his own work, he tells Cohn, will jeopardize his artistic integrity, without which the game is not worth the play. He simply cannot write an introduction or sign any more books, but maybe Edmund Wilson or Allen Tate, both of whom he trusts, would write one.[16] To temper his response, he says he will provide a page of unpublished manuscript which could be reproduced.

On Saturday, June 21, the *Lafayette* arrives two days early, delivering Jinny Pfeiffer and Ernest's son, nicknamed Bumby. The next evening, father and son are once again riding the train west, getting off in Cincinnati, where Ernest picks up his Ford roadster, which friends from Key West have ferried that far, and drives on toward St. Louis and finally Piggott, Arkansas. Stopping long enough to deposit some manuscripts in the Piggott bank, play son-in-law to Paul Pfeiffer's polite interest, and share a drink with Mother Pfeiffer, the Catholic center of the family, he walks dusty roads for morning exercise before the heat rises. It has been a dry, hot, early summer; cotton bolls are puny in the green fields, but he sees and counts the coveys of quail. Complaining to MacLeish of forty consecutive hot nights with little sleep, he is eager for the cool Wyoming mountains. "It will be fine in the mountains—need like hell to work too."[17]

Two days later, after leaving baby Patrick in Piggott with his grandparents and Aunt Jinny, Ernest, Pauline, and Bumby are off for Kansas City, where they stop with Ernest's cousins long enough for Dr. Guffey to say Pauline is well recovered from her cesarean delivery. When the journalist from the *Star* finds him, Ernest claims to be working on a new novel with bullfighting as the background.[18] After Kansas City, they disappear into the great American plains of corn, then wheat, then cattle, all languid under the summer sun, finally gaining altitude with the nights cooling. Making less than fifteen miles to the gallon at thirty to forty miles an hour top speed on two-lane roads, oiled or graveled, they bounce along, eye always out for the next filling station, a decent café, a likely tourist cabin for the night. They cross a sun-blistered Nebraska and drive into Wyoming's grass and cattleland—Casper, Salt Creek, Buffalo, Sheridan—looking for a place to write. But places that worked two summers before are now too civilized with eastern dudes who are charmed to meet an author. They move farther west up through Billings and into Yellowstone Park, through that wonderland and out the northeast corner, coming finally on a dirt road into Cooke City, Montana: end of the line; the only road in or out has grass growing between dusty ruts. Sometimes a load of whiskey on muleback comes over the Beartooth Pass from Red Lodge; sometimes, given a very good reason, a truck might make it southeast to Cody on rough ranch roads. But these few log cabins, frame houses, filling station, and general store are west of the mail, west of publishers, west of gossip, west of mothers, siblings, in-laws, west of almost everything. The Cosmopolitan Hotel, weather-beaten and largely empty, remembers better days. Surrounding this smattering of buildings, the Absaroka Range rises up like a rocky green and stone dream of mountains, with granite uplifts sheltering snow in the high crevices. In four weeks, by train and by car, Hemingway has traveled five thousand miles across the American landscape, arriving finally at this remote mining outpost on the edge of Yellowstone where there is no morning paper, no rail line, and no exit after the first snows fall.

———

L-Bar-T Ranch, July 13. Follow the ranch's station wagon east from town on a faintly etched road, crossing the Wyoming line and turning south along Clarks Fork with Pilot and Index peaks over the right shoulder, and then cross the river at the second ranch. The bridge of pine planks suspended on cables anchored to each side bucks, rattles, and sways beneath the car. Just beyond a smooth stone outcropping, the lodgepole barn and corrals with mustangs at rest, farther on the ranch house cum lodge with cabins fanned out above. Like every other building on the dude ranch, their double cabin—two bedrooms, one toilet, and a cold shower—is made of pine logs notched and fitted at the corners and caulked at the seams. Banked on the small porch, a pile of split wood is ready for the potbellied stove.[19]

———

For a month they disappear into the daily routine of the ranch: early breakfast in the lodge, writing all morning for Ernest, fishing on the river after lunch, early-evening supper in the lodge with Lawrence and Olive Nordquist attending to the several paying guests, and whiskey afterward in the heavy chairs around the fireplace. Situated at 6,800 feet on the floodplain of the Clarks Fork of the Yellowstone River, the ranch is sheltered by Squaw Peak rising to ten thousand feet behind it and the Beartooth Mountains at eleven thousand feet across the river. Along the Fork, creeks enter the flow, their names speaking of earlier days: Crazy Creek, Pilot Creek, Ghost and Beartooth creeks, Blacktail, Timber, and Hoodoo creeks. Here every turn and rise has its particular name, given to it by men and women now forgotten: Sugarloaf Mountain, Cathedral Cliffs, Painter Gulch, Beartooth Butte, Dead Indian Ranch. River and valley take their name from Lewis and Clark, whose expedition first brought eastern eyes to rest on this country whose richness exceeded all expectations.

Terrain maps, filled with detail, are Hemingway's travel companions, even in this newfound country where the geodetic survey is quite recent. Names of creeks, heights of mountains, distances between ranches, the direction of roads and rivers all matter to him. It is good to know where you are, where you have been, where you are going. It is even better to have some detail of it afterward: he records mileage driven, money paid, books read, and fish caught. He does not need a compass or a map to tell him the river runs east-southeast in front of the ranch. But afterward the map will be there to confirm memory and aid creation if he is writing. Having fished one steep canyon with gravel siding impossible to climb, he can read the map of a never-fished river canyon and understand it almost as well as the first. In his new fishing log, Ernest makes detailed notes on each day's catch, baits used, numbers taken, weights, and stream conditions. Rain or shine he fishes the river, horsing in the trout, netting small trout high out of the water without bending to meet them. His form is a little disappointing. When it rains, he notes how long it takes the river to clear. On his birthday, July 21, he and Pauline release fourteen and keep eighteen cutthroat trout. The next day, Pauline's birthday, returning from the river they see a fat black bear walking down the dirt road.[20]

On a marker tree beside One-Mile Creek where it passes a few hundred yards above the Hemingways' cabin, a bear's claw marks reach higher than a man's head. In mid-August, according to Hemingway's hunting log, a local rancher needed help with a "large old male bear" who was killing cattle high up off Crandall Creek. How much help was needed may be questioned, but that was the excuse for outfitting Ernest for a bear hunt out of season. On August 17, well attended by Nordquist's cowhand, Ivan Wallace, Ernest rode the now familiar pack trail southeast along Squaw Creek to the Crandall Ranger Station. From there the North Fork trail rising into mountains narrows as it passes under Hunter's Peak and into a rugged forest of fir, whitebark pine, and spruce based on volcanic rock. The trail, becoming little more than an animal path, crosses Blacktail and Cow creeks before it drops down through switchbacks to the North Fork of Crandall's Creek. Here Ernest and the redheaded Ivan shoot the old horse they brought in for bait and leave it to "rise." That was on Sunday. By Wednesday morning, predators are feeding on the carcass; in that rare air at eight thousand feet, odors intensify and the heart pounds, but no bear shows. By Tuesday night, Ernest is back at the L-Bar-T, without a bear but still eager for the hunt. Friday morning, reoutfitted with fresh supplies, his new Springfield rifle, Zeiss field glasses, and a raincoat, he and three ranch hands set out again for the bear bait. Before they reach the ranger station, Ernest's horse bolts, lurching him through a pine thicket that lays open the left side of his face, blood dripping and the horse spooked. A bandage won't do. He needs stitches, and the closest doctor is fifty miles away in Cody. By midnight, having traveled the unspeakable dirt ranch road through countless gates in a car rented from the ranger, they are in Dr. Trueblood's office, where the veterinarian turned doctor sews up Hemingway's wound with six stitches, using a little whiskey taken internally as anesthetic. A white bandage now swaddles his jaw and the left side of his face. The resulting scar will add to his bulging forehead scar from the falling Paris skylight, the one on his finger from the Key West punching bag, and the scars on his rebuilt right knee and his right foot from the war.

Returning through the Wyoming night, they are back at the ranger station by morning. That evening at the horse bait, as the light is about to fail completely, with the brown bear in the telescopic sight of his new rifle, Ernest is letting out his breath slowly and squeezing the Springfield's trigger with an even pull, and then the bear falling in slow motion. A week later, on the same ripe bait, he kills a second bear. Ernest, camera-shy and proud, stands beside the huge black pelt stretched upon the cabin wall. Admirers stroke the glossy fur.[21] Nine years later he will remember Clarks Fork Valley with trout rising to dry flies, remember waking in the cold night with coyotes howling. "You could ride in the morning, or sit in front of the cabin, lazy in the sun, and look across the valley where the hay was cut so the meadows were cropped brown and smooth to line of quaking aspens along the river, now turning yellow in the fall." The years blend together into one year with all the good days combined: "all the hunting and all the fishing and the riding in the summer sun and the dust of the pack-train, the silent riding in the hills in the sharp cold of fall going up after the cattle on the high range, finding them wild as deer and as quiet, only bawling noisily when they were all herded together being forced along down into the lower country."[22]

Evenly spaced along the Fork are ranches similar to Nordquist's, most of which were homesteaded at 320 or 640 acres: not enough land to raise cattle and too far from the market if you did. Some raised horses, but with little profit. Others, like Nordquist, caught hold of the dude-ranch craze bringing soft-seated East Coast families west for summer vacations. By putting on a little show for the summer dudes and picking up some hunters in the fall, a man could get by. Give the guests an evening cookout on the trail, ponies tethered and campfire smoking, or a makeshift rodeo in the high meadow where bangtails buck the boys about faster than a dude's camera can pan the field.[23]

Rising up under blankets to the odor of pine smoke and frying bacon, the air cool and resinous, Pauline standing there with her hands in her hip pockets, ready for whatever, Ernest watches the wranglers get dudes saddled up for the morning run, smells horse piss in the straw. This is country without a phone or electricity where the mail comes once a week, and no one particularly cares one way or another if Ernest spends his mornings writing, afternoons fishing, evenings reading. His contemplative and his active life are jammed together so tightly that only minutes separate them. By the end of July he is talking about having his bullfight book finished before the November snows force him out. Brave self-promises on a difficult book. He takes time to write Louis Cohn, promising that as soon as his "book trunk" arrives he will send a page of manuscript for the Hemingway bibliography Cohn is putting to press. "Thank you so much for the offer of the Galsworthy Conrad," he tells Cohn, "but it is doubtless too valuable for you to give. I'll take the Scotch or Rye and let the first editions go." Then he adds, "nor heed the rumble of the distant drums."[24]

The Nordquist ranch provides the conditions in which he works best and steadily, for he prefers to write in transient places, close to the natural world. *The Sun Also Rises* was written on the road in Spain, following the bullfights; *A Farewell to Arms* was drafted under transatlantic and transcontinental circumstances. At Nordquist's, five minutes after setting down his pencil he can be on a horse, or within twenty minutes his line is in the water. He arrived at the ranch with seventy-four pages of manuscript drafted on a book without a title and with problems to solve about the new edition of *In Our Time*. A month later he tells Max Perkins he is writing six days out of seven and has forty thousand words done, roughly another fifty pages of manuscript. By early September he is on page 174 or about sixty thousand words.[25] Max wants new material added to *In Our Time*, but Ernest is uncomfortable jazzing up an old book with new stories written in a different manner. Nor does he want Max Perkins rear-ranging the stories or grouping together all the vignettes which divide the stories: "Max *please believe me* that those chapters are where they belong."[26] However, his earliest story, which he was forced to cut out of the 1925 version of the book—"Up in Michigan," a brutal seduction story told from the woman's point of view—he tries to revise, but the scene with the drunken Jim Gilmore forcing himself on Liz Coates and her being left with the pain and the ignorance becomes less readable the more he fiddles with it. Finally he gives up, telling Perkins, "I know you will not publish it with the last part entire and if any of that is out there is no story." He has promised Max to have mailed the book with corrections, including the original, uncensored version of "Mr. and Mrs. Elliot" and "with or without a couple of short pieces of the same period depending on how these seem in the book between now and then."

But he cannot write the preface Max wants for the collection of short stories. "I am too busy," he said, "too disinterested, too proud or too stupid or whatever you want to call it to write one for it." Determined to resist as much of the whoring expected of "Professional Writers" as he can, Hemingway suggested Edmund Wilson for the job.[27] Looking for other material from the 1922–25 period which might honestly meld into *In Our Time*, Hemingway remembers "The Death of the Standard Oil Man," an unpublished story set during the Greco-Turkish War of 1922. But in August when his "book trunk" arrives from Piggott, the manuscript is not there. Instead he finds a story about the Greeks at Smyrna in 1922 when the Turks were about to burn that town, a story written in late 1926.[28] Its doubled narration—a reporter telling the reader what a British officer at Smyrna said—pulls the reader quickly through the page into the fiction. Ernest, who was never in Smyrna, knew reporters who saw and wrote of the Greeks breaking "the legs of the baggage and transport animals" and shoving them "off the quay into the shallow water."[29] It was a strong piece with refugees jammed on the quay and Greek mothers refusing to give up dead babies and "nice" debris floating in the water. It fit with the other stories like the Elliots trying but unable to have a baby, and the bloody cesarean operation at the Indian camp, war sketches with the dead in the street, and Nick having to return to the States because of his pregnant wife, the punchy boxer that night by the rail line, and Nick ending up after the war not quite right on Big Two-Hearted River.

On September 3, Hemingway mailed Perkins a corrected copy of *In Our Time*, including a somewhat sanitized version of "Mr. and Mrs. Elliot" and the Smyrna sketch, which he agreed to call "Introduction by the Author," which would follow the introduction he hoped Edmund Wilson would write because someone had to explain that this was an early book. His accompanying letter was a confusion of disclaimers: reissuing the book was Scribner's idea, not his, although it was a good book, but should not be called a "new" book; however, they could say it had new material, yet giving the readers an old book now would probably hurt sales of his bullfight book to follow (174 pages written). And Scribner's better check for libel, because they published this book at their own risk; he would give no guarantees against lawsuits. Sick of the interruptions caused by this reprint of *In Our Time*, he would take days to get back into the bullfight book.[30]

He was also working on an experimental story told in two voices and several parts, a story not unlike the bullfight book. The story began with a naturalist commenting, tongue in cheek, on the work of earlier observers of flora and fauna, complaining that war dead were ignored by natural historians. "Can we not hope to furnish the reader with a few rational and interesting facts about the dead?" he asked. The second paragraph, which he lifted word for word from Bishop Stanley's *A Familiar History of Birds* (1881), told of Mungo Park, on the brink of death in the African desert, finding God's fingerprints in a small moss-flower. Hemingway's naturalist asks, "Can any branch of Natural History be studied without increasing that faith, love and hope which we also, every one of us, need in our journey through the wilderness of life? Let us see what inspiration we may derive from the dead."[31]

Similar in theme to the vignette of the refugees on the Smyrna quay, which it references, but written in a different style, "A Natural History of the Dead" was an experiment in both structure and voice. The first half developed the premise; the second half illustrated the premise with an example. The narrator, a veteran out of the last war, speaks in a sardonic voice and with the detachment of a natural historian observing the dead bodies on the Italian front of 1918. Bodies left unburied go from "white to yellow, to yellow-green, to black." Left long enough in the sun, "the flesh comes to resemble coal tar," and swells inordinately, straining at the confining uniform. Everywhere there is paper of the dead blowing in the wind. And the smell of the unburied dead, mixed with the lingering odor of mustard gas, one cannot forget.

Nothing the narrator has seen gives him much cause to rejoice in God's presence in the natural world. Soldiers die like animals, some from wounds seemingly slight but deep enough to serve. Others "die like cats: a skull broken in and iron in the brain, they lie alive two days like cats that crawl into the coal bin with the bullet in the brain and will not die until you have cut off their heads." This observation leads him to an extended illustration: a mountain field station with wounded bodies and an overworked doctor. The dead are carried into a cold-storage cave; one of the badly wounded, "whose head was broken as a flower pot may be broken" and who was presumed dead, lies in the dark, moaning, like the cat refusing to die. Under pressure of the wounded crowding the station, the doctor refuses to move the dying man out of the cave, having no way of making his suffering less nor the faintest hope of saving his life. No, he will not give him an overdose of morphine, he tells a wounded artillery officer. He has little enough to operate with now. The officer can shoot the man if he wishes. Doctor and patient trade insults until the artilleryman loses all composure. "Fuck yourself," he said. "Fuck yourself. Fuck your mother. Fuck your sister. . . ." At which point the doctor throws iodine into his eyes, disarms him, and has him restrained. Meanwhile the moaning man in the cave of the dead has become permanently quiet. "A dispute about nothing," the doctor calls it.[32]

The story was not finished on September 13, when Ernest and

Pauline, preparatory to her going east with Bumby, signed new wills. His money went to Pauline, Patrick, and John, in that order. If they were dead, the estate was payable in equal shares to his first wife, Hadley, and his sister-in-law, Jinny Pfeiffer. His Italian war medals should go first to John and then to Hadley. The will did not mention Hadley's divorce settlement—all the income from *The Sun Also Rises*—nor did it mention what he expected her to do with the war medals.[33] Two days later in Billings, Pauline and Bumby boarded the Burlington train for Chicago and from there, connections to St. Louis. It was time for her stepson to return to his mother in Paris; Henrietta, their French nursemaid, would act as his traveling companion. That same day the fall hunting season opened, and Ernest's bullfight book was 188 pages of dense manuscript.[34] In two months at the ranch, he averaged about two pages a day. Over the next forty-five days, with only one fruitless hunt in the high mountains and customary afternoons of grouse shooting to take his mind off the book, Ernest completed another hundred pages of manuscript. He was close to the end: two more chapters and the appendix, he told Max.[35] Meanwhile, his public visibility was increasing dramatically: *A Farewell to Arms* was being translated into French and German; the Lawrence Stallings stage version of the novel was about to open on Broadway; and Paramount Pictures purchased the film rights to the novel for $80,000.[36]

———

November 1, Route 10 outside of Park City, Montana. Gently rising and falling as it follows the north bank of the Yellowstone out of sight in the dark, the two-lane road is empty except for a Ford roadster with two bearded men in the front seat and a third in the rumble seat. Hemingway drives. Next to him sits John Dos Passos, on his way to Billings to catch the night train east. Floyd Allington from Red Cloud is hunkered down in back. A diminished bottle of bourbon is shared against the cold, as the sun sets behind them and blue shadows go black. Fresh gravel laid down the day before is not yet properly rolled or settled, and the center line is not marked. With the lights of Laurel faint over the far hill, a car approaches, its lights bright; Hemingway, his night vision marred by a weak eye, blinks and moves the Ford as far right as seems safe. Someone is speaking, but with the noise of the engine and tires on gravel, it is difficult to hear.[37]

———

In the Saturday-night emergency room of St. Vincent Hospital, Dorothy Buller checks in for her night shift duties to find three strangers, two in pain, one of them seriously hurt. Bob Bass is telling someone how he helped pull the big fella from the overturned Ford out on the Livingston road and gave all three a ride into Billings. The Red Lodge cowboy, with a dislocated right shoulder and a few scratches, is taped up and sedated. The larger, darkly bearded man with the broken arm is being taken to x-ray. The third man, also bearded but unhurt, his glasses unbroken, wants to know if his friend's money belt is missing. Nurse Buller assures him that no one has touched anyone's money belt.[38]

On Sunday morning in Piggott, Arkansas, Pauline receives the telegram from Dos Passos telling her that Ernest is in the hospital injured. Packing quickly and putting her own problems on hold, she leaves Piggott Monday morning, reaching Billings on the Tuesday-evening train.[39] By this time Ernest is no longer in the three-person ward where he spent his first night. When Dr. Louis Allard, an orthopedic surgeon recognized nationally for his work on polio victims, discovered that his patient was Ernest Hemingway, he immediately moved him into a private fourth-floor room; when Pauline arrives, he moves him again, across the hall to 421, so that she can stay in the adjoining room. On Thursday, Dr. Allard operates to restructure the oblique spiral fracture three inches above Ernest's right elbow. Using kangaroo tendon to bind tight his bone work, the surgeon sews up his nine-inch incision and immobilizes Hemingway for three weeks to let the fracture heal properly.

That afternoon the *Billings Gazette* announces that Sinclair Lewis has won the Nobel Prize for literature, and off-year election results

are being posted across the country. Democrats are close to breaking the Republican control in both houses of Congress, and Governor Franklin Roosevelt of New York is returned to Albany by a
record plurality.[40] In steady, gnawing pain from the repaired fracture, Hemingway is not particularly interested in literary or political
prizes. After the fifth day, the doctor takes him off the morphine,
leaving him alone with the pain and his night thoughts.[41] For three
weeks unable to move for fear of ruining his writing arm, he has
plenty of time to think, too much time. He has been there before,
badly wounded in the Milan hospital twelve years earlier, worrying
then whether he might lose his leg, and sometimes now in the night
he wonders which hospital he is in this time. He is, Pauline says,
"pretty nervous and depressed from the pain and worry." Once again
he is sleeping fitfully by day and lying awake in the night. Not even
Pauline, with her seemingly inexhaustible capacity for tending to
his needs, can stay on his schedule. Tall, stately Harriet O'Day, the
special nurse assigned to him, provides the small bedside radio that,
along with a little prohibition whiskey from his well-stocked bar, gets
him through the nights.[42]

Three days after Hemingway's operation, two new patients, Martin Costello and Alec Youck, are moved into the ward across the hall
from Hemingway's room. In the Surita Café, Costello and Youck had
been shot by an unknown assailant. Youck, a Russian farm worker,
was hit in the thigh, but not seriously. The *Gazette* said that Costello,
a Mexican beet worker, might die from the bullet that passed through
his stomach. The newspaper said:

> *Two men . . . were arrested . . . Thomas Hernando, restaurant cook,
> and Joe Aglo, who lived in a room above the restaurant. A box of car-
> tridges was found in Aglo's room. . . . Arriving at the café, [Constable]
> Thomas found Youck on the floor in a rear room. At the foot of the
> stairs . . . Thomas found Aglo and Hernando supporting Costello who
> was bleeding profusely. . . . Costello . . . refused to talk of the shoot-
> ing. Officers recalled that three years ago when a bullet wounded the
> arm of a girl with whom he was walking and tore into his coat sleeve,*

he also refused at that time to name the person who fired the shot.
. . . Joe Diaz, operator of the Surita café and the rooms above . . . said
he knew nothing about any quarrel in which Costello might have
figured. Mrs. Diaz was at the café when Constable Thomas arrived,
but she, too, said she knew nothing of the shooting. Questioning of
persons in the vicinity elicited no further information.

The cartridges found in Aglo's room were .32 caliber, the same caliber as the slug removed from Costello's stomach, but no weapon was recovered. Four days later, the police gave up their investigation. The beet worker, the cook, the Russian, and the boarder all said they had no idea who the gunman might have been.[43]

Now Hemingway has something new to think about as he gets regular reports from the nurses on Costello's condition and his continuing refusal to name his attacker. The Russian groans a good deal the first few days, but Costello, with drain tubes hanging from his stomach, keeps his suffering to himself. Sometimes the wounded man's Spanish-speaking visitors share drinks with Ernest; sometimes they borrow his Spanish newspapers. Eventually they will all become part of his fiction, but then in the cold November, with the days beginning below zero and the light failing early, the wounded Mexican and his friends are a pleasant break in the monotony. By the end of the month, his pain has subsided enough for him to become difficult and abrasive: he dictates a querulous letter to Max Perkins, wondering if there is some special reason they are keeping Edmund Wilson's introduction from him, and where are the books he ordered?[44]

Hemingway's prominence and sometimes good humor, which he is able to maintain for the nurses and doctors, make him a remarked-upon and pampered guest for whom the Catholic Sisters of Charity who operate the hospital cannot do enough. Particularly drawn to him is Sister Florence Cloonan, who brings in his daily mail and who, in her "tin Lizzie," is well known on the streets of Billings. "When you saw her coming," one of the nuns said, "everybody moved to the other side of the street." With Ernest, Sister Florence speaks passionately about the baseball season past and the college football season just closing. Connie Mack's Philadelphia Athletics and Knute Rockne's Notre Dame are the two teams upon whose success her life seems to depend as she followed them religiously on the radio. "Because of a heart condition, she wasn't supposed to become excited. When a baseball game became particularly unnerving, she'd take refuge in the hospital chapel and pray until she was calm and could return to her post beside the radio."[45]

As November turns into even colder December, Hemingway is finally able to move about, his arm tightly wrapped and immobilized in a sling that looks as if it were made from bedsheets. The damaged nerves which have made his writing hand useless keep him ever edgy. By a low light, he reads late, devouring the book shipment from Perkins: Somerset Maugham's *Cakes and Ale*; Arthur Train's mystery *The Adventures of Ephraim Tut*; Dorothy Sayers's *Omnibus of Crime*; *The Real War 1914–1918*; and O'Flaherty's *Two Years*.[46] From Billings and Denver newspapers and from sketchy radio news, he is more in touch with his native land than he was during the previous four months at the ranch. In Cuba and Spain, revolutions flare up with the governments killing their own people in the streets. President Hoover, in his State of the Union address, tells the nation that it faces an enormous $180 million deficit, making any tax relief unlikely. Moreover, he asks Congress for an extra $150 million to spend on public works to reduce rising unemployment. Smelling fresh pork in the barrel, congressmen and senators bicker for almost two months over where the money will be spent. Meanwhile, no one in or out of the government can say exactly how many people are "idle," or how many banks have already closed.[47] In spite of which, radio crooners urge the country to sing "Bye, Bye Blues" and "Get Happy" because everything is "Fine and Dandy" "On the Sunny Side of the Street."[48]

Neither fine nor sunny could describe Hemingway's mood as the year's end approaches. His right arm remains splinted and useless in a sling, his wrist paralyzed from a stretched or pinched nerve, and the pain still a steady throb. Under the green fluoroscope, Dr. Allard shows him where the bone is mending, but when the feeling in his wrist will return is anyone's guess.[49] His few letters are dictated to Pauline, who types them as he speaks, but it is impossible for him to dictate the bullfight book.

Being a doctor's son, he always exaggerates his illnesses and is quick to project the worst possible scenario—traits which sometimes lead those who know him well to underestimate the seriousness of his condition. For the nurses he can always joke, but when Archie MacLeish, alarmed by the accident, flies into Billings from New York to comfort Hemingway, a hazardous two-day trip on Northwest Airlines, Ernest is surly and suspicious, accusing his friend of coming only to be present at his death. Maybe it was a joke, but Archie does not think so. The next day, he is a different Ernest, the one who would never have said such a thing and who carries on, in fact, as if he had not. A month later, MacLeish gave Max Perkins his report on Hemingway:

> He suffered very real & unrelenting pain over a long time. I went out because I know how his imagination works when his health is concerned & because I thought any normal event such as the arrival of a friend might give him some kind of a date to hold on to. When I got there the pain was largely over & the wound beginning to heal. . . . I think all his friends can do is to keep him cheerful in idleness—a hell of a job. Poor Pauline.[50]

A friend of Max Perkins who was visiting while Archie was there found Hemingway "pale and shaky although cheerful. . . . We drank a couple of bottles of Canadian beer. . . . I sent him up four mallards and some trout again."[51]

Facing what might be six months of physical therapy to rehabilitate his badly weakened arm, Hemingway finally admits to himself and MacLeish, whom he invited along all expenses paid, that he will not be able to go on an African safari in 1931. Gus Pfeiffer, his private banker, put up $25,000 of stock to underwrite Ernest's dream of African hunting, a dream he has nurtured since, as a ten-year-old, he followed in the magazines and on the movie screen the African hunting adventures of his hero Teddy Roosevelt. Now in Billings, with snow falling and Christmas decorations up in the halls, Africa is as remote as the moon. Ernest dictates a letter to Henry Strater, the New York painter, saying his promise of a paid-up safari is still good, but they will have to put it off for a year. In letters he can joke about being an "ex-writer," but it is a hollow joke.[52]

Early on the morning of December 21, Ernest and Pauline warm themselves in the Billings railway station, waiting for the eastbound Burlington train to arrive. Late the next evening they will be in Kansas City, and the following morning in St. Louis, to be met by Pauline's father, who will drive them on to a Piggott Christmas. Outside falling snow is accumulating in empty streets as the Zephyr pulls into the station. On Christmas Eve when they arrive in Piggott, he is running a fever; weak from two months in the hospital bed, he goes back to bed in his in-laws' house, where he never felt at home, not that feeling "at home" was ever a particularly calming experience for him. He cannot write left-handed, nor can he dictate. This he tells Owen Wister in a letter dictated to Pauline, who types as he talks. As for writing about a real person, as Wister did in his Roosevelt book, it could not be done well. "You can't recreate a person," Ernest says, "you can only create a character in writing. You can record an actual person's actions and recreate them in a sense, i.e. present them through this recording but it takes great detail."[53] As a constant reader of histories and biographies, he speaks as much to himself as to Wister, and speaking, perhaps, to others to follow. His book in progress, a study of the bullfight and a good deal more, is built on details small, numerous, yet selective, and didn't he always work that way, choosing the telling detail from the welter of possibilities?

Chapter Three

1931

ON THE ROAD AGAIN

Key West, Havana, Pamplona, Kansas City

ACROSS OLD AND new Spain that winter and early spring, revolutionists are at work. In Nicaragua, when the capital goes down in an earthquake, out of the ruins rise up the Sandinistas once again, killing nine Americans and several native sons. To the halls of Montezuma, President Hoover sends more U.S. Marines, and to Honduras where other American citizens are caught in a revolution, he dispatches the Navy. Bombs rock the colonial heart of Havana, where newspapers close overnight, their editors no longer to be found in the cafés. The university is shut down, and a young student, jailed on charges of attempting to kill President Machado, hangs himself in his prison cell. By the end of March, the streets of Madrid are stained with the blood of students in revolt.[1]

The Hemingways return to Key West, seeking shelter, a quiet place in which to recover the use of Ernest's writing arm and Pauline's composure. Very slowly, sometimes so slowly he does not believe in it, his arm improves, sensations returning to his fingers. Typing awkwardly with his left hand, he tells his mother-in-law that their next car will be one guaranteed to kill the driver when it goes into a ditch instead of leaving him a nuisance to everyone.[2] As for composure, Pauline's is sorely tested by too many visitors and the worst winter anyone in Key West can remember. January sets record low temperatures that keep their quarters continuously chilled. The old house on Whitehead Street, "out near the mullet seller," rents for only $25 a month, but its large, poorly insulated rooms are impossible to heat. The wettest February on Key West record is worse, crowding them and their guests too tightly together.[3]

During the six months since their last visit to Key West, the quality of life here has visibly declined. Some say that it cannot drop much lower, but that is before the best baker in town shoots himself, and someone, never named, ambushes one of the local dairy's cows to butcher a haunch of meat.[4] Elsewhere, out of sight but not far from mind, rural banks across the country close their doors, unable to refund deposits to bewildered citizens. Good times and bad always cycle, politicians say. Four million people may be out of work, but work will return. It always returns, Republicans promise. Any public relief program, according to President Hoover, is indefensible, for "federal aid for the distressed would strike at the root of government." He is certain that the Red Cross can "take care of the drought and the unemployment situation." And to prove it he gives $7,500 to the Red Cross relief fund.[5] Into the Key West harbor that January came a bounty of luxury yachts—the *Placida*, the *Arcadia*, and twenty-six others from the northeast—an addition to the economy but calling attention to the disparity between those with and those without means to make ends meet. By February, the town is on the verge of bankruptcy, unable to collect enough taxes to pay the firefighters whose intent to walk out is a serious threat to a wooden, windswept town. The firemen compromise, taking $25 and a promise of more when tax collection improves, which it does not. With a delinquent tax sale hanging over several Key West homes, fear of displacement is real. Boston, Newport, and New York money is moving into town, changing the faces and voices on the winter streets.[6]

Some locals leave town. Some despair. But if a man has access to a boat, he can make risky money during prohibition on the Havana run, ninety miles across the water, where liquor is cheap. Sometimes, in the dark of the moon, a man simply "borrows" a boat. In February, officials from the Key West customs house pick up a "missing" boat and 263 quarts of liquor. In a town where every boat's owner is widely known, this owner is never identified.[7] Key West protects its own. The grand jury might point out that over the last four years only eighty-five prosecutions involving gambling and prohibition laws have taken place, but that does not mean that anything is going to change.[8] As frequenters of the numerous small holes in the wall ("blind pigs") that sell Cuban rum, the sheriff's men occasionally make a show of rounding up a few locals, but not enough to slow business. Federal law out of Miami once in a while comes to town, but the grapevine intelligence system usually keeps the obvious places on Duval Street well warned. When the system fails, it is Key West news:

12 ARRESTED HERE TODAY IN

RAID BY U.S. DRY OFFICERS

RAIDERS COME IN BY BOAT AND TRAIN AND

SWOOP WITHOUT WARNING ON NUMEROUS PLACES[9]

Later that month, two well-known Key Westers—Henry Hollerich and Albert Taylor—are arrested in Havana for violating quarantine and maritime laws of Cuba. They were running booze and Chinese aliens through the Bahamas and into Miami. Ever since Congress, reflecting the national fear of "the yellow horde," reduced the Asian immigrant quota to near zero, Havana's Chinatown has exported illegals this way.[10]

———

Early March, Key West to the Dry Tortugas. From Garrison Bight, where small boats harbor, follow the ferry route out northwest channel, bearing west and passing just above the Marquesas Keys and across the edge of the quicksand where the *Valbanera* went down. On a clear day you can see her hull in the sand. Then bear west northwest from Rebecca Shoal until the brick fort appears low and square on the horizon. Watch the markers coming up on Garden Key, because it shallows up real fast around Fort Jefferson, and any storm can shift the bottom. It's fifty miles more or less. With wind out of the east, an easy trip going out, slow coming back.

———

All that winter while his arm healed and its damaged nerve restored itself, Ernest tended to guests who arrived, overlapped, and left entertained. To their rented house[11] came relatives and friends. From New York came Mike Strater, Max Perkins, Uncle Gus, and Aunt Louise Pfeiffer:[12] Strater and Perkins came for fishing and male camaraderie; Gus to check on his investment, encourage the postponed African safari, and suggest the Hemingways buy a Key West house for which he would put up the money. From Oak Park, Ernest's mother arrived for a two-day visit, the first time he has seen her since they buried his father;[13] his nineteen-year-old sister, Carol, a scholarship student at Rollins College, came down from Winter Park, Florida. Jinny Pfeiffer came, as did John Hermann and Josie Herbst, both writers wintering that year in Key West. From the L-Bar-T came Lawrence and Olive Nordquist for a visit, and their ranch hand, Chub Weaver, who drove the now-repaired Ford down from Billings.

They all come to see Ernest, who does not disappoint them. Until the nerve in his right arm regenerates, he can neither write nor fish, but he can take the citizens out in rented boats, work the line until he has a strike, then turn the rod over to one of them.[14] But the coldest January in twenty-five years makes it "a bad winter for fishing— one norther after another—never more than 2 successive fishing days between."[15] So when the big sailfish hit the teaser skipping on the surface, he is happy to see it; when it took the bait, he asks Chub Weaver to set the hook before giving the rod to Pauline. As with so much of their increasingly famous lives, the event does not go unnoticed:

Sailfish records for the present season were climaxed Monday when Mrs. Ernest Hemingway, wife of the noted author, captured one that upon accurate measurement showed a length of seven feet and one inch. Mr. and Mrs. Hemingway have spent a number of consecutive winters in Key West. They are credited with a number of remarkable catches.[16]

But he cannot turn over his book for someone else to reel in, the book he has not been able to write now for five months. All that late winter in Key West, as he instructs, arranges, and worries, the nerve slowly comes back, the arm recovers; the book of the bulls, however, remains dormant.

If some days he is surly, most visitors forgive him. But after what he said to John Hermann returning from the Dry Tortugas, Josie Herbst neither forgave Ernest nor forgot the way her husband folded before him; she was not a woman who accepted his "lord of the manor" domination with as much patience as the men. Nor had she particularly enjoyed the two previous weeks making small talk with Pauline, with whom she had little in common, and trying to be amused by young Patrick, who was fraying her nerves. She had not come to the moonlit island to be left alone by her husband. At thirty-eight, Josie Herbst, nine years older than John, looks even older. In the photograph, her pale eyes, once so attractive, are now sunken and circled; John looks more like her son than her mate. When he, who is quickly becoming an alcoholic, and Bra Saunders, who seldom refuses a drink, show up in a small boat from the Tortugas to fetch ice for three hundred pounds of fish about to spoil, Josie returns with them and later wishes she had not. Despite the four days it has taken John and Bra to make the one-day round-trip, John, Josie, Bra, and the ice arrive in time to save the fish but not the Hermann marriage, which crumbles under Ernest's sarcasm, mocking John's failures. "Look, the expert seaman afraid of a little storm. Look, the hero of Lake Michigan, stuck on a sandbar. Look, the famous handyman, can't even get the motor repaired." John smiles and keeps on steering the boat. That night back in Key West, when Hemingway starts in again on John, Josie walks out of the room in tears of rage. "Hemingway follows her, making excuses. His damn arm is bothering him, he tells her."[17] As they speak, an old Paris friend's essay in *The Nation* takes Ernest to task for the eccentricity and dullness of "the Hemingway school of writing." One student in that school, Josie Herbst, will never reach her potential, he says, if she cannot outgrow the fetish of simplicity Hemingway fosters.[18] Isidor Schneider could not have anticipated how quickly his advice would seem to take effect.

A visit to the Hemingways usually makes extraordinary demands upon all involved, but some visits, like that of their L-Bar-T friends the Sidleys, take the experience right to the edge:

VISITOR NEARLY DROWNED IN THE CITY PARK POOL

CHICAGO WOMAN, DRAGGED UNCONSCIOUS FROM
WATER BY MRS. ERNEST HEMINGWAY

> *Mrs. W. P. Sidley, of Chicago, narrowly escaped drowning this forenoon while swimming in Bayview park bathing pool with Mrs. Ernest Hemingway.*
>
> *Life was thought to have been extinct when she was brought ashore. After being rushed to the Marine hospital in an ambulance where restoratives were promptly administered by Dr. Lombard . . . Mrs. Sidley revived and in a short time was able to be conveyed to the home of Mr. and Mrs. Hemingway, on North Beach, where she is resting nicely this afternoon. . . . At the time of the near-tragedy Mr. Sidley and Mr. Hemingway were out on a fishing trip, not expected to return until late today.[19]*

But neither near-deaths nor afternoons on the water can long distract Ernest from how much his mending arm bothers him, both physically and in his head. The pain of the spiral fracture is past but not forgotten; the nerve slowly regenerates, but the arm is weak, his handwriting shaky, his letters few. Worse than the memory of pain

is the auto wreck's affirmation of a world that could, on whimsy, take
from him his ability to write. At the completion of each book there
was always that emptiness and silence when the machine inside him
shut down, and the fear that he might not write another book, might
have nothing left to say. In a note, he reminded himself that he had
survived periods like this before, periods between books when the
writing did not happen. As long as he was not dead, it would come
back. Finally, like an old friend, it always came back. All it took was
confidence and a good memory to weather through the hiatus, but it
was scary, the waiting, and worse each time the gift left him.[20] But this
time the fear is different: not his head but his body has failed him. He
can neither write nor fish, neither contemplate nor participate. In the
1918 Milan hospital, behind an infectious smile, he worried that his
wounded right leg might be amputated. Every day of his life, the rubber brace on his rebuilt knee reminds him of that fear.

Through visitors and winter storms, Pauline remains the self-
effacing family center, paying the bills, providing meals, tending
to the tedious. Sometimes autocratic, she does not mix much with
local Key Westers, nor does she have projects of her own. There is
no competition between them, for Ernest is her life. When they are
together, she purrs; when separated, she writes long daily letters.
When he wakes in the night with terrible dreams, she is there. Her
reward is his writing, for the well being of which she will sacrifice
almost anything. Like many fathers of his generation, Ernest takes
little interest in the rearing of his son who is too young to be interesting. Pauline accepts his disinterest, paying the nanny to keep little
Patrick occupied and meals cooked. Never thrilled with the hunting
life, to please Ernest she has become a fair shot and a competent
fisherwoman who encourages him always in his pursuits. Whatever
he wants, she wants. He wants a daughter; she will try to give him
one: by early February Pauline is once again pregnant. All that she
lacks is a permanent home, a place to make their own.

Not until April, five months after the wreck, is he able to write
Scott Fitzgerald that the paralysis is gone, the nerve returned, the

arm stronger, and the writing begun again on his unfinished book, four hundred words his daily limit.[21] That same day he writes Max Perkins, ordering a fresh supply of books to take with him in May when he and Pauline return to Europe: Baedeker's latest volume on Spain and Portugal came packed beside Dashiell Hammett's *Glass Key*, a biography of Whistler, the poems of Gerard Manley Hopkins, and Erskine Caldwell's *American Earth*. His arm is his own again, his mind again active and inquiring. He tells Max that he will outwrite all the competition, of whom only Faulkner is sometimes good enough to be taken seriously. The only true competition are the great writers dead and time itself: brave talk from a man picking up the pieces of a book five months cold.[22]

First he fiddles with "A Natural History of the Dead" to get the juices flowing, and has it typed, unable to say how much is enough with a story so strangely mixing genres—short fiction, reminiscence, and commentary. From the mountain field station where the Italian doctor has just thrown iodine into the officer's eyes to quiet his rage, the view shifts back to the narrator's memory of a sergeant on burial detail hacking gold fillings from the teeth of Austrian dead. "Now, as I write this, I think it is perhaps enough about the dead," the narrator says.

> *There is no need to continue and write accurate observations on a dead friend, a dead lover or a dead parent since a writer can deal at length with these in fiction rather than in natural history, an ill enough paid branch of writing. So perhaps the inspiration from the moss flower of extraordinary beauty, is to be derived not from the dead themselves, swollen too big for their uniforms in the heat, but from the contemplation of the sergeant at work on them. Let us learn from observing the industrious sergeant, let us take inspiration from the sergeant's researches, who knows how profitable the dead may be if we live long enough? Who knows how much gold may be extracted from them?*

It is a rough start, ragged, unfocused and eventually deleted, a warm-up before turning to the cold meat of the bullfight book.[23]

Writing, after such a hiatus, starts with Ernest talking to himself, saying what he needs to say to begin again—an apologia for his craft, stating his principles, laying out the rules he tries to live by. A writer, he tells himself, does not need to live in the country of his fiction, for if

> *he is a writer who deals with the human heart, with the human mind and with the presence of [or] absence of the human soul then if he can make a heart break for you, or even beat, make the mind function, and show you what passes for the soul then you may be sure he does not have to stay in Wessex for fear that he will lose it.*

Having vacillated between living in Spain and living in America, he now realizes that no matter what unpleasant changes are wrought on the American landscape, this is his home, the place he was born to. The new road into his Wyoming preserve may ruin the country and Key West may become another Provincetown, but "as you get older, privacy becomes internal and nothing can be spoiled from the outside."

Unlike an honest painter who can paint numerous variations on a single theme, a writer, once he gets it absolutely correct, must never repeat himself. The writer may be a less than admirable human being, he may cheat on his wife, disappoint friends, or have "this or that ugly sexual habit," but so long as he does not "lie to or deceive the innermost self which writes," he is still an honest writer. As such, he has the right to make whatever money from whatever market is available to him. If he is lucky enough to live on his income, he faces the danger that expenses will rise to exceed that income, compelling him "to write another book for money." Which is all right "so long as he does not consciously or subconsciously change one word, sentence, paragraph or chapter . . . from the way he wanted to write it."[24] Having said it, he tore the pages out of the old bound galleys he was using as a note pad and got on with his real book.

———

Deeds were filed yesterday transferring ownership of the fine home at Whitehead and Olivia streets, to Ernest Hemingway, whose summer home is his chateau near Paris, France. Mr. and Mrs. Hemingway have spent a number of winters in Key West. They like the climate here so well and enjoy fishing so much that they decided to invest in a residence. The place they have acquired is conceded to be one of the most ideally located home-sites in the city. With but little improvement of the large lawn and substantial building, the premises will become one of the most beautiful spots in Key West. Sale of the place to the Hemingways resulted in the payment of taxes amounting to $3,000 including city and county assessment. The county's share was slightly more than $1,000. Contract has been let by Mr. Hemingway for the immediately necessary repairs to the property at a cost of $500. Work on the proposition is under way today.[25]

—*Key West Citizen*, April 30, 1931

When they signed the deed on the "haunted house," as Lorine Thompson called it, Pauline was over two months pregnant and ready to adjust her expectations. They were not going to live in a French chateau, as the Key West paper called their Paris apartment. That part of their lives was finished. Nor would her husband choose any large city as a permanent home. He needed a secluded place in which to write, a place close to fishing or hunting grounds. She needed conversation and access to night life, music, a little dancing. Key West was not ideal for her, but Ernest wanted Key West, and she wanted Ernest. It was that simple. Miami was a train ride away, and old-world Havana's night life was only six hours by ferry. With air travel becoming a reality, the two-day train to New York would soon be unnecessary.

Although the pre–Civil War place was in terrible shape, she and Lorine settled on the Whitehead Street house, for which Uncle Gus put up $8,000 to pay off the bank and back taxes. Large enough for their purpose, with a huge yard, a few scraggly palms, and an enormous cistern, the old coral structure needed paint, plaster, and roof repairs. It needed a new kitchen and a second bathroom. It needed walls removed, rooms opened, windows glazed, tiles laid. It needed more work than any $500, as the paper reported, could buy. Pauline, accustomed to rented quarters and domestic help, had much to learn about the joys of homeowning, but they were largely postponed. Five days after signing the papers, Ernest was in Havana boarding the *Volendam* en route to Spain, where Pauline would join him at Hendaye later in May. If he needed to go to Spain to finish his book, she would go with him, remaining in Key West only long enough to have the roof patched and the wire-mesh fence contracted to be built. By May 16, boxes of Hemingway belongings were waiting for the drayman to move them into the new house, and Pauline was on the train to New York with Patrick and Henrietta; for months to come, nothing else was going to happen to the house on Whitehead Street.[26]

The day Ernest arrived in Havana, two army majors were indicted for commanding a "death squad" using wire garrotes to strangle victims. When he was seven days out of Havana on the *Volendam* bound for Spain, Monarchists in support of the abdicated King Alfonso took to the streets of Madrid. Before sunset, taxis and street-cars were on strike, two men were dead, and heads were bleeding.[27] The night before landing at Vigo, Hemingway told Waldo Peirce that he wanted to get to Madrid "before they set up the guillotine in the Plaza Mayor."[28] He arrived in Madrid to find the capital under martial law and Republican sentiment running so high that the Catholic Church, the long and avid supporter of monarchy, was in retreat. Cardinal Segura, the Primate of Spain, barely escaped across the Pyrenees en route to Rome, while at Loyola, reactionary Basques protected their beloved Jesuits.[29] It was all quite interesting to a writer looking for subject matter.

In Madrid, he settled into the Hotel Biarritz, where he could follow the street violence and the new season of corridas, beginning with Madrid's San Isidore feria, followed by weekly Thursday and Sunday cartels. On May 24, he watched his first son's namesake,

Nicanor Villata, perform at the Corrida de Abono. When he wasn't at the Madrid ring, he took the train out to Aranjuez on the river to preview Domingo Ortega, highly touted by his old Pamplona friend Juanito Quintana as "this year's revelation, and of whom it is said by those who have seen him that he is the best bullfighter born since bullfighting exists. . . . By what they say he must be a very serious thing."[30] Always there was a new revelation, a fresh savior born to restore the corrida's dignity, and always there was the disappointment, followed by more talk of the degenerate state of the art. Talk could be found in the cafés with Hemingway's new friend Sidney Franklin, who was in Madrid as a novillero, an aspiring but unfledged matador who talked a wonderful game and who gathered to his strange attraction "the ones coming to ask for work when he was fighting, the ones to borrow money, the ones for an old shirt, a suit of clothes; all bullfighters, all well known somewhere at the hour of eating, all formally polite, all out of luck."[31]

That summer, as Hemingway gathered new information and collected photographs for his book, there was plenty of blood in sandy bullrings and in the stone streets of Spain. As much as he missed Pauline, he was wise to have insisted she remain in Paris. All that summer revolution popped and simmered, angry men of all stripes waiting on the national elections. On May 27, six died in the San Sebastián streets, another twenty-five wounded when the Guardia Civil fired on striking fishermen.[32] On May 31 in the Madrid ring, the first bull hooked, catching Gitanillo in the thigh, tossing him against the barrera, where he was pinned to the wood with a horn through his back. Gitanillo took ten weeks to die slowly from meningitis.[33] The Republic took several years longer.

Since the early nineteenth century, the government of Spain had cycled through various constitutions regularly pricked by colonial wars and internal revolutions. The monarchy, the great landowners, the Catholic Church, and the military formed tenuous alliances to remain largely in power, until the 1930s. By 1931, the left side of the political spectrum included Republicans, liberals, socialists, syndicalists, communists, and anarchists; to the right were Monar-

chists, Carlists, fascists, Jesuits, and the military. Basques, Cata-
lans, Galicians, and Andalusians all wanted home rule. With King
Alfonso in self-exile and the military out of power, the left-leaning
elected politicians tried to assure the populace that "Spanish Communism is of slight importance. . . . We are as far from Muscovite
dogma as from that of the Socialist Second International. The dictatorship of the proletariat is continually mentioned. We want no dictatorship. Workers must be educated in freedom, not tyranny. . . .
Political revolution has been accomplished in Spain. Next should
come social revolution."[34] Nevertheless, fear of communist domination drove the peseta to new lows and kept middle-class bur-
ghers awake at night.

Throughout June, while Hemingway made brief trips to Hendaye
and Paris, the Spanish political stew simmered and thickened. In
midmonth, the provisional Republican government abolished the ruling system of military governors, who were told to retire. At the same
time Cardinal Segura, who slipped back into the country, was again
expelled, "garbed as a simple prelate, sitting stiffly beside a representative of the Department of Public Security. . . . A mob massed in front
of the Paulist monastery in Guadalajara, where he spent the night
'detained,' cried 'Long Live the Republic!' and 'Death to the clergy!'"
Meanwhile, Don Jaime de Bourbon, Carlist pretender to the Spanish throne, was exciting the Basque separatists of Navarra with promises of returning to Spain, where he had not been seen in twenty-five
years. The Pyrenees were "full of Jaimistas and Itegralistas who would
restore under the Carlist pretender a monarchy putting religion above
everything."[35]

Meanwhile in Catalonia, a young aviator on the separatist ticket
was making headlines:

*Madrid, June 25—Spain's revolutionary flyer, Ramón Franco, who
is now grooming himself as the savior of the masses, taking a flight
of oratory tonight, fell off the platform at village of Lora del Rio and
broke his leg.*

The Major could have broken his neck and thus made the pro-

visional government very happy. He has taken to stumping the cen-
ters of unrest like Catalonia and Andalusia where he has his little
"Republican revolutionary" party and has continually outraged their
finer sensibilities.

He told the masses in Barcelona that the revolution had to be
made safe for them even if they were forced to invade Parliament. . . .
Today the Government had to notify the energetic birdman . . . that
it wouldn't do for the director of the nation's aviation to fly about and
do any more dropping of electoral handbills from the air.

The next day, "the little aviator with the restless eyes, who last
December was willing to bomb Alfonso out of the palace," was dismissed as head of the nation's aviation and placed under informal
house arrest until after the elections.[36]

Two days before votes were cast, Hemingway wrote John Dos
Passos that twenty-three different political parties had "steamed up"
the country, which appeared heading for a Republican landslide.
Galicians, however, were on strike, refusing to vote, while Andalusia
would not "boil over" until it saw the new parliament's plan for land
reform. Navarra was enthusiastic for Don Jaime to restore the Carlist monarchy, and Catalonia was biding its time.[37] When votes were
counted, a left-of-center coalition was in control of the Cortes, the
Spanish parliament, but it was not a total victory. Nationalist parties
with their separatist agendas controlled Navarra and Catalonia. Die-
hard rightist Ramón Franco was elected in one of the Barcelona districts, although his forces were badly defeated in Madrid and Seville.
In a Madrid hospital, the airman himself was recovering from his
accident under guard.[38] A month later Ernest wrote Max Perkins,
"Wish there were some market for what I know about present Spanish situation. Have followed it as closely as though I were working for
a paper. Damned hard to break habits."[39] Socialists, Radicals, Radical Socialists, Catalonian and Basque Nationalists: all the pieces of
the political puzzle were out on the table, waiting to be formed into
the bloody picture they promised.

Fourth of July, 1931. At a London registry office, James Joyce and Nora Barnacle, after living together for twenty-seven years, were married. On that same day by the Swiss lake in the house for the mentally ill, Zelda Fitzgerald was waiting for Scott's phone call from Lausanne. At Bad Ausee, Austria, the Gerald Murphy family celebrated the day with their usual panache, pleased that Patrick's stricken lung remained under control by gas injections. At the beach of Hendaye where Ernest and Pauline had taken a small cottage, the American colony was too small to make much noise. In Berlin, Adolf Hitler was putting his shoulder to the wheel of German politics; in upstate New York, Governor Franklin Roosevelt, on crippled legs, was preparing to run for the presidency of the United States.

———

Five months pregnant, Pauline chooses to remain at the beach with Patrick and Henrietta while Hemingway takes his almost-eight-year-old son, John, to see his first bullfight in Pamplona. Juanito Quintana, their friendly hotelier, has saved them a room and secured "unsurpassable" first-row seats at the "place where the young lads with the swords place the capes."[40] When John Haldey Nicanor Hemingway saw his namesake, Nicanor Villata of the long neck, he hated him immediately. When the rowdy Pamplona crowd threw cushions at Nino de la Palma for a poor performance, the boy asked, "Can I throw mine, Papa?" It was at Pamplona during the now epic feria of 1925 that Hemingway first saw Nino de la Palma, a nineteen-year-old then hailed as the savior of the corrida. Having immortalized him as Pedro Romero in *The Sun Also Rises*, Ernest was always disappointed with Nino's performance after his first serious goring took away his valor. Nothing Ernest sees that day with his son causes him to revise his opinion: "If you see Nino de la Palma, the chances are you will see cowardice in its least attractive form."[41]

After the fights, Sidney Franklin, Ernest, and his son sit under the Iruña arcade, where they review the day's corrida, interrupted by well-wishers, old friends, and strangers. Winifred Mowrer is one of those at the table. Her reporter husband, Paul, is consentually elsewhere with Hadley Hemingway, with whom he has had an open affair for several years. Winifred has come to Pamplona with her two teenage sons as a rite of passage. They are almost of age, and she is almost ready to leave their father permanently for a different life. At Paul's request and with some difficulty, Ernest secured them rooms at the Perla and tickets to a corrida: anything for the man who is going to marry his former wife and provide for Bumby, now sitting at the table quite comfortably with his almost stepbrothers. The next morning as she and her sons continue on their walking tour across the Pyrenees, Winifred leaves a short, pleasant note of thank you. It is all very civilized.[42] Twenty-two years will pass before Ernest returns to the feria of San Fermin.

As soon as the last corrida is complete, Ernest rejoins his manuscript and his wife, complaining immediately that his writing could not go much worse.[43] Neither could the world at large. While the Hemingways are on the beach at Hendaye, banks in Germany, Hungary, and Austria close for twenty-two days as the old Hapsburg empire staggers beneath punitive war-debt repayments. While he and Pauline follow their usual Spanish itinerary to the Valencia feria, Seville is racked with syndicalist riots and martial law. In Havana, American intervention prevents yet another attempt on the life of President Machado; on Wall Street, U.S. Steel falls to 84 when directors reduce its dividend for the first time in sixteen years. The Bank of England raises its discount rate to staunch the flow of gold out of the country, and the great steamship lines make deep cuts in their transatlantic fares.[44]

Throughout July and into August when Ernest and Pauline once more retreat to the relative coolness of Santiago de Compostela, Spain bleeds. Strikes bring Bilbao and Cordova to a standstill. Catalonia votes to become independent, but the Cortes will not allow it. Elsewhere there are more transatlantic flights and more lost airmen. More screen stars romp in even briefer bathing suits at Cannes and Antibes. Charlie Chaplin thinks of building a house at Juan-les-Pins, but by August he is racing motorboats at Biarritz. In Germany four million are out of work, and in Great Britain the cabinet resigns, its budget unbalanced. In Cuba, sixty-six die in another failed attempt to bring down President Machado. After promising otherwise, U.S. Steel cuts salaries 15 percent, dropping its stock even lower. In Oklahoma and east Texas, five thousand wells are shut down in an effort to raise the price of crude oil, which has fallen below fifty cents a barrel. State militias are mobilized, and banks are closing in New York and New Jersey. President Hoover continues to maintain that no government "dole" is required; this crisis will pass.

While the world elsewhere churns and falters during the first week of August, Hemingway finishes an eighty-page glossary of bullring terminology, including a running commentary on Spanish custom, a curious collection of anecdotes, and related information on Spanish insults, shellfish, regional wines, street scams, and local beer. When Pauline returns to Paris to be more comfortable in her pregnancy and see to the shipment of apartment possessions, Ernest returns to Madrid to complete work on his book. The hundred or so photographs he has collected are being annotated, the glossary is almost finished, the first eighteen chapters have been revised and augmented, but the last two chapters remain as unwritten as when he arrived in May.[45]

His return to Paris at the end of August lasts only long enough to wind up some business with Caresse Crosby's Black Sun Press, balance his checking accounts, and prepare for the return to the States. For Pauline, now in her seventh month of pregnancy, the charm of Paris is waning, and three months of hotel life is enough. Their apartment furniture, en route to Key West, includes paintings by André Masson and Joan Miró's *The Farm*, which belongs to Hadley but is moving to Key West.[46] In a separate shipment, they send home their newly acquired oil painting—Juan Gris's *The Guitar Player*. Pauline completes last-minute shopping, while Ernest makes obligatory rounds. At Sylvia Beach's he buys D. H. Lawrence's novella *The Virgin and the Gipsy* and T. E. Lawrence's *Revolt in the Desert*, which is the very book for a man interested in violent political revolutions.[47]

The Hemingways avoid old Paris acquaintances and former haunts, but no matter how much they keep away from Montparnasse café life, their lives are never completely their own. A *Tribune* columnist and sketch artist catches them on the street and puts them in the paper:

The author of The Sun Also Rises, Farewell to Arms, Men Without Women, *and many brilliant short stories of the war and other subjects, has lost none of his enthusiasm for bullfighting and boxing.*

At the hotel near the Place Saint Germain des Prés where he is stopping he talked yesterday of Sidney Franklin the Brooklyn bullfighter . . . who is going into the arena at Madrid today for the first time in several months.

"Sidney is a marvelous fighter," he said. "He is absolutely courageous and keenly intelligent. He knows what it's all about. He's better than many of those boys who grow up in the tradition. They learn to go through the motions gracefully, but they don't know how to use their heads, as Sidney does. He's a regular Christy Matthewson."

Hemingway talked for about half an hour while he was posing for a sketch, but did not mention literature or himself, except to explain that he is ten pounds overweight because his arm was broken in an automobile accident and hasn't yet sufficiently healed. This keeps him from boxing.

He also had other worries. A young man who resembles him strikingly has been masquerading around New York recently as the original Ernest, telling wild stories of his adventures in the Italian ambulance service during the War, borrowing money and bumming drinks.

This has made Hemingway wary. When he signed the sketch which was made of him there, his wife remarked that the signature was hardly legible.

"Yes, I know, I wrote it that way purposely," he replied. "This town is full of chiselers. If I put a legible signature on this drawing and The Tribune prints it, there may be a half dozen bad checks at the bank by Monday morning. I'm taking no chances."[48]

Ernest's doppelganger continued to appear off and on in Paris, in New York, and later in St. Louis, casually saying he was on his way to Arkansas to visit his "wife's people."[49]

Three days after his interview appeared in the Paris paper, Ernest, Pauline, and Patrick take the afternoon boat train to Havre, where, along with the director of the Boston Symphony, the director of the Morgan bank, the Grand Duchess Maria of Russia, former Senator Guggenheim, Grant and Jane Mason, and old friend Don Stewart and his pregnant wife, they board the *Ile de France*, homeward bound. As they do so, Gerald Murphy is in Cherbourg boarding the *Europa* for New York, and Scott and Zelda Fitzgerald are disembarking in New York from the *Aquitania*.[50] That the Murphys, Fitzgeralds, and Hemingways were traveling simultaneously on separate liners, having made no attempt to group together, would have been unthinkable only a few years earlier.

Arriving finally in Kansas City to be close to Pauline's surgeon, Don Carlos Guffey, the Hemingways live first with Ernest's cousin Ruth White Lowry before moving into the Riviera Apartments when Pauline's delivery nears. On November 12, when her labor pains begin, Dr. Guffey waits twelve long hours before admitting Pauline cannot produce a natural birth.

———

Sedated and exposed on the operating table, the thirty-six-year-old white female in the ninth month of her second pregnancy is nearing the end of her childbearing years. Although her fertility will remain a potential for some time, after thirty-six the birth rate for white American women drops significantly. As the surgeon makes his lateral incision at the base of the uterus, he retraces the scar he left from her first cesarean section three years earlier. From the bloody opening he extracts a nine-pound male baby, slaps him to life, and sutures first the exposed uterus and then the mother's abdomen. (For every thousand such births, six mothers and sixty-one babies will die this year.) In the waiting room afterward the surgeon and the father congratulate each other on the successful delivery. He tells the father the twice-opened uterus will not stand the strain of another pregnancy.

———

They name their new son Gregory Hancock Hemingway: Hancock for Ernest's grandmother's family; Gregory "for any of numerous Popes, for Gregorian chant, and for Greg Clark of Toronto," he says.[51] But they cannot call him Pilar, the daughter's name they have saved since first using it as Pauline's nickname during their 1926 affair. "I want a girl very much," says he, having grown up in a house full of sisters, "but don't know how to go about it."[52] Soon he will be calling any woman younger than himself "Daughter," but there will never be a daughter.

While Pauline remains one month in Research Hospital recovering from her operation, Ernest lives alone, visiting her and working on his bullfight book. By Thanksgiving her wound is almost healed, the stitches out, and she is able to laugh again without fear of tearing something loose inside. For supper that night Ernest brings her wild ducks he shot on the Missouri River. On Thanksgiving day a year earlier, she was sitting in the chair, he lying in the Billings hospital bed. This day his writing arm is still crooked from his car wreck.

Outside, on the night streets of Kansas City, Christmas 1931 comes in chancy times. Corporate America is cutting wages, reducing inventory, limiting production; U.S. Steel falls to 59, down two hundred points over the last two years. In Manchuria, the Japanese invasion continues to move south against the hapless Chinese army. Guy Hickok predicts that in Germany, "Hitler [is] coming in, shoot up a few; then the [crown prince] will step out from behind him and restore peace and the dynasty."[53] With almost eight million Americans out of work, Ernest and Pauline have much to be thankful for: their bills are paid; their Key West home is debt-free; royalty payments from Scribner's continue; and Uncle Gus has added to Pauline's trust fund while setting $25,000 aside for a Hemingway African safari. Young Patrick is with his grandparents in Piggott in the keep of his new, enormous French nanny, Gabrielle, who was said to specialize in child care, veterinary surgery, cooking, and brewing.[54] Bumby has returned to his French boarding school; Jinny Pfeiffer is on her way to Key West, where Ernest's sister Carol will join her to install the furniture shipment from Paris for the Hemingways' arrival on Whitehead Street. After living well for several years in Europe on the strength of the dollar, Ernest and Pauline are now in the enviable position of having a little money when others have less or none. Prices are falling as businesses are sucked under. Coming through New York City on their way home from Europe, Ernest rents a safety deposit box, where he shrewdly caches several thousand dollars to hedge against the possibility of bank failures or government closures.[55]

Although Pauline's one-month hospital stay is lonesome for her and expensive for them, it gives Ernest the uninterrupted writing time he needs to bring his book of the bulls to conclusion. In the sterile furnished apartment, fortified by prescription whiskey, he finishes the penultimate chapter which began: "There are only two proper ways to kill bulls with the sword and the muleta and . . . both of them deliberately invoke a moment in which there is unavoidable goring for the man if the bull does not follow the cloth properly."[56] He might as well have written: "There are only two proper ways to finish a book like this and both of them risk unavoidable goring for the writer if the reader does not follow the story properly." For this book about the bulls and their matadors is equally a book about the writer, his writing, and the relationship of both to the reader. Writer and matador appear to be antithetical to each other: the one contemplative, the other active. But as artists, they bear metaphoric similarities. "Bull fighting," he wrote in the ninth chapter, "is the only art form in which the artist is in danger of death and in which the degree of brilliance in the performance is left to the fighter's honor."[57] The writer as artist takes similar risks, his art based on the same sense of honor, and his life as artist is equally dependent upon the response of his audience. While not literally in danger of death while writing, the author lives with the same possibility that his skills will diminish, that he will fall from the public eye, that his courage will fail. "Courage comes such a short distance; from the heart to the head."[58]

Having mastered his text as thoroughly as the matador his bull, having maneuvered it skillfully about the ring, leaving it finally stock still before the reader, he was now ready for the finish, the clean, honest ending that closes the text and opens the reader, an ending richer than anything he has ever written. It does not come easily, nor completely right the first time, but he gets it down on paper, saying what he needs to say, knowing he will cut it later where necessary. The hardest parts were always the beginning and the end, and he frequently starts too soon and just as often writes past the end. This book, for which no ending was obvious, came finally to close with the narrator admitting he is not able to get all of Spain between the covers:

> My God, you could not get in all the bootblacks; nor all the fine girls passing; nor all the whores; nor all of us ourselves as we were then. . . . the smell of olive oil; the feel of leather; rope soled shoes; the loops of twisted garlic. . . . There ought to be . . . the chestnut woods on the high hills, the green country and the rivers, the red dust, the small shade beside the dry rivers and the white, baked clay hills; cool walking under the palms in the old city on the cliff above the sea, cool in the evening with the breeze.[59]

The missing parts named, they were no longer missing, and the reader had the heart of Spain there at the end where it was most needed.

By the first of December, with the first draft of the book finished and Pauline still confined to the Kansas City hospital, Ernest went to Piggott for a week of quail hunting in the ruined fields of corn and peas: the hunter up early and out with the dogs, coming in after dark with his game bag warm and filled to the legal limit. When he returned to Kansas City, he began packing for their trip to Key West and answered letters. The book's last three chapters, he told Max Perkins, were so well written that the "hard times" surrounding them seemed not so hard. When his writing went well, nothing else mattered; when it did not, silly things became important. And when he was finished with a draft, he might have added, too many silly things began to matter, including other writers like Max Eastman, whose latest book, *The Literary Mind*, Ernest called "pretentious rubbish . . . cheap whoring articles . . . the fondler of the arts and unable to fornicate with them, the respectable radical—the revolutionary who never missed a meal."[60]

Earlier that day he wrote Archie MacLeish, "Believe made the god damn miracle we have to always make happen at the end happen again. Although may disillusion on it when see it in type. But if anything should happen to me it would be all right to publish it as it is."[61] In this book's conclusion, he says, "There is no security in any life that death is the end of, nor has economic security ever existed, nor is it possible."[62] At the same moment, Andrew Mellon, the richest Secretary of the Treasury in America's history, proposes a 1 percent increase in the federal income tax to offset the government's $1 billion spending deficit.[63]

———

Key West, Christmas. Plumbers in the kitchen, carpenters on the roof, the new nurse sick, the baby crying as his brother douses him with the flit can full of mosquito spray: another year ending. Winter is somewhere else; here it is as warm as early spring, southeast breezes holding steady, day and night. They sleep in the dining room until Pauline's scars can take the strain of the stairs; Ernest's throat is once more inflamed and raw, as are his nerves. On his writing table, amid the unanswered letters and various rubble of moving into Whitehead Street, is Archie MacLeish's new epic poem looking for a supporting blurb. In the living room, a typist hammers away on his manuscript. On the floor with other paper trash is the local paper, which says: "To 'Love at First Sight' for Key West, Ernest Hemingway Attributes His Coming Here."[64]

———

Chapter Four

1932

WINNER TAKE NOTHING

Key West, Havana, Cooke City

N O , H E M I N G W A Y S A Y S , no, he cannot become part of any as yet unnamed cooperative magazine where writers share profits, because like all writers, he writes alone, sells alone, gets turned down alone, is remembered or forgotten alone. Maybe there were some who could work together, but not him, not with twelve dependents counting on his income. (To a stranger, like George Albee, he feels such an exaggeration is permitted.) Tough times, he insists, may be "instructive" to a writer even if he has to stand in a breadline. Sooner or later, for God, country, or belly's sake, everybody must stand in line.[1] There in Key West plenty were out of work, and those he employed worked at half speed.

In the new year, Gabrielle, the Hemingways' recently hired cook and nanny replacing Henrietta, took to her sickbed, leaving little Patrick and baby Gregory to Ernest's visiting sister Carol's care. Pauline, not fully recovered from her cesarean, tried to do her part, but ended up back in bed herself.[2] That's when Patrick ate the ant poison and began to vomit. In the middle of this chaos, as roofers roofed and plumbers plumbed, Ernest continued to revise his typescript, which he now called *Death in the Afternoon*, a title jotted down the previous summer with notes for a story he never wrote:

> *Two boys—same town—same age—play bull in streets—one killed— Saragossa incident—one becomes matador—one becomes Revolutionist—/girl/—careers—matador takes girl—corrida—final——of ring*[3]

As those notes disappear into Hemingway's welter of saved paper, Max Perkins is forwarding an agent's unsolicited offer from Hollywood:

> METRO GOLDWYN MAYER HIGHLY RECEPTIVE MY SUGGESTION
> TO SECURE HEMINGWAY AT HIS PRICE FOR BULL FIGHT PICTURE
> TO BE WRITTEN IN HOLLYWOOD[4]

The next morning, having been up most of the night with Patrick, Ernest writes Max that he has no intention of whoring in Hollywood.[5]

All he wants to do is finish this book already three years in progress, but he cannot let it go. At the ends of chapters he inserts dialogues between a generic character called "Old Lady" and another called "Author," allowing him to speak as "I" in the chapter proper while moving the reader effortlessly from time past to present. Raising the book to another level, Hemingway takes an enormous risk: if the device fails, the book will fail with it. In Key West, as far removed from both bullring and publishing world as an author can be, he weighs the risk against the gain, but not without tongue in cheek:

> Old Lady: *Sir, I do not know.*
> Author: *Madame, neither do I and it may well be that we are talking horseshit.*

Old Lady: *That is an odd term and one I did not encounter in my youth.*

Author: *Madame, we apply the term now to describe unsoundness in an abstract conversation or, indeed, any over-metaphysical tendency in speech.*[6]

On January 14 at St. Mary's Star of the Sea, Father Dougherty baptizes the two-month-old Hemingway baby, whose name is misspelled in the parish index as Gregory Hancock Hemmingway, son of Ernest Hemmingway. That same day, Ernest wrote Archie MacLeish that the book was finished, his son properly blessed, and he a little drunk. But three weeks later, with the typescript in New York, Ernest was still fiddling with the text, adding more of the Old Lady.[7] He was also arguing with Max Perkins about serializing parts of the book. Alfred Dashiel, editor of *Scribner's Magazine*, wanted to publish a selection of his own editing, which Hemingway would not allow. Ernest was furious at Dashiel's paltry offer when *Cosmopolitan* offered $1,000 for first refusal on a story.[8]

With Gabrielle now a regular convalescent on Whitehead Street, Pauline could either nurse, nanny, and cook herself or find a replacement. It was not a real choice, for Ernest, who required a good deal of care, was always her first concern, her children second. Needing more than a nanny for their boys, she required a woman trustworthy enough to run the household when they were elsewhere, stable enough to deal with their unconventional life, and intelligent enough to be part of the family without intruding. Gabrielle was given a ticket home, and her replacement sought first in Miami and then in New York, where Pauline scoured the agencies before running an ad in the paper.

The morning of Pauline's departure, Ernest wrote Archie MacLeish that he should use Ernest's power of attorney to take some cash from Hemingway's Empire Trust safety deposit box—five hundred, a thousand, even two thousand if needed—whatever it took to get Archie and Ada to come to Key West. "I am a hoarder," Ernest said. "I made that money myself and I have as much right to keep it any damned place I please as to give it to a bank to pea away or to spend it. . . . there is 14 grand there and I want very much to put one or two in circulation . . . in answer to the President's plea." Six days earlier, President Hoover had appealed to the country to cease the hoarding of currency, which he estimated at $1.3 billion. "It is in the interest of the hoarders and it is their patriotic duty," the President declared, "to return this wealth to circulation."[9]

Hemingway put away his "small cash reserve . . . when they were planning to give us all the works last fall." Given that over two thousand banks failed in 1931, Hemingway has every reason to fear for his money. Nothing he has seen in Europe or at home gave him reason to believe deeply in government promises. President Hoover's Reconstruction Finance Corporation, designed to prevent bank failures, was only able to reduce them by a third. "If they think it will help them," he told MacLeish, "they will make the money worthless in which case we may have to spend it fast." *They* are the bankers, the money men, the government, the ones he saw turn the German mark to worthless paper almost overnight. However, as Uncle Gus taught him, times of great risk are also times of great opportunity; throughout the decade, he invests in blue-chip stocks at depressed prices. Because his hoarded money is earning no interest, he tells MacLeish that Pauline might need to "buy a few depreciated bonds" to make up for lost income.[10] Later that month when asked to move $5,000 to Hemingway's Key West account, MacLeish takes Max Perkins with him as a witness, knowing that for all Hemingway's generosity, money is serious business. "I didn't count the balance," he wrote Ernest, "but the envelope was sealed so I suppose it was all you left."[11]

By the time Pauline returned from New York with newly hired Ada Stern to care for the boys, John and Katy Dos Passos, on their way to Mexico, had stopped in Key West long enough for Dos to read and comment on *Death in the Afternoon*, always a tricky business with Ernest. While there is plenty in the book to praise, Dos has to tell Ernest that the attacks on living people are unnecessary and the philosophizing, at times, tedious. "And then later when you . . . give them the low down about writing and why you like to live in

Key West etc. I was pretty doubtful . . . it would be a damn shame to leave in any unnecessary tripe."[12] With the typescript in New York, already on its way to galleys, Ernest eliminated several of the passages that Dos Passos fingered. Gone was the discourse on the transient beauty of Spanish women, gone such passing comments as "It takes a long time to be a good whore and receiving visitors is a form of whoring." And the last chapter, the one he was so certain was the "miracle we always have to make happen at the end,"[13] he ruthlessly pared down to its solid core, leaving only the best parts about Spain.[14] "Have just finished cutting out all you objected to," he wrote Dos Passos, "and may god damn your soul to hell if it's not right. Seemed the best of the book to me."[15]

The curse was more good-natured than it sounded on paper, for Hemingway was riding a manic high not unlike the one in 1924 that produced *In Our Time*, his first book of short stories. Even at a distance Uncle Gus can sense the difference in Ernest's demeanor, a "radical and desirable change," he calls it.[16] Having gone five years while publishing only one story, Hemingway returns to that genre with skills honed, ready to push the limits of short fiction. In a six-week period tangled with intrusive carpenters, small children, and a recovering wife, he writes three new stories and brings several others to conclusion. On February 11, to *Cosmopolitan Magazine* he mailed "After the Storm," a story he heard from Bra Saunders about diving on the *Valbanera*, which sank during the 1919 hurricane in the Half Moon Shoals quicksand. None of her 488 passengers and crew survived, nor was Saunders able to retrieve any of her wine and liquor cargo. As a Miami paper told the story,

> *Greek sponge fishermen found her wreck first. She lay on her side, with the name visible from the surface. Her master apparently had been trying to guide his ship through the narrow channel between the Blue Moon and Rebecca shoals. Missing the deep water by a scant hundred yards, the Valbanera crashed on the bar.*
>
> *When she was found every port and door was closed. The spongers said they found some bodies in the ship as they searched for valuables*

*in her hold, but no bodies were ever found floating on the surface and
no wreckage from the ship came ashore. . . . Soon after the spongers
had salvaged everything they could find and moved on, the wreck was
officially found by the United States coast guard.*[17]

Hemingway's fiction, using all the reported elements of the *Valbanera* sinking, went through three drafts, each less discursive and
more focused. Without pity or fear for the dead trapped inside the
wreck, the working-class waterman tells matter-of-factly how he
failed to break the porthole through which he could see the face of a
dead woman: "Her hair was tied once close to her head and it floated
all out in the water. I could see the rings on her hands." His focus is
on her jewelry, for she is now an unimportant part of the food chain,
a meal for jewfish that feed in the wreck just as birds are feeding
off edible scraps that float to the surface. Without salvage equipment, the narrator leaves the wreck to Greeks who blow her open
with dynamite. "First there was birds," he says, "then me, then the
Greeks, and even the birds got more out of her than I did."[18] Devoid
of sentiment, it is a story for the times: when banks fail and jobs disappear, men on the edge cannot afford fine feelings.

At the end of February, Hemingway wrote Perkins that he had
seven stories done for a collection and two more in progress. Of
the seven, two were published—"Wine of Wyoming" and "The Sea
Change"—and "After the Storm" was in press; "A Natural History
of the Dead" he was now thinking of working into *Death in the
Afternoon* as counterpoint for his "Old Lady" to consider. The three
other stories were probably "God Rest You Merry, Gentlemen,"
"The Mother of a Queen," and "Homage to Switzerland," disturbing tales all. Set on Christmas day in a hospital "reception room,"
the first story has two Kansas City "ambulance surgeons" telling a
reporter about a young boy whose request for castration in order to
avoid sins against purity was refused by the doctors; the boy then
misperformed the operation on himself with a straight-edged razor.
In "The Mother of a Queen," a somewhat unreliable narrator unwit-
tingly exposes himself while telling about a homosexual bullfighter

who won't pay to bury his mother properly: "There's a queen for you. You can't touch them. Nothing, nothing can touch them."[19]

"Homage to Switzerland" is a triptych in which each part begins exactly the same way: a cold night at a Swiss rail station where an American man waits for the Simplon-Orient Express to arrive. The train is late. So is the hour. In the first part, Mr. Wheeler, who does not care for women, toys with the Swiss waitress, offering her money to go upstairs with him. "He had been in that station before and knew there was no upstairs to go to." In the second part, Mr. Johnson becomes slightly maudlin about his recent divorce, but talking about it "had not blunted it; it had only made him feel nasty." In the third part, Mr. Harris, whose father "shot himself, oddly enough," engages in a surreal conversation with a member of the National Geographic Society.[20]

Lesbian wife, homosexual bullfighter, castrated boy, divorce, suicide, and death by water: if a man at war with the genteel tradition wanted to make a statement to his publisher about full use of the English language, he might choose such characters and themes. Without using a single objectionable word, Hemingway opened new possibilities in American fiction, a part of the landscape which his reading audience was not quite ready to explore.

———

Dry Tortugas, March. Squalls forming out on the gulf; lightning flickers burnt orange on the horizon, too far out to hear its thunder; a thin moon is rising. At the Fort Jefferson dock, where prisoners once arrived, the fishing party is gathered. Bra Saunders has muttonfish frying; whiskey's in the glasses. Around the fire, Mike Strater with his sketch pad; Archie, Uncle Gus, and Charlie Thompson listening to Ernest; behind them the old brick fort rises up in the night black on black where men once died of yellow jack. Africa is all the talk, guns and shells, boots and baggage. Should they ship all the way to Mombasa or go overland from Cairo? Gus, the safari banker, listens and grins.

———

In the wake of the Tortuga trip, Archie MacLeish wrote Ernest that hard times had canceled all his dividend payments, making the safari impossible. But it was more than money that canceled Archie out: when a grass fire broke out, Ernest found fault with the way Archie responded to it. Shifting abruptly into his sarcastic mode, Ernest would not let loose of it; on the water going back to Key West, words were said not easily forgiven. As MacLeish remembered years later, "I told him somebody ought to prick his balloon and that led to ribald observations about my not having a big enough prick. . . . That began eating at him and he went on and on and on from there." Back on Whitehead Street, the argument continued, and Archie took the next train north.[21] Back in New York, he tried to say it clearly: "The thing that troubled me always was that you seemed to be on the defensive against me and not to trust me. I know that you do not believe in trusting people but I thought I had given you about every proof a man could of the fact of my very deep and now long lasting affection and admiration for you and it puzzled me that you should be so ready to take offense at what I did."[22] Not for the first time nor for the last, offense was taken, but this was the last time Archie left himself so vulnerable to Ernest's unpredictable rage: their seven-year friendship remained intact but never quite the same.[23] As with many another Hemingway contretemps, Ernest, who quickly forgot most of the incident, was surprised that Archie took it so seriously. "Bad weather but a grand trip," he told Max Perkins. "A fine trip with good storms."[24]

Perkins was probably happy to have missed the trip after reading Ernest's lecture about the photos for the bullfight book. Max's suggestion that they use only sixteen pictures was sound economics, but he was talking to the wrong author. Ernest was furious. Had he not promised the reader that the photos would show what he could not describe in words? Had he not spent the entire, expensive summer in Spain ruining his eyes looking at negatives? What did Max think he was going to do with two hundred photos? Had he not agreed to edit them down to only a hundred? Sixteen was ridiculous. Take out the color frontispiece, the paintings in color, but not the hundred photos.

Maybe he could compromise, but not sixteen, not thirty-two. Maybe sixty. Could they still sell the book at $3.50 with sixty photos?[25]

At this point in a new book's production, Max had come to expect such letters from Ernest, but this year he was sorely distracted by his promotion to Scribner's editor in chief and by his daughter Bertha's automobile accident resulting in mysterious convulsions. None of his authors was getting Max's full attention that summer of the deepening national depression. Once he had soothed Ernest by placing sixty-four pages of pictures behind the bullfight text, he tried to prepare his prize author for the possibility that Scribner's might publish Zelda's Fitzgerald's manuscript. "It was very much autobiographical," Max said, "about herself, and biographical about Scott. In fact, she even named her hero Amory Blaine. . . . This was written very recently, and I think when Zelda was ill with her breakdown, though that did not show in it in any obvious way." Scott was now involved with the revisions, raising Max's expectation that the "novel will be quite a good book when she finishes it."[26] Caught awkwardly between his two authors, whom he would never have published in the same season, Max tried to make the best of it. Two months later, *Save Me the Waltz* was under Scribner's contract for fall publication side by side with *Death in the Afternoon*.

About this same time, Hemingway's mother wrote from Oak Park, her letter beginning: "I won't bother you with any more letters after this as it will take you some time to answer the past six that I have written you."[27] It was the sort of jibe guaranteed to irritate him. Always uneasy with women who pushed their boundaries, he was never easy with Grace Hemingway, the mother with advice for all her children: "Surely we all need to be jarred out of our complacency and made to see life, only, as an opportunity for service."[28] He was sure, he said, that there was nothing personal in this advice, "but there is nothing makes it more difficult for me to write a letter than receiving one written in a noble moral tone. . . . I remember how you used to write me you would rather see me in my grave than smoking cigarettes etc. and I suppose—what is the use of writing like this? None and I won't do it. But it shows you why I don't write more."[29]

Grace Hall Hemingway, a woman born before her time, never let a man, much less a son, tell her what to do or say. One of the first women to vote in Oak Park, she was a self-reliant, ambitious, and articulate woman who loved to perform in public. When her contralto voice aged out, she taught herself to paint well enough to have Chicago shows and real sales. While most boys grow up in conflict with their fathers, Ernest's conflict was with his mother, whose every characteristic he shared without ever acknowledging the debt. After his father's suicide in 1928, Ernest chose to ignore the clinical depression of the Doctor and blame his mother for the loss. In October, responding to a review of *Death in the Afternoon*, Hemingway wrote, "There are no subjects I would not jest about if the jest were funny enough (just as, liking wing shooting, I would shoot my own mother if she went in coveys and had a good strong flight)."[30]

Havana, spring and summer. Dark painted doorways, yellow painted plaster of houses, the courtyard where the men were bowling, auto buses, trucks, men with sacks on their heads, shiny headed niggers, lottery ticket sellers . . . the land smell and the smell of the harbor, the brown water with the silver roll of the tarpon, the launches crossing, the spars of a smack sunk in the hurricane . . . the iron balconies and the iron grills, the stringy whores, the fat whores, the half niggers, the boxer training on the roof . . . the billiard room where the pilots play, the Cojo, the round tiles on the roof like poles of bamboo, the market, 100 radio police cars, 25,000 soldiers, the stool pigeons bar across from the Jefatura, view of Sloppy Joe's bar from the smooth stoned light and airy top windows.[31]

—Ernest Hemingway

On the 21st of April, after stopping by Thompson's chandlery for supplies, Ernest, his Kansas City cousin Bud White, Charles Thompson, and Joe Russell in Russell's thirty-two-foot *Anita* crossed to Havana under a full moon. Their plan for a ten-day trip was imme-

diately forgotten as soon as Ernest hooked his first marlin: days
turned into weeks, weeks into months. Wives came and left; others
appeared and disappeared, all taking their turns at the heavy rods:
Grant and Jane Mason, Ernest's sister Carol, Bra Saunders. Every
day but a few they fished early and hard, keeping a running account:
the log of the good ship *Anita*.

About the same time the *Anita*'s first marlin hit the trailing bait,
three Cuban university students were brought before a military tribunal for having tried six times to blow up President Machado with
a dynamite-laden car. At 8:45 a.m. Pauline's marlin ran her line out
three hundred yards, jumping and jumping, jerking her about for forty
minutes until Ernest pulled it to gaff. Before the marlin's colors faded,
the three students were sentenced to eight prison years on the Isle of
Pines.[32] Chugging back into the harbor that afternoon, no one on the
Anita noticed that the *Orizaba* had docked during their absence; they
were at dinner that evening when that ship departed for New York.
On board were the critic Malcom Cowley's estranged wife, Peggy,
and her sometime lover and troubled poet, Hart Crane, who at noon
the following day went over the fantail to his death by water.[33]

Each day began with the air foul around Arsenal Dock, the men
sleeping sometimes on the *Anita*, sometimes joining the women at
the Ambos Mundos, where a room with bath overlooking the harbor
and the cathedral was only $2 a day.[34] Sleeping wherever but rising
with the sun, they had their baits in the water before passing under
Morro Castle guarding the harbor. For those two months, Ernest's
intensity never lessened. His fishing partners came and left, but he
continued unsated. Once, with that same intensity, he was married
to trout fishing up in Michigan; then trout gave way to the corrida.
Now, with *Death in the Afternoon* in galley proofs, that ten-year passion is waning. These Gulf Stream days, pursuing fish as large as his
imagination, are the beginning of a new pursuit which will last him
the rest of his life. Hunting, of course, was always there in the fall,
but others, hunting before him when the country was new, had the
best of it. The purple Gulf Stream of huge fish is the new country. It

beats everything: hunting, flying, skiing, everything. He is "completely and utterly satisfied on this as sport, living, spectacle and exercise," he writes Mike Strater. For years commercial fishermen pulled in the marlin on handlines, but "we are the first to take them on rod and reel and have virgin fishing." Like the natural historian he dreamed of being as a boy, Ernest calls life in the stream "damn fine pioneering. Truly the most wonderful damned thing I have ever been on."[35]

Trolling in the stream, he sees the marlin smash his bait, take it in his bill, and run out a hundred yards or more with himself waiting, tensed to set the hook. Then long, impossible jumps, the sun glittering off a huge body completely out of the water, its weight on the line enormous, its head shaking like an angry terrier to throw the hook. Sometimes bringing him to gaff, sometimes losing him, twice to sharks who leave only the head and bill. Once, with the gaffed marlin almost pulled across the transom, another marlin "came to the boat and jumped high out of [the] water to look at what was happening to his partner . . . very strange."[36] Calm days and rough, squalls breaking over them, sun burning their backs, they fish fifty-four days out of fifty-eight, selling their catch at the dock or giving it away. For a few days in June, they were able to hire Carlos Gutiér-rez, captain of the fishing schooner *Paco*, to join them in the stream. When fishing slacks, Carlos tells stories of whale sharks 120 feet long, of a shark fighting a porpoise, and of a black marlin who took 495 fathoms of line three thousand feet straight down. He claims to have seen marlin leap over his small skiff, and once landed three of the four marlin hooked at the same moment on his handline.[37]

Soon after Ernest arrived in Havana, a reporter caught up with him, hoping for some pithy quotes only to be disappointed when "it was of fishing that he talked, ignoring totally the subject of Hemingway." Ernest told him,

The Cuban coast offers one of the best fishing grounds in the world to the fisherman who is looking for big game. Professional fishermen have brought marlin and swordfish to the local markets, which, even

after they are dressed, weigh more than the world record catch, and it is this size of fish we are looking for.

In three days of fishing we have caught four marlin and three sail-fish, one of which was landed by Mrs. Hemingway. . . . Professional fishermen in the harbor assure us that we would have to fish to a depth of fifty fathoms to catch them. And yet, yesterday, our teaser bait trailing behind the boat brought six of them to the surface. . . . I really shouldn't be telling this because as soon as fishermen learn the possibilities here and Havana prepares to care for fishermen, it will become famous and crowded. And when it does, we'll find some other fishing ground.[38]

They did not speak of Hemingway the author, nor did they speak of the unspeakable, the condition of martial law which ruled Cuba, criticism of which could close a paper and many a mouth. When a political prisoner "disappeared" from his cell shortly after Hemingway's arrival in Cuba, the secret police were asked to investigate. No one in Havana held his breath waiting for the unspeakable answer. On May Day, the *Havana Post* was not printed; whatever happened in the streets went unrecorded. Three weeks later, on the eve of the Republic's thirtieth anniversary, the secret police arrested sixty revolutionists from all walks of Cuban life. President Machado, surrounded in his palace by loyal forces, put extra police into the streets. Finally all official anniversary observance of the island's independence is suspended, and three hundred more Cubans are in jail. By June bombs are exploding here and there in the city while sons and daughters of prominent Cuban families are under arrest.[39] Unable to report the extent of unrest, newspapers are reduced to ambiguous statements:

Seven Spaniards and one Polaco were ordered deported by the president. Cleaning the riff raff out of Cuba in the form of these undesir-ables is claimed to be an excellent idea.[40]

The desperate ones do not get out so easily:

Found drowned in the harbor with his hands tied, Ignacio Iglesias,
skipper of the tug Providencia, is reported by his son to have suffered
from delirium of persecution for some time past.[41]

Having been a student of revolutions since his early Paris days,
Ernest tells Max Perkins that the new grist he has acquired for his
writing mill is not merely about fishing.[42]

On the 2nd of June, with the stream running strong to eastward
and no marlin striking, Hemingway came in early to answer mail.
Sending corrected galleys to Max, he said he was thinking of postponing his much-planned African safari for another year. Too much
was going on, he said, too many stories to write. The galleys were
revised with much eliminated; he is annotating photos by night,
fishing hard by day, learning more about his quarry.[43] To MacLeish,
he confirms his decision about postponing Africa: "My goddamned
conscience says not to go now. Too long away the way things are
going."[44] To Mike Strater, he suggests they hunt that fall in Wyoming
before the country is ruined by the road being built over Beartooth
Pass.[45]

"The way things were going" across America is not encouraging
unless you are a writer looking for subject matter: angry veterans
marching on Washington demanding their promised bonus; angry
policemen searching in vain for the kidnapped Lindbergh baby.
With millions out of work and the federal deficit approaching $1 bil-
lion, President Hoover insists on reducing government spending and
raising taxes to balance the budget. Unemployment, he argues, is not
going to diminish unless more credit is invested in private enterprise,
but when he asked for a manufacturing excise tax, Congress instead
raised the income tax. By early June, staggering under a $13 million
deficit of its very own, U.S. Steel watches its common stock fall to
24 1/4.[46] Ernest, who was thinking of putting part of his New York
cache into U.S. Steel preferred, chooses instead to buy ten shares of
Guaranty Trust and $2,000 of Belgium bonds.[47]

When she isn't in Havana with her husband, Pauline writes daily
letters, missing him always, but never petulant or complaining seri-

ously, never causing him worry. Greg's new tooth and Patrick's measles are fine; the house, fine. She is fine. (Her nagging Catholic conscience never lets her forget that Ernest is hers by virtue of her having destroyed his first marriage.) On Mother's Day she sent telegrams to both their mothers. Paying bills, supervising carpenters, forwarding galley proofs, she did not wish him home until the marlin stopped running. The good wife settled down with *War and Peace*, while in the yard Jane Mason's gift of peacocks preened beneath the fig trees.[48] Pauline knew what Ernest expected and when, knew his moods and methods. It was she who balanced the bank account, paid the bills, and managed the children. While he fished through the month of May, she was planning their excursion to Wyoming: what to do with the house, the children, their clothes, the car. She did it all, giving Ernest the room to roam and to write, for she knew that his writing, which fed off his enormous energy, mattered most. He is her husband, her lover, her project, her satisfaction, and she does whatever is necessary to protect his gift and to keep herself on his mind.[49]

———

Key West, June 26. Fifteen hours coming back across the Gulf sick, running a fever, finally making the American Shoals light, returning to the house empty except for the odor of Pauline's perfume and her letter from Piggott, where she missed him, wanted him. Hurry, she said, hurry. He could not hurry the fever, and at night he woke sweating, sheets damp, the lighthouse across the street playing off the bedroom wall and the peacock screaming in the yard. Page proofs on the desk carry a running head: Hemingway's Death.

———

After leaving Patrick and Gregory with Pauline's parents in Piggott, she and Ernest return like migratory animals to the high country, living that summer and early fall once again in a log cabin at the Nordquist ranch. Their new Ford roadster, having carried them safely cross-country against the tide of displaced, road-weary Americans, rests while they ride horseback, fish, and hunt. Rising up early in the morning, he passes the cabin of Josie Merck, calling out, "Up, up, Daughter!" on his way to the lodge breakfast. While he corrects page proofs for *Death in the Afternoon*, Josie and Pauline take long walks in the woods, returning with small flowers and wild strawberries that stain their hands bloody red.[50]

In August, before invited friends arrive, Ernest finishes a story about young Nick Adams, the boy he invented in Paris, giving him many of his own experiences: summer fishing in upper Michigan, parents like his own parents, fears like his own fears. The story began abruptly with Nick and Tom, teenage road boys, walking into a small-town bar: "When he saw us come in the door the bartender looked up and then reached over and put the glass covers on the two free lunch bowls," Nick tells us. On their way out of town, with the sharp smell of tan bark in the night air and water beginning to freeze in the puddles, they stop at the railway station, where five whores, six white men, and three Indians are crowded into a hot waiting room reeking of stale smoke. As soon as they enter, they notice one of the men with a white face and white hands. Another man asks them, "Ever buggar a cook? . . . You can buggar this one." As the boys listen and watch, two of the whores, Alice and a peroxide blonde, begin to argue over which of them actually knew a once famous but now dead boxer, shot down by his own father. Nick becomes fascinated with Alice, an enormous woman with a pretty face, "but my God she was big." As the boys move toward the door, the cook asks, "Which way you boys going?" Tom tells him, "The other way from you." "What the hell kind of place is this?" Tom asked. Night visitors in a surreal world of words without action, threats unrealized, temptations unanswered: it was an enigmatic story whose center lay just beyond definition. Hemingway called the story "The Light of the World."[51]

Pauline typed the story between trout fishing and bird hunts from which they never returned empty-handed. Two days in alfalfa fields full of sage hens, they killed twenty-five birds for the Nordquist dinner table. On the second day, Ernest, pumping his 12-gauge as fast it would fire, brought down three hens and a running jackrabbit with four shots. Pauline, with her double-barreled 28-gauge, brought down three winged cripples. Both of them, having grown up among men who hunted, accept blood sport as a natural activity; what they kill, they customarily clean and eat. Pauline participates because it is Ernest's passion. Her witness at his kills gives him pleasure, and in the fields, she is his pupil just as she was at the bullrings in Spain. She loves him and what he loves as hard as she is able, but there is a part of him that goes beyond her ability to follow, a need to kill so long as birds flew or marlin rose to the bait. During that fall season, his hunting log recorded: 32 sage hens, 2 rockdogs, 1 porcupine, 2 elk, 11 rabbits, 2 bears, and 1 eagle shot on the wing.[52]

Ernest arrived at the L-Bar-T slim, dark, and confident if a little weak from his bronchial infection. Two months of heavy hauling against huge marlin built new muscular structure across his back and forearms. Turning thirty-three, he is approaching his physical and literary prime, stretching his limits. Nothing he can imagine is out of reach. Soon after arriving at the Nordquist ranch, he sent Bill Lengel, editor at *Cosmopolitan*, "Homage to Switzerland" in response to his request for a new story. "Homage" was a new form for the short story, Ernest told Lengel, three stories in one, all opening the same way.[53] Unwilling to run such an experimental story in his mass-market periodical, Lengel declined the story. Smarting from the rejection, Ernest immediately offered "Homage," "Light of the World," and "Mother of a Queen" to Perkins for *Scribner's Magazine* at a cut-rate price of $2,100 for all three. He would like them to run in three successive issues "to bitch Cosmopolitan—they have offered $1.00 a word up to 3500."[54] No need to tell Max about Lengel's rejection.

That same day he responded at his virulent best to Paul Romaine, whom Hemingway allowed, in a moment of weakness, to reprint in a limited collector's edtion an early poem. When Romaine suggested that Ernest might benefit from the current leftward swing of literature, Ernest told him that was "so much horseshit." He did not follow fashions, then or ever. The only ones disillusioned by the state of the nation were not paying attention to what was happening all through the Twenties. Left and right were equally despicable, along with limited-edition publishers, who should be shot when the revolution started. Romaine, sorry to have touched an exposed nerve, said he knew that Ernest, restrained from going left for "reasons we both understand," would stay to the political right. Ernest dismissed the reply as the "same presumptuous poppycock," refusing to state his political beliefs, which, if published, could put him in jail.[55] Having never voted, never supported a political party, and having never believed any poltician since his postwar education as a reporter in Europe, Hemingway was, if anything, a passive anarchist who wanted all government, except tribal, out of his life.

In August, possibly with a hint of malice, MacLeish sent Ernest the summer issue of *Hound & Horn*, which felt obliged to "condemn" Hemingway for defects in his imagination, sincerity, and virtuosity. "Laziness," claimed Lawrence Leighton, "confines Hemingway's attention to primitive rudimentary beings." His "sincerity and appeal exist only for the tabloid mind." Addicted to the first-person narrator, Ernest was "not playing fair." His characters did not live. "They are nervous instead of passionate." His vision and imagination were defective; his attitude toward life revealed his spiritual poverty. If only Hemingway might learn what Henry James had to teach him about the life of the mind. But it was a hopeless case. Ernest's sentimentality, "his desire to obtain emotion without earning it," was barely "concealed by his habit of saying as little as possible. If only Hemingway, who was such an influence on contemporary American writers, could write more like Raymond Radiguet, whose "qualities of mind and ways of thinking" Mr. Hemingway lacked. Radiguet's strength was his ability to use his inherited tradition. "One feels behind Radiguet," the long article said, "Mme. de Lafayette, Benjamin Constant, Proust, even Racine."[56]

Furious, Ernest promised Archie that the next time he was in New York he was "going to beat the shit out of" Lincoln Kirstein, the editor of the magazine. But he did find Leighton's arrangement of who stood behind whom sexually amusing. Possibly Radiguet, a homosexual, might stand behind the lady, but he would certainly "have felt the others behind him and well up into him, doubtless, if it would have helped him to get along."[57] Having said it to Archie, he immediately wrote a letter to the editor, calling the essay "very interesting," but taking exception to the arrangement of the French tradition:

> *Surely this should read "Radiguet behind Mme. de Lafayette." The rest of the sentence might stand although it would be more just to place Cocteau behind Radiguet and give Racine the benefit of the doubt. But perhaps Mr. Leighton has a feeling for Racine and would not wish to deprive him of his place.*[58]

As a footnote in *Death in the Afternoon*, Hemingway included a dialogue in which the "Author" explained to the "Old Lady" that the meaning of decadence depended largely upon who used it. For example, he told her, Cocteau found it decadent when he discovered that his young lover, Raymond Radiguet, was having a clandestine affair with a woman.[59]

With five bank accounts in three states and one foreign country, their Key West house paid for and clear, and no outstanding debts, the Hemingways were floating easily with the depressed economy. If book sales fell, so did the price of gasoline. If royalties were reduced, so were transatlantic fares. The "American Earthquake," as Edmund Wilson called it, was not threatening their lives. While the political rhetoric of President Hoover and freshly nominated Democrat Franklin Roosevelt heightened toward the fall election, Hemingway, whose distaste for both parties was acute, listened to coyotes where no radio could reach him. On his birthday (July 21), while police were telling the Bonus Expeditionary Force to evacuate Washington, Ernest deftly dropped his MacGinty fly onto Sealey's pool, and the cutthroat trout rose to it as in a dream.[60]

Visitors arrived early in September. First came the tribe of Murphys: Gerald, Sara, Baoth, and his sister, Honoria; Patrick, who seemed to be recovering from his tuberculosis, was still hospitalized. The two families fished and camped out, Ernest and Gerald a little uncomfortable with each other but trying to be decent. As Ernest told Archie, "I always get along well with Gerald and like him when I'm with him. But the countries you love best are the ones you miss when you are away from them."[61] Gerald, of course, complained amusingly about the food: all that beef and not a decent chef in sight. When canned fruit salad appeared on the table with a dollop of mayonnaise and a maraschino cherry on top, Sara laughed. High up at the lake campsite, Ernest took their daughter in hand, teaching Honoria how to catch a trout and how to clean it afterward, explaining the beauty and function of all its parts.[62] As the Murphys were preparing to depart, Gerald explained by letter to MacLeish that Ernest was "never difficult with the people he does not like, the people he does not take seriously." To those who did not matter, like Gerald himself, he was indifferent "to the point of open inattention." Murphy also found him "more mellowed, amenable and far more charitable and philosophical than before—and more patient also. But the line has been drawn between the people whom he admits to his life and those he does not. . . . He is fast taking on the qualities which are necessary to a working artist,—and he *is* of the race."[63]

As the Murphys left, Charles Thompson arrived to join Ernest on a strenuous, frustrating hunt for mountain goats too wary for the novices. When they came down from the mountains, Pauline left for Piggott and Key West, torn as she frequently was between her duties as mother and wife. On September 23, while Ernest was killing a seven-point bull elk up on Timber Creek, *Death in the Afternoon* was published in New York. Reviewer Lawrence Stallings, who adapted *A Farewell to Arms* to the stage, caught the complexity of the book:

> *Certain books, notably ones in which authors are constrained to follow their daimon, are definitely without calculation. . . . They remain forever out of literary categories and become, according to the depth of originality in the writer, a work unto themselves. Their influence is not to be calculated. So it is with "Death in the Afternoon." It is one of the great vagaries and we have not had another such in a long time.*[64]

The *New York Herald Tribune* review urged readers with no taste for bullfights to read the book anyway, for it was "teeming with life, vigorous, powerful, moving and constantly entertaining."[65] Other reviewers, less open to experiments, were not impressed. The *New York Times* found the subject matter too technical and the prose style beneath Hemingway's best: "Action and conversation . . . are his best weapons. To the degree he dilutes them with philosophy and exposition he weakens himself."[66] *The New Yorker* called the book "suicidal" on Hemingway's part. Granville Hicks could not stand the book; at great length, Malcolm Cowley avoided the question.[67]

A week after the book's publication, with the first heavy snow already fallen, Ernest and Charles Thompson rode into the Closed Creek and Pilot Creek wilderness, where a Nordquist horse had been shot to ripen for bear bait. The two men were pushing their luck, for winter snow would soon close Cooke City and the Clarks Fork Valley until the following spring. Just before an October 7 storm dumped more snow thick on the trails and deep in the woods, Charles killed his black bear feeding on the bait. Despite the now heavy snow, Ernest would not give up. Four days later, as the light was failing, a hulking bear approached the frozen bait. Unable to see the front of his open sight against the bear's black mass, Ernest breathed out slowly, squeezing off a shot that hit the animal high on the shoulder with a solid thump. Wounded and angry, the bear thrashed off into the woods, trailing dark blood on the luminous snow. With a fresh round in his chamber and a moon rising overhead, Ernest, alone, followed the ragged tracks and blood spoor black against the snow into the thickening darkness. He could not see the bear until, separated by only twenty feet, they were on top of each other. When Ernest's quick shot struck the animal, he "bawled like a bull," collapsing dead in the snow. Leaving his kill to skin the next day, Ernest rode twenty-five cold and dark miles beneath the risen moon back to the ranch. By the next day's light, the stiffened hide fetched out at eight feet between back and front paws.[68]

Three days later, Ernest and Charles packed up to run in front of a fresh storm coming out of the west. In his last letters before departing, Hemingway said they have "killed enough meat for two guides to get married on." Early the next morning, Ernest paid the month's bill with a check for $1,620.[69] By that night, he and Charles are in Cody with the smell of snow in the air and winter setting in thickly behind them.

———

Key West: Election Day, 1932. Black-habited nuns lead schoolchildren into the Convent of Mary Immaculate. Up Whitehead Street, searching for truants, comes Cayo Hueso, the two-wheeled ice cream seller's boat, its black funnel curved backward. In Grunt Bone Alley, a pushcart loaded with yellowtails and grunts will sell you a "bunch" for twenty-five cents. Down Duval Street, the Hard Times Drag, hauling freight in a handcart, nickels-and-dimes its way across town. Papayas, sea grapes, sapodillas, and Spanish limes are bunches of color on the sidewalk display next to Demerrit's corner market, selling "fresh fish" to customers who cannot imagine any other. In "jungle town" where colored folk live, Welter's Coronet Band is marching a funeral party to the graveyard.[70]

———

The day began with no rain falling out of a gray scudding sky, but water is standing in pools and puddles from yesterday. At the First Precinct polling station, Hemingway's neighbors cast 131 votes for Roosevelt and 32 for Hoover. Charles Thompson's brother Karl is elected county sheriff by a two-to-one margin; Norberg Thompson, the eldest and wealthiest brother, is unopposed for county commissioner. Three thousand citizens of Monroe County vote, but not Pauline, who this day is riding the train to Memphis, where her father will meet her. In Piggott both of her boys are sick with whooping cough. Ernest and his visiting first son, Bumby, are in the almost renovated and half-redecorated Key West house. If he voted, he makes no mention of it. At Taiku, China, in the province of Shansi, his uncle Willoughby Hemingway, medical missionary for thirty years, dies quietly this day from influenza.[71]

By the time Hemingway joins Pauline in Piggott, Mr. Stitt, a publicity man for Paramount Pictures, is hounding him with telegrams, wanting to set up a showing of *A Farewell to Arms* right there in Arkansas. Ernest, more interested in jumping coveys of quail with the dogs, Hoolie and Jack, declines the offer. When the second telegram announced

> *You and guests are cordially invited to the World Premiere of Farewell to Arms Strand Theatre Piggott Wednesday December Seventh (Stop) Kindly advise number seats you wish reserved regards.*[72]

Ernest asked if there was something about his first answer, no thanks, that Mr. Stitt had not understood. He is absolutely uninterested in being Mr. Stitt's publicity project. Paramount purchased the film rights, but they did not purchase the book's author. Moreover, he has heard that the nurse, Catherine Barkley, was miraculously restored to life in the film version, ruining the end of the book. Would Mr. Stitt kindly stop annoying him. By December 6, the AP wire service in Little Rock spread the story that Ernest was "indignant over the traditional 'happy ending' in the screen version of his book," and would not attend the Piggott showing of the movie.[73] Mr. Stitt wired his reply:

> *Interpreted your first answer correctly I am sure and since I followed the advice showing of film in Piggott naturally off stop my endeavors were plainly for your reaction publicity-wise to help put picture over stop I may add if you call a woman dying in childbirth a happy ending then the picture has just that stop with all regards.*[74]

Two days later, well-meaning Uncle Gus, having attended the film's New York premiere, wired Hemingway that the film was faithful to the book's conclusion and quite moving, with Gary Cooper and Helen Hayes giving excellent performances. A Mr. Stitt had called Gus, wondering how to get Ernest to see the movie, for he was anxious to have a private showing so that the author might make suggestions for improving the film. As politely as he could, Ernest explained to Gus Pfeiffer that he simply was not interested in Paramount's using him to make more money for themselves. Gus wired back that he understood Ernest's position and that he should "stick to it."[75]

The Paramount effort to use Hemingway was not an isolated incident, for increasingly his private life was becoming public domain. When he invited Max Perkins to come to Arkansas for a pre-Christmas duck hunt, Ernest also asked Max to issue a statement which, in part, said:

> *Mr. Ernest Hemingway has asked his publishers to disclaim the romantic and false military and personal career imputed to him in a recent film publicity release. . . . While Mr. H. appreciates the publicity attempt to build him into a glamorous personality like Floyd Gibbons or Tom Mix's horse Tony, he deprecates it and asks the motion picture people to leave his private life alone.*[76]

Such statements, of course, merely fired the public's curiosity to know more about his life, which would never again be private. The persona he created to narrate *Death in the Afternoon* would, before the decade was finished, displace the sometimes shy, frequently reserved, and always observant private man. Recognition translated into income from book sales, which allowed him the luxury of his expensive pursuits, but that same recognition came at a stiff price. Part of him understood the cost, but once he was seated firmly in that saddle there was no way to dismount short of shooting the horse.

Between telegrams to New York and afternoon quail hunts in the ruined fields of the river bottom, Hemingway was part-time nurse to Pauline, Jinny, and Bumby, who were down with the flu, a virus which always frightened Ernest. About that same time the Pfeiffers' barn, converted into a guesthouse, caught fire from an overheated woodstove. Before the blaze could be quenched, it and the firemen's water destroyed Ernest's typewriter, his boots, several of his guns, books and letters, and most of their clothes. Only his manuscripts and his cherished Woodsman pistol were rescued.[77] By December

15, Ernest was more than happy to leave the cares of the Piggott Christmas to the Pfeiffers while he headed for Memphis to meet Max Perkins's train.

Their week's hunting trip began on the coldest day of the year, the temperature in the twenties, snow and sleet turning the road into a nightmare with Ernest driving. Telephone lines were down all along the route to Watson, where they were booked into the *Walter Adams*, a houseboat on the Arkansas River with hunting guides provided. The next day was so cold that ducks were found frozen on the ponds, so cold no one who was there ever forgot it. The eerie silence is regularly broken by tree limbs crashing down in the woods, now on one side of the river, then on the other. All the while the men squint against weak sunlight glittering through iced branches, their breath hanging in the air before them. Given the number of minor crises he has recently faced, Ernest is in remarkable form, shooting well, sleeping well, waking in darkness eager to crouch in the duck blind waiting for the first flight to come into the decoys with the sun rising behind them. Sometimes drifting on the river, jump-shooting singles they scare up, sometimes hunkered down in the blind with retrievers at their feet, he and Max share the days so intensely that if they never hunt again, it does not matter. Despite cold weather and what passed for poor hunting in that part of Arkansas, Hemingway shipped fifteen ducks to Charles Thompson in Key West and another fifteen to Piggott.[78]

At Helena, Arkansas, four days before Christmas, Ernest put Max back on the train for Memphis and New York, his editor's flawed hearing unimproved by a week of shotguns blasting over frozen duck ponds and rivers. Chilling in the baggage car were Max's seven mallards and several of Ernest's. In his hand luggage, Max also took with him the typescript of a new Hemingway story so spare and oblique that nothing seemed to happen, no action, no overt conflict, little but dialogue. In a late-night Spanish bar, two waiters, one younger than the other, discuss an old man, past eighty, drunk in his customary cups, their last customer, who won't go home. Their conversation reveals that the old drunk, who has plenty of money, tried to hang himself the previous week, but was cut down by his niece. Finally the younger waiter refuses to refill the old man's cup, forcing him out into the night, "a very old man walking unsteadily but with dignity." The younger waiter goes home, leaving his older friend to turn out the lights. As he does so, he assesses his own condition and that of the world where a clean and pleasant café can be a haven against the nothingness that is everywhere. "It was a nothing he knew too well. It was all a nothing and a man was nothing too. It was only that and light was all it needed and a certain cleanness and order." To himself he mutters a parodic version of the Lord's Prayer, beginning "Our nada who art in nada, nada be thy name." He would go home to a narrow bed where he would lie awake until daylight came. "It is probably only insomnia," he tells himself. "Many must have it."[79] Ernest called the story "A Clean, Well Lighted Place," a phrase so apt that it would become a permanent part of the American vocabulary.

Many did have "it" that year of Hoovervilles cobbled together out of packing crates, loose tin, and cardboard boxes. Many had "it" in high-rise buildings with windows opening conveniently onto nothingness; others had "it" on high bridges, in lonely alleys, among strangers. That previous fall, over Wyoming whiskey, Ernest upset Charles Thompson by saying that one day, like his father, he would have to kill himself.

Chapter Five

1933

ONE   TRIP   ACROSS

Key West and Cuba

M OST MODEST OF all American writers is Ernest
Hemingway whose half-dozen published books have
set a new style in contemporary literature, but who,
nevertheless, shuns personal publicity as an owl shuns daylight.
Hemingway . . . does not even care to have any biographical material about himself made public. . . . Though hundreds of thousands of persons know his works, however, very few know anything
about the man himself. With what amounts almost to a mania, he
avoids personal publicity of every kind.

—*Key West Citizen,* February 11, 1933

In the first week in January, Hemingway loaded up his Ford,
kissed his family goodbye, and drove over the gravel road out of Pig-

gott, heading east. Pauline and his three sons would take the train to Key West; he is on his way to New York, driving through Nashville and Knoxville and up over the Blue Ridge Mountains to Roanoke, Virginia. With only two weeks having passed since Max Perkins's return to the city, there is no single, compelling reason for this trip. He has a contract to sign for his as yet untitled book of short stories and some tax business with his lawyer, Maurice Speiser, all of which could be accomplished by mail. Call it road work, a trip to clear his head after too many in-laws, too many sick children. As much as he needed an orderly family life for refuge, sometimes he simply needed to be on the road again counting miles; sometimes he needed the rush of New York: take in a fight, see Strater, buy some books, have a little hotel life, which he truly enjoyed. Leaving Knoxville on Saturday, he sent Max a telegram: "Arriving Sunday morning." Passing through Marion, Virginia, without calling on Sherwood Anderson, his old mentor and no longer friend, he arrives in Roanoke, stores his car, and catches the night train into New York.[1] By the time he reaches Penn Station, skies are gray, the temperature hovering in the thirties, not quite freezing.

At his Scribner's office on Fifth Avenue, Max and a tall, gangly Thomas Wolfe are waiting when Ernest arrives. The two authors, meeting for the first time, are wary but friendly. In 1929, Wolfe's staggering first novel, *Look Homeward, Angel*, ran cheek by jowl with Hemingway's *A Farewell to Arms*. Born within a year of each other, they, along with Fitzgerald, are the headliners in Max's stable of bright young writers. For lunch, Max walks them up to Cherio's, where his customary table is waiting in the downstairs dining room, his martini on the table, and his customary order of guinea hen's breast in the offing. If he hopes, as he once said, that Hemingway's restrained style may somehow exert an influence on Wolfe's gargantuan appetite for words, the lunch is a failure. But the two writers seem to enjoy it, Hemingway talking, Wolfe listening.[2]

Later in the week, having signed copies of *Death in the Afternoon* along with his Scribner's book contract, Hemingway shopped for new phonograph records, ate lunch with acerbic Dorothy Parker, dined with Uncle Gus, visited Sara Murphy, talked safari with old African hand Dick Cooper, bought and shipped books to Key West, and attended the Sunday-evening fights. With Gus Pfeiffer, he discussed the African trip scheduled for late December. He also found time for Sidney Franklin, the Brooklyn bullfighter he met in Spain: "He looks sort of shoddy in Spain sometimes," he said, "but by god he looked awfully good in New York. I believe he is the best story teller I've ever known." During the second week, he paid the taxidermist bill on his black bearskin rug with head attached, picked up presents for Pauline at Bergdorf Goodman, and bought a Friday-night train ticket back to Roanoke.[3] One afternoon with no Paramount publicity men hounding him, he took Josie Merck, his friend from the L-Bar-T, to see the movie version of *A Farewell to Arms*. At the end, when Gary Cooper carried the dead Helen Hayes to the hospital window and white doves fluttered past, Ernest whispered, "Josie, those are just damn sea gulls."[4]

New York was never his town, but he was sometimes its darling. Not only was *A Farewell to Arms* playing on the screen, but at the newsstands, *The Nation* carried Clifton Fadiman's essay "Ernest Hemingway: An American Byron"—claiming the author was more of a public hero than an artist.

> *Hemingway is a man born in his due time, embodying to perfection the mute longings and confused ideals of a large segment of his own and the succeeding generation. He is the unhappy warrior that many men would like to be. About him has sprung up a real contemporary hero-myth.*

Any publicity is good publicity if you are selling books, but if you are the writer of those books, it might not help to be told that you court violence, darkness, and death, that your work embodies "a kind of splendid, often very beautiful, disease of the imagination."[5] Previously, he was a talent to be nurtured, a discovery to be worn on the critic's watch fob, a young writer of promise. But this is the new territory where it is open season on his life and his art.

Between business and pleasure, he found time to have a disagreeable confrontation with young John Gardner, who presented himself as the would-be husband of Carol Hemingway, Ernest's younger sister, who was on a writing scholarship at Rollins College. Ernest was pleasant but firm: without his permission, no one married Carol, and John did not have his permission. Ernest became threatening; John stood up to him. "I was indifferent," he said later. "I really was. I didn't hold him in some kind of awe, and I was in love with Carol." Studying abroad that winter in Austria, Carol, with a mind of her own and a will equal to her brother's, was determined to marry Gardner. Ernest, behaving more like a father than a brother, became increasingly furious with the sister who looked more like him than anyone else in the family. When the young couple married in Kitzbühel on March 21, Ernest responded like a jilted lover, angry and hurt; he never let Carol back into his life and never forgave her for leaving it.[6]

Despite the Gardner confrontation, Hemingway's two weeks in New York were a flurry of reasonably pleasant encounters with old friends and new, the most important of which took place in Louis Cohn's House of Books. On Friday, January 20, he visited with Cohn to discuss a limited edition of "God Rest You Merry, Gentlemen," which Cohn was to publish in April. Quite accidentally, a Hemingway collector from Chicago was also at Cohn's to purchase a $75 copy of Hemingway's quite rare *Three Stories & Ten Poems*, three hundred copies of which Robert McAlmon once published in Paris (1923). Cohn introduced the author to his admirer Arnold Gingrich, publisher of *Apparel Arts* and soon to be publisher of a new, as yet unnamed magazine for men. Gingrich explained that back in Key West, Hemingway would find his letter asking Ernest to sign an enclosed copy of *Death in the Afternoon*.[7]

That Friday evening, Hemingway boarded the southbound Seaboard train with a one-way ticket for a lower berth, arriving early Saturday afternoon in Roanoke, where he retrieved his car. On Sunday, leaving the boys with Ada, Pauline took the night train out of Key West to be in Jacksonville when Ernest drove in that afternoon.[8]

————

Miami, February 15. In the shirtsleeve evening, Giuseppi Zangara pushed his way forward to within fifteen feet of the open automobile. As he climbed up on the bench beside Lillian Cross to get a clear view, she saw him pull a revolver from his pocket. "He was aiming right at the President," she told reporters afterward. "I saw him. That's when I caught his arm and forced the gun up." The first bullet missed President-elect Franklin Roosevelt and struck Chicago mayor Cermak in the stomach. Four other bystanders were wounded, two shot in the head, as Zangara wildly emptied his pawnshop pistol. On March 20, thirty-two days after he pulled the trigger, Zangara went to his execution, shouting, "I'm no afraid that chair. Put me in electric chair."[9]

————

Hemingway was interested enough in the attempted assassination to purchase the verbatim testimony of Zangara, whose "beautiful but expensive beliefs," Ernest said, demanded atonement.[10] The surface of the country, however, only rippled with the shock of Roosevelt's close encounter with death, for there were more immediate fears loose in the land. Gold coins and certificates disappeared into private places, forcing banks to close, one by one, then in pairs, in coveys, and finally they all closed, taking a "bank holiday." When Monroe County taxes went unpaid, first Key West garbage collectors, then street cleaners went hungry. A pound of flour sold for three cents, a pound of pork shoulder for nine cents. To pay workers, city governments began printing scrip. No one knew how many people were out of work, on the streets, riding the rails, standing in breadlines, or shivering under city viaducts. No one could afford to count them. Over the radio, between comedy shows laughing in the lap of despair, came the plaintive lyric "Brother, can you spare a dime?"

"Don't worry about me," Hemingway told a young man trying to become a writer, "I have a damned good time—all of the time—or nearly all." Whatever critics said about his work now did not matter. A writer's final reward came after his death: ten lines of poetry or a hundred pages of prose could make any writer immortal. Meanwhile he had the best of life now: fishing, hunting, riding, taking in all of life. As long as he was writing, he never felt "low." "Evidently," he concluded, "I only write you when I'm laid up or low because you don't want to ever worry about me being sad."[11] Now he was writing steadily, every day and well, but he was working so close to the bone that someone should have worried about him.

The usual round of visitors came, fished, drank, and departed: the rich, like young sportsman Tommy Shevlin, flew in by private plane; the less affluent, like the Jesuit priest Father Tom McGrath, arrived by bus.[12] All come to a meal equally set and leave having seen only Hemingway the host who always has an afternoon free for fishing, an evening for food and drink, a commodious man. They do not see him at his writing, nor do they read the handwritten manuscript that is piling up almost too rapidly. For reasons he neither understood nor wished to question, the long summer and fall pursuing marlin and bear refilled the well from which he drew his fiction. Between the end of January and the first of April, he finished the Billings hospital story, wrote two drafts of a disquieting war experience which he gave to his old character Nick Adams, and completed five chapters of a new novel set in Paris.

In the morning he wakes early to return to the hospital story where his fictional Mr. Frazer, the phraser with a broken writing arm, contemplates against his pain the various opiums of the people: religion and music, economics, patriotism, sex and drink and gambling, ambition and new forms of government. "What," he asks himself, "was the real, the actual, opium of the people?"

> He knew it very well. It was gone just a little way around the corner in that well-lighted part of his mind that was there after two or more drinks in the evening; that he knew was there (it was not really there of course). What was it? He knew very well. What was it? Of course; bread was the opium of the people.[13]

So intense are Hemingway's mornings that not even heaving against afternoon fish can take away the churning inside his head where stories keep writing themselves, summoned or not. Like Mr. Frazer, he needs at times like this a sovereign touch of gin, a few fingers of evening whiskey to take the edge off, to put his mind at rest, letting him sleep.

In the novel, which no one saw but himself, pages multiply quickly: the story of a writer who can no longer write, wants to paint but cannot paint in the cold Paris studio, where not so many years ago he, Ernest, once lived when first separated from Hadley. In one draft he called the character Philip Haines; in two others, James Allen: by whatever name, the man is a writer separated from his wife, who still loves him, while he is in love with Dorothy Rodgers, the "other woman," who has returned to the States until his divorce is final. The setting for the story Ernest knew by heart, but as his writer-cum-painter settled deeper into lonely depression, the fiction began to twist. One James Allen version begins, "For two weeks James Allen had wanted to kill a girl." In the Philip Haines version, the estranged wife, Harriet, called "Harry," is planning to remarry. When Dorothy finally returns, Philip, before driving to Havre to meet her, buys a pistol for protection on the road. As Hemingway writes about the fictional Harriet, Hadley Richardson Hemingway, eight years divorced from him, is planning to marry Paul Mowrer, a prominent journalist with whom she has maintained an open affair since Ernest divorced her and whom Hemingway's visiting son Bumby now regards as a second father. Had Pauline been reading the story in which the "other woman" so closely resembled herself, she might have worried when the writer/painter found Dorothy's letters unsatisfactory, found her refusal to return before the divorce maddening. "She'd said she would come if he asked her. Hadn't he asked her? He couldn't have asked her any plainer."[14] Before the end of February, Hemingway wrote Perkins that he was going well on a novel they had not discussed. He had four chapters written and, unlike early going in *A Farewell to Arms*, he knew how this story was going to end.[15]

At the same moment, Arnold Gingrich was writing Ernest about a new quarterly magazine he was starting which would be "to the American male what *Vogue* is to the female. But it won't be the least damn bit like *Vanity Fair*. It aims to have ample hair on its chest, to say nothing of adequate cojones." When Gingrich decided to call the magazine *Esquire*, Ernest found plenty of fault with such an elevated title, but Gingrich held his ground. Without saying he wanted to use the Hemingway name to secure other writers, he asked Hemingway to contribute to the first issue anything he wanted to submit. "No editing whatsoever," he promised. "You write and I print." The offering price for an essay was $250, maybe more if he found he could afford it.[16] Hemingway's initial response was guarded: $250 was not worth negotiating, for he could get ten times that much for a story, but it was interesting pocket money for something less than a story. Maybe he would send something, but Gingrich should not count on it.[17]

It was not paucity of money offered that changed Hemingway's mind. By February he was picking up information that Harcourt Brace was publishing Gertrude Stein's *The Autobiography of Alice B. Toklas* and that *Atlantic Monthly* was serializing parts of the memoir that were less than flattering to Ernest. In March, he kept Gingrich on the hook, saying he might have something for the first issue.[18] In April, before he had read *Atlantic*'s first installment, he was telling Gingrich that Gertrude was "a fine woman until she went professionally goofy complete lack of judgment and stoppage of all sense lesbian with the old menopause. . . . Then she got the idea that anybody who was any good must be queer, if they did not seem to be they were merely concealing it."[19] He went on to promise four "letters" for Gingrich's quarterly. Without telling Gingrich, he secured a platform for his own ends: if every former friend, like Stein, was going to put his private life on public display, he needed a forum to set things right. The writer who abhorred personal publicity, who would not attend the Paramount movie premiere, who would not talk about his writing with the *Havana Post*, that writer is about to enter the public arena with only the barest fictive mask between himself and his audience.

———

Dear Mr. Hemingway:
I would like to be a man and to write the way you do. The last chapter of Death in the Afternoon makes me sadder than anything I ever read. . . . it makes me remember that I can't ever live the whole of life, that I can't have the beautiful soundness of domesticity and the rightness of three children . . . and the deep fine delight in the color and drama of a quick, moving, unsettled life . . . because having one would give an edge of guilt or unrightness to the other. . . . it makes me sad because it reminds me I am a woman and can't possibly get the savor out of life a man can— because a woman always has the feeling that she musn't lose an ounce of what she hates to call "womanliness."

Mary Post[20]

———

The way he wrote was early and often, every day when it was going right. Sitting in bed with several sharpened pencils, he wrote in cursive on legal-size sheets of unlined paper with a flat surface beneath them. That morning in the bedroom on Whitehead Street, he began a new story: "As I came into the town walking the bicycle along the street to avoid the shell holes." Then he crossed it out, and started over with shattered trees and dead bodies floating in the ditch and the narrator pushing his bicycle along that Italian road.[21] The handwriting runs for several lines smooth and parallel to the bottom of the page before it begins to slope down from left to right as he picks up speed only to break it off and start over.

The second draft told the whole story of the American narrator returning to visit his old battalion along the river that he remembers too well. Drawing on fragments discarded from "A Natural History of the Dead" and his own still vivid war memories, Hemingway opened this draft with a dispassionate review of a battle's aftermath left in the fields of Fossalta, the village where he was blown up that

night fifteen years earlier.[22] Still writing in the first person, he raced
through the story, scribbling revisions between lines and up the margins. As he writes, the story splits into two parts: the narrator's shaky
return to the front Italian lines to raise troop morale by walking
about in an American uniform, and an embedded story of a "hysterical" Italian lieutenant, who first appears charging two enlisted men
with sexually perverse activity, for which he says they should be shot.
The Major, who cannot afford to lose soldiers unnecessarily from his
thinly defended position, sends the men back to their posts with a
reprimand. That same day, when shells fall on the Italian lines, the
"hysterical" lieutenant, whom we learn behaved badly during a previous attack, shoots himself through his palm, pretending it is a shrapnel wound. The Major, perfectly willing to lose a useless officer, puts
him under guard to face charges later. On either side of these two
incidents the narrator and Major Paravicini reminisce about early
days in the war when they both faced attacks fortified with grappa
laced with ether. The story ends with the narrator being sent on his
way by the Major.[23]

Thematically the story is about the failure of courage, a condition
with which the narrator says he has some experience, having been
unable to face an attack sober. But never getting inside the narrator's
head keeps the story at a distance, which no amount of piecemeal
revision could fix. In the next draft, composed on the typewriter,
Hemingway threw out the hysterical lieutenant, salvaged all useful details, and focused the story completely on the narrator's now
clearly unstable mental state, a condition vaguely suggested in the
first draft. On the first page of the new draft, he changed the point of
view so that his character had a name—Nicholas Adams—and the
new, offstage narrator could tell the reader what was happening in
Nick's head. Keeping the same structure as the first draft, the author
used two views of Nick's shell-shocked behavior, in and out of his
head, to replace the two incidents with the lieutenant. What began
as an unpleasant but not threatening story, told with little comment,
became a complex, disturbing trip into that other country of the
mind where

some did not get down but we went up and we went back and we came down, we always came down, and there was Gaby Delys, oddly enough, with feathers on, you called me baby doll a year ago tadada you said that I was rather nice to know with feathers on with feathers off the great Gaby and my name's Harry Pilcer[24] . . . those were the nights the river ran so much wider and stiller than it should and outside Fossalta there was a low house painted yellow.[25]

Having known the Paris weirdness of shell-shocked, death-loving, war-wounded veterans, having observed up close the erratic behavior of Zelda Fitzgerald and Jane Mason, and having lived with his own bad dreams and night sweats, he let the words run free, writing a prose beyond his previous limits.[26] Nick, speaking in tongues about the efficacy of grasshoppers as fish bait, is a mind clearly out of control. Paravicini thinks that Nick's head wound should have been trepanned—core drilled and drained. "It's a hell of a nuisance," Nick says, "once they've had you certified as nutty. No one ever has any confidence in you again." He called the story "A Way You'll Never Be."

As he was working on the second full draft, Jane Mason dropped into Key West for several days of fishing, drinking, and storytelling. In the Hemingway yard, her gift of peacocks preened in the sun, and on Duval Street that week, the Strand Theater, with unintentional irony, featured *Ladies They Talk About.*[27] As the stunning wife of the Pan-American Airlines man in charge of the Caribbean, Jane was accustomed to being talked about, partied around, photographed, and remembered. At eighteen, she married Grant Mason, a bright, athletic, moneyed Yale graduate who spurned Wall Street for the excitement of the new airline industry. Now seven years into their marriage, Jane's sometimes erratic behavior was a continuing puzzle and sometime irritant to Grant. "If only she had been at rest with herself, with her own talents," her son said years afterward.[28] Hemingway would later say that he wrote "A Way You'll Never Be" to distract a young woman who was losing her mind. Everyone took the woman to be long-legged Jane of the golden hair, the graceful young

Jane of the magazine ads, but if Ernest thought she was going crazy in March of 1933, he kept it to himself, not that he wasn't keenly attuned to aberrant behavior lurking beneath smooth surfaces.

———

Censorship of all the Cuban domestic press, of all incoming papers from abroad and of all outgoing cables . . . a reign of terror is operating under the direction of President Machado. Political assassinations of opponents are the order of the day. Criminals let loose from jails have been given authority to inaugurate a regime of the bludgeon. Freedom of the press, assembly, and petition is dead. . . . Secret police infest the island. Misery is almost universal and the rumbles of approaching revolt are swelling.

—*Key West Citizen*, March 3, 1933

———

Pushing hard to finish a book of short stories for the fall season, Hemingway wrote almost every morning that March. When Lent began, he took his list of sins to confession and received communion on Ascension Day, fulfilling his Easter Duty.[29] At St. Mary's Catholic church, he was not the most regular parishioner, but he and his family attend Mass when they are in town, and he supported with modest donations the various causes of the resident Jesuits, whose order he admires. When attending Mass, he stands at the back of the church, never taking a pew, for his right knee, which is still braced from his war wounding, cannot take the hard kneeling. His parish priest, Father Dougherty, said, "Oh, yes, he never misses Sunday Mass. . . . Easter duty? Most assuredly. Lovely wife and children, all of them Catholics, good Catholics too."[30]

By the middle of March, most of the nation's banks are once more open, President Roosevelt's new regime having certified them sound, and hoarders of gold are surrendering it under threat of punishment as the United States went off the gold standard. On March 15, the stock market, closed for twelve days, reopened. In Germany, Chancellor Adolf Hitler's government refused to buy from Jews; in the universities Jewish professors were barred from their classrooms. In

Key West, *Mädchen in Uniform*, the talking German picture that broke all New York movie-run records, opened at the Strand.[31]

The nation, the President said, has nothing to fear but fear itself; Hemingway was less certain. A few days before the stock market closed, he invested part of his Scribner's advance money in blue-chip stocks to hedge against what he thought would be inevitable inflation.[32] Also rightfully worried about Cuban repression becoming a threat, he asked Max Perkins to provide a letter signed by Charles Scribner on his "most impressive stationery" that might, in time of revolution, keep Ernest from being shot.[33] The resulting insurance letter said that Hemingway was "preparing for publication by us a work on the migratory fish of the Gulf Stream, their habits, and capture, with a special reference to the fishing in Cuban waters from the sporting standpoint."[34]

On Wednesday afternoon of Holy Week, Ernest, Charles Thompson, and Joe Russell on board the *Anita* waved back to their wives as they motored out of Garrison Bight, heading for Cuba. As they passed beyond the Sand Key light, a large school of porpoise were leaping from the water in front of a refinery tanker. By eight o'clock that night, with a new moon rising, they picked up the white glare of Havana on the horizon; at 1:30 a.m. on Holy Thursday, they passed under the battlements of Morro Castle and into Havana harbor. The three men slept late that morning, cleared their papers with the harbormaster, lunched at the Florida, and caught dolphins that afternoon with Grant Mason on board.[35] In the early evening of Good Friday, while the fishing party is eating supper, explosions rock Havana, marking the beginning of "Red Week," as the student ABC Revolutionary Society has threatened. All through the night, bombs detonate at fifteen-to-thirty-minute intervals, emptying the streets; by morning, troops armed with revolvers and rifles bring Holy Saturday traffic to a standstill as they stop and search anything moving. On Easter Sunday morning, church bells speak of the risen Christ, but in city jails and prison, chemists, doctors, lawyers, students, and many university faculty are in holding cells, some never to be seen again.[36]

Neither that day nor the next did the *Havana Post* speak of bombings, or of martial law, or of "La Porra," as government death squads armed with bludgeons are called. Reprisals came as swift, public applications of *ley de fuga*, the law of flight. In a residential neighborhood, two young brothers are pushed from a Secret Service car and told to run for their lives. As they flee in opposite directions, government sharpshooters posted above the street open fire. From his apartment balcony, a newspaper correspondent sees what happened to one of the students:

> *The first fusillade missed the boy and he started running, shouting, "Don't shoot any more." Despite his cries for mercy, a second volley followed. The victim, hit in the head by bullets, staggered, ran some twenty feet and collapsed as a third volley poured into his body. The uniformed Negroes who had done the fatal shooting came down the side of the cliff, with rifles and revolvers in their hands, to inspect the body, after which they sauntered off, unmolested by the uniformed national police, who arrived on the scene immediately.*[37]

On Easter Sunday, waiting for Uncle Gus and Karl Thompson to come over from Key West, Ernest went to Mass and then out to the Masons' house for lunch, where he stayed through supper. In his day log, he noted that he drank too much.[38]

For the newspaper, Hemingway maintained and amplified his intentions of writing a book on the marlin:

> *Ernest Hemingway returned to Havana yesterday for 65 days of deep-sea fishing in adjacent waters. An avocation of long standing, fishing in the Gulf Stream will be the subject of another epic comparable to "Death in the Afternoon." . . . A deliberate study, Hemingway has assembled quantities of material on the subject which will be amplified during his stay here. At the same time he is working on another novel; and a volume of short stories will be published by Scribner's during the coming autumn. . . . As is their custom, the party is stopping at the Hotel Ambos Mundos.*[39]

The week after Easter, as bombings and nightly gunfire diminished, the Hemingway party fished hard by day and did nothing to attract attention when ashore. The following Friday night, bullet-riddled bodies of four students were brought to the Havana morgue, and the American manager of a local theater, informed by police his life was in danger because of his associations, departed immediately for New Orleans.[40]

———

In the photograph a young Cuban lies face-up on the pavement. His head is turned to the left facing the camera, which is quite close. On the left cheek is an almost perfectly round, black spot, too dark to be a birthmark, perhaps either a bruise or dirt. Across the right cheek are fainter stains that seem to be the residue left after a hurried washing. Black hair, neither long nor short, cushions the head and spreads into shadow. The white shirt has been pulled down, exposing smooth shoulders. Because the mouth is slightly open, one can see small, even white teeth. The eyes are closed, as if sleeping. From the left corner of the open mouth a thin trickle of dark blood runs across the cheek, past the ear, and blends with the mass of darker hair.[41]

———

The face of Jane Mason was a study in white and gold, a face to turn any man's head, an effect in which her husband took pride. Her beauty was, in fact, a business asset for Grant Mason, who was busy extending Pan American's network of airlines throughout South America. At their home looking out on the exclusive Jaimanitas golf course, they gave parties so exhilarating that old men remembered them thirty years later. Jane and Grant were the Murphys and Fitzgeralds of the Anglo-Cuban Havana establishment: he the clubbable Yale man, she the young beauty whose wild streak added to her excitement. Tallish, big-boned, and athletic, she wanted all her life to be remembered for something more than her beautiful face, but most of her life she belonged to some man. The tombstone inscription she wrote for herself years later reads, "Talents too many, not enough of any." She was an active sportswoman and sometime daredevil, danced so well the floor cleared to watch her, at one time owned and managed a Havana art gallery, and was fluent in three languages.

That summer of 1933, while the Machado regime tottered, the Masons, like most of the Anglo-Cuban establishment, lived as if nothing were different. Their English nanny, Haitian houseman, Chinese cook, Italian butler, German gardener, and Cuban chauffeur maintained order, managed the house and grounds, fed and cared for the family and the animal menagerie: honey bear, monkey, peacocks, flamingos, fox, parrots, Doberman, Dalmatian, and Great Dane. Cuban revolutions were, after all, not exactly a novelty: there had been dicey times before and they would come, no doubt, again, but that did not mean that their lives would be affected. When Cuban soldiers during an uprising actually threatened the Masons and American Ambassador Guggenheim, who lived next to them, Grant stood on the front porch with a megaphone telling the soldiers that he was armed with two shotguns, "and that if they dared trespass on American soil, he was going to shoot the hell out of them."[42]

Despite street killings and bombs in the night, despite rumors which exaggerated both, Jane and Grant were occasionally on board the *Anita* in search of marlin, but almost always with Pauline at hand. Later many would say that a torrid affair took place that summer between Ernest and Jane, but letters, the *Anita* log, and the *Havana Post* show that Hemingway had little time for adultery. Between April 14 and 27, while Charles Thompson and Gus Pfeiffer were both in Havana, Ernest could not risk encouraging Jane, no matter how interesting he found her. During the following two days, Pauline arrived with Bumby and Patrick, staying until May 13, when Jane and Grant left for Miami. The Masons returned to Havana on the morning of May 23; that evening, young Patrick and Ada Stern returned on the ferry from Key West to join Bumby and Ernest; the three boys and Ada became guests at the Masons' house at Jaimanitas. The following afternoon:

HAVANA WOMAN,

THREE CHILDREN

IN AUTO CRASH

Mrs. Grant Mason and

Hemingway's Sons Escape Injury

Mrs. G. Grant Mason, Jr., her 3-year-old son Tony, and John and Patrick Hemingway, sons of Ernest Hemingway, the writer, narrowly escaped serious injury and possible death yesterday afternoon at 4:45 p.m. near El Cano when Mrs. Mason's car left the road and plunged over a 40-foot embankment, turning over three times and landing upside down.

Extracting themselves from the car which was almost totally wrecked, they found that except for minor bruises and scratches, all had escaped unhurt.

En route from Finca Milagras to Jaimanitas, Mrs. Mason had just passed through El Cano when she met a bus coming at high speed and pulled out of its path to the edge of the road. The shoulder of the road gave way and the car, traveling at a slow speed, slowly turned over, gathering momentum as it rolled down the embankment. Aware of the possible danger of fire from broken fuel lines, Mrs. Mason shut off the ignition as the car started to overturn. The doors of the sedan were jammed but a small opening in the window of the front door enabled them to crawl to safety. The bus for which they had turned out continued on its way with the driver and the passengers unaware of the accident. Passing motorists, employees of the Pan-American Airways, brought Mrs. Mason and the children to Havana.[43]

Years later, her son remembered Jane's Chevrolet with the yellow wire wheels slipping off the road and rolling down into an earthen amphitheater dug out for baseball games.

Patrick was on my right and Bumby was in the backseat. And I remember the car sliding, and then started to head down the hill. . . . it rolled over and over. And I remember . . . the door jammed so that Patrick held on to me and I held on to my mother . . . Bumby had put his hands on the ceiling. . . . He sort of cartwheeled inside the car down the bank.[44]

The same day the story appeared in the *Havana Post*, Grace Hemingway in Oak Park read the wire service version. She wrote to Ernest: "We are all so shocked to read in the papers this morning of your near tragedy. God is so good to have spared their lives and kept them safe and sound, apparently. I shall pray that no after effects come to them. I just could not spare my two oldest grandsons."[45] From Key West, where she was probably informed by phone, Pauline, still dazed from the news, said it would take her a while to "grasp" the accident, but Jane, who had grasped it completely, had all her sympathy.[46]

The following morning at nine-thirty, Jane appeared at the dock with a terrible hangover, but apparently unhurt, ready to fish. As the paper reported and the *Anita's* log confirms, she landed two marlin, fishing that day and the next two.[47] Afterward the story turns opaque. Some say that Jane tried to kill herself by leaping from the low balcony of her Jaimanitas home, but the lawn and shrubs that were then below the balcony made it an unlikely choice for a suicidal jump. One newspaper said she was shot in the back by a revolutionary—a story quickly denied. For certain, there was the auto accident followed by two strenuous days of fishing, followed by the newspaper story: "Mrs. G. Grant Mason, Jr., is a patient at the Anglo-American hospital undergoing treatment for shock brought on by an automobile accident several days ago."[48]

At which point Jane's summer came to an end. She remained in the hospital, where "treatment for shock" may have been the case, or it may have been a polite phrase to obscure the causes. In his logbook, Hemingway noted at least one hospital visit to Jane before Grant sent her to New York for extended treatment:

MRS. GRANT MASON WILL SAIL TODAY

En route to New York, Mrs. G. Grant Mason, Jr., will sail this after-noon on the Morro Castle.

Mrs. Mason has been in the Anglo-American hospital recuperating from nervous shock resulting from an automobile accident several weeks ago; and upon the advice of her Havana physician will remain in the Doctors' hospital in New York for a few days before going to Tuxedo Park to visit Mr. Mason's family.

Their young son, Tony, went north three weeks ago.[49]

Three weeks later, Hemingway, thanking Archie MacLeish for visiting Jane in the New York hospital, tried to explain about her husband, Grant, who, five days after placing his wife in the Havana hospital, left for Miami to buy a new motor launch.[50] Any husband tolerated long enough became the wife's own fault, Ernest said.

All women married to a wrong husband are bad luck for themselves and all their friends. . . . Mr. M. is a man of great wealth and will have more[,] none ever as yet having been spent. People seem to put up longer with a rich than a poor twirp. Also people put up with each other beyond our understanding. . . . I tried to write a very short story about it by saying Every spring Mrs. M. wanted to marry someone else but in the spring of 1933 she broke her back. That's a little too simple too.[51]

It was not until early September that Jane Mason, having spent months in a body cast, was able to write the Hemingways that in another two months she would be fitted with her "iron virgin" back support which she would have to wear for the next year. With more back treatment a possibility, she was continuing sessions with a psychoanalyst, apparently at Grant's insistence. Nothing like it, she said, for diminishing what small ego was left. Down the middle of her back was a seven-and-a-half-inch scar, and another on her leg where the bone graft was taken to repair her fractured vertebrae. She hoped to go to Europe and maybe meet the Hemingways on safari, but it seemed unlikely.[52]

———

Cabanas. In a small hotel miles from Havana, they sleep beneath mosquito netting to wake at four to the grinding of morning coffee; breakfast at six: tortilla, guava paste, soft-boiled eggs in a glass, chorizo, cider, black coffee. Sun rising on a calm bay, royal palms dark-leafed, their white trunks rising out of mist white on the water. Behind, dark mountains, and closer, green wooded hills of mahogany and cedar. The surface of the bay ripples with a rising school of small fish; an alligator slides off the bank. Flocks of white egrets and herons along the river and the water turning from brown to blue where it meets the sea. The writer and his wife drift through this day and another, and one other outside of time.[53]

———

Max was pleading with him for the book title so they could set up the salesmen's dummy, but Ernest could not find one—not in Baudelaire, the Bible, or in Old English poetry. *The Twelve Good Joys* was ironic but misleading; *Strange Countries* was no better. When he and Pauline, that first week in June, motored down the coast to Cabanas, the missing title was on his mind as he rearranged the stories in various sequences. In unlikely places, like Thomas Browne's *Urn Burial*, he is reminded of what he knew, forgot, and always relearned: nothing lasted—neither friends nor places—they all went under. In forty years, Browne told him, a man's gravestone is no longer legible. Putting aside the reference books, he finds the title within himself: *Winner Take Nothing*. Before he returns to Havana to put Pauline on the Key West ferry, he adds a neomedieval epigraph of his own device:

> *Unlike all other forms of lutte or combat the conditions are that the winner shall take nothing; neither his ease, nor his pleasure, nor any*

*notions of glory; nor, if he win far enough, shall there be any reward
within himself.*[54]

As effusive as he ever got, Max Perkins said it was "a very fine title. I
wish you would tell me where that quotation came from."[55]

Max also wanted the stories as soon as possible, for the deadline
on fall publication was close. Hemingway resists. With thirteen stories being typed, he still does not have the anchor, the story at the end
that will hold the others in place. Two days after Pauline returned to
Key West, Ernest woke well before dawn and while still in bed began
writing a story about his father's suicide, a story he has tried to tell
several times, a story that is now coming out right. Often his writing process, which he did not like to analyze for fear of "spooking" it,
worked that way: some fragment of an idea, broken off, shelved but
remembered, and then when he least expected it, the story was there
because it had been writing itself somewhere in his head.

The story about his father's suicide he first tried to tell at a distance, using a young boy discovering his father's hunting death was
no accident. After ten pages, he quit it, unable to deal with the real
issues: the dead father and the dominant mother. Years before Clarence Hemingway pulled the trigger that ended his life (1928), Ernest
wrote "Indian Camp," in which an Indian father, unable to bear his
wife's protracted labor pains, slits his own throat with a straight razor
while Dr. Adams delivers the screaming woman by a primitive, jack-
knifed cesarean section without anesthesia. In the rowboat coming
back across the lake with his father, the doctor, Nick asks, "Do many
men kill themselves?" It was too prophetic to think about, the death
of the father, the inquiring son, sex and death. The hunting father
who kills and cures; the screaming mother, all bloody in birth: the
secrets were out. What else was there to think about? Hemingway
returns now to that father/son impasse: the knowledge of sex and
death.

He wants to blame the father's death on the mother, his own
mother, because that is easier than admitting his father's "nervousness" is like his own: highs and lows, cycling each time a little farther

down that dark road he will one day call "black ass." He needs to blame his mother, whom he cannot forgive for being alive.[56] So there in Havana, he writes:

> *There is only one thing to do if a man is married to a woman with whom he has nothing in common, with whom there can be no question of justice but only a gross fact of utter selfishness and hysterical emotionalism and that is to get rid of her.*[57]

But when he said it, he knew he could not let it stand, because she will read it. No matter how much he wants to hate his mother, and he insists he does hate her, tells everyone what a horror Grace Hemingway is, but no matter, he cannot hurt her that directly. Having said it, he takes out the page and never uses it.

With idyllic Cabanas days with Pauline fresh in his mind, and with memories of his father rising up while his own son, Bumby, is with him on the boat, roles flicker in and out of focus: father, husband, son, and lover—a continuum. He is now the father, the self-named Papa, and he is still the grieving son. The story begins in a car with Nicholas Adams driving through a small, depression-era town where the traffic lights "would be gone next year when the payments on the system were not met." As the town gives way to harvested fields of corn, soybeans, and peas, Nick hunts them in his head, thinking which way the quail would fly. These fields take him back to hunting fields of his youth with his father as instructor. About hunting, the father's advice was always useful, just as it was unsound on sexual matters.

> *His father had summed up the whole matter by stating that masturbation produced blindness, insanity and death, while a man who went out with prostitutes would contract hideous venereal diseases and that the thing to do was to keep your hands off of people.*

This memory leads Nick to his father's suicide, which he needs to write about if he is ever to put it to rest, but it is too soon, too many people still alive. He remembers his father's face, repaired by the undertaker, a face that had been making itself for a long time. "We all betrayed," Hemingway wrote, "some more than others, in our several ways."

That reverie takes Nick back to his own sexual education with the soft and pliant young Indian girl in the summer woods of his youth. As he fondly remembers their naive and innocent coupling, the light begins to fail, and Nick's mind returns to his father, who was with him always "in thickets, on small hills, or when going through dead grass, whenever splitting wood or hauling water." The father he loved, admired, and even hated, hating enough once to draw a bead on him, holding the shotgun loaded and cocked, thinking, "I can blow him to hell. I can kill him." At this point Nick's son, silently riding beside him through this remembrance of things past, asks Nick what it was like when he was a boy hunting with the Indians. He cannot tell his son that the Indian girl "did first what no one has ever done better." The boy wants to know about his grandfather, but Nick can only say he was a fine hunter with amazing eyesight. The boy wants to discuss where the grandfather is buried, when they will visit his "tomb," and where Nick will be buried.[58]

Stories embedded inside a story: Nick and his father, sex and death, Nick and his son, past and present—it was a rich story but not the whole story. Stories never were the thing itself. Nick was never himself but someone he remembered in the mirror. He left out his mother and the way she seemed to dominate his father, left out their arguments, said nothing about his father's moodiness, erased the pain when his father's depressions left the puzzled son hurt and isolated in a house full of women. He might never be able to write the whole story.

He first called it "The Tomb of My Grandfather" before finding its final title: "Fathers and Sons." With it, his book of stories was focused as clearly as he could make it. On July 13, he mailed Perkins thirteen stories, with this anchor story to follow as soon as he had it revised. He wanted to lead off with young Nick and the whores in "The Light of the World" and end with Nick and his son driving past the darkening fields of autumn.[59]

———

But what a book, they both agreed, would be the real story of Hemingway, not those he writes but the real story of Hemingway. . . . they both said, it is so flattering to have a pupil who takes training . . . he looks modern and he smells of the museums. But what story that of the real Hem, and one he should tell himself but alas he never will. . . . Hemingway although a sportsman was easily tired. He used to get quite worn out walking from his house to ours. . . . Ernest is very fragile, whenever he does anything sporting something breaks, his arm, his leg, his head.[60]

—Gertrude Stein

———

Gertrude Stein got in the first blow, but he was always a counterpuncher, promising to write his own memoirs, funny and accurate, when there was nothing else to write.[61] Then in June, Max Eastman, another old friend, got inside his guard with an essay review in *The New Republic* of *Death in the Afternoon* that hurt his pride. "Romantic gushing and sentimentalizing," Eastman called Hemingway's descriptions of the bullfight, "child's fairy-story writing."

To drag in notions of honor and glory here . . . [is] rather sophomoric. But to pump words over it like tragedy and dramatic conflict is mere romantic nonsense. . . . It is of course a commonplace that Hemingway lacks the serene confidence that he is a full-sized man . . . [he has] a continual sense of obligation to put forth evidences of red-blooded masculinity. . . . and it has moreover begotten a veritable school of fiction-writers—a literary style, you might say, of wearing false hair on the chest.[62]

On June 11, Ernest, having read the essay in Havana, wired Max Perkins, "Tell your friend Eastman will break his jaw."[63] Perkins's reassurances that Ernest was invulnerable to his critics did nothing to soothe his anger. "The swine aren't worth writing for. I swear to christ they're not. Every phase of the whole racket is so disgusting that it makes you feel like vomiting."[64]

Taking Eastman's jibe about being a "full-sized man" to be a question about his sexual potency, Hemingway wrote *The New Republic* a sarcastic letter, inviting Eastman to "elaborate his nostalgic speculations on my sexual incapacity. Here they would be read (aloud) with much enjoyment (our amusements are simple) and I should be glad to furnish illustrations to brighten up Mr. Eastman's prose if you consider them advisable."[65] In private he was less restrained. "I suppose it is good to see while you are alive the process that takes place after you are dead," he wrote MacLeish, "but I have so god damned much pride (and it is all I have) that I can't watch it with pleasure."[66] There was another alternative, of course: don't wait for others to write your life.

The first week in July, Pauline returned briefly to Havana to pick up Bumby, and was back in Key West packing for their African safari when the giant marlin began their annual run. On July 6, Ernest hooked and fought a huge marlin for over two hours, only to lose him while changing rods. The following day, Ernest, his back muscles sore and knotted, tied into another enormous marlin that pulled the *Anita* stern-first, while he fought the fish to a standstill. Fearing that his back and hands would give out before he brought the marlin to gaff, he promised a hundred Hail Marys, a hundred Our Fathers, and $5 to the Church.[67] It was not the record fish that he came for, but it was the biggest fish he'd ever brought across the transom.[68] On July 18, three days before his birthday, Ernest and Joe Russell called it quits for the marlin season with a total catch of fifty-four. Shortly after midnight, having been guests of honor at an Ambos Mundos farewell party, they took the *Anita* out of the harbor and set a course for Key West, ninety miles away.[69]

As soon as he got unpacked, he began writing "A Cuban Letter," for the first edition of Arnold Gingrich's *Esquire*, the quarterly which quickly became a monthly. Accompanied eventually by seventeen photos, the "Letter" took its reader from the Ambos Mundos out through the harbor and into the Gulf Stream where marlin rose to the teaser baits. The reader learned what to eat for breakfast and lunch, how to fix baits, the feeding habits of marlin, when to slack and when to strike, how to fight the fish, tire him, bring him to gaff. By the time the essay appeared in print, Ernest would be in Paris on his way to Africa, each stop becoming another "Letter." For the next two and a half years, his life was a continuing serial, reaching an expanding, largely male readership. The first edition of *Esquire* sold out its 105,000 printed copies. Two years later, it was selling half a million copies a month, reaching the largest audience ever afforded an American author.[70]

Chapter Six

1933—34

AFRICAN GAME TRAILS

Spain and East Africa

HAVING LEFT GREGORY in the care of Ada Stern, Ernest, Pauline, her sister Jinny, and his sons John and Patrick arrived in Havana on August 4, just as the lights were going out. During the three days before they sailed for Europe, the Hemingway party in the Ambos Mundos had a good view of the streets where the Machado regime was reaching its violent conclusion. After all the political maneuvering, the student ABC underground, bombs in the night, and assassination attempts on Machado, what brought down the Cuban dictator were the drivers for a local bus company striking over wages and working conditions. Slowly, other trades across the city joined the drivers, until the machine stopped. By August 4, before its typesetters joined the shutdown, the *Havana Post* ran a banner headline: GENERAL STRIKE THREAT SPREADS. The Hemingways arrived with no buses, no streetcars, no taxis running. On the docks, longshoremen and stevedores let fruit rot and freight sit. No food came into the paralyzed city. Machado bargained with the leftists, thinking they controlled the workers, but the strike was beyond anyone's control. On August 7, the Hemingways' ship—*Reina de la Pacifica*, with unloaded freight for Havana still on board—managed somehow to leave port, but not before a false rumor was in the streets that Machado had resigned. The riotous mob that poured into the Boulevard de Prado was met with gunfire from a loyal cavalry detachment; when the streets cleared, forty were dead, two hundred wounded, and the army occupied Havana under martial law.[1]

Three days out of Havana, Ernest wrote Max Perkins, furious that galley proofs for *Winner Take Nothing* had not reached him in Havana. Despite the general strike closing the post office, Hemingway held Scribner's to blame for insufficient postage. Angry over Gertrude Stein's accusations of his fragility and Eastman's slurs on his manhood, he took out his anger on Max, accusing Perkins of disloyalty to him and to *Winner Take Nothing*. His detractors, whom he called Max's friends, could not touch this new novel he was writing. Gertrude and others so eager to pronounce him finished would break, but he, Ernest, would outlast them, outwrite them, be there when the final counting was done.[2]

By the time the Hemingways docked at Santander, Spain, the Cuban government was in shambles. In the predawn darkness of August 12, President Machado, his retinue, and twenty-eight pieces of luggage were ferried out to a Pan Am seaplane waiting in the harbor by arrangement of the U.S. ambassador to fly them to safety.[3] It was the age of revolutions in Russia, Germany, Spain, South America, Cuba—some at the ballot box, some at gunpoint, and Ernest's interest in revolutions was neither lukewarm nor recent. One of his earliest sketches (1923) became a one-page story he called "The Revolutionist," and in the fall of 1927, he had begun a novel ("A New Slain Knight") about a professional revolutionist which he broke off, admitting in a note to himself that he did not yet know enough to write that story.[4] In 1934, a character in *Green Hills of Africa* would remember:

I was crouched down behind a marble-topped table while they were shooting in Havana. They came by in cars shooting at everybody they saw. I took my drink with me and I was very proud not to have spilled it or forgotten it. The children said, "Mother, can we go out in the afternoon to see the shooting?" . . . I don't want to just hear about revolutions. All we see or hear is revolutions. I'm sick of them.[5]

After disembarking at Santander on August 17, the Hemingway party made its way first to La Coruna to decompress and then by train to San Sebastián, where Hadley's telegram of greetings was waiting for them.[6] Having recently married Paul Mowrer, her longtime friend and lover, Hadley was as happy as Ernest to turn the care of Bumby and Patrick over to their old nanny, Henrietta. This arrangement left Ernest, Pauline, and Jinny free to spend two months in Spain, where their dollars were worth more than in Paris.[7] True to Ernest's prediction, President Roosevelt was devaluing the dollar in an effort to pull American industry out of the depression. On Uncle Gus's advice, Ernest did not sell the depressed Warner stock Gus had given them to finance the safari. Instead he borrowed money from Gus against the stock's future value while making nominal interest payments on the loan.

By the end of August, Ernest, Pauline, and Jinny were registered at the Hotel Biarritz in Madrid, where he was correcting the finally delivered galleys for *Winner Take Nothing*. Still worrying over story placement and titles, Hemingway changed "Give Us a Prescription, Doctor," as it was printed in *Scribner's Magazine*, back to its original title, "The Gambler, the Nun, and the Radio." Uncertain about "Fathers and Sons," he invited Max to cable him if one of the alternates he proposed sounded better. The book's dedication should be "To A. MacLeish." He also asked that a note be added as inconspicuously as possible to "A Natural History of the Dead" saying that it was being reprinted at the author's request. Perkins honored the request with a footnote probably more detailed than Hemingway had in mind.

This story was published in a rather technical book called Death in the Afternoon, *which sold, or rather was offered for sale, at $3.50. It*

is reprinted here in case any one not caring to spend that appreciable
sum for a rather technical book should care to read it.[8]

More significant changes were made at Max's urging: three "anglo-
saxon phrases" eliminated and other possibly offensive phrases
revised. When the bartender in "Light of the World" challenges
Tom's attempt to sample the "free lunch," Tom no longer replied,
"Up your ass." Now it was "You know where." And in "God Rest You
Merry, Gentlemen," Doc Wilcox's advice to the sexually tormented
young boy—"Oh, go and jack-off"—was reduced to a blank. In
"A Natural History of the Dead," Ernest told Max he could either
leave "fuck" as "f--k" as it was printed in *Death in the Afternoon*, or
change it to "f----." Max, given that opportunity, took out the "k."
In his "small" campaign to reform the genteel tradition, Hemingway
always argued for full usage of the English language, but without his
publisher's strong support, he could not afford to lead a one-man
crusade. In Paris, Henry Miller was writing furiously on books that
would not be published in America for another twenty-five years.[9]

Hemingway completely ignored Perkins's inquiry about the new
novel Ernest said he was writing. Never mentioned again by Hemingway, the James Allen (failed writer) novel was abandoned but not
forgotten. Once centered in Madrid, with Pauline next to him and
Hadley remarried, he probably realized that the James Allen story
would deeply hurt both women, who were easily recognized as the
wife and lover in the story. Like his 1927–28 attempt to write about
a revolutionist, the Allen exercise served its purpose of keeping him
writing when he did not know what to write next. Another reason to
abandon the story was the question it raised—had James Allen made
a mistake in leaving his wife for another woman? Unresolved but not
forgotten, the issue would reappear in Hemingway's Paris memoir
begun at least fifteen years later.

With no book-length effort in mind, Hemingway turned to a number of minor projects, the sort he often agreed to do when he was at
loose ends. He wrote a tongue-in-cheek dust-jacket blurb for James
Thurber's *Life and Hard Times* which was also his first counterpunch

in the Stein-Hemingway match: "Even in the days when Thurber was writing under the name of Alice B. Toklas, we knew he had it in him if he could get it out."[10] For Sidney Franklin, who was translating a Spanish novel of the bullring for Scribner's publication, Ernest read typescript, "cutting, re-doing some of the conversation and straightening out the sentences." It was a "trashy" book, Ernest said, but with a flashy book jacket and Sidney's picture on the back it might sell well. Hemingway tried to pressure Perkins into a better royalty payment for Franklin while he himself was paying for the operation to repair Franklin's intestinal damage from a rectal goring suffered in the bullring three years earlier. Franklin, as always, was an expensive friend, both emotionally and financially, but Ernest enjoyed Sidney's theatrics and his flair for storytelling.[11]

By the end of September, the Franklin typescript was revised and the promised "Spanish Letter" for Gingrich was in the mail.[12] Loosely structured, the *Esquire* piece was a lament for the politics of the failing Republic and for unfulfilled promises of the Spanish bullring, the two issues being metaphors for each other. Bullfighting, always in decline from some previous golden age, was as depressing as the seashore, where the newly affluent "did not seem to know whether they were having any fun or not." The best matadors lacked style, killing in a monotonous manner; the worst lacked intelligence or courage or both. Like the Salamanca feria bulls who were "without force, bravery or style," the governing politicians rooting in the tax trough gave no one confidence in their performance. "People are traveling," Hemingway wrote, "who never traveled before; people go to bull fights who could not afford it before; and many people are swimming who never took a bath before." Spain's developing middle class was rubbing the charm off Hemingway's special places. An office building now stood where the old café Fornos once catered to those in the know, and the Aquarium café looked "like the last phase of Montparnasse."[13] Always more comfortable with either wealth or poverty, Hemingway, like Yeats, Pound, and Eliot, had little sympathy for the plodding middle class from whom he sprang and who were, in fact, the buying audience for his work.

Not quite as generically anti-Semitic as Pound and better than Ezra on revolutions, Hemingway tried to arrange a meeting with his early mentor, asking him to come up from Rapallo, Italy, to Paris in the fall. Ezra's replies were disoriented and ragged. He might come as far as Toulon, because Ezra was worried about the safari. If Ernest was determined to be a naturalist, Ezra approved, but if he was merely going to Africa to slaughter lions, well, that was hardly a worthy task when so much intellectual work remained to be done. "Y'orter take a little mental xercise now'n again," Pound advised. Ezra jokingly suggested that instead of butchering defenseless animals, Ernest assassinate one or two on Pound's growing list of exploitive villains, the tracking and finishing off of whom Ezra thought might appeal to Ernest's sporting interests. "Yew are getting too lazy to think," he warned, signing off as "Yr fexshunate unkl."[14]

As soon as he had finished revisions on Franklin's translation, Hemingway began a Cuban story that started: "You know how it is there early in the morning in Havana with the bums still asleep against the walls of the buildings; before even the ice wagons come by with ice for the bars?" Speaking was Harry Morgan, sometime fishing guide out of Key West, sometime rumrunner, a common man with uncommon nerve, a man down on his luck. When his insufferable fishing client leaves Morgan unpaid and broke in Havana, the story changes dramatically. Out of options, Morgan contracts with a Mr. Sing to smuggle Chinese aliens into the Florida keys. The price is $1,200; the risk is ten years in prison if caught; the scam allows Morgan to dump the illegals anywhere: Mr. Sing does not care. After picking up his passengers, Morgan cuts his risks to zero by taking the payment, breaking Mr. Sing's neck, and dumping the Chinese back in Cuba. It was a brutal, depression-era story about money: those who had it and those who needed it. Coming on the edge of Pound's needling, it was also Hemingway's first extended proletariat fiction. Jinny Pfeiffer was certain the story, which Hemingway called "One Trip Across," was true, which amused Ernest, who always insisted his best stories were the ones he made up.[15]

When Jinny and Pauline left for Paris that first week in October,

Ernest was not exactly isolated, but there were no women in his vicinity, a condition which put him alone in his night bed, where he did not sleep well. By day he was not much better. Almost immediately he began worrying that his pulse was too fast, his heart failing. Real or imagined, the condition drove him to the doctor, who assured him he would die but not from heart failure and not anytime soon.[16] Before leaving Madrid, he sprained his wrist falling on the stairs in his new hunting boots, and was back at the doctor's office for his chronic strep throat.[17] There were, of course, several good reasons for Hemingway to remain in Madrid. His new hunting boots of Spanish leather needed more fitting, and he was waiting for the final page proofs to arrive. Another good reason for being in Madrid rather than in Paris was *The Autobiography of Alice B. Toklas*, partially serialized in *Atlantic Monthly* and now in hardcover, which the Paris *Tribune* headlined as the "Season's Most Brilliant Book."[18] Gertrude Stein "was a good psychologist," as Ernest readily admitted: "She knows I don't get sore at being called any damn thing that I am, truly. But blow up like a set piece of fireworks if accused of anything I'm not. . . . It's damned intelligent malice."[19]

With equally intelligent malice, Hemingway wrote a short response which he called "The Autobiography of Alice B. Hemingway." The six-page sketch is told by the wife, Alice, but written by her husband, Ernest. "Listen," he tells his wife, who tells us he always starts with "Listen," a less than endearing characteristic. Listen, he says, no matter how excellent a critic of his stories Gertrude may be, she is already the past. No longer willing to be critical of her own work, she never corrects anything she writes. Lazy to a fault, she cannot lose because nothing is at risk. He should write about her, Alice tells Ernest, but he says no, he still likes Gertrude. But he could tell some stories about the Polish woman who lives with her, the disciplinarian who runs their life. Arriving unexpectedly one day, he once overheard things about their relationship that he will someday tell Alice, but not now. He still likes both of the women too much for that.[20]

Waiting for page proofs and with nothing left to write, Hemingway went to the bullfights with Luis Quintanilla, an artist he admired, scheduled a private estate hunt to break in his new boots, read books, and answered letters.[21] To one of his readers who thought Hemingway should write more decorously, Ernest explained:

> I am trying to make a picture of the world as I have seen it, without comment, trying to keep my mind as open as a doctor's when he is making an examination, and am always trying to concentrate rather than elaborate. Naturally much will be unpleasant, much will be obscene and much will seem to have no moral viewpoint.[22]

To his mother-in-law, Hemingway wrote a long letter about his hatred for Hitler's warmongering and about the dishonesty of Roosevelt's inflation of the dollar. He also cautioned her that *Winner Take Nothing* might not be as well received as his earlier books. If she (an ardent Catholic) did not like it, she should not make an effort to be polite about her response. He was afraid the stories would be distasteful to many readers.[23] His calculated frontal attack on the genteel tradition—stories of whores, homosexuals, suicide, castration, and insanity—no matter how well written were now giving him second thoughts. Torn between desire for broad audience acceptance and his need to maintain credentials as a serious artist, he may have written a book doing neither.

And every day they are apart, even when there is nothing to say, Ernest and Pauline try faithfully to write each other. Alone, he is lonely, given to moping and worse. Pauline, knowing his condition from much experience, punctually responds lovingly and anxiously, filling in with small talk. He tells her how exhausting it is to live in another language, trying to please everyone. Relating an incident in Spanish leads to his departing "consistently and utterly from the truth" for the sake of the story. The exhaustion he feels after such ordeals is the same as he felt when he was writing fiction; in fact, it is the "same damn business as writing really."[24] Underneath that observation lay the disturbing truth that Hemingway was never completely at ease with the idea of fiction. Like most of his contemporaries, he was raised to tell the truth, and punished for telling lies. Fiction, by definition, was telling a story not factually true; any story not true was a lie. The syllogism might be logically flawed, but emotionally it carried its weight. More than once Hemingway categorized his stories as those that actually happened and those he made up. When he told Pound that he was training to be a naturalist, he returned to his earliest dream of being a natural historian. He told one critic that he was going to write a book on the Gulf Stream and its migratory fish, about which he had acquired a good deal of knowledge. "Knowledge of a thing is like hours in the air in flying," he said. "I study what I'm interested in and have a damned good time doing it. Anyway it's always valuable if it's true. [The book] will be true."[25] Hemingway never stopped believing that there was a truth to tell.[26]

This moral dilemma was made worse by overly zealous Catholics wondering how Ernest could claim to be of their faith while writing such immoral fiction. He had to admit that the two parts of the equation appeared to be at odds with each other. He told one inquisitor, "I would not wish to embarrass the church with my presence. You may state . . . that Ernest Hemingway, the writer, is a man of no religion. My beliefs I cannot change but I have no right at present to practice them."[27] He sent the letter to Pauline to critique, saying the church might kick him out for writing *Winner Take Nothing*, but if he could keep Hemingway the writer separate from Hemingway the private man, he would still say his "prayers, go to mass, contribute to support and anywhere not known officially can go to confession."[28] Pauline's reply was noncommittal, saying only his letter might be shorter. On the issue of his having no right to call himself Catholic, she was silent, mentioning only that she was attending Mass once again at St. Sulpice, their former parish church.[29] If she worried about her husband's increasing paranoid fears that others were trying to ruin his writing—old friends, his publishers, the critics, the Church—Pauline kept her concern to herself.

––––––

Madrid, Oct. 15—Madrid will miss Ernest Hemingway, who showed himself a more knowing bullfight fan than many a native in his *Death in the Afternoon,* when he leaves next week for Paris with big plans in view. Paris is only the stepping-off place for an adventure in Africa. Mr. and Mrs. Hemingway and a friend named Thompson from Key West, Florida, will sail from Marseilles next month on the first stage of a big-game shoot. Mr. Hemingway has been staying some months in Madrid and the torrid summer heat has not prevented him from keeping busy on a new short novel.[30]

—Paris *Tribune,* October 16, 1933

By the time he reached Paris, Hemingway was long reconciled to hunting in Africa with only Pauline and Charles Thompson, but plans for the safari did not begin that way. Originally, the safari was going to be an all-male affair with Pauline waiting in Paris for the hunters' return. As another of Hemingway's attempts to reassemble the "summer people" of his youth, the expedition first included Archibald MacLeish and Mike Strater, both of whom backed out of their commitment: Archie because of money problems, Strater because of family problems. Replacements were invited, but none could accept Hemingway's invitation to a cost-free adventure. Uncle Gus, who paid for the safari, looked on the $25,000 as an investment in the book that would result from the experience.[31] Pauline's parents were not enthusiastic about her trekking in primitive Africa, but Hemingway promised them he would take good care of their daughter. Among the entourage of drivers, trackers, cooks, and hunters who were to be her close companions for sixty days, Pauline would be the only woman. Because it was important to her husband, Pauline, neither an outdoors woman nor an avid hunter, tried to match and verify his enthusiasm for the adventure; Ernest, disappointed that the men would not be with him, tried to be a considerate husband.

In the Paris-Dinard Hotel on rue Cassette,[32] Ernest and Pauline were based in their old neighborhood, close to Place St. Sulpice and St. Germain des Prés. With less than a month left before their departure for East Africa, they made lists of what remained to be done. The tailor must be paid for Ernest's safari jacket and shirts, but the buttons were wrong, the cartridge loops unsatisfactory, and the shirt sleeves too tight. They bought more film for the 4×5 Graflex and priced a telephoto lens; they found mosquito boots and sunglasses. The "Indian" needed to be paid for the tin trunks, and Pauline needed a nail brush. Money was moved from New York to Paris to pay for the necessaries, and the tin trunks filled with clothes and books. With the dollar worth 30 percent less than when they last lived in Paris, Ernest's thriftiness was continually challenged, but he did buy Pauline's Christmas present, one of those new dustproof, waterproof watches she wanted.[33]

When he arrived in Paris, Ernest found in the stack of mail the first edition of *Esquire*, leading off with his "Cuban Letter," retitled by Gingrich "Marlin Off the Morro." With full-page color cartoons of barely clothed women saying to each other, "Yeah, and then after he insulted you, what else did he do?" the magazine was a splash of then familiar names: Gilbert Seldes, author of *The Seven Lively Arts*; George Ade, writer of humorous fables; John Dos Passos; Dashiell Hammett; Erskine Caldwell; James Farrell; Gene Tunney, retired heavyweight boxing champion; Douglas Fairbanks, Jr., film star and writer. With a 10×14 format, color ads, men's fashions, and Chicago breeziness, *Esquire* was more than Hemingway expected. Along with the magazine was a long letter from publisher Gingrich, telling about his troubles with U.S. Post Office censors who would not allow Dos Passos to write "get your ass kicked," nor would they allow Gingrich to print clear photos of a burlesque stripper. They rejected a cartoon "showing nude shoulders of man leaning over dividing wall of two roofs to speak to nude girl lying face downward taking sun bath—gag line reading, 'Perhaps I'd better introduce myself.'" Gingrich also explained that he wanted to expand immediately from quarterly to monthly production; could Ernest supply twelve such letters a year at the same $250 rate? A letter a month was asking a lot from a man going on safari, miles from a post office, paying $100 a day to hunt. Maybe he could write more letters, but Gingrich would have to take them as they came. "I deliver what I promise," Ernest told Gingrich, "and you must see—what ever your need—that I can't promise now."[34] In the Paris-Dinard, Hemingway, as was his custom, rented a separate room to write the "Paris Letter" for which Gingrich had already deposited payment.[35]

The Paris of his early years was much diminished, a time and place already legend but no longer recoverable. Half the Americans who once lived in Paris had gone home; the half that remained were all too serious. That summer, Wambly Bald gave up his *Tribune* chronicle of the Left Bank, saying that Montparnasse was no longer a handkerchief to wave at friends: "It is a filthy rag one drops into the nearest garbage can." Having become the haven of dilettantes and fakes, tourists and poseurs, the Quarter had lost its charm and its heroes— the unknown painters and writers who graduated to greatness. "The world," Bald wrote, "is leveled off. Montparnasse is Main Street. . . . Even automobiles are going Picasso. The staunch army may disband. Gertrude Stein has crashed (of all things) *The Atlantic Monthly*, and her autobiography is accepted for publication by the Book-of-the-Month Club."[36] The modernist revolution was now mainstream.

Informal, discursive, and personal, Hemingway's "Paris Letter" opened with memories of Wyoming hunting, moved on to Paris, where old friends had disappeared, reminisced about French boxers from seasons past, and ended with two disparate points: a warning that there was another war coming, which America should avoid; and a closing nostalgic paragraph on Paris:

> It was a fine place to be quite young in and it is a necessary part of a man's education. We all loved it once and we lie if we say we didn't. But she is like a mistress who does not grow old and she has other lovers now.[37]

Along with praise for Hemingway's letter from Spain, Gingrich included unsolicited advice in response to Hemingway's comments on Gertrude Stein and critics in general:

> Your growing cynicism about human relationships in general is understandable . . . but I regret it just the same. You get too set in this

attitude and you can't help, before long, beginning to hurt yourself by
adding needlessly to the number of your ex-friends. . . . people who
knew you when you were fairly far down on the way up are always
prone to resent the fact that you didn't stay there. But the inevita-
ble outcroppings of professional jealousies are doubly unfortunate if
they're going to make you feel that the world is peopled exclusively by
bitches and their sons.[38]

Like most prophetic advice, Gingrich's perceptive remarks did little
to deflect Hemingway's anger with the critics' response to *Winner*
Take Nothing, which was published on October 27, the day after he
arrived in Paris.

Max Perkins's telegram was waiting: "First review Tribune very very
good think prospects excellent."[39] Archie MacLeish's followed soon
after: "Deeply gratefully affectionately moved magnificent book unwor-
thy dedicatee incommunicable sentiments."[40] In the third year of the
depression, when good books selling fewer than five thousand copies
were thought a wonder, Perkins wired on November 11, "Plenty speak
well sale eleven thousand will push till Christmas."[41] The reviews,
however, even Max found "unsatisfactory and a good many are absolutely enraging."[42] Written as if a group project, the reviews uniformly
recognized Hemingway's impact on contemporary writing: "He has
created a fashion, almost a tradition." All acknowledged that his distinctive and much-imitated style was a marvel: "I take for granted that
his prose always reaches certain levels of excellence, that his art has
always been deliberate." Most found one or more stories in the collection to praise. But, and the "but" loomed large, the Twenties were
over, the postwar generation's say had been said; New York critics
wanted something different, something more compassionate in hard
times.[43] The *New York Times* review said the writing was superlative:

the dialogue is admirable; . . . [the] picture is vivid, whole; the way
of life is caught and conveyed without a hitch. . . . It is not that the
life they portray isn't worth exploring. But Hemingway has explored
it beyond its worth.[44]

Taking out his anger as usual on Max, Hemingway said that Scribner's was trying to ruin him by not advertising the book effectively, by giving up on him, by using damning quotes in what ads they ran. The critics were shits, demanding better stories than the best he had written. "God damn it there can't be better ones. . . . I'll be goddamned if I like to have to say how good my stuff is in order to give the business office confidence enough to advertise it after they have read an unfavorable review and think I'm through."[45]

There is not enough time to vent all his spleen, for with his departure for Africa upon him, Hemingway has plenty of items remaining on his checklist. Two days are spent gathering visas from the consulate offices of Egypt, Ethiopia, and Great Britain.[46] A deposit is paid on return tickets in March; trunks are packed, books selected, guns oiled, and last letters mailed. On November 22, Ernest, Pauline, and Charles Thompson (who joined them in Paris on November 15) sail out of Marseilles on the *General Metzinger* bound for Mombasa to fulfill the African dream he has nurtured from his boyhood.

———

Madame Bertrand de Jouvenel, the former Martha Gellhorn of St. Louis, Mo. has a first novel, *Nothing Ever Happens*, appearing shortly on London bookstands. Critics who have seen it in manuscript or proof describe the novel as sensational for its literary quality and for its subject matter. Madame Jouvenel has already started a second novel and is leaving shortly for the United States in order to gather material for it with her husband, brilliant young French journalist and economist. While Jouvenel is making a lecture tour, Madame Jouvenel will study at close range the reaction of American youth to the New Deal. Her work in progress deals with the problem presented by the moral and social disintegration of the depression generation, particularly the new poor.

—Paris *Tribune*, November 20, 1933

———

The *Metzinger*, lacking the amenities of a large liner, is a time traveler, chugging away from rainy Europe and into an earlier world of colonial governors, dust and flies, slow sailing dhows, and strange tongues. Ten days it takes to clear the Mediterranean and pass through Suez, where heat rises, food worsens, and the French close curtains to what small breeze blows. Finally, seventeen days out, they reach the lush green island of Mombasa with its huge-trunked baobab trees, coconut palms, white lime-washed houses, shaded verandahs, shuttered windows, palm-thatched roofs, and ebony faces. They come down the gangplank: Pauline in a white dress, gloves, and parasol; Charles in suit and tie, sweating in the heavy heat; Ernest, with white shirtsleeves rolled and wearing a wide-brimmed Stetson. "Pauline and I looked like missionaries," Thompson said, "while Ernest had the distinct look of whiskey drummer." Everywhere Indian businessmen hurry along, heads bobbing, and the rich odors of curry flow from the alleyways. At the Palace Hotel, rooms are clean, the bar is open.[47]

Next afternoon at half past four, with legs still wobbly from the sea voyage, the hunting party, paying the baggage bill, boarded the Kenya and Uganda Railway bound for Nairobi, 330 miles inland. At dusk, with coastal jungle beginning to thin, they eat a five-course supper in the new dining car, and afterward bed down in compartments with small washrooms.[48] The overnight journey, taking them from sea level to mile-high Nairobi, passes through storied country which Ernest knows well from reading, in his youth, J. H. Patterson's horrific *The Man-Eaters of Tsavo*. For most of a year, two lions so terrorized Indian and native laborers that construction of this railway came to a halt. At night these lions, slipping into boxcars where workers slept, killed and ate more than twenty-eight men before Patterson was able to shoot them. At Chicago's Field Museum of Natural History, young Hemingway stood more than once before the infamous Tsavo lions, now permanently poised on their sandstone lair, tails almost twitching. One lion crouched, ready to spring; the other stood with right foot expectantly raised.[49]

They sleep as one can to the clackity-click of rails and wake to wonder on the prairie rolling in sunlight toward distant blue mountains. Farther away than seems possible, Mount Kilimanjaro, domed with fresh-fallen snow, hovers in the western sky. Everywhere there is game: giraffe, antelope, zebra, kongoni, eland, and jackals. "Nothing I've ever read has given any idea of what this country is like," Hemingway said. Covered with fine red dust and farther from home than could be measured in miles, the Hemingway party reaches Nairobi, where most of the city seems to be waiting the once-a-day train's arrival. In midmorning heat, Ernest, Pauline, and Charles, along with heavy luggage, are transported down tree-lined Government Road to the New Stanley Hotel, which claims to be the only establishment north of Johannesburg with a bathroom attached to every bedroom.

Armed with letters of introduction, Hemingway went the next day to Tanganyika Guides to make a second payment on the safari. In his hotel room a letter from Jane Mason warned him that Dick Cooper "is afraid you may get one of those 'no-good white hunters' which abound in Africa. They promise you all the game in the kingdom and end you up with nothing but a few reels of pictures of the country."[50] The requested guide, Philip Percival, forty-nine-year-old director of the company and legendary safari man, once worked on Theodore Roosevelt's epic 1909 safari, which young Hemingway followed in magazines, and in Oak Park watched the jerky moving pictures of the Colonel's expedition on the silent screen. More than anyone else, Roosevelt, his earliest hero, was responsible for opening East Africa to Hemingway's imagination.[51] At the age of six he stood in awe beside two gigantic stuffed elephants in the Field Museum; at sixteen, he promised himself to do "exploring work" in Africa; at twenty-six, he gave his character Jake Barnes the dream of hunting in British East Africa. Now, at thirty-four, Ernest was there on Roosevelt's ground.[52] Percival, graying, understated, and very British, agreed to lead their safari, but could not go into the field until December 20.

This delay was actually a blessing, giving the group time to acclimatize, not only to the surroundings but to the altitude, which demanded more red blood cells for the thinner air. Tanganyika Guides provided hunting excursions in the Nairobi area, where

Ernest and Charles shot Grant and Thompson gazelle, kongoni, and impala, which were almost at their front door. Days were no hotter than in Key West in winter, and by night they slept beneath hotel blankets. When not exploring the nearby countryside, Hemingway was in the company of two young, wealthy sportsmen, Winston Guest and Alfred Vanderbilt, introductions provided by Jane Mason. Guest, twenty-seven-year-old Ivy League lawyer with a huge inherited fortune, played world-class polo and was an avid hunter. With two large ivory tusks already taken on his license, he was in Nairobi eager for more elephant hunting. Young Alfred Vanderbilt was also in Nairobi waiting for Bror Von Blixen, Percival's partner, former husband of Karen Blixen (aka Isak Dinesen) and reputedly the best white hunter in East Africa, to lead his safari. To Gingrich, Hemingway recommended Vanderbilt as a "good young kid" who knew horses and racing, spending most of his time with the fabled Vanderbilt stables, and who wanted to write for *Esquire*. "I don't know whether he can write or not but he knows racing and horses and would be the TOP in insiders for you to have writing for you."[53]

With not enough information to write his "African Letter" for Gingrich, Hemingway used the Nairobi layover to fulfill his promise of an introduction for the Montparnasse memoirs of Jimmy Charters, the Paris barman at the Dingo. Still smarting from Stein's portrait of him, he began the somewhat carelessly written introduction: "Once a woman has opened a salon it is certain she will write her memoirs." No matter how useful one might be to the salon keeper, once no longer valuable, he was certain to be slandered by her.

> *The memoir writer will usually prove that a lady's brain may still be between her thighs—but let us not make jokes about thighs—and will treat you in her memoirs as any girl around the Dôme or the Sélect would; imputing this to you, denying you that.*

In the last paragraph he finally got around to Charters, whose memoirs Ernest took to be another sign of western civilization's decline. He wished Jimmy luck, but also wished the book were not about

"Montparnasse because that is a dismal place."[54] He mailed the handwritten draft to a Paris friend, who typed it, making minor corrections before sending it on to Charters.[55]

While waiting for Philip Percival to arrange their safari, the hunters were not without local distractions to pass the time. Nairobi was a small town halfway between pioneer squalor and urban sophistication. Wild and sometimes dangerous animals were as close as the edge of town and often closer. At the Indian bazaar all manner of exotic objects were for sale: snow leopard and fox furs, dik-dik skins, drums, stools, spears and shields, a "beautiful walking-cane made of one piece white rhino horn, gold mounted in London."[56] At the New Stanley bar, the talk was about a murder trial being argued in the Nairobi courthouse and across much of the colony. Henry Tarlton, whose native name meant "The Man Who Was Never Wrong," had his Caucasian skull smashed by a heavy blade. Doomed by witnesses and strong circumstantial evidence, the accused African native had "horrified the whole country," raising dark fears and prompting letters to the editor:

> *Deep distress is felt amongst the old settlers in the district at the death of Henry Tarlton. . . . strong action needs to be taken to protect the white settlers and their womenfolk from the truculent attitude of the native, which, if unchecked, may culminate in an attack.*

Meanwhile, Y. A. Hunter of Nairobi was quietly appealing the eighteen-month suspension of his driver's license for his reckless driving which killed a native. Having paid the fifty-pound fine, Hunter argued that temporarily being unable to drive was an undue hardship.[57]

On December 20, after delays about trucks and supplies and much midmorning beer-drinking, the Hemingway safari departed from Percival's farm, making straight for the Tanganyika border, riding easily across rolling plains and bush country green from recent rains. Game abounded, but they did not shoot that day or the next, which took them to the customs shed at Namanga. While the men passed guns through inspection and stamping, Pauline sat partly shaded in the noonday sun watching a bare-breasted Masai woman flirting with a tall black man—shiny and shapely she found them. With her khaki trousers and bush jacket, her small close-cropped head dwarfed by a wide-brimmed hat, only her orange-and-yellow neck scarf distinguished Pauline from the men around her. As she watched, the Masai man picked up the woman and carried her into a hut, from which laughter and wrestling noises were heard.

From Namanga on through Arusha, stopping over at a hotel with a swimming pool, trucks and hunters stepped off finally into the great Rift Valley, moving north toward the Masai game reserve in the Ngorongoro Crater. With heat waves rippling the plain, Pauline watched Ernest humiliate himself all of one morning in pursuit of a Grant's gazelle. Firing repeatedly low and away, stubbornly refusing to make corrections, he missed and missed again. They chased in the car, stalked on foot, but never got the prize head. After five or six shots at a smaller Grant, he wounded and finally killed it. Percival told him that everyone's shot was a bit off when first out. Pauline, detached, observing, making notes, infrequently shooting, did not much care for hunting by car: too hot, too dusty. As she watched, her nail polish faded in the sun.

Getting laden trucks up the wet, slippery dirt road to the crater rim took most of the morning before Christmas, leaving Pauline alone staring out into the mist of the huge, flat, green caldera beneath her, where famous lions were said to roam. When the men came up after pushing and cursing the trucks, Ernest asked her to go somewhere else, for he was having an attack of diarrhea. He didn't want to go into the three-foot grass because there might be snakes. That afternoon they took one car down into the crater, where she and Ernest saw their first lioness, driving to within fifty feet of her. After killing two zebra for bait and driving back toward the lioness, Percival, Pauline, and Ernest were stunned by an explosion beside Ernest's head. His rifle, strapped to the car top and supposedly uncocked, had fallen to the ground beside his door and unexplainably fired. Visibly shaken, Pauline's first thought was that Ernest had been killed.

The day after Christmas, wearing her new wristwatch, Pauline got her first clear view of the Serengeti Plain, full of game moving in all directions. Here their day's pattern became more regular, taking on the rhythm of their quarry: early breakfast of tea and whatever; morning hunts ending when the heat became oppressive; in the shade a cold lunch from the chop box; back to the hunt in late afternoon; returning to whiskey, a sit-bath, more whiskey, and dinner in pajamas. Antelope, guinea fowl, and potatoes became their daily fare, quickly leaving Pauline and Charles constipated from too much meat and not enough water. Constipation, however, was not Ernest's problem. No sooner had they begun the safari than his attacks of diarrhea became more and more frequent. What began as a joke quickly became a nuisance that passed into real concern. While Ernest took doses of chlorine salts administered by Percival, Charles and Pauline complained of piles. Either way, riding over bumpy terrain on stiff seats became more and more painful for the Key Westers. Between internal difficulties, heat and dust, biting flies, disturbing night noises, and her certain knowledge that she was not brave regarding wild animals larger than herself and far more deadly, Pauline's enthusiasm for the safari was hard pressed to match Ernest's.

On the morning of December 29, Pauline took her first shot at a lion and missed. As she noted in her journal, her "characteristic" shooting was always a little low, a little high, a bit to the left or right. Always splendid shots, according to Percival, but always leaving her disappointed. Ernest, shooting his relatively light Springfield .30-06, flattened the lion with a single shot, followed by another shot for safety. Word went out from her guide M'Cola to the truckers, cooks, and bearers that Mama had killed her lion, which resulted in much shouting and dancing. Chagrined and wishing that she had killed the lion, Pauline distributed traditional shillings all round. Later the day turned hot, dusty, and disappointing, with the plain stretching out endlessly and no camp where camp was supposed to be and driving on for more than two hours to find it finally with tents up in proper sequence and whiskey waiting for them.

The last day of the year went out to a chorus of missed shots and curses. The morning began with Ernest missing a roan antelope, fol-

lowed by three missed shots at a leopard. Later he wounded a cheetah, which everyone tracked up and over the hill for more than a
sweaty hour without finding him. That afternoon Charles fired six or
seven shots at an impala, finally bringing him down. Next morning,
the first of the new year, Pauline, worn out from hiking in the brush,
stayed in camp while Ernest was out redeeming his sorry shooting of
the previous day. Before noon he had killed a warthog and a cheetah, and then he and Charles killed three buffalo, which Pauline had
to see. So they sent Ben Fourie, the mechanic and driver, an hour
back to camp to haul her to the killing ground, where she admired
the dead buffs with ticks still crawling on them. Too much heat, too
much dust, too much male talk; Poor Old Mama, as they were now
calling Pauline, had reached her limits. Gloom descended upon her,
and down she went into it, taking supper that night in bed alone.
Making strenuous demands upon her in the field, the men, who
apparently did not understand either her disappointments or her
fears, frequently added to Pauline's melancholy. A long way from St.
Louis, she was trying, almost desperately at times, to be the outdoors
wife Ernest so wanted her to be, but at heart's core she was addicted
to city pleasures and convenience.

Three days later, approaching by car a mated pair of lions on a
slight hill, the group was surprised when the two predators came
toward the vehicle, the lion to one side, his mate to the other. To
Pauline's rising anxiety, the men agreed that she should shoot the
male lion, which had grown huge in her eyes by the time they got
her out of the car. As she took aim, Percival said, "For Christ sake
don't shoot the lioness!" She looked up, wondering if she could
be shooting the lioness, which, of course, was on the opposite
side of car. As she resighted down the rifle barrel, she could hear
Charles struggling to get out of the car. Afraid the lions would
spook, she hurried her shot, apparently missing. The lions quickly
disappeared into a dry streambed thick with brush. No amount
of beating about the edges of the donga could bring them back
in sight. Pauline returned to camp in silent despair. Ernest, she

noted later, had remained inside the car, unable to save her if the lion charged.

Changing camps every two or three days, the hunting party shot its way further into the Serengeti, living off the land and taking trophies. By January 8, Ernest and Charles had killed their lion, buffalo, cheetah, and leopard, leaving only the rhino to complete the five truly dangerous animals. With Percival as their guide and mediator, Pauline as their audience, and several natives as appreciative chorus, an increasing rivalry was beginning to create tensions between the two men. Ernest was by nature competitive to a sometimes unpleasant degree; Charles, the less talkative of the two, was the invited guest who had no intention of being the designated loser in this passage of arms. For amusement the two men kept track of the hyenas they shot at every opportunity.

Adding to the tension was a growing awareness that Ernest's quickly multiplying diarrhea attacks were actually dysentery. By January 11, he was taking chlorine salts continuously, but his evening drinking undermined any good the medicine might have done. By January 13, he was too weak to stay out in the field and too uncomfortable sitting in the car. On the evening of the fourteenth, driving back to camp over a punishing road, Ernest, in terrible pain, was clearly in need of medical attention. Percival sent Ben careening over bush roads 115 miles to Lake Victoria, the closest telegraph station, to arrange for an airplane to fly Hemingway to the Arusha hospital, which was three days away by car. All the next day, Hemingway remained in bed, moving to the campfire only in the evening for a bowl of mashed potatoes. Through that night of wind and rain, awakened by biting bugs and her own anxiety, Pauline tosses about while Ernest sleeps through the commotion. When Ben returns the morning of the 15th, they learn the plane will arrive at two that afternoon. All morning and afternoon, they wait in camp, listening for the motor, but no plane appears. Hemingway spends the day reading magazines, apparently feeling better for the rest and for two days of not drinking. Somehow a radio message comes through: no plane today; plane tomorrow. The next morning at ten, the small silver plane lands in the road, loads a smiling Hemingway aboard, and takes off for Arusha at the foot of Mount Kilimanjaro and the government doctor.

————

Your amebic dysentery correspondent is in bed, fully injected with emetine, having flown four hundred miles to Nairobi via Arusha from where the outfit is camped on the Serenea river on the far side of the Serengeti plain. Cause of the flight, a. d. Cause of a. d. unknown. Symptoms of a. d. run from weakly insidious through spectacular to phenomenal. I believe the record is held by a Mr. McDonald with 232 movements in the twenty-four hours although many old a. d. men claim the McDonald record was never properly audited.[58]

—Ernest Hemingway, "a.d. in Africa: A Tanganyika Letter"

————

Unbeknownst to Pauline and Percival, Ernest landed at Arusha and then continued on to Nairobi, where he registered at the New Stanley Hotel. There a Dr. Anderson treated him with regular injections of emetine, whose efficacy was most apparent in Hemingway's bar bill, which rose from four shillings for mineral water his first night to sixty-four shillings and fifty pence four nights later, when he apparently was well enough to entertain guests at dinner.[59] He used the days in bed to arrange an end-of-safari fishing trip on the coast, to write his promised "African Letter" for *Esquire*, and to answer mail.

The day after he arrived in Nairobi, he was writing Max from his hotel bed, thanking him for royalty and sales statements (over thirteen thousand *Winner Take Nothing*s sold), telling about the pleasures of amebic dysentery ("Feels as if you were trying to give birth to a child"), recounting the game bagged, and bitching about the state of public letters. His present unpopularity, which he insisted on despite healthy sales, was to be expected, for a writer's stock always rose and fell with current fads like "this present damned YMCA economic hurrah business." Having once belonged to the YMCA in his Oak Park youth, he often used it as a shorthand way of demeaning trendy salvationists,

which was his view of Roosevelt's attempts to revive the nation's economy. He assured Perkins that when the economic slump passed, he,
Ernest, would be better than ever, having remained a writer while others followed the ideological trend to the left. But he could not expect
the public to believe in him when his own publisher appeared to have
given up on him. This now familiar accusation followed every book he
published with Scribner's. No matter what the sales, there would have
been more if only his publisher had pushed harder, taken out more
ads, done more to promote the book.[60]

While Hemingway recovered, the safari degenerated badly. The
morning after his departure, Pauline and Charles poured shot after
shot in the direction of an antelope they stalked relentlessly for what
seemed like hours before killing him. By the next day, Percival was
running a fever as he led the trucks back up to the top of the Ngorongoro Crater, where Pauline and Charles hunted to no great end while
Percival remained in camp. On January 20, Pauline and Percival drove,
hot and dusty, into Arusha to surprise Ernest, but only surprising
themselves when they learned he was actually in Nairobi. Telegrams
were sent, but not knowing whether his client was fit for more hunting and feeling somewhat sick himself, Percival repaired to the hotel
bar alone. On Sunday morning, Arusha church bells ringing, Pauline
thought of going to Mass, but without stockings or proper shoes, she
could not face her religious duty in trousers.

After spending an awkward Sunday with Percival, whose drinking
did not relieve his gloom, Pauline was delighted on Monday when
an apparently cured Ernest, smiling, weak, and handsome, stepped
off the small plane on the Arusha landing strip. The three of them
spent another day in town, waiting for truck parts, drinking at Luigi's
bar, the men telling war stories. By January 24, they were back in the
field, camped on the Mosquito River, ready to begin the final month
of the safari in pursuit of rhino and kudu.

———

Waking in the dark, still weak and thinking maybe not to go out,
but after breakfast with the light beginning to break, it all looked

better. Sitting on the hill with M'Cola, Pauline, and Percival, the day heating up as the beaters circle behind the hill, when here comes the rhino, breaking cover fast, heading for the river. "Not awfully good," says Percival, "but we'll shoot him." Three shots at an impossible distance and one snort from the rhino before he's out of sight. Every one running now with Droopy Lids tracking, finding blood, and then we could hear heavy breathing and then nothing but the birds. The rhino down in the grass, dead, with everyone gathered about for the photograph, one of the trackers touching the horn for luck.

———

Unfortunately the safari has become a matter of measurements: Ernest's rhino carries a seventeen-inch horn, and Charles's rhino, killed two days later, sports a twenty-three-inch horn. Nothing can change these numbers, not even the magnificence of Ernest's remarkable shot. For good reason, therefore, Percival keeps the two men separated as much as possible during the day, sending Charles off with Ben, the mechanic, and his own trackers while he stands watch over Ernest and Pauline. Much better that way. But there is always the evening rendezvous with whiskey by the fire, where every shot is rehashed. Charles's trophy heads, somewhat larger than Ernest's, out of sight but never out of mind, color all their conversations.

With rhinos taken, the safari spends two days at Dick Cooper's place near Babiti within view of Lake Manyara's miles of pink and rose flamingoes. There they shoot ducks for the supper table, sleep in real beds, bathe in comfort, and rest for the final push. With less than two weeks remaining before the rains make the dirt roads of the Serengeti impassable, the men turn to the last animal on their list: the greater kudu. Day after day, they rise early to breakfast in the dark, returning weary and late from the bush empty handed. On February 9, they drive all day and part of the next to fresh country around Kijungu where the antelope is said to abound. Lured on by tracks, they hunt in blinds by the salt lick, but no kudu appears.

With the men getting testy, Pauline waits with Percival in the camp rather than spending the day in the field with Ernest. On February 11, Charles brings in the first kudu with grotesquely twisted thirty-eight-inch horns; the next morning before dawn, Pauline wakes to see a sad-looking Ernest preparing to leave for the salt lick. Only five days are left for the hunt.

This day's hunt is spoiled by the clanking truck of a short, round little German, who remembered from the mid-Twenties reading the poet Hemingway in a German magazine. Four years later Herr Kortischoner wrote Hemingway, reminding him that he was the man

> you found one day with a broken down motor car, who was a reader of the Querschnitt. . . . You pulled this man out of his awkward situation; he spent two days in your camp at Kijungu, where he met Mrs. Hemingway who kept a diary in which you may find his name.[61]

On Valentine's Day, Percival sends one truck off with a tow rope to pull Kortischoner and his truck over a hundred miles into Handeni. Meanwhile, Ernest finds one salt lick under water from the now falling rains, another spoiled by native hunters. Back in camp, Pauline feels as despondent as the cows mooing outside her tent. Should have stayed in bed longer, she tells herself.

No kudu that day nor the next, but rain is now falling regularly, slicking the surface of the dirt roads. In another week or less, dirt will be mud, and trucks will be unable to get the safari to the coast. Philip Percival, against best judgment, pushes his luck to satisfy his clients. On February 16, Ernest and his tracker take food and mattress by car into a far salt lick in order to be on the killing ground at first light and all next day if necessary. The morning he leaves, Charles and Ben, who have, for two days, been on their own at another likely spot, kill an enormous kudu. When Percival moves their camp to Kibaya, there are the horns, lovely, long, dark, and spiraling. Sad that Ernest has apparently not gotten his kudu and none too glad about Charles's getting one, Pauline goes to bed early. Thirty minutes later, she awakens groggy to shouting and banging. Dashing out in pajamas, she sees Ernest there in the car lights with natives singing and Percival clapping him on his shoulder. Then she sees the horns, two pairs of lovely kudu horns and a sable for good measure. The next morning in a group photo, Ben, Charles, Philip, and Ernest kneel, smiling, each holding vertical a set of horns on a still-bloody skull: three kudu and Ernest holding his sable. Ben looks pleased, Philip relieved; Ernest grins. Charles, his face covered by one of the horns, seems to be looking somewhere else. Measurements are taken: the horns of Charles's kudu extend fifty-seven inches; Ernest's measure fifty-one and a quarter. The safari is finished.

———

Of the antelope family, they killed four Thompson gazelle, eight Grant, seven wildebeest, seven impala, two klipspringers, four roan, two bushbucks, three reedbucks, two oryx, four topi, two waterbuck, one eland, and three kudu. Of dangerous game, they killed their licensed limit: four lions, three cheetahs, four buffalo, two leopards, and two rhinos. They also killed one serval cat, two warthogs, thirteen zebra, and one cobra. Animals wounded but never found included two cheetahs, two warthogs, one eland, one buffalo, and one dik-dik. For amusement forty-one hyenas were also killed. There may have been more but these are the recorded kills.[62]

———

Chapter Seven

1934

PURSUIT REMEMBERED

Key West, Havana, and Key West

O N   T H E   A F T E R N O O N   of April 11, as Hemingway
stepped off the Havana Special from New York, a Key
West jazz band hired for the occasion struck up a raucous
march and a throng of greeters surrounded him: Pauline and five-
year-old Patrick, Ada MacLeish, John and Katy Dos Passos, Charles
and Lorine Thompson, and other assorted well-wishers.[1] In his luggage is a copy of Scott Fitzgerald's recently published novel, *Tender
Is the Night,* for whose heroine Sara Murphy, standing beside him,
was one of the models. Two weeks later, when Ernest wrote Gerald Murphy, thanking and repaying him for the train ticket, he said
that Scott's book was not much good. "There's been too bloody much
flashy writing," he said. "There is almost no true writing and people
do not like to read it."[2] As he wrote that sentence, on his shelf there
were twenty-three rare volumes on African hunting, recently purchased in Paris, background and reference books for his next work, a

story which was to be as true as he could make it to his African experience. When Hemingway's interest focused on new material or a new genre, he first read broadly and deep to find what not to write.[3]

Hemingway also brought with him from New York a catalog from the Wheeler Shipyard advertising a thirty-eight-foot Playmate cabin cruiser which, with some modification, could become the fishing boat he dreamed about but could no longer afford, having sloughed off too much of the $7,000 he'd saved to buy it. Arnold Gingrich, seeing a chance to keep Hemingway's name on his magazine's masthead, offered him a $3,000 advance against twelve future *Esquire* "letters." Hemingway quickly agreed, promising that Pauline would pay off the debt should he die before fulfilling it, but adding that the debt would be canceled if the magazine went under.[4] Six days later Hemingway signed and mailed a contract for the boat with a $3,000 down payment to Eugene Wheeler, specifying several modifications:

> *more gas tanks for longer cruising*
> *transom lowered twelve inches for pulling in big fish*
> *a live fish well*
> *a second deck chair*
> *an auxiliary motor independent of the main engine*

The hull was to be painted pirate black, and on its stern in white letters the name should read *Pilar* of Key West.[5] During their 1926–27 affair, "Pilar" was Pauline's code name, and more recently the name they saved for the daughter they now knew they would never have.

Hemingway quickly arranged with Max Perkins to borrow another $2,500 from Scribner's to pay off the *Pilar* when it arrived in Miami. This loan would become part of an advance when Hemingway delivered his next book, a plan for which was forming in his mind. Taking an earlier advance, he rushed *Winner Take Nothing*, a mistake he said he would not make this time. (Somehow a 4 percent loan was not the same as an advance.) Talking to himself more than to Perkins, he said that

my idea of a career is never to write a phony line, never fake, never
cheat, never be sucked in by the y.m.c.a. movements of the moment,
and to give them as much literature in a book as any son of a bitch
has ever gotten into the same number of words. But that isn't enough.
If you want to make a living out of it you have to, in addition every so
often, without faking, cheating or deviating from the above give them
something they understand and that has a story.[6]

And his idea of how to write was to get up every morning, go to
the spare room over the garage, sit down to the table, and put penciled words about Africa onto bond paper. At the start, there was no
plan, only the joy of recreating the zebra shoot on the hot, dusty plain,
and the flamingos turning the lake all pink at one end. Like many
simple things, it was difficult work: much detail to be left out; scaf-
folding to come down when the story stood on its own. Sometimes he
was only saying things that he had to see on paper before removing
them. On his return from Africa through Paris, he used up part of his
safari experience in two more *Esquire* letters, one on lion hunting,
the second on other dangerous game. He intended to write at least
two more: one on rhino hunting, one on kudu and sable.[7] But as soon
as he was back in Key West, reading in the old safari books, he told
Gingrich that there would be no more African letters for *Esquire*.[8] By
May Day, he was already twenty good pages into a story of the kudu
hunt, not knowing how long it would be and not really caring. It was
to be as true a story as anything remembered can be true.[9]

While he was living mornings in Africa and afternoons on the
water, other, less local Americans were reading his story "One Trip
Across" in the April *Cosmopolitan*, and the April *Esquire* featured his
"a.d. in Africa: A Tanganyika Letter." Many of these same readers
were amused by *Vanity Fair*'s full-page spread of the Ernest Hemingway paper doll. Centered on the page was a caricature of Ernest as
Neanderthal wearing a leopard skin and holding in one hand a club
and in the other a dead rabbit. Four cutouts framed him: the Lost
Generation Hemingway seated at a sidewalk café table covered with
wine bottles; the Isaac Walton Hemingway in the rowboat *Anita*

loaded with six marlin; the Unknown Soldier Hemingway in uniform and on crutches; and the Toreador Hemingway in a suit of lights holding a bull's head in one hand.[10]

While most of Hemingway's generation were moving into their midlife course with their notoriety behind them, he was just hitting his stride. (Scott Fitzgerald, once the darling of *The Smart Set*, was no longer a madcap youth driving cars into public fountains; the once lovely Zelda, her mouth hardened and her blue eyes more vacant, was spending quiet evenings in the sanitarium.) Almost thirty-five years old, Ernest Hemingway was a newsworthy figure whose every public act was grist for the media; his broad shoulders, and his round, mustached face with its pronounced widow's peak becoming as widely recognized as some movie stars. Where once his fiction drew attention to his active life, now that life drew attention to his writing. His sportsman's adventures also drew the attention of natural historians. On his way back from safari, Hemingway answered the Philadelphia Academy of Natural Science's questions about game fish in Cuban waters—classifications, life histories, food, and migrations. Hemingway said he would be happy to cooperate with the director, Charles Cadwalader, for "it would be very interesting to have a complete collection of these fish and determine scientifically which are truly different species and which are merely sexual and age variations of the same fish." His own theories, he said, were "too extensive to put in a letter."[11] After Hemingway stopped for an afternoon in Philadelphia on his train trip back to Key West, Cadwalader and Henry Fowler were eager to join Ernest in Havana for the summer marlin run.[12]

Back in Key West with his "extensive" marlin theories fresh in mind, he wrote his seventh *Esquire* letter, in which he raised questions of the sort that interest natural historians. Why won't a mako shark eat a hooked marlin when other sharks will? What is the purpose of the sailfish's sail? Why do marlin always travel against the current? Why do the great fishing years in California and Cuba coincide? Could the white, the striped, and the black marlin be variations of the same fish? He admitted that he would fish marlin "even if it were of no scientific value at all and you can't expect anyone to subsidize anything that anybody has a swell time out of. As a matter of fact I suppose we are lucky to be able to fish for them without being put in jail. This time next year they may have gotten out a law against it." (There should have been a law against editor Gingrich's having the letter illustrated with a woodcut of Hemingway fishing with one hand and swigging from a liquor bottle with the other. Protruding over the stern of the *Pilar* are sixteen bottles of liquor, one of which is being guzzled by a marlin in the water.)[13]

Three days after Ernest arrived in Key West, E. B. White's poetic jibe about Hemingway the African hunter appeared in *The New Yorker*. Taking off on a newspaper story in which Hemingway was quoted as having shot only lions who were utter strangers to him, White advised "friends" to "cling to Ernest Hemingway"

> *Who writes by night and hunts by day,*
> *Whose books with gore are fairly ruddy*
> *But not with gore of pal or buddy,*
> *And who, in time of darkest danger,*
> *Will only dominate a stranger.*[14]

Old and former friends like Sherwood Anderson who read these lines must have winced, knowing that strangers were, in fact, frequently better treated than themselves. At that moment, Ernest was assuring Sara Murphy by mail that he had stopped treating John Dos Passos so meanly.[15]

Having been in Key West only one month out of the past twelve, Hemingway was returning to a visibly diminished island where three out of every four citizens now qualified for government relief, where property taxes were not paid for lack of cash, and where trash uncollected by unpaid workers was piling up. Under President Roosevelt's Federal Emergency Relief Act (FERA), a few hundred men were employed clearing land for an airport and building a saltwater aquarium to attract tourists, but most of the have-nots were living off fish and small cash handouts from the government supplemented by free flour, beef, butter, and vegetables delivered on an irregular schedule. With the Army and Navy bases closed, even bars and prostitutes were short of customers. Before the summer was out, every New York train was met by a welcoming band working for FERA, hoping to lure Havana-bound tourists into stopping over in Key West.[16] This was the summer that the midwest drought finally turned west Texas and places north into a hopeless dust bowl; the summer of garish bank robbers, made famous by the media, going down in bloody shoot-outs: Pretty Boy Floyd, Bonnie Parker and Clyde Barrow, John Dillinger; a summer of riots, strikes, and discontent.

———

His "method" is dictated by his own physique, his raw masculinity, and the type of experience he constantly seeks in life. The success of his works is to be attributed to their possession of qualities not usually found in "literary" writing. . . . The legend of Hemingway is modern-Byronic. It is made up of tales of drinking, bull-fighting, carnal experiences in the war, rough talk and bad manners, and then wine and more wine. . . . People who have had only a glimpse of him are forever bragging about his athletic prowess and his shocking manners. It is easy to attribute to him all of the experiences that are in his books, for he has penetrated perfectly and even sympathetically all of the most abandoned types of human beings. . . . his weakness as an author is the eternal sameness of his material and of his method.[17]

—Lawrence Conrad, August 1934

———

The morning before he and John Dos Passos took the P&O ferry to Havana for May Day, Ernest was writing Max Perkins about Fitzgerald's *Tender Is the Night*, eight years in the making. Angry with Scott for arbitrarily mixing characters—first the heroine is Sara Murphy, then Zelda, then back to Sara—and for not understanding the emotional complication of Gerald Murphy but only his exterior, Ernest complained that despite Scott's beautiful prose style, he still could not consistently think straight. Loaded with talent, always readable, Scott never grew up, never learned his trade, was "never a man." All that Hemingway said about Fitzgerald's use of prototypes others once said about his own practice in *The Sun Also Rises*. He was lecturing to himself as much as to Perkins: "Using actual stuff is the most difficult writing in the world to have good. Making it up is the easiest and the best. But you have to know what things are about before you start and you have to have confidence."[18] There was no way for Max to know that Hemingway was describing his own concerns about the African story he was writing—a story about which he said little to anyone.

Late on May Day when Hemingway and Dos Passos arrived in Havana, the shooting was over and the wounded counted. That morning, as 25,000 workers, labor leaders, communist agitators, and spectators gathered in a park, police confiscated banners considered slanderous to the American ambassador and Colonel Fulgencio Batista, who was the military power behind the post-Machado government. With intimidating Cuban army planes stunting noisily overhead, the crowd began its procession through the streets toward Cristal Stadium. Then snipers opened fire from rooftops, panicking the marchers, who disappeared into side streets never to regroup. Only eleven were wounded; no one died. Afterward the working class claimed the government was responsible for the shootings; the government argued that communists pulled the triggers so they could blame the government. The snipers were never caught.[19]

The two authors went to Havana for fresh observations of revolution in action, for the abdication of Machado did not bring peace to the troubled island only one president away from the Batista dictatorship. Havana did not disappoint them. On May 2, transportation workers shut down the city for an hour in protest over the snipers. The next day, when high school students gathered in front of the Havana Institute to protest the May Day shootings, soldiers sent to suppress the affair opened fire with rifles, killing one student and wounding six others. A government investigation, as usual, was said to be under way, which meant nothing would come of the outrage.[20] A more personal reason for Hemingway's visit was to secure a preferred docking site for his new fishing boat, which he intended to bring over in July for the marlin season. (Hemingway and the Masons seem to have viewed revolutions as a spectator sport, no more threatening than a summer baseball league.) It took him four days to get six different required signatures on the required forms.[21]

Hemingway returned from Havana just in time to help bury Father Dougherty, the parish priest who had baptized Gregory, and to ride the train to Miami to take command of the *Pilar* on delivery. Bra Saunders, who knew boats, motors, and the protected Hawk's Channel route back to Key West, accompanied Ernest; in Miami they picked up the Wheeler shipyard representative, who motored back with them on the *Pilar's* shakedown cruise, making sure everything worked properly. At the Key West Navy submarine base, which was being opened to visiting yachts, a welcoming party met them at the dock: Pauline, children, and household staff; the Thompsons; Arnold Samuelson, a young would-be writer Hemingway was feeding; and Ernest's nineteen-year-old brother, Leicester, and his shipmate Al Dudeck, who had sailed their tiny, homemade *Hawkshaw* from Mobile into Key West on their way to Venezuela. As if this were not entourage enough for a man trying to write, Ernest, over the next month, entertained Archie MacLeish and Archie's father-in-law, followed by Father MacGrath, a Jesuit fisherman out of Miami, who hooked an Atlantic record sailfish that Ernest landed.[22]

Waiting for Hemingway in the stack of letters was Scott Fitzgerald's plaintive question "Did you like the book?"[23] It took him two weeks to send an answer, beginning: "I liked it and I didn't like it." It wasn't Scott's use of the Murphys that he disliked, it was the liberties he took with them that resulted not in real characters but "faked case histories." Sara and Gerald were characters ready-made for a novel, but first you had to understand them, you had to see and listen. Scott saw them clearly enough, but he had stopped listening. Being a "rummy" married to a crazy woman bent on destroying his work was a hell of a handicap, but one that Scott might overcome if he would only write honestly. He signed the letter, "Always your friend, Ernest."[24] With that out of his system, he wrote Perkins that

Tender Is the Night, aside from its essential weakness, was much better than he first said it was.

———

At the Thompson fish company that May, when they opened the shark to remove its hide, they found a slipper with bones from a human leg and foot. Eight days later, a mirage of Havana hovered in the evening sky over Key West: hundreds could see the Morro Castle, the Hotel Plaza, and the crowded Prado with pedestrians walking along it. Four days later a strange animal, something like an alligator, was seen swimming in the Key West harbor, and the keeper of the Fowey Rocks lighthouse caught an even stranger sea animal eight feet long with three rows of teeth and curious pale green stripes. That these oddities were signs few doubted, but as to what they meant, even fewer could agree.[25]

———

On the Fourth of July, citizens of Key West celebrated as if their property were not at risk for unpaid taxes. Opening with a morning parade, the day expanded with races—on foot, horseback, in boats under power and under sail—a bathing beauty contest, and fish fries that culminated with a jitney dance and fireworks in the dark. That night, those with a little money continued dancing to a small combo at the Cuban Club. Around midnight, as the last dance began to the strains of "Good Night, Sweetheart," the typesetters at the *Key West Citizen* were preparing a banner headline:

> KEY WEST NOW UNDER STATE CONTROL
>
> PASSES INTO HANDS OF FERA
>
> IN REHABILITATION PROGRAM
>
> STATE ADMINISTRATOR JULIUS F. STONE ACCEPTS
>
> GOVERNOR SHOLTZ'S INVITATION TO TAKE
>
> CHARGE OF AFFAIRS IN EMERGENCY OPERATIONS[26]

Not every townsman was thrilled with this unprecedented move by the federal government, but alternatives were limited: either move most of the population off the island or rehabilitate Key West into a tourist attraction. Food handouts and piecemeal FERA projects were reducing islanders to the status of beggars while barely keeping their families from starvation. Within ten days, beautification of the island began. On government money, piled-up garbage and trash were collected for burning, and free flowering plants were distributed to every household. In an appreciative gesture, the city council immediately renamed Main Boulevard as Roosevelt Boulevard.[27]

If cities have phases to their extended lives, one of Key West's was over, another begun, but Hemingway was not there to watch the transformation. On July 18, leaving his wife and three sons (Pauline had gone to New York, picked up Bumby, and returned) in Key West, he signed clearance papers, oath of manifest, and shipping articles to pilot the *Pilar* to Havana. He listed himself as master, Charles Lunn of the P&O Steamship Line as seaman, and Arnold Samuelson, who knew nothing of engines, as engineer.[28] Stowed in lockers and under the deck were thirty-two cases of canned vegetables, fruit, soups, chili, tamales, pork and beans, coffee, and sardines, a gallon of vinegar, three quarts of mustard: enough supplies to feed them for months. Along with motion-picture and Graflex film, anchor and line, thirty-five gallons of motor oil, and a half-dozen bottles of Saniflush was a copy of Zane Grey's *Tales of Swordfish and Tuna* and 201 pages of Hemingway's handwritten manuscript of what had started to be an African story and was now neither a novel nor exactly a safari narrative but something else.[29]

With Lunn aboard to give navigational advice on the *Pilar*'s maiden voyage to Cuba, the ninety-mile trip went smoothly enough until, within sight of Havana, the cooling pump failed, overheating the main engine. Using the four-cylinder auxiliary engine for emergency power and bucking the current, Ernest and company spent two hours covering the last three miles into port, an inauspicious start to their summer expedition.[30] Clearing customs and health inspection the following morning, the *Pilar* was allowed to put into the San Francisco docks within spitting distance of Ernest's favored Ambos Mundos Hotel, its crew free to go ashore. Lunn was given his certificate of discharge in time to catch the return ferry and was replaced as planned by Carlos Gutiérrez, dedicated Cuban friend and experienced fisherman, who signed on as seaman (age fifty-two) and found a man who could rebuild the water pump. On the Friday evening, after meeting Pauline at the P&O ferry slip, Ernest registered at the Ambos Mundos, where they would celebrate his thirty-fifth birthday the next day and her thirty-ninth the day after.

On Saturday morning, the *Havana Post*, with its usual inaccuracies, made their presence public:

> So quietly and unheralded, however, did Mr. Hemingway make his return to Havana this year that only a few were aware of his presence yesterday morning when he put in for the clearance papers on his piping new motor yacht Pilar, in which he entered Havana Bay Thursday night. . . . Designed by Mr. Hemingway, the trim 38-foot yacht . . . is named after his daughter. . . . Mrs. Hemingway, prominent American sportswoman and a well known writer in her own name, arrived in Havana last night on the P&O liner Florida to join her husband. . . . Mr. Hemingway recently returned . . . from an African expedition which rivaled the most thrilling jungle adventures of the late "Teddy" Roosevelt.[31]

Three days later Pauline returned to Key West, Grant Mason came back from Miami, Havana phones went dead during a brief operators' strike, and the natural historians from Philadelphia joined the *Pilar* to gather specimens for their collection.[32]

With Charles Cadwalader and ichthyologist Henry Fowler aboard along with Samuelson, Carlos, Juan the cook, and a steady stream of guests, Ernest was kept busy being host, instructor, captain, owner, and principal fisherman on a new boat. In wicker deck chairs offering no substantial help against large fish, the men butted thick rods into the crotch cups of leather harnesses that left their back muscles knotted and sore after an afternoon's excursion. Doing that every day for a month, two months, three months, back muscles begin to harden and swell, calf muscles to bulge, shoulders to fill out. Fishing without Josie Russell at the helm was a learning situation for Hemingway, for Russell knew from years of experience when and how to maneuver the boat to the angler's advantage. On Hemingway's new fishing team, Carlos manned the gaff and Juan took the wheel; every command was in Spanish. As Ernest wrote for *Esquire*:

> *In Spanish you cannot tell a man just to put her ahead. You have to tell him to put her ahead for the love of God and his mother or he does not believe in the existence of an emergency. When you want her thrown out, the clutch, that is, you must say throw her out, disengage her, remove her from functioning, for the love of God such stupidness, throw her out.*[33]

For almost three weeks no amount of Spanish cursing or English vernacular produced anything like a sizable "needle fish," as Carlos called the marlin. The big fish were someplace else.

That first month in Havana, between frustrated fishing and too many guests, Ernest wrote almost nothing on his African book. Five days after the Philadelphians arrived, Sidney Franklin, his sister, and her husband came in on the largess of a local public relations group trying to promote live bullfights in Cuba. With his usual flair, Franklin drew attention to himself and his sometime profession through newspaper interviews, public lectures, and a radio talk show, all of which resulted in a month's worth of letters to the editor pro and con on the ritual killing of bulls. When he was not being interviewed, Sidney spent time on or around the *Pilar* just as marlin began to feed on the surface.[34]

On the Havana dock encompassed by young Cubans in white shirts, an enormous blue marlin hangs from the hoist head down, mouth open, spear almost touching the wet concrete. Ernest, in moccasins, white trousers, and work shirt, one hand resting on a fin, the other holding a fishing rod. Between Ernest and the marlin's head, Carlos crouches; behind him, Cadwalader is framed in the open space between Ernest and the fish. To the left of the marlin and behind its full dorsal fin, Juan, in an undershirt, is framed by the hoisting ropes. And there beside Juan is Sidney Franklin in a buttoned suit, tie, and black *boina*, standing with his hands clasped at his crotch, looking oddly formal and vaguely out of place.[35]

———

Between July 20 and August 25, Pauline came four times to Cuba, leaving her children in Key West, far from the Havana polio epidemic, not to mention the virulent outbreak of malaria. In the first week of August, forty cases of polio were reported in Havana; seven children died. All that month, confusion and anomalies were the rule. In the harbor, a man-eating shark took down a young swimmer and then another before being caught and beaten to death by fishermen. On August 7, Pauline and her cousin Ward Pfeiffer Meriner were met at the dock by Sidney and Ernest, who after supper entertained them and other guests on board the *Pilar*. That same day, the government announced the capture of three Americans, including soldier of fortune and veteran of earlier Cuban revolutions Arthur Hoffman. With the arrests a rumor spread that a large arms shipment had come ashore close to Havana.[36] Bombs continued to explode in the sultry night, "wrecking the home of a high government official, slightly injuring his son, and damaging buildings within a radius of four blocks."[37] Conspirators, regularly arrested, disappeared into ancient prisons. Briefly striking workers just as regularly brought the streetcars, the telephones, or the postal service to a standstill.

If all of these excitements and intrusions were not enough to disrupt Hemingway's vulnerable writing schedule, worrying about his younger brother kept the African story on hold. On August 14, Leicester Hemingway and the *Hawkshaw*, forty-eight hours out of Key West, were overdue in Havana. Ernest, keeping a composed face for the press, said he wasn't worried. That was on Tuesday. When the top-heavy home-built sailboat that could not point up into the wind had not made port by Thursday morning, Ernest put the *Pilar* out to sea, half fishing while scanning the horizon. As the light was failing that evening, he found Leicester and his new sailing companion, Bob Kilo, twelve miles off the coast without a hope of reaching port that night. Tying on to the *Pilar*, the young sailors were towed without ceremony into the harbor in time for supper.[38]

Because Hemingway was now fishing both mornings and afternoons until the squalls break, he returns to port too tired to write. A month after arriving in Havana, he has added less than three thousand words to his manuscript, but he knows where it is going and how to get it there.[39] Working from memory, photographs, and his own notes, he began with only a ragged notion for a good story—the kudu hunt. What is developing is the story of a hunt, a meditation on writing, a semifictional autobiography, and a discourse on aesthetics. Like so many modernists—Joyce, Pound, Stein, Yeats—Hemingway is consciously creating a handbook for his readers, explaining how to read his texts. He is also creating a prose more complicated than any of his earlier writing, a prose that stops time, twists time, escapes outside of time. If Einstein could imagine more dimensions than three, just maybe a writer can work through the fourth dimension of time and into a timeless fifth dimension: a continuous present tense both *now* and *then*, *here* and *elsewhere* simultaneously.

Using the last month of the safari as his narrative line, Hemingway is able to flash back to earlier episodes without having to retell everything. The story began close to the end when the little Austrian in his noisy truck ruined the day and the kudu hunt looked hopeless. Then it moved the reader back "to the time of Droopy, after I had come back from being ill in Nairobi and we had gone on a foot safari to hunt rhino in the forest" (p. 46). "I" was a character who looked and spoke as Ernest spoke, but was a creation, both better and worse than his creator. This semifictional "other," this man in his mind's mirror, made wonderful shots on running animals at great distances (true) but, unlike the hunter in Pauline's journal, never missed so badly, never left wounded animals unfound in the field. This man living in the manuscript was recovering from "being ill," but without the graphic details Ernest described in the *Esquire* letter on dysentery. Quite deliberately, Hemingway was creating an exaggerated man with all faults exposed, a man afraid of snakes, a sometimes cruel man who bragged excessively, a man like himself who was always teaching someone, a lecturer, an authority on literature ("it all started with *Huck Finn*"). This mirrored man's wife was ever supportive, never bored or depressed; Charles Thompson's avatar, "Karl" in the book, was almost invisible except when he brought down trophies larger, better, more splendid than Ernest's. The competition between his two male hunters, which Hemingway was using to teach his created self and his readers a lesson, was exaggerated. What emerges is and is not the safari of record, for the very act of storytelling inevitably transforms what is remembered.

Writing once more on the run or back in Key West, jamming it all in—smells and sounds remembered, daydreaming at the noon break, whiskey talk at day's end—this writing is a joy unlike any pure fiction. Stopping at midday on the rhino hunt to read in Tolstoy's *Sevastopol* leads him back to riding his bicycle down rain-slick Boulevard Sevastopol in Paris, and now remembering that early apartment above the sawmill (*its parenthetical sounds and smells italicized*), and eventually taking him into the Luxembourg Gardens past Flaubert's bust. This dreamy stream of consciousness takes him finally and appropriately back to Joyce, who patented the process and whose fiction is for Hemingway a sovereign measuring stick.

"All I wanted to do now was get back to Africa," he wrote. "We had not left it, yet when I would wake in the night I would lie, listening, homesick for it already" (p.72). Revising this passage, he worried that the reader might miss the point. Loving the country, he explained, gave a happiness that was like being with a woman, postcoital, spent but recovering and wanting more:

You can never have it all and yet what there is, now, you can have, and you want more and more, to have, and be, and live in, to possess now again for always, for that long, sudden-ended always; making

time stand still, sometimes so very still that afterwards you wait to
hear it move, and it is slow in starting. (p. 72)

That was how he broke time apart until the reader is inside and outside of it all at once, but never getting too removed from the hunt.

During the night of September 4, more than a dozen bombs
exploded in Havana and surrounding towns. The next morning,
Hemingway put Arnold Samuelson and Carlos Gutiérrez to work
scraping and varnishing the *Pilar* while he returned to Key West during the dark of the moon, waiting for Carlos to send word that big
fall marlin are again feeding on the surface.[40] In Key West, young
Patrick fawns upon him, hungry for attention; Pauline he finds
transformed, her hair turning blond for the second time. It was the
year of the blonde: Mae West's and Jean Harlow's platinum screen
images are being imitated by housewives across America. Ernest, for
whom blond hair was an erotic adventure, could not have been more
pleased to be home.[41]

For eight working days in Key West, he lived in the Africa of
memory while penciled manuscript piled up on the table: twenty-
two pages one day, thirty the next, then another twenty.[42] It was a
book with no name, only a working title, *The Highlands of Africa.*
(The title almost always came last.) All that remained to tell was the
trekking down dusty roads, fruitless waiting, tempers strained during
the last days of the kudu hunt. And always there was counterpointing discussion, Ernest saying that if he ever wrote about Africa "it
will just be landscape painting until I know something about it" (p.
193). So simple to say, but time melted and bent: the writer writing
about an African hunt in which his narrator, a writer like himself,
says he is not ready to write about this African hunt.

Trying to reach a prose beyond his earlier work, Hemingway uses
the hunt, the quarry, and the hunter as metaphors for his trade.
Hunter and writer are both professionals whose ground rules are
stringent, whose conduct at parallel activities is meticulous, whose
expectations for performance are high. The hunter pursues the
lovely kudu, the promise of whose impossible spiraling horns makes

the hunt valid. The writer is equally driven to write a book beyond anything he has done before, and in doing so exhausts an experience he can never again write. The greatest joy is in the pursuit of both kudu and book; the successful hunt puts one trophy on the wall, the other on the bookshelf. Leaving out most of the safari's killing and using the kudu hunt as a guise, Hemingway is writing a book about writing a book.

On September 14, in response to an urgent message from Carlos, he returned to Cuba only to find the giant marlin already come and gone.[43] He fished another month, but it was all over this season. He has not boated the thousand-pound marlin of his dreams, but at the Ambos Mundos, he is finishing his manuscript. During the rest of September and into October, writing beautifully clean pages that need little revision, he doubles the length of the manuscript. By October 3, he tells Max Perkins that he has fifty thousand words written "on this long thing," and three new projects: a collection of all his previously published stories; a collection of the *Esquire* letters; and a novel, the content of which he does not specify.[44] Perkins's immediate response must have worried Hemingway a good deal. Thinking that Ernest referred to the book at hand, Max replied that the novel was wonderful news. "I'd felt morally certain," he said, "you were doing a novel, but not quite, because when you were here you spoke of having written a great deal on a narrative and of thinking you might reduce it to a story. . . . You do a novel and we will strain every muscle for it. . . . For God's sake don't get to be too much of a naturalist or you won't have time to write."[45]

In late September, Pauline spent ten days in Havana, her hair having reached what Ernest called "the fine South American white gold color."[46] Two days after she took the ferry back to Key West, Ernest towed three enormous sharks into the harbor to distribute at the dock, where a crowd, expecting his customary free marlin, had gathered.[47] First the marlin left, and then he sliced his finger open on a bait, producing a swollen hand that acted like blood poisoning, and then the rains began, ending everything but the writing in which the African rains threatened the hunt. The only excitement on the Gulf

Stream was a rare pod of whales that appeared one afternoon. Before using the experience for *Esquire*, he wrote Charles Cadwalader:

> *I harpooned one using over fifty fathoms of line . . . but the harpoon pulled out. Had all the life belts tied on one end and were going to let the line go over if we had to. . . . I thought by working on him with the Mannlicher whenever he came up we could kill him. We had a very exciting time. When I struck the whale the spout of another one along side went all over us.* [48]

The next day, John and Katy Dos Passos arrived in Havana, Dos sick and Katy distraught over the recent death of her father. From Hollywood, Dos had a Paramount paycheck for working on the Marlene Dietrich film *The Devil Is a Woman*, and a bad taste in his mouth from the experience.[49] Accustomed to being upstaged by Hemingway, he was not surprised by his interview in the Sunday *Post*:

> *John Dos Passos, eminent American liberal organizer and writer, is extremely interested in Cuban political developments, but has not had time thus far to study the situation. . . . Ernest Hemingway was a visitor in the room of Mr. Dos Passos during the interview. . . . has been in Havana more than three months . . . disclosed that he has succeeded in landing at least 12 of the giant fish this year.* [50]

The day after revolutionaries bungled an assassination attempt on the U.S. ambassador, Hemingway put away his fishing gear for the season. With fall storms regularly churning the Gulf and the prospect of more "northers" on the way, it was time to give up on the marlin. On October 26, at five in the morning, he and Arnold Samuelson motored the *Pilar* past the Morro Castle and headed back toward Key West to finish his African book. In his suitcase he packed a copy of the *Havana Post* with stories on twenty-four accused terrorists being freed from the Havana jail and a local man arrested for having two rifles and ammunition. Navigating by compass and adjusting for the current, Hemingway, on his first unaided trip across, raised Sand

Key nine hours and forty minutes after clearing Havana. The long summer was over.[51]

Another good reason for Ernest's return was the family's diminished Key West checking account, for which he, like his father before him, required a strict accounting of all expenditures except his own. Pauline managed their local bills, took care of wages for their hired help, balanced the books, and felt guilty when funds ran low. On the first of October, after moving $200 from their New York City account to Key West, Pauline sent Ernest a detailed accounting of expenditures ($306) so he would not think she was "throwing money away." Not included were groceries, for which she usually signed and paid for only when the total became significant; nor was her monthly deposit to Ina Hepburn's savings account for washing included. ("You look just like a devil standing out there," Ernest told Ina as she boiled clothes in a blackened backyard kettle.) Nor did the $306 include wages to their cook (Isobel), their "house boy" (Lewis and/or Nathaniel), or their gardener (Jimmy). One hundred dollars of the total went to Ada Stern as salary and expense money for keeping Gregory, who had been with Ada in Syracuse, New York, all summer and into the fall.[52]

When Isobel left cooking in the Hemingway kitchen, her friend Miriam Williams replaced her. Years later Miriam recalled that she was hired despite her inexperience: "Between Miss Pauline and Ada Stern, the housekeeper, I learned, but I'll admit the first year was rough. They were good to me and very patient. After that I could cook almost anything. I learned how to tend bar, too." Miriam learned to prepare Hemingway's favorite dishes: baked fish, black beans laced with salt pork, garlic, and onions, with either broccoli with hollandaise sauce or string beans. In the formal dining room, dress was casual and the wines French. On weeknights Ernest and Pauline were in bed by ten o'clock, but on weekends after dinner they would go downtown to drink and dance. Every morning at seven-thirty, Miriam took two full trays upstairs to the Hemingways, who always breakfasted in bed. "There was some kind of happiness over there [in the Hemingway house]," Ina remembered. "You never seen anything like it. . . . Some people didn't think Mr. Hemingway dressed very nice, but when he did get dressed up, it was something grand."[53]

Like most white Americans of their generation, when speaking to other whites Ernest and Pauline could refer to their black household staff as "niggers" while trusting them with the well-being of their children and the safekeeping of their possessions and treating them as part of the family, albeit less privileged. In the same way, Ernest and Pauline were both generically anti-Semitic while having close Jewish friends. Ernest, for example, could genuinely embrace Sidney Franklin while saying that he might move his children to Africa rather than have them grow up "in this F.E.R.A. Jew administered phony of a town."[54] This contradictory behavior was not peculiar to the Hemingways; it was deeply embedded in the American grain. In Key West, as in most of America, anyone born white between the end of the last century and several decades later grew up in a society so prevalently racist that the racism was invisible to the dominant class. In fact, most white Americans from this period would have been offended to be called racist. Yet in Key West, African-Americans sent their children to a "colored" school, swam at the "colored" beach, picnicked in Nelson English park for the "colored" where "colored" bands gave concerts. At the Dixie Theater, they could see motion pictures never advertised in the paper; when one of them died, the *Citizen*'s headline always read "Colored Man to Be Buried." As Teddy Roosevelt, hunting through East Africa, exclaimed time and again, "This could be a white man's country," as if the black Masai and Wanderobo natives were inconsequential.

———

Here in Key West we have a national rehabilitation project running everything. I am dragged by the house-renting clerk before the Rehabilitator in Chief to see if I will do, that is to say, measure up to his idea of what the new citizenry must look as if it thought, felt and acted on under God and the President in Washington. The Rehabilitator is a rich young man in shorts with hairy legs named Stone. . . . The town has been nationalized to rescue it from its own speculative excesses. The personal interest of Roosevelt in his second coming has been invoked and both mayor and governor have abdicated. . . . It is tropical all right but it is rather unsanitary and shabby. It has a million dollars worth of concrete sidewalks with no houses on them. It has three races not very well kept apart by race-prejudice, Cubans, Negroes and Whites.[55]

—Robert Frost, 1934

———

Ernest returned to a Key West transforming itself into something new and strange. Under the demagogic eye of FERA-man Julius Stone, the island outpost, without ever taking a vote, was becoming by default a government tourist attraction. His hairline receding, his mustache clipped, Stone ruled the island. "With a scratch of my pen I started this work in Key West," he said, "and with a scratch of my pen I can stop it—just like that!" (But he could not keep the old-time "conchs" from laughing at his hairy legs: what sort of grown man would walk about publicly in his underwear?) Vacant lots of trash disappeared; houses were painted, flower gardens planted, a Garden Club in full stride. Onetime fishermen were employed to round up stray dogs and cats for extermination. Two hundred homes, whose owners six months earlier could not pay property taxes, were being refurbished with FERA loans to be paid back from vacationers' rents. On Rest Beach, thatched-hut cabanas were being constructed. Even bars and nightclubs were getting a paint job on government loans. A mattress factory was under way, and coconut palms were being planted along the main thoroughfares. Between the island and Miami, an FERA-subsidized airline was scheduled to fly in tourists. Up on Matecumbe Key, an advance team was building camps to house the World War veterans being sent there to construct bridges for the overseas highway.[56]

Hemingway was appalled. His wire fence could not keep tourists from staring at his house on Whitehead Street, and nothing could keep them out of Josie Russell's bar. In his African book, when Percival asks what is happening in America, Ernest replies: "Damned if

I know! Some sort of Y.M.C.A. show." Later he adds, "Starry eyed bastards spending money that somebody will have to pay. Everybody in our town quit work to go on relief. Fishermen all turned carpenters. Reverse of the Bible."[57] Actually, there was no work to quit, no market for fish, no money for food, but that is easy to ignore if the self-reliant strenuous life is your moral guide and your diminished bank account is in no real danger of failing, not with money in Paris and New York accounts, money coming in from Pauline's trust, gift money from Uncle Gus, advance money from Scribner's. There was always money somewhere, or if things got too tight, he could write for the magazines. *Cosmopolitan* was begging for a story.

On November 3, when Ada Stern returned from Syracuse with Gregory in time for his third birthday, their younger son saw Ernest and Pauline almost as strangers; in the previous year and a half while almost exclusively in the care of Ada, Gregory saw his parents only in passing, leaving him understandably confused. Patrick said later he always knew Pauline was his mother, and Ada, whom he hated for her terrible cooking, a mean woman who could roast in hell. Jack, as Bumby grew up to become, was old enough (ten) to deal with Ada: he abetted her secret drinking with supplies from Ernest's liquor cabinet. But Gregory, delivered at three months into Ada's care, had no defense against the woman who used his fear of being unloved to control him.[58] In Pauline's letters to her frequently absent husband, Patrick's deeds and sayings appear over and over; Gregory, or "Gigi" as they called him, is largely missing.

Ernest, so eager to be called "Papa" by adults older than himself, was never comfortable with his own children until they were old enough to fish and hunt. Then he was their instructor, showing them the way water changes color over the reef, teaching them to clean their kill, instructing them on the importance of terrain. He loved his sons, but having grown up with a father who could not express his emotions, Hemingway was not good at communicating this love when they were small, nor did he let them interfere with either of his two driving interests: the outdoor life and writing. As they grew old enough to accompany him in the hunting fields and on the *Pilar* fishing, their bonding improved, except for Gregory, who remembers still his overpowering tendency to seasickness the moment the *Pilar* left the harbor.[59] All three of his sons needed desperately to please Ernest, a need not easily fulfilled.

Neither his children nor tourist traffic generated by the rejuvenating island distracted Hemingway that mild fall as he pushed the African book to its conclusion, trying to bring all the elements together: killing the kudu, pursuing beauty, the writer writing, memories and projections. M'Cola asking for beer from the African chop box and brown beer remembered "sitting at the wood tables under the wisteria vine" with Chink Dorman-Smith twelve years earlier and Alsatian beer at Lipps in Paris: all remembered in the Key West heat, which was not in the story but was leaving sweat stains on the paper. Freely associating *then* and *now* produced amazing time warps: time past always shifting, sometimes Paris, sometimes earlier in the hunt; time present equally fluid, sometimes at the African salt lick, sometimes removed without saying where, the narrator making judgments and connections.

On African roads, escaping the drought and locust plague along the coast, African natives trudge past the safari truck; unmentioned are the towering west Texas dust storms freshly embedded in the American mind through newsreels. From associations stated and silent, the narrator tells us that "the earth gets tired of being exploited." The promise of America, fulfilled for earlier generations, is no longer real:

> *Our people went to America because that was the place to go then. It had been a good country and we made a bloody mess of it and I would go somewhere else as we had always gone. (p. 285)*

Whether he is referring to the streets of Key West or the American dust bowl, the narrator's conviction that the American dream is a dream gone by spoke to the gnawing fears of a country now entering the fifth year of the depression.

Hemingway's increasing need to pontificate, which even tolerant friends began to question, led to excesses in the manuscript, some of which Hemingway eliminated, some he retained. As Katy Dos Passos, who had known Hemingway since he was a twelve-year-old at Walloon Lake, told the Murphys:

> *Did I tell you Ernest was translated when seen in Havana? Remember how irascible and truculent he was before. Now he's just a big cage of canaries . . . He was sweet, but had a tendency to be an Oracle I thought and needs some best pal and severe critic to tear off those long white whiskers which he is wearing.*[60]

On November 10, Perkins, who still had no idea what Ernest was writing, said that if Hemingway's novel was ready for publication, they should put "The First Fifty-seven" collection of stories on hold.[61] Four days later, Hemingway began telling Max and other correspondents that the new book was finished (492 pages of holograph), and that he was starting another story. "Might as well take advantage of a belle epoque while I'm in one."[62] Max convinced himself it was the novel begun before Hemingway went to Africa. Because Ernest never told Max any details about the abandoned Philip Haines/James Allen chapters, the assumption was understandable.[63]

On November 20 at the Pierre Matisse Gallery in New York, Hemingway helped his Spanish friend Luis Quintanilla with the opening of his first American show. Impressed with Quintanilla's Goyaesque etchings and his radical politics, Hemingway arranged for the show, fronted money to pull the etchings, and contributed, along with Dos Passos, a statement for the catalog. He was now asking his New York friends to support the opening because Quintanilla was in a Madrid jail, charged with "being a member of the revolutionary committee" fomenting a riot against government policy. Hemingway asked Perkins to put the Scribner's publicity department to work on the show, perhaps pulling the two introductory pieces he and Dos Passos wrote into some sort of press release. What Max and *Time* magazine found in the catalog was good copy but not about the etchings. Hemingway wrote:

Now this may possibly be a good time to suggest that a small tax be levied on the use of the word revolution, the proceeds to be given to the defense of, say, such people as Luis Quintanilla, by all those who write the word and never have shot or been shot at; who never have stored arms nor filled a bomb, never have discovered arms nor had a bomb burst among them; who have never gone hungry in a general strike, nor have manned streetcars when the tracks are dynamited; who never have sought cover in a street trying to get their heads behind a gutter.[64]

Having seen most of it, he wrote as the insider angry with those who had not borne actual witness to violence.

Riding a manic high, when words came easily and nothing touched him, Hemingway put aside the African story long enough to rip off an *Esquire* letter making fun of Gilbert Seldes, Alexander Wollcott, and William Saroyan, all of whom appeared in the magazine:

Now a lot of us weren't as bright as you, Mr. Saroyan, see I'm giving you a break. You're bright. So don't get sore. But you're not that bright. You don't know what you're up against. You've only got one new trick, and that is that you're an Armenian.[65]

Having called New York writers "angleworms in a bottle, trying to derive knowledge and nourishment from their own contact and from the bottle," Hemingway was gratuitously baiting much of the literary establishment, alienating potential reviewers of his next book.[66]

With the *Esquire* letter in the mail to Gingrich, Ernest tried to explain for the first time to Max Perkins about the African book, which, starting as a story, grew into something like "Big Two-Hearted River," his long, controlled land- and mindscape with fisherman from 1924, only better. It had the landscape painting in it, "but a hell of a lot happens in this one and there is plenty of dialogue and action. . . . plenty of excitement. . . . I've written it absolutely true—*absolutely* no faking or cheating." He tried to say it three times, but words did not explain the book, which he knew Max expected to be a novel and which he insisted was "the best thing I've written—True narrative that is exciting and still is literature is very rare." Worried over Max's possible disappointment and Scribner's risk of having put up a loan against this book, Ernest suggested publishing it as a long story to lead off a collection of all his stories. They could even let this African book wait, publish the stories and the essays, and then he might do an Oak Park novel, except his mother and his father's brother were still alive.[67] By this point in the letter, Max was thoroughly confused about what it was Hemingway had written. So was Ernest, for the book, which he was still calling *The Highlands of Africa*, defied generic categories. In his cautiously understated reply, Max said that these were tough questions raised by Ernest which required careful thought.[68]

After working through the possibilities, and discussing it with Charles Scribner himself, Max said they should publish the long story as a freestanding book, without appendages, for readers resented padded books, and added stories would distract the reviewers. Putting it as a lead story to "The First Fifty-seven" would make too large a book for the market, and the new story would not get the reviewers' full attention. "I see that you regard this as a story, not a novel," Max wrote, still not understanding what Ernest was telling him, "but that makes no difference." If Hemingway could only modify the title to *In the Highlands of Africa*, implying that something happened there. Otherwise people might think this was merely a travel book.[69]

Hemingway chewed on Max's advice while he worked on revisions, inserting sections, chopping out others, all the while dealing with winter visitors. Unexpectedly, Alfred Vanderbilt and Dick Cooper flew in one day and out the next in the Vanderbilt amphibian. *Esquire* editor Arnold Gingrich, at Hemingway's invitation and lured by the scent of the new book, flew in on the FERA airline, fished with Ernest and Dos Passos, and flew out two days later.[70] Working steadily every morning, Hemingway wrote Perkins that he could "beat the present title," but first there was a Piggott Christmas to attend.[71] Leaving Gregory (three) behind with Ada Stern in Key West, Pauline departed by train for Miami while Ernest and Patrick (six) followed in the car, picking her up and driving north to Memphis and into Piggott two days before Christmas.[72]

Chapter Eight

1935

HEAVY WEATHER

Key West, Bimini, and Matecumbe

DURING THE SIXTH year of the economic nightmare, thieves begin breaking into Key West homes where a few years earlier no one had anything worth stealing. Nevertheless, the Key West city council remains optimistic. Having made Duval Street a "Great White Way" with streetlights which they could only afford to turn on for weekends, they now order two electric traffic lights to control the anticipated tourist traffic. They also put out a handbill on good driving manners which include not stopping the car in the middle of the street to speak with friends. In the Navy harbor, expensive wintering yachts now dock with some regularity—*Placida, Sylvia II, Minoco, Alva, Azara, Kallisto, Mariposa*—bringing new money to town. Each day, more vacationers are renting winter quarters in Key West. Winter guests staying at the Casa Marina are catching toothy barracuda, which, to the amusement of the locals, they are having mounted for their northern homes. Three new clubs open with live music and featured entertainment on weekends. For the three to four to five hundred weekenders coming in by train, car, and plane, Key West provides band concerts, parades, flower shows, semiprofessional boxing matches in the high school gym, the town's first art gallery for WPA artists, and a saltwater aquarium. Where once the Dry Tortugas were available only to dedicated fishermen in seaworthy boats, now for $10 anyone can fly round-trip to see Fort Jefferson, leaving at 11:00 a.m., returning at 2:30 p.m. The government men, pleased with their progress in Key West, are thinking of turning the Tortugas into a tourist attraction.[1]

Not everyone, however, is prospering. By the time the Hemingway family returned from their Piggott Christmas, rowdy war veterans were creating problems. Sent in by the WPA to construct bridges linking all the Keys with a continuous highway, many of the vets are displaced and disgruntled "bonus marchers" run out of Washington by the U.S. Army. Eight hundred and seventy-five of them are housed in hurriedly constructed camps, men carrying war memories and bad debts, men without women and without much hope, reassembled with others of their kind. Before Christmas, Sheriff Karl Thompson (brother of Charles) sent deputies to Lower Matecumbe to preserve order and reduce the sale of bootleg liquor. In Key West, citizens complain that vets on liberty arrive drunk, get drunker, and make a public nuisance right there in the front yard.[2]

On the last day of February, Key West's Battery E of the Florida National Guard is mobilized and sent up to Matecumbe to quell a strike already three days in progress. Despite rumors of violence, the Guard found the strikers playing baseball or sitting around swapping stories. The strike was

> *brought about by a number of agitators, or camp lawyers, who were undesirables. . . . the disturbers were men who had stressed a demand for improved sanitary conditions, the reinstatement of certain committee members who had been rejected from the camp and . . . a scale of wages for skilled labor equal to that being paid civilian workers.*[3]

A week after the strike began, a vet stepped up on a Duval Street front porch, took off all his clothes, and began telling a gathering crowd how bad things were on Matecumbe. Police soon took him off to jail to sober up.[4]

When the National Guard came home, a regular patrol of Key West auxiliary deputies remained stationed on the island to maintain order. On March 21, two vets were brought into Key West in irons, arrested for "interfering with an officer." Three weeks later they brought in two more, one behaving "strangely," the other with his wrists slit in a botched suicide. The quickly convened lunacy commission, which found both men insane and dangerous, exported them to a veterans' hospital in Tennessee.[5] And on any Key West Saturday night in the Silver Slipper or Sloppy Joe's, drunken vets not yet annoying enough to be arrested or crazy enough to be exported curse, carouse, and brawl, leaving the floor slippery with spilled beer and blood.

———

Don't be surprised when you see the town—There's been changes. The New Dealers are here . . . and Key West is now a Greenwich Village Nightmare—They have stirred up all the old art trash and phony uplifters that sank to the bottom after the war, and they're painting murals on the café walls, and weaving baskets, and cutting down plants and trees, and renting all the homes (with Washington money) and arranging sight-seeing tours, and building apartments for tourists so they can observe the poor Hemingways. They even wrote to Jed Harris' sister that she would have an apartment "with a view of Ernest Hemingway," and all the dreary international smart-alecs are turning up as they always do about six years later, "discovering" the place, . . . you can't stir out of your house without being run over by a little Jewish woman on a bicycle. . . . The little Jewish women are always either circling around the Hemingway house or else taking their book reviews to the post office. It's a paradise of incompetents, all floating around in a rich culture of humanitarian graft. . . . There is even a band of fake Cubans with velvet pants and red sashes that meets the train every day and the sky is full of aeroplanes and the speakeasies are jammed with drunk and cynical newspaper men. They are putting in Tea Rooms painted in black and orange . . . and those fearful cork candlesticks and fishnets.[6]

—Katy Dos Passos, January 1935

While Ernest revised his African book and fed it to his typist, Pauline worked feverishly on the house, preparing for the usual spate of winter guests, invited and otherwise; young Patrick, avoiding adults as much as possible, went about singing softly to himself a song he'd learned from a Victrola record sent by the Murphys:[7]

> *Cellophane, Mr. Cellophane*
> *Ought to be my name.*
> *You walk right past me,*
> *Look right through me,*
> *And never know I'm there.*

Every morning Ernest secluded himself, sometimes in the bedroom, sometimes above the garage, changing, inserting, moving words about and reliving Africa. In Gregory's earliest memory of his father, Ernest looms enormous on the second-floor porch glaring down at him in the yard below, where he is beating on tin pans. Ernest shouts at him: "Will you please be quiet! I'm trying to write."[8]

On January 16, Ernest wires Scribner's that he is delighted that Max Perkins and his wife, Louise, are coming to Key West. He wants Max to read the manuscript, rough as it is, hoping that *Scribner's Magazine* will serialize it as it did *A Farewell to Arms*. Timing is delicate: if the serial runs six or seven monthly issues, to publish the book version in the fall they will have to begin in April, May at the latest. Four days before Max arrived, Burt MacBride, an associate editor from *Cosmopolitan*, registered at the Casa Marina, carrying a personal letter to Ernest from editor in chief Harry Burton. The word on the New

York street says that Hemingway has a new novel finished; maybe this time he will give *Cosmopolitan* the first look for a serial.[9]

MacBride gave the African book a quick read, made enough notes to talk to Burton, and put Hemingway on hold for two days until a decision is made in New York. As Perkins arrives in Key West on the Havana Special, MacBride is leaving on the flight to Miami, where he wrote Hemingway that Burton was not going to agree to a four-part serial of nonfiction, sight unseen. "Due consideration" was required. He had to think of his audience: would this African book appeal to them? A Hemingway novel was a sure thing, but Burton would not take MacBride's word on nonfiction, which he "to be quite frank" could not recommend anyway, despite thinking it "a swell performance. . . . Better luck next time."[10]

For eight days, Max and Louise Perkins stay at Casa Marina, fishing afternoons on the *Pilar*, and dining at Whitehead Street more than once. Max also spends several days reading what he thought was going to be a novel, while Ernest, suffering from a recurrence of amebic dysentery, manfully plays host between doses of emetine and castor oil. At the Key West dock next to two suspended swordfish, Max stands, almost smiling, with his ever-present hat oddly in hand, his tie tightened against his collar, his striped suit double-buttoned. Erl Roman, editor of the "Rod and Reel" section of the *Miami Herald*, stands to the right, more casually dressed in working pants and a windbreaker. On Max's left, Ernest grins broadly, hair blowing in the wind, wearing an open collar, buttoned sport coat, white pants, and bedroom slippers.[11]

Before the Perkinses leave for New York, Max tells Ernest the book, for which there is no generic term, is wonderful and *Scribner's Magazine* might serialize it for maybe $5,000, which was more hesitant than Ernest needed to hear just then. Two days later, Max wired:

> *All keen about idea of serial but as arrangements depend on number of issues will need to study manuscript stop send as soon as you can stop writing all about it tomorrow stop grateful to you and Pauline for fine time.*[12]

Without waiting for further explanations, Hemingway immediately wrote Arnold Gingrich, trying to interest *Esquire* in the serial version. *Cosmopolitan*, he said, offered him big money but asked him to reduce the text by almost half, which was not possible (nor was it true, but this was business). At the very least he needed a minimum of $10,000 for the serial; less than that would not help. As soon as Max returned the typescript, he would send it to Gingrich on spec.[13]

When word came from Perkins that the *Scribner's Magazine* offer was $4,500 for the serial, Ernest was furious, reminding Max how loyal he had been to Scribner's. Were they offering so little because they wanted him to turn it down? "We do not intend there shall be any hard feeling about price," Max had written. What was that supposed to mean? Hemingway's response was an old story that Perkins knew by heart. Negotiating between Ernest's demands and Scribner's accountants, Max raised the offer to $5,000, which Hemingway reluctantly accepted.[14] With the first installment scheduled for May, there was little time to waste. Having decided not to use his photographs in the magazine or in the book version, Hemingway immediately sent moving pictures and safari photographs for the illustrator, Edward Shenton, to use for models, but he insisted there be no illustrations of dead animals. Hemingway's brittle moodiness, which kept family and visitors tense, was made worse by his touch of dysentery and the effects of emetine taken to cure it.[15]

About that same time Sara Murphy, arriving without Gerald, rejoined John and Katy Dos Passos to share a Key West house, frequent the Hemingways, and spend occasional afternoons on the *Pilar*. From New York, Gerald sent breezy news along with new Fats Waller phonograph records for Ernest to enjoy. Patrick Murphy (fourteen), still fighting the tuberculosis contracted seven years earlier, was under constant care at Saranac Lake; Baoth Murphy (fifteen) was recovering from measles at his Massachusetts boarding school. On February 20, Gerald's telegram said Baoth was "mending," and that Sara should "get some rest." The next day Baoth's measles became a double mastoid infection, rushing Sara northward in the night to a connection with the plane to Boston.[16] What followed were days and nights of dull horror, one operation after another with hourly telegrams carrying bad news south to Key West:

> *Blood transfusion tomorrow morning to combat toxemia and replenish depleted condition stop holding his own we are hopeful stop feel your prayers much love.*[17]

Two days and two transfusions later, Baoth Murphy, fifteen years old, died from meningitis with Gerald beside him and Sara, bending over him, pleading, "Breathe, Baoth, please breathe."[18] Ernest tried to say it several ways, none of them worth a damn, but still saying it: "Very few people ever really are alive and those that are never die; no matter if they are gone. No one you love is ever dead."[19]

———

The house at present occupied by your correspondent is listed as number eighteen in a compilation of the forty-eight things for a tourist to see in Key West. So there will be no difficulty in a tourist finding it or any other of the sights of the city, a map has been prepared by the local F.E.R.A. authorities to be presented to each arriving visitor. Your correspondent is a modest retiring chap with no desire to compete with the Sponge Lofts (number 13 of the sights), the Turtle Crawl (number 3 on the map), the Ice Factory (number 4), the Tropical Open Air Aquarium containing the 627 pound jewfish (number 9), or the Monroe County Courthouse (number 14). . . . Yet there your correspondent is at number 18 between Johnson's Tropical Grove (number 17) and Lighthouse and Aviaries (number 19). This is all very flattering to the easily bloated ego of your correspondent but very hard on production.[20]

—Ernest Hemingway, April 1935

———

Once painter and fisherman Mike Strater arrived in Key West, Hemingway was ready to leave for Bimini, where Mike swore there were tuna larger than Ernest's imagination, not to mention marlin well over a thousand pounds. With Dos Passos and Charles Thompson rounding out his latest version of "summer people," Hemingway planned to take the *Pilar* twenty miles out in the Gulf Stream by day, letting the current carry them up the Florida coast, fishing as they went. At night they would pull inside the coastal barrier reef to anchor safely in Hawks Channel. By the second night they would reach the Carysfort light, and from there next morning steer east-northeast into the Atlantic toward Gun Cay and Bimini. The fishing team included Albert "Bread" Pinder, who knew engines and something of navigation. "Saca Ham" Adams was signed on to cook for the group. On Sunday morning, April 7, having loaded aboard navigation charts, two months' worth of canned goods, extra water, rods, reels, and plenty of line, the Mannlicher rifle, and Hemingway's favorite .22 Colt Woodsman, the six men waved goodbye to the women at the dock and headed out toward blue water.[21]

That evening they returned to the dock, Ernest nauseous from having accidentally shot himself with the Woodsman. While Pinder was gaffing Ernest's shark and Ernest was standing by with his pistol to finish him off and Dos Passos was trying to film the event, the shark twisted, the wooden gaff snapped, the pistol fired, and two holes appeared in Ernest's left calf. "I'll be a sorry son of a bitch," Hemingway said. "I'm shot." The soft-nosed lead bullet had ricocheted off a brass railing, splattering as it did so, one small piece entering below Ernest's kneecap, a larger piece farther down, and tiny fragments smaller than birdshot elsewhere. Back in Key West, Dr. Warren "removed the fragments, probed, had an X-ray made, decided not to remove the large piece of bullet which was about three or four inches into the calf."[22] A week later, the crew and the fishing team without Dos Passos put to sea once more, reaching Bimini on Tuesday evening, April 16.

Lying south from Grand Bahama Island and northwest of Andros, and forty-five miles east of Miami, the Biminis are a cluster of small green-and-white islands, only three of which, North and South Bimini and Cat Cay, are inhabited. On North Bimini, barely seven miles long and less than five hundred yards wide, two tiny villages exist; on South Bimini, a sheltered harbor for fishing boats, four hun-

dred souls, several bars, and Mrs. Duncombe's boardinghouse, The
Compleat Angler, with ten rooms and decent food. During prohibition, two liquor barges anchored in the harbor ready to fill the steady
orders from Miami bootleggers. Now a pilot boat out of Miami, cap-
tained by George Kreidt, freights in supplies every Tuesday, and Pan
American seaplane service brings in passengers and mail to nearby
Cat Cay on Mondays and Fridays. Without phone service, the only
direct communication is by telegraph: Ernest Hemingway, Bimini,
BWI. On protected beaches there are shells and pristine white sand;
above high tide line, windblown royal palms. The Gulf Stream passes
so near the shore that one could not harbor closer to it.[23]

When the Dos Passoses came over to visit for a week in May, they
found "a wharf and some native shacks under the coconut palms and
a store that had some kind of barroom attached where we drank rum
in the evenings . . . and a couple of sun-eaten bungalows screened
against the sand-flies up on the dunes." With miles of shallow, clear
water between and among lightly wooded, uninhabited islets, day
sailing could not be better.[24] Katy called Bimini "a crazy mixture of
luxury, indigence, good liquor, bad food, heat, flies, land apathy and
sea magnificence, social snoot, money, sport, big fish, big fishermen,
and competitive passion."[25] In the evening with the rum flowing,
Nattie Saunders would be singing his homemade songs with Ernest
listening and remembering long afterwards:

> Oh, they got John in jail
> No one to stand John bail
> Oh let's go see Uncle Sonny
> Ask if he got any English money
> English money can stand John's bail
> English money can take him out of jail.[26]

Over on Cat Cay, where the Pan Am plane splashed down, the very
rich were building a private development the way the rich always do:
find the place, import a lifestyle theretofore unknown, and leave it
when the flavor is gone.

Bimini was not Cat Cay. Bimini was barefoot country where a man did not have to shave unless he wanted to, did not have to do anything. "It's like the end of the world," Ernest said, his kind of place where rules were local and negotiable.[27] Visitors came, fished, and left: Charles Thompson, the Dos Passoses, Bror and Eva Von Blixen, even Uncle Gus. In May, Pauline was back and forth, without children, staying with Mrs. Duncombe while the men slept on the *Pilar*. It was, Hemingway wrote MacLeish, the best summer he could remember: clear water in the harbor, huge tuna in the stream, and good whiskey afterward. A man need not change clothes for a month if he starts the morning by diving into the harbor in lieu of a bath, and in the evenings the gentry tell fishing stories and drink.[28] Sometimes they drink too much, like the evening when Joe Knapp called Ernest a phony, fat slob and then had to back it up; three bare-fisted left hooks and a looping right put Mr. Knapp flat on the wooden dock, and Ernest not even breathing hard, his first real brawl in a long time. Nattie Saunders, who sees it all, is soon singing:

> *Mister Knapp look at him and try to mock*
> *And from the blow*
> *Mister Knapp couldn't talk*
> *At first Mist Knapp thought*
> *He had his bills in stalk*
> *And when Mister Ernest Hemingway walked*
> *The dock rocked*
> *Mister Knapp couldn't laugh*
> *Mister Ernest Hemingway grinned*
> *Put him to sleep*
> *With a knob on the chin.*[29]

It was not like Havana; Ernest's companions in Bimini were the very rich, men who liked to wager on the day's fishing, men like Tommy Shevlin, Mike Lerner, who had a grand house on Cat Cay, and Bill Leeds, whose huge yacht, *Moana*, was too large for the harbor.[30] In Oak Park, where Hemingway grew up comfortably among families wealthy enough to hunt big game, he was always on the outside look-ing in at a lifestyle that part of him admired and wanted for his own. Now in Key West he owned a house as fine as those in Oak Park and with more servants. But there was also a part of him that despised the very rich as a class, for they had, in Oak Park, made him much aware that he was outside, and he never forgave them. Without being ter-ribly rational about it, Hemingway could despise the class but not the representative, just as he was raised to be anti-Semitic but was great friends with Mike Lerner, whose house he sometimes used.[31]

Warm, starry nights; hot, sun-drenched days: Bimini in summer was a fisherman's dream and an editor's nightmare if the fisherman was Ernest Hemingway with a serialized book in production. There were more isolated places than Bimini in the western hemisphere, but Max Perkins was not going to mention them to Ernest for fear he might go there next time they had a book to produce. With only three chances a week to get magazine and book proofs into Bimini and out again, trusting the U.S. mail to convey them to the pilot boat captain or to the seaplane pilot who had to remember to take the proofs to the island, and then trust that the process would work twice in a row to get them back in time to meet deadlines—all of these worries put an edge of anxiety on Max Perkins's summer of 1935.

Somehow it worked. Swahili words get corrected by Bror Von Blixen, who mislays sections but not permanently; the illustrations by Shenton are completed and approved; magazine installments appear as advertised; lost corrected proofs arrive in the nick of time.[32] By July 9, Max can almost rest easy: the fifth magazine installment is still between here and there, but they are setting book proofs. Some corrections made for the magazine probably don't get into the book; some of the book doesn't appear in the magazine. Hemingway sel-dom compared manuscript to typescript, typescript to galley proofs, magazine proofs with book proofs. Mistakes happen. Given the cir-cumstances, the author, and the times, there should have been more.

Through all that summer, a tension runs beneath and between Hemingway's letters: after disappointing sales of *Death in the After-noon* and *Winner Take Nothing*, he is certain *Green Hills* will turn everything around. From the beginning, he establishes ground rules: no photographs, he makes his own word pictures; keep the price at $2.50; never advertise it as a novel or a travel book.[33] May, June, July—the installments in *Scribner's Magazine* appear, giving potential book reviewers plenty of time to pick their shots, for Hemingway's running remarks about the worthless writers and critics of the new-found American left were guaranteed to offend. For a writer desperately wanting his work to be well received, Hemingway was almost daring the reviewers to trash *Green Hills*. To Perkins, Ernest insists that Von Blixen and Charles Curtis, both of whom know Africa, are wildly enthusiastic; if Scribner's will only do a decent advertising job, they should sell twenty thousand, enough to repay his $3,500 loan/advance money and put another $2,500 in the bank. Added to the $5,000 serial payment, he would be ahead of his expenses. It is a good story, he says again and again, a true, straight autobiography, taking people places they would never be able to go on their own.[34] Max, having prepared salient points for the salesmen on the road, promised that advertising would be good and persistent. "There's one thing I shall not worry about," he wrote Ernest, "and that is your giving up writing for sport. I do not believe you would give up sport for writing, either, although I'll bet you would that first if it came to a show down." Then, almost as non sequitur, he added, "You must finish a novel though before long."[35]

As usual, there are offensive *words* to discuss, words like "condom." Floating prominently in Hemingway's longest ever metaphor for the relationship of the temporary to the timeless, the condom was crucial to a passage he could not cut. Remembering how Havana garbage scows dump their traffic into the Gulf Stream and how bits and pieces—palm fronds, corks, bottles, light bulbs, condoms, a corset, dead dogs and cats—surface for pickers to pluck out with their long poles:

> *and the palm fronds of our victories, the worn light bulbs of our discoveries and the empty condoms of our great loves float with no significance against one single, lasting thing—the stream.*[36]

There were other words, he told Max, that he might employ—used rubber, safety, French letter—but "condom" was the "most dignified" word for this "very serious passage."[37] Max, so sensitive about some words that he could not bring himself to say them, balked: "I think we shall have to go against you on that word." It was one of the finest passages Ernest or anyone else ever wrote, but fanatics sought the least excuse to attack an author's work.[38]

By the end of July, with the last magazine page proofs in the mails to Bimini, Max was waiting on Hemingway's decision about chapter titles before laying out the book itself. At the same time Ernest was writing Max about his bare-fisted boxing matches on the Bimini docks: four fights, four knockouts. Island life was so good he wanted to stay, but could not leave the *Pilar* so exposed during the hurricane season. Book galleys 25 through 36 arrived, were being read, and would be flying to the mainland the next day. No chapter titles would be used because that was too much like a novel, but he was making divisions, calling them "Part One, Part Two, Part Three," each with a subtitle: "Pursuit and Conversation—Pursuit Remembered—Pursuit as Happiness."[39]

On his birthday, July 21, Hemingway caught his biggest marlin of any season (540 pounds), but no one was interested in the meat. Unwanted marlin was never a problem in Havana, where locals waited at the dock for Ernest to photograph his catch and then give it away. Killing the large fish only for the pleasure of it bothered Ernest, whose original but futile plan was to salt the meat down in wooden kegs for future consumption. "Killing fish for no useful purpose, or allowing their meat to waste wantonly, should be an offense punishable by law," he wrote for *Esquire*. "But those who should make the law should also provide a means of disposing of the fish." *Should* upon *should*, he tried to ease his conscience: there was no law; he was not responsible.[40]

———

Sunday, midmorning on Matecumbe Key, some vets washing clothes, writing letters home, others with hangovers exploding in the heat, trying to remember where they hid their postal savings books. Crossing the bridge where Snake Creek cuts through Windly's Key, an unscheduled train, filled with National Guardsmen, is trailing smoke, bound for Key West. As she hits the Matecumbe straightaway, Munn Norwood opens the throttle, blows the whistle twice. Up ahead he sees a man walking toward him on the right-of-way. Munn blows the whistle again, pulls the bell cord, and the man still walking. Four hundred feet away, doing sixty, Munn watches, unbelieving, as Fred Griset, veteran of the Argonne, quite deliberately steps into the middle of the track, faces the train, and raises his right hand. What is left of Fred's body is found in the bar ditch, his brains splattered across the front of the engine, a piece of his skull on the drawhead.[41]

———

In mid-August, Ernest and his crew motored twenty-six hours back to Key West, where he planned to stay only long enough to answer mail and write an *Esquire* letter before leaving for Havana. However, the *Pilar*, burning too much oil, needs to have her piston rings replaced. First the rings don't arrive from Detroit, then the local mechanic goes on vacation, putting Havana on hold until another season.[42] It was probably all to the good, for tropical storms are beginning to flare up in the Caribbean. On August 20, an advisory warns of a tropical disturbance moving toward the Bermudas. But with no better tracking information than wireless reports from Atlantic shipping and island stations, hurricane landfalls are seldom predictable. On Whitehead Street, Hemingway studies his hurricane charts showing the patterns of September storms past. That Saturday of Labor Day weekend, just as the circus is arriving in Key West, the paper says the storm is east of Bermuda, heading for the Florida keys, but not yet at hurricane force.[43] Forty-eight hours later, in the middle of the night, the veterans' camps on upper and lower Matecumbe Key disappear when a fifteen-to-twenty-foot storm surge sweeps across the low island.

First reports and rumors say the vets were evacuated on a train sent down from Miami. It is almost true. On Monday afternoon, at 4:24 p.m., when someone remembers that hundreds of vets are exposed on the keys, a train is dispatched with Jim Gamble at the throttle. Three hours later, passing through Tavernier, over Windly's Key, and heading for Matecumbe, he stops at the Islamorada station to pick up stragglers when

> *suddenly the entire train blew away . . . six coaches, two baggage cars and three box cars. . . . Every car in the train was turned on its side. There were quite a number of people in the coaches and the water came up in the coaches. In some of the cars it nearly drowned the people there. All of the people succeeded in getting out, . . . [the] depot and the commissary of the Florida emergency relief administration all blew to pieces suddenly and blew around over the engine and the coaches.*

On Windly's Key, women, children, and forty men, half of them vets, have taken shelter against rising water in the hospital when they see the relief train pass. Forming a human chain in now waist-deep water, they try to make their way two hundred feet to the slightly elevated Snake Creek rail crossing, hoping to board the train on its return. No sooner are they out into the raging night than the hospital disintegrates, disappearing behind them. Only three make it to the crossing, where they climb a tree as water covers the rail line.[44] In Key West, Ernest Hemingway watches the barometer at his bedside fall to 29.55; at midnight he bulls his way on foot through driving wind and rain to keep watch over the *Pilar*'s moorings until morning.[45]

On Lower Matecumbe Key, which is so narrow a man can almost throw a rock across it, hundreds of veterans wait in ragged groups around the rail line. A train is coming, they are told. As the wind howls, tents blow away, wooden buildings implode in the dark. There is no place to hide when the storm surge rises, no high ground. Next morning, when the sun is full up, Fred Johnson flies his single-engine plane low over the island to report: "Matecumbe is flat. Nothing is left standing in all that . . . [fifteen-mile] section except one building at Tavernier." Of the relief train, only the engine is on the track; some of the boxcars are four hundred feet from the right-of-way. It looks like thirty miles of track are washed out, steel rails warped and twisted.[46] On Windly's Key, the three survivors in the tree climb down, exhausted and alone. On the bank of Snake Creek, a body is turning green in the early-morning sunlight. At the north end of Islamorada, all that remains of Camp No. 1 is four smashed houses blown far off their foundations. The other twenty buildings have either disappeared or become debris. On the lee side of the key, bodies are beginning to bloat in the mangrove thickets.[47]

After a reeling night of heavy winds, Key West wakes Tuesday morning relatively unscathed: trees and limbs are twisted and torn, some roofs damaged, but no casualties. All that day, high winds and rough sea prevent anyone from going north; the ferry schedule is canceled. With all telephone and telegraph lines to the mainland down, nothing but static-ridden radio news comes in. One rumor says Tavernier has been destroyed by a tidal wave, killing seventy-five persons, but no one wants to believe it, hoping that the train evacuated the vets. By Wednesday morning, food, water, medical supplies, and a portable transmitter from Key West are being assembled at the ferry slip on No Name Key, where relief parties board Coast Guard and Navy cutters, a lighthouse tender, and a geodetic survey vessel bound for Lower Matecumbe, forty-five miles up the lee side of the keys. No one is prepared for what is found there:

> Matecumbe Hotel at Upper Matecumbe was in ruins. . . . The Caribbee colony . . . was completely swept to sea. Where the No. 5 Veterans camp had been on Lower Matecumbe Key, the territory was leveled almost to the ground, only chewed off stumps of palms and pines showed sparsely. There was no sign of the camp.[48]

Offshore the sea is calm, almost smooth in the light breeze; across the landscape, blue bedsteads are splattered like a rash. Where woods once stood, there are blasted stumps leveled as if by an artillery barrage. Here, there, in the mangroves, in ditches, some in blue dungarees, some stripped naked by the water, lie battered, bruised, and twisted bodies. Of the three camps, nothing remains alive but seventy veterans who clung in the howling dark to a tank car filled with water. The odor of several hundred other veterans, beginning to rot in the blazing sun, fills the air.[49]

On Thursday morning, more than two days after the disaster, Monroe County Sheriff Karl Thompson, who now realizes the enormity of the problem, assembles two hundred volunteers, including Ernest Hemingway, to attend to the dead on Lower Matecumbe. All that day, Key West boats go back and forth between No Name Key and Matecumbe. Equipped with axes, machetes, rubber gloves, and gas masks, the men face the stench and horror of bodies so ripened in the sun that some burst open when lifted. The living periodically stop lifting, remove the gas mask, and vomit in the sand. Where possible, the vets are named by their pay disks, but many go unidentified as bodies accumulate, some buried where they are found, some cremated in piles like cordwood. Some dead vets, once run out of Washington for bonus marching, are now dropped stinking into wood coffins for burial in Arlington Cemetery. At Camp No. 5 only eight out of 187 are left alive; two sun-swollen women are found stripped naked by the storm and deposited in a tree, as in some Goya etching. All along the keys, in shallow bays, on sandbars, in mangrove thickets, the sickly aroma of the dead arises. By Saturday, September 7, over six hundred bodies are accounted for; another four hundred remain missing. Two months later, eight civilians and three vets are cremated on the north end of Matecumbe.[50] After that they stop looking.

The Key West that complained about drunken vets pissing in residents' yards, that arrested them for vagrants but took their money, that Key West now mourned with public ceremonies and newspaper poems for the dead, twice dead, whose spirit went first, killed by those who forgot their sacrifice, and then

> *The storm killed them,*
> *And scattered their broken bodies.*
> *How could we know*

(We were so sure!)
They were "worthless drunken bums"?
Weep twice for them,
Those Vets who've gone
At last to find their rest.[51]

When *New Masses*, the left-wing magazine that was home to political rebels of the Thirties, asked Hemingway to write a dispatch covering Matecumbe, he was of several minds about it. First, he was busy correcting the last set of book galleys for *Green Hills of Africa*, and *New Masses* was not his sort of venue. Neither left nor right, but opposed to government of any sort, he trusted working-class people, but not those who would lead them to the barricades and not the masses en masse; he befriended the rich on a selective basis but not as a class, nor did he trust demagogues, left or right, whose names were put up on street signs and monuments. (Huey Long was dying from an assassin's bullet in Baton Rouge and Key West was contemplating a statue of Franklin Roosevelt.) Closer to home, Hemingway had no use for *New Masses'* book reviews denigrating his work for political reasons. But his anger got the better of his judgment: what he had seen on Matecumbe he thought he could never use in his fiction. It was too gruesome and too important. So he wrote a piece he titled "Panic," which *New Masses*, without consulting him, retitled and printed a week later.[52]

––––––

You found them everywhere and in the sun all of them were beginning to be too big for their blue jeans and jackets that they could never fill when they were on the bum and hungry. I'd known a lot of them at Josie Grunt's place and around the town when they would come in for payday, and some of them were punch drunk and some of them were smart; some had been on the bum since the Argonne almost and some had lost their jobs the year before last Christmas; some had wives and some couldn't remember; some were good guys, and others put their pay checks into

the Postal Savings and then came over to cadge drinks when better men were drunk; some liked to fight and others liked to walk
around the town; and they were all what you get after a war. But
who sent them there to die?[53]

————

Having already spent too much of Scribner's advance money to
go to Cuba or Wyoming for the fall, Ernest was at loose ends, looking for some way to celebrate the completion of *Green Hills*. Page
proofs were corrected, including his reference to Gertrude Stein as
"some bitch he's tried to help get published." What would be better,
he asked Max: "Fat bitch? Lousy bitch? Old bitch? Lesbian bitch?
What is the modifying adjective that would improve it?" Having gotten that out of his system, he changed the word to "female." ("That
will make her angrier than bitch.")[54]

That was when Gingrich asked him to report on the Joe Louis–
Max Baer heavyweight championship fight scheduled to take place
just one month before Hemingway's African book would be published. Never having been in New York when one of his books was
released and certain that *Green Hills* was going to be a critical success, Hemingway decided to spend a couple of months visiting East
Coast friends while taking full pleasure in his accomplishment. It
seemed like a good idea, but Max Baer probably thought the Louis
fight was a good idea until he actually stepped into the ring.

From Ernest's vantage point, it was not a pretty fight, as young
Louis took his opponent apart in three rounds and put him to sleep in
the fourth. Outclassed, outhit, outboxed, the more experienced Max
Baer looked like a frightened amateur who should never have been in
the same ring with the fighter they were calling "Dark Lightning." It
was, Hemingway wrote, "the most disgusting public spectacle, outside of a hanging, that your correspondent has ever witnessed. What
made it disgusting was fear." A natural and protective reaction, fear
was not an unknown experience for Hemingway, but not something
he expected to pay $25 to witness. Having described the fight and its
peripherals, he closed his *Esquire* letter with a contemplation of Joe

Louis' future: someday an older, heavier, balding Louis would take a beating from a younger fighter, but Hemingway was willing to bet that anytime Louis lost in the next fifteen years, his opponent would have to get up off the canvas to beat him. Max Baer "does not get off the floor with any such projects in mind," he said.[55]

The boxer, the writer, the matador: age eventually diminishes their skills, judgment, and timing. Eventually the best of them are crushed if not defeated by age and death. Professionals trapped in a holding action they cannot win was ever Ernest's interest from his Paris days forward. Unwilling to relinquish self-reliance, yet knowing how the story must conclude if followed far enough, Hemingway always sees the end of the road. If one loves this world, there are no happy endings. Most readers saw only the masculine world he described so clearly; those who understood what he was saying were not always happy to be reminded of their vulnerability.

As Ernest and Pauline watched the boxing match, across the country a hundred thousand *Esquire* readers were absorbing his "Notes on the Next War," written on Bimini amid whiskey talk of wealthy men who battened on war. Hemingway advised his readers:

Not this August nor this September; you have this year to do in what you like. Not next August nor next September; that is still too soon; they are still too prosperous from the way things pick up when armament factories start at near capacity. . . . But the year after that or the year after they fight.

It would be a European war which America, having no European friends, should avoid. The only country worth dying for was one's own. Sooner or later, Hitler would have his war, but "of the hell broth that is brewing in Europe we have no need to drink. . . . We were fools to be sucked in once on a European war and we should never be sucked in again."[56] Because he went to the wars, studied and wrote about them, did not mean that he was their lover: a point never well understood by his readers.

Between the Louis–Baer fight and the release date of *Green Hills*,

Ernest and Pauline visited with her relatives at Uncle Gus's "Home-stead" in Connecticut and with Sara Murphy at upstate Saranac Lake, drinking by the fireplace, listening to "Begin the Beguine." ("Shall we beguine?" asks Sara.) By October 17, the Hemingways return to New York, perhaps not wanting to be at Saranac for the fifteenth birthday of Patrick Murphy, who is slowly losing his fight with tuberculosis.[57] On Friday, October 25, Ernest opened the *New York Times* to read John Chamberlain's review, which began: "Ernest Hemingway went to Africa to shoot the bounding kudu and the ungainly rhinoceros and to reply to his critics." *Green Hills* was, he said quite accurately, "the most literary hunting trip on record."

Chamberlain, like many New York reviewers to follow, could not stand the narrator's lecturing nor his skewering critics and other writers. The writing, Chamberlain admitted, had its moments, but many of them were spoiled by characters all speaking in Heming-way's pidgin English. Chamberlain doubted Hemingway's prefatory statement that he was attempting "to write an absolutely true book to see whether the shape of a country and the pattern of a month's action can, if truly presented, compete with a work of the imagina-tion." Could people really speak this way, and would they keep ask-ing the narrator to lecture them? Five months later in the English edition, Hemingway omitted this statement, substituting a letter to the book's white hunter, asking him not to take offense at the dia-logue put into the mouth of Pop. "Remember you weren't written of as Pop. It was all this fictional character."[58]

Many reviewers disagreed with what they took to be Hemingway's personal views on life and letters while admiring his landscape paint-ing and narrative. That was not enough for Ernest. Bernard DeVoto found long parts of the book dull, but enjoyed the humor and clown-ing, thought Hemingway's self-exposé delightful. Charles Poore, in the Sunday *Times*, recognized the experiment of the writing, but it wasn't a novel. Reviewers wanted a novel. Van Doren in the Sun-day *Herald Tribune* saw it was structured like a novel complete with Hemingway characters; he also saw that many had misjudged Hemingway: beneath what appeared tough and hard-boiled was "a

very sensitive man, subtle and articulate beneath his swaggering surfaces." Clifton Fadiman never got past the bleeding animals, as if
that were the whole of the book, but *Time* magazine thought the
best parts were "Hemingway's comments on politics, revolution, literature and man's fate." Never had Hemingway's reviews been so
disparate: he had written a book of several parts, any one of which
was offensive to someone. No one saw clearly what he was trying for
in his multidimensional prose, but if he did it well enough, no one
on first reading should have noticed.[59] On balance, these reviews
would have delighted many a Thirties writer, but not Hemingway.
To seek unqualified praise from the very critics his book professed
to despise was, he now saw, a game he was bound to lose. No one, it
seemed, wanted natural history from a novelist whose last novel was
published six years ago.

———

My Dear Mr. Hemingway,

What do you do, when it is like milk in the breasts? And will
not come. And you want it to come, or else how is the baby going
to get it? And it hurts not coming. Then, you are not sure it is
there except you know it must be there. You feel that it is there, if
it would only start. And you look around for remedies to make it
come. You will try anything to get it started, no matter how foolish you know what you are doing is. And it hurts and hurts and is
on your mind and you can't think of anything else. But you don't
know what to do. You never know, so far. You just wait for it to
come. Not really knowing if it is there. But believing it is. What do
you do, when you do this?

Sincerely,
Rose Blucher[60]

———

Ernest and Pauline returned to Key West too late to help their
friend J. B. Sullivan, who was running unsuccessfully for the town
council. "Sully" needed twenty-six more votes, so two votes more
would not have mattered, even if the Hemingways had paid their

poll tax and were registered to vote, which they were not.[61] As politically astute as Ernest was, he was equally uninvolved, asking only for
the absolute minimum of government. A writer, he insisted, should
never be bound to any government, should always be on the outside, critical and wary, for government was never his friend.[62] He was
much more interested in revolution itself than in the government
established by a successful revolution.

Smarting from wounds inflicted by the critics, he reentered Key
West unnoticed and morose. Early-winter weather, one norther after
another, kept the *Pilar* in port and himself anxious with no outlet for
his anger but his pen. He began writing long responses to critical letters from both friends and strangers, a sure sign that he was at loose
ends. To one friend, he said he would like to take a tommy gun into
a couple of New York establishments and wipe out some of the critics along with himself; to a stranger, he said he sometimes felt like
"climbing into the stands when somebody gets snotty" but his hide
was tough enough to take "chickenshit" attacks without flinching.[63]
To Fitzgerald's less than enthusiastic critique of *Green Hills*, Ernest
replied that he was happy to see Scott was no better at recognizing
good work than he ever was. "You are like a brilliant mathematician
who loves mathematics truly," he said, "and always gets the wrong
answers to the problems."[64] The next day he wrote Dos Passos about
Fitzgerald's "supercilious" letter telling him how bad *Green Hills* was.
It was a good book, Ernest insisted, a book killed by the critics. What
was the point in writing if no one could tell a good book when he read
it?[65] That same day he wrote Perkins that *Green Hills* failed for three
reasons: (1) the price of $2.75 was too high; (2) he had "without even
thinking about it" managed to insult the reviewers; and (3) Scribner's
had not pushed hard enough with advertising.[66] The faults with his
publisher were the same ones he used to explain the failure of *Death
in the Afternoon*. Max replied that he might have warned Ernest about
attacking New York critics, "but I did not think you wanted it, and I
do not believe you have heeded it for an instant. Nor do I think you
should have."[67] Max, ever careful, always had it both ways.

When a Mr. Harris questioned the value of Hemingway's *Esquire* "letters," Ernest responded with a three-page, single-spaced apologia, defending some, explaining others. The *Esquire* pieces might have kept him from writing stories as Mr. Harris suggested, but he was now "trying an experiment" with four short stories; if *Esquire* writing interfered, he would "cut out" the letters, which is what Pauline was advising him.[68] In the writing room, his notebook said:

> *Finish Happy Ending*
> *Write hurricane short story*
> *Write story of boat broken down in Gulf*
> *Story of revolution in Cuba*[69]

The Matecumbe hurricane story he never wrote as fiction; the boat broken down in the Gulf would appear later in the Harry Morgan saga. The Cuban revolution was longer than a story, maybe many stories that fit together, a scheme that was forming in his head but not yet on paper. There was also an unmentioned but unfinished story about a young Madrid waiter, full of illusions, who bleeds to death from a severed artery. Much concerned with death—the dead on Matecumbe; Baoth Murphy dead, Patrick Murphy dying—the question raised in the manuscript was "When is death a misfortune?" In March, trying to comfort Sara Murphy on the death of Baoth, he said that by dying young, the young boy was spared the disillusionment of discovering "what sort of place the world is."[70]

First, he finished the second Harry Morgan story—"White Man, Black Man, Alphabet Man"—which he sent to *Esquire* in lieu of his December letter, in effect giving away what he might have sold elsewhere: "a really expensive present," he told Gingrich.[71] The working title referred to rumrunner Harry, his black crewman, Wesley, and a government official with one of the new agencies, FERA, WPA, CCC, take your pick. It was a story of self-reliance, of friends helping each other outside the law, defying the powers transforming Key West into a respectable tourist attraction.[72] *Esquire*, not allowed to say that a person was "kicked in the ass," had no trouble printing this story's numerous references to Wesley as "the nigger."

As the year was closing, Hemingway offered by letter to take Fitzgerald on a tour of Havana, where revolutionaries were now financing their cause through kidnapping and bank robberies. He was writing a story about this next revolution; Fitz could find some material in Havana as well. If nothing else, he could heavily insure himself and Ernest would arrange to have him killed: "All you'll have to do is not put your hands up quick enough and some nigger son of a bitch will shoot you and your family will be provided for and you won't have to write any more." It was supposed to be a joke, but the joke of a mind gnawing on its own dilemma: what to write when his best had not been good enough. In six years he had published three books so rich that general readers had no taste for them. He took his readers into the new country, but they did not enjoy the trip. The day before Christmas, reassessing his writing life, he decided to take his name off the masthead of *Esquire* as a contributing editor. *Green Hills*, he explained to a Mr. Green, was worth the effort if only for learning to write about terrain, a skill which would pay off if he could ever write a "big novel." "But I have worked hard enough," he said, "to be entitled to live my life for a while because you are dead so damn soon."[73] On the last day of the year, critiquing stories sent to him by a novice, Hemingway's advice was good for both of them: "Write what you know about."[74]

Chapter Nine

1936

BOXING THE COMPASS

Key West, Havana, Bimini, Wyoming, Key West

ENTERING THE SEVENTH YEAR of a depression without precedent, Key West was more isolated than ever. When local boatmen were arrested for running illegal Turks and Armenians into the Keys from Havana for $200 a head, Key West understood why "conchs" took the risks, but not why aliens wanted to come. Pan American seaplanes were flying tourists in from Miami once and sometimes twice a day; freighters brought passengers from Tampa and Havana on a regular basis, but the storm-ravaged railroad was not being repaired; remains of the highway, still showing a fifty-mile water gap at the end of Matecumbe, were ripped, torn, and washed out in places. Almost a year after the hurricane swamped bridges, wrecked ferries, and destroyed the rail line to Key West, state and federal congressmen were still debating what to do about the situation. While one Washington committee wondered why the weather bureau could not track something so large as a hurricane, another discussed a $10,000 memorial to the dead veterans whose names were already past remembering. Key West men without money, watching luxury yachts arriving in the submarine basin, could neither grin nor well bear it. Men working on relief whistled and catcalled at tourists, who complained that a woman wearing shorts should "be able to step out of her car . . . without being made the center of attraction and comment by a group of laborers whose race and blood range from Caucasian to negroid."[1]

Behind the wire fence on Whitehead Street, where a gaudy peacock preened by day and screamed in the night, Hemingway is in a period of reassessment, melancholy and morose, waking in the dark to write in his upstairs room until dawn. In private he is moody, quick-tempered, difficult to please. In public with strangers and visiting guests he remains ever the smiling host, keeping glasses filled, hooks baited, and his eye on the water. Invited and otherwise, winter guests arrive: Dick Cooper and Seward Webb; Burris Jenkins, cartoonist with the *New York American*; Ursula Jepson, his married sister, with her daughter, Gayle; Harry Sylvester, New York writer, and his new bride; film actress Nancy Carroll with writer Quentin Reynolds; Russell Akins of *Fortune* magazine; Tommy Shevlin; Waldo Peirce with wife, three children, and nanny.

Still smarting from reviews that wanted him to be more concerned with the working class, Hemingway speaks with increasing frequency about his future death. To a Russian critic, he says he hates "the shit that will be written about me and my stuff after I am dead."[2] To Pauline's mother he writes that laurels did not come to the living: "So I am going to work for success after I am dead."[3] While caught up in fears that he can no longer write, he tells Sara Murphy that he is "going to blow my lousy head off."[4] The last time he was so preoccupied with his demise was during his separation from his then lover, Pauline, while waiting for his divorce from his first wife, Hadley. Here is no separation, no other woman offstage, but the restless, distracted condition is real enough. In his writing room, two short stories are taking shape. One is about a possibly accidental shooting death on safari in which a bitchy woman, who looks a lot like

Jane Mason, kills her husband, who looks a lot like Grant Mason, with a rifle bullet through the back of his head. In the second story, a bitchy writer, dying of gangrene on the Serengeti Plain, harasses with sarcasm his faithful wife, who sounds a lot like Pauline.[5]

Adding to Hemingway's uneasy melancholy is the February *Esquire*, which carried his story "The Tradesman's Return," and the first part of Scott Fitzgerald's personal essay "The Crack-up." Writing lyrically, if somewhat vaguely, about "cracking like an old plate," Fitzgerald repented of being "a mediocre caretaker" of his own talent, and one who let himself "be snubbed by people" with no more ability or character than himself. He was through with caring about others, he said, for he was no longer able to stand the sight of former acquaintances, particularly writers. For moral support he had only childhood dreams of heroic deeds on fields of sport or war.[6] When Ernest read Scott's essay, he could joke about it even though he was, presumably, one of the writers no longer to be tolerated. "Once a fellow writer always a fellow writer," Ernest writes Dos Passos, telling him that Perkins "says he [Scott] has many imaginary diseases along with, I imagine, some very real liver trouble."[7]

In letters, Hemingway diagnosed his own insomnia and depression as the effects of not exercising while writing too hard. The experience, he said, is instructive, making him more tolerant of his father's suicide.[8] But this newfound tolerance does not carry over to immediate family, who walk softly during these touchy weeks, realizing that Ernest is explosive. When his sister, Ursula, came in one evening in tears over Wallace Stevens's disparaging remarks about Ernest, he raged out into the rain to settle the matter as he had in Bimini. In the dark, wet street by lamplight, he confronted Stevens, a large man, a little drunk, a little belligerent, twenty years Hemingway's senior. In the following flurry, Hemingway popped Stevens several times before pausing to take off his own spectacles. Then Stevens got in a solid right to Ernest's jaw before Hemingway put the poet down on the wet pavement, ending the fight. The following evening Stevens, who tended to drink too much on his Key West vacations, came to Whitehead Street to apologize to Ursula and to

Ernest, but could not use his damaged right hand.[9] Promising to tell no one of their fight, Ernest was soon writing the details to Sara Murphy, excusing himself from his vow on the grounds that Sara will not tell anyone else. He told Dos Passos to get the story from Harry Sylvester, which would not violate the promise: "As I say am a perfectly safe man to tell any dirt to as it goes in one ear and out my mouth."[10] His exhilaration, however, was short-lived.

When the second part of Fitzgerald's essay, "Pasting It Together," appeared, Hemingway was depressed and appalled. Not only was Scott wallowing in self-pitying rhetoric, but he was also referring to Hemingway by implication if not by name. "I saw honest men through moods of suicidal gloom," Fitzgerald wrote, "some of them gave up and died; others adjusted themselves and went on to a larger success than mine." Ernest must have seen allusions to his own "suicidal gloom" during his 1926 divorce, after which he wrote Scott that he was "all through with the general bumping off phase."[11] Fitzgerald went on to refer to a contemporary "artistic conscience," whose "infectious style" he was barely able to avoid imitating.[12] Hemingway, who did not want to be remembered as Fitzgerald's artistic conscience, wrote Max Perkins that he "felt awful about Scott," whose public whining he took as the act of a coward. "It is a terrible thing for him to love youth so much that he jumped straight from youth to senility without going through manhood. But it's so damn easy to criticize our friends and I shouldn't write this. I wish we could help him."[13] Honest work is the only treatment Hemingway can recommend.

In April of 1936, shortly after reading Fitzgerald's third installment in *Esquire*, Ernest finished his story of the dying writer in disrepair, "The Snows of Kilimanjaro," in which Harry berates himself for the same kinds of failure that haunt Fitzgerald: squandering talent which never creates the fiction of which it was capable. While waiting on the African veldt for a rescue plane to arrive, Harry remembers stories he was saving to write and now never would, each interlarded story told as a fragment. The result is a collection of unwritten short stories inside of a short story about a writer who failed his talent by not writing these very stories. One of Harry's memories is of "poor Scott Fitzgerald and his romantic awe" of the very rich:

> . . . *how he had started a story once that began "The very rich are different from you and me." And how some one had said to Scott, "Yes, they have more money." But that was not humorous to Scott. He thought they were a very glamorous race and when he found they weren't it wrecked him just as much as any other thing that wrecked him.*[14]

When Scott found himself so skewered in the August 1936 *Esquire*, he asked Ernest to "lay off" him in print; not wanting "friends praying aloud" over his corpse, he asked Ernest to take him out of the story when it was reprinted.[15]

Despite Ernest's complaints about insomnia and melancholy, he was writing well, "using his hurt," as he called it. Developed in tandem with "The Snows of Kilimanjaro," the safari story about the wife shooting her husband, begun in November of 1934, was gradually reaching its final form. As was his habit when finishing a story, he made a list of sixteen possible titles, many of which might have worried Pauline had she seen them:

> *A Marriage Has Been Arranged*
> *The End of a Marriage*
> *Marriage is a Dangerous Game*
> *A Marriage Has Been Terminated*
> *Marriage is a Bond*
> *Through Darkest Marriage*[16]

While Ernest was making last revisions to the story, which he finally called "The Short Happy Life of Francis Macomber," Grant and Jane Mason, prototypes for the fictional Francis and Margot Macomber, motor their *Pelican II* into the Key West yacht basin for a few days' visit.[17] While the Masons dine at the Hemingway table, out in the writing room sits the manuscript describing Margot as "an extremely handsome and well-kept woman" who "five years before, commanded five thousand dollars as the price of endorsing, with photographs, a beauty product which she had never used." In Ernest's clipping file is a three-year-old face-cream ad from *Ladies' Home Journal* in which Mrs. George Grant Mason's stunning photograph appeared purporting to have said, "I could enthuse indefinitely over the creams I use. I do believe they take care of your skin more effectively than any others."[18]

When not writing in the early mornings or fishing in the afternoons, Ernest works out with Harry Sylvester, a visiting New York writer and former Notre Dame boxer. Over at the Navy Field Arena, the two writers are training young Emory Blackwell, reputedly the best light-heavyweight on the island, for a bout with Baby Ray Atwell. On March 19, more than six hundred people, many of whom have side bets riding on the fight, pay money to enter the arena. The evening began, as most matches did in Key West, with a battle royal in which five skinny black kids in ill-fitting trunks bashed each other simultaneously about the ring until only one lad was left standing: "a fair exhibition," the paper called it. The main event was "short and sweet." In the second round, with Hemingway and Sylvester in his corner shouting instructions, Blackwell began connecting with heavy blows, counterpunching Atwell, who left himself open every time he threw his right. In the third round, Blackwell staggered Atwell with a right, jabbed him into a neutral corner, and knocked him out with a right hand to his unprotected stomach. Ernest and Harry help carry the defeated boxer back to his corner, where he does not regain consciousness for almost ten minutes. In the semifinals, the two writers take turns refereeing a six-round match between Bobby Waugh and Kid Pelican. "At the end of the fight," the newspaper reports, "Mr. Hemingway raised the hand of Bobby Waugh as the winner." In his next letter to Max Perkins, Hemingway says, having "made quite a lot of money gambling," he is not yet asking for more advance money.[19]

———

Hemingway's home is a block or two back from the water and occupies a city square. Smothered in huge palms, it is more than

100 years old, of Spanish Colonial type with two-story porches on all sides. The ceilings are fifteen feet high and the floors are of oak plank and Spanish tiles. . . . At strategic points on the walls various heads of animals shot by the Hemingways on their African safari have been strikingly mounted. . . . Hemingway writes from early morning until lunch and refuses to be disturbed. His studio is on the second floor of an outbuilding which once served as slave quarters. He reaches it by a bridge swung from the second floor balcony. A large square room lined with bookcases to the ceiling, it contains no furniture except a flat top desk and a chair. The floors are strewn with skins of lions and tigers [sic] shot in Africa. . . . At the moment he is working on a novel dealing with the contemporary scene.[20]

—*Kansas City Star*, June 2, 1936

By mid-April, Hemingway was run down with the flu, emotionally uneven, overly sensitive to criticism, and, at 208 pounds, overweight, a sign of his lassitude. Defending himself in letters to friends and strangers, he resented being told he was selling out his talent (having just finished a story about a writer who felt guilty about selling out his talent). To whom and for what? he wanted to know. Money from his first two novels went to his former wife and his mother's trust fund. "Am probably the only living son of a bitch who is universally believed to have sold out and who did not sell out nor get any dough for it," he protested to Gingrich. The "chickenshit communists," who wanted him to write about labor strife, ought to know that his books were selling well in Russia. Defensively, he told one critic that he wanted to write three more novels, a book on the Gulf Stream, and a "study in the mechanics of revolution."[21] To Perkins, he complained about ideologists like Malcolm Cowley, "as dull as cold tallow and as permanent." The New York bunch, who wanted to destroy him, could not tell "literature from shit," and he would never again "notice them, mention them, pay any attention to them, nor read them. Nor will I kiss their asses, make friends with them, nor truckle to them."

From now on he was working by and for himself and the judgment of the future.[22]

Clearly distressed and out of joint, he knew it was time to get out of town: too many visitors, too many distractions, too much food. On April 23, the *Key West Citizen* reported, with its usual inaccuracies:

> *Ernest Hemingway is planning a trip to Cuba soon. Then he is going to Africa [sic] again for fishing and hunting. That chap has done a lot for Key West, entertains every personage that comes to town, has had most of the important newspaper and magazine men here as his guests, and writes a Key West Letter and other articles advertising this locality.*

The next day, Pauline and Gregory took the steamer north to Tampa en route to Piggott to give her parents a dose of their youngest grandson, leaving Patrick with Ada. The following evening, Sunday, the *Pilar* left for a night crossing to Havana with Ernest at the wheel, Josie Russell in charge of the engine, and Jane Mason along for the ride home.[23]

Not having been in Havana since October of 1934, Ernest returned to a city changed, its power structure shifted: new names on doors and mastheads. Many Havana reporters had taken up less dangerous trades or moved on. The *Havana Post*, having forgotten how to spell his name, could not remember exactly what Ernest had once done to become famous:

> *Ernest Hemmingway . . . got in yesterday from Key West. . . . years ago he obtained the winning prize among thousands of competitors of $56,000 for a striking title to a picture, Farewell to Arms. . . . Greetings are also to be made extensive to Mrs. George Grant Mason . . . a guest on the Pilar on the trip from Key West to Havana.*[24]

There were more clubs, more Americans, more bars, movies, gossip, gambling, and soldiers. The military, controlled by former sergeant Fulgencio Batista, kept their violence out of the papers, but in dark alleys and on country roads, revolutionists still died, if not so publicly as in the old days; bombs still exploded, but no one officially heard them. Tourists—playing the horses, betting on the jai alai, overpaying the whores—were not to be disturbed.

On May 4, at Ernest's invitation, Sara Murphy and John and Katy Dos Passos flew into Havana's harbor on the Pan Am seaplane from Miami for an eight-day visit; two days out of the next six on the *Pilar* they catch marlin, the bill of one becoming a letter opener for bedridden Patrick Murphy. With Sara, whom Hemingway admires and whose affection he values, Ernest is the considerate host, wanting her Havana experience to be perfect. After a hard night's drinking, she gave him "bromoseltzer and whiskey sours" for breakfast, and he took her up the coast to his favorite cove, where the party lunched on an untouched beach. In the cool of the evening at the Ambos Mundos café, Sara delighted in musicians who played "No Hubo Barrera en El Mundo" at their table, and in the morning when the *Pilar* left the harbor in the wake of the odoriferous garbage scow, she assured Ernest that their late start was not his fault. On Saturday night before his visitors flew back to Miami, Ernest accompanied them out to the Masons' expensive home in the wealthy Jamanitas enclave for a dressy dinner party. "What wonderful places you live in," Sara told Ernest later, "and what a good life you have made for yourself and Pauline, and what a lot of people you have made love you dearly!" The following Monday, Jane Mason, Sara, Dos, and Katy boarded the morning Pan Am flight for Miami, where two days later Sara, in her ever-present pearls, met Pauline, who was en route to join Ernest in Havana.[25] Pauline "went on to the Havana plane looking like a delicious, and rather wicked little piece of brown toast," Sara wrote Ernest, "and the opinion was unanimous that she, & her hair, had *never* looked better & that she is a divine woman."[26]

Having been den mother to many writers, painters, and musicians of the "lost generation," Sara Murphy was nobody's fool when it came to reading between the lines of a letter or a face. If her praise of Pauline seemed a little thick, it may have been that she sensed that something was changing in the Hemingways' life. In fact, Ernest's dark moods were becoming more erratic and unpre-

dictable. As one friend remembered, "There were days when he was
absolutely a malevolent bastard, full of self-loathing. But the awful-
ness would leave him after a couple of hours. Generally, before he
lost that black mood someone caught hell for it."[27] Even his trusted,
aging mate Carlos Gutiérrez was not exempt from Hemingway's sarcasm. Deeply unhappy with his writing career, angry with critics,
and under pressure to produce a successful novel to redeem himself,
Hemingway was not made less bitter by Dos Passos's spending his
time in Havana correcting galleys for his new novel, *The Big Money*.
Ernest's genetic inheritance of cyclical depression and insidious
paranoia that led to his father's suicide was surfacing in his own life,
most obviously in disturbing mood shifts.

Pauline, whose antennae were as finely tuned as Sara's, must
have recognized that Ernest's moodiness was similar to his behavior in 1926–27 when he was caught between herself as lover and
Hadley as wife. This time the only other woman in sight was Jane
Mason, whom Pauline at one time likely saw as a threat, but no
longer. She and Ernest, both of whom enjoy Jane's company, recognized her as a woman dangerous to herself and those around her.
Like Zelda Fitzgerald before she was confined to sanitariums, Jane is
too intense, walks too close to the edge. Her stunning beauty, with
which Pauline never thought of competing, gives Jane no protective cover from the eyes of men. More than one of the Hemingways'
friends thought Ernest was having an affair with Grant's lovely wife,
but Pauline knew them both too well to be overly worried. When
Ernest had an affair, it did not take a private detective to discover
the evidence. Yet this angry and sometimes self-destructive moodiness of his, striking out at people closest to him, herself included,
is very like the dying writer in his recently finished short story: "I'm
crazy as a coot," he tells his wife, "and being as cruel to you as I
can be." Harry Walden, watching his leg rot on the African plain,
hates himself for abusing his talent, for betraying himself, for dull-
ing his perceptions with alcohol, for letting his rich wife provide him
with too many comforts. Harry is not Ernest Hemingway; Pauline is
not that fictitious wife. Nevertheless, she can not deny the piece of

their life there in text, nor does she know what to do about it except wait it out, keep her nest attractive, and remind Ernest of their joint resources. When she returned to Key West after her ten-day visit, she wired Ernest that the chandelier they admired in Havana would be perfect for their bedroom.[28]

Intending to return to Key West the day Pauline left, Hemingway instead spent five days at the Ambos Mundos, waiting for heavy weather to clear. On May 23, Pauline warned him by telegram that strong winds were blowing steadily over the Keys. Ferryboat captains, sticking to their daily schedule, confirmed high seas and dangerous winds. Finally on May 27 at 11:00 p.m., believing the worst to have passed, Ernest and the *Pilar* clear port, making the night voyage alone under scudding clouds. At the same time the S.S. *Florida*, en route between Key West and Havana, found herself, without warning, wallowing in huge seas that crashed over the bow, ripping out her port railing and twisting steel support stanchions. Three hours out of Havana, the first big wave, unseen in the dark, hit the *Pilar* from the starboard side, forcing Ernest to turn upwind, steering northeast, forty-five degrees off course up the Florida Straits. All that dark night, he hangs on the wheel as the *Pilar* goes up, up, and over rolling walls of water, catching the full blast of gale-force winds at the top before crashing down into the next trough. Seams creak, and the bilge pump strains to stay ahead of salt water in the hold.

With the night storm demanding Ernest's every resource, there is no time to check the engine oil or the packing on the pumps. During that long night, the engine block cracks, but Ernest does not know it. Every time he hears the intake pump sucking air at the top of a wave as the *Pilar*'s bow noses over into the trough, his heart skips a beat. In the gray dawn that takes forever to appear, he can finally see enormous waves dwarfing his tiny fishing boat, and fear returns. Unsure of his position and steering by guess on a quivering compass needle, Hemingway turns the *Pilar* ninety degrees back to the northwest, barely heading her up before the wave that would have swamped her catches the stern and pushes her ahead. For the next three hours, he travels with the wind, riding up and down the black slopes like a roller coaster. At 8:00 a.m., he turns the bow as far into the north as possible, and at eleven-thirty "coming out of a blind squall had Sand Key dead ahead." This trip across, taking Ernest as close to death by water as he has ever been, has lasted almost fourteen hours, pushing him and the *Pilar* to their limits. He wrote Archie MacLeish, that he had a "recurrence of the old difficulty of keeping voice sounding normal. It scared you somewhere between your ankles and your balls. My balls felt very small. When the Capt. of the Cuba heard we'd left to cross that night he told Sully they'd have to give us up."[29]

He is very bitter about the critics, and very bold in asserting his independence of them, so bitter and so bold that one detects signs of a bad conscience. . . . Would Hemingway write better books if he wrote on different themes? "Who Murdered the Vets?" suggests he would. . . . I should like to have Hemingway write a novel about a strike, to use an obvious example, not because a strike is the only thing worth writing about, but because it would do something to Hemingway. If he would just let himself look squarely at the contemporary American scene, he would be bound to grow. I am not talking about his becoming a Communist, though that would be good for the revolutionary movement and better for him. I am merely suggesting that his concern with the margins of life is a dangerous business. In six years Hemingway has not produced a book even remotely worthy of his talents.[30]

—Granville Hicks, November 1936

Everyone knew exactly what he should be writing, and was quick to tell him so. Harvard wanted him to write a check for its 300th Anniversary Fund.[31] Max Perkins was desperate for a novel. *Cosmopolitan* wanted short stories like the ones he'd written ten years earlier, only without offensive words. Ezra Pound, despairing, he claimed, of interesting Ernest in serious subjects, wanted him, for unclear reasons, to write an *Esquire* piece on *The Life and Letters of Walter Hines Page*.[32] Abner Green pleaded with Hemingway to take up the cause of political refugees who were being denied asylum in United States. Hemingway eventually agreed to lend his name to that cause, and his tactical compass led him to the heart of the issue: find a legal way to get them into the country. "Otherwise you are simply going to publicize an endless series of deportations which is O.K. if anybody wants martyrs but God damned unpractical as tactics."[33]

In the face of these various well-meaning suggestions, Ernest instead wrote out an order list for the Bimini pilot boat: 2 tins of candy, 1 caviar, maple syrup, vegetables, fruit, 2 dozen lemons, a dozen tomatoes, dill pickles, 2 jars of goose paste, walnuts, pecans, barbecue sauce, crackers, cookies, jelly, tripe, mustard, a jar of pickled onions, and a tinned ox tongue.[34] No sooner was he back from Cuba than he and Pauline, with Patrick, Greg, and Bumby in tow, moved into Mike Lerner's spacious summer home at Cat Cay in early June for a month's fishing. Bimini itself was still recovering from the same hurricane that had destroyed Matecumbe a year earlier. The small rental cabins had lost their thatched roofs, coconut palms were stripped, shrubs devastated. Among the five hundred blacks and the handful of whites who lived through the storm, typhoid and malaria were commonplace.[35] None of which deterred the rich and the dedicated when large tuna began their summer run: Tommy Shevlin, Kip Farrington, Dick Cooper, and Jane Mason were there to compete as members of teams and as individual boats. Very much with them was Ernest. When Arnold Gingrich flew in for a consultation on "The Snows of Kilimanjaro," Ernest remarked, "You and I are the only peasants here."[36]

All that June, Pauline, her sister Jinny, the three boys, and Ada Stern lived on Cat Cay in the lovely home above the beach, collecting shells, swimming in the shallows, and occasionally accompanying Ernest on the *Pilar*. Bumby, now Jack (twelve), kept four birds flying loose in his room; Patrick (eight) set fire to the house, resulting in expensive smoke damage; and Gregory (five) refused to swim out over his head. In the cool of the evening by the Bimini dock, with the children in bed, Pauline and Ernest gather with the wealthy sportsmen to talk of tuna tactics and the fall presidential election. The Barbados rum is heady, night breezes fair, and Fats Waller, singing on the phonograph, insists he is not misbehaving, saving all his love for someone.[37]

———

I'd heard so many tales in Bimini of his going around knocking people down, that I half-expected him to announce in a loud voice that he never accepted introductions to female novelists. Instead, a most lovable, nervous and sensitive person took my hand in a big gentle paw and remarked that he was a great admirer of my work. . . . the day before I left he battled six hours and fifty minutes with a 514 pound tuna, and when his Pilar came into harbor at 9:30 at night, the whole population turned out to see his fish and hear his story. There was such a mob on the rotten dock that a post gave way, and his Cuban mate was precipitated into Bimini Bay, coming to the surface with a profanity that was intelligible even to one who speaks no Spanish. . . . As the Pilar made fast, Hemingway came swimming up from below-decks, gloriously drunk, roaring, "Where's the son of a bitch who said it was easy?" The last anyone saw of him that night, he was standing alone on the dock where his giant tuna hung from the stays—using it for a punching bag.[38]

—Marjorie Kinnan Rawlings, June 1936

———

Hemingway went to Bimini intending his next publication to be a complete edition of his short stories, followed by a novel, but Arnold Gingrich's visit to Bimini changed that plan. As Ernest explained later to Max Perkins, the novel would come first, the collected stories to follow; the Harry Morgan stories would become part of the Key West–Havana novel, which contrasted the two settings, including all Ernest now knew about revolution and its effects on its constituents. Back in 1923 when he first wrote about a revolutionist, he stayed outside the sketch, barely knowing enough to get it right with the young kid riding the train into

Swiss exile. Two years later he tried a story about Spaniards plotting to overthrow the monarchy from a Paris café, but broke it off before completing the first page. In 1928, he wrote twenty or more chapters about a soldier of fortune taking his young son to Europe for his first revolution. That novel never got to the war zone before he gave it up, admitting he needed more data, more experience, to tell the story.[39] About this planned novel, he told Max, "I got the last stuff I needed for it on my last trip across." He spared Max the details: the friend whose ankles were broken, his testicles smashed, gas poured over him and set aflame.[40]

He explained to his editor that the themes of this newly conceived novel were "the decline of the individual" and his "re-emergence as Key West goes down around him" and "a hell of a lot more."[41] His private notes were rough, hurried, and contradictory, not an outline but a working through of ideas. There were three themes running sometimes in parallel, sometimes, in counterpoint, reinforcing each other. The first was local: the rise and fall of Harry Morgan in tandem with the decline of Key West into penury and its resultant destruction by government bureaucracy. The second theme would contrast the two islands—Cuba and Key West—both tropic, both aquatic, both Hispanic and Anglo but with their power structures reversed. The third theme was the overview pulling the two stories together: the dream of what might have been in the new world, the promise of Eden so quickly destroyed by greed and politics. He would include the lost dream, the death of the Cuban revolution that began so idealistically, and the rise of oppressing army control. Inside this plan, there were to be other parallels and contrasts of characters and events, enrichments and further complications. He would give his readers the Matecumbe vets in their darkest night going under as the hurricane's surge swept across the island, give them the revolutionists in the same storm running dynamite out of Key West and into Cuba, and give them finally the betrayal that brought everything together: the bridge that had to be blown, the Key West and Cuban revolutionists betrayed but not defeated, and it all going down to failure. It was an ambitious, complicated plan, a *War and Peace* in miniature.[42]

On July 16, with the barometer falling, Ernest and his son Bumby left Bimini on the *Pilar* to return to Key West. While the two Hemingways sailed from one island to the other, in the Canary Islands, General Francisco Franco sailed from his virtual exile on Tenerife toward the island of Las Palmas, where he immediately declared martial law. With coordinated right-wing uprisings in Morocco and Andalusia, the fratricidal Spanish war was beginning, which would make ephemeral Hemingway's outlined novel. On July 18, Ernest apologized to his mother for having missed writing her on her birthday, professing to have had neither calendar on Bimini, nor her address, nor any way of getting a letter off the island. As he prevaricated, Madrid radio was assuring the Spanish public that no one on the mainland was part of the Moroccan plot, which would soon be crushed.[43]

On his thirty-seventh birthday, Ernest wrote Gingrich that he was unable to cut the remarks in the Macomber story about not shooting lions from the car. He missed Gingrich, he said, and missed Jinny, who was still on Bimini. In fact, the only people he really cared about were Pauline, Jinny, and his kids. Katy had changed Dos Passos, "shifted his compass a little." Ernest was about to leave Key West for the L-Bar-T ranch, where he planned to work on the novel just as the two of them had discussed on Bimini. Four days later he wrote Lawrence Nordquist to expect himself, Pauline, Bumby, and Patrick in about two weeks: "Am sending some express out, my book trunk with manuscript of a book I'm writing in it." The following day, by seaplane, Pauline, Gregory, and Ada Stern flew to Miami, where nanny and child boarded the next train north to Ada's home in Syracuse for the rest of the summer and fall. Leaving Key West on the same day by car, Ernest, Bumby, Patrick, and a chance acquaintance, English professor Harry Burns, met Pauline that night in Miami just as a hurricane out of the Bahamas was making its way up the Florida coast, delaying them three days waiting for Jinny to fly in from Bimini. By the time the group arrived at the Hotel Monteleone in New Orleans for a hard week's partying, Harry Burns, now nicknamed "Professor McWalsey," was on his way to becoming a prototype in Ernest's incipient novel. As he warned in *Death in the Afternoon*, "It is always a mistake to know an author well."[44]

––––––

The kudu was a good 470 meters away. I grabbed up my Mann-licher, muttering to the Laconic Limey, "Thoreau is lousy—Willa Cather is a bum—Josephine Johnson is an illiterate brat." I threw down the Mannlicher and grabbed up my Sharp's. The n.g. with his usual native-guide surliness said, "N'bo?" which meant, "Why, in the name of the crocodile god, don't you try a Thompson submachine gun—that's the only wagon you can hit that kudu with now!" . . . By now the kudu was 516 meters away. I aimed pretty carefully. "You're a swell woodchuck killer!" jeered the L.L. I went on aiming. It was swell. I felt fine. The o.l. shouted, "It's certainly swell! I feel fine! You're a swell shot!" And maybe I was, for the kudu, hit in the belly, was crawling, his guts dragging, while he made a foolish noise like a woman dying in agony.[45]

—Sinclair Lewis, October 1936

––––––

All that late summer and early fall, Ernest and Pauline lived in the Sidley cabin, where river music from Clarks Fork of the Yellowstone played in the background. Close to the L-Bar-T lodge for social comfort when needed but distant enough to avoid Lawrence Nordquist's other paying guests, they have the best of the dude ranch. Until mid-September, when his Chicago Latin School called him home to Hadley, young Jack was with them, riding and fishing, Patrick trailing in his wake. Chub Weaver returned to the ranch on Ernest's payroll ($75/month) as cook, factotum, and outdoor instructor for the young. Ernest also paid a crewman ($60/month) to keep the *Pilar* in shape, and Ada Stern ($100/month) to care for Gregory in Syracuse.[46]

In September, after fishing hard with Ernest at Bimini, young

Tommy Shevlin and his wife, Lorraine, joined the Hemingways at the ranch. About Hemingway, Shevlin later said:

> He was a complex, very difficult man with a tremendous zest for life, and when he did anything he did it absolutely up to the hilt, no half measures. . . . Although I greatly admired him, I was always on guard because of his hair-trigger temper. . . . He was self-confident about everything in the field and in fishing. But he was terribly shy if he had to go out to dinner. . . . He had a terrific sense of humor, but he hated jokes on himself. . . . At times he was very much a bully, mostly when he was drinking, although I never told him so.[47]

About Shevlin, Ernest said he was "a nice kid, but he can't shoot. He has known so many big game hunters he became a big game hunter without ever burning the necessary cartridges."[48]

Hemingway, however, came to the ranch neither for the hunting nor the fishing but to finish his novel. During the first two weeks he wrote almost every day, adding eighteen thousand words to the manuscript, finishing the section where Cuban revolutionaries rob the Key West bank. Over the next month, interrupted by a three-day antelope hunt and one high-country fishing excursion, he wrote another twenty thousand words.[49] Writing in almost discrete sections, he was telling the story of Harry Morgan's fall from economic grace in the Key West depression; counterpointing Harry's principles of self-reliance with the self-indulgent lives of the very rich yachtsmen in the Key West harbor, Hemingway was writing a natural historian's view of the species. The rich were spoiled rich, lazy rich, but not oppressive, merely careless; the poor were hardy poor, blunt and basic, but far from noble. In between the two classes were a college professor and a writer, each with his own point of view. The several story lines intersected and diverged, commenting on each other as they did, and coming back together in the aftermath of a bank robbery.

Among the many characters were more than a few drawn from local Key Westers and Hemingway's visiting friends. Jane Mason was blatantly portrayed among the idle rich as the collector of interesting men, Helene Bradley: a tall, blonde, lovely, small-breasted woman with her shining hair drawn back and her cocktail gown trailing behind, hips moving as she walked, gracious, vital and lovely. She is said to collect writers, painters, and big-game hunters as sexual trophies. "The big slob," as Hemingway refers to his own persona, is said to be the only best-selling author who was never in Helene's bed.[50]

Joe Russell, fishing friend and owner of Sloppy Joe's, was in the story running Freddy's Bar, and George Brooks, a prominent Key West lawyer, was pinned on the page like some interesting specimen as "Bee-lips," the middleman who helps the Cubans stage the bank holdup. Harry Burns became MacWalsey, a genial, hard-drinking academic who ends up by default with the wife of Richard Gordon, proletariat author of *The Ruling Classes*, *Brief Mastery*, and *The Cult of Violence*. Taking a page of the poet Yeats, Ernest has Gordon, bicycling past the Hemingway house on Whitehead street, say to himself that the overweight writer who lives there has betrayed his promise, letting down a whole generation of young writers who once admired him. After that one great novel, nothing followed. All he was writing now was tripe for *Esquire* when there were plenty of stories in Key West bars about the drunken vets and the poor fishermen, but in six years, the "slob" had not written a thing about them. Probably he was too drunk to write.[51] While Gordon, in his Joycean consciousness, thinks these thoughts he passes the heavy-set author on the street without recognizing him, a moment at once ironic and satiric, but eventually deleted.

In his first draft, even Hemingway's old friends John and Katy Dos Passos are skewered. Nameless but recognizable, Katy is characterized as a "charming" woman with one defect: "She likes to steal as much as a monkey does." Her husband is said to live off loans given him by rich friends while he attacks the very rich in his fiction: "In a year he'll borrow about what the average writer makes." Earlier he repaid his debts, "and was really incorruptible." Now he no longer feels obliged to pay the debts.[52] The words, vicious and unnecessary, vent some of the anger boiling up in Hemingway, anger over critics and publishers, anger with himself, unfocused anger that is as liable to strike old friends as enemies. There was also professional jealousy in Ernest's caricature: the August reviews of Dos Passos's *The Big Money* were wonderful. They said that Dos was "the most incisive and direct of American satirists." To find his equal the reader must look to *War and Peace* or Joyce's *Ulysses*.[53]

The fictive Tommy Bradley, Helene's strangely permissive husband, who sounds like Hemingway but looks more like Waldo Peirce, spices the novel with extraneous literary gossip about the demise of writers. Speaking of Harry Crosby's suicide, Bradley says rather callously that Crosby was a crazy, terrible writer who should have killed himself sooner. Another suicide, the homosexual Hart Crane, had a talent for picking the wrong sailors, who regularly beat him up. Having already received the request not to use Scott Fitzgerald's name in his fiction, Hemingway lets Bradley say that Fitzgerald, who lacked good sense but was all charm and talent without brains, had gone straight from youth into senility without passing through manhood.[54]

August, September, October, he wrote steadily in the Sidley cabin, wasting no time with *Esquire* letters and very little with correspondence. The exception was fellow Scribner author Marjorie Rawlings, whom he had met briefly on Bimini. Inviting him to stop at her Cross Creek farm on his drive to or from Key West, she said she was stunned by the artistry of "The Snows of Kilimanjaro," a story sure to last. Quite shrewdly she suggested that he has "taken some sort of hurdle" in his own mind—"being done with something that was bothering you—being ready to be free." His sports writing she thought "gorgeous," but those who most enjoyed it were, in her mind, not his true audience. She wanted to know if there was conflict within himself "between the sportsman and the artist."[55] The day her letter arrived, Hemingway answered it, something he rarely did when immersed in his fiction. He agreed that most sports fishermen were a dull lot, old-maidish men who never excelled at baseball and who now reeled in fish by using mechanical advantages. As for the active life of sportsman versus the contemplative life of writer, he could not choose one

over the other. Without the fishing and hunting, he "would probably go nuts."[56]

In that same letter he said, "Lately, I have felt I was going to die in a
short time . . . so I have been haveing more fun maybe than I deserve."
For a thirty-seven-year-old man at the height of his physical and mental powers, Hemingway was inordinately drawn to the contemplation of his own demise. A few days earlier, he had written Pauline's
mother that the Pfeiffer bloodline was what his children needed "to
try to breed some of the suicide streak" out of them.[57] Tommy Shevlin,
remembering that fall at the ranch, said, "It's extraordinary the number
of times he mentioned suicide."[58] Six weeks after his letter to Rawlings, he told MacLeish, "Me I like life very much. So much it will be a
big disgust when have to shoot myself."[59]

A world away, General Franco's rebel army was consolidating
early gains as it moved toward the capital of Madrid. On September
26, Hemingway wrote Perkins that he wanted to finish the book in
time to reach Spain before the fighting ended, pledging to revise
the novel when he returned. Seeing such a trip as a real threat to
his prize author's life, Perkins hoped that Madrid would fall and the
war end before Ernest got there.[60] On October 27, after writing a
$1,934.73 check to pay their bill at the L-Bar-T, Ernest, Pauline,
and Patrick packed up for the drive back to Piggott and Key West.
Ernest's trophies included three grizzly-bear hides, two prize elk
heads, and 352 pages of typed and handwritten manuscript of his
still untitled novel.[61]

The Hemingways did not vote that November when Roosevelt
swept Arkansas and forty-five other states, but they stopped off at
Piggott long enough to discuss the President they and the Pfeiffers
despised for his socialist tendencies. Ernest was son-in-law-polite,
and Pauline made arrangements with Ada Stern, still in Syracuse, to
return with Gregory to Key West on November 12. When Ernest and
Patrick left Piggott with their newly hired driver, young Toby Bruce,
at the wheel, Pauline remained at the Pfeiffer home for a few more
days before going first to her St. Louis dentist and then on to New
York City. After three months in the high country of male camarade-

rie, she was ready to spend a couple of weeks in New York visiting Jinny, shopping for Christmas, and seeing some theater. While she is watching John Gielgud's performance of *Hamlet*, dining with the MacLeishes, and visiting with Jane Mason, Ernest is in Key West showing a reporter where he was going to build his trophy room and Key West's first swimming pool.[62]

He has become the legendary Hemingway. He appears to have turned into a composite of all those photographs he has been sending for years: sunburned from snows, on skis; in fishing get-up, burned dark from the hot Caribbean; the handsome, stalwart hunter crouched smiling over the carcass of some dead beast. Such a man could not have written Hemingway's early books. . . . It is hard not to wonder whether he has not, hunting, brought down an even greater victim.[63]

—John Peale Bishop, November 1936

By the time Hemingway reached Key West, the first international brigade was arriving to stop Franco's troops at the gates of Madrid. Men he knew, men like Hadley's journalist husband, Paul Mowrer, were already in Spain and back again, reporting the war. In the Key West paper, Spain's turmoil barely rippled the water, but in the New York paper that came in the mail, Ernest followed the war closely as he rushed to finish his novel. Having waited until he knew enough to write the stories of Cuban military revolution and American social revolution, he may have waited too long. American attention was turning back to Europe, where armed violence was taking on new dimensions.

Spain had to wait until he brought this complex novel to conclusion, which he once thought he understood but now was not so certain. Using multiple voices, jump cuts from place to place, and differing views of high life and low, he was trying to write beyond his previous limits, pushing the edge of possibility. Lives were crossing in his fictional Key West streets like those in Joyce's *Ulysses*. The very rich on their harbored yachts, the vets smashing each other mindlessly at Freddy's Bar, the Cuban revolutionaries dead, and Harry Morgan redeemed but dying from stomach wounds: these several strands required "the old miracle you always have to finish with," as Hemingway wrote Gingrich.

The "miracle" Hemingway had in mind for his fiction was going to take wealthy Tommy Bradley into Cuba with a load of dynamite to blow up a crucial bridge. Before leaving Key West the previous July, Ernest asked his journalist friend in Havana, Dick Armstrong, to collect newspaper or eyewitness accounts of specific events that he might use as source material for the Cuban theme. He planned to alternate revolutionary violence and Batista atrocities with Key West chapters, leading to Bradley's conversion to the revolution's cause.[64] Unable to find back issues of the newspapers Hemingway requested, Armstrong sent thirteen typed pages of information on the splintered revolutionary groups—CONC, Joven Cuba, various communist cells—and specific details on places and events: the floor plan of the police station at Monserrate and Empedrado; the killing of Antonio Mesa and his three sons; the retaliation by *deconocidos*; the curious death of Octavio Seigle.[65] By early October, with the necessary ending half clear in his head, Hemingway was planning to return to Havana to finish the novel: "There is some stuff I would like to see again. Some places seen at night [I] would like to see in daytime and viceaversa."[66] Given the length of his manuscript, he must have realized he could not encompass as much of the Cuban revolution as he once planned, not without another six months of writing.

When Pauline flew into the Key West seaplane basin on November 29, Ernest, having worked hard on the novel for three solid weeks, was ready to cross to Havana. Harry Morgan, after killing the fictional Cuban bank robbers, was gut-shot and dying in the Key West hospital; the rich and idle yachtsmen were pinned on the page; and Tommy Bradley and Richard Gordon were en route to Cuba with the explosives. As a Cuban voice explained, it was crucial to blow the bridges across the Almendares river to delay government troops from counterattacking. If the bridges were blown, a very few revolutionists could hold up the troops for a long time. But without the dynamite, there was no way to take out the bridges, and their attack would be hopeless.[67] In the remainder of this "Interlude in Cuba," as he titled it, Hemingway used up most of the information Dick Armstrong had provided. Now he needed more site information on the bridges and a way to make the operation fail.

On December 6, Dick Armstrong and Sidney Franklin met Ernest at the P&O ferry dock; nine days later, without giving any details, he wrote Perkins that he had all he needed to finish the book. On December 15, he returned to Key West, having spent over $400, including a $50 loan to Franklin and another $50 to the Friends of Spanish Democracy's ambulance fund. The siege of Madrid, complete with artillery shelling and regular bombings, was putting a daily casualty count in the Havana paper, but not in Key West.[68] The war in Spain, where Loyalists (to the elected leftist government) were said to be killing Catholic priests and Franco's troops were killing the wounded in their hospital beds, that war was making everything more difficult for writing the book and for maintaining Hemingway's Catholic marriage. Trying to keep an apolitical stance, he was caught emotionally between Franco's fascist rebels, supported by the Catholic Church, and the leftist reform government, which included anarchists, syndicalists, socialists, and communists.

His young friend Harry Sylvester, having listened too closely to their sometimes drunken Key West conversations, had recently written a long apologia for Hemingway in the very Catholic *Commonweal* magazine. Repeating some tall tales about Hemingway's courage in the Great European War, Sylvester defended Hemingway as a once and now returned member of the Church. Sylvester speculated that Hemingway's war experience of having drunken troops under his command rape village women with the blessing of his commanding officers—not true—may have caused him to doubt God's existence, but his faith had been restored:

One hears by word of mouth that Hemingway has become a Catholic. This is inaccurate: Hemingway has returned to the Roman Cath-

olic Church, in which he was baptized some years ago. . . . although Hemingway has come . . . to accept again the spiritual body of the Church, he is still distrustful of at least part of the corporal body of the Church. He goes to Mass every Sunday. . . . He is of the Church, but not dedicated to it. He is dedicated to nothing but his family and his art. He will never be dedicated to the Church in the same way that Communist writers are dedicated to Communism. But someday he may write the first great Catholic novel in the English language.[69]

As soon as Hemingway returned to Key West, he asked Sylvester to stop talking about him as a "Catholic writer" or the Church would throw him out. "When I write," he said, "I try to have no politics nor any religion nor any friends nor any enemies but to be as impersonal as a Wasserman Test. Of course nobody ever is." As for Spain, he was trying to reserve judgment until he got there, but he could never support fascists trying to "exterminate the Spanish working class" even if "the government had killed every priest in Spain."[70] Such a position was going to be difficult to defend to Hemingway's Catholic wife or to his mother-in-law in Piggott, where the priest came once a month to say Mass in the tiny, private Pfeiffer chapel.

————

Pauline seemed sharp-edged, too eager, brown and desperate. Her confessionals, her rosaries, that kept her head up during the bad years (so that she amazed everyone with her poise) do not after all fill the major gap in her life and give it a frittering quality that does not flatter. She should have a cause, beyond Saks Fifth Avenue, and a philosophy, instead of a religion.[71]

—Dawn Powell, 1942

————

Some say that when the mother, the brother, and the tall, lovely daughter walked into Sloppy Joe's in late December, Skinner, the bartender, and every other open male eye watched with admiration as the daughter crossed the room to where Ernest was sitting at the bar. Others remember she wore a black dress that did nice things for her legs and that her blond hair was a wonder. That's what they say about Martha Gellhorn's entrance into Hemingway's life. They say that she had Ernest on her mind when she walked in the door, that he drank with her through the afternoon and into the evening, missing his supper and telling Pauline to meet them at Pena's Garden of Roses club. They say that when she left the city, Ernest, unable to get her out of his mind, followed her the next day to Miami.

Certainly Martha was there, and she certainly was beautiful. That much is as true as a photograph can document. But the last five days of December when many who were not there remember all of this to have happened, Ernest and Pauline were in Miami, and when Martha left Key West, Ernest was already booked for his trip through Miami to New York.[72] So maybe Ernest was not as overwhelmed by her long legs as the bartender remembers, and maybe Martha was not bent on destroying his marriage from the moment she walked in the bar. Intentional or not on her part, stunned stupid or not on his, it did not matter. The effect was the same, only it took longer than the barroom memories rightly recall.

Chapter Ten

1937 — 38

A STRICKEN FIELD

Spain, Bimini, Key West, Havana

W HATEVER HAPPENED THAT afternoon in Sloppy Joe's, Martha Gellhorn remained in Key West for several days after her mother and brother departed, for she was flattered that Ernest took an interest in her. However, Martha was not a star-struck novice from the midwest looking for tutelage. Since 1929, after walking away from Bryn Mawr in her senior year without graduating, she had been writing professionally, first for *The New Republic*, then six months for the *Albany Times Union*, before leaving for Europe and a variety of writing jobs, including Paris *Vogue*. In 1934 she published her first novel, *What Mad Pursuit*, with epigraphs from the two contradictory writers she most admired: Ernest Hemingway and Thomas Wolfe. Two months before she arrived in Key West, Martha's second book, *The Trouble I've Seen*, with a preface by H. G. Wells, put her on the cover of *The Saturday Review of Literature*. Martha fashioned stories based on field interviews with destitute Americans gathered for the WPA that moved the President's wife, Eleanor Roosevelt, to do a public reading from the collection in New York and to recommend the book to readers of her newspaper column.[1] Unlike either of Ernest's wives, Martha was a professional, a dedicated writer. Years later she would say: "When I was young I believed in the perfectibility of man and in progress, and I thought of journalism as a guiding light."[2] As unlikely as it seems, Martha, Pauline, and Ernest's first wife, Hadley Richardson, were all well-educated St. Louis women from prominent families. Martha's recently widowed mother, Edna Gellhorn, helped found the League of Women Voters, and had recently given an invited lecture at the meeting of the American Academy of Political and Social Science. Martha was her mother's daughter, born, it would seem, with a need to help others, particularly the victims of war.

That Ernest was attracted to Martha from the moment he saw her was never in question. That Pauline was aware of his interest was equally obvious; she was accustomed to tolerating women, more beautiful than she, attracted to her husband. That Martha, a twenty-eight-year-old writer savoring her first national recognition, found Ernest, at thirty-seven and ten years famous, "an odd bird, very loveable and full of fire and a marvelous story teller"[3] was almost predictable; many women did. But Martha Gellhorn was not desperate to have a man in her life. She had done that once, married some say to a French writer, Bertrand de Jouvenel; if not married, certainly she was with Jouvenel for four years in Europe, long enough to know what she did and did not need from a man. What Martha needed was a cause of her own, one untouched by her mother. Unlike Pauline, whose sympathy for the working class was *noblesse oblige*, Martha was a born political activist whose social conscience, with its acute sense of right and wrong, fair and foul, was both her shield and her weakness. She came to Key West already interested in the Loyalist Spanish government and its fight against Franco's Nationalist rebels. She left Key West on Saturday, January 9, determined to go to Spain. She also left interested in the Harry Morgan story, which Ernest allowed her to read in Key West, and in his anecdotes about various revolutions in Cuba. After reading one of Martha's stories, Ernest gave her advice about her writing: don't overthink it; get it on paper and have the courage to throw it away if it stinks. A writer, he told her, must push her limits, risking failure in the privacy of her workroom.[4]

The night Martha left town, Rudy and his Swing Band at Sloppy Joe's was playing rumbas, and Georgie Brooks, the diminutive lawyer and master of ceremonies, sang "Love in Bloom." The next afternoon, Ernest boarded the Pan Am seaplane for Miami, where he supped that evening with Martha and Tom Heeney, the heavyweight boxer.[5] Two days later, Hemingway arrived at Penn Station for a whirlwind New York visit with Max Perkins (promising the novel by June), with the American Friends of the Spanish Democracy (promising to chair the committee to buy Loyalist ambulances), with the Murphys at Saranac Lake (making bearskin promises to young Patrick, dying), with Harry Burton at *Cosmopolitan* (trying without luck to sell a piece of the novel), with Prudencio de Pereda (rewriting narrative for a documentary film, *Spain in Flames*), and with John Wheeler (signing on as a North American News Alliance journalist). For $500 per cabled dispatch and $1,000 per mailed feature story, Ernest was going to report on the Spanish war for NANA's numerous clients.[6] Like his *Esquire* articles, his prominently bylined NANA dispatches, thirty over the next seventeen months, would keep his name in front of the nation's readers.

In Key West, Pauline was writing Ernest newsy letters about an evening at Sloppy Joe's, a morning tennis match, a pheasant meal with the Thompsons, cute things Gregory was saying.[7] In St. Louis, Martha was writing Eleanor Roosevelt that she was eager to get to Spain, which appeared to be the beginning of the next European war that would make everyone's life less important.[8] While she was reading Martha's letter, Mrs. Roosevelt's husband was preparing his second inaugural address, in which he said, "The test of our prosperity is not whether we add more to the abundance of those who have much, it is whether we provide enough for those who have too little."[9] Martha Gellhorn's passionate concern for the welfare of those with too little and those oppressed was sincere and idealistic; in Ernest Hemingway, whose love of Spain was equally passionate, she thought she had found a fellow writer as dedicated as she to the sad plight of others. Martha could not have been more mistaken.

————

Pauline always tried to be very tolerant of Ernest and any of the girls that sort of made a play for him, or that he seemed entranced with. I don't think he fell in love with other women. He was nice and maybe a lot of women thought he was giving them more attention than what there was; his was in a kidding way. . . . There was no question about it: you could see she [Martha] was making a play for him. Pauline tried to ignore it.[10]

—Lorine Thompson

————

On January 24, Pauline flew to Miami to meet her husband's train and to motor with him on the *Pilar* back to Key West.[11] Accompanied by Sidney Franklin, who was ready to go anywhere at Hemingway's expense, Ernest was home only long enough to pack his bags and answer mail. The hardest to write was the letter to the Murphys when Patrick (seventeen), ghostly white and tired, finally died from tuberculosis.[12] Equally difficult to write, perhaps, was the letter to Pauline's parents, thanking them for Christmas money and explaining that he was supporting the Loyalist government in Spain's civil war because it represented the working class and not absentee landlords or fascist mercenaries, a conflict in which he had previously never shown much interest. Without mentioning to his Catholic in-laws the Church's support of Franco-led rebels, or the killing of Catholic priests by Loyalists, he said his goal was antiwar journalism to keep America out of the European war to follow. On his desk lay the formation papers of Contemporary Historians, a group formed in New York by MacLeish, Ernest, Dos Passos, and Lillian Hellman to support a documentary of the Spanish war to be filmed by Joris Ivens, a Dutch filmmaker.[13]

In the margin of his letter to the Pfeiffers, Ernest added a note whose past tense seemed almost elegiac: "I'm very grateful to you both for providing Pauline who's made me happier than I've ever been before."[14] A day earlier in St. Louis, Martha Gellhorn was writing Ernest that she hoped they were "on the same ark when the real deluge begins."[15] Given the gap between Pauline's semiautocratic and deeply Catholic sensibilities and Martha's footloose idealism, Hemingway's now nagging social conscience was leading him into difficult waters. Pauline, having made her husband her life's work, tended him as carefully as her garden, writing the checks, arranging the house, managing the hired help, and raising their children. Almost forty-two, she was not interested in boarding any ark in a deluge, but she would have followed Ernest anywhere he would permit, war-ripped Spain not being one of those places he allowed. Within a month, Pauline, angry with herself for not going to Europe with him, was writing Max Perkins from what she referred to as "The Widow's Peak." "I am told," she said, "that when I was a very young baby I could be left alone on a chair and would never fall off. I seem to be still on it." To take her mind off Ernest and to keep his on her, Pauline began planning a trip to Mexico City with Key West friends.[16]

Pauline Hemingway came to the door wearing slacks, with her black hair brushed back in a boy's haircut. She was built like a boy and wore no makeup. Her face was tanned from being out in the sun and there was nothing you could see she had been doing to make herself beautiful except keeping her weight down. . . . like a boy, never sitting around, always on the move.[17]

—Arnold Samuelson

Martha Gellhorn, not yet twenty-nine, was not a tender of men, nor did she require much attendance. Whereas Pauline, who by her own admonition traveled badly, was often seasick on liners or fishing boats, Martha traveled easily, gladly, and often. She was, in this trait, almost too much like Ernest. Never willing to suborn herself or her writing for anyone, she might enjoy being on the same ark with Ernest, provided both arrived with their independence intact and with their own life vests. Many would say she followed him to Spain, but Martha never saw it that way. In her last letter to him before he left Key West, she asked him to leave word in Paris for her and to give her love to Pauline. "Please don't disappear," she said. "Are we or are we not members of the same union?" Using one of his high school nicknames with more familiarity than one might expect from a recent acquaintance, she told him, "Hemingstein, I am very fond of you."[18]

By March 10, registered at the Paris Hotel Dinard with Sidney Franklin and poet Evan Shipman in tow, Hemingway was at work gathering a correspondent's visa to Spain, securing diplomatic safe-passage letters, provisioning his two unlikely volunteers, and filing his first NANA dispatch. He also rendezvoused with Joris Ivens at the Deux Magots to discuss the documentary film.[19] From a Republican official, Hemingway carried a safe-conduct letter saying that he was "staunchly loyal" to the elected Spanish government and "was not much interested in politics."[20] This was also Ivens's initial take on Hemingway, who would be with him in Spain, where not being interested in politics could be mortally dangerous. But Hemingway's avowed disinterest was no indication of his political knowledge of how revolutions worked, a subject he had studied for over fifteen years, in books and out of books, and sometimes in Havana dry-mouthed and up very close. Ivens later said that he "set the task to make Hemingway understand the anti-fascist cause. I felt he would be an asset to our cause because he wrote such good articles."[21] Hemingway required little or no indoctrination to despise fascism, for which he harbored no illusions, but Ivens's cause was the communist one. Although Hemingway would never be a communist any more than he would support any political party, his support for the leftist Republican government of Spain was the strongest political statement of his life thus far. It was also a step further away from the politics of his Pfeiffer in-laws and their daughter, his wife, Pauline.

On Sunday, March 14, Hemingway visited with his old friend the soldier of fortune Charles Sweeny, before catching the night train to Toulouse. Two days later, when Ernest was boarding the Air France flight from Toulouse to Valencia, the provisional capital of Republican Spain, Martha was in New York, her credentials as a *Collier's* correspondent and a liner ticket to France in hand, but no word from Ernest about how to get to Spain. Nor had he left any messages for her in Paris, no directions, no encouragement. Being a resourceful woman with several years of European experience, Martha gathered the necessary documents, took the train south to the Andorran-Spanish border, and made her way on foot across the frontier, carrying in her knapsack all a woman needed to go to a war. In Valencia, Martha quite accidentally ended up in the same government car with Sidney Franklin driving to Madrid, where they found Ernest at supper in the Hotel Gran Via. "I knew you'd get here, daughter," he said, "because I fixed it up so you could." When Martha finished correcting him, it was clear that this was a self-sufficient woman.[22]

For better or worse, Ernest and Martha were together in Madrid on the edge of a war more cruel and more politically complicated than historians would ever sort out. The forces of the elected government called Republicans or Loyalists were a rare collection of regular army troops, newly trained civilians, five volunteer international brigades composed of men from all over Europe and America, most of whom spoke no Spanish, and a cadre of Russian professionals, political commissars, and field tacticians. Within this loosely organized amalgamate were Stalinists, Trotskyites, anarchists, syndicalists, and three varieties of socialists who never felt obliged to agree with each other on the course of politics or the war. Because France, England, and America, refusing to support the leftist Spanish government, would not allow arms sales to the Republic, the government turned to Russia for aid. Franco's Nationalist army of Spaniards and Algerian mercenaries, supplemented with Irish, Italian, and German "volunteer" brigades, was aligned with Hitler and Mussolini, whose fascist governments used the war to field-test their new weapons systems. Franco's Spanish support was politically divided among monarchists, fascists (Falangists), Agrarian Republicans, and Popular Agrarians. Seething within these political divisions were the separatist movements of Cataluna, Navarra, and Galicia. By the time one counts the several trade unions, youth organizations, and the full spectrum of political agendas, over forty political factions divided Spain. For whatever happened, on or off the battlefield, during the three-year bloodletting, there were always two versions and frequently more.[23]

That 1937 early spring in cold Madrid, where they lived at the Hotel Florida, Ernest and Martha fed off the emotional rush of public violence and private romance. Madrid, having repulsed at its very gates the bloody Nationalist attack, was under steady siege from Franco's artillery and bombers. "Cold, enormous, and pitch black," Martha remembered her entrance into the city, which "was a battlefield, waiting in the dark. There was certainly fear in that feeling, and courage. It made you walk carefully and listen hard and it lifted the heart."[24] For freeing the human spirit from the tedium of responsibility, there is, ironically, nothing quite like war. As Josephine Herbst said, remembering Spain: "The unknown is dear to us, and, contrary to opinion, security is not the heart's true desire."[25] When the possibility of death is no farther away than the next incoming artillery round, past and future tenses are diminished, and *now* is as *always* as life can be. Under these conditions and despite Martha's resentment of Hemingway's need for paternalistic control, their relationship, tentatively begun, rapidly became a full-blown love affair.

———

There was never a secret about Hemingway living with Martha Gellhorn at the Florida Hotel. . . . Hemingway had a room on the sixth floor. . . . The seventh and eighth floors had been destroyed by shell fire. My wife and I lived on the fifth floor. When the hotel was shelled our great fun, Helen and I, was to stand at the foot of the stairway to see who was running out of what room with what woman. I don't need to tell you who came out of Hemingway's room.[26]

—George Seldes

———

Somehow Evan Shipman moved a load of canned food, bought in Paris and paid for by Hemingway, to Madrid, where it supplemented their restaurant fare, badly reduced in quality by the war.[27] Evan himself was now a volunteer infantryman being sketchily trained at Albacete on his way to the George Washington Battalion.[28] Sidney Franklin, who lived at Hemingway's expense in the adjoining hotel room, scavenged the markets for secondhand bullfight apparel at a bargain, always keeping his eye out for edibles, a ham here, a sausage there. Ernest, equally resourceful, was never without whiskey for his oversized canteen or the occasional wild hare for supper. Nor was he without friends and admirers. Because he always had good maps, inside information, and outrageous stories, his rooms in the Florida were frequented by an assorted cadre of journalists and writers: Herb Matthews (*New York Times*), Virginia Cowles (Hearst papers), Sefton Delmer (*London Daily Express*), Henry Buckley (*Daily Telegraph*), George Seldes (*New York Post*), John Dos Passos, Josephine Herbst, Joris Ivens.

Most of the Madrid journalists were sympathetic to the Republican cause, seeing Franco's fascist rebellion as the first act in the drama Hitler and Mussolini were preparing for Europe. Living in a city bombarded, their hotel rooms within walking distance of the front lines, these writers became an informal brotherhood for whom this war was the initiation. Twenty years after the Battle of the Somme, there was finally a cause in which to believe, a battleground upon which to decide the future. Matthews would later write: "In those years we lived our best, and what has come after and what there is to come can never carry us to those heights again. . . . We left our hearts there."[29]

Much of the world, however, saw the war as Russia's effort to export its communist revolution, a twenty-year fear of western conservatives. In their endless "Red scare," corporate powers never met a fascist they could not support if he would only promise them to keep communism at bay. Propaganda machinery supplied lurid stories of "Red" atrocities, real and imaginary: brutal executions of priests and nuns, churches burned with parishioners inside, night vigilantes terrorizing the streets, young girls forced into whoredom, spies and counterspies, horror and counterhorror. What the world believed of Spain increasingly came from movie theater news that favored the fascist side of the war. Contemporary Historians, founded by MacLeish and company, was producing the Ivens film as a counterweight to the mainstream newsreels. Hemingway, who invested considerable time and money in the venture, was regularly on location with Joris, carrying equipment, scoping terrain, observing and listening. Because Ivens's political contacts allowed his small film crew access to the war zone, Hemingway was, during his first month in Spain, absorbing more timely experience than most of the journalists. On the Guadalajara front, he walked the battlefield with the field commander, reviewing tactics and observing dead Italian volunteers left behind by retreating Nationalists. That evening, March 22, in his fourth NANA dispatch he wrote:

> *Over the battlefield on the heights above Brihuega were scattered letters, papers, haversacks, mess kits, entrenching tools and everywhere the dead. Hot weather makes all dead look alike, but these Italian dead lay with waxy grey faces in the cold rain looking very small and pitiful. They did not look like men, but where a shell burst caught three, like curiously broken toys. One doll had lost its feet and lay with no expression on its waxy stubbled face. Another doll had lost half of its head. The third doll was simply broken as a bar of chocolate breaks in your pocket.*[30]

While he was writing this dispatch in his hotel room, another artillery round crashed into the abandoned top floors of the Florida.

Ten days later, Ernest was with Ivens filming a tank and infantry attack at Morata outside of Madrid, and on April 9 the crew was forced out of its filming position by incoming shells at the very edge of the city.[31] Not since the night of July 8, 1918, when an Austrian trench mortar shell left him badly wounded on the Italian river, had he been this close to war. Then on April 26, while Ernest and Martha were touring the Republican front lines in the Guadarrama Mountains, miles away on the Basque coast Junker bombers piloted by the German Condor Legion killed or wounded a third of Guernica's population while destroying much of the village. Neither the first nor the last time civilians were indiscriminately bombed in this war, Guernica would be the most remembered. Hemingway, who tried to report only what he observed firsthand, never wrote about Guernica, but on April 30, returning to Madrid he found the city

> *late at night with the air still full of heavy granite dust and high explosive smoke, the sidewalks scattered by new round jagged holes with blood trails leading into half the doorways you passed.*[32]

After twenty consecutive days of Nationalist shelling, three thousand madrileños were wounded, 312 dead.

Sometimes with him on dangerous film locations, in the mountains, and always in Madrid, was the tallish blond woman who looked like an angel to men in the trenches. Young, attractive, and congenial, with a sense of humor, from the moment she arrived in Madrid, Martha Gellhorn was very much with Hemingway. That is how most of the journalists remembered her: an intelligent woman who was not actually a journalist and who required much teaching. Less attractive women remembered Martha's always fresh appearance, her Saks Fifth Avenue slacks, and her access to Hemingway's largess. No one seems to have remembered that she had written WPA essays, a novel, and a collection of short stories. She may never have been to a war, but she was as professional a writer as anyone in Madrid. If her credentials from *Collier's* were a favor, given with no expectation that she would actually write for the magazine, the editor had no trouble printing her several essays from Spain. Less interested than Ernest in battlefield details and military strategy, Martha focused on the effects of war on the wounded, the women, and the villages, and on Madrid:

> *Women are standing in line, as they do all over Madrid, quiet women, dressed usually in black, with market baskets on their arms, waiting to buy food. A shell falls across the square. They turn their heads to look, and move a little closer to the house, but no one leaves*

her place in line. . . . An old woman, with a shawl over her shoul-
ders, holding a terrified thin little boy by the hand, runs out into the
square. . . . She is in the middle of the square when the next one falls.
A small piece of twisted steel, hot and very sharp, sprays off from the
shell; it takes the little boy by the throat. The old woman stands there,
holding the hand of the dead child, looking at him stupidly, not say-
ing anything.[33]

Having long admired and selectively employed Hemingway's style
before she ever met him, Martha was later said to be his creation,
which she resented as deeply as Ernest resented its being said that
he was Gertrude Stein's creation.

After two months of reporting the Spanish war for NANA, Ernest
returned to Paris, where café life in St. Germain seemed totally
unreal and absurd after the broken streets of Madrid. On May
11, the *Tribune* announced that Ernest Hemingway and Stephen
Spender would give a public reading the following evening at Sylvia Beach's Shakespeare and Company bookshop, Spender from his
poems, Hemingway from his unpublished novel. Reservations were
recommended.[34] That next evening, Ernest slipped into Sylvia's
place, gave her a hug, claimed he'd never read in public and would
not again, sat down at the small table with the pages of his Harry
Morgan manuscript, and said, "I don't know whether I can do this."
But he did, slowly at first, and in a slightly flat tone, but when he
reached the third chapter

his voice had lost the monotonous pitch, his mouth and half-moon
mustache twitched even more. He began to put expression into the
clean, terse phrases. . . . The picture of him which must have been
taken some twelve years ago, when he was twenty-seven and very
handsome, could be seen on the wall behind. He continued on about
Mr. Sing and the twelve Chinks.

When he stopped at the end of the fourth chapter and the
applause died down, James Joyce, "who had been sitting in the back

of the room got up and walked out," not waiting for Spender's read-ing.[35] Early the next morning, Ernest boarded the boat train to the coast, where the *Normandie* sailed that afternoon with his name at the head of the published passenger list.[36]

————

Morata was crowded and full of excitement. Several brigades have their headquarters there in the houses which remain standing. Besides the brigades there are a certain number of typhus germs in the neighborhood. Nearby is the front, and a little while ago there were plenty of Rebel airplanes flying over and dropping bombs very accurately. It is not a healthy place, and as a village it is no longer attractive to look at. Flies swarmed over the soldiers and camions in the main square. We asked about the road to the first-aid station: Was it safe? Well, who could say? It had been shelled off and on all morning, probably by mistake. The only way to know about it was to try.[37]

—Martha Gellhorn

————

When Pauline received Ernest's telegram that he is arriving in New York on May 18, she has been back from Mexico City almost a month. Every other day she wrote him wistful, chatty letters, feed-ing anxiously off his telegrams and rare responses. She wrote about money paid out and paid in, about children growing and friends drinking. They were lonely letters, trying to make jokes but sound-ing to herself dull and flat.[38] Probably she has not yet heard about the importance of Martha in her husband's life, but soon enough she will hear it from Katy Dos Passos, or Sara Murphy, or Josie Herbst, for too many people only one or two removes from Pauline also know about the affair. Around the perimeter of the Key West house, Pau-line has Toby Bruce, chauffeur and handyman, building a brick wall to keep strangers out, or perhaps to keep family in.

What Pauline hoped for was an Ernest come home sated with the Spanish war and eager to return to Bimini for summer marlin, to Wyo-ming for fall hunting. But Pauline did not know how war can make once treasured routines seem ephemeral and dull. Having lived with artillery rounds exploding in the Madrid streets, awakened to rifle fire only two thousand yards away, and having heard machine-gun bullets pinging off the armor plating of his transport in the Guadarrama Mountains, Ernest has difficulty putting Spain away for the company of the rich on Bimini.[39] Overweight from too much alcohol and too little exercise, Ernest returned to Pauline overcommitted and strangely discontent: little things that once pleased him are now uninteresting. Early morning of May 26, Ernest takes the *Pilar* out of Key West with Toby Bruce and Josie Russell's wife on board bound for Bimini, where Pauline, Ada, and the boys join them by plane via Miami.[40]

In New York, Joris Ivens is sweating out the final cuts of *The Spanish Earth*, for which Ernest promised to create narration to match the scenes. Martha, having returned separately from Ernest to New York, is arranging with Eleanor Roosevelt for a White House screening of the finished film sometime in July.[41] In their rented house on Cat Cay, Ernest revises the thematic statement for the Spanish film, worries over a speech he agreed to make at the Second American Writers Conference, and struggles with final revisions to his Key West–Havana novel, tentatively titled *To Have and Have Not*. Gone is most of the Cuban revolution along with clear references to John Dos Passos and Donald Ogden Stewart; on Arnold Gingrich's advice, Hemingway removed from Helene Bradley's character many of Jane Mason's more obvious characteristics. The once-planned Matecumbe hurricane section was never written, and literary gossip about Scott Fitzgerald, Harry Crosby, and Hart Crane is taken out. Also excised is a fictional account of finding his father's dead body, his head blown in and blood soaking the bed covers.[42] An entire chapter with Tommy Bradley and Richard Gordon trying to transport dynamite to the Cuban rebels is deleted, along with the details of how Harry Morgan lost his arm. Reshuffling the remains, inserting new bridges between disparate parts, Hemingway does his best to counterpoint the "haves" (the very rich and the supercilious writers) and "have nots" (working poor and displaced vets). With the typist's version completed, he reads it over one final time, and then inserts eight new pages culminating with Harry Morgan's dying words:

"One man alone ain't got. No man alone now." He stopped. "No matter how a man alone *ain't got no bloody fucking chance."*

He shut his eyes. It had taken him a long time to get it out and it had taken him all of his life to learn it.[43]

Leaving Pauline with their children in rented quarters on Cat Cay, where screens were oiled to keep flies away, Ernest on June 4 flew out of Bimini to attend the American Writers Congress on a puddle-jumper flight with several stops, arriving in Newark barely in time for him to reach Carnegie Hall at 10:00 p.m. to see an excerpt from *The Spanish Earth* and to make his promised speech. When Hemingway rose to the podium, he was greeted by thunderous applause from the 3,500 who jammed the hall for this, his first public political statement in defense of his craft. In hard, terse tones, he told them that no true writer could live with fascism, for

Fascism is a lie told by bullies. . . . It is condemned to literary sterility. When it is past, it will have no history except the bloody history of murder that is well known. . . . It is very dangerous to write the truth in war, and the truth is also very dangerous to come by. . . . But there is now and there will be from now on for a long time, war for any writer to go to who wants to study it. It looks as though we are in for many years of undeclared wars.[44]

Writers on the stage with Ernest remembered him as nervous, perspiring, and overweight, reading awkwardly from a loosely organized speech. The writer Dawn Powell, who knew most of the speakers, including Hemingway, was able to view the evening through comic glasses: "about ten thirty all the foreign correspondents marched on each one with his private blonde led by Ernest and Miss Gellhorn, who had been thru hell in Spain and came shivering on in a silver fox chin-up." (How could she know the fur was a gift from the Abraham Lincoln Brigade?) Dawn liked Ernest's speech, which she said summed up "that war was pretty nice and a lot better than sitting around a hot hall and writers ought to all go to war and get killed and if they didn't they were a big sissy. Then he went over to the Stork Club, followed by a pack of foxes."[45] From young writer and friend Prudencio de Pereda's view from the balcony, Ernest appeared sleek and happy. "Yes, there was some awkwardness—both vocal and physical—but he faced and beat them both. . . . it was the speech of the meeting. The audience had come for Ernest; he was there for them. He lapped up the warm acceptance."[46] No matter where they were sitting, however, Hemingway's message was clear. Neutral, middle ground was no longer viable, no longer on the map; those who would not choose would be branded sympathetic to the cause they most resembled. Hemingway, after years of insisting upon his political disinterest, was now publicly committed to antifascism, if not to communism itself.

Two days later while flying back to Bimini, Hemingway worried about the Harry Morgan book as discussed with Max. One option which Max did not like was taking out the vets and the very rich, leaving only a shortened version of the Morgan stories as a novella followed by "The Snows of Kilimanjaro," "The Capital of the World," and "The Short Happy Life of Francis Macomber." Ernest now suggested giving the reader even more for his money, something new, a "living omnibus" of his writing: Harry Morgan, the three stories, "Who Murdered the Vets," several news dispatches reedited and revised if necessary, and his Carnegie Hall speech. For titles, he suggested *The Various Arms* or *Return to the Wars*. Promising a typescript by July 5, he confirmed that he was returning to Spain for the fall. Should anything happen to him, Scribner's could recoup its advance money with his collected short stories. When he returned, he promised, "I will write you a real novel. I wish I had the time to write it now. But after this fall will be better. I'll have the end of summer, fall and winter then in it. Have winter, spring and early summer now." Max, who seldom told Ernest no, was unenthused about mixing genres into an "omnibus."[47]

For ten Bimini days in June, Hemingway fished little and wrote late, trying to patch together the Morgan novel, finish the narrative for Ivens's film, and caption Spanish war photographs for a *Life* magazine special. On June 20, leaving Pauline angry, worried about his health and his behavior, he returned again to New York, this time for the Orson Welles recording of the narrative for *The Spanish Earth*. No sooner had he left than Pauline wrote him from Cat Cay to absolve his promise to return in four days and to encourage him to let the Morgan book rest before making any more revisions. For years his best critical reader, Pauline says the writing is wonderful, the substance perfect; it is the "form" that needs some thought. The next day, she again urges Ernest not to hurry home, closing with a curious admonition: Ernest should remember that tragedy comes from within, not from without, and he also should remember her without him "within limits." Martha Gellhorn is never mentioned, nor would she be, but in New York the affair is now a loosely kept secret.[48] If Pauline does not know about Martha, it is because she does not want to know.

When Ernest returned to Bimini, there is barely enough time to prepare for the July 8 White House screening of *The Spanish Earth*. He leaves again on July 6 and flies to New York, rendezvousing with Martha and flying with her and Joris Ivens south to Washington on July 8. As the three guests sit down to eat that evening with the President, Mrs. Roosevelt, and Harry Hopkins, the U.S. Navy in the western Pacific is about to give up the search for another of Eleanor's friends, the missing Amelia Earhart. While they are eating "rainwater soup followed by rubber squab, a nice wilted salad and a cake some admirer had sent in, an enthusiastic but unskilled admirer,"[49] Pauline was writing to Sara Murphy in Paris that she is leaving in two days to join Ernest when he and Joris take the film to Hollywood on a fund-raising effort for the Republican cause. Ernest, she said, was returning to Spain in August.[50] At the White House, dressed in his formal dinner clothes and sweltering in the heat, Ernest noted Mrs. Roosevelt's unexpected height and deafness and the President's restricting paralysis. The visitors are all three delighted that both hosts want the film to be an even stronger statement for Loyalist Spain's condition. The following Sunday, July 11, Martha responded for the group, thanking Mrs. Roosevelt for her hospitality and apologizing for being so distracted during the evening, worrying about her two prodigies. The film, she promised, would be improved; the Orson Welles narration, which all found too theatrical, would be replaced at Ernest's expense.[51]

Afterwards when it is all over, you have a picture. You see it on the screen; you hear the noises and the music; and your own voice, that you've never heard before, comes back to you saying things you'd scribbled in the dark in the projection room or on pieces of paper in a hot hotel bedroom. But what you see in motion on the screen is not what you remember. . . . you remember how cold it was; how early you got up in the morning; how you were always so tired you could go to sleep at any time; how hard it was to get gasoline; and how we were always hungry. . . . Nothing of that shows on the screen except the cold when you can see the men's breath in the air.[52]

—Ernest Hemingway

In Spain, Republican losses, including three of Hemingway's friends, mounted over the summer of 1937, and in America, personal losses were also mounting. Hemingway's behavior with old friends was erratic, combative, sometimes intolerable. Before he returned to the Spanish war in mid-August, his relationship with Archie MacLeish was once again strained, this time over the production of the Joris film, and his relationship with John Dos Passos was ruined beyond repair.

During the previous spring in Spain, Dos Passos sought in vain to find out what had happened to José Robles, his friend and translator of his books. Hemingway urged Dos to give up his inquiry because he would bring suspicion down on all of them. Josephine Herbst, having learned from a ministry source that Robles had been executed, told Hemingway, who finally confirmed what Dos Passos had heard rumored: his friend had been executed for treason. It was not Hemingway's information that so irritated Dos Passos, but the manner of his imparting it: too knowing, too officious, too ready to accept Robles as a traitor to the Republic. Dos Passos also had no stomach for Hemingway's ability to accept whatever the leftist factions did as necessary for the war effort. When Ernest warned John that he should not write about the Robles affair, Dos said he would only write the truth about Spain when he knew what that was. Five months later in New York, there was an acrimonious evening in the Murphy penthouse apartment, Hemingway's sarcasm clouding the air and Dos Passos walking out.[53]

In December 1937, Dos Passos published in *Common Sense* an essay, "The Communist Party and the War Spirit: A Letter to a Friend Who Is Probably a Party Member," written to former friends whose too ready acceptance of Stalinist methods in Spain Dos Passos could not accept. In March 1938, Hemingway sent Dos Passos one of his most scathing letters, accusing him of attacking for money those he once supported, of not having his facts straight, of not being able to tell the difference between a Russian and a Pole, and of not telling the truth. Ernest suggested that if Dos ever made any real money, he might repay some of the several loans made to him over the years. "Always happy with the good old friends," he said. "Got them that will knife you in the back for a dime. Regular price two for a quarter. Two for a quarter, hell. Honest Jack Dos Passos'll knife you three times in the back for fifteen cents."[54] After all the Paris nights and Key West days, after Havana and Pamplona together, after all the shared meals and friendships, it was over between these two, leaving them only their future journalism and fictions to denigrate each other.

By August 10, 1937, Hemingway is back in New York with Martha Gellhorn, preparing to return to Spain. Pauline, once again convinced that Spain is too dangerous for her to accompany Ernest, prepares in Key West to take nine-year-old Patrick and teenager Jack Hemingway to a Mexican bull ranch with Sidney Franklin as guide and dubious father figure. Gregory, approaching his sixth birthday, is going once again to Syracuse with his surrogate mother, Ada Stern.

Other than his growing need for Martha and the difficulties inherent in a duplicitous life, there is no pressing reason for Hemingway to return to Spain. With *To Have and Have Not* already galley-proofed and set for October 15 publication as a novel, and Scribner's ready to talk about his collected short stories, he does not need the NANA money, and his marriage is already severely stressed. He writes explaining the situation to his mother-in-law, who suggested rather pointedly that he might spend more time looking after his sons. He tells her in twisted syntax that he "promised them I would be back and while we cannot keep all our promises I do not see how not to keep that one. I would not be able to teach my boys much if I did." Mary Pfeiffer's charge that his extended absences were hard on Greg and Pat led him into an even more awkward defense:

> *After the first two weeks in Madrid had an impersonal feeling of haveing no wife, no children, no house, no boat, nothing. The only way to function. But now have been home just long enough to lose it all; to value all the things again; and now go back knowing I have to put them all away again. So don't point out how much harder it is on them because have a little imagination too.*[55]

Mary Pfeiffer, already worried about her daughter's marriage, is not reassured by Ernest's nostalgia for a life without responsibilities, nor with his fractured logic. She is also picking up mixed signals from her daughter, Jinny, who knows more gossip about Ernest's extramarital life than any sister-in-law should know.

High-strung and emotionally erratic, Ernest is in New York long enough to provoke a silly fight in Perkins's office with Max Eastman, whose jaw Hemingway once promised to break after Eastman's review of *Death in the Afternoon* seemed to question Ernest's virility. Hemingway, stirring up that old disagreement, exposes his hairy chest before blows are exchanged. Gossips pick up the fracas, then newspapers and finally magazines until it reaches mock-epic stature.[56] As *The New Yorker* finally put it,

> *There was no very good way of telling who won the fight in the Scribner office because one man said one thing and the other man said something different and the one man who wasn't in the fight [Perkins] hadn't much to say about it perhaps because he wasn't a writer himself and therefore not especially interested in the dramatic life.*[57]

On August 14, Ernest left on the *Champlain* for Cherbourg, reaching Paris on the 21st. Martha, traveling for propriety's sake on the *Normandie*, arrived a day later in Havre, joining him on the 23rd in Paris at the Hotel Foyot, where Ernest was reading page proofs for Jonathan Cape's British edition of *To Have and Have Not,*[58] and replenishing his various accounts at the Guaranty Trust: $3,000 into a new dollar account; one hundred pounds from Cape; and thirteen thousand francs into another account. Complaining of what he diagnoses as liver problems and insomnia, he also visited Dr. Robert Wallach, who advised him to stop eating eggs and rich sauces, to cut his drinking by half, to take two doses of Drainochol, morning and night, to improve his liver functions and one Belladenal Sandoz tablet at night to help him sleep.[59]

If Hemingway reduced his drinking that fall in Spain, none of his fellow journalists noted it, nor did they remember ever refusing a swig from his battered silver flask that seemed miraculously to refill itself. Not that there was much to celebrate if you leaned left in this messy war, for the summer was one disaster after another for the Republican government. After the fall of Bilbao and the Basque provinces to Franco's forces in early July, the Republic was internally torn by communist purges of splinter groups in Spain and by wholesale Stalinist purges of the Russian military at home. Many of the best Russian field tacticians, on loan to the Republic, were called back to Moscow, never to reappear. In midsummer, Republican forces began an offensive to take the pressure off Madrid; the attack drove a wedge into rebel lines at Brunete but with terrible losses and stopping short of its objective. Meanwhile Franco's force overran the defenses of Santander, taking the port and encircling large numbers of its Basque defenders, who were forced to surrender. Rebel armies now controlled the entire Atlantic coast and the middle of Spain; if they could drive a corridor through to the Mediterranean coast, they would be able to split what remained of the Republic in two.

———

Now we learned to know the wounded, the various ways of broken flesh, the limbs sliced off clean and left whole on the ground, or blown into a red pulp stuck with white fragments of bone and still hanging by throbbing veins to living bodies. We saw bared flesh splashed with a crimson wash mixed from the wound-spoutings of half a dozen men; we saw jerking limb-stumps with the blood gushing from them bright and sparkling in the sunshine; we learned the shape and color of spilled entrails palpitating amongst rags of torn underwear; we learned the faces of men dying and not knowing it, greenish, livid, with impersonal, gaping mouths.[60]

—John Sommerfield, 1937

———

En route to Madrid, Ernest and Martha stopped first in Valencia, where they traveled out by car to survey the aftermath of the Republican offensive along the Aragon front, talking to the brigades who fought the bloody battles at Quinto and Belchite. Hemingway's dispatch, filled with precise details and close analysis, included a brief reference to Robert Merriman, who,

a former California history professor and now chief of staff of the 15th brigades, was a leader in the final assault [on Belchite]. Unshaven, his face smoke blackened, his men tell how he bombed his way forward, wounded six times slightly by hand-grenade splinters in the hands and face, but refusing to have his wounds dressed until the cathedral was taken.[61]

Having the luxury of sending in typed stories rather than foreshortened cables or telephone reports like Ernest, Martha's version of this same encounter with Merriman was more detailed. Dusty, tall, shy, and a little stiff, Merriman explained the offensive to them,

> *drawing the plan of it on the dirt of the floor, going over every point carefully as if it were his freshman class in economics back in California. Forty kilometers march . . . Quinto encircled . . . Belchite surrounded . . . then the fighting in the town itself, from house to house, cutting through the walls and bombing their way forward with hand grenades . . . rushing the cathedral where rebel machine gunners held out to the last . . . the dead piled eight feet deep in the streets. . . . "The boys did well," Merriman said.*[62]

Using details from the briefing without attributing them, Hemingway carefully studied Merriman, who would not survive the war but whose presence would be recognized in Ernest's next novel.

From Valencia, Hemingway and Gellhorn continued on to Madrid, returning to the war zone old hands at the game. Their rooms on the second floor of the Hotel Florida[63] were amply stocked with basics—corned beef, cheese, coffee, soups, tamales, and chocolate bars brought with them from Paris—and with extraordinary tinned treats sent in by Sara Murphy: *poulet rôti, confit d'oie, jambon, saumon, boeuf aux haricots, tripe à la mode de Caen*, and 3 Kraft Welsh rabbit.[64] For two and a half months in Madrid there was sufficient food but little to report. Between September 23 and December 19, Hemingway filed only two NANA dispatches, one of which NANA variously headlined as "Madrid Front Is Quiet" and "Life Goes On in Madrid."[65] Pauline heard from him barely at all—occasional cables, a few letters. Increasingly it would seem that his inviolable promise to return to the war was made more to Martha than to any Loyalist cause. On October 15, when the New York critics began to dissect *To Have and Have Not*, Hemingway was happily writing in Madrid with a sign on his hotel door—Working, Do Not Disturb—which became the working title of his play in progress.[66]

Since writing a parody and a farce in his Oak Park high school days, Hemingway, like many novelists of his generation, always wanted to write a play.[67] His manuscript trunk in Key West held several outlines, fragments, and opening scenes for plays which never matured.[68] Now in Madrid, living through the siege of the city and having picked up various stories about Falangist spies, some caught and executed, he began a play about a counterspy, Philip Rawlings, and his tall, blonde lover, Dorothy Bridges. Rawlings appears to others as a comic, brawling man who drinks too much. Nothing serious, as the Spanish might say. Posing as a journalist to cover his dangerous shadow life, he spends his nights in counterespionage trapping Madrid's fifth columnists. A modern Scarlet Pimpernel, Rawlings is the product of Hemingway's lifelong fascination with spies, revolutionists, and guerrilla warfare. In recent years, he has read, for example, everything he can find about T. E. Lawrence (of Arabia)—his two books on the desert war, his published letters, and several biographies.[69]

With Martha in the room adjoining his own (113/114) and the fictional Dorothy Bridges sleeping in the room adjoining Philip's (109/110), the drama was developing on two levels—public and private. He was not Philip Rawlings, counterspy living some wonderfully dangerous life, and Martha was not Dorothy. In fact, the real action of the drama needed no Dorothy. She was there because between the lines Hemingway was using the play to work out his own sexual dilemma. In a discarded fragment, he wrote that Dorothy caused Philip's problem by wanting to marry him. Had she remained a contented mistress, Philip could return all the more loving and tender to his wife for having been unfaithful to her. Of course Dorothy had not intended to marry him, and was quite distressed when she found that she was fated to do so.[70] In the introduction for the published version, Hemingway said that if the play "has a moral it is that people who work for certain organizations have very little time for home life. There is a girl in it named Dorothy but her name might also have been Nostalgia."[71] How else explain to Pauline the beautiful blonde in Rawlings's life when Philip looked so much like Ernest?

But what was Martha to make of her pale shadow, who was so compliant, dependent, and ornamental? How to explain Rawlings's analysis of Dorothy's character: "Granted she's lazy and spoiled, and rather stupid, and enormously on the make. Still she's very beautiful, very friendly, and very charming and rather innocent—and quite brave."[72]

Wanting it both ways and neither, wanting a mistress and a wife, wanting a home but not wanting to be home, Ernest wanted both women, both worlds, in much the same way that he once kidded Scott Fitzgerald about his, Ernest's, idea of heaven, which would be having

> *two lovely houses in the town; one where I would have my wife and children and be monogamous and love them truly and well and the other where I would have my nine beautiful mistresses on 9 different floors . . . there would be a fine church like in Pamplona where I could go and be confessed on the way from one house to the other.*[73]

Now, in the hotel room, the occasional incoming round rocking the Florida, Hemingway's counterspy completes his dangerous mission, resulting in the arrests of hundreds of fifth columnists. Exposed as a counterspy by the arrests, Philip Rawlings must transfer out of Madrid for the good of the "cause." "We're in for fifty years of undeclared wars," he says prophetically, "and I've signed up for the duration." Dorothy, still without a clue to his late-night life, begs him to go with her to St. Tropez or St. Moritz. Philip tells her she must follow the soft life on her own. "Where I go now I go alone," he says, "or with others who go there for the same reason."[74]

With the curtain coming down on *The Fifth Column*, as the play was eventually titled, Hemingway's painted portrait was appearing on the cover of *Time* magazine, which ran a lengthy retrospective of his life and work while reviewing *To Have and Have Not*. Warning its readers that this novel, with twelve gory killings, "all the four-letter words extant," as well as scenes of copulation and masturbation, would offend the "strait-laced," *Time* called Harry Morgan the author's "most thoroughly consistent, deeply understandable character." Following a long synopsis of the novel, the review concluded that those who had written Hemingway off as a has-been were premature, for this novel reaffirmed his place in the front rank of American writers.[75]

Other reviews were divided among those who could not stand a proletarian Hemingway at any price, those who were offended by Morgan's "no fucking good," those who loved the action, the many who boggled over the fragmented telling of the story, and those who loved the politics. Sinclair Lewis begged the writer, "Please quit saving Spain and start saving Ernest Hemingway." *The Nation* perceptively saw the novel as "a transition to the kind of book that Hemingway will write in the future." Malcolm Cowley, who blew hot and cold over Ernest's work, now believed him "just beginning a new career." *New Masses* hailed Hemingway's "increasing awareness of the economic system and the social order it dominates." Impressed or distressed by *To Have and Have Not*, no reviewer ignored it. Riding the wave, the book was reprinted twice in October and once in November, selling 38,000 copies in five months, a depression-era best-seller.[76]

Paris burned with a million lights last night—in the cafés of its boulevards, on the altars of its churches, in the eyes of its excited children. . . . If anybody got to sleep before dawn, he must have been someone far out in the suburbs, well away from the night-club districts, away from the chimes bells of the churches, the bedlam of shouts and songs from the bistros and brasseries. It was a Paris Christmas Eve.[77]

—Eric Sevareid, 1937

On December 20, two Atlantic liners passing in the night—Pauline inbound for France on the *Europa*, Martha homeward bound on the *Normandie*—bring the distressed wife to Paris and return the lonesome lover to America while Ernest remains in Spain.[78] On December 21, Pauline's boat train arrives in Paris during a snowstorm that blankets the city for Christmas; at Teruel, Spain, where a five-day blizzard has left troops frozen in their slit trenches, her husband watches Loyalists attack through the snow, taking the city:

> *All day long we moved forward with the steady merciless advance the Government troops were making. Up the hillsides, across the railway, capturing the tunnel, all up and over the Mansueto, down the road around the bend from kilometer two and finally up the last slopes to the town whose seven church steeples and neatly geometrical houses showed sharp against the setting sun.*

When he wires the story from Barcelona, Hemingway asks his NANA editor to "cable my wife now Paris waiting me Christmas there correspondents credentials . . . enabling her procure visa projoin me here Christmas rush."[79]

In November, Katy Dos Passos said that Pauline "seemed worried about Ernest, and no wonder—she was very cute and nervy, I thought—but couldn't sleep."[80] By the time Pauline was sitting alone in the Paris Hotel Elysée Park, mistakenly certain Ernest was Christmasing with Martha, "nervy" was no longer an apt description. "Angry" and "hurt" were closer to the mark. When Ernest finally arrived in Paris, frazzled from days of exposure to near-zero cold in the taking of Teruel, Pauline exploded. Bill Bird, an old Paris friend from the earliest days, called at their expensive Right Bank hotel, to find them as dark and gloomy as the Paris weather.[81]

Ernest and Pauline remained in Paris for twelve days into the new year, quietly meeting a few friends, arranging for foreign translations of *To Have and Have Not*, buying books, and tending to Ernest's list of physical complaints. He returned to Dr. Wallach, who prescribed more homeopathic medicines for insomnia and liver problems.[82] On January 12, they left France and crossed the channel to Southampton, where they picked up the *Gripsholm* on its way to New York. There were more convenient liners leaving from French ports, but the *Gripsholm* offered a single advantage: before reaching New York, it stopped in Nassau. Earlier, Pauline had suggested that Ernest come back through Cuba to avoid New York publicity. Now, with their relationship in conflict, neither wanted to answer reporters' questions.[83] Their storm-tossed Atlantic crossing triggered Pauline's usual seasickness, temporarily taking her mind off marital problems. When the *Gripsholm* arrived in Nassau, the couple disembarked and caught the Pan Am flight to Miami, where Pauline flew on to Key West and Ernest picked up the *Pilar*, arriving at No Name Key the evening of January 28. Pauline met him with their car, taking him home to Key West, where he had been less than three weeks out of the previous thirteen months.[84]

On edge and ill-humored, Ernest found it difficult to be enthusiastic about the brick wall around their property or the excavations for the newly begun swimming pool he once wanted. Part of him was with Martha, another part brooding over the Spanish war, in which Teruel was lost, retaken, and lost again. Domesticity, with its confusion of unanswered mail, competing children, squalling peacocks, and local gentry, was small beer after the shelling of Madrid and the fierce slopes of Teruel. In a black mood with his paranoia rising, Ernest was like a decommissioned combat veteran still possessive of the war, angry with NANA for cutting his dispatches short, and furious with the *New York Times* for crediting Matthews as the only journalist in Teruel. Still brooding over the way the *Times* had reported his fight with Max Eastman and "completely sabotaged" his journalism, he railed against critics ganging up against *To Have and Have Not*. For the Key West reporter, he put on a different, slightly false face:

> *Expressing concern at the local criticism of his latest novel, "To Have and Have Not," Mr. Hemingway regretted that this is so and said, "I am delighted to be back in Key West. It is my home and where my family is. My best friends are here. No one has more admiration for the town, and appreciation of its people, their friendliness, the fine life and wonderful fishing here than I have."*[85]

That same day he wrote his former wife, Hadley, he did not give "a good goddamn" about anything, but was not suicidal. Someone else would have to shoot him.[86]

While he was writing Hadley, Martha Gellhorn, on a national speaking tour, was telling Hemingway's mother and other members of Oak Park's Nineteenth Century Club about the history of the Spanish war, its effects on civilians, and the need for all to oppose fascism:

> With a short black dress setting off her taffy-colored hair hanging childishly about her face in a long bob, Miss Gellhorn looked sixteen but spoke in a luscious, deep, free flowing voice with words of maturity and an emphasis of authority.[87]

Ernest read the newspaper account sent to him by his mother, who noted in the margin how happy she was to meet Martha: "She knows Ursula [one of his sisters] and you."[88] His mother could not see him there on the shaded side porch, reading the newspaper account and remembering the softness of that taffy hair, nor could she know how very well he did know Martha.

Chapter Eleven

1938 — 39

A PIECE OF THE CONTINENT

Paris, Barcelona, Madrid, Key West, Havana

THE SEASON'S SHIFT is so mild on the island, winter blooming so lovely, Key Westers hardly notice the early changes of spring. On Whitehead Street, however, where the surface of the southernmost swimming pool in North America shimmers in the sun, a pair of pet raccoons, three pairs of peacocks and hens, two small boys, five employees, and a hurt wife are aware that the house has changed, its moody master sometimes wretched, frequently indifferent. In the coral basement, once dug out to provide building blocks for the old house, two French racing bicycles are rusting in the tropical climate. Their india-rubber tires, flattened from disuse, are melting into the stone floor. On these same bikes Ernest and Pauline, honeymooners at Grau-du-Roi, once traveled the dirt roads of the French Camargue, once pedaled together on

Paris streets. To reach the racks of wine, Ernest must now step carefully past the bikes in the dimly lit cellar.[1]

Across the Atlantic, on the bare hills and plains of Spain, spring comes much later, but the war has never stopped; outsupplied, the Republic entered the third year of battle with its ravaged brigades short of men, its air force in disrepair. On February 21, Teruel was retaken for the last time by Franco's forces. Two weeks later his offensive in Aragon began the push to the Mediterranean to split what was left of the Republic in two. Lightly opposed Italian planes from the Balearic Islands were regularly dropping bombs on the civilians of Barcelona. On March 29, Hemingway and Martha return to Paris en route to Spain. That morning, he telephones the American ambassador, Claude Bowers, concerning the need for an evacuation plan for Americans in Spain should the Republican government suddenly collapse. He and Edgar Mowrer (Paul's brother on the *Chicago News*) are raising money for emergency medical help in Marseilles for those too badly wounded to move further, but the United States must be ready to send ships into Spanish ports to evacuate American medical teams and wounded who, if captured by Franco's troops, will be executed. The ambassador thinks enough of their concern to forward the plan to Washington.[2]

Two days later, at Gare d'Orsay in Paris, war correspondents Hemingway, Vincent Sheean, and young Jim Lardner (humorist Ring Lardner's son) await the night train for Perpignan on the Spanish border. Martha Gellhorn may or may not be with them, for in the memoirs of various reporters she sometimes disappears out of deference to Hemingway's marriage. On Sheean's train she is not there in the compartment with the men sharing whiskey from Ernest's silver flask. Nor does Sheean remember her sitting beside Hemingway during the Barcelona showing of *The Spanish Earth* when the "film was stopped in the middle by an air raid and we sat in the theater for about an hour until the alarm ended."[3] But in Martha's letter to Eleanor Roosevelt, dated Barcelona, April 24, she has been in the city as long as Sheean and Hemingway, has covered the Loyalist retreat in the first week of April, and tells of seeing *The Spanish Earth* again. (Martha says they were five minutes into the movie when the air raid siren sounded.) When Nationalist forces broke through the Republican defenses to reach the sea, Hemingway and Sheean are with Herb Matthews in his recollection, but Martha is invisible. Yet how clearly she is able to describe to Mrs. Roosevelt the twelve black German bombers followed by the same silver Italian planes bombing Tortosa that Matthews describes along the same road Hemingway speaks of in his April 5 dispatch datelined Tortosa.[4] Male memory or good manners notwithstanding, Martha is there with Hemingway all that April and May when he appends to his cable dispatches love to his family in Key West.

Later, trying to clarify what happened in Spain, Martha said,

> *There was plenty wrong with Hemingway but nothing wrong with his honest commitment to the Republic of Spain and nothing wrong with his admiration and care for men in the Brigades and in the Spanish Divisions and nothing wrong with his respect for the Spanish people. He proved it by his actions.*[5]

His coolness under fire, his humor and generosity, and his skills at living in another country make him a boon companion in the fields of war and at the bar afterward. That they are lovers is not as important to Martha as that they are friends. That she respects his writing is clear from the start; that he is possessive of her is equally clear to all who saw them together in Spain; that she, a woman who insisted on her independence, allowed that possessiveness is part of an old story: Ernest got what he wanted.[6] That he was not as idealistic about the needs of mankind as she, or as dismayed at the stupidity of politicians, or as committed to social justice, was not so obvious in those early days of commitment to a single cause.

Hemingway's third trip to the Spanish war was a less happy relationship with his employer, North American News Alliance. No sooner were he and Martha in the field with Herb Matthews and young photographer Robert Capa than NANA requested that he separate himself from *New York Times* correspondent Matthews so their stories would not overlap. Hemingway was furious. A Jesuit plot, he called it, certain that Catholics at the *Times* resented his pro-Nationalist point of view. In mid-April, NANA wired him "suggesting future stories emphasize color rather than straight reporting." A few days later they asked him to "restrict cables to vitally important developments until further notice."[7] Having taken risks beyond those expected of a correspondent, exposing himself to artillery, rifle fire, and strafing, Ernest was understandably piqued, for he had given the news agency what it asked for: stories at once personal and timely, accurate and detailed, stories that take the reader onto the killing ground. Six weeks later, back in Key West and settling accounts with NANA, Hemingway told John Wheeler, his NANA employer, "My stuff on Spain has been consistently accurate. . . . I gave full accounts of government disasters and criticized their weaknesses in [the] same measure I reported their success."[8]

Hemingway vented his anger in a series of essays for Arnold Gingrich's new magazine, *Ken*, which allowed him to be more openly political than Wheeler would allow. On April 7, the first issue of *Ken* appeared with Hemingway's essay "The Time Now, The Place Spain." Writing for what he still considered paltry pay ($200 per essay), Hemingway was personal and direct, telling his reader a truth that was becoming obvious to many journalists: the world's democracies must defeat the fascists in Spain or eventually fight Hitler and Mussolini across Europe. U.S. State Department bureaucrats and British Foreign Office diplomats with their neutrality nonsense and appeasement policies would have much to answer for when the main feature began.[9]

———

Pear trees were candelabraed along the grey walls where picks had opened holes for snipers. Trenches angled through kitchen gardens full of peas, beans, cauliflower and cabbage. Poppies were bright in the green wheat between the almond trees, and the bare grey white hills of Madrid seemed far away. Then a soldier peering

through the wall fired twice and you saw his cheek punched back
from the kick of the long-stocked ugly Mauser. . . . Through a gap
in the wall you saw with the field glasses the cone-shaped muzzle
of a light machine gun looking at you through a little break in the
garden fence less than a hundred yards away.[10]

—Ernest Hemingway, April 29, 1938

When Ernest and Martha came out of Spain on May 16, the war
zones had stabilized, and he was still predicting that Franco's fascist rebellion would be defeated by the Republic. The lovers lingered
several spring days in Paris before Ernest took the *Normandie* back
to New York.[11] On May 31, Pauline was waiting at the Key West
airport when Ernest's flight from Miami landed, bringing him back
for the third time from Spain unscathed. Angry with her husband
for his continuing affair with Martha, but not wanting to begin their
reunion with an argument, she brought Patrick, Gregory, and Toby
Bruce with her, hoping for a quiet homecoming.

Five minutes after he lands, Hemingway's Ford convertible with
its smashed fender is centered in the intersection of Simonton and
United streets; WPA worker Samuel Smart's jalopy, having been
knocked across the intersection into the curb, has turned over and
skidded another ten feet. Hemingway and Smart are standing toe to
toe in the middle of the street shouting at each other. Toby is measuring skid marks when police officer John Nelson arrives. Unable
to settle the argument, Nelson arrests both men and takes them to
Police Court, where Judge Caro hears the evidence.

Facing a judge for the first time since a teenage game law viola-
tion up in Michigan, Ernest is concerned enough to have his lawyer
Georgie Brooks, so roundly satirized as the shyster Bee-lips in *To
Have and Have Not,* in court with him, hugely enjoying Ernest's discomfort.

*Young Patrick Hemingway, Hemingway's son, testified and said his
dad was going 15 miles an hour. How did he know that? He looked*

at the speedometer. Attorney George Brooks tried to make the child realize that the testimony was important and began with "You go to Sunday School, don't you?" but Mr. Hemingway stepped in with "No, No!"

Unable to fix blame, Judge Caro finally dismisses the case as being too minor to prosecute either way. Smart, glaring at Hemingway, demands damages, over which Caro says Police Court has no jurisdiction. Hemingway snaps, "I will not pay damages. I'll counter suit any suit he brings up. I was struck." The next day while being interviewed about the Spanish war, Hemingway says, with humorous exaggeration:

It's much more dangerous to be in Key West and have an old jalopy without brakes crash into you than it is to be under heavy fire from airplane bombs, artillery fire, and machine guns, as I was 24 hours a day.[12]

Two weeks later, Hemingway purchases a new eight-cylinder Buick convertible. After ten years of Fords, he is moving up to a heavier car.[13]

Neither the accident nor Ernest's reaction to it is particularly amusing to Pauline, whose tolerance for her husband's explosive behavior is wearing thin. In Key West, because Ernest was so frequently someplace else, their friends—J. B. Sullivan, the Thompsons, the Cates—when forced to choose in the Hemingway marital arguments, support Pauline, who is now ready to take Jinny's advice: be tough. To the new friends of Pauline's who are strangers to Ernest, there is no question that he is acting like a son of a bitch. This time back from Spain, Ernest's only loyal support comes from Josie Russell. At home, he and Pauline snipe at each other over little irritations, and he retreats to his writing room, where a story set in war-torn Madrid is taking shape. Begun in Paris before his return, "The Denunciation" is a story of friendship and betrayal in Loyalist Madrid: the writer-narrator Henry Emmunds tells of assisting a Chicote's bar waiter in "denouncing" an old friend turned fascist to government security. Following as it did hard on the heels of Hemingway's own denunciation of John Dos Passos in a *Ken* essay, "Treachery in Aragon," the story is ambivalent.

From the old days before the war, both Emmunds and the waiter know Luis Delgado, a fascist who has inexplicably shown his face at Chicote's bar where he is most likely to be recognized and arrested. Emmunds only supplies security's phone number to the waiter, who makes the call. Delgado, having taken a foolish and unnecessary risk, is arrested and will be shot. The waiter feels guilty for denouncing an old client of Chicote's. The writer, who says he does not want the fascist aviator to die thinking a Chicote waiter betrayed him, asks his friend Pepe at security to tell Delgado that he, Emmunds, made the phone call. In Key West, where old friends are speaking to Ernest in guarded tones and where he is something of a stranger in his own house, "The Denunciation" cuts several ways at once. Dos Passos's friend Robles was denounced and shot by Loyalist security; Ernest has denounced Dos Passos for betraying the Loyalist cause; and Jinny Pfeiffer is denouncing him to Pauline for betraying their marriage. Even at Sloppy Joe's, old customers are looking at Ernest in a different way, for a number of them were recognizable characters in *To Have and Have Not*.[14]

In the summer heat of Key West, with a thousand tourists a week streaming in from Miami over the newly completed highway bridges, Hemingway isolates himself in his writing room, which now has a window air conditioner. Edgy and unpredictable, in public and on paper he is abrasive. He wants to write an exposé of the *New York Times* Catholic bias which he feels ruined and restricted his NANA dispatches.[15] He argues in long, redundant letters with Max Perkins about the fall publication of his collected short stories. (He wants "Up in Michigan" included; Max wants the story's sexuality toned down. He wants *The Fifth Column* to lead off the collection; Max has serious doubts.)[16] Then the question of who owes whom how much for *The Spanish Earth* puts him into a seething rage. Quick to misunderstand and take offense, Hemingway thinks that Archie MacLeish is somehow cheating him out of money spent on the film; detailing his expenses in long letters, some of which are never mailed, he warns Archie:

> *You can make me out something better than average vile when I am not around. But when I am around Mac you will keep your long Scotch mouth shut and if you want another nice friendly suggestion: try to keep your nose clean too about other people's affairs.*[17]

Almost deliberately, he seems bent on alienating his friends and his family. What once gave him pleasure, lil.e fishing on the *Pilar*, has temporarily lost its appeal. When not writing, he turns to the Blue Goose arena, where he referees semiprofessional boxing matches and spends afternoons training Mario Perez for his next local fight. Mario, who was knocked down nine times in his last fight, needs all the help he can get. Hemingway, the paper reports, was once an amateur boxing champion, a new twist to the fictive life he some-times creates in humorous moments, sometimes defensively when depressed. That the foremost male writer in America needs to retail such fictions says nothing good about the state of his mind.[18]

On Whitehead Street, tension sits at the table like some uninvited guest, refusing to leave. Arguments, over anything but Martha, are daily fare, and the evening meal a battleground. Once he finishes arranging stories for a collection to be called *The Fifth Column and the First Forty-nine Stories*, Ernest pulls out of Key West with Josie Russell to fish in Cuba while avoiding the throng gathering to cele-brate the formal opening of the Overseas Highway. Pauline, keeping up public appearances, plans a costume party at the Havana-Madrid club, only to have Ernest return early, angry, refusing to go to the party. The argument heats up when he cannot find the key to his locked writing room. Charles and Lorine Thompson arrived at the house as the argument peaked. "He was like a crazy man," Lorine said later. "Waving the pistol around. I didn't know what he was going to do." Suddenly, while Pauline reasons with him, he fires the pistol at the ceiling, then shoots the lock off his writing-room door, slamming it behind him. Pauline and the Thompsons send Ada with the children to the Thompson house for the night while they go on to the party. Later in the evening, Ernest appears at the club and gets in a brawl with a drunken guest, ruining Pauline's evening, not to speak of humiliating her in public.[19]

Beneath the surly surface of their clearly cratering marriage is always, unspoken, Ernest's affair with Martha, about which most of his friends are by now aware and unsupportive. On July 22, an unsigned wire from Europe arrives in Key West:

Arrive Cherbourg twenty-eight auto Aquitania April first Colliers okay if anything ever stops our working together then future nix.[20]

Half-coded by Martha from England, where she was on assignment for *Collier's* after doing a feature on the plight of the Czechs, it was a dangerous telegram to send to Whitehead Street: she was taking the *Aquitania* to New York; her *Collier's* feature on besieged Madrid, "City at War," was "okay"; and if anything came between herself and Ernest, "then future nix."

Despite the public and private arguments of the summer, Pauline refused to give up on her marriage. Shortly after their birthdays (she forty-three, he thirty-nine), she made her to-do list for another cross-country drive to the L-Bar-T ranch in Wyoming: pack "Papa's western gear," two rifles, three shotguns, one pistol, and four different sizes of ammunition; have the new Buick road-checked; fix the cork for the water jug.[21] They got no farther than West Palm Beach when Gregory, who is going once again to Syracuse with Ada for the summer, accidentally scratched the pupil of Ernest's eye, forcing a stop in the George Washington Hotel.[22] Two days later, wearing an eye patch and dark glasses, Ernest and family are back on the road, his attitude unimproved by the incident. Patrick, too young to understand but old enough to remember, listens in the backseat as his parents argue and pick at each other across the country.[23] They arrive at the L-Bar-T with rain falling steadily, which keeps them cabin-bound for the next week.

They came to the ranch planning to remain through the fall hunting season, but the world intrudes. By August 18, Ernest, at NANA's request, is planning to leave Pauline at the L-Bar-T to make her own way to New York while he goes to France, where it appears that Hitler is about to start the next great war. By the inexplicable chemistry that can temporarily smooth out a troubled marriage, Pauline agrees to his leaving. He promises that he won't engage in combat; she is excited about spending two months in a New York apartment waiting for his return. Explaining his behavior to his mother-in-law, he says that he could not have run his life any worse than he has, admits to being intolerant, righteous, and many times ruthless and cruel; he needs the Catholic Church's discipline, but has not been able to accept it when the Church supports Franco. Without speaking of his marital difficulties, he tells Mary Pfeiffer that Toby Bruce will pick up Pauline and the boys, driving them back to Piggott.[24] He tells neither his wife nor his mother-in-law that he plans to dedicate his collection of stories to Herbert Matthews and Martha Gellhorn.[25]

———

August 14, Paris. Martha is back from Corsica, where she went for writing peace (but there was no peace, only a man drowning on the beach). Sitting at the writing desk in her small rented room, she tells Mrs. Roosevelt how strangely cool she finds Paris in August, the waiters kinder, the trees so lovely in the Bois de Boulogne. On the dead-end street not far from the Arc de Triomphe, she spends quiet summer days working on her fiction. Along the French border, the German army's summer games pump up rumors of a war to begin before the end of September. Should Hitler, who is mad enough to do it, bomb Paris, she tells Eleanor, then mankind deserves to be doomed. Hemingway's name is unspoken, for now that they are separated lovers, she must be circumspect.[26]

———

On August 31, the *Normandie* leaves New York with Ernest on board, he having sent Pauline two wires with the promise of a thirteen-page letter and Evelyn Waugh's new book, *Scoop*. At the

Nordquist ranch, Pauline writes long letters filled with the boys catching trout, the wounded baby owl eating mice, and her missing him deeply. After being berated by Ernest in front of Key West guests, humiliated by him at her costume party, and arguing with him cross-country, she is now writing him loving letters. Whatever was agreed upon between them, Pauline says she is serene about their future together. By September 6, Ernest is in Paris, rejoined with Martha, and Pauline, packing up for the trip to Piggott, writes him not to worry about her. She misses him but is confident their future together will work out just fine. Whatever he told her in his long letter leaves Pauline reassured. From Piggott she speaks of sending him a "golden key" to her New York apartment, certain that he is returning quite soon. Three weeks later, Pauline, Patrick, Gregory, and Ada are all in New York ready to move into an apartment at East 50th Street on a two-month lease; Ernest is in Paris, with and without Martha, who makes an extended trip along the Italian and Spanish borders for another *Collier's* feature. Ernest has finished a new short story and is beginning a novel, which was the supposed point of the trip as far as Pauline is willing to believe. She hopes that it is going well.[27]

His writing is the only thing going well. In Spain in late September the international brigades, their ranks now composed largely of Spaniards, were withdrawn from the front lines. In New York on October 14, Scribner's published 5,350 copies *of The Fifth Column and the First Forty-nine Stories* with Hemingway's short preface, but the reviewers concentrated their attention on the play, which few found interesting. *Saturday Review* was excited about the collection, but the *New York Times* thought it monotonous, and *The Nation* said *The Fifth Column* was "almost as bad" as *To Have and Have Not*, "by far the worse book" Hemingway had written. Even *Time* magazine called the play "ragged and confused." *New Masses* predictably praised Hemingway's newly developed social conscience; Malcolm Cowley, riding the fence, said Philip was interesting but Dorothy Bridges was another "Junior Leaguer" who prevented the play from becoming a tragedy: "If Philip hadn't left her for the Spanish people, he might have traded her for a flask of Chanel No. 5 and still have had the best of it."[28] Two weeks after the book was published, Hemingway was complaining once more about reviewers "ganging up" on him and threatening his livelihood, and bitching to Max Perkins that Scribner's was not countering the reviews with large ads. He said that Pauline could not see a copy of the book in the Scribner's Book Store window on publication day. The complaints were his customary ones, but the tone was mild, even jocular, for when he was writing well, little else mattered, not even the sickening "conflicting obligations" which he said, without naming them, were in great supply.[29]

Growing up surrounded by four sisters, Ernest enjoyed the presence of many women, preferably admiring ones, who not infrequently created "conflicting obligations." He liked nothing better than having Sara Murphy, Katy Dos Passos, and Jinny Pfeiffer all hovering around his house in Key West. There was about him a sexual magnetism which his first wife to-be, Hadley Richardson, recognized, asking, "You don't have lots and lots of infatuations do you? What could I do if you did? Course if you do I guess you can't help it."[30] What he could not help was his Jekyll and Hyde alternation between needing a wife and feeling restricted by that wife. He wanted a home, but could not remain there long without it chafing him. He loved his children, but was seldom with them. He wrote better on the run, living in monastic hotel rooms, than he did in the Key West house. In September he arrived in Paris half believing that his marriage to Pauline was permanent; on November 24, he arrived back in New York half believing that he could possess both women. He should have known better.

By early December, when Ernest and Pauline return to Key West, the arguments resume, lasting through Christmas. While Ernest keeps much to himself, revising new short stories and missing the excitement of Martha, Pauline still refuses to give up on their marriage. She remembers how he used sarcasm, tears, and melancholy to drive Hadley away when he was having an affair with her. Now, twelve years later with her role reversed, she sees it all happening again. They drink too much these days and share too little, but she is

Mrs. Hemingway still. On Christmas Day, his mother writes, thanking him for a generous check and also for his letter, the first she has received in almost three years. Perhaps suspecting that something is wrong with her oldest son, she mentions the possibility of visiting Key West in February.[31] No sooner are Christmas gifts put away than Ernest flies to New York, to work on revisions to *The Fifth Column* for its possible stage production; from St. Louis, where she has spent Christmas with her mother, Martha returns to New York on January 14. The next morning she reads about Ernest in the New York tabloids:

> HEMINGWAY BY K.O. IN BIG NIGHT CLUB CARD
>
> *Ernest Hemingway, who has hair on his chest, two attorneys and two society brokers gave the night club sector one of its busiest fight sessions in weeks early yesterday.*
>
> *Hemingway was accosted in the Stork Club by a man who insisted on rubbing his hand over the writer's face while muttering, "Tough, eh?"*
>
> *Quintin Reynolds, magazine writer, advised Hemingway to "give him a poke, but don't hit him too hard."*
>
> *The author of "Death in the Afternoon" arose and clipped the unwelcome visitor on the chin. When he was lifted off the floor he gave his name as Edward Chapman, a lawyer. Hemingway previously proved his claim to a hairy chest in a scrap with Max Eastman in the fall of 1937.[32]*

Two days later, Walter Winchell in his syndicated "On Broadway" column, deflated the story:

> *A Former Chicago reporter . . . and several working newspapermen were at the next table to Hemingway's when Eddie Chapman (Hemingway's alleged victim) fell from his chair from too much woofle-water. The next day the front pages related how Hemingway and Chapman "went to it." . . . the former Chicago reporter, when he encountered us that sundown, [said,] "so these night club fights aren't*

framed, eh?" . . . *Bill Corum, in the same group when the phony battle
took place, also exposed the inside yesterday in the Journal-American
column. . . . It just didn't happen.*[33]

Real or imagined, the story added to Hemingway's growing public
legend, which he once cultivated but was now firmly rooted and
flourishing with a life of its own.

When Jack Hemingway came into the city from his Hudson
River boarding school to see *The Spanish Earth*, he was surprised
to find on his father's arm an incredibly lovely woman with a fur
coat and a flair for obscenities.[34] After ten days laboring with theater people by day and being with Martha by night, Ernest flew out
of New York in a snowstorm on January 24, arriving back in Key
West barely in time to greet Pauline's Uncle Gus and Aunt Louise,
who are concerned about their niece's marriage, in which they have
so much invested.

Pauline continues to invite old friends, like Sara Murphy, down
to share the winter sunshine as if nothing were wrong between
herself and Ernest, but Sara can read between the lines. Thanking
Sara for her gift of Gregory's sailboat, which lives in their swimming
pool, Pauline says the boat in the pool is a metaphor for a man's life:
everything goes smoothly, when without warning it changes direction, runs up the side of the pool trying to get out to a larger body
of water, then settles back into its familiar pool to begin the pattern
over again. In the next paragraph she says that Ernest is home from
New York, contented and relaxed.[35] From this distance one cannot
tell if Pauline is simply keeping up appearances or if she actually
believes Ernest to be settling in.

On February 5, he writes a late Christmas thank-you letter to
Mary Pfeiffer, complaining about New York "Jews" ruining his play
("It should be called the 4.95 Column marked down from 5 now")
and politicians letting the Republican cause in Spain go down in
defeat. Patrick was confirmed in the Catholic Church; Pauline is
fine, never looking better. (He does not say that Martha is vacationing with her mother a hundred miles due north at Naples, Florida.)[36]

Two days later, Grace Hemingway drove herself into town, registering at the Casa Marina, Key West's most expensive hotel, at her
son's expense. For six days, Ernest is on his best behavior, solicitous of Pauline, the good father all round, which probably does not
fool Grace, who keeps her own counsel. On February 15, the day
after Grace leaves for Oak Park, Ernest steps on the P&O ferry to
Havana; his second marriage is all but finished, but it will take the
principals some time yet to admit it.[37]

He arrived in Havana with five new stories finished, four set in
the Spanish war, one set in Havana. They were some of the best stories he had written, he said, but that's what he usually said. He had
two more planned, one using his experience at Teruel and another,
which had been on his mind for some time, about fishing:

> . . . the old commercial fisherman who fought the swordfish all alone
> in his skiff for 4 days and four nights and the sharks finally eating it
> after he had it alongside and could not get it into the boat. . . . Every-
> thing he does and everything he thinks in all that long fight with the
> boat out of sight of all the other boats all alone on the sea. It's a great
> story if I can get it right.[38]

In Havana, he collects his mail from Pauline and Max Perkins at the
Ambos Mundos desk, but he is registered at the Sevilla-Biltmore. As
he explains two months later, the only way to find peace to write is to
"tell everybody you live in one hotel and live in another. When they
locate you, move to the country."[39]

From Key West, Pauline writes perfunctory letters, refusing to
beg, getting in her points, but not closing the door: the boys have
been to the dentist; the male coon is sick, perhaps dying; visitors are
there and others on the way. Referring to revisions New York is asking for Ernest's play, Pauline says that when younger she might have
"taken a stand about love," but she has found she knows nothing
about it. The letter closes with her hoping that he has everything he
wants. Yet she can invite Sara Murphy to come visit in April when
Ernest would be home and life would be "VERY nice."[40] Meanwhile

Ernest is stocking his Sevilla-Biltmore room with a twelve-pound ham and four pounds of various cured sausages, recreating the Madrid larder for a writer who does not want to stop for lunch.[41] At his desk sits his beat-up typewriter and two stacks of paper, the smaller of which holds pages covered in his typing: inconsistent double spaces between words and consistent spaces between the end of the sentence and the punctuation.

The typed first page begins:

We lay on the brown ,pine -needled floor of the forest and the wind blew in the tops of the pine trees . The mountain side sloped gently where we lay but below it was steep and we could see the dark of the oiled road winding through the pass . There was a stream along the side of the road and far down the pass I could see a mill beside the stream and the falling water of the dam white in the summer sunlight.[42]

By the time he reached the third page, he went back with a pencil to revise every "we" and the single "I" to "he," deciding almost from the start to write this story in the detached third person.

The man lying on the pine-needle floor is a Loyalist saboteur, Robert Jordan, who, like Robert Merriman, is a college professor, not at Berkeley but Montana. In his heavy backpack he carries sticks of dynamite to blow up a strategic bridge during a Republican attack in the Guadarrama mountains. The time is three days at the end of May of 1937, three days when Hemingway was in New York City. It is all there on the map, the road winding down along the river, the stone bridge across, thick pines above, even the cave where the guerrilla band was hiding. He has been there in his imagination, but he was not there when the actual La Granja attack failed. Because the stone bridge is too sturdy for his story, Ernest changes it to steel girders, ones that carefully placed dynamite can bring down. This is the same bridge he eliminated from *To Have and Have Not*, the boatload of dynamite here reduced to what Jordan can carry on his back. Jordan himself owes much to Ernest's reading, particularly *Revolt in the*

Desert, T. E. Lawrence's autobiographical study in guerrilla warfare. Like the real Lawrence, the fictional Jordan has earlier specialized in blowing up trains.

After five weeks alone in the Havana hotel, Hemingway returned to Key West to be there when his son Jack came down for his Easter vacation, which coincided with arrival of several visitors: Ben Gallagher (a Paris hunting friend), Sara Murphy with daughter Honoria, and Jinny Pfeiffer. Reporting to Perkins that the first two chapters of the novel were in draft with heavy revisions, he gave elaborate explanations why he was going back to Havana to finish the book: wonderful place to work; no telephone to bother him; no intrusions; no matter what personal problems he had, writing was more important. He was ridiculously happy as he always was when the writing went well. His weight, another indicator of his mental state, was below two hundred pounds, another good sign. It was, he told Max, a story he did not think he was ready to write, but once he started it went along beautifully.[43] Perkins was finally to get the novel for which he had waited so patiently these last ten years. On April 5, Hemingway motored the *Pilar* out into the Gulf and returned to Havana.

When, at Ernest's invitation, Martha joined him in April at the Hotel Sevilla-Biltmore, she was not impressed with his messy room: the Hotel Florida while artillery rounds fell on Madrid was one thing, but cramped quarters in peacetime Havana were not acceptable. Although working on her own novel, she immediately began searching for a rentable house. On the outskirts of Havana in the village of San Francisco de Paula, she was shown a run-down estate called La Vigía, "The Lookout," perched on a low hill, its fifteen acres of grounds overgrown with tropical green and its swimming-pool water equally green. While Ernest wrote mornings in the hotel and fished in the afternoon, Martha hired with her own money carpenters, painters, two gardeners, and a cook to make La Vigía livable.[44] By May 17, she and Ernest were living quietly on her hilltop[45] where she wrote slowly on her novel and managed the house, for which Ernest was now sharing expenses.

In Martha's novel, Mary Douglas contemplates what marriage with her lover John might be like:

What difference would it make . . . marriage is for living in one place, and tennis with the neighbors on Sunday afternoon. We aren't like that, we'll never be settled. Maybe marriage is also for absence.[46]

———

Perhaps no American talent has so publicly developed as Hemingway's: more than any writer of our time he has been under glass, watched, checked up on, predicted, suspected, warned. One part of his audience took from him new styles of writing, of love-making, of very being . . . another section of his audience responded negatively, pointing out that the texture of Hemingway's work was made up of cruelty, religion, anti-intellectualism, even of basic fascism, and looked upon him as the proponent of evil. Neither part of such an audience could fail to make its impression upon a writer. The knowledge that he had set a fashion and become a legend may have been gratifying but surely burdensome and depressing, and it must have offered no small temptation.[47]

—Lionel Trilling, 1939

———

In Key West, Pauline is packing for a trip to New York with Jinny; Ada will bring the children up if she finds a suitable place to rent. Pauline's letters continue to arrive at his Ambos Mundos mailing address, and Ernest continues to write others as if nothing were changed, but from the moment he moves into Martha's country place, his marriage with Pauline is finished. At the end of May he tells his mother that Pauline and his children are "fine." In a birthday letter to Patrick, he speaks of Martha's houseman, Reeves, as if the man worked for him. In July when Pauline abruptly leaves with friends on an extended European trip, her first in their marriage without him, she tells him that other than his few unsound ideas, there is no one like him, and he is certain to figure out what is best for them. Writing as if there were no Martha in his life, Pauline signs the letter with love and luck. Ernest writes of Pauline's spur-of-the-moment trip to his mother-in-law as if it were nothing unusual. It will be "jolly," "fine," and "great fun" for Pauline.[48] Out of sight in Cuba, where it is easy to keep up appearances, he and the world are at the end of one period and the start of another.

The Great Depression is coming to a close, as is the twenty-year grace period since the Treaty of Versailles ended the Great European War. Ernest entered the decade a young writer on the wave of a best-seller; he is going out of the decade as the best-known male writer in America, but without the momumental book for which he was reaching. In Key West the FERA plan has succeeded in turning fishermen into local color for tourists to photograph, and Sloppy Joe's now features live music every night of the week. The Overseas Highway is bringing in a steady stream of middle-class Americans to displace the wealthy yachtsmen. Even if Martha Gellhorn had not appeared in his life, Ernest would have soon left Key West to its gaudy future, just as he always moved on.

In choosing Martha, he is leaving behind the burden of house and family, the intrusive friends whom he, of course, invited but complained about, and the burden of money. Life is much simpler with only the *Pilar*, his fishing gear, his typewriter, and his faithful editor, Max Perkins. No more Spain, no more ferias at Pamplona for seventeen years. No more Bimini with his crew wearing white uniforms and the *Pilar*'s name across their chests. One last trip to the L-Bar-T ranch before it is packed away, photographs in a box. No more safaris paid for by Gus. For the first time since 1920, there is not a woman's trust fund to help pay for his traveling life. (To ease the transition, Hollywood replaces Pfeiffer money by paying handsomely for the *To Have and Have Not* film rights.) Also for the first time in his adult life, he is living with a woman younger than himself: his Red Cross nurse during the war and Hadley Richardson were both eight years his senior; Pauline was four years older; Martha is nine years younger.

Changing women means changing habits and habitats. When he

left Hadley, he and Pauline moved from Montparnasse to St. Germain des Prés, changing cafés just as the great tourist throngs descended on the Dôme and the Sélect looking for characters out of *The Sun Also Rises*. He is leaving Key West behind just as the next generation of tourists arrives looking for characters out of *To Have and Have Not*. In Paris his affair with Martha moved Hemingway, for the first time, to the other side of the Seine: the Left Bank is abandoned, too many ghosts, too many cafés where he once sat with other wives. He is also leaving behind Joe Russell, Charles and Lorine Thompson, the Murphys, Mike Strater, Waldo Peirce, Bra Saunders, the MacLeishes, and John and Katy Dos Passos. With some he will stay in loose touch, but none of them will again play a significant part in his life. All whom he touched remember him, not always kindly or accurately, but more vividly than many closer friends. Archie MacLeish once said that Ernest sucked the air out of a room as he entered it. Now turning forty, his hair thinning, his beard grayed, he remains the center of any circle in which he lights. His weight is no longer so easily managed, his metabolism no longer able to handle heavy drinking so handily, but he still retains his magic, his humor, his intensity for life that exhausted so many who tried to burn at his level.

Whatever the costs of this expensive decade, Hemingway is now the consummate writer, having mastered through steady work in a variety of genres a full repertoire of skills, voices, and structures. Finally he is ready to bring all his talent to bear on this book at hand, whose action is exactly realized and whose time is perfectly now. All that summer and fall of 1939, he writes the story of the dynamiter, the girl, and the band of partisans on a hopeless mission in a world turned inside out by civil war. Finally he can write of his revolutionist, the one he did not know enough about in 1928 nor in 1936, the one he has studied, invented, lived with these ten years and more in his head and in abandoned manuscripts. Now he knows the country and the people, in peace and war, knows the taste of fear in the high country when planes fly overhead, the smell of cordite in the morning, the way men die under bombardment and how their bodies twist against the earth. He knows so much that he can leave out everything but these few men, two women, and a steel bridge that must be destroyed, even if the attack is betrayed, because beyond all politics, a man finally must do his duty, just as a writer must write.

To create his characters, he needed all those Spanish days of *Death in the Afternoon*, studying the bullring and the faces surrounding it. He needed the African book to learn about moving people through terrain. He needed all those experiments with structure before he could write this story which has within it several other stories, each in a separate voice. He needed his affair with Martha before he could write of his fictional Maria. He needed the strength and purpose of Pauline to create the older woman, Pilar, whose name once belonged to her. He needed to watch the Italian bombers on the Tortosa road before he could describe the bombing of the lonely hilltop. This is any war, every man, a simple story as old as history. Before this book is finished, Poland is ravaged by the Nazi blitzkrieg; by the time it has a title—*For Whom the Bell Tolls*—Denmark and Holland are reeling under invasion, and death bells are tolling once again for the western world.

BOOK II

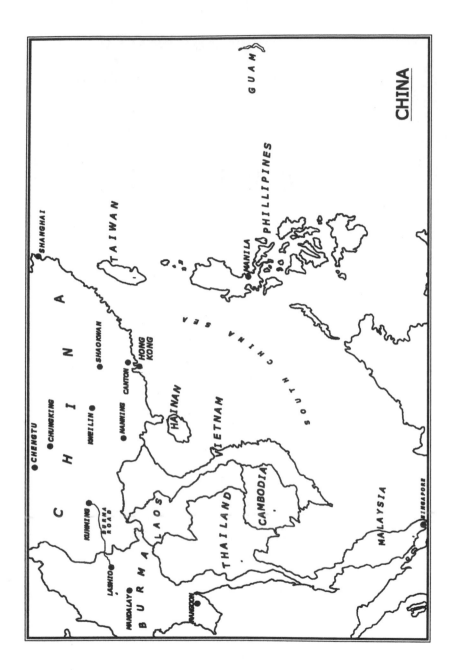

CHINA

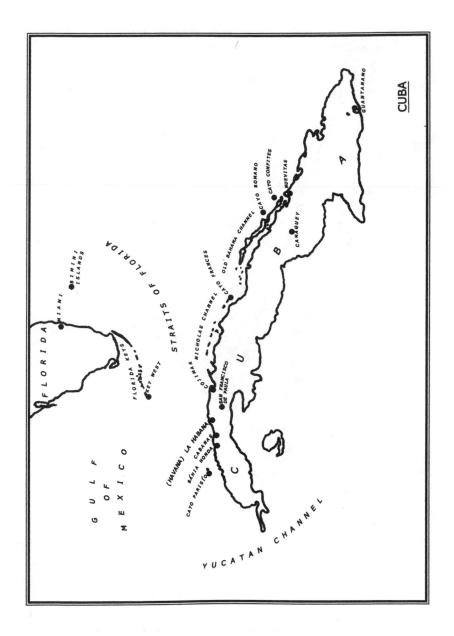

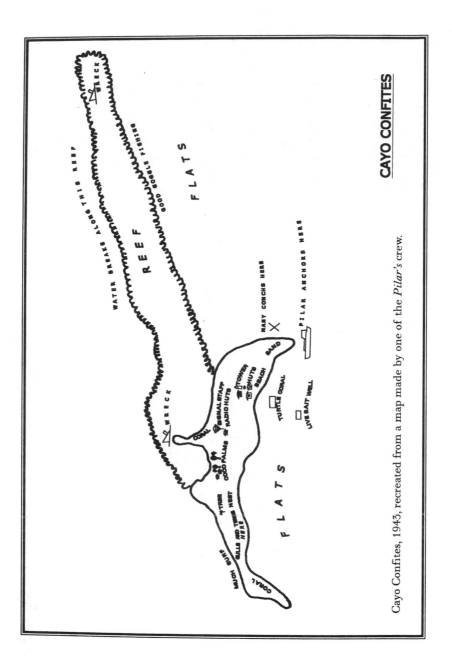

Cayo Confites, 1943, recreated from a map made by one of the *Pilar*'s crew.

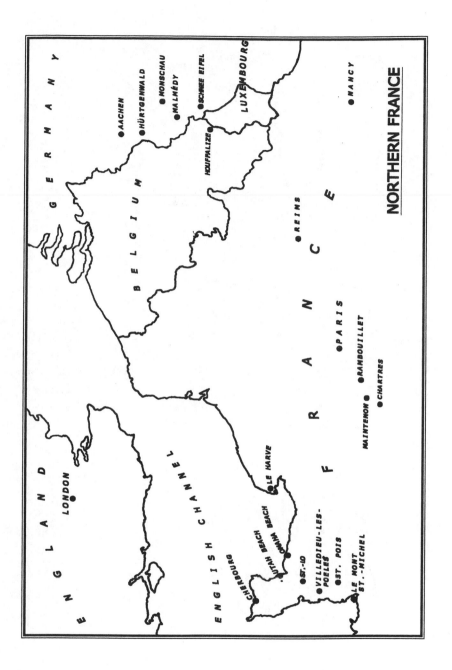

NORTHERN FRANCE

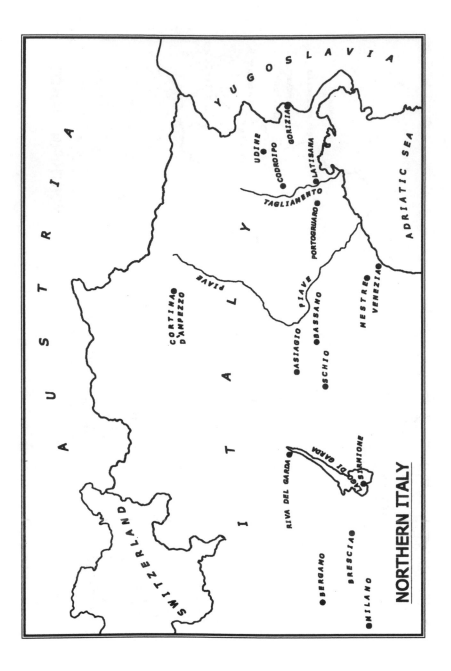

NORTHERN ITALY

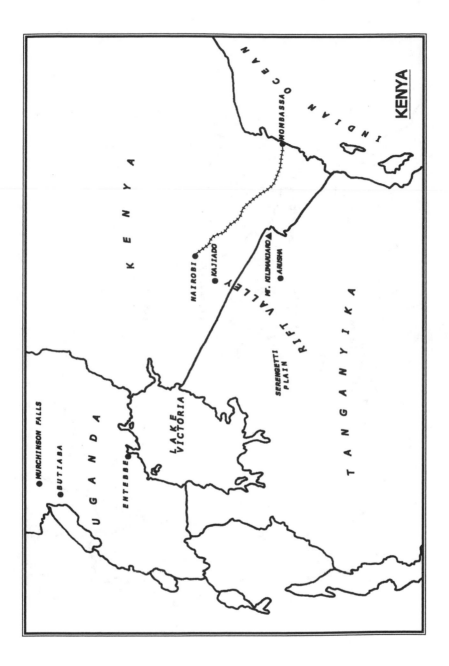

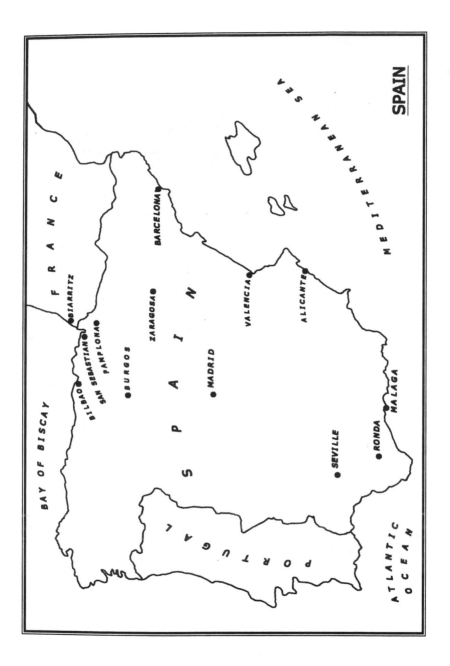

PART ONE

THE FORTUNES
OF WAR

JULY 1940 TO NOVEMBER 1944

And while I am talking to you mothers and fathers, I give you one more assurance. I have said this before, but I shall say it again and again and again: Your boys are not going to be sent into any foreign wars.

Franklin Delano Roosevelt, October 30, 1940

Chapter Twelve

RINGING THE CHANGES

July to Early Winter 1940

WITH THIGH BONE snapped by his falling horse and pain now beading his face in sweat, Robert Jordan lay as quietly as possible, calling on all his reserves for one last effort. It was not a question of would he survive or not. As soon as the bone splintered, his death was certain. The only question was whether he could hold off the pain long enough to do one last thing well. His small flask of absinthe was lost in the fall, and no matter how he tried, he could not think past the pain. He could not think about the girl, nor his father dead by his own hand, nor even his Civil War grandfather. At that last moment when he felt himself slipping into unconsciousness, the Nationalist cavalry officer came into view below him. Positioning his extra clips close at hand, Jordan sighted quite calmly down the barrel of his submachine gun at the moving target. "He was waiting until the officer reached the sunlit place where the first trees of the pine forest joined the green slope of the meadow. He could feel his heart against the pine needle floor of the forest."[1] Having come full circle, he was back where he started three days earlier, before he had received the incredible gift of the girl, Maria, before El Sordo's death on that other lonely hilltop, before Pablo stole the dynamite plunger but came back with the extra horses, before the bridge was blown.

On paper, only three days had passed between the typescript's opening page and its last one, but it had cost seventeen months of Ernest Hemingway's life and the end of his second marriage to create those three days. In March 1939, when he started the story of the dynamiter and the band of Loyalist partisans, the Spanish Civil War was all but over. The elected government's effort to defeat Franco's fascist revolution was doomed when America, England, and France refused to support a leftist government being helped by the Russians. No matter that Hitler's Nazi Condor Legion was bombing Guernica; no matter that Mussolini's Italian troops were in the Spanish trenches; no matter that sound journalists warned, time and again: if the world did not fight fascism in Spain, it would have to fight it across Europe later. Now in steamy late July 1940, as Hemingway read through his typescript one last time in his New York hotel room, the European war was edging ever closer to American participation, despite President Roosevelt's campaign promises to the contrary. The Nazi blitzkrieg, having rolled over Poland, Norway, Belgium, Holland, and most of France, was now poised to invade England itself. Meanwhile, as if the mounting war with fascism were not the issue, the ever vigilant congressional investigating committee of Martin Dies continued to worry the nation about the communist threat to American values. Stories spread that Reds operating the radios on U.S. ships, and other communists, were slipping into the United States through Cuba.[2]

Five years earlier, as a lover of military history and a hater of war, Hemingway laid it out as bluntly as possible, telling his *Esquire* readers that a European war was brewing in which America should play no part. "Never again," he wrote, "should this country be put into a European war through mistaken idealism, through propaganda, through the desire to back our creditors."[3] That was the disillusioned Hemingway speaking, the young man sucked in by propaganda during World War I. Spain changed his point of view. After ten years of following Spanish politics more closely than what was happening in the United States, Hemingway believed in the Spanish earth, its working class, and its rituals, without ever embracing the politics of socialism or its radical left, the Communist Party. Seventeen years after idealism died in the muddy trenches of the Somme, Passchendaele, and Verdun, it resurrected in the Spanish conflict only to die a different death when fascism triumphed while democracies refused to help.

Now, with German troops marching down the Champs-Elysées, German U-boats once again shutting down the British island, and the Luftwaffe bombing London, Hemingway's warning to America seemed far away and long ago. If the war came to him, he would fight to save his homeland and his people, but never to save the politicians who started the war. Soon, he knew, there would be no choice, but on this day, his mind was completely absorbed in the story of Robert Jordan's last few hours on earth. As he told his editor, Max Perkins, after living with Jordan for seventeen months, he hated like hell to kill him off.[4] With Jordan's death, of course, Hemingway killed off, once more, a piece of himself. That's how he felt about his writing: each book a little death, another story he could never again write. All that was left him to do were tedious revisions of the galley and page proofs, arguments with his editor over certain words, and then the reviews that his clipping agent collected for him, reviews he always read and never liked.

Alone in the Hotel Barclay, it was easier for Hemingway to lose himself in his book than to think about his personal life, which had become incredibly complicated. His first wife, Hadley, and their son, Jack, were in Chicago, where she was remarried to Paul Mowrer, her income supplemented by Ernest's parting gift of all royalties from *The Sun Also Rises*. His second wife, Pauline Pfeiffer, and their two sons, Patrick and Gregory, were in the Key West house waiting for her divorce from Ernest on grounds of desertion to become final. For the last year and a half, he had been living in Cuba with Martha Gellhorn while still married to Pauline, whose strong Catholic conscience resisted the idea of divorce. Mixing more debris into already muddy waters, Ernest enlisted Pauline's uncle, wealthy Augustus Pfeiffer, to ask Pauline for a reasonable divorce settlement, for she had more than enough money of her own. Fooling no one but keeping up a facade, Hemingway posted and received his mail at the Hotel Ambos Mundos but lived with Martha first in the Hotel Biltmore Sevilla and later in a run-down, rented farmhouse, La Finca Vigia, on the outskirts of Havana. While Ernest labored over his typescript, Martha was working on a *Collier's* magazine exposé on German fifth columnists in Havana.[5]

Having worked all morning on his typescript, Hemingway gathered a roomful of friends, for he hated to be alone when he was not writing. Outside in the streets the temperature hung at 88 degrees with humidity to match; inside the Barclay, it was not much better. When Robert Van Gelder from the *New York Times* arrived, he found the room crowded with a lawyer, a Spanish Civil War veteran, and others unidentified, circled around a bucket of ice, soda water, and a fifth of Scotch. Van Gelder, taking it all in, caught the scene in a thumbnail sketch:

> *Hemingway looked elephant-big, enormously healthy. His talk is unevenly paced, a quick spate and then a slow search for a word. His chair keeps hitching across the floor toward the other chairs, and then as he reaches a point, a conclusion, he shoves the chair back to the edge of the group again.*[6]

Gustavo Durán, an old friend and admired combatant in the Spanish war, was sitting on one of the beds, listening to the conversation as it easily shifted from English to Spanish to French. Four months earlier, Hemingway told Durán in a letter that he was finally writing the really good book that he once thought he might write in his old age, which he imagined would not be quite old because Hemingways usually shot themselves or someone did it for them.[7] When talk turned to the lost war in Spain, Durán said, "The world now is very confusing. It is amazing how sure we once were, Ernest, that our ideas were right." Hemingway replied, "The fight in Spain will have to be fought again." Durán said nothing.

Those conspicuous by their absence at the Barclay were faces once mainstays in the entourage Hemingway customarily gathered about himself. Poet and old friend Archibald MacLeish, who once flew through winter storms to be with Hemingway when he was hospitalized in Montana, was no longer part of the inner circle. After accepting President Roosevelt's nomination to be Librarian of Congress, MacLeish said publicly that the postwar writers, like Hemingway, in their disillusionment with the "war to end all wars" had "educated a generation to believe that all declarations, all beliefs are fraudulent, that all statements of conviction are sales-talk, that nothing men can put into words is worth fighting for . . . those writers must face the fact that the books they wrote in the years just after the war have done more to disarm democracy in the face of fascism than any other single influence."[8] Two weeks later, in response to *Life* magazine's request for authors' rebuttals, Hemingway accused MacLeish of having a bad conscience while Ernest had fought fascism every way he knew how and had no remorse, "neither literary nor political. . . . If the Germans have learned how to fight a war and the Allies have not learned, MacLeish can hardly put the blame on our books."[9]

Even more conspicuously absent were Gerald and Sara Murphy, owners of the Mark Cross department store and two of Hemingway's earliest and most ardent supporters. When Ernest was distraught with the agony of leaving his first wife, Hadley, for Pauline Pfeiffer, it was Gerald and Sara who gave him comfort. Gerald told him, "We love you, we believe in you in all your parts, we believe in what you're doing, in the way you're doing it. Anything we've got is yours." During his separation from Hadley, Ernest lived in Gerald's cold-water Paris studio. When Gerald feared Ernest was living without funds, he put $400 in his Morgan Guaranty bank account without being asked.[10] The day after Van Gelder observed Hemingway and friends, a letter from Sara at the Murphy summer place in East Hampton arrived at the Barclay: "Dear Ernest—I hear you are in N.Y.—& it would give us such pleasure if you would come down here to spend a few days . . . it's very peaceful, & cool seabathing."[11] For five months, Ernest was unable to answer the Murphys' letter, unable to face them when he was separated from Pauline and living with a much younger Martha.[12] Always looking for others to blame for his problems and quandaries, Ernest usually found a woman to be the responsible party: his mother deprived him of his college education, threw him out of the house, and drove his father to suicide; Pauline separated him from Hadley as if he were a sack of potatoes; Jinny Pfeiffer, by telling Pauline of his affair with Martha, had ruined his second marriage.

During the days following the Van Gelder interview, the heat wave that was killing hundreds across the Midwest continued to stultify New York. There in the Barclay hotel room with the window open, Ernest was sweating heavily, his wire-rimmed glasses cutting into the bridge of his nose, his eyes blurring from the marathon reading. The electric fan on the coffee table waved its head, moving warm air from one part of the room to another. As sections were finished, they were rushed to the printer, who was hurrying them into galleys for an October publication. Hard-pressed to stay ahead of the typesetters, Hemingway stuck to his task. Wednesday, July 31, Hemingway's editor, Maxwell Perkins, told him that they had only enough copy for one more day's work. That morning the *New York Times* reported that 3.6 million aliens in the United States were being registered and fingerprinted by the FBI, and the book page noted:

> *Ernest Hemingway up from Cuba where he has been rounding out his new novel "For Whom the Bell Tolls," has been in New York the last few days. The new novel which Scribner's will bring out in October, is a love story with the Spanish Civil War for a setting. Mr. Hemingway will return to Cuba in a few days.*[13]

On top of his dresser was the signed contract, dated July 15, calling for Hemingway's royalties to be 15 percent on the first 25,000 copies sold; thereafter they rose to 20 percent, higher rates than most authors received, but Ernest Hemingway in 1940 was not most authors. He may not have published a best-selling novel during the entire 1930s, but through his nonfiction, his *Esquire* articles, his

Spanish Civil War journalism, and his personal exploits hunting in East Africa and marlin fishing in the Gulf Stream, he had become the most widely read male author in America. On Thursday, Max asked for another two hundred pages if it were at all possible.[14] Anything was possible, of course, if Ernest worked hard enough, long enough.

No matter what else happened in his life—sick children, angry wives, broken arms, bad weather, petulant friends—the one thing which he never scanted was his writing. If he was a less than attentive father, an uneven friend, a faithful or unfaithful husband, the one standard of self-measure that remained constant was the quality of his writing. So long as his writing ethos remained inviolate, he was true to himself: whatever outrageous fortune might assail him, that certainty was his shield. Seldom leaving the hotel room, he finished the typescript revisions for the printer, who set the galleys in record time; this book would go from typescript to the public readers in only three months. As soon as the galleys were packed, Hemingway was on the train to Miami, where he boarded a Pan-American clipper for the quick flight to Havana. Martha and her mother, Edna, met him at the boarding dock.

Her coiled blond hair now grayed at sixty, her blue eyes still brilliant, Edna Gellhorn was standing on the dock beside her daughter, the two of them startlingly alike, both beautiful and both equally independent. Edna may have deferred more to the dominant males of her era than Martha ever did, but the older woman was also more adept at getting her way. To Hemingway, who was vulnerable to older motherly women, Edna was more like the mother he wished his had been. Ernest "loved my mother," Martha said later. "Both of my husbands loved my mother, always . . . they loved her more than me . . . and they were absolutely right."[15] The feeling was guardedly mutual. Edna appreciated Ernest and was tolerant of his casual lifestyle. Although she caught Ernest on an emotional high, his book finished and galleys arriving, Edna nevertheless saw something beneath his surface that made her feel sorry for him, something that eluded Martha at the time. Whatever she saw led her to advise her daughter not to marry the famous author; advice Martha did not easily ignore.

As a younger woman in St. Louis, Edna Gellhorn marched with suffragists seeking the vote, and three months before the Nineteenth Amendment was ratified, she organized the St. Louis League of Women Voters.[16] With her, quite frequently, was her small daughter, Martha. During the 1916 Democratic Convention in St. Louis, Edna was on the planning committee that lined the streets leading to the Coliseum convention center with seven thousand women; at a strategic corner, a tableau was arranged of women draped in white, gray, and black representing states with full suffrage, partial suffrage, or no suffrage for women. "At the top was . . . Miss Liberty. Down in the front . . . were two little girls . . . who represented future voters."[17] One of those little girls was Martha Gellhorn.

Having grown up at the side of her politically progressive mother, Martha was herself an activist but not a joiner. "A self-willed, opinionated loner . . . never a team player," was how she later characterized herself.[18] Rather than organize the voters, Martha's goal was to prick their consciences through her journalism and her novels. It was Martha's personal friendship with Eleanor Roosevelt that allowed her to arrange for a White House showing of *The Spanish Earth*, the Joris Ivens film supporting Loyalist Spain, with Hemingway reading his own narrative. In November 1938, Martha was in Prague when the Czech government capitulated to Hitler's claim on the Sudetenland. Among the journalists on the last free flight out of Prague, Martha carried with her testimony of the Nazi terrorist tactics. In December 1939, she left Hemingway at the Sun Valley Lodge in Idaho to take a *Collier's* assignment in Finland, arriving there as the first Russian bombs were falling on Helsinki. Ernest may have commanded more money for his journalism, which he often viewed as a means of support while gathering experience for his fiction, but Martha was the more dedicated journalist. Almost to a fault, she was passionate about the downtrodden, the war-torn, and the victimized. That May of 1940, she wrote a friend, "It is extremely pretentious to take the world's troubles as your own, but I must say they concern me more gravely than anything else."[19] In Ernest Hemingway she thought she had found a man of the same ilk. She could not have been more wrong.

No sooner had Hemingway returned to Cuba than galleys arrived from Scribner's, keeping him happily busy while Martha planned their trip to Sun Valley for the fall season. At the same time Hemingway received his proofs, Scribner's sent a set for consideration to The Book-of-the-Month Club (BOMC) along with Perkins's addendum: "Two short chapters, amounting to 1,500 words in all, will bring the book to a conclusion." These chapters, which Hemingway had outlined, were meant to tie up loose ends. Max assured the BOMC that "These chapters are written, but not yet to the complete satisfaction of the author. He wished to wait until after reading the proof up to this point before perfecting the end."[20] Perkins also marked up another set of galleys which he sent to Hemingway on August 14, suggesting a number of changes, some typographical, some substantive, none so onerous as revisions Hemingway was forced to make a decade earlier.[21] This time Ernest, in anticipation of censorship, avoided the problem up front by either not translating Spanish obscenities or by creative use of English. In *The Sun Also Rises* (1926), Mike Campbell wanted to say, "Tell him the bulls have no balls," but in the reactionary climate of 1926 America, Perkins told Hemingway "balls" was not a word Charles Scribner would print. Instead, the bulls were said to have no horns.[22] In *For Whom the Bell Tolls*, when Robert Jordan is asked by a needling Pablo what a Scot wears under his skirt, Jordan tells him, "*Los cojones*" (206). When Jordan says that the girl, Maria, was put in his care, one of the partisans replies, "And thy care is to *joder* with her all night?" (290). Max Perkins, who himself was never known to say "fuck" in anyone's company, either did not understand or did not object to the word in Spanish. Nor did he protest when Hemingway used abstractions in such a way that only the purest of mind could not translate them:

> "*Thy duty,*" *said Augustin mockingly. "I besmirch the milk of thy duty." Then turning to the woman, "Where the un-nameable is this vileness that I am to guard?*"

"In the cave," Pilar said. "In two sacks. And I am tired of thy obscenity."

"I obscenity in the milk of thy tiredness," Augustin said.

"Then go and befoul thyself," Pilar said to him without heat. (92)

On August 26, while Perkins was writing to say how pleased Scribner's was that the Book-of-the-Month Club had taken *For Whom the Bell Tolls* as its November selection, Ernest was packaging the first 123 pages of galleys for air-mail shipment to New York, keeping the last 18 for more work. All the requested corrections and revisions, he said, were made or answered, grammar improved, and references to masturbation toned down. But he remained uncertain about the book's conclusion. He had additional scenes after Jordan sighted down the submachine-gun barrel, but they seemed like talking about the boxing match after it was over, or like his several failed endings to *A Farewell to Arms* where he tried to tell what happened to the survivors after the war. That tendency to tidy up loose bits, he said, was always a problem for him; but the book "really stops where Jordan is feeling his heart beating against the pine needle floor of the forest." Two days later, Max's telegram confirmed that they should leave off the epilogue.[23]

While submerged in final corrections, Ernest's emotional center took a heavy hit when Martha began questioning the wisdom of their marrying. At four in the morning Ernest wrote her a note, saying her news busted his heart and left him with a first-class headache. He knew that for the last eighteen months he had been "no gift to live with," as she put it, but she must remember how he helped her with her book—*The Heart of Another*. But if she was not going to marry him, she should tell him before he took the *Pilar* alone to Key West giving himself too much time to think: another veiled threat of suicide. He closed his in-house note telling her that Mr. Scrooby (his penis) now referred to himself as "us."[24] In these and other private letters, Hemingway's ardor and frustration reached levels similar to his courtship of his first two wives. Martha was his "Mookie," his "Chickie"; he was her "Bongie," or her "Bug." Words did not always move another writer like Martha so easily, but she did reaffirm her intention to marry Ernest.

The problem was not that Martha loved him too little but he loved her too much. To Rodrigo Diaz, his pigeon-shooting companion and sometime doctor, Ernest was always at risk in his relationship with Martha. Easily hurt, he was tremendously vulnerable beneath the tough exterior with which he faced the world. Diaz thought Hemingway was born either too soon or too late, a man who would have been more comfortable in another era. A practicing psychiatrist, Dr. Franz Stetmayer, was an interested observer of Ernest's behavior with Martha. His conclusion was that she was the less committed of the two and that Ernest was terribly afraid of losing her.[25] Separately, the two left Cuba—she to St. Louis to see her mother; Ernest to Key West—to rendezvous at Sun Valley.

As soon as galleys were in the mail, Ernest motored his fishing boat, *Pilar*, ninety miles across the Gulf of Mexico to Key West for winter safety and repairs. The Hemingway house on Whitehead Street was empty. Pauline was in New York; their sons, Patrick and Gregory, were already in Sun Valley, Idaho, with their stepbrother Jack (Bumby), awaiting Ernest's arrival. With little delay, Ernest picked up a new Buick convertible from the Key West dealer and spent a day selecting half the books out of his Key West library for eventual shipment to Cuba.[26] Leaving Key West with old friend and factotum Toby Bruce at the wheel of the Buick, the two men made good time driving the almost three thousand miles to Union Pacific's resort at Sun Valley, arriving as the fall hunting season opened. At the same time, Martha took the train to St. Louis to tell her mother that she and Ernest would marry as soon as his divorce was final, although she also told Clara Spiegel, a Ketchum friend, that she felt somewhat trapped by the idea of marriage.[27]

The Sun Valley Lodge, which the wealthy railroad financier and now diplomat Averell Harriman opened in 1936, was one of the first multi-use western resorts catering to the moderately wealthy, the famous, and those on the rise. When guests stepped off the Union Pacific train at Shoshone, they were met by the Lodge station wagon to be driven up the valley past smooth brown hills, through the old mining town of Hailey, past Club Rio and the Alpine where sheepherders, miners, and Sun Valley dudes could gamble and drink. Turning right at Jack Lane's Mercantile store, they did not stop because Jack was not fond of outsiders. "Hell, he wouldn't even get up to wait on 'em," Bud Purdy recalled. A mile east of Lane's was the well-modulated western world of Sun Valley. There eastern dudes found hunting and fishing guides at the ready, a skating rink with instructors and visiting stars like Sonja Henie, a ski basin with chairlifts, live music in the evenings, a comfortable bar, airy rooms, sleigh rides in winter, a rodeo in summer, cook-outs in the fall, a movie theater, a first-class dining room, Basque cooks, an in-house photographer, and a public relations staff. In Silver Creek, trophy trout lurked in the eel grass; in the fall fields, pheasant were abundant, and on the irrigation canals ducks were plentiful. Antelope and elk hunts were available in season. In the main dining room on almost any fall evening, one might see a Hollywood movie star, a famous musician, or even a best-selling author like Ernest Hemingway. In an effective publicity effort, Sun Valley offered well-known personalities like Hemingway free use of the facilities providing they allowed their names and pictures to be used to promote the resort.

That fall of 1940, when Paris was occupied by German troops and London was burning, Ernest and others arrived at Sun Valley for what many thought would be the last Christmas before America was involved in another war. On the dance floors of the country, fools rushed in to find their love on Blueberry Hill, while Glenn Miller's swing band took the young through Tuxedo Junction on moonlit serenades. Two former vaudevillians—Bob Hope and Bing Crosby—took their movie fans on the humorous road to Singapore, which by February 1942 would be occupied by invading Japanese. On the front page of American newspapers, there were plenty of signs: the U.S. Navy was building two hundred new ships; the first peacetime draft in the nation's history became law; the defense budget received a second

$5.25 billion supplement. Before the year was out, Ernest would be suggesting that seventeen-year-old Jack ought to delay college to spend a year fishing and working, because war was coming: "A man might as well catch a steelhead [trout] in this life if there's only one life."[28]

Whatever the future held, Ernest was more concerned with his novel, the last eighteen galleys of which he air-mailed to Max Perkins on September 10, along with its dedication: "This book is for Martha Gellhorn." Scribner's and The Book-of-the-Month Club were advertising the book heavily in trade publications and on newspaper book pages. When the novel was published to rave reviews on October 21, Ernest and his publisher knew they had a best-seller. The *New York Times* called it "the best book Ernest Hemingway has written, the fullest, the deepest, the truest." *The Nation* said the novel "sets a new standard for Hemingway in characterization, dialogue, suspense, and compassion." *The New Yorker* found it touching "a deeper level than any sounded in the author's other books." *Saturday Review of Literature* thought it to be "one of the finest and richest novels of the last decade." Even Edmund Wilson, once his early champion but afterward disappointed with the 1930s Hemingway, was able to say, "Hemingway the artist is with us again; and it is like having an old friend back."[29]

Ten days later, BOMC increased its initial order to an astounding 200,000 copies, and the book was already in its third Scribner's printing for a total of 360,000 copies. In the following six months, 491,000 copies of the novel were sold.[30] Full of himself, expansive, joking, surrounded by all his sons and his wife-to-be, Ernest was riding an emotional high further fueled by Paramount Pictures paying $110,000 for the film rights to his book. In such a mood, he was already fabricating stories of the novel's inception. To Gustavo Durán, he claimed that the novel rested on his experience commanding a company with Kemal in the Greco-Turkish War, and on his participation in various Cuban revolutionary movements, as well as being a descendant of Major Colquhoun Grant, who fought with Wellington in Spain during the Napoleonic Wars.[31] None of which was true in the sense of having taken place; all of which was true in the sense that each claim was what Hemingway wished had happened.

As a *Toronto Daily Star* reporter, Ernest was not present when Kemal and his Turks ravaged Smyrna, but he once wrote about it as if he were a witness. Nor had he yet been directly involved with any of the numerous Cuban revolutionary movements, although he watched them develop with great interest, writing about them in discarded portions of *To Have and Have Not* (1937). From his youthful admiration for Teddy Roosevelt, Hemingway developed his need for both the active and the contemplative life, neither satisfying without the other. But reality was never quite able to match his expectations. When the trench mortar shell ruined his right knee and killed men standing next to him in World War I, Hemingway was decorated by the Italian government as a war hero. Ashamed afterward to have been only a Red Cross ambulance man and not an active combatant, Ernest made up fantastic stories of being an Italian officer with the Arditi troops. In Spain during the 1920s, he followed the bullfights with religious fervor, but knowing bullfighters and watching from the *barrera* was not enough; he had to create the impression that he himself had been in the bull ring. Intrigued with revolutions, spies, and clandestine operations through reading, watching, and talking with Charles Sweeny, a professional soldier of fortune, Ernest always wanted to be a revolutionist. During the Spanish Civil War, he reported accurately from the very edge of battle, but with his deep reading in military history and tactics, he yearned to be a field commander, preferably one operating beyond the reach of higher authority.

When not writing, he was happiest outdoors with some novice whom he could instruct, for in any situation, Hemingway was the teacher of others. As friends would testify, Hemingway placed novices in the best position for the first shot, or in the chair for the first marlin strike. Hemingway was always organizing small groups of friends to participate in some outdoor activity. That fall, after hearing farmer Frees's complaints about the abundance of rabbits, Ernest organized the great rabbit hunt. Gathering together some fifteen shooters—Greg and Patrick, movie stars Gary Cooper and Merle

Oberon, rancher Bud Purdy, Sun Valley employees Don Anderson and Taylor Williams, among others—he positioned them in a semicircle, herding the rabbits through brush toward an irrigation canal. As Bud Purdy remembered it, "we lined up there and pushed all those rabbits back toward the canal and when they couldn't cross the canal, they'd come back. I'll bet we shot five hundred rabbits that day. . . . Cooper and I kinda got out of the way after a little bit. I was scared of too many people shooting. . . . Hemingway was a great guy to organize, you know, where you'd be sneaking up on a duck, he'd always tell us where to stand and what to do, you know. He was the general."

No one who met Hemingway ever forgot him. He was the strange attractor around whose light all manner of men and women circled: movie stars, millionaires, cooks, crooks, bartenders, writers, soldiers. Forty-one years old and at his physical peak, he was not the most handsome man in the room, but he was the most magnetic, a sometimes shy man who listened intently, enjoyed good stories, and spoke carefully. Bud Purdy's wife, Ruth, remembered him as a man who "had a kind voice, was always nice to people, and made you feel important."[32] He studied terrain the way some men study the stock market; his reading in history, military tactics, and biography was considerable. In early October, while awaiting publication of *For Whom the Bell Tolls*, Hemingway ordered from New York a typical spectrum of bedside books: *The Ox-Bow Incident*; a Margery Allingham murder mystery; Van Wyck Brooks's new literary history, *New England, Indian Summer*; Edmund Wilson's *To the Finland Station*; *Audubon's America*; Raymond Chandler's *Farewell My Lovely*; and *How to Play and Win at Poker*.[33]

With ducks thick in neighboring creeks and canals, and out on Tom Gooding's ranch pheasants fat with grain, Hemingway could not have been happier. Hunting frequently with Gary Cooper, who was more a Montana cowboy than a Hollywood movie star, Ernest posed for countless pictures, holding the day's bag. Cooper, he found, was a better rifle shot; Ernest was best wing-shooting with his over-and-under shotgun. Both men had come of age in an America so abundant with game that bag limits seemed onerous, and predators were to be eliminated. On his 1933–34 African safari, Hemingway had amused himself shooting hyenas; Cooper did the same with hawks on telephone poles and coyotes in the field.[34] The two were both artists and outdoorsmen, fitting comfortably together in the field and at supper. Hemingway complained that Martha was so impressed with Cooper that she wanted Ernest to dress better, but nothing, he said, was going to make his face any better.[35] Both men knew and admired each other's work: Cooper had portrayed Frederic Henry in the 1932 film version of *A Farewell to Arms*. Already there was talk between them that Cooper might become Robert Jordan for the movie version of *For Whom the Bell Tolls*.

In November, *Life* magazine sent Hemingway's friend from the Spanish Civil War, Robert Capa, to Sun Valley to photograph Ernest as part of a feature on the filming of the movie. In the photo-shoot, he was to include Martha, news of whose pending marriage to Ernest was in the wind, Walter Winchell having said so to "Mr. and Mrs. America and all the ships at sea" on his syndicated radio show. The volatile Hungarian photographer, whose specialty was war coverage, covered the pheasant shoot as if it were a battleground. When Hemingway's divorce from Pauline became final on November 4, and Edna Gellhorn arrived at Sun Valley for a pre-wedding party, Capa was standing on a bar stool, blasting away at Hemingway and company, spent flashbulbs popping off the camera like empty shells.

On November 21, in the Union Pacific dining room in Cheyenne, Wyoming, Ernest and Martha were married by a justice of the peace.[36] The next day from Key West, Pauline wrote, thanking him for pheasants he sent to her when Patrick and Gregory returned home, thanking him also for the mounted warthog head from their safari, and wishing him happiness with "Mart," whom she no longer called "Miss Einhorn."[37] Two days later the newlyweds stopped briefly in Kansas City's Hotel Muehlbach to visit Luis Quintanilla, artist in residence at the University of Kansas City. Hemingway had supported Quintanilla's artwork in New York and his counterespionage work in Madrid during the Spanish Civil War. In the hotel room a local reporter caught up with Ernest as he mused about what he might write next: "one a story of the Gulf Stream. That would be factual like *Death in the Afternoon*. And I would like to write a book for my boys." Martha, who was on her way to New York to accept an assignment from *Collier's* for feature stories on the Japanese war with China, closed off the interview, saying, "Right now I'm the war correspondent in the family."[38]

On December 21, 1940, while Hemingway was on his way back to Cuba for Christmas, Scott Fitzgerald died in Sheila Graham's Hollywood living room, a simple failure of the heart. On his bookshelf was a copy of *For Whom the Bell Tolls*, signed: "To Scott with affection and esteem, Ernest." In response Fitzgerald had praised the book, telling Ernest it was "better than anybody else writing could do. . . . I envy you like hell and there is no irony in this." In his notebook, he thought otherwise: "It is so to speak Ernest's 'Tale of Two Cities' though the comparison isn't apt. I mean it is a thoroughly superficial book which has all the profundity of Rebecca."[39] Within three months, three of the men most influential to Hemingway's early career were dead: Scott Fitzgerald, James Joyce, and Sherwood Anderson. Modernism, whatever that word meant, had become a historical period, and what would follow was not yet written.

Chapter Thirteen

TO MANDALAY AND BACK

January to September 1941

O N   T H E   L A S T   D A Y of January 1941, Martha with her
Collier's assignment, Ernest with his *PM* journalist's credentials boarded the *Matsona*, bound for Hawaii. Eager
to see the Asia of her reading—Manila, Hong Kong, Chungking,
Singapore—Martha was ill prepared for the months that followed.
Hong Kong appeared to her "as if nailed together hurriedly from odd
lots of old wood and sounded like a chronic Chinese New Year." Encir-
cled on three sides by invading Japanese and teeming with refugees,
the Crown Colony was throbbing at an hysteric pitch. Martha was
appalled by the poverty, the hopelessness, and the lack of sanitation.
"The sheer numbers, the density of bodies," horrified her. "There was
no space to breathe." She could not believe the ease with which Ernest
picked up enough local patois to make himself understood by waiters,
rickshaw coolies, and street vendors. He loved the Chinese food that
made Martha's stomach queasy; he was like a small boy lighting fire-
crackers in their hotel room until she made him stop. But she could
not stop the reality of the Hong Kong streets: "Why do they have to
spit so much? . . . You can't put your foot down without stepping on a
big slimy glob! And everything stinks of sweat and good old night soil."[1]

In Hong Kong, the China News Agency reported the couple were collecting materials for a new novel.[2] In fact, Ernest and Martha were going into China not only to report on the Sino-Japanese War, but also to collect intelligence for the U.S. government. Through Martha's connections with the White House, they were asked to observe closely the politics of the China war. In Hong Kong, they were briefed by Lauchlin Currie, whom Roosevelt had sent to study the China situation where a quasi-democratic Chiang Kai-shek was or was not using U.S. military aid to suppress the communist left for his own purposes while also fighting the Japanese. Carl Blum, the general manager of the Rubber Company of the Far East, also briefed them on the strategic importance of the Orient.[3]

A month later, from the inland vantage point of Shaokwan, where her hotel bed was a plank and the latrine a "stand-up hole-in-the-floor toilet down the corridor," Hong Kong looked much better to Martha. Desperate to keep somewhat clean, she was depressed when Ernest told her she was a fool to touch the water and never to use it to brush her teeth. Later, when her hands developed "China Rot," a highly contagious fungus, Martha was forced to wear awkward gloves over a "malodorous unguent." "Honest to God, Martha," Ernest said, "you brought this on yourself. I told you not to wash." On their way from Shaokwan to the front lines of the Chinese war, the Hemingways traveled by motorized sampan and then small ponies through mud and rain, arriving finally at the Seventh War Zone:

> Headquarters were sometimes a new wood house, sometimes a house made of lashed mats on stilts above the duck pond. The pond water was rotting garbage and mud . . . pigs rooted in the muck, flies swarmed, and over all villages hung the smell of China: night soil. We passed through slatternly villages, each adorned with a triumphal arch for us and a duck pond with malaria for them.[4]

Day after sodden day filled with such squalor left Martha despondent. There in a cold stone house, bedded on the stone floor, mosquitoes and flies circling overhead in the dark, Martha said, "I wish to die." "Too late," answered Ernest. "Who wanted to come to China?" Finally, having seen their fill of Chiang Kai-shek's army in the field and having toasted themselves to the point of oblivion, the conspicuous couple began the trip back down the river.

Forty-three hours later, they arrived back in Shaokwan, road-weary and almost resigned to whatever came next. The evening of April 3, they bedded down on the train to Kweilin in what was advertised as a first-class compartment. What Martha found was dirt, cigarette butts, orange peels, and cinders. There was no dining car, no food. They ate oranges and hard-boiled eggs washed down with boiled water. Twenty-five hours and four hundred miles down the track, they got off in Kweilin, where their expected military flight to Chungking was not awaiting them. Someone had not sent the message. They checked into the Palace Hotel, where bedbugs reigned and the down-corridor toilet was overflowing. "The sight was more appalling than the stench," Martha said later, "though the stench was superlative."[5] By late the next afternoon, Ernest's explosive tirade (his first on the trip) produced the Douglas DC-3 that flew them to Chungking, the working capital of Free China.

The next morning they were greeted by the finance minister of China, H. H. Kung, with whom they ate breakfast, lunch, and supper. Kung was an old friend of Ernest's uncle, Dr. Willoughby Hemingway, a medical missionary who died in China in 1932, and who was responsible for Kung attending Oberlin College. While a student, Kung was several times a guest at the Hemingway family home in Oak Park. Now he was able to open doors for Ernest and Martha that would otherwise have been closed. He asked them to stay at his house, but Ernest begged off; instead, they stayed at the unoccupied house of Kung's brother-in-law who was in Washington, D.C.[6] With the Kung connection, road life was somewhat easier for the Hemingways in Chungking, and Ernest continued to gather intelligence, including a somewhat clandestine interview with the communist political figure, Chou En-lai. A major difference between Ernest and Martha was by now quite apparent. Ernest was able to accept whatever the local social conditions were as a given, while Martha was almost always angered and appalled by the same conditions:

> *grey, shapeless, muddy, a collection of drab cement buildings and poverty shacks, the best feature a lively market. . . . Crowds of thin cotton-clad expressionless people swarmed in the streets. Lepers abounded. They were beggars and forgivably spiteful; you hurried to find money in your purse; if not quick enough, they touched your shrinking skin.*

Ernest thrived in Chungking, developing contacts, gathering information, and making the most of his opportunities. As Martha later admitted, "He did not value cleanliness far above godliness like me, and wasn't reduced to despair by all the manifestations of disease."[7] Soon he was alone on a flight to "Chengtu in north Szechwan Province where the caravans come down from Tibet and you walk past yellow and red lamas in the dust-deep streets of the old high-walled city." There he saw and obtained photographs of the 100,000 workers who, without machinery, were building an airstrip over a mile long, one hundred and fifty yards wide, and five feet deep, capable of landing an American B-17 Super Fortress, building it from scratch in three months time. "China," he learned, "can do anything China wants to do."[8]

On the evening of April 14, a Chungking farewell party for the Hemingways was hosted by various organizations—the Chinese Journalist Association and the Sino-American Cultural Interflow Association among others. At the Chialing Hostel, more than three hundred people were gathered when

> *Dr. H. H. Kung led Mr. and Mrs. Hemingway into the hall. . . . Ernest Hemingway has a rosy face with brown mustache. Colossal and muscular, he is apparently much taller than Dr. Kung, the Vice Premier. He shakes hands, politely and elegantly, with his greeters. Oh, each finger of his seems thicker than the stalk of a pen which produces panic when grabbed. . . . With golden hair and a*

*water-melon seed shaped face, Mrs. Hemingway looks like a blonde,
but without blue eyes. Of light color, she is beautiful, wearing an
exquisite wrist watch and ring of jade. Moreover she is graceful and
charming as Jeanette MacDonald, the famous movie star. . . . [The
guests were] served peanuts, cakes, steamed dumplings, spring rolls,
and goblets brimming with wine whose color resembles that of Mrs.
Hemingway's golden hair.*[9]

From the capital, Martha went south to Java and Singapore; Ernest
flew south, following the vulnerable Burma Road, which supplied
the Chinese Army, to its source at Lashio. From there, first by car
and then by slow train, finally arriving in Rangoon, Hemingway filed
four stories for *PM* newspaper, by which time Martha was in Bata-
via on her *Collier's* assignment. Ernest's return flight went back up
to Kunming, where a storm had most of the passengers vomiting,
and from there to Hong Kong, which was socked in with a two hun-
dred-foot ceiling. Three times the pilot tried to land before finding
a way down to the tiny landing strip across the bay.[10] Five days later
Ernest was in Manila awaiting passage on one of the transpacific
flying boats. While there he reported to the Army Intelligence team
for debriefing. On May 13, he had gotten as far as Guam, where the
plane landed to refuel and rest the pilots. The next day they took
off for Wake Island, but four hours later at the point of no return,
they turned back because headwinds were too strong: they did not
have enough fuel to reach Wake. On May 16, they launched once
more for Wake, refueled, and rested long enough for Ernest to get
sunburned on that tiny wishbone before continuing on to Midway,
where rough weather almost grounded them. Finally they reached
Hawaii, where there was another two-day break before flying on to
San Francisco. By the time he set foot on American soil, Hemingway
had spent twelve days crossing six thousand miles of the Pacific.[11]

In June 1941, when Hemingway's stories were featured in *PM*, a
majority of his American readers were unconcerned with the war in
China and deeply opposed to sending U.S. troops, planes, or ships
to the European War.[12] Charles Lindbergh told an America First

rally in Chicago that Britain had already lost the war; on university campuses college students were holding "peace" rallies and strikes against participation in a foreign war. The American Youth Congress heralded the demonstrations as evidence of student opposition to Roosevelt's plan for convoying ships to rescue England and Russia. The Youth Committee Against War said, "Mr. President, we hold you to your pledge against involvement. Convoys mean a shooting war. We oppose war."[13]

Isolationist or aggressive, the nation's eyes were focused on England, not China. Hemingway's analysis of the four-year Sino-Japanese War did not turn many heads, but it was extremely accurate. He said that an American war in the Pacific would begin when Japan attacked the Philippines, or the Dutch East Indies, or Malaysia. "But the real reason for fighting Japan will be that if she moves south in the Pacific, she will be attacking the control of the world supply of rubber." No rubber, no tires; no tires, no trucks or airplanes. But there were other needs that would drive the Japanese south: Philippine iron ore and Dutch oil fields. At present, Japan's oil and iron were supplied by England and America. "Japan has not enough iron to manufacture armament and munitions. She has not enough oil to refine gasoline for her planes or to fuel her battleships. . . . If the U.S.A. and Great Britain shut off her gasoline and oil she would be forced to move south toward oil at once."[14] His analysis of Chiang Kai-shek's army was equally astute: with two million troops well armed and trained to fight defensively in the mountains where Japanese artillery and tanks were ineffective, the Chinese would fight as long as America supplied resources and money. But without a competent air force or an influx of serious artillery, Chiang would not be able to mount an offensive. Having seen the Chinese pilots fail miserably against the superior Japanese Air Force, Hemingway said, "Any real American aid . . . would have to include pilots."[15] When Hemingway's story ran in *PM*, General Claire Chennault was conducting closed and confidential briefings with the best military pilots in America, explaining his venture for a volunteer force to fly P-40 Tomahawks against the Japanese along the Burma Road. His band of adventurers, who would not fly their first missions until December 1941, became the legendary "Flying Tigers."[16]

In late May, Ernest and Martha were together once more in Washington, D.C., to be debriefed at the Office of Naval Intelligence (ONI) and to report to Secretary of the Treasury Henry Morgenthau. Hemingway emphasized the strategic importance of support to Chiang Kai-shek: a long ground war in China would engage a majority of the Japanese Army, delaying their drive into Southeast Asia and the Philippines. By building two less battleships and using the money to support the Chinese, America could buy a year's grace in the Pacific, enough time to build up the two-ocean navy so crucial to its national defense. Such a navy "can destroy any Eastern enemy . . . a powerful enough navy imposes its will without having to fight."[17]

At the time, he did not dwell on the issue of the communist presence in the war, but a month later, he wrote Morgenthau a six-page, single-spaced, typed letter detailing the conflict between the Kuomintang wing (Chiang Kai-shek) and the communists (Mao Tse-tung and Chou En-lai)—a conflict which he prophesied was going to produce a civil war unless a defensible geographic division of the huge country gave each side its own territory. The communists would continue fighting the Japanese, but they were also extending their sphere of influence, just as Chiang was doing. Chou En-lai, Hemingway reported, was brilliant, charming, and intelligent—the only communist with direct access to Chiang. In Chungking, "window-dressing" communists were allowed to move about freely; elsewhere they were hunted down and imprisoned, as were any liberals critical of Chiang's government. While Chiang said he wanted the communists to become part of a unified China, he also kept a large reserve army out of the front lines to contain the communists should they start a civil war.[18]

En route to Havana, Ernest and Martha stopped in Key West long enough for them to pick up the *Pilar* and Ernest's sons Patrick and Gregory for their summer vacation at the Finca. On June 6, Ernest was sitting on a familiar bar stool at Sloppy Joe's while the owner and close friend, Josie Russell, put his place in order before taking a fishing vacation with Hemingway in Cuba. Since their first trip to Havana in 1932, the two hard-drinking compatriots fished together for marlin every summer it was possible. Joe Russell, onetime rum-runner and now revered Key Wester, was immortalized by Hemingway in *To Have and Have Not* (1937). The local reporter caught Hemingway holding forth, but could not get him to talk about his China trip. "You see how it is, kid," Hemingway explained. "I'd like to give you this China story and let you write it, but it's coming out in *PM* Monday, and they'd call me a louse if I gave it away now." He and Josie planned to fish hard for six weeks, stopping only for a quick trip to New York to see the Joe Louis–Billy Conn heavyweight championship fight. "Louis may knock him out in a round and you're robbed," Ernest explained, "or it may turn into a battle you'll want to tell the kids about." What was he going to write next? "Well I can't say. No, it isn't about China, just about some of everything." Before sundown, Josie and Ernest were on the water for the night passage to Havana; Martha was in Miami with his sons catching the Pan-Am flight to meet the fishermen there the next morning.[19]

Josie and Ernest never made it to Madison Square Garden for the Joe Louis–Billy Conn fight, missing one of the "Brown Bomber's" most exciting title defenses. On June 21 in the *Pilar's* irregular log book, Hemingway wrote, "Mr. Josie died." The *Key West Citizen* gave more details:

> *Joe Russell . . . died at 3 o'clock yesterday afternoon in a Havana hospital. Ernest Hemingway . . . telephoned Joe Russell, Jr. here last night to tell him of his father's death. The elder Russell had gone into the hospital for a minor operation and was said to be recovering only a few hours before death came, apparently from a stroke.*[20]

Another death close to the bone, another reason not to look back. "Losing Mr. Josie was no fun for Mr. Josie," he told Pauline. "And I was riding with him somewhere in it all only should have protected him better and truly. Though he always had so much sense and judgment and so I didn't worry."[21] After assisting Russell's son with the paperwork involved in moving a dead body from Cuba to Key West, Hemingway kept his hurt to himself. The loss was an irreplaceable one. Josie Russell at fifty-one was the older brother Ernest never had, the drinking and fishing companion he needed, the salty, red-faced bootlegger who was the real thing.

Back at Finca Vigia, which Ernest had purchased outright with $12,500 of his money from Paramount Pictures before leaving for China, Martha and he faced the usual problems created by lengthy absences: a leaky roof here, a malfunctioning pump there—the housekeeping problems that neither relished. Yet there was plenty of ready money to pay for repairs, to loan to relatives, and to pay for a new Lincoln Continental convertible in August.[22] By the first of April, the Book-of-the-Month Club paid Scribner's for 252,000 copies of the novel, and Scribner's had sold another 239,000 copies. Although Ernest, as always, said he was disappointed his publisher had not pushed the book harder, his complaint was halfhearted.[23] The Hemingways' only financial worry was their joint income tax for 1941. Under the progressive tax rates, Ernest and Martha might owe 60–70 percent of their net income. He said his children, when asked what their father did in "Mr. Roosevelt's war," could say that he had paid for it.[24]

Another pressing problem was the mountain of unanswered mail that piled up during their trip. Martha hired a young woman, Patricia Cahill, two afternoons a week to take Ernest's dictation and type it up, but she proved to be very slow. One of her first letters was dictated to Ernest's younger brother, Leicester, for whom Ernest was a role model and hero. For Ernest, his twenty-six-year-old brother was a source of worry. A year earlier, Leicester and a British friend, Tony Jenkins, had sailed a leaky boat through the Caribbean in search of clandestine Nazi activity. The results of their amateur espionage, published in the *Baltimore Sun*, reported suspicious caches of diesel fuel which might one day be used for Nazi U-boats, furtive men who sounded a lot like fascists, and letters arriving in out-of-the-way places with German postmarks.[25] That diesel fuel was used by

most of the small freighters in the Caribbean did not keep the two spies from assuming it was destined for German U-boats. Sailing their schooner *Blue Stream* further into the maze of small islets, they heard waterfront gossip that in 1938 Germans scouted the uninhabited Miskito Keys, a perfect site for fuel dumps and anchorage for seaplanes, but the two "snoopers" found no hard evidence. Further down the coast, they thought they were propositioned to run fuel oil to a Nazi submarine. The offer came to naught, but for the two adventurers it "confirmed the fact that the Nazis have honeycombed the waterways and cays off the wildest and most remote part of Central America and can use their preparations at will in a Blitzkrieg of the Caribbean."[26] In a Puerto Rico post office, they discovered ahead of them in line two men speaking German. "One received mail with the postmark Berlin, the other Dusseldorf."[27]

Ernest was less than impressed with the feature stories, realizing how thin the evidence and how inexperienced Leicester was as reporter or spy. Trying to find his brother some employment, Ernest set up an interview for him with the Office of Naval Intelligence in Washington, where Leicester worked in radio intelligence for the next two years. Worried that he might not understand the difference between newspaper journalism and intelligence work, Ernest advised him to control his imagination, stick to verifiable facts, and not try to interpret them until he was fully trained.[28]

In late July, when it was obvious that Ernest's stenographer was far too slow, Martha wrote her friend in Havana, Jane Armstrong, at the American Consulate, who found a replacement; but at the end of August the new secretary, Miss Sherbine, was forced to return to the States.[29] One of the last letters she typed was Hemingway's angry response to his Scribner royalty statement where he found that he was bearing the entire legal cost of a spurious plagiarism suit, a deduction Hemingway felt should be shared by his publisher. He closed the letter questioning Edmund Wilson's *The Wound and the Bow* analysis of his fiction, saying he could not tell what his purported wound actually was, but he had a helluva bow, and when he wrote his memoirs, Wilson would get its full effect.[30] Eight years ear-

lier, smarting from Gertrude Stein's portrait of him in *The Autobiography of Alice B. Toklas*, Hemingway had threatened to set the record straight with his own memoirs "when I can't write anything else."[31]

That summer of 1941, Hemingway was a writer without a book to write, for he had used up most of his material from the 1930s—Key West, Africa, Spain—and he did not know enough about China to use it as a setting for anything beyond journalism. Four days earlier, Martha told Jane Armstrong that Ernest was on the edge of writing his memoirs, but the word—memoirs—put him off. Too pretentious. Martha suggested calling it something else and get on with it, but evidently the time was not right. She was certain the book would eventually be written.[32] Using his own experiences, a writer gets his first two or three books free before his writing catches up to the present moment. After that, he has to create his fiction based on the lives of others and his own imagination. Hemingway's readers and critics thought that his fiction came straight from his own life, which was only true for large parts of *The Sun Also Rises*, less of *A Farewell to Arms* and some of his early stories. His 1930s fiction was set in places he knew well, but the characters were never himself, and the plots were all invented. Never having been a bootlegger, never having killed anyone, never having been gut-shot, he was not the one-armed tough guy, Harry Morgan, in *To Have and Have Not*. Never having been a counterespionage agent in Madrid, he was not Philip Rawlings in *The Fifth Column*, nor was he ever Robert Jordan in *For Whom the Bell Tolls*. Since finishing the manuscript for the *Bell*, a year had passed in which he had written nothing but the feature stories for *PM*. Now, in the August heat of the tropics, he was sweltering in that purgatory reserved for writers with no idea of what to write next.

When Ernest was irritable, nothing went right in his near vicinity, particularly his relationship with Martha. At some point in the summer, he left her an in-house note quoting Rilke: "'Love consists in this, that two solitudes protect and touch and greet each other.'" He suggested that they begin again to be the friends they knew they could be.[33] Through the humid Cuban summer, while Martha put

finishing touches to her collection of stories, *The Heart of Another*, Ernest's predictions about the coming of a Pacific war appeared less theoretical as America's neutrality became more fictional each week. The public might want to avoid war, but their president and Congress, using massive deficit appropriations, were arming the nation as quickly as possible. The Selective Service program for a peacetime draft was in place for all men between twenty-one and twenty-eight, and the Army Air Force was recruiting pilots to man its newly acquired planes. While the East Coast worried about German air raids should war erupt, and the FBI made headlines arresting German spies, the potential war in the Pacific edged closer. On July 24, President Roosevelt suggested that the United States might stop selling oil to Japan. By August 1, the new Gallup Poll said 51 percent of Americans favored checking Japanese expansion in the Pacific even if it meant war. In midsummer, Pan-American pilots began ferrying American-built bombers to England, and Roosevelt froze all Japanese assets in the United States, warning Japan, whose army now occupied Saigon, to stop its expansion in Southeast Asia. Surreptitiously and apparently without the president's knowledge, Assistant Secretary of State Dean Acheson imposed a de facto embargo on oil being sold to Japan. What followed was now inevitable.[34]

With his usual emotional mood swing toward moroseness following a book's publication, Hemingway was more angry with his publisher than his president. Despite the enthusiastic reviews of *For Whom the Bell Tolls*, Hemingway focused on the handful of critical responses. When the Pulitzer Prize Committee announced there would be no award in fiction for 1940, Hemingway acted as if it did not matter to him: "If I'd won that prize," he said, "I'd think I was slipping. I've been writing for twenty years and never have won a prize. I've gotten along all right."[35] But beneath the nonchalance he presented to the world was an ego as fragile as any writer's: the prize did matter, but not in public.

In case Max Perkins and Charlie Scribner had missed his point earlier about his anger over the legal costs of the false plagiarism suit, on the last day of August, Ernest repeated it in a lengthy night telegram, ending it:

TELL CHARLIE IF HE NEEDS ANY MONEY WILL BE GLAD TO LOAN IT TO HIM RATHER THAN HAVE HIM STEAL IT FROM ME AND IN THE END WE WOULD BE BETTER FRIENDS AND HE WOULD HAVE MORE MONEY.

The next morning, he sent another telegram asking Max and Charlie to disregard what he said.[36] The issue was past, but not forgotten; it would continue to flare up in Hemingway letters for the next three months. Within days of sending the telegrams, Ernest and Martha headed north for Sun Valley, where Toby Bruce was waiting for them with Ernest's newly purchased "paradise green" Lincoln convertible.

Like the migratory birds he loved to hunt, Hemingway, when unimpeded by events beyond his control, moved with the seasons: spring through late summer there was marlin fishing in the Gulf Stream; in the fall, bird hunts in the West; then warm winters at the Finca. By the time Ernest and Martha reached Sun Valley that September, the coming of war hung like a shroud across the country. In his Labor Day radio broadcast to the nation, President Roosevelt pledged that "we shall do everything in our power to crush Hitler and his Nazi forces." Three days later, a German U-boat fired two torpedoes at the U.S. destroyer *Greer*. On September 11, Roosevelt ordered the Navy to destroy on sight any hostile submarines or surface raiders found "in the waters which we deem necessary for our defense." Those waters now extended in the Atlantic as far as Iceland, and in the Pacific all the way to the Philippines.

Chapter Fourteen

VOYAGERS

<hr>

September 1941 to Christmas 1942

ALL THAT FALL, Ernest and Martha lived at Sun Valley, once again nonpaying guests of the resort, along with several Hollywood faces. Robert Montgomery and his wife, Barbara Stanwyck, were something of a disappointment to Ernest. Montgomery was too tiny to be taken seriously, Hemingway said, and Stanwyck, his "tough mick" wife, was ugly, but nice and intelligent.[1] Gary and Rocky Cooper, director Howard Hawks and his stunning wife, Slim, were there at Ernest's request so that Hawks and Cooper might discuss the possibility of Hawks directing Cooper in the filming of *For Whom the Bell Tolls*. Cooper was as "aw shucks" plain as ever, a good man in the field and around the table afterward. Slim Hawks was something else: young, beautiful, and attracted to Ernest in what she thought of as a nonsexual way. "I had never known anyone so intelligent," she explained. "His mind was like a light . . . illuminating corners in your own head that you didn't even know were there. He had a tremendous influence on my thinking, my literary taste, my enjoyment of things simple and open, my recognition of and distaste for pomposity." She found the physical side of Ernest less attractive. Wearing the same clothes for days in a row,

Ernest never seemed quite clean to her, a chronic female complaint since his high school days when potential dates complained that his fingernails were never clean and his hair unkempt.[2]

Other guests included Robert Capa, whose camera seemed to follow Hemingway; Leland Hayward, a prominent Hollywood agent; and his wife, the actress Margaret Sullavan. There were dances and parties at Trail Creek Cabin, gambling at the rough tables in Ketchum, and bountiful hunts of whatever was in season—antelope in the Pahsimeroi Mountains, ducks on Silver Creek, pheasant at Dietrich. Hemingway's three visiting sons were pampered by Martha, went hunting with Ernest, and returned to their respective mothers. Elsewhere, the world was moving inexorably toward the war Ernest told his hunting companions would begin in the Pacific. "We'll probably get it for a Christmas present," he said. "Or maybe wake up New Year's morning with an unshakable hangover."[3] On October 30, the U.S. destroyer *Reuben James*, on convoy duty off Iceland, was sunk by German torpedoes, killing a hundred American sailors. On November 1, without revealing their secret December 1 deadline, the Japanese warned that if the United States did not halt its economic blockade, Japan would seek vital resources farther south.

On October 27, Martha's book *The Heart of Another* was published by Scribner's under her own name—not as Martha Hemingway, as Ernest asked, although it was copyrighted by Martha Gellhorn Hemingway.[4] Ernest worried over the book like an expectant father, advising their mutual editor, Max Perkins, on the contract, design, and marketing, taking the dust jacket photo of Martha himself. Reviewers, who generally liked the collection of stories, were all too quick to see the Hemingway influence, which Martha seemed to accept as fair response. Early in their relationship, Martha, who was no novice, was open to Hemingway's paternal instruction; later she deeply resented his saying that she was now the writer in the family and he her manager.

Between hunts and children, Hemingway took time to read Scott Fitzgerald's posthumously published *The Last Tycoon*, edited in its unfinished condition by Edmund Wilson, and published with as much fanfare as Scribner's could muster. Stephen Vincent Benét's review advised, "You can take off your hats now, gentlemen, I think perhaps you had better. This is not a legend, this is a reputation— and, seen in perspective, it may well be one of the most secure reputations of our time."[5] Hemingway, however, could find little good to say about the almost novel or the short stories that Wilson included in the volume. He told Perkins that Scott "still had the technique and the romance of doing anything, but all the dust was off the butterfly's wing for a long time even though the wing would still move until the butterfly was dead."[6]

Hemingway was somewhat rankled that Fitzgerald, once his close friend, was entering the literary pantheon to the beat of such memorial drums. The *New Republic*'s "In Memory of Scott Fitzgerald"—a collection of authors' anecdotes—was extended over two issues, featuring John Dos Passos, Budd Schulberg, John O'Hara, and Glenway Wescott, among others, remembering poignant Fitzgeraldean moments. Wescott's rather long and self-promoting essay repaid Hemingway for his satirical portrait of Wescott in *The Sun Also Rises*. Recalling the early days in Paris, Wescott described a conversation with Fitzgerald when Scott was urging Hemingway on all his acquaintances:

> *Hemingway had published some short stories in the dinky deluxe way in Paris; and I along with all the literary set had discovered him, which was fun; and when we returned to New York we preached the new style and peculiar feeling of his fiction as if it were evangel. Still, that was too slow a start of a great career to suit Fitzgerald. Obviously Ernest was the one true genius of our decade, he said. . . . What could I do to help launch Hemingway . . . my enthusiasm was not on a par with his; and looking back now, I am glad for my sake that it was not.*[7]

By the time Wescott wrote this piece, he was no longer a promising young writer, and Hemingway's own reputation had taken on a life of its own. In 1941, eight anthologies reprinted eight different

Hemingway stories, several with apparatus for study. In November, Robert Penn Warren requested reprint permission for "The Killers," which, along with a stunning interpretation, would be part of an influential college text, *Understanding Fiction* (1943).[8] In his mid-November letter to Max Perkins, Hemingway offhandedly said he could not come to New York for the Limited Editions Club award to him of their Gold Medal for fiction. On the same day he apologized at some length to Sinclair Lewis for not being able to attend the ceremony where Lewis would make the presentation, but promised that Scribner's would provide a stenographer to record the event. Never having had any awards for his writing, he said this one made him feel "damn good," especially when a writer whom he admired, like Lewis, was one of the judges.[9]

But he did not tell Lewis that it was almost as difficult for him to accept public adulation as it was to bear critical attacks. In Oak Park, where Ernest grew up, they said that "praise to the face was open disgrace." Yet when Max Perkins failed to have the requested stenographer at the award ceremony, Ernest was furious and hurt, saying he wanted never to see the medal. Instead it should go to Scribner's to remind the firm how carelessly and callously they had treated him. It would have been useful to have reprinted Lewis's speech as a pamphlet, but now that would never happen. He would never read the speech. His children would never see it. Nothing his publisher might now do would mollify him.[10]

By the time he wrote those letters, the December 7 Japanese carrier attack on Pearl Harbor had sent the heart of the United States Pacific Fleet to the bottom of the bay. The USS *Arizona* along with seven other battleships and ten other naval vessels were sunk or badly damaged. Hickam Field and its aircraft were bombed out, and bloody Scofield Barracks was filled with wounded Marines. As the smoke cleared, two hundred American planes were smoldering and three thousand men were dead or wounded. The war that had been blowing in the wind since November 1919, the war consuming most of Europe and half of the Pacific Rim, that war was now sitting down to breakfast all across America. Whatever plans people had for next year were

as useless as the *Arizona*. Young men, whose president once promised they would never die on foreign soil, were about to leave home,
many for the first and last time. Their sweethearts would receive letters from Army Post Offices; their parents, telegrams beginning: "We
regret to inform you." Americans would learn a new vocabulary, a new
set of values; new icons would become part of their collective memory. New graveyards would be arranged in exotic places; new songs
would echo forever in the heads of the survivors, along with images too
hard to bear. The intensity of the next four years would reduce the two
decades between wars to vague memories and faded photographs. The
generation who came of age with the Great European War (1914–18)
was leading its children into another one, a war that would once more
change the surface of American society.

In time for Christmas, Ernest and Martha returned to Finca
Vigia, which Martha continued to resuscitate from its fallen state,
and where both writers, as soon as their joint tax returns were finished, began new work.[11] Centered on a young Caribbean girl, Liana,
whose beauty was both her power and her misfortune, Martha characterized her work as "a simple unambitious novel, just a story about
some people on a small Caribbean island. It has nothing to do with
the war or with current events."[12] Ernest was working on two long
short stories, which he interrupted to write an introduction for a
Crown Publishers collection of fiction and nonfiction to be called
Men at War. What started as a simple task became more complicated
when he disagreed with many of the selections, insisting that some
be dropped, others added. In New York, Max Perkins began making suggestions, and Hemingway's military friends—Colonel Charles
Sweeny and Marine Colonel John Thomason at the Office of Naval
Intelligence—also became involved. Before the book was completed,
Ernest was grousing that Scribner's should have published the book
so they could have made some money on it; instead, the collection
was his first contribution to the war effort, a "weapon" that might "do
some good."[13] Without referencing Archie MacLeish's charge that
his fiction had undermined the values of his 1920s readers, Ernest
was putting his shoulder to the war wheel as best he could.

Using quotations from Karl von Clausewitz's *On War* for his thematic divisions of the anthology, Hemingway's finished selection would open with Julius Caesar's invasion of Britain and close with the Battle of Midway (June 1942). In between there were over a thousand pages of fiction, history, and firsthand accounts of what war can do to the warrior. Several of the selections were double-edged, not only telling about man's experience in battle but also telling Hemingway's readers something about his own writing. Having written crucial parts of *A Farewell to Arms* from secondary sources, Hemingway included all of Stephen Crane's *Red Badge of Courage*, his precursor for creating believable fiction out of research. Juxtaposed with Livy's classic account of "Horatio at the Bridge" he placed his own account of El Sordo's last stand in *For Whom the Bell Tolls*. In a left-handed acknowledgment of sources, Hemingway reprinted T. E. Lawrence's description of blowing up a train in *Seven Pillars of Wisdom*, a book that echoes throughout the *Bell*. After calling attention to Fabrizio's experience at Waterloo in Stendhal's *Charterhouse of Parma*, he placed Victor Hugo's "Waterloo" up against Frederic Henry's retreat from Caporetto in *A Farewell to Arms*.[14] These selections and their placement were not accidental. By juxtaposing his work with that of Tolstoy, Stendhal, Lawrence, and Crane, Hemingway set the terms of the competition, asking to be judged against the best of the best.

Still seething from the so-called Allies' refusal to help Loyalist Spain in its heartbreaking fight against the fascist rebels, Hemingway made his political position as clear as possible:

> The editor of this anthology, who took part and was wounded in the last war to end war, hates war and hates all the politicians whose mismanagement, gullibility, cupidity, selfishness and ambition brought on the present war and made it inevitable. But once we have a war there is only one thing to do. It must be won.[15]

As much about the responsibility of the writer as about the effects of war, Hemingway's introduction was personal and blunt:

The last war . . . was the most colossal, murderous, mismanaged
butchery that has ever taken place on earth. Any writer who said
otherwise lied . . . writers who were established before the war
had nearly all sold out to write propaganda during it . . . a writer
should be of as great probity and honesty as a priest of God. He is
either honest or not . . . after one piece of dishonest writing . . .
which he knows in his inner self is not true, for no matter what
patriotic motives, then he is finished. . . . And he will never be
at peace with himself because he has deserted his one complete
obligation.[16]

Reviewers found Hemingway's personal commentary and lecturing
discursive and badly put together, but they were unaware of its sub-
text. Already Hemingway was being asked why he was not involved
with the war effort. In a defensive response to a *Time* magazine journalist who wanted to know what he was doing to help America win
the war, Hemingway said only his children had the right to ask such a
question.[17] It was to those three sons—John, Patrick, and Gregory—
that *Men at War* was dedicated.

All across America, men and women were asking the same question of themselves. Men, draftees or volunteers, were being trained
in sometimes tedious routines and physical drills, preparing them
for the invasion of beaches months away. As the government took
more and more control of Americans' daily lives through rationing,
blackouts, air-raid drills, and volunteer programs, housewives began
saving bacon fat in coffee cans for the nitrates that would eventually
become part of war-bound ammunition; their husbands, by day, sub-
scribed to war bond drives, pledging part of their monthly salaries; at
night they worked as air-raid wardens; their children collected tinfoil
and scrap iron. Then the whole family helped dig up the side yard for
the "Victory Garden," trading fresh corn with the neighbor who was
raising pullets.

All through the summer of 1942, while Ernest was rearranging
the contents and writing the introduction for *Men at War*, the war
was close at hand, but he had no way to get to it. Too old for the

draft, too controversial for the government, and too far from Key West, his options were limited. In April, the U.S. Marines at Bataan surrendered to the Japanese Army, the worst U.S. military humiliation since the Sioux destroyed Custer. In May, the German plan of Admiral Doenitz, Operation Drumbeat, began its attack on the American pipeline of war material flowing to England and Russia. Knowing how crucial oil, gasoline, and aviation fuel were to fighting a war, the German U-boat commanders focused on three refining centers: Aruba in the Caribbean; and New Orleans and Houston in the Gulf of Mexico. Knowing that without bauxite there was no aluminum, without aluminum no airplanes, the German raiders also centered on the British and Dutch Guianas, which then produced most of the ore in the western hemisphere.

On the evening of February 16, at the entrance to Lake Maracaibo, where Venezuelan crude oil came across the bar in shallow draft tankers to be refined at Aruba, it was a calm, warm night. At the Lago refinery on Aruba, the graveyard shift came to work with the night lights fully lit and flare gas burning. Each month this refinery, the world's largest, was producing 7.1 million barrels of gasoline, aviation fuel, and lubricants, most of which was going to support the British war effort. At 1:30 a.m. in a coordinated attack German U-boats turned seven tankers into burning hulks, shelled the refinery with surface guns, and left without a scratch on their gray hulls. Observing the smoking ruins the next morning, the Chinese crews refused to sail without protection, forcing the refinery to shut down and Lake Maracaibo oil production to stop, having no more storage space. Nineteen ships went down that month in the Caribbean; nineteen more the next month; eleven in April; thirty-eight in May. Between February and November 1942, almost twice as many ships were sunk in this confined area as were sunk on the North Atlantic convoy routes. By the end of November 1942, 263 ships were on the bottom of the Caribbean Sea.[18]

To enter the Gulf of Mexico, the U-boats had only three routes, all of them narrow and thus dangerous: the Straits of Florida, the Old Bahama Channel at the northeast end of Cuba, and the

Yucatan Channel at the southwest end of the island (see map). Once safely into the hunting ground, the German subs found little effective opposition. The U.S. Navy's Gulf Sea Frontier Command had only recently implemented a convoy system between Key West and Norfolk, Virginia, for which it had minimal protection. American antisubmarine warfare (ASW) was on-the-job training.[19] Because of news censorship, the general population never knew the extent of the losses at their peak, nor when the losses slackened.

By May 1, the submarine threat was so intense in the Gulf of Mexico that all shipping was stopped along the north coast of Cuba until convoys could be established.[20] Seventeen days later, a further order came down from the Naval Commander of the Gulf Sea Frontier: "Movements are stopped between Gulf or Caribbean ports and U.S. Atlantic Coast . . . and from Gulf and Caribbean ports to east coast of South America."[21] In those first eight months of 1942, when attack ships and planes were few and their crews inexperienced with new electronic gear, U-boat commanders were earning Iron Crosses on every trip west. Although Havana and other Cuban ports did not contribute to the tanker traffic, the island, which barricaded a major section of the Gulf, had primary shipping lanes on all sides. In June and July 1942, over thirty ships were torpedoed within easy reach of the Cuban coast. No longer an American protectorate, the coming of war put Cuba's neutrality in a precarious position, which it swiftly resolved in its own best interests by declaring war against the Axis powers and cooperating with the U.S. antisubmarine efforts. Quickly, small tent outposts were established on remote islands and keys off the north coast to support U. S. Navy seaplanes and to act as supply bases when antisubmarine cutters were in the area. By mid-April, Army Air Force planes using bases in Cuba were patrolling the Yucatan and Old Bahama Channels by day and later by night.

Initially undermanned and outplanned, the United States did what Americans have always done best: it improvised solutions with whatever materials were at hand. Less than a month into the war, the Coast Guard began organizing East Coast yachtsmen and small boat owners into auxiliary units. Larger private sail- and motor-driven ships were "rented" at a dollar a year for submarine patrols in coastal waters.[22] In late June, with ships being sunk at unsustainable rates, the Navy took desperate measures:

> *Washington, June 27 (AP)—In a move to put a great fleet of small boats into the war against submarines off the Atlantic and Gulf coasts, the navy called today for all owners of seagoing craft to volunteer the services of themselves and their vessels. . . . Approximately 1,200 small boats are in such service now . . . [and] it is hoped that upward of 1,000 additional small boats for offshore navigation may be added to the auxiliary. . . . Boats found to be qualified will be equipped with radio, armament and suitable anti-submarine devices as rapidly as possible.[23]*

Soon the recruitment for the auxiliary patrol was intensified. Secretary of the Navy Frank Knox issued a call for "patriotic yachtsmen and small-boat owners" to come to the aid of their country, offering them

> *the opportunity which they have been so earnestly seeking: to serve their country and combat its enemies in the sea-going manner for which their experience fits them. . . . These boats are needed right now—not only for . . . Harbor Patrol duties but for actual offensive operations against enemy submarines.[24]*

By the time Secretary Knox issued his plea, Ernest Hemingway's private war against the U-boats was well underway.

From his reading about World War I Q-ships, Ernest saw immediately the possibilities for an armed auxiliary boat the size of the *Pilar* patrolling as a fishing craft. If such a secretly armed ship could lure a German submarine to the surface, it might be able to get in the first shot, crippling the raider.[25] Early in the war, German submarines operating in the Caribbean and the Gulf of Mexico were, in fact, liable to attack on the surface, using their deck guns to conserve torpedoes. The long-range Type-XI U-boat common in the Gulf was formidably armed for surface combat: a primary 105mm deck gun, a 37mm auxiliary gun, and two 20mm machine guns.[26] On May 2, Ernest read in the local paper of a running battle between a lightly armed tanker and a U-boat off the north coast of Cuba. Attacking on the surface with its deck gun, the submarine sank the tanker after a two-hour exchange of fire.[27]

The only impediment to Hemingway's joining the auxiliary was his location, Cuba, where no such opportunity existed. The island-nation was at war with the Axis powers—Germany, Japan, and Italy—and the Fulgencio Batista government cooperated with the United States, barring Axis nationals from entering Cuba and interning aliens on the Isle of Pines. The Cuban Navy and Air Force, using obsolete American ships and aircraft, were patrolling Cuban territorial waters, but that did not mean that an American national, not even Ernest Hemingway, could form his own auxiliary under the Cuban flag. Nor, of course, had Hemingway any intention of going to war under the Cuban flag. Instead, he worked through the American Embassy, where First Secretary Robert Joyce was helpful in putting Ernest and his fishing boat *Pilar* into the war effort; but it took several months for the idea to become reality.

About this same time, the new American ambassador to Cuba, Spruille Braden, became worried about the loyalties of the 300,000 Spanish residents of Cuba, as many as 10 percent of whom were thought to be dedicated Falangists and therefore potential sources of aid to the Nazi cause. Until the FBI could find the right men for the Havana station, Braden recruited Hemingway to organize a make-shift intelligence service, which Ernest set to enthusiastically. As Braden remembered it, Hemingway "enlisted a bizarre combination of Spaniards: some bar tenders; a few wharf rats; some down-at-heel pelota players and former bullfighters; two Basque priests; assorted exiled counts and dukes; several Loyalists and Francistas. He built up an excellent organization and did an A-One job."[28]

Although Martha and others thought the "Crook Factory" something of a joke, the new Ambassador Braden thought Ernest's reports on the activities of Spanish Falangists in Cuba significant enough to include them almost verbatim in several long reports to the State Department.[29] The crucial diplomatic question was, what would Cuba do if Franco's Spain joined the Axis in the war?—a very real possibility given the German-Italian support of Franco's successful rebellion. In October 1942, Spruille Braden's cogent review of the Cuban situation documented the Spanish Embassy's clandestine support of the Falange, which was generating Axis rumors and propaganda. There was also the strong possibility that the Falangists were gathering information on military installations, communicating with and refueling German U-boats, and planning and executing "attempts at sabotage." Despite being outlawed by the Cuban government, the pro-Nazi Falange was both active and dangerous to American interests.[30]

Ernest's long-standing fascination with spies and counterspies was, for this brief period, completely in synch with prevalent American war fears. America was a nation on edge, expecting the worst. When crude sound detection gear picked up what seemed to be two flights of unidentified aircraft, the entire San Francisco Bay area was blacked out all the way to Sacramento for almost an hour. When Jacob Steinberg's lights failed on the Williamsburg Bridge, he made the mistake of stopping his truck. Unable to fix them, he continued on toward his Brooklyn home, never hearing the warning whistle from the soldier on guard duty at the bridge. Jacob did hear the five warning shots, however, one of which flattened a tire, another almost hitting him. In Indiana, the Civilian Defense Headquarters was asked by a county official, "Would it be possible to have a bomb dropped in our county to have the people realize this country is at war?" He was told, "We're saving all bombs for Tokyo."[31] On June 13, the fears became a reality when a Nazi U-boat landed four saboteurs on the south shore of Long Island. Four days later, another group of German agents was put ashore close to Jacksonville, Florida. On June 27, J. Edgar Hoover, head of the FBI, called a late evening news conference to announce all eight agents were under arrest, their caches of explosives recovered, and the safety of the nation for the moment assured. Their objectives, he said, were the bridges leading into Manhattan, three major aluminum plants, the New York City water supply, the hydroelectric plant at Niagara Falls, and key rail centers. Shortly after noon on August 7, six of the eight German agents were executed in a portable electric chair installed at the District of Columbia jail.[32] By the time the saboteurs were dead, 250 enemy aliens, many of them naturalized American citizens, were in jail, charged with various subversive goals, most particularly blowing up the Pennsylvania Railroad's horseshoe curve outside Altoona.[33] And the British-Honduran businessman suspected of refueling German U-boats in the Caribbean and smuggling spies into the Panama Canal Zone was arrested by the U.S. Navy at sea.[34]

With its large international population, its critical location, and its long history of revolutionary activity, Cuba was not immune to the war fears on the mainland. In April, the *Havana Post* reported that "almost fifty Germans, Italians and Japanese were rounded up and arrested in a swift and simultaneous action by agents of the Enemy Activities Section of the Cuban Bureau of Investigation. . . . [charged with] espionage and other illicit activities on behalf of the Axis powers . . . most of those arrested are on the U.S. blacklist." Among those arrested were several associated with the German spy ring at Nuevitas, "from which port several freighters have departed during recent weeks and been later sunk by enemy subs off the Cuban coast."[35] On July 14, as Hemingway's "Crook Factory" was being formed, the FBI sent Raymond Leddy to the Havana embassy as an attaché to replace the FBI agent who could not "tell fact from rumor."[36]

On June 26, all three of Hemingway's sons—Jack (eighteen), Patrick (thirteen), and Gregory (eleven)—arrived on the Pan-Am flight in time for Patrick's fourteenth birthday two days later. Martha at thirty-three—blond, lithesome, and lovely—was more like an older sister than a stepmother. For Jack, still called "Bumby" or "Bum" by his father, Martha was his second stepmother, replacing Pauline Pfeiffer, the mother of his two stepbrothers. Having hunted with her at Sun Valley the previous fall, all three sons seemed at ease around this lovely woman who treated them with unaffected kindness and amazed them with her ability to say "fuck" in a way so ordinary as to be inoffensive. They were also impressed with the renovations she had made at the Finca. When she found the farm in 1939, it was overgrown with weeds and badly in need of repairs. After Ernest bought the house and property, Martha had refurbished the six large and airy rooms into a tropical haven.[37] Ceiling fans moved the humid air, cool in the morning, warm by noon. Slowly, Martha came to accept the constant battle with the insect life. Through open windows came the *comejen*, a flying white ant with a termite's taste for wood. The *traza*, small and wormlike, preferred books, silks, and linens, while out of the bread box trailed a company of small, mahogany-colored ants. In an effort to disrupt if not control the ant problem, small cans of kerosene were placed under the legs of stoves and cupboards. Compounded by mosquitoes in several sizes, scorpions, tarantulas, and centipedes, the insect war was never won, nor was it ever finished.[38]

As Jack remembered that summer, the Finca's swimming pool was filled and functioning; next to it was the crushed coral tennis court, and at the front of the house, "an enormously old ceiba tree . . . with its large, high-reaching roots extending from the bulbous trunk like sinuous flying buttresses of smooth, gray bark. Many orchid plants live on its trunk and among its broad branches." Greg remembered the view from the hilltop, the lights of Havana seen in the night, and the lush greenery and tropical flowers where hummingbirds made their nests.[39] With a cook taking care of meals, a driver for the three cars (Plymouth, Buick, and Lincoln), tennis matches, live pigeon shoots, and deep-sea fishing on the *Pilar*, summertime life at the Finca was a boy's dream.

For Martha, that summer at the Finca may have been a dream, but not a completely pleasant one. On the tennis court with her stepsons or at the Floridita for supper, she was perfectly delightful, but beneath the surface her impatience with the war, with the slow Cuban life, and with her stalled novel festered. As she told Eleanor Roosevelt, the president's wife and her close friend, she needed to understand the characters better. She also needed to get away from the Finca, where she was the designated housekeeper, a role that held no joy for her. As she said later, "During that terrible year, 1942, I lived in the sun, safe and comfortable and hating it."[40]

Martha was an incurable traveler who preferred road life to home life, not unlike Ernest. If she had to be at home, she wanted more solitude than the Finca provided that summer. Hemingway's three sons crowded the six-room house; his coterie of Basque jai alai players were constant visitors; the butler, the cook, and the gardener needed continuous attention in a language she could not speak well; and the Crook Factory, with its overly dramatic secrecy and its operatives arriving at the Finca at all hours, was an impediment to her writing.[41] What she had not understood about Ernest during their four-year affair was his need to assemble groups to participate in the activity du jour: fishing in Michigan; skiing in Austria; bullfights in Spain; marlin fishing in the Gulf Stream; hunting in Wyoming—whatever his seasonal interest, it required a loyal group of fellow travelers, preferably one or two of whom required mentoring. That summer he was teaching his sons the finer points of wing-shooting live pigeons, the rituals of the cockfights, and the intricacies of betting on the jai alai matches.

What Ernest did not understand, or appreciate, about Martha was her need sometimes to be alone, sometimes to follow her instinctive impulse to be at the heart of the action elsewhere. In 1938, leaving Ernest in Paris, she had struck out to cover the Nazi takeover of Czechoslovakia, barely making the last flight out of Prague with her story. During Christmas 1939, she left Ernest at Sun Valley to cover the war in Finland. As biographer Bernice Kert has written:

> *When she was away she longed for him. When she was home she found it difficult to put up with his exasperating habits. At the same time she scolded him for not bathing, or for drinking too much, or for telling some silly lie about his exploits, she would make an impressive effort with his sons, his cats, his parties, his guests. When nothing changed she boiled up with frustration and knew only one way out, to get away for a while.*[42]

Soon after the arrival of the Hemingway sons, Martha, needing respite from being Mrs. Hemingway, reverted to Martha Gellhorn journalist at large, traveling albeit on Mrs. Hemingway's passport.

She convinced her *Collier's* editor to pay her expenses in the Caribbean for a series of articles on the effects of the submarine war. By July 20, she was writing Ernest a birthday greeting from Port-au-Prince, Haiti. For the next three months, she traveled the Caribbean by plane, motorboat, and sailing sloop during the heart of hurricane season; she fought off mosquitoes, rescued a cat, slept on plank floors, survived dengue fever, fractured her wrist, flew on a submarine patrol, was disappointed with a bauxite mine, and traveled by dugout canoe up a jungle river until she fell off the map.[43] She talked her way into and out of restricted areas, visited a French penal colony where the convicts, "dead-eyed skeletons in red and white striped pajamas, cut wood in the jungle until they died of exhaustion and disease." But Martha never saw a submarine, never realized due to censorship how many ships were going down around her. For her three-month adventure, *Collier's* paid her expenses and bought two feature stories: one that detailed the poverty and squalor of Puerto Rico's poor; the other describing the boredom of American troops guarding an equally boring bauxite mine in Surinam.[44]

While she was gone, Ernest was the good father and even better companion to his sons, but he was also enlarging his counterintelligence activities to include sub patrols with the *Pilar*. On July 28, Ernest took young Patrick and Gregory with him as part of his crew to investigate alleged German sympathizers resupplying submarines out of nearby Matanzas. Part of the assignment included investigating a coastal cave reported to be a supply drop point. When the cave narrowed to the point that Winston Guest could not squeeze through, he sent Patrick and Gregory crawling back into the space where they found nothing at all—a false lead. But Ernest wrote Martha that they came close to intercepting a "tin fish."[45] Into August, while Martha continued on her Caribbean fact-finding trip, Ernest and his *Pilar* crew carried out short patrols within easy reach of Havana while they waited for clearance from Navy Intelligence to patrol around Cape San Antonio, the southern tip of Cuba. All through September and into October, they waited for orders that never came.

Finally in early October, with Martha not yet returned, Ernest and his crew began working with hand grenades, machine guns, and satchel charges on practice targets out in the Gulf Stream.[46] His first mate, Winston Guest, whom Ernest met on his 1933 African safari, had checked into the Hotel Nacional in early September, ostensibly to tend to his mining interests in Santa Clara.[47] At six foot five, "Wolfie" was an easygoing man, a ten-goal polo player, an excellent athlete, and a Columbia University law graduate. Like Hemingway's counterparts on the east coast of the United States, Ernest's objectives were basic: keeping track of coastal traffic, particularly small ships that might be refueling U-boats; investigating floating debris; and if possible locating U-boats on the surface. U-boats, however, rarely surfaced during the day, preferring the cover of darkness for their attacks and for the necessary recharging of batteries.

While accepting all of the objectives assigned to the coastal patrol, Hemingway was also dedicated to a risky plan of actually disabling a U-boat at sea. Without radar, sonar, or MAD gear, the *Pilar* could not patrol at night, nor could it locate a submerged submarine. The slight wooden structure of the fishing boat would not support the twin 50mm machine guns Ernest hoped to install, leaving him with only light machine guns for his crew and a bazooka incapable of penetrating a U-boat's conning tower. Undeterred, he hoped to arouse the curiosity of a German commander to the point he would surface to inspect the *Pilar*. If they could get close enough to the submarine, they would attack with grenades and light machine guns to clear the deck, and a satchel charge encased in a fire extinguisher would be tossed onto the conning tower and with luck down the open hatch, where its explosion would prevent the U-boat from submerging. Then by radio the *Pilar* would call in U.S. Navy cutters to finish the job. Highly risky, perhaps even suicidal, the plan was grounded in the reality that U-boats did sometimes stop small boats at sea to relieve them of fresh fruit and fish.

Ambassador Braden was sufficiently impressed with Ernest's counterintelligence efforts and his enthusiasm for the sub patrols that he "scrapped the regulations, got him what he wanted, and sent him on his way." Hemingway's uncanny ability to outdrink the ambassador and his guests also impressed Braden:

> [Hemingway] could consume an astonishing amount of liquor—any kind of liquor—without appearing to feel it. . . . I don't know how many cocktails we had before dinner; but Ernest didn't take cocktails, he took absinthe drip. During the dinner we had white and red wine, followed by champagne. When [the wives] . . . left the table, he ordered another bottle of champagne, just for the two of us. . . . [Afterward] I had highballs, but Ernest went back to his absinthe drip. And he remained cold sober.[48]

Or so it seemed to the ambassador, who was trying to hold his own.

FBI Agent Leddy reported to Washington that Hemingway convinced Ambassador Braden to finance "certain coastal patrol and investigative work on the south coast of Cuba." Braden had "acceded to HEMINGWAY's request for authority to patrol certain areas where submarine activity has been reported. . . . [censored] . . . he has secured from the Ambassador a promise that his crew members will be recognized as war casualties for the purposes of indemnification in the event any loss of life results from this operation."[49] Wary of Hemingway's clandestine activities, but not yet worried about them, Agent Leddy's main concern was keeping the bureau informed. Hemingway, as Leddy noted, had an abiding distrust of the FBI, dating back to early 1940 when the FBI charged several Americans with participating on the Loyalist side of the Spanish Civil War. In an August letter to his old friend and sometime poet, Evan Shipman, Ernest said he did not write "personal things because we are at war and anybody who thinks indiscreetly or criticizes in time of war adds to whatever dossiers or photostatted letters he has assimilated."[50] As his FBI dossier would one day reveal, Ernest did well to keep this advice in mind.

After a Washington, D.C., briefing with new American Ambassador Spruille Braden, Martha, back from her dangerous excursion, flew on to New York on October 11 for a medical checkup, a hair session at Elizabeth Arden's, lunch with Charlie Scribner, and a little shopping before returning to Washington to visit at the White House as Mrs. Roosevelt's guest. About this same time, Agent Leddy at the Havana embassy was writing a follow-up letter to Director Hoover about Ernest's counterintelligence activities:

> Of further interest in this matter is a visit of Mrs. ERNEST HEMINGWAY (the former MARTHA GELLHORN), to Washington . . . to be the personal guest of Mrs. ROOSEVELT . . . the Ambassador [Braden] outlined to her certain aspects of the intelligence situation in Cuba in order that she might convey the same, in personal conversation, to the President and Mrs. ROOSEVELT. This has specific reference to the Embassy's request for approval of financing by the American Government of internment and investigative programs brought out by the Cuban authorities.[51]

When Martha returned to the Finca at the end of October, she reported to Ernest the kinds of military gossip rampant in Washington and in Miami: wives and girlfriends who knew exactly when convoys were leaving, troops arriving, and airlifts to West Africa departing. Out of her conversations came a report to Spruille Braden detailing the lax security on the mainland. One friend gave her "the date that 150 U.S. bombing planes, loaded with U.S. troops, took off from Brazil to West Africa, and I believe he told me it was a daily occurrence."[52]

Each morning in November, Martha and Ernest ate breakfast with Gustavo Durán and his wife, Bonte, who were houseguests at the Finca. Durán, a former Loyalist officer and friend of both Hemingways, had been called in to take over the Crook Factory operation, leaving Ernest free to concentrate on changing the *Pilar* from a fishing boat into a Q-boat. All of which was immediately reported by Agent Leddy directly to J. Edgar Hoover.[53] Each morning at 6:30

a.m., planes took off from mainland bases and San Julien (Cuba), to begin their daily patrols of a body of water littered with the flotsam and jetsam from sunken ships, bombings, and convoy traffic. Up and down the trafficked channels, oil leaked from the bowels of old and new wrecks. The sea itself was littered with lost oars, fragments of cargo, loose mines, tattered life jackets, and empty life rafts with no story to tell.[54]

In newspapers and on the radio, the war on all fronts appeared desperate, its outcome in doubt. In fact, the war in Europe and the Pacific had, without full fanfare, reached turning points. Deep in Russia, the German Army was bleeding itself to death at the gates of Stalingrad. In the Pacific, the Japanese Navy was devastated at the Battle of Midway. In the Solomon Islands, U.S. Marines, despite heavy casualties, were taking the island of Guadalcanal away from Japanese defenders. On both fronts, counterintelligence was quietly changing the odds in favor of the Allies. At home, American code-crackers broke the Japanese Purple Code; in England, their counter-parts solved the German Enigma Code that directed its U-boat wolf packs. In the last four months of 1942, Germany lost almost fifty U-boats to Allied attack. Over the next five months, over one hun-dred U-boats were destroyed, and the Battle of the North Atlantic was all but finished.[55] In September, the trial of two German spies began in Havana. For both men, the death penalty was being asked. "One was making drawings of the new air base being built outside Havana. The other was arrested with a radio transmitter and secret codes." Both were found guilty, and one sentenced to die.[56]

While Ernest turned over his Crook Factory operation to Gustavo Durán, he was busy in Havana arranging for the voyage of the *Pilar*. Beginning his late morning in Havana at the Hotel Ambos Mundos to check his mail drop, he then walked a few doors up to the Ameri-can Consulate, later lunching at El Floridita with consulate friends, and perhaps finishing his rounds with a browse in the International Bookshop—all situated on Obispo Street. These conveniently grouped locales were his base of operations in those days of 1942, establishments where he was known on sight and where he trusted the proprietors. For drink and fresh seafood, Ernest most favored the golden-friezed Floridita, its metal shutters up, its eleven doors open to the busy street life. Inside the café overhead fans were turning, and the great mirrors behind the bar kept the room under observation from Hemingway's habitual seat at the left-hand corner of the bar where Constantino mixed the daiquiris. In those days before air conditioning, the only refrigerated part of the Floridita was the seafood display case, where one could choose fresh shrimp, crawfish, or stone crabs served with slices of tart lime and a small bowl of mayonnaise. The Floridita was a safe place to leave or pick up a message, use the phone, or listen to the waiter's report of curious Americans speaking fluent German.[57]

On November 2, Hemingway reported to Colonel Hayne Boyden at the U.S. Embassy that he and his crew were prepared to leave for a shakedown cruise no later than November 11, providing all the "materials" required arrived in time. Though her pirate black hull and newly painted dark green deck were out of the water for anti-fouling paint and a new stern bearing, the Pilar in four days would be ready for outfitting. It was vital, Hemingway said, that the training exercises with guns, grenades, and satchel charges be conducted in an area to the west of Havana if their first armed patrol was going to be along the northeast coast.[58] Four days later, with the Pilar still out of the water, a late tropical storm of near-hurricane strength came out of the Gulf, hitting Cuba broadside and delaying the final outfitting of his Q-boat at the Casablanca shipworks. Finally, on November 20, Hemingway; Winston Guest; Gregorio Fuentes, the cook and most experienced sailor; Pachi, the Basque jai alai player; and two other Cubans passed under the battlements guarding Havana Harbor, moved out into the Gulf Stream, and turned westward.

Nineteen days later, while anchored for lunch inside the Colorado Reef, the crew spotted a large, white-hulled ship moving rapidly eastward toward Havana, thick smoke pouring from her stacks. Identified as the Spanish ship Marques de Comillas, the freighter appeared in the Zeiss field glasses to have a smaller boat in tow. Keeping the ship under observation for forty-five minutes, Hemingway became suspicious as the *Comillas* appeared to slow down. At a trolling speed of seven knots, the *Pilar* moved into deeper water on a NNW course to close with the ship when she turned due east. At a distance of three miles, the smaller gray ship in tow seemed to be a submarine, which turned away from the *Comillas*, picked up speed, and quickly left the *Pilar* behind. Immediately their observation was reported via shortwave radio in code to the American Embassy in Havana.[59] From there it went to the Commander of the Gulf Sea Frontier, who requested Havana authorities to keep track of a possible spy arriving on the SS *Marques de Comillas* that afternoon, adding:

> *Lt. Dr. Duffy, Aide to the Naval Attaché Havana, advised that reliable parties reported to have observed the Marques de Comillas slow down and stop while a smaller vessel, suspected of being a U-boat, went alongside. At 22-53/83-25 in a cove on the east side of Punta Alacranes near the village of La Mulata. Occurred on Dec. 9. The observers, two reliable Americans and four Cubans, state they were within five thousand yards of the boat in question when the incident occurred.*[60]

When the *Comillas* docked in Havana, Agent Leddy, with the "cooperation" of the Cuban police, interviewed the forty crew members of the Spanish ship and

> *some fifty passengers . . . most of the latter known as anti-fascists repatriated from Spain. None of the persons interviewed would admit sighting a submarine. . . . The negative results of this inquiry were reported. Thereupon Hemingway submitted a memorandum stating that it would be a tragedy if the submarine were carrying saboteurs . . . and that the Legal Attaché discounted Hemingway's report because it had not come from an FBI agent.*[61]

Careful to report any information that might undermine Hemingway's counterintelligence work or his coastal patrols, Agent Leddy had never forgiven Hemingway for introducing Leddy at a jai alai match as a member of the Gestapo.

Soon after Hemingway's memorandum suggesting that the FBI bungled the *Pilar* report on the *Comillas*, a flurry of FBI documents were generated out of Agent Leddy's office and at the bureau. In Washington, Agent D. M. Ladd, to whom Leddy reported, compiled a four-page report for Director Hoover, reminding him first that Hemingway was on the side of the Spanish Republic in the Spanish Civil War, and that he had been accused of being a communist. He explained that Hemingway's Crook Factory was, in Leddy's opinion, getting out of hand. Expanding from an investigation of the Falange to include the "involvement of Cuban officials in local graft and corruption," Leddy feared that Hemingway's activities "were going to be very embarrassing unless something is done to put a stop to him." If the Cuban press ever figured out that Hemingway, with the embassy's blessing, was investigating General Benitez, the head of the Cuban police, "serious trouble may result." Ladd ended his report with Leddy's assurance that he could "handle this situation with the Ambassador so that Hemingway's services as an informant will be completely discontinued."[62] That same day, in response to Ladd's memorandum, Hoover wrote Leddy suggesting that he "discuss diplomatically" his misgivings about Hemingway's intelligence operation, adding: "Any information which you may have relating to the unreliability of Ernest Hemingway as an informant may be discreetly brought to the attention of Ambassador Braden. In this respect it will be recalled that recently Hemingway gave information concerning the refueling of submarines in Caribbean waters which has proved unreliable."[63]

Two days later, Hoover sent an interoffice memorandum to Agents Ladd and Tamm, warning them to put distance between the agency and Hemingway. Anything critical that the FBI might report to Ambassador Braden would be repeated immediately to Hemingway. "Hemingway has no particular love of the FBI," Hoover wrote, "and would no doubt embark upon a campaign of vilification." As for Hemingway's value as a counterspy, Hoover said Ernest was "the last man, in my estimation, to be used in any such capacity. His judgment is not of the best, and if his sobriety is the same as it was some years ago, that is certainly questionable."[64]

With his crew dispersed for Christmas, Hemingway returned to the Finca to await the December 26 arrival of Patrick and Gregory. As soon as the boys moved in, Martha packed her unfinished novel and flew to St. Louis to visit her mother. The tension between husband and wife over the Crook Factory and the sub patrols was temporarily deflated but not forgotten. On the last day of 1942, she typed Ernest a sweet, melancholy letter, made the sadder from reading Dostoyevsky's letters to his wife. She hoped that his next patrol, scheduled to begin on January 12, would be successful.[65] As the year closed out, it was becoming obvious the tides of war were turning: the Russians were slowly and at great cost pushing the Germans out of the Caucasus; the Japanese thrust in the Pacific had been stopped; in North Africa, the British were holding their own against Rommel. When Naval Intelligence said there were no U-boats operating in the Gulf of Mexico, the usual night patrols of the sealanes out of Miami were canceled for Christmas Eve. In Japan, Prime Minister Tojo told the Japanese Diet that the real war was just beginning. Much the same might have been said about the married couple living in Finca Vigía.

Chapter Fifteen

AMERICAN PATROL

January to July 1943

TRAPPED IN CHICAGO by foul weather, Martha explained to Ernest by letter that she could not be back at the Finca before he left on his January 12 patrol. Given that circumstance, she would spend a few more days with her mother, whom she realized was more important to her than even her stalled novel. "The story is safe inside," she said. "All that is necessary now is the discipline to finish it and I know I will do it." The letter was full of love for Ernest, which seemed to burn in Martha more fiercely when they were separated than when together. With miles between them, not knowing when she would see him next, Martha admitted their last year had been less than perfect, but there was a cathedral candle burning to protect him and the boys.[1]

The *Pilar*'s departure was also delayed until January 20. Fully outfitted with small arms, grenades, a high-frequency direction finder (Huff Duff), submarine recognition guides, code books, and a sophisticated radio complete with a Marine sergeant to operate it,[2] Ernest and his crew—Winston Guest, Gregorio Fuentes, Pachi, and Sergeant Don Saxon—put out from Cojimar in winter weather to patrol the north coast west of Bahia Honda. One of their specific charges was to relay information of the *Marques de Comillas*, which the U.S. Navy, despite Agent Leddy's assurance that the *Comillas* was not in contact with U-boats, wanted to keep under surveillance.[3] For three months now, there had been no ships sunk in the Gulf of Mexico, but "a new school of Eyeless fish," as the cautious embassy letter called the submarines, "was expected in these waters."[4]

The *Pilar* and her crew, only a tiny blip in the larger defense picture, conducted themselves as if the war depended upon their vigilance. Reports are filed on the time tables assigned; codes used; watches kept during the night hours. A running evening poker game eased the boredom of men living in cramped space and without the amenities of home. Periodically who owes whom how much is totaled up in the log book as faithfully as the expenditures of gasoline and the barometer readings.[5] Gregorio, part-time steersman and full-time cook, can with equal dexterity read water depths without reference to charts and prepare a dinner of mutton fish sautéed in lime juice, onions, and garlic. To maintain their cover story of being on a scientific expedition, the outriggers are always mounted, baited or not, as they patrol outside the coral reefs at trolling speed. Not fast enough to close on a surfaced U-boat heading away from her, the *Pilar* relied on their opponent's curiosity or his need for supplies to bring the sub to them: they were the bait. Three days after they left Cojimar, word of two possible U-boat contacts came down the intelligence chain—one on the eastern edge of the Frontier; one in the Old Bahama Channel, close enough to the *Pilar* to raise the crew's adrenaline level.[6]

Their first patrol was in bits and pieces, returning to Cojimar periodically for fuel and supplies and a few days ashore. Ernest dropped in and out of the Finca, where Martha's story of the mulatto girl's loveless marriage to the island patron was filling out. Ernest kept up with her work in progress, and also found time to reopen old wounds at the embassy. On the evening of February 8, while he and Martha were eating supper in the Floridita, they were joined by some embassy people, including the newly arrived assistant legal attaché, Ed Knoblaugh, whom Ernest and Martha once knew as a fellow journalist during the Spanish Civil War. Hemingway also knew Knoblaugh from reading his book *Correspondent in Spain*, which he felt supported Franco's revolution. Because Knoblaugh worked under the legal attaché, Agent Leddy, Ernest knew without being told that he was also a special agent for the FBI. After polite dinner conversation, Hemingway spent the next two days preparing a lengthy typed indictment of Knoblaugh, which he sent directly to Ambassador Braden.

By giving Knoblaugh oversight on Falangist activities in Cuba, the ambassador was, Ernest thought, assigning a sympathizer to report on fascist subversives. Without questioning Knoblaugh's patriotism, Hemingway cited numerous passages from *Correspondent in Spain* quoted by pro-fascist writers. He concluded that the new assistant legal attaché was "unsuited for any operations which might involve his having to investigate any Falangist or Spanish Fascist activity."[7]

Hemingway's demands that Knoblaugh be transferred were countered by Agent Leddy's defense of Knoblaugh, after which the ambassador decided that the issue was not as critical as Hemingway insisted. As Leddy informed the bureau, "It is known that Hemingway and his assistant, Gustavo Durán, have a . . . personal hostility to the FBI on an ideological basis, especially Hemingway, as he considers the FBI anti-Liberal, pro-Fascist and dangerous as developing into an American Gestapo."[8] The Civil War in Spain, supposedly finished in 1939, was still being fought in less violent ways among its several constituents. Hemingway backed off from this confrontation, returning to sea for another six weeks.

The remainder of February and all through March 1943, the *Pilar*'s crew kept uneventful watch of the bays, cays, and surface traffic in their assigned area. For almost five months now there had been no U-boat activity in the Gulf, but no sooner did they return to home port for replenishment and repairs than the German *U-155* at the end of its Caribbean patrol came through the Yucatan Channel and up the north coast of Cuba. On April 1, almost within sight of Hemingway's favorite port of Cabañas, the *U-155* torpedoed and sank the Norwegian freighter *Lysefjord*. A day longer on station would have put the *Pilar* in the rescue operation that saved eleven of the freighter's crew. Two days later the American tanker

Gulfstate was sent to the bottom of the Florida Straits by the same U-boat. While Hemingway caught up with correspondence and his crew enjoyed shore leave, the Gulf Frontier Command made every effort to trap and destroy the German raider. Armed blimps and aircraft flew day and night over the three escape routes out of the Gulf. The Cuban Navy sent three newly acquired cutters to patrol the Old Bahama Channel. After a week of false leads and no hard contacts, it was assumed the U-boat had slipped through the net and was on its way back to Germany.[9] During the six weeks the *Pilar* was re-outfitted for an extended patrol, two merchantmen were torpedoed in the Old Bahama Channel, triggering an intense response from the Commander of the Gulf Sea Frontier. On May 15, five miles behind a passing convoy, a positive sub contact was made in the heart of the Nicholas Channel, redoubling the search, which yielded no further results but cost four planes that went down in the Gulf during the operation.

Hemingway used the down time to write his old friend, Archibald MacLeish, now heading President Roosevelt's Office of Facts and Figures, about their mutual friend and longtime expatriate, Ezra Pound. Since January 1941, Pound had been making regular radio broadcasts from Rome, spewing vitriolic anti-Semitism and supporting the Fascist government of Mussolini while belittling the British and American war efforts. MacLeish himself was targeted by Pound, who characterized Archie's new appointment as "a gangster's brief and he has been entrusted with the defense of a gang of criminals and he is a-doing his damnedest."[10] In April, Hemingway asked MacLeish for the timetable and wavelength of Pound's broadcasts, thinking to listen in on the *Pilar*'s sophisticated shortwave receiver. Certain that Ezra would eventually face an American court, Hemingway wanted to be informed, for he and Archie, as old friends of Ezra from their Paris days, might have to testify.[11] On May 5, writing from the Finca, Ernest thanked MacLeish for the Pound information and asked for photostats of Ezra's broadcasts. "If Ezra had any sense," he said, "he would shoot himself."[12] After Pound was indicted for treason by a federal grand jury, Hemingway wrote Allen Tate that those whom Ezra once helped must do all they could to prevent his postwar hanging even if it meant climbing up on the gallows with him.[13]

On May 20, the daily intelligence report from the Gulf Frontier Command alerted its several components that the Hemingway crew was back on the water:

> COMGULF *advised that . . . Havana had reported that the American 38 foot motor boat* PILAR, *black hull and green deck, was operating from Havana eastward along the north coast of Cuba on a scientific mission and identifies herself on aircraft approach by an American flag during the day and flashing "V" at night.*[14]

Passing quickly through the Nicholas Channel to the hunting grounds of the Old Bahama Channel, the *Pilar* ran inside the reefs, checking the bays and inlets; somewhere along the north coast of Cuba, Gulf Command said a U-boat was lurking.[15] On May 29, Hemingway and crew set up rough camp on Confites, a flat disk of sand with a few palm trees, a wooden shack with a radio antenna, and the Cuban colors flying from a flagpole. A bored Cuban officer and two enlisted men who manned the isolated station were an unenthusiastic welcoming party. The next morning Hemingway sent Winston Guest in their auxiliary boat into Nuevitas, where there was an American consul and a U.S. Navy liaison office which would be their supply depot for the next two months. Two days later, Wolfie returned with twelve live chickens, two turkeys, one small pig, soda water, and eggs. On Confites, the crew established their menagerie, fattened the pig on corn and garbage, and conserved water, for it would be almost two weeks before they could be resupplied.[16]

Each morning they were up and out on the channel before nine, running at trolling speed and noting down any passing traffic for their evening radio report. Each evening they came into Confites with the light failing, measured their port and starboard fuel tanks, and cleaned up the *Pilar* for the next day's patrol.[17] While Gregorio prepared supper, Don Saxon made his coded radio report of the day's observations and took down instructions for patrol duty. Almost every evening Ernest wrote Martha back at the Finca, even though the letters might wait for days before being sent ashore. After supper, the evening poker game by lamplight commenced. If the sea breeze died, mosquitoes would end the game early. When the once-a-week mailboat came by, a new chapter of Martha's novel in progress would arrive for Ernest's critique: Liana, the native wife of a rich, white patron who treated her as a possession, was deeply in love with a French tutor hired by her husband to civilize her. Caught between two worlds—a dirty shack in the hills where her mother lived in poverty and the white world of her husband—Liana was no longer happy in either. Winston Guest remembered Hemingway sitting "up late with an oil lamp reading and correcting" the manuscript.[18] On most nights, the captain and crew were asleep before ten and up with morning sunrise.

Later, some acquaintances would say that it was all a lark, a way to get rationed gasoline for the *Pilar*; but none of those people were on Confites that June of 1943 when the U-boat war resumed, and Ernest never told them about it. After months of comparative quiet, during which the Gulf Command in no way relaxed its vigilance, intelligence reports indicated that the Germans were sending subs back into the Gulf. All that June at Cayo Frances, the twelve Navy officers and seventy-eight enlisted men were on constant alert, their seaplanes on daily patrol. The *Pilar* was sent into isolated cays to search for transmitters alerting U-boats of convoys passing through the Old Bahama Channel. June 8–10, Operation Friendless, as Ernest had named the operation after one of his Finca cats, went ashore on Cayo Chico and Cayo Megano Grande, assuring the Gulf Command there were no *fugaze* (fugitives) on those islets.[19] On June 8, ASW Group 5 at Cayo Frances was ordered to intensify its search for a U-boat entering the Old Bahama Channel at the edge of the *Pilar*'s patrol area. On June 14, while the *Pilar* was on patrol for sixteen hours, the planes of ASW-5 dropped "mouse traps" and depth charges on a U-boat in 400 fathoms of water off nearby Cayo

Fragoso, producing an oil slick five miles long with enough flotsam to call it a "likely sinking."[20]

After the early June flurry of action, silence descended on the channel: no German voices broadcasting late at night; no U-boats reported in the close vicinity. The convoy system and heavy patrols had accomplished their mission. On June 16, Hemingway's two vacationing sons, Patrick and Gregory, in the tow of Winston Guest, joined their father on Confites. During eleven days with no children to bother her, Martha was able to finish the novel, which was called *Liana* for lack of a better title.[21] Liana's tutor and lover, Pierre, after promising to take her away with him to Martinique, gives in to her husband, Marc Royer, who convinces Pierre that he could never take a Negro wife back to France, nor does he have any way to support her in Martinique. Consoled with Marc's promise that he would not send Liana back to live in a shack, Pierre slips away from the island in Marc's motorboat. Liana, seeing herself as merchandise at the mercy of white men, uses Marc's last razor blade to slit her wrist.[22] On one of his return trips to Finca Vigia, Hemingway referred to Martha's fiction and their own lives, saying that she had him mixed up with Marc Royer. There was no need for Martha to destroy the love they shared to take a foreign correspondent's job, although he thought she was foolish to pursue her irrecoverable youth.[23]

On Confites, his young sons sometimes went out on the daily patrols, but most often were left ashore with Gregorio as guardian.[24] With his new telescope Patrick bird-watched by day, star-watched by night. Greg collected shells, swam inside the reef, fished, and watched the palms blow. The high point of any week was the arrival of the supply boat, the *Margarita*, carrying blesséd ice, fresh bottles of water, canned fruit, sometimes a bottle of McCallum's Perfection Scotch Whiskey, sometimes even Coca-Colas. Each day Winston Guest diligently took their live pig out for a swim, so diligently in fact that one day Gregory, out goggle-fishing, looked up to see the pig swimming out to sea, finally disappearing over the horizon. At night, as often as not, Ernest could be seen beneath his kerosene lamp rereading *War and Peace*. Back at the Finca, Martha was threatening to have two of the male cats castrated in order to control their violent night fights. Ernest hated the idea, saying he would rather have the vet kill them or that he would kill them himself when he returned. He promised Martha that as soon as he got his submarine, he would help her get wherever on the war front she wanted to go.[25]

After forty days at sea, working in cramped quarters, the *Pilar's* captain and crew were beginning to get on each other's nerves. No matter how tasty, Gregorio's cooking was now boring. They never had enough ice, beer, or gin. On July 4 their permit to operate from Confites expired, but they had no message from Naval Intelligence to return to Havana. Bored and on edge, Hemingway wrote Martha a seven-page, lonely letter asking her not to give up on him and reminding her how easily and deeply she was able to hurt him with threats of leaving the Finca, whose exterior was now pink over faded yellow. Maybe he was as ugly as she said he was, and maybe he could not dance because she said he could not, but inside he felt as if he was still in his twenties. And Mr. Scrooby, his faithful penis, was eager to return to her. Two nights before, he dreamed that he had made love to a lovely, silver-colored bear, which was a sure sign it was time for him to come home.[26] Finally, on the morning of July 9, Don Saxon copied out the coded orders telling Hemingway that his patrol was over, his permit to return to Havana arriving on the supply boat along with future plans for Operation Friendless.[27]

After months of heavy duty, the *Pilar's* engine was in bad shape, intake and exhaust valves loose, piston rings badly worn, gaskets corroded, prop damaged, and her drive shaft out of alignment.[28] The next day she began her slow trip back to Havana, the crew weary but ready for shore leave, and equally ready to be set free from the malodorous feet of Don Saxon, festering with jungle rot, which had not responded to Ernest's treatment of sulfa drugs. On July 18, the *Pilar* limped into Cojimar harbor, Ernest fully bearded and his two sons much browner than when they left. The day after they returned, a Navy blimp while attacking a U-boat in the Florida Straits was shot down by the sub's 20mm guns. Nine of the blimp's crew survived; one man was eaten by sharks.[29]

A year later, *Saturday Evening Post* would publish "The Battle of Florida," making public, in a small way, the story of the Gulf Frontier Command's war with the U-boats. Explaining how initially ill prepared the United States was for battling the raiders and how the magnitude of the sinkings was kept secret in 1942–43, the article gave examples of civilian yachtsmen performing heroically against the U-boats. The quickly formed Coast Guard Auxiliary had men like Willard Lewis who encountered a U-boat on the surface and was nearly successful in his effort to ram it with his forty-five-foot fishing boat. When asked what he expected to accomplish by ramming a steel submarine with a small wooden boat, Lewis replied, "I aimed at her conning tower, and I might have messed up something. That sub was trying to get men ashore. I thought so then, and I was sure of it when it turned out that saboteurs had been landed later on that night farther up the coast." Actions by civilian volunteers, operating mostly at their own expense, were kept secret by the government in order to make the effort effective and for fear of turning every small fishing boat into a Nazi target. "The minutemen in motorboats did not greatly affect the formidable course of the struggle itself," the *Post* story said. "They were a mere stop gap—the 'something' that was better than nothing."[30]

Upon returning to Havana, the first thing Hemingway did was order a new marine engine for the *Pilar*.[31] The first thing Don Saxon did was get roaring drunk, arrested, and bailed out by the naval attaché. Patrick and Gregory helped Martha and the embassy crowd plan Ernest's forty-fourth birthday and welcome-back-from-the-sub-wars party. It began at the Club Cazadores del Cerro where the best wing shots in Cuba gathered to test each other against the flight of *tira pichon* (live pigeons) with sizable bets riding on the side. For the party, "the most unorthodox collection of targets were set before shotguns . . . pigeons . . . a covey of quail . . . six [Mexican] tree ducks . . . a half bushel of Cuban oysters with mangrove steamers . . . a dead guinea pig, seven clawless lobsters, and four small tuna. Constantino, the bar tender at the Floridita, contributed an immense . . . moro crab . . . [which] would be saved for Ernest's last shot."[32]

After considerable drinking at the club, shooters and shouters regrouped at the Finca beneath the enormous ceiba tree for a pig roast that started with a priest's blessing, at the end of which one of the Basque jai alai players beaned another Basque with a hard roll. Ernest rose to his feet, and from his patriarchal beard came the judgment: "That was wrong. On my birthday you can't throw rolls until dessert. *No hast'el postre.*"[33]

Chapter Sixteen

INTERMEZZO

August 1943 to May 1944

T HEY HAD BEEN a couple now for seven years, the first four clandestine, the next three married. Their affair, begun in war-torn Spain, was cathartic for both; their exhausting trip to China, a bonding experience. But their life at the Finca became a Jekyll and Hyde marriage that neither Martha nor Ernest nor anyone else understood very well. Apart, they wrote each other loving letters. Together for longer than a week, they embarrassed their friends with loud arguments. Living in comparative luxury in a peaceful setting while the wider world was burning pricked Martha to her very core. She was too comfortable, too safe, too domesticated. In one of her last letters to arrive at Confites, written in that bittersweet sadness of having finished her novel, she tried to explain her condition:

I wish we could stop it all now, the prestige, the possessions, the position, the knowledge, the victory. . . . You have been married so much and so long, that I do not believe it [marriage] can touch you where you live and that is your strength. It would be terrible if it did because you are so much more important than the women

*you happen to be married to. . . . I would like to be young and poor
and in Milan and with you and not married to you. I think I always
wanted to feel in some way like a woman, and if I ever did, it was
the first winter in Madrid. There was a sort of blindness and fervor
and recklessness about that sort of feeling which one must always
want. I hate being so wise and so careful, so reliable, so denatured,
so able to get on.*[1]

She was certain he would not understand her letter, which he did
not. They could not go back: the past was irretrievable except with
words on paper.

No sooner was Ernest back from Confites than he was talking
about the *Pilar*'s next extended cruise. At the same time, *Collier's*
asked Martha to go to England as their correspondent. After having
spent six months as lady of the Finca with its attendant responsibilities, Martha felt as if she were becoming someone she never wanted
to be: a housewife. More and more their arguments centered on
Ernest's failure to commit to the war as a journalist, which was the
only role that Martha could envision. Ernest could not or did not
want to understand his wife's need to reaffirm her identity as Martha Gellhorn. Martha never understood his morbid loneliness when
left alone, particularly at night. All that late summer and early fall
of 1943, they sniped at each other in vicious ways that usually wors-
ened the more Ernest drank. Gregory, who remembered his father
as a heavy drinker in Key West but seldom drunk, was surprised to
see Ernest drunk at the Finca, where he also allowed both Greg and
Patrick to drink. Ernest's theory was that the boys would learn their
limits and remain within them. "Papa would be just drunk out of his
mind, but able to do it because Juan (the chauffeur) would drive the
car home. So he could get as drunk as he wanted. . . . He'd have all
these drinks at the Floridita . . . just unbelievable drinking." Or so it
seemed to a twelve-year-old Greg.[2]

There was no easy answer to his father's drinking, nor to his irrational arguments with Martha, but Greg had seen it all before in
the Key West house when his father's second marriage was com-

ing apart because of Martha. This time there was no other woman. There was only the war to which Martha longed to go, and about which Ernest had mixed feelings. Because neither Ernest nor Martha felt connected to the war in the Pacific, their eyes turned only toward Europe. Ernest had been to a European war in 1918 when he believed that the world could be made safe for democracy; he still had shrapnel in his legs and a rebuilt right kneecap to remind him of that war and the death he almost bought there. Taking serious risks with little apparent fear or forethought, Martha never seemed to consider her own mortality; Ernest lived with his like an old friend.

For a year now he had been fighting this war as best he could—counterintelligence and submarine patrols—living largely in a male world with occasional spots of domesticity. It was a world cut off from Martha except for the rowdy shore leave drinking at the Finca between cruises. During that year, the global war had changed. Rommel and his Panzer forces were run out of North Africa; Allied troops had invaded Sicily; from forward bases, bombers were systematically destroying Nazi ports, factories, rail centers, and airfields. In the mid- and North Atlantic, the German U-boats were so decimated during the first six months of 1943—151 U-boats destroyed—that the Gulf of Mexico was no longer threatened. Martha, who put little credence in her husband's tales of the north Cuban coast, urged him to give up the submarine patrols and come to England with her, for in his absence, she had accepted the *Collier's* ETO (European Theater of Operations) assignment. As Ernest admitted in letters, they needed the income *Collier's* offered, for he was living on savings and advance loans from Scribner's, and Martha insisted on paying for her share of their household expenses. For Martha, the assignment was more than a paycheck: if she could get Ernest to England, together again with the "chaps," they might recapture the excitement of Madrid when life was a day-to-day proposition and artillery shells rattled their hotel.

Martha misunderstood Ernest's lack of interest in going to another war as a journalist, but then she misunderstood the *Pilar* patrols also. Having spent six weeks as a Red Cross man in World War I (1918), and having covered the Greco-Turkish War (1922) as a reporter for the *Toronto Daily Star* and the Spanish Civil War (1937–39) as a journalist for NANA (North American News Alliance), Ernest was loath to repeat the frustrations of watching the action without being able to participate, and not since his brief experience as a reporter in Toronto (1923–24) had he written news stories. He was a feature story writer whose personal perspective was always a key ingredient in the story. Already there were hundreds of competent journalists supporting the U.S. war effort, younger men without bum legs who, when the time came, would go ashore with troops, leap out of airplanes with the paratroopers, and give America's newspapers the stories the censors wanted them to read. That was their job, but it was not Hemingway's job. Having grown up as a boy with a grandfather who commanded troops in the Civil War, having observed the deployment of troops at close range in Spain, and having studied battlefield tactics in books from the time of Napoleon forward, Ernest wanted to command troops in battle, but with the freedom that independent ventures like the *Pilar* patrols allowed. His story of the dynamiter and the partisan guerrillas in *For Whom the Bell Tolls* was a fantasy close to his heart. He did not want an honorary commission to feed the U.S. propaganda machine, nor did he want to become a cog in some huge operation over which he had no control. In May 1942, he explained to Max Perkins that he was willing to go to the war, send his sons to the war, and give his money to the war effort. The one thing he could not do was write propaganda.[3] With the exception of his introduction for *Men at War*, as Ernest reminded his editor and his publisher, he had not written anything in three years. This hiatus, the longest of his career, made him prickly and short-tempered, which did nothing to improve his relationship with Martha.

A year earlier, in response to an irritating inquiry as to what he was doing for the war effort, he replied that in 1945 he would be glad to match war records with the questioner "for a nickel a side. We can also put in all our children's war records at a nickel apiece (ones who get killed count a dime). At that point we will also match Martha's war record (all time) against Mrs. Grovers. Then we will take all the nickels and melt them up to be cast into a medal to honor the winner."[4] He told Archie MacLeish that he once considered asking for a commission as friends of theirs had done, but gave it a pass, preferring to operate without any officer's insignia on his collar. Due to the secrecy of his patrol and wartime censorship (the FBI was reading some of his mail), he could not tell Archie about the *Pilar*, but after the coming summer he thought he might "be of some use in China."[5] In August, Hemingway asked MacLeish if there was any possibility of the government sending writers to war, not to write journalism or propaganda, but to gain the firsthand experience to write the books that needed to be written when the war was over. Maybe the Library of Congress could send him over as its correspondent?[6]

All of August and September, Ernest fretted over the redeployment of the *Pilar*, but one delay after another kept him ashore, where he listened to war news on the radio and answered letters in which he was frequently talking to himself. To a fellow writer who recently broke through an inactive period to write again, Ernest quoted Martha saying that "stalled" periods were an occupational hazard. All a writer needed to do to feel right about himself at day's end was to write well that morning. "Biting on the old nail never feels good," he advised, "[but] that is what we have to do and if we do not do it we end up as bad fathers and everything else."[7] The "old nail" of which he spoke was three years rusting on his writing desk, and two more years would pass before he put it between his teeth again.

At the beginning of September, Jack Hemingway, a newly commissioned lieutenant in the Military Police, visited briefly at the Finca before going on to his first duty station at Fort Custer, Michigan. At the same time Ernest was receiving letters from Oak Park neighbors advising him that his mother, Grace, was sick and becoming worse. "Your mother does not feel she is going to get well," a friend of his mother told him. "If it is at all possible for you to come, do so. A mother's first born son has a very close place in her heart." By the time Ernest received clearer information, Grace (seventy-one) had been in and out of a coma and was on her way to recovery, but the reminder of being her firstborn son produced the usual equivocal responses in Hemingway.[8] His mother, whom he blamed for his father's suicide, whom he reviled as an "all-American bitch," and from whose creative nature came much of his own drive, was a constant irritant to Hemingway. Scarcely a friend or passing stranger escaped without hearing of his horrible mother. If he resented ambitious, creative, independent women, that resentment linked directly to his feelings about Grace. That he married just such a woman in Martha was a conundrum, as were so many of his mixed feelings about married life. He wanted a home, but spent little time there. As soon as a passionate woman became his wife and mother to his children, he began to feel trapped; but should that woman leave him alone for longer than a week, he became morose, vulnerable, and began to speak of his own death. If he exploded in senseless arguments with Martha, he first learned that behavior listening to his parents in the far room, his mother usually dominant. What young Gregory witnessed that summer at the Finca were arguments rooted in Oak Park.

On September 20, Martha left for New York to begin her *Collier's* assignment, and the *Pilar* should have put to sea soon after, but Ernest and Martha both faced delays. It took Martha a full month of bureaucratic red tape before she could depart for England. In New York, while she waited, she saw the film version of *A Farewell to Arms*, and while visiting Eleanor Roosevelt at the White House, she saw a private showing of *For Whom the Bell Tolls*, with Gary Cooper playing the leads in both films. Before leaving New York, she wrote Ernest a long letter, professing her love for him and hoping that she was not too bad a wife. She was happy to be back in the thick of things, but "like woman, and your woman, am sad; only there isn't anything final, is there? This is just a short trip and we are both coming back from our short trips to our lovely home . . . and then we'll write books and see the autumns together and walk around the corn fields waiting for the pheasants."[9]

That October in the Gulf Sea Frontier, fifty-three convoys passed back and forth without a single loss, in fact, without a single attack.

The Command lost seven planes and two blimps to the usual kinds of errors in judgment, but raised not a single German U-boat.[10] War in the Gulf of Mexico, which only a year before was irregular and dangerous, had become systematic and boring, but demanding no less vigilance. Hemingway looked elsewhere for action. Walking down Obispo Street to wait for Winston Guest at the Floridita, he was not eager to tell his executive officer that the *Pilar* still lacked clearance from the U.S. Navy and the embassy to begin its patrol. With nothing happening in the Gulf, they had requested permission to operate the *Pilar* in Caribbean waters, using the base at Guantanamo for supplies. They should have been on their way at the end of July. Now, three months later, Ernest and Wolfie were still ashore winning side bets at the skeet and pigeon range. All the exciting possibilities came to nothing. They led a makeshift crew out for short cruises in early November, but the patrol log of the *Pilar* was closed, never to reopen.

With no more sailing to do and left too much alone at the Finca, Ernest was not at his best. Facing a Christmas Day without his wife, he lived in an empty house with cats his only company. Drinking too much, too often, and feeling too sorry for himself, Hemingway complained to almost every correspondent about Martha's absence. The day after Christmas, he told Archie MacLeish that being without Martha was like having his heart cut out. With so much of his love invested in her, he "would be in a bad place" should anything happen to her.[11] Unfortunately, he was less tender in his letters to Martha. In London, weak but recovering from multiple viruses, Martha still hoped to hear that Ernest was coming to the war zone. Everyone she met asked about him, wondered where he was, when he would be there. Every time she begged Ernest to come be with her, he responded that he was doing his assigned job in Cuba. She predicted that he would regret his decision later, but she would not ask again. "I have to live my way as well as [you] yours or there would not be any me to love you with. You really wouldn't want me if I built a fine big stone wall around the Finca and sat inside." Nine days later, after reprofessing her love for him, Martha admitted to Ernest that life at the Finca now seemed to her "remote and somehow awful." Dreading it, she compared it to being strangled "by those beautiful tropical flowers that can swallow cows!"[12]

Whatever the reasons, the equation for Hemingway changed: the Gulf Frontier Command no longer needed an irregular Navy; the Allied invasion of France was clearly going to happen; and Martha was not coming home soon. Winston Guest, at the age of thirty-seven, joined the Marines; John Thomason was in the Pacific; Jack Hemingway was transferring from the Military Police to a newly formed group called the Office of Strategic Services (OSS) where Winston's brother, Raymond, and David Bruce were players. On January 13, 1944, Ernest grudgingly wrote Martha that he was closing down the *Pilar* patrols, closing down the house, and coming to England as soon as his present cruise was completed.

After playing in the outfield of the war game, albeit a very remote outfield, going back to journalism was like throwing down his glove to take a seat in the stands. Her arguments for being in the war zone were, he agreed, all sound for her, but as for being a part of history, well, fuck history. When the war began, he said he never thought he would outlive it, or that he would ever have to write another book, implying that a death foreseen awaited him, if not on patrol then perhaps in Europe.

She should blame his bitterness on his inability to sleep soundly, his enforced celibacy, and his frustration of having to give up active participation in the war. When he did sleep, his dreams were filled with frustration. Recently he dreamed that her luggage, was left at a metro station where she was embarking on a ship. He cut across the electrified rail, picked up the luggage, and with great effort got it to Martha, who was unimpressed, aloof, and critical, telling him that if he wanted to be with her that he needed to respond quicker. He signed the letter as her loving husband.[13]

Seventeen days later, the *Pilar* returned to Cojimar, her career as a clandestine naval auxiliary finished. The following day, Ernest wrote Martha, repeating that he would soon be joining her, but not to expect him to take any special interest in the venture. He was like an old horse being forced to take the steeplechase jumps against his better judgment. Being a professional he would jump as well as he was able, but he would take no joy in it. Had she allowed him to remain on patrol, a fine novel would have come out of his experiences, but now he would lose the story, for journalism would erase it from his head.[14]

Two days later, writing to an old friend, Hemingway casually announced that he expected to be in New York in about two weeks, for he was too lonely at the Finca without Martha. "Now I hope I will meet her where I go," he wrote, without saying where he was going. As soon as he took care of the thirteen cats, five dogs, fighting cocks, and pigeons, he would be on his way. The anger inside him, at a boil without a focus, needed direction. A married man with family responsibilities could not afford "the luxury of being killed," he said, unless he left his dependents well provided.[15]

Ernest's deliberately oblique and vague references to his plan for getting to the war are puzzling. He may have already begun his negotiations with *Collier's* magazine to sign on as their front-line correspondent. Who made that first contact is not clear, but for certain the possibility was discussed with Charles Colebaugh, Martha's editor at *Collier's*, and Martha must have known about it, if not in London, certainly in New York when she passed through en route to Cuba. On March 10, Colebaugh wrote Hemingway that he would have to embark for Europe via New York, but it would take two weeks in the city to arrange all the documents.[16]

The week of March 13, when Martha returned to the Finca, her husband's unfocused anger found a target. For public consumption in *Collier's*, Hemingway remained his wife's professional admirer: "When she is at the front or getting there, she will get up earlier, travel longer and faster and go where no other woman can get and where few could stick it out if they did. . . . She gets to the place, gets the story, writes it and comes home. That last is the best part."[17] With Max Perkins he could make rough jokes about how a bossy woman, once given the rank of captain, would never give it up; his only choice was to get a higher rank so he could say, "Roll over captain, a period of strenuous calisthenics is about to begin."[18] In the privacy of their bedroom, his demeanor was alarmingly different. Having sent her succinct telegrams—"ARE YOU A WAR CORRESPONDENT OR MY WIFE IN BED"—he now opened up with heavy artillery. As Martha told Bernice Kert some years later,

> *Ernest began at once to rave at me. . . . He woke me when I was trying to sleep to bully, snarl, mock—my crime really was to have been at war when he had not, but that was not how he put it. I was supposedly insane, I only wanted excitement and danger, I had no responsibility to anyone. I was selfish beyond belief . . . it never stopped. . . . I put it to him that I was going back, whether he came or not.*[19]

Having never seen her husband behave like this, Martha, even at several years remove, did not consider that Ernest might be suffering from something other than loneliness. The charges of being insane, of seeking out danger, or acting selfishly and irresponsibly applied as much to himself as to her. His son Gregory firmly believed that his father changed during that 1943–44 period into a different person. Hemingway's last wife, Mary Welsh, would experience the same sort of abuse that Martha reported. It was as if some inner, furious animal was set loose, an animal over which Hemingway had some control in public, but little at home. Anyone looking backward from 1960–61 might say that his behavior was a manifestation of the depression that eventually destroyed him. But that March of 1944, no one around him, least of all Martha, had the experience, training, or clinical knowledge to understand Hemingway's behavior as anything but outrageous and intolerable.

At the end of March, Hemingway wrote Colebaugh at *Collier's* that he and Martha were booked to fly into New York on April 23. In the letter he enclosed a commendation from Ambassador Braden, thanking Hemingway for carrying out "highly confidential intelligence activities" which he could not spell out until the war was over. Braden went on to thank Ernest for doing "certain other work, likewise of a confidential nature, involving personal risks and ever-present danger."

Ernest asked Colebaugh to keep the letter confidential, for he wanted no publicity for this work.[20] When the syndicated columnist Earl Wilson found Hemingway in New York—fully bearded and overweight at 220 pounds—working out with the trainer, George Brown, Ernest was all sweetness and light with regard to Martha.[21] Like many manic-depressives, he could be as nice as pie in public and a son of a bitch in private. He could also keep a secret. Neither Martha nor Colebaugh knew that Hemingway had volunteered for assignment to the recently formed OSS, perhaps offering his journalist's credentials as his cover story—a scenario imagined seven years earlier in his play, *The Fifth Column*. On May 1, that offer was declined in a once secret document that read:

> *MECATO 3> OSS Will Not Use Hemingway. (GB-002-425, Shepherdson to Joyce.) Decided in the negative about Hemingway. We may be wrong, but feel that, although he undoubtedly has conspicuous abilities for this type of work, he would be too much of an individualist to work under military supervision.*[22]

When the Hemingways arrived in New York, Ernest became *Collier's* front-line correspondent—each magazine was limited to one—and Martha took an assignment that confined her, in theory, to the rear of that line. Later Martha would say that Ernest "automatically destroyed my chances of covering the fighting war."[23] If that was Hemingway's intention, Gellhorn's credits with *Collier's* in 1944–45 document his ineffectiveness. Martha forgot to remember the War Department ruling that female correspondents could "go no farther forward than women's services go," restricting Martha and fellow female correspondents to hospital areas. "Women were accredited to the war zones. They did not have accreditation to military units, as required for admission to press camps at the front." To defy these limits made a female correspondent liable to lose her credentials and even face court-martial. The U.S. Army, which had not wanted any female correspondents in Europe, specifically forbade them from covering the Normandy invasion. When Martha was on the beach with a hospital unit at D-Day +1, the Army press officers punished her for defying orders by not allowing her to accompany the other women when they were finally allowed ashore.[24] Ernest or no Ernest on their payroll, *Collier's* could not send Martha to the war as their front-line correspondent; had Colebaugh not hired her husband, he would have hired some other man.

If he did not exactly take her job, Ernest certainly did his best to punish Martha for being Martha, who acted, he claimed, with the willfulness of a spoiled child, but "always for the noblest motives."[25] When he refused to arrange a seat for her on his scheduled flight to England, Martha, angry and determined, found passage on a dynamite-laden freighter leaving New York on May 13. Ernest spent the following afternoon at Port Jefferson, Long Island, in writer Dawn Powell's beach cottage, where she noted in her journal: "Hemingway down all day yesterday—exhausted by his immense gusto—someone who gives out more in six hours than most people do in a lifetime— leaves you groggy."[26]

Arriving by military plane in England on May 17 two weeks before Martha's freighter docked, Hemingway quickly caught the war fever that made each moment potentially the last, each embrace a possible farewell.[27] In New York he had berated Martha, saying he would probably be killed in Europe, hoping that would satisfy her.[28] But at London's Dorchester Hotel his old journalist friends found him affable and expansive. Meanwhile, Martha was experiencing frugal life aboard a wartime freighter slowly convoying its way across the still dangerous Atlantic, where Nazi wolf packs were decimated but not yet out of business. In her notes she called the eighteen-day voyage "a fine rest cure," but she also remembered the food was terrible; there was nothing alcoholic to drink; with a habit of two packs of cigarettes a day, she, the only passenger, could not smoke. If she arrived in London a bit testy, there were good reasons.[29]

While Martha was at sea, Hemingway was busy cultivating RAF pilots for a story about their night raids on German targets. He was also cultivating a small, lovely, American journalist whose British husband was out of the country. In those last, mad days before the great invasion, Mary Welsh, whose by-line appeared in both *Time* and *Life*, did not lack for male attention. Novelist Irwin Shaw and *Time/Life* correspondent Bill Walton were both her frequent companions at the White Tower restaurant, and more than one senior officer was taken by her midwestern confidence, curly hair, and blue eyes. One day at lunch, Shaw pointed out the bulky figure of Ernest Hemingway across the room. Mary, whose sweater made it clear she was wearing no bra, was being greeted by every passing male acquaintance: "Nice sweater," or, "The warmth does bring things out doesn't it?" When Hemingway, who knew Shaw, came to their table asking for an introduction, Shaw obliged, and told Mary afterward that it had been nice to know her. She didn't understand, but she soon would. Before Martha Gellhorn ever stepped ashore in England, Ernest was telling Mary Welsh, "I don't know you, Mary. But I want to marry you. . . . I want to marry you now, and I hope to marry you sometime. Sometime you may want to marry me." [30] Mary did not know what to make of his sad face or of his voice filled with loneliness, nor could she imagine the emotional maelstrom into which she was being drawn.

At three in the morning a few days later, Hemingway pulled his face back from the shattered windshield of a friend's car to find warm blood running into his eyes. Drunker than he should have been but no drunker than the driver, neither of them saw the steel water tank in the blacked-out London street. Hemingway's scalp was neatly parted in a shallow but ugly gash that put him once more in a hospital emergency room. Already he carried plenty of scars from other woundings: his right foot and knee were scarred from the 1918 trench mortar shell on the Piave River; his forehead bulged from the night emergency-room visit in 1927 Paris when he accidentally pulled the bathroom skylight down on top of himself; beneath his beard there was a scar from the veterinarian stitching up his face when his horse bolted through the Wyoming thicket in 1930; and his right arm bore scars from repairwork to a compound spiral fracture from a 1930 auto wreck outside Billings, Montana.

Arriving at Liverpool on May 31, Martha soon discovered that

Ernest was a London patient in St. George's Hospital. The first news releases reported him dead, but the next day, May 25, *The Times* said he "was slightly injured early yesterday . . . when a car crashed into an emergency water tank at Lowndes Square." The slight injury required over fifty stitches, not to mention the ear-ringing concussion that Hemingway carried with him for weeks afterward. But when Martha arrived at his hospital room, she found her husband holding court with a roomful of visitors who were making ample use of his liquor supply, reconstructing his Milan hospital room from a world war earlier. Having had plenty of time at sea to review their relationship, Martha entered the room half sure their marriage was over; when she left, she had no doubts. "If he really had a concussion," she explained to Bernice Kert, "he could hardly have been drinking with his pals or even receiving them. He did not look the least ill anyway."[31] The concussion was real enough, and drinking was a sure way to make it worse. Ernest, garrulous and full of male-bonding jokes ("I never had a WAC shot out from under me"), was with Martha in the war zone as she had so fervently desired, but it was a husband she hardly recognized. If war released her from life at the Finca, it set Ernest free in ways she had not imagined. Before the ground war began on the beaches of Normandy, the private war between Martha and Ernest was finished. There was no acknowledgment of defeat by either party, but that was only a formality.

Chapter Seventeen

PUTTING ON THE RITZ

June, July, August 1944

I N   T H E   P R E D A W N   H O U R S   of June 6, 1944, Hemingway
was wide awake, his head still ringing from his recent concussion, his scalp wounds not yet completely healed beneath the
bandage. He was not the only man wide awake aboard the *Empire
Anvil* and the hundreds of other transports crossing the English
Channel toward France. The great crusade to liberate Europe,
the most complex military maneuver in history, was closing on the
beaches of Normandy, its outcome uncertain. Like his shipmates',
Hemingway's view of the operation was limited to his line of sight.
He could not see the incredible size of the Allied armada, but he
could hear salvos from battleships, cruisers, and destroyers pounding the German fortifications. On Hemingway's briefing map, the
Normandy beaches were labeled "Sword," "Juno," "Gold," "Omaha,"
and "Utah." The narrow sector on which Hemingway focused was
labeled "Fox Green" on the left flank of Omaha Beach, where 34,000
soldiers were about to go ashore under fire.

His head wound still fresh and with both knees swollen, Hemingway climbed down his ship's rope ladder into a landing craft, only
to be transferred to another ship, up and down another rope ladder,

and finally into the small, crowded landing craft. Here his vision was even more limited. In the first gray light of dawn, hundreds of landing craft wallowed in the rough sea, trying to group for the charge toward the beach. Hemingway described the scene for his *Collier's* readers:

> *As the boat rose to a sea, the green water turned white and came slamming in over the men, the guns and the cases of explosives. Ahead you could see the coast of France. The gray booms and derrick-forested bulks of the attack transports were behind now, and, over all the sea, boats were crawling forward toward France.*[1]

Some men were praying, some seasick and puking, no one was talking. On that same sea 5,000 ships were sending 150,000 men onto beaches from which there was no retreat. If they could not break through the German defenses, they were lost souls.

On paper and in practice sessions, the Normandy invasion went smoothly enough considering its complexity, but in briefing rooms the sea was calm, no smoke obscured key landmarks, and there was no confusion among the landing craft. At the Fox Green sector of Omaha Beach, reality was far removed from theory. As naval historians later assessed:

> *The resulting difficulties of the boat teams were heightened by the frequent separation of sections of the same company. Whether because of delays suffered by individual craft, straggling on the way in, or disagreement between coxswains in recognition of landmarks, some unit formations of landing craft were broken up enough to result in widely scattered landings. Under conditions prevailing at the beach, separation of craft by as little as 200 yards could easily bring about the complete isolation of a section.*[2]

Before that day was done, one thousand soldiers died on Omaha Beach. Some were wounded to drown in the surf. Some were blown up with their landing craft. Many died facedown in the sand of Fox Green and Easy Red where German gunners had easy targets.

From the landing craft Hemingway scanned the horizon with his field glasses, picking out the Coleville church steeple as a guide. The coxswain could not decide if the route into the beach was clear of mines; the lieutenant was not sure if this was Fox Green or if they should put ashore. Finally, confused and frustrated, they began the run into the beach where Hemingway could see that "the first, second, third, fourth and fifth waves [of landing troops] lay where they had fallen, looking like so many heavily laden bundles on that flat pebbly stretch between the sea and the first cover." When the German machine-gun fire picked out their landing craft, Hemingway dropped down, and the lieutenant took the LCVP back out to sea. If that was Fox Green, it had not been cleared of mines in the water, nor had the tanks, two of which were burning on the beach, done their job. Later, when Navy destroyers blasted out some of the German guns, Hemingway's landing craft finally got its men and supplies into the surf and quickly backed out again, picking its way through underwater obstacles tipped with contact mines. Bearing evidence of the German machine guns, the LCVP made it back to the *Dorothea Dix,* where Ernest climbed back up the rope ladder unscathed.[3] Ten other landing craft that morning were blown up in the water before reaching shore.

Because of the uncertainties of the Normandy invasion, few correspondents were allowed ashore that first day. Late that night, Hemingway and most of the correspondents returned to English ports and from there to London. Ernest, not yet assigned to a specific unit, had yet to fulfill his commitment to *Collier's* for a story on the RAF's sky battles with the Germans. Working out of the Dorchester Hotel, he talked to RAF pilots based on Salisbury Plain about their secret aircraft, the Tempest, which flew fast enough to intercept the V-1 German buzz bombs that were now falling on England in random patterns. At Dunsford, on June 15, Hemingway was in the officers' mess of the 98th Squadron when a V-1 dropped out of the sky at the edge of the base. Flight Lieutenant R. G. Teakle soon received a reprimand asking him to be more careful regarding security matters, for the group captain had learned that "certain parts of a Flying Bomb were taken by Mr. Ernest Hemmingway [sic] while he was under your charge. I now learn that the parts have been restored to the Security Branch."[4] A few days later Hemingway was flying with the 98th on an afternoon mission to bomb V-1 launch sites at Drancourt in France. Eight groups of six B-25 Mitchell bombers came in low enough that Ernest could see plane wreckage left behind by earlier attacks, and then the black flak bursts from antiaircraft guns began blossoming alongside Commander Lynn's aircraft. Ernest watched the nearest B-25's bomb bay open, and "the bombs all dropped out sideways as if she were having eight long metal kittens in a hurry." When he asked Lynn to go back over the target to check the damage done by the 500-pounders, the commander refused, of course, not willing to risk any more flak. The leading bomber in the second group was reported shot down at the target.[5]

On June 29, flying with RAF Group Captain Peter Barnes, Ernest went up on a practice flight in a Type-VI de Havilland "Mosquito," whose Rolls-Royce engines could push the aircraft to almost 400 miles an hour. Built of specially treated plywood, the plane relied on speed and maneuverability, not armor, to stay alive. Late that night Barnes took Hemingway on a coastal patrol run which came across several V-1s inbound for Portsmouth. At Hemingway's urging, Barnes dove on one of the buzz bombs from above, but was unable to get into position before they were in the middle of the Portsmouth antiaircraft barrage. Barnes fired a short burst from his 20mm guns, and then

> *pulled away before we reached the barrage balloons. Ernest seemed to love the fireworks bursting all around us, and urged me to press on. . . . I was already in a state familiar to those who tangled with Ernest—I was acting against my better judgment. . . . I knew I was supposed to keep Ernest out of trouble. If you did blow one up, particularly at night, it was touch and go for yourself. . . . We dived even more steeply on the second V1 . . . gave it two long bursts . . . and then we were in the Portsmouth barrage again. I pulled away*

*in a confusion of search lights and intensive flak. As we winged
over, there was a huge flash behind us, and the aeroplane danced
around like a leaf in a whirlwind. Someone got the V1, but not us.
. . . Ernest seemed to have loved every moment of it.*[6]

Unwinding after their return to base, Hemingway and Barnes got
into a deep discussion on stress and strain, courage and bravery—
conditions and traits about which Barnes knew too much from over
four years of combat experience. When Ernest claimed that combat
fatigue was a lack of courage, Barnes told him he had a lot to learn.

Hemingway was not the only correspondent who flew bombing
missions or risked his life at Normandy, but he may have been the
most prominent. To the combat troops and RAF pilots, he seemed
almost shy, a man asking questions, listening intently to their
answers. Anyone familiar with his depressed and petulant moods at
the Finca would not have thought him the same man. On the surface
it would seem that his concussed and bleeding head had somehow
pushed his demons back down below the surface of his mind. The
soldiers and airmen admired the cool eagerness with which he faced
the dangers they encountered, but they sometimes wondered why a
man so famous would take such risks. That question had no easy or
simple answer. Part of Hemingway wanted to be the warrior he imagined himself as a young boy listening to his grandfathers' stories of the
Civil War. Part of him was half in love with an honorable death, not
one that he sought, but one that found him. Yet another part of him
simply no longer cared if he lived or died. This year or next, as Shakespeare said, a debt owed to God that he would be quit of. Were this
not wartime, his behavior would have raised more questions. Because
it was wartime, no one was dumbfounded by his acts, nor did anyone
think it strange that this famous and married man returned to Mary
Welsh's bedroom, behaving like a figure from a romantic novel.

Twice married, once divorced, Mary was no novice in the field of
love; her current husband, the journalist Noel Monks, was sent to
France immediately after D-Day, leaving her a "target of opportunity," as Ernest described his own heart at the time. Exactly when

they became lovers is a movable date, but maybe it happened as he described it in his first poem for Mary. He is sitting lonely and alone in his hotel room, watching the electric clock move "toward the hour when she will come opening softly with in-left key. Saying 'May I come in?' Coming small-voiced and lovely to the hand and eye to bring your heart back that was gone; to cure all loneliness and bring the things we left behind upon the boat."[7] That they were lovers was nothing strange in that London of 1944, nor, if rumors have any substance, was he her first or only lover. She also did not seem to be bothered that his hotel room had evidence that other women came and went.[8]

The first week in July, Hemingway shaved off his sub patrol beard, leaving only a mustache. On his head, stubble was growing back after the hospital stitching. Catching a seat on a small plane flying into the half-cleared Cherbourg peninsula, he gathered there with fellow correspondents Bob Capa, Bill Walton, Charles Collingwood, Bill Paley, and others. After a rainy week spent visiting liberated villages—Ste. Mère-Eglise, Valgones, Barfleur, and others—he and Collingwood paid their homage at Château de Tocqueville, where *Democracy in America* was written and where the two correspondents left their initials—EH CC 7 44—"etched discreetly in the soft stone to the left of the main door of the *Pavillon* wing."[9] Still assigned to covering the RAF, Hemingway returned to London, where he soon got himself reassigned to George Patton's Third Army grouping at Néhou, well behind the front line. Flushed with the initial success on the Normandy beaches, the Allied armies were now engaged in bloody hedgerow fighting against well-trained, entrenched German troops. It was not yet clear that the invaders would be able to move off their several beachheads. A month after the D-Day landings, they were less than ten miles inland; somewhere along the loosely connected seventy-mile-front an opening had to be blasted.

When Hemingway arrived in France on July 18, General Patton's tank corps was being held in reserve while General Omar Bradley's First Army was assigned to force a wedge in the German defenses at St. Lô. On July 24, Hemingway transferred to the First Army at the very moment Bradley's forces broke out of their coastal confinement. That afternoon and the following morning, Eighth Air Force bombers, laying down a wall-to-wall carpet of fragmentation bombs to open the German lines, misread the bomb line and bombed their own troops, killing 136 and wounding over 500 American soldiers. Later, Hemingway's bitter character Colonel Cantwell recounts what happened when the wind blew the smoke marking the bomb line back into the American positions: "They bombed us the same way they bombed the Krauts. First it was the heavies, and no one need ever worry about hell who was there that day." [10]

Four days later, Hemingway found his semipermanent field home with the 22nd Infantry Regiment whose commander, Colonel Charles "Buck" Lanham, was too busy fighting the war to worry much about what Ernest was doing or where he was going. That was just as well because from that point forward Hemingway was sometimes a journalist, sometimes an irregular soldier, and sometimes a gatherer of intelligence. His driver, Archie "Red" Pelkey, would take him anywhere, no matter what the road conditions. Their jeep carried rifles and grenades; Ernest was never without his Zeiss field glasses or his liberated German case full of battle and road maps. He was there in the France that he knew and loved early in his career, coming back now in the crusade to free her, following the old pilgrimage routes toward Paris.

On July 30, Hemingway liberated for his own use a German motorcycle with sidecar, and a Mercedes convertible, which was immediately repainted olive drab; he also liberated a well-stocked château's wine cellar: Château Lafité, 1915; Châteauneuf du Pape, 1929; Rudesheimer, 1915, which he, Ira Wolfert, Duke Shoop, and other journalists enjoyed that night, washing down K ration chili with rare vintages.[11] The following night in his letter to Mary in London he sounded tired but happy, fighting the war as best he could and to the extent his circumstances allowed. His headaches, he said, were much better.[12] On August 3, Reuters news service reported that Hemingway and Pelkey captured six German prisoners: "The private, with Mr. Hemingway, tossed hand grenades into the house and six of Hitler's supermen piled out and surrendered to Hemingway."[13] That same day, as the 4th Division mopped up German resistance at Villedieu-les-Poêles, Colonel Lanham remembered seeing Hemingway at a street corner, "standing poised as always on the balls of his feet. Like a fighter. Like a great cat. Easy. Relaxed. Absorbed. Intent. Watchful. Missing nothing."[14] With rifle and machine-gun fire only buildings away, Hemingway's street corner stance put him once more in close proximity to death. He was either very sure he would not be killed (a foolish thing of which to be sure), or he simply did not give a damn.

Two days later, at the outskirts of St. Pois, he lay flat in a ditch, head throbbing and ears ringing beneath his steel helmet pulled down tight. His liberated German motorcycle with sidecar was upended in the middle of the road. Somewhere ahead, he could hear Germans talking, but he did not raise his head to look because the first time he did, machine-gun fire splattered dirt in his face, and the antitank gun that knocked him there let loose with more rounds. For two hours he lay, not moving, listening to the noises in his head, and knowing the London concussion was back in business, not that it had ever gone far away. The rest of his band was safely hunkered down behind the protective curve in the road, watching the exposed inch of his butt sticking up from the ditch. It was a long afternoon.

The news story said the first German shell "fired at point-blank range exploded in the middle of the road three yards from Hemingway, who was blown into the ditch." Robert Capa (one of the men behind the protected curve) thought the first shell hit about ten yards in front of the motorcycle. Three yards or ten, it did not matter much to Ernest in the ditch. Capa, well known for his stunning battlefield photographs from the Spanish Civil War, was said to have "continued to take pictures until a second antitank shell swished close to him. Then he also took cover."[15] Capa remembered only the tracer bullets hitting the dirt above Hemingway's head, "and the popping, which came from a light German tank . . . continued without let up." When the tank pulled back, Hemingway ran to join Capa and his driver, Red Pelkey, and two other soldiers. Capa wrote that

Hemingway "was furious. Not so much at the Germans as at me, and accused me of standing by during his crisis so that I might take the first picture of the famous writer's dead body."[16]

Traveling that unsecured back road into St. Pois, Hemingway was taking the sort of risk that became his trademark all that year in France. When he first showed Capa the way into St. Pois on the map, the photographer was dubious. "Papa looked at me in disgust," Capa wrote later, "and said I could stay behind. I couldn't do anything but follow him, but . . . I told him that Hungarian strategy consisted of going behind a good number of soldiers, and never of taking lonely short cuts through no man's land."[17] Hemingway would take more and more shortcuts, pushing the laws of probability to their limits.

The next day, Hemingway and Bill Walton were crossing the mile-long causeway connecting the mainland of France to Mont-St.-Michel. Rising up out of the tidal flat before them was the ancient abbey with its Gothic visage and its surrounding ramparts. The register of the Hôtel de la Mère Poulard was filled with the names of recently departed German officers, le Mont having been liberated only five days earlier.[18] By the time reporters John Carlisle and Charles Collingwood arrived, Ernest seemed to be in charge of the place, having completely charmed the *patronne*. Collingwood said, "He chose the wine, decided on menus. He had great force of personality and a gift for organization."[19] For Carlisle, Ernest was "one of the happiest men I ever knew, a guy with a great zest for life and who enjoyed every minute of it." Bill Walton, who loved and admired Ernest without overlooking his faults, found him always "marvelous company. . . . He made me laugh more deeply than anyone else I'd known." John Ford's camera crew caught Ernest dining with A. J. Liebling. Not every fellow correspondent was so taken with Hemingway's ability to be always at the center of the action, to speak with commanding officers like Buck Lanham in their own language, and to speak with the locals in their own patois. For William Randolph Hearst, Jr., Ernest was "a pain in the ass" and no gentleman. "He was only a reporter the same as us, but he thought he was the Second Coming and acted like it. . . . I don't think anyone liked him."[20] Some, like Hearst, resented Hemingway's freelancing out along action's edge. Some accused him of "playing soldier."

They could not have been more wrong about Ernest Hemingway, who had not "played soldier" since he was a small boy armed with a wooden gun. After his wounding in World War I, Hemingway viewed armed combat as the most central experience of his century. Here a man could see his species stripped down to a primal level; here he could test his own emotional resources. This was Hemingway's fifth war since 1918; when not at the front lines, he was continuously reading the masters of war from Caesar to Clausewitz. Years of hunting in broken fields and rough terrain, facing dangerous game in tight places, all of it was good practice for the hedgerows of France and the forest at Hürtgen. His ability to read a topographic map as if it were a three-dimensional photograph let him anticipate where the Germans would or would not move. His familiarity with weapons, his proficiency in French, and his ability to shut down the normal response of fear made him invaluable to officers like Buck Lanham and a source of worry to officers more bound to the official book of war.

Soon after leaving Mont-St.-Michel, Hemingway himself threw away the book. At St. Michel he had made contact with an OSS officer, and by August 15, Hemingway carried a brassard of the Free French of the Interior (FFI) inscribed: "A Mon Ami et liberateur, un Francais Reconnaisant." By the time his old Havana embassy friend and now OSS colonel David Bruce met him outside Chartres on August 20, Ernest was working under contradictory compulsions: as a correspondent he was supposed to be a noncombatant gathering printable war news; as unofficial liaison officer with the French Resistance while working with the OSS, he was an irregular combatant who must never write of his activities. Much later, one who was there confirmed that "Hemingway was fighting with the Resistance before the liberation of Chartres. I saw him with the FFI right after we left le Mont." An OSS operative saw Hemingway in Chartres "during the liberation battle, at the site of a mass grave while the fires were still burning and the last Germans surrendering."[21] Between August 18 and 20, Hemingway was back and forth between Chartres, which was being liberated, and Rambouillet, which controlled one of the routes into Paris and which was tenuously held by a handful of Maquis, French Resistance fighters.

When David Bruce regrouped with Hemingway at the command post of the 5th Division, Ernest was carrying a handwritten note directing dynamite units to "provide Mr. Ernest Hemingway with small arms, grenades or other captured articles he desires." It was signed by a major from Army Intelligence.[22] Although General "Wild Bill" Donovan, founder of the OSS, was said to be arriving in Chartres that evening, Bruce thought it more important to join Hemingway in Rambouillet. If the town were as vulnerable to German counterattack as Hemingway said it was, firsthand intelligence would be needed by the forces at Chartres where the liberation of Paris was being planned. One of the two routes into the French capital ran through Rambouillet. Any rearguard action the Germans might mount there would cost lives, delay the highly charged and symbolic liberation, and embarrass its planners.

When Bruce arrived at the Hôtel du Grand Veneur, he found Ernest's two rooms on the second floor were an arsenal for the Maquis as well as a reporting point. "Agents and patrols kept rushing in with reports, some of them contradictory, but all indicating that the Germans were laying mines . . . about eight miles away with a force of approximately 150 men. . . . there were no American troops in Rambouillet." Bruce set off to gather reinforcements from the Resistance group twenty-two kilometers away at Maintenon. By midnight, Rambouillet was occupied by thirty volunteers, "including two very drunken AWOL paratroopers, ten Resistance people, fourteen gendarmes, and a few machine guns." Around midnight, Bruce organized the night patrol, password "France-Orléans," and bedded down in a private home to the sound of heavy rain on the roof.[23]

The next day, wet and overcast, Bruce and Hemingway were holding the town and "sending out small patrols along all the roads." The American reconnaissance team was gone, leaving Bruce and Hemingway defending the key crossroads with a handful of OSS men and a few Maquis. Both men found it incredible to be thirty miles from Paris with reports "that even a very small task force could easily move in," and to be forced to wait for unstated reasons. The report in Paris of imminent liberation caused Resistance fighters to rise up prematurely, resulting in "considerable losses." (Over the next five days, 901 Free French of the Interior and 582 Paris civilians were killed in the liberation, another 3,500 wounded.)[24] That afternoon Bruce moved into the Hôtel du Grand Veneur, where he, Hemingway, and a French secret service operative, Mouthard, interrogated patrols, settled local disputes, and received German prisoners brought in by armed civilians. That night the three combatants led an excursion to receive an arranged air drop of munitions, returning with "a number of bazookas, rifles and grenades."[25] For the next two days, Bruce, Hemingway, and Mouthard provided some semblance of order in the confusion that was Rambouillet, where German forces were still active on the perimeter. Later, Bruce recalled the scene in Ernest's bedroom:

> Within, Ernest, looking like a jolly, dark Bacchus, dispensed high, low, and middle justice in English, French and broken German. His language was strong, salty, and emphatic. Army gear littered the floor. Carbines stood in each corner, revolvers of every nationality were heaped carelessly on the bed, the bathtub was filled with hand grenades, and the basin with brandy bottles, while under the bed was a cache of Army rations and whisky. . . . At one point we had a Polish private, a Ukrainian corporal, and an Austrian sergeant all shivering before Ernest. He dealt with them in summary fashion—the Pole was sent to the kitchen to peel potatoes, the Russian to a broiling greenhouse under guard, and the Austrian to clean jeeps.[26]

On August 22, Bruce recorded in his diary that "ten German tanks up the road were active again today. One of our Resistance men was killed, another captured, and they [Germans] took fifteen hostages away with them." The following day, correspondents poured into Rambouillet, hot on the track of General Jacques Leclerc, who arrived that afternoon at Château de Rambouillet, the summer residence of the president of the republic, to command the French column that would officially liberate Paris. Bruce recorded that General Leclerc was "tall, spare, handsome, stern-visaged, and a striking figure. . . . I was . . . asked by him to give all the intelligence I could to his G-2 Commander Repiton. This, with the assistance of Hemingway, Mouthard, and Mowinckle, I did."[27]

Early the next morning, August 24, Bruce and his OSS compatriots joined Leclerc's move toward Paris. On the outskirts of Versailles, they "found Hemingway and the Private Army, including Mouthard, had been engaged in a battle between French tanks and two Bouche 88 guns. The latter were demolished, and prisoners taken."[28] (Ernest's account sounded less heroic: when the German 88s opened up on the column, he dove for cover.) In Hemingway's shirt pocket was a ragged-edged note ripped out of Bruce's memo book. Written the previous night, it directed Hemingway to arrange transportation for the Resistance men into Paris, where Bruce would pay their reasonable expenses. "I feel," Bruce wrote, "that it is important to keep them together to be used for certain future purposes that I have in mind."[29] In the early afternoon of August 25, the feast day of St. Louis, patron saint of France, General Leclerc's column crossed the Seine and entered a Paris gone crazy with joy. By late that night, having weathered the thousands of Parisians who besieged them with flowers, kisses, and wine, having come through the sporadic sniper fire from rooftops and the celebratory firing of weapons in the streets, Bruce, Hemingway, and his band of men settled down in the Ritz Hotel on Place Vendôme, where the manager provided them first with an enormous round of martinis followed by a superb dinner. Outside, as Bruce recorded in his diary, "the streets are really dangerous, for everyone with a firearm is trying to use it."[30] The following morning, Hemingway and the FFI paid a call at the Shakespeare and Company bookstore where the younger Hemingway's Paris education began twenty-two years earlier. Sylvia Beach, the owner, came running down the stairs to greet him, and her enduring friend, Adrienne Monnier, offered wine to the men and her next-to-last bar of soap to Hemingway. The bookstore itself, earlier under threat of confiscation by the Germans, was bare, its five thousand books, photos, letters, and records spirited away to safekeeping.[31]

While Hemingway enjoyed the liberation of Paris, readers of the *New Republic* a world away caught the first wave of the postwar Hemingway critical industry—Malcolm Cowley's "Hemingway at Midnight." While editing the Viking *Portable Hemingway*, Cowley, a member of the Lost Generation turned critic, spun off essays that brought Hemingway's work into a clearer focus for general readers and young college instructors, who would, in turn, write their own academic essays. Cowley, seeing the patterns emerge, linked Hemingway to "the haunted and nocturnal [American] writers, the men who dealt in images that were symbols of an inner world." That there was an inner world to Hemingway, a world beneath the surface of his fiction, that one needed to read all of his stories to see it—these suggestions moved Hemingway's work out of the category of popular fiction and up to the level of American classics. Cowley, of course, did not get it all right the first time out, but here was the start of something new.[32]

Hemingway was too busy living in the intensity of Paris revitalized to be concerned by his literary reputation. Very quickly the appetites of its liberators reduced the Ritz kitchen to paltry fare, but its magnificent wine cellar continued to produce a steady flow of champagne. Most legitimate restaurants were closed while black market cafés flourished; the Métro remained immobile; and electricity was scarce. The swarm of American correspondents were billeted at the Hôtel Scribe, where an Army kitchen was set up to feed them, but Hemingway and his FFI men remained at the Ritz, operating out of room 31. That's where Mary Welsh found him with a half-finished letter to her on the table, telling her that he felt his luck had run out and asking her to find a *Time/Life* assignment in Paris, which she had already done without his urging.[33]

Mary registered for room 86, but as often as not she and Ernest either shared his bed or hers, a liaison which did not escape the eyes of Mme César Ritz, the proprietor's mother, who refused to recognize Mary's presence. The lovers rediscovered the Hemingway haunts from his early Paris days—old Montparnasse and St. Germain cafés, the Luxembourg Gardens, the St. Sulpice apartment— the two of them walking alone through all his old familiar places. The Louvre and other museums were closed; Gertrude Stein and tiny Miss Toklas were in the country; and at Cafés Select, Lilas, and du Dôme the answer was the same: no whiskey, no gin, no cognac. They found Picasso alive and painting in his chilly studio, undaunted by the Nazi occupation. For Ernest, those Paris days with Mary were a re-creation of his affair with Martha Gellhorn eight years earlier in Madrid. He was back in a grand hotel, in a war-ravaged capital city, sleeping with a lovely young woman while married to someone else. Not only was Mary sexually creative, she was also, and even better, a woman who had not heard all his stories of being poor in Paris. They lived existentially: "This is it," he told her, "our one and only life."[34]

Chapter Eighteen

DOWN AMONG
THE DEAD MEN

September to November 1944

ASMALL BUT WELL-ARMED Hemingway convoy—two cars, two jeeps, and a motorcycle—left Paris the morning of September 7 with Archie Pelkey once more assigned as Ernest's driver. With them were three of the remaining FFI men, one Army officer, and two other correspondents, all en route to rejoin Lanham's 22nd Infantry Regiment for the push into Germany. The rest of September was a blur of road blocks, blown tires, friendly villagers, and retreating Germans. That Hemingway's convoy came unscathed through minefields, dangerous crossroads, and the possibility of German ambush is a matter of sound maps, good fortune, and battle-tested judgment. As they reached the Belgian border, Germans were counterattacking a few kilometers ahead at Paliseul, leaving ten Americans dead and twenty-three wounded. Ernest is warned to expect increased ambushes and traps, for Germans with captured American battle plans are trying to get their retreating troops and artillery safely behind the vaunted Siegfried Line of defense. Before sleeping that night, Ernest writes Mary, professing his love, wishing her good luck, and hoping that he is not in too much trouble, for he knows that disgruntled journalists have filed charges accusing him of carrying and using weapons at Rambouillet. If a full-blown court-martial results, he could be stripped of his correspondent's credentials and summarily sent back to Cuba.[1] When Ernest wakes in the night to a mortar's cough, he writes Mary that he thinks of Tom Welsh's lovely daughter, the look, touch, and feel of her. His almost daily letters are ardent and insistent, increasingly so, as he re-creates the paper passion of earlier separations from his previous muses—Hadley, Pauline, and Martha. Since meeting Mary in London, he has forgotten Martha except when drinking enough to bring out his wicked tongue. Once again he is living by his own rules of behavior, rules he will soon be calling tribal.

On September 9, Lanham's forward command post was situated on a hillside overlooking the Belgian town of Houffalize; the 22nd's tank destroyers were picking off retreating German armored vehicles as they crossed the town's bridge toward Liège. German artillery, in turn, was laying down protective fire on the approaches into the village. In the woods to the left, one of the 22nd's tank destroyers hits a mine: two men are wounded. On a foolish bet as to who can reach the village center first, Lanham and Hemingway depart on separate routes: Ernest, with Pelkey driving, follows another jeep of FFI men down the main road; Lanham's group takes a back route following a goat path. Delayed by a series of felled and booby-trapped trees blocking the road, Hemingway's group divides, Ernest and Pelkey going one way, the FFI jeep another. By the time Ernest arrives, the Germans have blown the bridge and Lanham is staring across the swift stream at the retreating enemy. He and Ernest, perched on a fence, survey the situation. It will be nightfall before his engineers arrive to repair the bridge, and Lanham is not going to advance on foot without his armored support. Once the liberated villagers understand the problem, they begin clearing debris, building buttresses, hauling and nailing plank flooring: in forty-five minutes they put up a wooden bridge that supports jeeps and tank destroyers.[2]

Three days later, the 22nd Regiment splits into two columns, entering Germany to seize the high ground above Hemeres. Hemingway follows the northern column through heavy woods, making his way up a high hill to see two German tanks racing out of the village chased by artillery shells sending up yellow clouds of smoke. Down the hill and across the slabstone riverbed, Hemingway touches down on German soil to be greeted by two villagers offering him schnapps while others come out with hands above their heads to surrender. On the right flank, Avel is burning, and the 50-caliber machine guns hammer away in the distance. Outside the village, Hemingway stops for the night at an abandoned farmhouse. There in the kitchen, with artillery fire punctuating the conversation, Ernest watches the interrogation of prisoners. The first one has fine yellow dust covering his face, his long hair tangled and clotted with it. The youngest, barely eighteen, tells of desertions, of Panzer tanks firing on their own troops, forcing them to attack, and of American bombs leaving him partially buried. Outside the farmhouse, American P-47s are laying down close air support, driving off another German counterattack.[3]

For several days afterward, Hemingway retires to the warmth of division headquarters to clear up a chest cold while Lanham's troops fight their way through the woods of the Schnee Eifel. When Hemingway returns to the front on September 18, Lanham walks him over the battle terrain, pointing out where the German 88mm opened up on his troops, explaining how he and Captain Blazzard rallied the men and took the hill. Ernest listens hard, interviews Blazzard, taking detailed notes, and writes it up as "War in the Siegfried Line," which due to *Collier's* editing sounds as if he were actually there as an eyewitness.[4] (From years of writing based on numerous sources, Ernest can take his reader into places he has never been, and everyone is certain that it is firsthand experience until anomalies appear.) That night at Buchet, where Lanham has set up his command post in a large farmhouse, Ernest is invited to a steak dinner celebrating his return to the regiment.

When the first German shell comes through one wall of the farmhouse and out the other side without exploding, ten of the twelve men at the dinner table disappear into the potato cellar. At the door Lanham turns back to see Hemingway "quietly cutting his meat." The colonel orders him into the cellar, but Ernest refuses and they begin arguing.

> *Another shell came through the wall. He [Ernest] continued to eat. We renewed the argument. He would not budge. Another shell went through the wall. I told him to put on his goddamned tin hat. He wouldn't so I took mine off. . . . We argued about the whole thing but went on eating. He reverted to his favorite theory that you were as safe in one place as another as far as artillery fire was concerned unless you were being shot at personally. I pointed out that was precisely what was being done.*[5]

When the shelling stops and the dinner guests, officers and correspondents, return to find Lanham and Hemingway still sitting at the table, some call their behavior bravery. Lanham called it foolhardiness, emphasizing that he and Ernest knew the difference between the two.

There in the village of Buchet within a thousand yards of Hitler's Siegfried Line, Hemingway added to his legend without revealing anything about his inner condition. If he believed, as he told Mary, that his luck had run out, his act could be seen as suicidal. Externally, he appeared during this entire period to be extraordinarily happy, and said he was in letters—happy to be with front-line fighting troops, happy to see and understand the battlefields. He also continually took risks that amazed and worried the 22nd's riflemen. In a poem for Mary, he wrote:

> *Repeat after me.*
> *Do you take this old whore*
> *Death for thy lawful*
> *Wedded wife?*
> *Repeat after me*
> *I do, I do, I do.*[6]

After returning from division headquarters, where he may have heard more bad news about the investigation into his Rambouillet activity, Hemingway's letters to Mary became more ardent and more lonely. Words are repeated over and over—away from her, he is sick, lonesome, missing her, loving her, writing sad, dull letters, needing her letters, needing her next to him in bed desperately. She is his "Pickle" or his "Small Friend," as bomber pilots refer to their fighter escort as "Little Friend."

At Buchet the advance of the 22nd stalled for lack of supplies, ammunition, and gasoline. For almost two weeks, Lanham's troops laid mines and booby traps to protect their overextended lines, but still the Germans slipped through at night to lay their own mines. Vulnerable and a long way from home, it was a narrow time for the 22nd and for Hemingway. Lanham said later that he and Ernest were "both convinced that the Germans would jump us some dark night and would be back in our rear areas in nothing flat. . . . [Hemingway] told me repeatedly that he slept with his clothes on and his weapons beside him." During those tense evenings, sweating it out, Ernest and the colonel told each other tall tales of their youth. Lanham remembered hearing about Ernest's mother, Grace, "whom he hated and to whom he invariably referred as a bitch." He listened to Ernest's increasingly elaborate story of how his first wife, Hadley, "lost his volume of short stories. . . . He said it nearly did him in. Even in the retelling of the story I could see his rage mount." When Ernest told Buck about his married life with Martha, "his hatred of her was a terrible thing to see."[7] Increasingly, Hemingway's life was becoming his story, which he rehearsed and refined, embedding it with such vivid details that it would be difficult later to sort out his fictions.

On September 23/24, writing to Mary, he still worried about charges filed against him, furious to be in trouble over action of which any man should feel proud. The "liars" and the "phonies" are ganging up on him while the politics of war sicken him. After fourteen pages the letter breaks off, followed by two more pages the next day, and stuffed into an envelope marked: "Please Deliver (In case of

CASUALTY)." In those added pages, he says no matter who has loved her, he loves her more; please love him, trust him.[8] On September 26, Ernest received permission from the 4th Infantry Division to "be present in Paris an indefinite period for the purpose of writing articles for Collier's Magazine."[9]

Returning to the Ritz, now reserved by the military for Very Important Persons only, Hemingway had no trouble in securing a room while continuing to share Mary's bed. She soon made clear her misgivings about their relationship. In a letter to Ernest, she admitted that her second marriage was finished. Noel had written that he was sorry he "had not the qualifications to stay the distance" with her. She, in turn, was made to feel inadequate by Ernest, whose manic ardor at times overwhelmed her, demanding nothing less than everything. She admitted having avoided him at the Ritz one day, "wanting [a] four hours pass from your domination because you are so big and you absorb me so that I lose myself, wanting only the soft easy business of flattery and admiration and gaiety that matters not, and nothing intense, a whole evening cut right down to my small stature with no effort and nothing at all clutching at my throat and chest and stomach."[10]

On October 3, orders came from Supreme Headquarters Allied Expeditionary Force (SHAEF) directing Hemingway to report to the Inspector General, Third Army.[11] There was no need to specify the reason: charges of being an armed combatant had come home to roost. On October 5, at Nancy, officers Ernest knew on Patton's staff advised him to deny the charges. The Inspector General's hearing on October 6 was an inquiry to determine if the charges had any merit; it was not a court-martial. The hearing began with Ernest's rehearsed and sanitized version of Rambouillet, where he served only as an interpreter and conduit between the handful of OSS officers and the French Maquis. When Colonel Bruce arrived, Ernest said, "I offered my services to him in any way in which I might be useful provided that my actions did not violate the Geneva convention or that any of them should in any way prejudice my fellow war correspondents." In helping with the problems Bruce faced, Ernest said that he "served only in an advisory capacity to Colonel Bruce . . . I did not command troops nor give orders but only transmitted orders." The Inspector General then listed the specific charges:

> *That Mr. Hemingway stripped off correspondent insignia and acted as a colonel [of] French Resistance troops; that he had a room with mines, grenades and war maps; that he directed resistance patrols.*

Hemingway admitted to being without his correspondent's insignia only when he was in shirtsleeves in the warm August weather. As for being called a colonel, "it was in the same way that citizens of the state of Kentucky are sometimes addressed as colonel without it implying any military rank." Any arms seen in his room were "stored there by French Resistance men who were operating under orders of the proper authorities." As for war maps, he always traveled with maps, and he never directed any patrols.

> *Q. Were there mines in your room?*
> *A. There were no mines in my room. I would greatly prefer not to have mines in my room at any time.*

When asked if he ever "fought with the men," he responded somewhat mendaciously that he "didn't fight with the men."[12] As he explained years later,

> *I swore I was not armed in Rambouillet. There was not need to state I was armed outside of the city limit. I swore I did not "fight with the men." Who would fight with the men, i.e. not get along with them. Not me. . . . I denied and kidded out of all of it and swore away everything I felt any pride in.*[13]

Ever since the summer of 1915, when he was pursued by a game warden for shooting a blue heron and eventually standing before a county judge to pay his fine, Hemingway had a profound, almost irrational fear of the law, its enforcers, and the courtroom. He might joke about his sworn testimony at Nancy, but at the time there was nothing humorous about it until the Inspector General found no cause to pursue the charges. When Ernest sent *Collier's* his story on the 22nd attacking the Siegfried Line, he wired changes to a photograph, advising them to paint out the protruding ammunition clip from his pocket, which he was carrying for a sergeant and which "might be misconstrued."[14] By the end of the day, the Inspector General could report that there were no grounds for a court-martial, letting Hemingway off the hook. The finding should have elated Hemingway; instead it left him dark and moody, angry with the "phonies" and suspicious of higher authority.

His erratic behavior on returning to Paris may have been related to the interrogation. At the Ritz with Mary and his old friend, Marlene Dietrich, Ernest alternated between considerate, boyish lover, humming tunes off-key, and the dark, violent man who slapped Mary for insulting his drunken friends from the 22nd. She carped too much; he drank too much. Mercurial, impulsive, but eventually and always endearing, Ernest was never boring that October in Paris. Then, as the month was ending, he was told that his son Jack, while on an OSS mission behind enemy lines, had been shot, captured, treated, and moved to a German hospital in the Vosges. Ernest was helpless, fuming, determined to effect a rescue while knowing such action would further endanger his oldest boy. The next day he convinced Mary to use her connections to apply for front-line coverage in the Vosges so that she might find better information about Jack. At the same time, he began packing up to rejoin the 22nd Infantry, leaving Paris on November 9.[15]

The day was drear when Ernest walked back into Lanham's command post, a plywood trailer in a far field facing an impassable forest. The 22nd's battalion commanders were already briefed for the morrow's attack on the Hürtgenwald, a battle from which none who were there would emerge whole. Lanham was happy to see Ernest's face. Over bottles of wine supplied by Hemingway, the two men talked until almost three in the morning. Lanham said, "We told each other about our childhood[s], our parents, our dreams, our hopes, our education, our women, our friends, our enemies, our triumphs and our disasters. . . . It was one of those rare occasions when two human beings suddenly find themselves in complete rapport and their separate worlds meet and merge."[16] Lanham, short and thin, was the field commander that Ernest would like to have been. In the Schnee Eifel, when his troops began to fall apart under murderous German fire, Lanham, armed with a pistol, led them back into the fight, telling them, "Goddamn, let's go get these Krauts. Let's kill these chickenshits. Let's get up over this hill now and get the place taken."[17] Hemingway, large in manner and bulk, was the writer that Lanham, who wrote poetry, would like to have been. They made an unlikely pair that night, each needing the other to be whole, a Laurel-and-Hardy tableau without slapstick, a "species of brotherhood," Lanham called it. It was a night spent whistling past the graveyard, for the soldier and the writer both knew the pending battle would be a bloody one.

The next morning, before the attack began, Hemingway wrote a quick note to his editor at *Collier's*, naming Mary Welsh as the sole beneficiary of the magazine's insurance policy on him. Martha, he said, was "fully provided for."[18] Shortly after noon on November 16, Hemingway watched the first riflemen of the 22nd Infantry wade across the Roter Weh and into the dark woods of Hürtgen Forest. Lanham's men who went across the stream and into the trees were a tight unit, battle-tested, operating smoothly with confidence in their leadership and in their own abilities. About three miles away lay their objective, the tiny village of Grosshau. Thirteen days later, when they pushed into the village, 87 percent of the men who crossed the Roter Weh were casualties, and those few who remained, including Ernest, could not say why.

Across the stream, the infantrymen made their way up the facing hill to the Rabenheck (Raven's Hackle), where terrain and German fire stopped them by sunset. Firs and hardwoods in orderly, tightly packed rows were impossible to see through. Firebreaks and logging roads were puddled with rainwater and deep with mud under which German mines were planted. Private First Class John L. Page, squad leader, said: "I never dried out, and neither did most of the rest of us for the next two weeks. The heavy mud caused most of the boys to throw away their galoshes and the constant rain and sleet made us that much colder and wetter." The gorge below their front line was filled with chest-deep water of the Weisser Weh; in the draw to their left was a German pillbox surrounded by log bunkers and barbed wire. That evening, the 22nd took out the bunkers and the pillbox, leaving twelve dead Germans and taking four prisoners. Lanham's losses that day were four officers and sixty-nine enlisted men. That night, riflemen carried their wounded back one thousand yards through inky woods to the closest transport, at every step hoping they were still on the mine-cleared path.

Then rain began to fall, turning to sleet, and the German artillery barrage began to burst in the treetops, sending splinters and shrapnel slicing through the Americans below. Technician 5th Grade George Morgan said,

> *You can't get protection. You can't see. You can't get fields of fire. The trees are slashed like a scythe by artillery. Everything is tangled. You can scarcely walk. Everybody is cold and wet, and the mixture of cold rain and sleet keeps falling. They jump off again and soon there is only a handful of the old men left.*

Every trail is mined, every intersection zeroed in upon, every night a nightmare. Some men break down from the noise, some from the blood, some from fear. Replacements pouring into the staging area are frequently dead men before ever reaching their platoons. Battalion commanders disappear at an unsustainable rate; lieutenants go down like birds in a shooting gallery. Field commissions raise sergeants to the officer ranks where they are chewed up as so much fodder. On the second day of the battle, the 22nd lost 10 officers and 129 enlisted men without advancing across the Weisser Weh. Each day ended with the thought that the fighting could not get worse, and each morning that hope faded.

The men of Fox Company, reduced to fifty riflemen, no sergeants, and two lieutenants, were looking across a hundred yards of open ground to the wood line beyond.

> Lieutenant Fitzgerald stood up and shouted, "Come on all you riflemen, let's go," and about thirty followed. This poorly organized group of soldiers reached the edge of the woods without opposition, but instead of holding there continued into the woods, became disoriented, and turned to the south. In a draw outside the battalion sector, Fitzgerald halted the platoon and had the soldiers begin entrenching. Just as they began to dig, a small German unit counterattacked them. Only four of the platoon made it back to the main body of the company.

By the time the report reached Lanham, all that remained of Fox Company were two officers and twelve enlisted men.[19]

Each day Hemingway writes Mary about close encounters with that "old whore, Death," unable because of the military censor to give details. Each day his notes to her become grimmer, as the woods deteriorate into a shambles of splintered stumps, shell holes, and body parts of dead men. To take his mind off mortar bursts that seem continuous, he writes about their future life in Cuba, living at the Finca, fishing on the *Pilar*, writing well, being a good husband and father. A recent hurricane that devastated parts of Cuba could not have destroyed everything; the Finca will be their command post. Mary's first letters back from the Vosges tell him that his son Jack is a confirmed POW with a shoulder wound that is not serious. She has applied for extended leave to return with him to Cuba, telling her boss that "we thought we had something that deserves a chance." Not so emotional as his letters to her, Mary's closes with: "I am your woman my dearest Only One for as long as you'll have me, and I will try to make that forever."[20]

The next day she told him of encountering Martha while lunching at the Hôtel Scribe. As Mary walked the length of the dining room, she passed Martha's good friend Virginia Cowles on one side and Mrs.

Hemingway on the other. When Bob Capa was asked where Mary was sitting, he said, "Just follow the daggers," referring to the looks given her by the two women. It was Mary's first encounter with Martha, whom she fairly assessed as "very pretty . . . the line of her nose was quite different from mine, and her skin nicer. It made me wish I were a tall slim sultry brunette . . . for you must be a little tired of blondes. And knowing she is very slim and straight-legged and lovely, I was terribly conscious of my damned old can. There was no face-to-face nonsense or anything stupid like that."[21]

Ernest had little time to savor Mary's account. Eight days into the woods, Lanham's command post trailer was now sitting on the edge of a firebreak, unsafe from artillery fire by day and from an unlocated German mortar by night. Returning one day from the area dubbed "The Valley of Death," Lanham found a rearguard fight going on in his clearing. "Men were firing and advancing and dropping and firing . . . then I saw E. H. . . . He was standing bolt upright watching the fight with intense interest. He was moving with the moving wave but I never saw him hit the ground. And this time there was no question at all that he was armed and using those arms."[22] That night Ernest tried to explain to Mary the cleansing effect of the violence surrounding him:

> You know how I was spooked of it [the battle] before it started. . . . But then about yesterday and the day before just like a gift . . . I get the old feeling of immortality back I used to have when I was 19—right in the middle of a really bad shelling—not the cagey assessment of chances—nor the angry, the hell with it feeling—nor the throw everything away feeling . . . just the pure old thing we used to operate on.[23]

Thereafter his letters begin to speak more frequently of his future writing, of collecting information, observing closely, seeing again the telling details. Absorbing and digesting the experience, he will "be able to invent a good battle for a book sometime out of my knowledge."[24] His book will not compete with the new young writers coming out of battles like this one, the ones "that we hope will write better and sounder than we can. That we blast the trail for. . . . I will just take my small piece of a tiny part of it and buttress it with the forgotten sometimes punchy knowledge and the new will work the mess so the old magic will work—and then we will have [the] book, a day at a time."[25]

Hemingway spent his days with Lanham and his troops, sleeping at night in the relative safety of a woodcutter's hut closer to division headquarters. His mornings began with General Raymond Barton's daily briefing on yesterday's action and the plans for the day, an affair Ernest disparagingly called the "ballroom bananas." By the time the 22nd got out of the dark forest, "Tubby" Barton was being referred to as "Our Lost Leader," after he stopped coming to the front lines to see what was actually happening. After several profane conversations between Lanham and Barton, the general did his best to have his regimental commander relieved, sending a psychiatrist to probe for signs of combat fatigue. Caught between entrenched Germans in front of him and a less than supportive commanding officer to his rear, Lanham sorely needed Hemingway as his "bitching post." The disparity between the infantrymen dying in the splintered, dripping forest and the military politics going on at division headquarters left a permanently bitter taste in Ernest's mouth.

Hemingway's own encounter with the psychiatrist did nothing to improve his attitude toward the profession or General Barton. Fellow journalist Bill Walton remembered the psychiatrist calling courage and cowardliness false values with which people kidded themselves. An argument developed, which led to the psychiatrist saying, "Every damn one of you is going to break sooner or later. . . . Including you, Hemingway!"

Hemingway exploded. He flushed deep red and pounded on the table so hard the wine bottle jumped around. . . . The captain was an ignoramus, an uneducated fool, a pervert, an enemy spy, and anything else unpleasant he could think of. . . . Something that was very deep in him had been touched. He couldn't forget it.[26]

On November 26, eleven days into the death factory, the 22nd Regiment finally reached their second-day objective: the village of Grosshau. The next two days were a horror show: infantry crossing an open field caught in murderous fire from entrenched Germans. Baker Company stalled at the edge of the woods, losing fifty-four out of seventy-nine soldiers. Suddenly, in one of those selfless acts that sometimes happen in battle, Private First Class Marcario Garcia went into the woods alone to destroy the enemy machine gunners with hand grenades and his rifle. Wounded in his assault, he nevertheless wiped out a second machine-gun pit, allowing what remained of his company to reach the woods. When Easy Company arrived with fresh support, they found "a picture of real carnage—arms, equipment, dead and wounded, Jerrys and GIs strewn all through the woods. Blasted trees, gaping shell holes, and the acrid smell and smoke of small arms and mortar fire completed the terrain. Company B remnants—2 lieutenants and 15 to 20 enlisted. . . . This was no picnic."[27]

Eventually Grosshau was taken by the 22nd in bloody house-to-house fighting that further diminished Lanham's already weakened regiment. For days afterward German artillery continued to bombard the American troops occupying the village until little was left above ground but rubble. When the 22nd was finally relieved from front-line duty on December 3, the regiment had cleared the enemy from six thousand yards of forest and one small village while sustaining over 2,700 casualties. The 22nd Regiment's Chaplain Boice said, "A part of us died in the forest, and there is a part of our mind and heart and soul left there." Two days after the 22nd stood down, Ernest wrote a bleak, tense letter, clearly disturbed by the Hürtgen experience, telling Martha that she had destroyed him with her demands to be free of him. In passing he said that a fellow correspondent related that Martha told him that Ernest's taking away her *Collier's* job was the worst thing ever done by one journalist to another. Ernest said the man would not believe that she had sent him to *Collier's*.[28]

Hemingway, Pelkey, and Walton were almost added to the list of those who did not get out of the woods. On the last gray, chilly day, driving down an exposed stretch of muddy road, Hemingway told Pelkey to stop the jeep. Listening to a faint hum, Ernest yelled, "Oh, God, jump!" The three went crashing face down into the muddy ditch, Ernest on top of Walton, while overhead they heard a plane stitching their jeep with its machine guns. In the dead quiet that followed, Ernest sat up and unhitched his canteen, offering Walton and Pelkey a roadside gin. They were alive only because Ernest recognized the aircraft motor from the Spanish Civil War. While they remained in the ditch, the plane reappeared out of the overcast sky to riddle the road one last time.[29]

Patrick, Bumby (Jack), and Gregory summering on Cat Cay while Ernest fished for tuna. (John F. Kennedy Library)

Financial angel to the Hemingway family, Uncle Augustus "Gus" Pfeiffer on board the *Pilar*. (John F. Kennedy Library)

Sara Murphy with her three children, Baoth, Patrick, and Honoria. (John F. Kennedy Library)

Photo taken from the lighthouse across from Hemingway's Key West home on Whitehead Street before the brick wall and swimming pool were built. (Library of Congress)

Having moved his bar from Greene Street to Duval, Josie Russell began featuring free live music on Saturday nights. (Library of Congress)

Martha Gellhorn in Cuba in the late 1930s. (Toby and Betty Bruce Archives)

The *Pilar* cutting a wake with teasers in the water and lines baited. (John F. Kennedy Library)

Hemingway's Cuban mate, Carlos Guitiérrez, rigging fishing lines on board the *Pilar*. (John F. Kennedy Library)

Hemingway and his Cuban mate displaying a twelve-foot marlin on the Bimini dock. (John F. Kennedy Library)

ABOVE: Left to right, Ben Fourie, Charles Thompson (obscured), Philip Percival, and Ernest Hemingway at the end of a kudu hunt: "great, curling, sweeping horns, brown as walnut meats"—from *Green Hills of Africa*. (John F. Kennedy Library)

LEFT: His characteristic glasses in hand, Ernest resting at the Percival home waiting for the safari to begin. (Wright Langley Archives)

Serengeti Plain, Pauline's lion that she almost shot: "No I didn't. Don't lie to me. Just let me enjoy my triumph"—from *Green Hills of Africa*. (Wright Langley Archives)

"We rolled the rhino into a sort of kneeling position and cut away the grass to take some pictures"—from *Green Hills of Africa*. (John F. Kennedy Library)

LEFT: Nattily dressed, bullfighter Sidney Franklin and Ernest Hemingway on the *Paris* en route to the Spanish Civil War. (John F. Kennedy Library)

BOTTOM: Spanish Civil War photos from Hemingway's collection. Woman in the middle is dead; man on left is a heartbeat from death; the man on the right watches the executioner put a hood on the hanged woman. (John F. Kennedy Library)

West of almost everything: Ketchum, Idaho, ca. 1940. Until the Sun Valley Lodge dominated the scene, Ketchum was a rough ranch and mining town with open gambling and several saloons. The sign for Jack Lane's Mercantile store, barely readable in the middle of town, marks the right turn toward the Lodge. Hemingway's house, bought in 1959, was located in the woods north and slightly to the left of Lane's. (The Community Library, Ketchum, Idaho)

Celery stalks at midnight: December 1940, New York City. A month married and not yet antagonists, Ernest and Martha are sipping martinis at the Stork Club, Martha with her habitual cigarette. *For Whom the Bell Tolls* has become a bestseller, and they have booked trans-Pacific passage to the war in China. (Sherman Billingsley's Stork Club)

Over there: July 1944, somewhere in France. Ernest studies battle maps with his jeep driver after the breakthrough at St. Lô. Noticeable are his wire-rimmed reading glasses. Noticeably missing are any insignias designating him a correspondent. (John F. Kennedy Library)

RIGHT: The Blond Venus reprised: ca. 1950. Mary Hemingway, her short-cropped hair bleached the smoky shade of blond favored by Ernest. (John F. Kennedy Library)

BOTTOM: The eyes have it: December 1950, in the Floridita Bar, Havana. Gianfranco Ivancich with his arm around Mary watches Ernest bask in Adriana's light; Mary Hemingway smiles at Adriana; Dora Ivancich looks back toward her son, Gianfranco, while Adriana looks elsewhere. (John F. Kennedy Library)

In the middle of the night: late spring, 1952, Finca Vigia. Scary photo of Ernest armed and rampant at the Finca during the period of break-ins. (John F. Kennedy Library)

After the fall: January 23, 1954, near Murchison Falls, Africa. The remains of Roy Marsh's Cessna after the first crash, from which Ernest and Mary walked away relatively unhurt. (John F. Kennedy Library)

PART TWO

A FALL FROM GRACE

1945 TO 1952

Like one
Who having into truth, by telling of it,
Made such a sinner of his memory,
To credit his own lie.

William Shakespeare, *The Tempest*

Chapter Nineteen

STARTING OVER

March to December 1945

WITH THE WAR in Europe moving toward its
now inevitable conclusion, Hemingway was suddenly
eager to return to Cuba where Mary agreed to meet
him for a trial union. On March 6, 1945, in her Ritz Hotel box she
found his hasty farewell note promising to be faithful to her and
love her always. He was her Mountain; she was his Kitten. A week
later from New York, he sent her detailed instructions for getting to
Cuba, where he would meet her at the airport. Displaced and out of
step with the home front, he was discovering the chasm separating
combat vets from state-side civilians: they no longer spoke the same
language. Those who had not been there did not understand about
Hürtgenwald. When not with others like himself, he felt strange and
vulnerable. After a week in the city tending to chores—his publisher,
his lawyer, his banker, his former wives, his children—he was on
the train to Miami with sixteen-year-old Patrick, and from there to
Havana. With him he carried two new shotguns and his bank statement showing a $20,000 balance.[1]

He was returning to domestic problems long deferred and to a
life so quiet by comparison to the Schnee Eifel or to wartime Paris

that it seemed hardly to move at all. By the time he reached the Finca, he had lost his temper twice with his second wife, Pauline, in phone conversations about their two boys. By letter she asked him to erase their arguments; she would be more considerate of his time if he would do the same for her. Knowing how incapable he was of dealing with a woman as an equal, she gave in on which boy would be with her for Easter. Pat was already with him; Greg would join them in Havana in a week.[2] Assessing the damage to the Finca and to himself, Hemingway found his numerous cats starved thin, many of his mango trees destroyed by a hurricane, and a good night's rest requiring a sleeping pill. Cats could be fattened and trees replanted, but his writing or the lack of it was a more difficult problem. For five years now he had written no fiction. In his writing room was an almost forgotten fragment of a Bimini story that referred back to the island's heyday as a rumrunner's haven during prohibition. Other than that, he had used up most of what he knew from the previous decade, but his recent war experiences were filled with usable material. So the difficulty was not the subject matter, it was the act itself—sitting down alone with pencil and paper to put down words in their effective order. It was an old problem that he had solved several times before. After each of his novels, he had experienced that emptiness that comes with having completed the work, followed by uncertainty of what to write next. Sometimes it had taken him as long as six months or a year to return to his trade, but never had he gone five years. It was going to be very difficult, he wrote Mary, but somehow he would get through it. The writing appeared impossible, but he would get in shape to fix that. He promised her that he was not drinking at night to fight off loneliness, nor was he drinking in the morning. For a man who began his mornings in Paris with a bottle of champagne, this was a large promise.[3]

On April 12, with the defeat of Germany in sight, Franklin Delano Roosevelt died of a massive hemorrhage, shrouding the nation in a cloak of mourning. Across the United States there were banner headlines, grieving civilians, special church services, and flags at half-mast, but at Finca Vigia, Hemingway did not weep. Despite having once met and dined with the president at the White House for a private showing of *The Spanish Earth*, Hemingway always resented what Roosevelt's programs had done to Key West. The quiet fishing village which was Ernest's haven went bankrupt in 1934, turning itself over to the Federal Emergency Relief Act. The island was transformed into a tourist resort, completely managed by federal bureaucrats and soon overrun with gawking mainlanders looking for a glimpse of Ernest Hemingway. Two days after Roosevelt died, with Havana flying flags at half-mast, Hemingway went out to supper with a friend; in his several letters written that day, the only mention of FDR was to Buck Lanham:

> *They talk about our Lord haveing [sic] a bad time on that tree and everyone in mourning for the death of the Chief Executive but nobody has ever been anywhere that hasn't been with Infantry. Catch him, men. Sentiment is about to over-come him.*[4]

In those same several letters of mid-April, what Hemingway did not mention to anyone was the doubt that he could write a better book than *For Whom the Bell Tolls*. In the previous twenty years he had published three collections of short stories, a satire (*The Torrents of Spring*), a roman à clef (*The Sun Also Rises*), a semihistorical novel (*A Farewell to Arms*), a book of natural history (*Death in the Afternoon*), a safari book (*Green Hills of Africa*), a semiproletariat novel (*To Have and Have Not*), and a play (*The Fifth Column*). *For Whom the Bell Tolls* was his epic novel just as "The Snows of Kilimanjaro" was his epic short story: in both, he gave the reader a story within which was embedded an entire collection of short stories. The critics who said he repeated himself were missing the obvious. Always experimenting, always reaching beyond his last effort, Hemingway had never repeated the form, and he was not about to start. The bone upon which he gnawed was old, bearing teethmarks of every artist who ever created a masterpiece: how to make a better one when the last one was the best he could make.

Following his old prescription for beginning again, Hemingway started by writing letters and reading background books: Buck Lanham's book on infantry tactics and the biographies of two generals—Nathan Bedford Forrest from the American Civil War, and Michel Ney, Napoleon's faithful field commander.[5] When his Havana doctor, José Luis Herrera, came by the Finca to discuss Ernest's recurring headaches and insomnia, Hemingway told him about his two concussions and their aftermath: a ringing in his ears, loss of verbal memory, temporary impotence, and sometimes erratic behavior. After listening to his patient's symptoms, Herrera explained that his first concussion in London should have been trepanned and drained, and that his post-accident drinking could have triggered a fatal hemorrhage. The doctor recommended that Hemingway rest, do a little intellectual work each day, but not force it.[6]

Before Mary arrived early in May, Ernest had the Finca ready for inspection: the maid, cook, chauffeur, and gardeners at attention; the heavily chlorinated pool water as clear as possible; the house airy and bright; the Capehart phonograph restored to action. At Cojimar, Gregorio was almost finished with repairs to the *Pilar*, returning her from sub hunter to fishing boat. Having carefully prepared his bower, Hemingway was a little anxious: what if Mary did not like the house, his friends, the country, or his children? His loneliness, much detailed in every letter, sorely required a wife in bed beside him. He was convinced that Mary was ready to give up her career in journalism to be Mrs. Hemingway full time, to be the wife to him that Martha never was.[7]

Her arrival could not have been more propitious: on May 8, Germany surrendered unconditionally. The war in Europe was over. Simultaneously Ernest learned that his son, Jack, was safely liberated from a German prison camp. A month later, Hemingway told Buck Lanham how happy Mary was at the Finca, and how active they were together in bed: fifty-five times in May, he bragged.[8] When Jack arrived on thirty days leave for rest and rehabilitation, he found Mary lovely to look at and supportive of his dad. Greg, at fifteen, was wary at first, having given his heart to Martha; but Mary won him over with her apparent devotion to fishing, her ability to command the Finca staff, and her quickness in learning to wing-shoot. Every one agreed: Mary was the perfect fit for Ernest. She loved the Gulf Stream, enjoyed fishing, swimming, and boating, was taking Spanish lessons, and adored the Hemingway cats.[9]

In her journal, however, Mary chronicled a far less satisfactory life, one that she kept below the surface as well as she could. "Nothing is mine," she wrote. "The man is his own with various adjuncts— his writing, his children, his cats. . . . The strip of bed where I sleep is not mine. The room belongs to Marty—my heart belongs to Daddy." Martha's picture remained on the wall of Mary's bedroom because Ernest said he did not want to upset his sons who loved Martha. Martha's furniture filled the room, her presence hung in the air like perfume. "About your picture of Marty," Mary told him on an inter-house note, "I will try from now on not to be offended by such considerations for the children . . . [but] I cannot help but wondering whether or not you kept pictures of Pauline around for the sake of the children when Marty was here."[10] The Finca became for Mary "a lovely place for a prison," and her bracelets, gifts from Ernest, felt like "chains to this place by the wall." Alone in a strange country whose language she did not yet speak, she was terribly vulnerable and too aware of her differences, knowing nothing "of pursuit of fish, animals and birds," the house religion. Ernest wanted a daughter with Martha's blond hair; Mary resisted becoming "an old brood mare." She wept for the future "which looked good, tasted good and went sour in my stomach."

At the Club Cazadores, Ernest organized a shoot to welcome Jack back to Cuba, but Mary found the following luncheon raucous and disorderly, the only other woman in sight being some man's mistress. When a firecracker went off close to her ear, she burst into tears, and was driven home, where she wrote in her journal:

> Can only conclude I'd be an idiot to stay here and marry Papa. . . .
> Our values—most of them are antipodal. . . . He puts a premium on
> bad manners, on violence, on killing (man, animals, birds, fish), on
> toughness, on death. I begin to realize how highly I value gentleness,

*conversation, non-violence. . . . I'd better go while the going is pos-
sible and can be without too much bitterness.*[11]

Without fully understanding how accurate his guess, Ernest referred
to Mary's journal as her "Horror Diary."[12]

On June 19, Ernest wrote Mary's father, thanking him for the gift
of religious books and professing his love for Mary whom he would
marry as soon as possible. The next day, Ernest drove Mary to the
airport to return to Chicago to complete her divorce from Noel
Monks. On the mud-slippery road, Ernest lost control of the Lincoln
convertible, which left the road, smashing into a tree. Ernest's forehead banged into the rearview mirror, four of his ribs were damaged
against the steering wheel, and his left knee was badly hurt. Jack
was safe in the backseat, but Mary was covered with blood streaming from her left cheek. At the hospital, Ernest quickly arranged for
a plastic surgeon to repair Mary's face, but could do nothing about
her placement in the women's ward where the cries of those in labor
went on all night long.[13]

A violent crash, bloody heads, wailing women: omens too ominous to dwell on, perhaps, but a determining accident nonetheless. Given her state of mind, had Mary left Cuba that day, she may
never have returned. During the extra two months she remained at
the Finca, Ernest was more solicitous of her well-being, listening
to her ideas for organizing the household and to her requirements
for a more orderly life. By the Fourth of July, Mary was writing to
Pamela Churchill that life at the Finca was "so idyllic, so lush, so
leisured, with everything so plentiful" that she sometimes felt guilty.
"I can sun in the altogether with only the Finca dogs, cats, servants,
and children to disturb my privacy." There were, she said, twenty
cats, five dogs, and a parrot who said, "Wanna be a fighter pilot." She
ended the letter saying, "I know why they always have the films ending with the two lovers riding into the sunset . . . felicity is so dull to
all except its immediate participants."[14]

Before leaving at the end of August to complete her divorce, Mary
wrote Ernest a good-bye note that pledged her love no matter what

adjustments they needed to make.[15] While she was gone, Ernest bombarded her with letters and gifts pledging his ardor and his good intentions. She was his full partner in the Hemingway venture, and his best lover always. Her suggestions for the Finca were underway: gutters were being improved to gather water; the cats would no longer sleep all over the house; the new furniture she wanted to replace Martha's was being built.[16] The two of them, he said, were a country of their own beyond the rules and prejudices of institutions. Needing no organized religion to guide them, they must only believe in each other. As always, Ernest was a more persuasive swain on paper than in person; his written words, which were his art, were always able to move a woman's heart closer to his own.

Mary returned in October, her divorce final and her previous unhappiness at rest. She found Ernest to be constantly polite, loving, and open to her needs to work. She would help him with his typing, take care of marketing, oversee household expenses, learn the routines of gardens and pool, and most importantly keep Ernest's "privacy absolutely intact for whatever hours each day he works and let nobody get at him." After six weeks in Chicago, the Cuban weather, the ease of country life complete with servants, and the beauty of the Finca were a soothing balm.[17] One of the first things she did was answer a telegram from Time/Life asking if she planned to return. She telegraphed back: "With much nostalgia for Time . . . I [am] nonetheless eager [to] continue current career of loafer fisherwoman housewife . . . so strike me off the rolls."[18]

Her euphoria lasted about a week. Soon she complained of Ernest's need to control all that he surveyed. He might speak of sharing, but in fact he continued to make most of the everyday decisions: what food to buy, what meals to prepare, what jobs needed to be done. He even took to "supervising" Mary's letters to her parents. In her journal, she noted:

> *Whatever else the critics say about him, they certainly [are] right about him and women—he wants them like Indian girls—completely obedient and sexually loose. That I think I might learn to handle. But the*

*. . . criticism and long intelligent speeches about [the] inadvisability
or expense of something—after about 3 samples in one day—I get that
smothered feeling. . . . I wish the hell I were out of here and running
my own household and my own life—with no dictatorship. . . . This is
like being a high-priced whore.*

It was that kind of relationship—erratic and volatile, with little
middle ground between adoration and revulsion. On a bad day in
October, Mary could find fault with everything about her circumstances:

1. *On being alone 5 out of 7 mornings.*
2. *On cultivating sports which bore the shit out of me.*
3. *On having so little company I don't know why the hell I try to stay
   here.*[19]

At this same time, Mary wired Time/Life asking if her position there,
which a week earlier she had given up, might be reinstated as a leave
of absence until December.[20]

Yet in December she remembered the previous two months as
idyllic as she gradually understood that Ernest's "supervision" was
largely to protect her until she became confident in this other country. To please Ernest, she bleached her brown hair blond, painted
her nails a darker red, and exercised herself thinner. She swam daily,
read his writing regularly, criticized little, manicured his hands and
feet, and cut his hair. She was going to Spanish classes, learning to
wing-shoot a 20-gauge shotgun, studying navigation, and cooking
Sunday-night suppers when the kitchen staff was off. Ernest was
"seldom over-drinking," and "in bed he has certainly been better for
me than any man I ever had."[21] He was also a mercurial man whose
temper could explode without warning, a demanding man given to
emotional highs and lows. A part of him could spend money without a second thought. The same man wanted a detailed accounting
of every penny spent on the Finca. It galled Mary that he gave her
money as a gift, as a reward, as a bribe. It doubly galled her that,

unlike his first three wives, she had no income of her own, nor would she ever if she gave up journalism.

As the sultry heat of summer faded and the hurricane season passed, life at the Finca settled into a reassuring if unexciting routine for Mary. Whatever money worries there had been disappeared when the film rights for Hemingway's "The Killers," and "The Short Happy Life of Francis Macomber" sold for $112,000. Even with the staggering monthly upkeep of the Finca at $3,000, they had a comfortable margin. Mary might complain that she did not see Ernest in the mornings, but it was because he was rising early and writing, which meant he was completely happy for the first time since returning from Europe. After seven months of "getting in shape," and beginning rough starts that floundered, Hemingway was writing easily once again. A year earlier, riding the rush of the Paris liberation, he told Max Perkins that he would write a war novel encompassing sea, air, and land action, but his attempts to begin that epic did not jell. This time he began with a war correspondent, called Hudson, who looked a lot like Ernest Hemingway, complete with concussed head and healing wounds, who covered RAF raids along the Somme. The story quickly turned into conversation, and the action moved to London where Mary, the Irish maid at the Dorchester, could barely wait for Hudson to bolt the door of his bedroom before undressing.

He wrote two drafts of another story called "The Faker," which never got past its opening few pages once more set in London. At the White Tower, Hudson introduces a British flight surgeon, Blakely, to two female correspondents—Pam, short and dark; and Jan, a tall blonde with long legs who sounded a lot like Martha. In the course of their acidic conversation, it becomes apparent that Hudson and the blonde have known each other for some time, and coincidentally Blakely performed a curettage on her when she miscarried after a jeep accident in Greece. The accident for Martha was actual, but not in Greece, and the miscarriage was a fictional reminder that Martha did not give him the child he wanted from her.[22] Despite a friendly exchange of letters with Martha, Ernest had not yet forgiven her, as he saw it, for leaving him.

From a brief meeting with her in London on his return trip to the Finca, Hemingway also knew that Martha and Virginia Cowles (a dark-haired journalist) were writing a play about male and female correspondents during the war. Under various trial titles—*Men Must Weep, Take My Love Away*, and finally *Love Goes to Press*—the comedy centers on two female journalists—Jane Mason (blond and British) and Annabelle Jones (dark and American)—who connive to prevent Annabelle's onetime husband, Joe Rogers, from marrying a touring British movie star. Annabelle tells Jane that Rogers married her "to silence the opposition," by stealing her stories. "You can't tell from the outside that he's got the character of a cobra," Annabelle explained. "From the outside he's a beautiful, funny, fascinating man."[23] Nor could you tell from Martha's letters to Ernest that she still smarted from his treatment of her.[24]

Having flown only a few actual missions as an RAF observer, Hemingway found he did not know enough to write the air war, and put it aside about the same time that Mary returned from Chicago in October.[25] With his drinking cut down to a minimum, his weight down to 202 through his daily regimen of thirty laps in the pool, he returned to the Bimini story begun before he went to England. The eight typed pages started with a narrator questioning whether the story he wants to tell will hold together. An odd story, some of it unprovable, its beginning known to only a few people and its conclusion confused, it was still a story worth telling, he assured the reader, once he straightened it all out. Picking up the thread of the story, Hemingway continued, writing quickly and easily. Within a week he had forty-seven pages done; five days later, more than seventy pages written. By the end of the month, he reported to Max Perkins that he averaged 750 words a day through October. By then he knew he was writing a novel, but had no idea where it would end. It was a strange enough story, mixing memory and desire on the cool sea breeze coming through the open doorway and windows of a painter's island cottage. The time is 1936; the two male characters—the older painter and the younger novelist—are old friends who carry heavy personal baggage. The theme was remembrance of things past, but most par-

ticularly it would detail the condition of the artist played out against the backdrop of twentieth-century conflicts. In fact, it was a story he had been writing obliquely for some time now, and would continue to write for the rest of his life.[26]

By December, Mary's nostalgia for the "helter-skelter of journalism and politics" was fading as she became more accustomed to life at the Finca. Although Ernest had no love of Havana night life, he did take Mary to an occasional concert, including one given by Yehudi Menuhin. Jack Hemingway, who was visiting his father, took Mary to the Sunday-night movies in the tiny adjoining village of San Francisco de Paula. Ernest's divorce from Martha was now final, making Mary feel more like a fiancée than a camp follower. Patrick and Gregory, who seemed to accept her without question, were arriving on December 28 for a delayed Christmas, for which Mary was desperately trying to translate holiday recipes for the Chinese cook.[27]

Chapter Twenty

RULES OF THE GAME

1946

DESPITE RECURRING ARGUMENTS with Mary and internal conflict with his own erratic moods, Hemingway in the new year wrote like a man possessed. Going to sleep at night with two Seconal tablets, he woke before dawn and was at his writing pad when the light broke. Remembering all the monumental authors he ever read—Homer, Proust, James, Joyce—Hemingway loosely envisioned a book that would bring together everything he had learned about structure, landscape, and character. The first part—Bimini before the war—was begun years earlier. Returning to it now with a more complex vision, he would use Bimini as the foundation for a multivolume work that would span the decade 1936–46, encompassing the land, air, and sea war—earth, air, water, and fire. What started as a monumental but straightforward project became over the next fifteen years more complex and introspective. In its metamorphosis, the sea war became what is now called *Islands in the Stream* and *The Old Man and the Sea*. The air war was eventually abandoned, and the ground war would become the memories of a bitter Army colonel dying in Venice—*Across the River and into the Trees*.

He poured himself into the fiction, reliving the summers on Bimini with his sons, catching and losing the big fish, scaring the hell out of himself when the boys were in the water with the feeding shark. Embedded were memories of early days in Paris where the artist learned his trade. For the next fifteen years, Hemingway's memory and his fiction would return again and again to the apartment above the sawmill on rue Notre Dame des Champs where he first found his voice. Finally, remembrance of things past would produce his Paris memoir—*A Moveable Feast*. Out of the same matrix came a different story of a Paris writer, David Bourne in *The Garden of Eden*. By July 1961, the book that began as a study of the artist at war had become a multivolume portrait of the artist/writer in the first half of the twentieth century, "complete with handles," as Hemingway might say.[1]

While his Bimini painter and the visiting writer had their problems with fictional ex-wives and new lovers in Hemingway's writing room, Ernest's attention was continually distracted by Mary's unhappiness. With his previous three wives, each marriage entailed a change of venue: with Hadley he left Chicago for the Latin Quarter of Paris; with Pauline he moved into the St. Germain area and then to Key West; with Martha he moved to the Finca in Cuba. With each marriage he had given up certain favorite spots and more than a few friends closely associated with the preceding wife; none of the first three wives was asked to live in the house of her predecessor. With Mary, none of the above applied: she moved into Martha's house, ate off Martha's china, looked at Martha's photograph on the wall, and lived with Martha's servants. Every old friend of Ernest's who came to the Finca was once there while Martha was wife; every Havana bartender made unspoken comparisons. The only place Mary did not feel like an intruder was on the *Pilar*, which had survived Pauline and Martha because it was always Ernest's boat.[2] Wherever she turned, except in bed, she felt inadequate: she was not the lady from St. Louis as were the first three wives, nor was she able to give Ernest children as Pauline and Hadley had. She did not know the Paris of the 1920s, had not read all the books, met all the famous faces. She did not have Hadley's or Pauline's trust fund; she did not have Martha's poise or stunning beauty; she did not bring a rich uncle to the marriage as had Pauline.

In Mary's recurring dream, she is in a large house filled with people "all jolly and gay," eating from tables of food. Suddenly the guests all depart for a picnic, leaving Mary behind, uninvited. Wandering through the house, she finds Ernest and "another woman, unidentifiable, but older and bigger" than she, sitting on a stone bench. Ernest and the woman go for a walk, asking Mary to join them:

> We walk along a sort of country road with deep smooth ruts, and you and [the] woman take the ruts. . . . You are very tall and your legs are very long and because you are both much taller than me, I cannot keep up with your conversation because you talk across my head, and I cannot keep up with you in speed because you are walking fast and you have good foothold in the ruts, and I am walking between the ruts, and the ground there and the fields beside the road are of shiny slippery white porcelain so that I slide back with every step.[3]

It is not surprising that their relationship was filled with misgivings, misunderstandings, and violent arguments.

As was his habit learned early as a boy in Oak Park where angry parents left notes for each other, Hemingway preferred to state his case or make his apologies in letter form. Throughout the mild late winter of Cuba and into early spring, the interhouse mail was in steady use. Please forgive him, he asked, for he could not imagine why he behaved so badly over the glass of water. He was both ashamed and apologetic for smashing the glass, and would try very hard to be good. Ernest's fierce temper was liable to explode when Mary was least expecting it, sometimes scaring her with its violence. When their milk cow died and no one came to haul the carcass, he turned on her, having no one else to yell at, and afterward wrote another apology. These abject, remorseful exercises sounded more and more like the young boy in Oak Park writing out his apology to parents for misbehaving at a church function. Always he would do better. Mary accused him of making her into a bitch, but he claimed it was just not so. When he wanted to hurt her, Ernest paraded the men in her life before her—Noel Monks, Irwin Shaw, the General—they all loved her, maybe not as completely as he did, but then it was not his fault that the General found her in bed with Shaw while she was still married to Noel. What seemed like a non sequitur was a reminder of Mary's recent history of fornication, implying Ernest was not alone in contributing to her bitchhood.[4]

At the end of February 1946, Hemingway wrote Buck Lanham that he was deeply depressed, "black ass to end all black ass," what with Bumby's unsuitable girlfriend and Mary being more difficult that he ever anticipated.[5] Mary's misgivings about their relationship, in which she bore the brunt of his "black ass" moods, had steadily increased. No, he argued, he was not jealous of her friends, was not keeping her from seeing them, nor was he trying to be anything but gentle when he woke her in the morning. To prove it he paid for her week's trip to Miami in January to see old friends and shop for clothes. Meanwhile, he said that he would find a way to cope with the terrible loneliness her absence caused in his heart. In fact, he would not even mention it because that would be whining.[6] She quickly answered that she also was missing him badly, wishing "very much could curl into your arm and leg and neck and be very close to you. Please don't stop loving me dearest and please let's give ourselves another chance to both be good."[7]

Before their marriage that spring, they had, through several rounds of play, established the house rules for this game of love: Ernest initiated the attack; Mary retaliated; Ernest apologized; Mary, if unmollified, threatened to leave him; Ernest begged her to stay; Mary professed her continuing love. It was a game heavy on manipulation, with each player aware of the other's vulnerabilities, a game Ernest had played successfully with earlier wives. His arsenal of verbal abuse included irony, sarcasm, ridicule, vulgar insults, public embarrassments, and temper tantrums. When all else failed, he relied on petulance and sulking before playing the last card in his hand, the threat of suicide, which he used so often that his friends became inured to it. When he wanted to repair the damage, he wrote loving in-house letters, made sure that Mary slept late and undisturbed, gave her money, or, after seriously behaving like a bastard, gave her an expensive gift. These various tactics worked well with his first wife, Hadley, and his second wife, Pauline. Martha simply refused to play the game. Mary, who was more of a street fighter than her earlier avatars, played the game as if she had invented it. To spectators, the game was embarrassing, but they were not privy to the excitement each round could produce later in bed.

To call this serve-and-volley relationship a game is to minimize the hurt of any actual moment, and at the start, with no pattern established, Mary's distress reached intense levels. On March 13, the day she and Ernest were to pledge their brief wedding vows before the Cuban civil authority, she told him that she did not want to marry him. With plans set, a few select guests invited, his fishing and sub-hunting friends Tommy Shevlin and Winston Guest in attendance, Ernest was furious. Mary, finally relenting, went through the civil ceremony, while Ernest was barely civil and guests cringed. In her journal at 3:00 a.m. on their wedding night, Mary recorded her impression of the day:

> He came out with only a few of the nasty ironic resentfulness he usually accords me, then spent most of the day giving me that highly formal treatment, pretending I would be unreasonable about everything— thus clearly indicating to Tom Shevlin and Bumby what a heel I am. So phony, so cheap, so chickenshit. . . . But pinched by circumstances (Wolfie being here) we went to the lawyers and signed declarations to marry. I was certainly not gracious, and from then on he took it out on me—making jokes as we went back to the Florida about "Have a glass of hemlock"—and on the way home working himself into a fine rage and calling me "Rather-Out Welsh!" . . . What infuriates him most apparently is that he thinks of our life as some kind of game war and tonight that he thought I had won it. That was what started him. Tonight he has made the concession of allowing me to sleep alone— which is a relief.[8]

The next morning when the sun rose over the grounds of the Finca, the woodpecker was busy digging insects out of the huge ceiba tree, Ernest was at his writing pad, and Mary slept late. When they and their houseguests gathered later beside the pool, it was as if the previous night's embarrassment had not happened. Two weeks later, Mary was writing an ecstatic letter about the "simple-minded happiness" of her life with Ernest.[9]

Over the next three months, Hemingway's routine did not vary: wake early, write through the morning, swim in the afternoon or take the *Pilar* out from Cojimar to fish, return to an early supper, listen to music on the Capehart, and retire early to read. It was not an exciting life for Mary, but at least there was some harmony in the garden over which she was now the mistress. Gradually she brought about needed changes: the cadre of house servants and gardeners was somewhat reduced; the expense receipts were organized; the vegetable garden planted; and cows were brought in to produce milk for the family, the staff, and the cats. Within a month Mary was confident enough in her new role to write Martha about shipping to London the Gellhorn monogrammed silver, china, and crystal left behind. Light of voice and pleased to bring her former life to a distinct close, Martha replied that she was looking forward to the shipment.[10] Two months later, her china and silver having arrived in London, Martha replied to Mary's questions about other possessions. There was no need to be facetious, she said, about sending things as mundane as a box of corn pads. If Ernest thought he could needle her with the suggestion, he was wrong. "I feel," Martha wrote, "that I have been completely mild and entirely modest, though I know how prone E is always to feel that he is being robbed. In all cases, let us cut out such nonsense, as it is a bloody bore all round." As for her papers at the Finca, her letters to Ernest had been returned long ago. "He wants the record, I do not."[11]

At the end of April, another woman out of Ernest's recent past appeared at the Finca to undermine Mary's self-confidence in her newfound role as Mrs. Hemingway. Slim Hawks, wife of renowned movie director Howard Hawks, called from Nassau to tell Ernest that she was a new mother and an unhappy wife. Urging her to fly into Havana, Ernest said, "You need to be with people who love you." He was speaking for himself, for Mary did not love the tall beauty who walked into the Finca trailing clouds of Hollywood gossip. Nor was Slim particularly taken with Mary, whom she found to be

> *a fidgety banty hen of a woman, always scurrying around, doing need-less things that she thought made her indispensable . . . she didn't have a clue how to run a house with Ernest Hemingway in it. She was tatty-looking . . . [with] a deep, affected voice that wasn't hers at all. And she wasn't sophisticated enough to disguise her displeasure at my having been invited to Cuba because of her husband's great affection for me.*

Having appeared on the covers of several fashion magazines and recently been named "Best Dressed Woman in the World," Slim Hawks, with her natural blond streak, her wit and carriage, and her long list of prominent friends, was Mary's antithesis. Slim prided herself on never having worked in her life; Mary was born working and felt diminished when she was not.

Bemused by Hemingway's disregard for his newly married wife's feelings, Slim enjoyed his attention. When she returned to him a borrowed shirt, he gallantly told her that he would never wash it, for now it smelled like her. It did not take Slim long to figure out what Mary was learning the hard way: Ernest needed a wife and needed another woman with whom to flirt: "He didn't have to consummate the flirtation; in fact, it was the key that he didn't . . . although he might be having a silent love affair in his head, he was faithful to his wife."[12] From his first marriage to his last, Hemingway needed the presence of more than one woman within range of his magnetism. His wives were not always at ease with this need, but all coped to varying degrees. Before his first marriage with Hadley Richardson, she asked rhetorically, "Ernest, you don't have lots of infatuations do you? What could I do if you did? 'Course if you do I guess you can't help it."[13] The one gift that neither Hadley nor Pauline nor Martha was able to give Ernest, the one gift by which Mary could consolidate her position, was the gift of a daughter. By the time Hemingway met Mary, he was calling any woman younger than himself "daughter." As soon as their vows were spoken, Mary did everything her Chicago doctor advised in order to become pregnant. When she did not miss her April period, she wrote Dr. Gough for further advice, saying his pills were no help.[14]

As a largely absentee father, Hemingway went for long periods without being particularly concerned about his three sons. Then, on a mood swing, he could become overly parental. On June 21, Ernest's concentration on his writing was broken by his concern for his three sons, who were driving cross-country with Jack at the wheel bound for a California vacation. Angry to be told so little about their plans while he was trying to organize a family rendezvous at Sun Valley in August, Ernest wrote them that they needed a little discipline, which he was happy to provide: from this day forward he expected two letters a month (written on the first and fifteenth) from each son—letters neither hurried, sullen, nor forced. Further into the letter he changed the dates to the first and third Sundays of the month, coupling this duty with Pat and Gregory's religious duty to attend Mass. If these letters were not forthcoming, Papa Hemingway threatened that steps would be taken. As he was writing his sons, his mother in Oak Park was writing him in care of his publisher, for she had no idea what his Cuban address was.[15]

Two days after he began his letter to the boys, Mary precipitated another argument, locking herself in her bathroom and refusing to speak to him. Afterward in writing she explained to him her sense of diminished worth and entrapment resulting from her total dependency, a condition she had never before experienced. She knew that financial provision for her aging parents fell entirely on Ernest's largesse, for she was earning no money of her own. She was lonely, insecure, and bored. "I have no life of my own," she wrote, "only odd functions which provide you with companionship . . . and release of your sex functions which has long been almost totally mechanical." For the past month, Ernest had gone directly to bed after supper, leaving her too much time to consider her situation. Having given up her independence and her profession to face the challenge of being Mrs. Hemingway, she realized her job's longevity depended solely on his whim.[16] Whether it was Mary's despondency causing Ernest to pay more attention to her or the doctor's pills, a month later, a delighted Hemingway told Buck Lanham that Mary thought she was pregnant. Maybe this time he would get the daughter he longed for, and by the time she was old enough to be trouble, he would be dead.[17]

By July 21, Hemingway had almost a thousand pages of manuscript, revisions, and inserts done on the book that he refused to plan. As he explained to Lanham, he never knew precisely what was going to happen in any book he wrote; whatever plans he had always went astray when the story got away from him. So he lived in the book, inventing it day by day, letting it develop organically. If it did not "get away" from him, he would be worried.[18] Taking a day off from writing, Hemingway celebrated his forty-seventh birthday at sea on the *Pilar* with Mary and one or two friends, followed by a small gathering at the Finca. On that same day, his mother, vacationing on Walloon Lake with his sister Marcelline's family, wrote her son a birthday letter, reporting on the condition of the Hemingway cottage where Ernest spent his first eighteen summers and which was the setting of his first mature fiction. Years earlier, his mother had transferred ownership of the lake property to Ernest's name. Not having seen the cottage in four years, Grace was upset by what she discovered.

> *I walked over to Windemere, and thought of all the happy days we spent there. I grieved to realize that you cared nothing for the place and had never been even to see it in the past eleven years. I left it clean and perfectly furnished to the last detail. . . . For some time it was broken into almost every winter by marauders . . . the mice have gnawed holes in the house . . . the front porch floor and roof are fast disappearing. The steps . . . have rotted away. The neighbors call it the haunted house.*[19]

Windemere was, indeed, filled with ghosts from Hemingway's youth, memories still tender on the mind. There his father taught him to hunt and fish, taught him about the woods and the water, taught him to be resourceful. There on his birthdays beside the decorated birthday tree, his father would ceremoniously give him the five-dollar gold piece, heavy in his hand. In the lake shallows at the foot of the cottage, Ernest and his young sisters bathed naked in the water. Windemere was his first Eden, the clearest part of his life. And like Eden it was lost to him in various ways, some his own doing. When he was twelve, his father Clarence stopped coming to the lake during the summer as he retreated into progressive depressions that the young boy did not understand then and the man did not want to understand. When Ernest was twenty-one, Grace threw him out of the cottage, calling him a menace to youth, telling him not to return until he cleaned out his mouth and could respect his mother. Two years later, he and Hadley spent their wedding night at Windemere, the last time he was in the cottage. In his dreams and fiction, he returned there more often than his mother could know, nor would he tell, for he had nothing good to say to or about Grace Hemingway, holding her responsible for his father's strange moodiness and eventual suicide. Grace, he said, would be more dangerous dead than most women alive. If he ever went to her funeral, he would fear she was booby-trapped.[20] The older Hemingway became, the larger his mother's guilt grew in his mind; from Normandy to Hürtgenwald, he told friends and strangers that he was, in truth, a son of a bitch.

A week after Hemingway's forty-seventh birthday, he learned that Gertrude Stein, his literary mother and godmother to his first son, had died in Paris, leaving tiny Alice to nurture her memory. Cancer took the "mother of us all," leaving the garbage pickers of history her literary remains and the memories of those who once paid her homage. Sweet, sweet, sweet Gertrude, as a doer she was done. Having had her say on Ernest in *The Autobiography of Alice B. Toklas*, she made the singular mistake of leaving him alive after her passing, for he too would have his say, as he often promised. The following Monday, a biting letter arrived from Martha that caused Ernest to explode in a three-page typed diatribe, berating Martha for her ingratitude, reminding her that he titled her books, *A Stricken Field* and *The Heart of Another*, and wondering if he should copyright "A New Slain Knight" before she stole that one. He wished her luck in finding someone of his caliber to correct, rewrite, replot, and tone down her penchant for melodrama as he had. Having vented his spleen, he said, in a metafictional moment, that he would not send the letter, for it was too fine a piece to waste on her. He signed off, calling her a phony, pretentious bitch, and never mailed the letter.[21] There was more than one way to make his point for future literary historians.

On August 7, with a thousand pages of drafted manuscript in hand and Mary two months pregnant, the Hemingways left Cuba for Sun Valley, Idaho, where they would be joined by his three sons for a fishing and hunting vacation. Having wormed his way through the Cuban restrictions on moving guns or ammunition in or out of Cuba, Ernest checked a small arsenal in baggage and boarded the Pan-Am flight to Miami, where their Lincoln convertible was being road-checked and outfitted with five new tires, difficult to find in an America not yet returned to prewar conditions. It was the summer of a deadly outbreak of polio and the disappearance of most of the Bikini atoll during the testing of a new atomic bomb. The trip was one of rediscovery, for Ernest had not driven the route since 1941. On the highway and in the small towns, not much had changed except around military bases where Quonset huts had mushroomed along with nearby signs for used cars, cold beer, and hamburgers. The cars on the road were all prewar vintage, for new models were not yet in production. Prices for goods and services were in flux. The Office of Price Administration (OPA), which froze prices and imposed ration stamps on basic goods during the war to prevent inflation, was gradually letting America return to a free marketplace.

As the price of everything from sugar to silk began to rise, organized workers demanded better pay. Rail travel was in chaos due to a Pullman porters' strike; in Detroit, Packard automobile was closed by union strikers. Everywhere they stopped for food, gas, or a night's sleep, they found returning servicemen trying to assimilate into the almost too quiet life of Wabulla, Apalachicola, and other sleepy towns all across the South. On static-ridden radio stations and nickel jukeboxes, songs from the war years were giving way to new nonsense—"hubba, hubba, hubba" and "hey baba rebop." The long cross-country Route 66 that once carried the dust-blown and destitute west during the Depression was now being immortalized as the place to "get your kicks." Skinny Frank Sinatra pleaded with someone for "only five minutes more" of her kissing, while others, bags and reservations in hand, were "gonna take a sentimental journey home." Franklin Roosevelt, dead and buried, left his little known vice president, Harry Truman, to deal with out-of-work veterans, Russians in Berlin, higher Social Security taxes (now 1%), and a resurgence of the Ku Klux Klan.

On the road again, Ernest was not bothered by the stifling August heat burning West Texas and southern Colorado dusty brown, nor by the Lincoln's occasional vapor lock as they gained altitude. In no particular hurry, they drove up through Denver and Cheyenne and on to the open Wyoming plains, stopping August 18 in the Mission Motor Court's tiny, un-air-conditioned room in Casper, Wyoming. From Casper through Yellowstone National Park to Sun Valley, where they were scheduled to rendezvous with Ernest's sons, was an easy drive, but they would not reach the resort until almost a month later. On the morning of August 19, Mary woke alone in the cabin with an excruciating pain in her stomach, tried to stand, and doubled over screaming. Ernest, outside the cabin packing the car, found her writhing in pain. An emergency ambulance carried her to the county hospital, where the doctor on duty determined she was hemorrhaging from a burst fallopian tube resulting from an ectopic pregnancy. The hospital surgeon, away on a fishing trip, did not arrive until that evening, by which time Mary had been given several transfusions of whole blood and plasma. Finally, late that night, as she was being prepped for surgery, Mary's veins collapsed on the operating table. The doctor told Ernest it was hopeless; if he operated, Mary would die from shock. It was time to tell her good-bye. Ernest, who had seen enough battlefield transfusions in Hürtgenwald to know what he was doing, took charge. He ordered the intern to cut for Mary's vein and insert the needle, but the plasma would not flow. Ernest "cleared the line by milking the tube down and raising and tilting" until he got it flowing. With a fresh pint in her, Mary fluttered back to life, and Ernest told the surgeon to operate. Four bottles of plasma later and her ruptured tube removed, Mary was out of danger. Before dawn, she received two more blood transfusions under an oxygen tent, where she remained for a week.[22]

Quite literally, Ernest's quick and effective decisions brought Mary back from the edge of death. As ample evidence attests, he could be an impossible man to live with, a sarcastic drunk, a self-centered adolescent, but no one was better in an emergency than Ernest. For all their bickering and all of Mary's threats, past and future, to leave him, she never forgot that he saved her life. For the following two weeks, when Mary woke from her drugged sleep, either Ernest or a private nurse was at her bedside. Nine days after the operation, her stitches were removed, but Mary remained in the hospital until September 3 and could not travel for another week after that. As she gained strength and was clearly recovering, Ernest became restless and bored in Casper. He bought a Royal portable typewriter to write letters, but did not want to work on his novel until he could give it his full attention. At the end of August, he went fishing, probably with Mary's surgeon, but mostly he was taking care of his wife. After a week back at the motor court, Mary was finally able to travel. With Ernest driving and Mary napping in the Lincoln's front seat, they left Casper the morning of September 12, crossing through Yellowstone bound for Sun Valley and his sons.[23]

Sun Valley Lodge was not yet returned to service from its war duty as a rest and rehabilitation center for wounded soldiers. Instead, the Hemingways booked into two of the McDonald log cabins, which included a small kitchen, a fireplace, and a separate writing room for Ernest, where he returned to the novel he now titled *The Island and the Stream*. Although the Lodge was not yet back in the entertainment business, most of Hemingway's Ketchum friends remained in place, and the local bars and eight gambling establishments were wide open. Ernest, who would place or accept a bet on almost anything, favored the Alpine ("homey and nice"), where he claimed to be "well ahead." The bird season was abundant with quail, Hungarian partridge, and pheasant in the fall fields and ducks on the irrigation canals. Patrick Hemingway, who remained on in Ketchum when his brothers returned to school, added to the larder with a prime buck, his first big game kill. Between afternoon bird hunts, late evening suppers, and visiting friends, Hemingway's writing mornings were shorter than usual and less productive. At the Sun Valley theater, producer Mark Hellinger premiered for invited guests a director's cut of his film based on Hemingway's short story, "The Killers." Hemingway, who hated most films made of his work, so enjoyed this one that he acquired his own copy to run at the Finca.

In the hunting fields, with a cold wind blowing and stubble dry underfoot, Ernest and Mary shared their days with Gary and Rocky Cooper, with Hemingway's old mentor Charles Sweeny, and with Slim Hawks, who arrived at Ernest's invitation to escape the gossip columnists hot on the trail of her adultery with Leland Hayward. Hemingway advised her to answer no questions, ignore the publicity, and take none of it seriously. She should escape to Ketchum, where he would put her up in the cabin he used for writing, asking her to bring "a little seconal for Papa."[24] Mary, more secure in her relationship with Ernest after her ordeal in Casper, was less resentful of Slim's presence than she had been at the Finca, and could not have anticipated the near horror that Slim almost wrought. Returning to Ketchum with a nice bag of partridges, Hemingway suddenly stopped the Lincoln when he spotted another partridge; he, Mary, and Slim piled out, loading their shotguns, but no wings beat the air. Slim, sitting on the fender of the car, pumped two cartridges out of her 16-gauge automatic, forgetting that she had removed the plug to allow more shells. Thinking the chamber empty and not wanting to leave the weapon cocked, she pulled the trigger. Just as Ernest was bending over to tie his shoelace, the gun fired, sending a load of birdshot zinging past his head, singeing the hair on the back of his neck. He rose up livid with anger just as Slim shrieked and began to cry. Ernest quickly swallowed his anger to console her, trying to make a joke of the near miss, but no one was laughing.

By early November, snow was falling in the Idaho high country. Knowing that the two-lane roads south would soon become dangerous or impassable, Ernest and Mary, completely recovered from her near-death experience in Casper, drove south to Salt Lake City. There they hunted briefly with Charles Sweeny, who had fought in a half century's worth of revolutions and wars. From Utah, the Hemingways continued south to Arizona, spending the night of November 19 at the Grand Canyon on their way to Tucson. Turning east, the dusty road followed the old trail through Apache country into Lordsburg and down to El Paso. A long, hard day's drive south and east took them across Texas and then into New Orleans for Thanksgiving. Mary's parents, plain and basic folk, were charmed by their new son-in-law, who provided a complete turkey meal served in their spacious hotel suite. By train, Ernest and Mary traveled on to New York, where they booked into the Sherry-Netherland on December 1. It was there that Buck Lanham found a Hemingway much altered from Hürtgenwald days. Unshaven and overweight, his paunch bulging over his German belt buckle, Hemingway was dressed in bedroom slippers, tight pants, and a loose shirt with missing buttons. Speaking in what sounded to Lanham like Indian dialect from a bad western movie, Ernest was clearly drinking too much and behaving badly.

Contrary to his usual policy of refusing to talk to unknown reporters, Hemingway was feeling so good about his writing that he gave three interviews, each filled with inaccuracies, many of his own making. Mary Harrington erroneously reported that Hemingway ran away from home to become a prize fighter, but was persuaded to finish high school by his father. At the Stork Club with Mary, the columnist Leonard Lyons, and Buck Lanham, Ernest saw the prominent actor Charles Boyer seated close by with Ingrid Bergman. Ernest, residually possessive of any attractive woman who passed through his province, began "to ask loudly whether or not he should give that small green-faced character [Boyer] the back of his hand." Before the week was out, he left a pointed message for the editor of *New Masses*: "Tell Mike Gold to go fuck himself."[25]

After a miserable duck shoot with Winston Guest and Lanham on Gardiners Island, a short distance from the city, Hemingway returned to New York, where he gave interviews to the *Herald* and the *Post* at the Sherry-Netherland. Yes, he was working steadily on a long book that would "touch on the war." With twelve hundred pages of manuscript finished, it might take another nine months. "It's a big book," he said, "I've broken the back of it now." The war novels he anticipated would not be the "disillusioned realism" like that of the Twenties. "Some very excellent writing is going to come out of this war by writers who are completely unknown right now," he said, "but it's going to be entirely different from what we had before." He recommended Jean-Paul Sartre's *The Wall*, but backed shyly away from accepting the compliment of being "the best living American writer." He said that "William Faulkner is the best living, and Nelson Algren." Soon afterward *The New Yorker* caught up with him for a martini and snails lunch:

> *His resemblance to a handsome, playful, and potentially violent bear was heightened by the way his hair ran down over his coat collar like a shaggy gray pelt . . . he looks and acts indestructible—a state of affairs that neatly supports his theory that no Hemingway ever dies a natural death.*[26]

By the time the interviews were in print, Ernest and Mary were back in Cuba putting away the remains of Christmas celebration at the Finca. On the desk was a gossipy letter from Paris telling them that Ernest's journalist friend from Hürtgenwald, Willy Walton, was now involved with Martha Gellhorn.[27]

Chapter Twenty-One

YEAR OF THE DOG

1947

ORTY-SEVEN YEARS OLD and aging quickly, his hairline receding, his liver slowly betraying him, Hemingway had not published a book in six years and would not for another three. In 1940, he was a lion among writers; in 1947, he was becoming an historical artifact, a relic from the Lost Generation whose early work was entering the academic literary canon. Soon biographers would be at his door, ready to entomb him. Elsewhere, a new moon was rising on the cultural landscape of America. On the dark side of New York the Beat apocalypse of Allen Ginsberg, William Burroughs, and Jack Kerouac was evolving underground. In Chicago, Nelson Algren was about to take a walk on the wild side, and in Brooklyn, a young veteran named Norman Mailer was finishing *The Naked and the Dead*. In his studio reeking of automobile paint, Jackson Pollock was dripping abstract colors in wild profusion, making ancient Miró's *The Farm*, which presided over Finca Vigía. Fats Waller with his rolling eyes was dead, and the new young beboppers were playing a jazz the white boys could not steal. "Papa, papa," pleaded the pop recording, "won't you dance with me? Won't you dance?"

Ernest did not bother to answer. Having gone his own way

always, he was confident in the long book piling up on his work table. A thousand pages into it, he began revising, typing the opening section to see how it looked, paring down the manuscript. He had not yet reached the air war over England, much less the invasion of France, but was under no pressure to hurry. Mark Hellinger, pleased with the money made from his film *The Killers*, was offering Hemingway a lucrative deal on four unwritten short stories: $50,000 a year for four years, plus 10 percent of the film profits, guaranteed minimum $25,000 per film.[1] Scribner's was about to reissue his three best-selling novels—*The Sun Also Rises, A Farewell to Arms,* and *For Whom the Bell Tolls*—in a boxed set, perhaps with illustrations. *A Farewell to Arms* was coming out in a college edition with an introduction by Robert Penn Warren, and Jonathan Cape, Ernest's British publisher, was keeping his work in print. Publishers in Germany, France, and Russia were returning to the marketplace with Hemingway translations, all of which would provide steady income for the rest of his life.[2] Despite the high cost of maintaining his lifestyle at the Finca and his penchant for equally expensive travel, Hemingway could afford to lay down books in his bank vault if he chose, leaving them to his heirs to publish.

He was also leaving heirs, friends, and scholars the complex and contradictory legacy of his life. It was never the same story twice, never quite the same mood. Chiding William Faulkner for writing while drinking, he prided himself on not taking a drink before noon when he was working. For a man who belittled alcoholics, Hemingway spent a lot of time in letters congratulating himself on not being one. At eleven in the morning when he was through writing for the day, one of the servants would bring to poolside a shaker of martinis— "Montgomerys," Ernest called them in sarcastic reference to Field Marshal Montgomery's need for a fifteen-to-one advantage on the battlefield. Hemingway would tell a guest, "Eleven o'clock. What the hell it's noon in Miami. Let's have a drink."[3] When he drank too much, which was more and more often, he was liable to say almost anything to anyone, and the less he respected someone, the more outrageous his mouth became. How many Germans did you kill,

Papa? The number increased in direct ratio to his drinking. When the figure went past one hundred, most listeners stopped believing the stories. Thus he denigrated and devalued his long days on submarine patrol, the tense moments at Rambouillet, and the dark night of Hürtgen. Unable to explain his sudden mood shifts and excessive drinking, those who loved him looked the other way, made excuses, remembering always the man sober, intense, and magnetic.

Yet in an emergency, he remained the one who never panicked, the cool head who assessed the situation quickly, organized the response, and took control. In April at the Finca, he was faced with a tense and emotional crisis when his son Patrick arrived from Key West with an undiagnosed concussion from a car accident. As Ernest explained to Mary, who was in Chicago where her father was undergoing hospital tests for prostate cancer, Patrick's behavior exhibited all the signs of mental disturbance: excited and slurred speech, disjointed conversation. That evening, when Patrick explained about the accident, Ernest was certain he was suffering from a concussion. Five days later, with Patrick running a high fever and behaving violently, doctors were running blood tests, and Ernest was organizing all available hands for round-the-clock watches, he himself sleeping outside Patrick's door. Patrick's mother, Pauline, came from Key West to help with the nursing and cooking, glad to be of use and pleasantly surprised by Ernest's considerate behavior. Erratically better, Patrick had brief lucid periods followed by relapse; for three weeks, the Finca team kept watch, feeding their patient, bathing him daily, and restraining him when violent. In his deliriums, Patrick fought valiantly with the devils he found at his bedside. When lucid, he did not remember the fiends who tormented him. By May 2, Ernest was worn out from going sleepless and from worry; he passed in and out of dark, gloomy periods, but his responsibility for Patrick kept him from going over the edge.[4]

Unable to work with any consistency on the prewar Bimini novel, he wrote daily loving letters to Mary, assuring her that he could pay her father's hospital bills and giving her detailed medical advice on prostate cancer. From his recent reading of Paul DeKruif's *The Male*

Hormone, Ernest explained that injections of testosterone would some-times arrest prostate cancer. (Soon he would be taking injections him-self for his flagging energy level.) He also reported on Patrick's slow progress and life at the Finca. Blue poinciana and eucalyptus were flourishing; alligator pears were forming on branches by the hundreds. His letters frequently carried some private reference to their sexual life which he and his penis—"Mr. Scooby"—were eager to resume. Much of the eroticism was connected with Mary's brown hair, now bleached and dyed blond. While in Chicago, he urged her to go to a professional beautician to turn it smoky silver, which would complement her tan. She could tell how excited he was about her return, he said, because he usually did not write about their private sexual games. She might, he suggested, really surprise him by returning as a redhead, which would please Papa as well as *Catherine* and *Pete*.[5] The latter two were the names they invented for the characters they sometimes assumed in bed—he was "Catherine," Mary was "Pete." Her girl "Catherine," he wrote her, had not been around much since she left, but he was cer-tain she would turn up as soon as "Pete" (Mary) returned."[6] Eight days later, Ernest turned his own hair a bright copper tone to amuse Mary on her return to the Finca. Trying for the color that "Catherine" wore, he was shocked the next morning to see the results in the mirror. He wrote Mary that so long as their games hurt no one, it was nobody's business but their own. Then her letter came, asking him to bleach his hair exactly as he had already done it.[7] Soon these games would become part of his fiction, which in turn would enrich the games. In the beginning he could move easily back and forth between the fic-tional world of his characters and the less fictional world outside his writing room. Later that dividing line became so porous that it was dif-ficult to say on which side of it he stood.

On May 18, Mary returned to the Finca, and Pauline, who had taken a break from nursing Patrick, returned five days later, for her son was not yet "lucid" and still required constant care. Bemused, delighted, and sexually stimulated to have both women in the house at once, Ernest wrote Buck Lanham on May 24, "that he and Mary had made love eighteen times since her return."[8] Twelve days later, Mary came down with a virulent flu that put her in bed for two weeks, running a high fever; Pauline again returned from Key West to nurse Mary so that Ernest would not carry the flu to Patrick, but also because she knew how the threat of flu terrified Hemingway ever since he listened to the death rattle of flu-stricken soldiers in World War I.[9] Mary, in her fever, tore off part of a brown paper bag to scrawl out a quick will stating she wanted her cremated remains to be dropped into a "clean part" of the Gulf Stream. She also assigned her London flat's contents to Pauline, with whom she was now close friends.[10]

Frustrated by the hiatus in his writing, worn out from nursing duties, Hemingway took another heavy blow on June 17 when Charles Scribner's telegram told him that Max Perkins had died suddenly from pneumonia. "What awful luck," Ernest cabled back, unable to say in a few words the magnitude of his loss. Max, the caretaker, was no longer there to run Ernest's long-distance errands, deposit the Scribner loans, and deflect Hemingway's angry outbursts after each book was published. For twenty years, Max was there for Ernest, mediating between the needs of the author and the exigencies of the publishing house, counseling wisely and always sympathetic. For Max's leaving, Hemingway was the poorer, having lost a voice of reason that no one could replace. Missing Max with his well-worn hat, Max so proper in the face of whatever nature sent his way, Ernest had no one left from the old days to lean on, to talk the literary talk. By deaths and disputes more and more isolated from his old literary friends, Ernest was vaguely aware that the postwar age was passing him by. Always overly sensitive to constructive criticism, his tolerance for it was now almost nil.

On June 26, Ernest put Mary, still feverish, on the plane to Key West, where she recuperated for another two weeks with Pauline, who moved back and forth between the two sick bays. On July 7, Patrick began new treatments three times a week, which immediately improved his condition.[11] Through all of the late night watches, worry for his son, lost sleep, and the strain of remaining calm, Ernest's own physical condition was deteriorating. With only erratic exercise and almost no fishing, his weight ballooned up to

256 pounds, and though he did not yet know it, his blood pressure was approaching fatal numbers. When, in a "black ass" mood, he read a William Faulkner statement seemingly questioning his courage, Ernest was stung to the quick. Rather than respond himself, he asked Buck Lanham to send Faulkner a detailed testimonial to Hemingway's behavior under fire and in close quarters. Faulkner had, in fact, used the word "coward," saying that of the leading American writers, Hemingway took the fewest risks in writing, not trying for the impossible. Chagrined by Lanham's lengthy documentation of Hemingway's courage, Faulkner wrote directly to Ernest, apologizing for not insisting on looking at the interview before it was published. "I have believed for years that the human voice has caused all human ills," it said, "and I thought I had broken myself of talking. Maybe this will be my valedictory lesson."[12]

Hemingway's friendly response said he was sorry Faulkner had been misquoted, and that nothing Faulkner said mattered now that he knew how it happened. That was on a good day. Time and again, when the paranoia, lurking beneath the surface of his reason, became full blown, he would come back to Faulkner's inadvertent insult, reopening the old wound. Faulkner took Hemingway's letter at face value, saying he hated literary gossip, particularly having started it himself by testing out an idea of no value anyway. Some of Hemingway's stories, like "An Alpine Idyll," were so complete that there was "nothing more that even God could do to it; it's hard, durable, the same anywhere in fluid time; you can write another as hard and as durable if you are good enough but you can't beat it. . . . I wish I had said it that way . . . what I wish most is I'd never said it at all."[13]

Slightly miffed that Faulkner chose an early story rather than something more recent to declare durable, Hemingway pointed out several parts of *For Whom the Bell Tolls* where he was taking the sort of chances that Faulkner praised Tom Wolfe for attempting and failing. But the real test was not their contemporaries, but the durable writers from the past: Dostoyevsky, Turgenev, de Maupassant. Faulkner was, Ernest said, a better writer than Fielding; they both had beaten Flaubert, the "honored master." Filled with military metaphors and earthy language, the letter played more to Hemingway's public image than to that inner part of him where the writer lived.[14]

On September 20, in a year already filled with pain, worry, and loss, Hemingway received news of the death of his old friend, Katy Smith, the wife of John Dos Passos. Driving westward into a setting sun, Dos crashed headlong into a truck parked on the road's shoulder; when he regained consciousness, he found his car's top almost sheared off and Katy dead in the seat next to him. Dos himself was badly bruised, and his right eye permanently damaged beyond repair. Hemingway sent a telegram of sorrow and loss, silently remembering the long-ago summers at Walloon Lake when Katy, with her teasing eyes, was the sexiest woman he knew.[15]

All that summer and into the fall, while Hemingway's attention was largely familial, the political intrigues of the Americas were bubbling on all sides of him. In Costa Rica, violent labor strikes left dead and wounded in the streets. In Paraguay, a civil war was raging, and in Chile, civil liberties were suspended to deal with communist-led strikes. In August, a bloodless coup replaced the president of Ecuador; in September at Rio de Janeiro, President Harry Truman was one of the nineteen endorsers of the Inter American Treaty of Reciprocal Assistance, but on the same day the new dictator of Ecuador was himself overthrown. On September 12, an armed coup attempt in Venezuela was suppressed.

Then came the Dominican Republic fiasco. The first story broke in Havana on August 6, when the minister of defense announced the capture of four pilots and their airplanes presumably belonging "to the group that is preparing the much publicized revolutionary expedition against Santo Domingo."[16] Two weeks later the recently reelected president of the Dominican Republic, Rafael Trujillo, asked Cuba "to intervene to stop revolutionary preparations . . . being made in Cuban territory against the Dominican Republic."[17] There was, in fact, a ragtag army being formed and trained to overthrow Trujillo, and one of the revolutionists' supporters was Ernest Hemingway, who had foolishly given money to the cause in the form of personal checks. As with any political activity in Cuba, someone in the government had to be complicit in the effort, either for money or for idealism, for it to succeed. In this case the minister of defense had given guarantees that Cuban President Ramón Grau would be kept uninformed of the revolutionists and that the government would not interfere. Either not enough money changed hands, or the minister found it more advantageous to betray the project. Whatever his reason, his betrayal left Hemingway liable to arrest as soon as his checks surfaced. His doctor, José Luis Herrera, could not believe that Ernest had been so naive as to give them checks, or to have ever believed that the minister of defense would keep his word. Had Hemingway not noticed that none of his Cuban friends who hated Trujillo were involved in the plot? Herrera assured Hemingway there would be arrests: he must flee the country immediately. If they hurried, they could just get him on the afternoon flight to New York. René, who oversaw the Finca staff, packed a suitcase, while Ernest left hurried advice for Mary, who was remaining at La Vigia along with Pauline, Patrick, and Gregory.[18] Cursing the politicians, Hemingway was driven into town by his chauffeur, Juan Lopez, reaching the airport just in time to trot up the boarding ladder.

On September 26, the *New York Times* reported that Cuban military and naval units had trapped "about 1,500 Dominican revolutionists on Confite Key off the north coast near Nuevitas . . . former United States fliers, said to have been engaged to pilot planes, now are reported to have been returned to the United States." Four days later, a front-page *New York Times* story confirmed that eight hundred revolutionists had surrendered and were now in Cuban prison camps. They were now being charged with "action against the security of Cuba," and the minister of education was under arrest as a conspirator. "Large quantities of arms and ammunition were captured."[19] It was rumored that the government sweep missed one of the organizers, young Fidel Castro.[20]

When the Cuban government finally admitted the suppression of a plot on Cuban soil to overthrow Rafael Trujillo, Hemingway, with Toby Bruce driving, was miles north entering Yellowstone National Park en route to Sun Valley.[21] Thus he was not at the Finca when the

Diario de la Marina said that the planning committee met at Finca Vigía where Hemingway reportedly held out for token bombing of the Dominican capital. A second story said that Ernest was heading a revolution against Cuban President Grau.[22]

When further details were made public, Hemingway's name was prominently featured:

> *[Mercenary pilots] were given lodging in the home near Havana, Cuba of the American novelist, Ernest Hemingway, who on several occasions acted as spokesman for the revolutionaries. The American aviators implicated in the plot . . . [said] that although they had been well fed and provided with drink in Hemingway's home, they had not been paid the sums they had been promised for their part in the adventure . . . an agent of the Dominican government was informed by the revolutionary spokesman, Ernest Hemingway, that the invasion army "had grown to seven thousand men," and that their training was being carried out publicly in several places in Cuba.[23]*

How involved Hemingway actually was in the failed revolution depends upon who is telling the story. One of his doctors said, "Hemingway gave some money for the Confites thing. But we heard he was going to be arrested, so I . . . got him a ticket for Miami. . . . We got to the airport just a few minutes before the plane's departure."[24] In a letter to Buck Lanham, Hemingway's knowledge of the foiled plot indicated that he had inside information: the group had no security, pitiful logistics, and no sense of priorities. He himself was too busy nursing Patrick to become involved, but was tempted because it would have been easy to bring off. All he did was give advice and make recommendations.[25] Whether Hemingway left Cuba on the run, or leisurely as planned, did not matter to Mary when Lieutenant Correa and his squad arrived to search the property and question Ernest. When she ordered Correa out of the house, he pointed his pistol at her as if to shoot. Mary quickly invented a pregnancy and a U.S. Army captaincy to protect herself. Not finding Ernest, the lieutenant and his men confiscated all weapons, but returned them next day. On October 3, speaking to Mary through a patchy phone connection from Sun Valley, Ernest learned about the frightening house call, and apologized to her for having to go through it alone. Guilty or not, his known interests in revolutions made him a likely suspect; but five months later when he returned to Havana, the whole affair had blown over.

When Mary arrived at the Sun Valley Lodge, she found her husband dieting, restraining his drinking, and exercising daily in the hunting fields, but his blood pressure (215 over 125) remained high, creating a steady, irritating buzz in his ears. Comfortably ensconced in the "Glamour House" suite with two bedrooms, a living room with fireplace, and two sun porches, each morning Ernest was up early, invigorated by the altitude and the perfect Indian summer weather. For the first time in months, he was once again writing steadily on the Bimini book. With a rich supply of ducks on Silver Creek, fat pheasants at Dietrich, the World Series on the afternoon radio, he was happier than he had been for many months. The string of deaths, sicknesses, and setbacks seemed at an end. At Thanksgiving, he urged Mary to accept Pauline's invitation to join her in San Francisco for Christmas shopping, which she did. There was no problem about money because the second payment of $25,000 was due from Mark Hellinger. By mid-December his weight was down to 220, and his blood pressure, with the help of Nitrotonal pills, fell to 150 over 110.[26]

When his three sons arrived for a Ketchum Christmas, Ernest moved the entourage into three of the McDonald Cabins, where they were joined by Juan Dunabeitia and Roberto Herrera, who were there as Hemingway guests, their reward for having faithfully helped when Patrick was sick. Mary cooked and baked, listened and laughed, correcting her husband's exaggerations and keeping track of expenses, which were significant. Mark Hellinger's check arrived, which, even after setting aside $20,000 in his tax account, would leave the Hemingways in reasonable financial shape. Because of the high tax rates imposed during the war and not yet rebalanced,

Hemingway's seemingly large tax reserve was not without reason, for he was in the 90 percent bracket. Unfortunately, a few days before Christmas, Hellinger died and Hemingway returned the uncashed check to his widow.[27] The long-term deal promised by the Hollywood producer went up in smoke along with any future payments. It was an appropriate end for a year filled with disappointments and loss. New Year's Eve at Trail Creek Cabin, Ernest in coat and tie took up a defensive position in a corner of the room, where he spent most of the evening talking with Ingrid Bergman and Gary Cooper. There was a good deal of joking about the lovemaking in the sleeping bag scene in the *For Whom the Bell Tolls* movie, but by midnight, levity was muted. Watching the limbo dancers trying to slither under the low bar, Hemingway told Bergman, "Daughter, this is going to be the worst year we have ever seen."[28]

Chapter Twenty-Two

ENTER BIOGRAPHERS, STAGE LEFT

December 1947 to September 1948

A s ALBERT CAMUS was beginning to formulate, there comes a midpoint to a man's life beyond which time is no longer on his side, a point at which he knows, perhaps for the first time, the absurdity of the universe. Uncommonly aware of this absurdity since being blown up at eighteen, Hemingway was existential long before the word was current. When drinking with people he knew, he often regaled them with scenarios of his own death, sometimes demonstrating with an unloaded rifle or shotgun exactly how he would place the muzzle against his palate and trigger the shot with his naked toe, or any object at hand. That friends were not amused by this demonstration in no way lessened the delight he took in the performance. The specter of his own death was never far from his consciousness; "the old whore," as he called her, was always there, rocking the cradle.

For the previous thirty years, this relationship with the absurd heightened his experiences, making them more valuable because they were momentary. One never knew if this was the last fish, the last Scotch, the last pretty woman, or the last book. Each time he changed wives, he moved on to new homes, new cafés, new territory—moving westward until he passed a different sort of midpoint than the one Camus would describe. The previous September on his way to Sun Valley, he took a long detour up the lower Michigan peninsula to the "haunted" cottage on Walloon Lake. Around the old store at Horton Bay, some say he stopped, asking directions, because everything was changed.[1] He had not been there since 1921, and this visit was the beginning of his many returns, going back to once familiar places: Fossalta where he was first wounded; Pamplona with the bulls in the street; the Serengeti of his first lion. Each return would be a disappointment. He should have listened to T. S. Eliot who said "old men should be explorers," not returnees. But by 1948, Hemingway stopped his explorations to revisit and reassess a life that was already a legend. The only newfound lands left to him were in his fictions. He entered, unannounced, into his final period, a holding action against all kinds of physical and emotional problems, but writing with renewed intensity.

This period was also characterized by the appearance of Hemingway's chroniclers, the first of whom, Lillian Ross, arrived at Sun Valley early the day before Christmas to gather information for a *New Yorker* "Profile" on Sidney Franklin, the Brooklyn bullfighter and Hemingway's friend. She met Ernest at the McDonald Cabins:

> He was standing on hard-packed snow, in dry cold of ten degrees below zero, wearing bedroom slippers, no socks, Western trousers with an Indian belt that had a silver buckle, and a lightweight Western-style sports shirt open at the collar . . . he looked rugged and burly and eager and friendly and kind. . . . I was absolutely freezing in the cold.[2]

Although dubious of her ability to write convincingly about a ritual for which she had no *afficion*, Hemingway was a gracious source of information. Ross spent most of the day with Ernest and Mary, talking, Christmas shopping, eating and drinking. In the process, she picked up interesting inside information on Hemingway as well as on Franklin, information that would lead eventually to her *New Yorker* "Profile" on Ernest a year later. No sooner was she on her way back to New York than those around Hemingway realized that Ross's appearance had upset him. Maybe it was his high blood pressure; maybe one of those sudden mood changes which were becoming more frequent. Ross, he said, was bright enough, maybe even a sound journalist, but he did not trust her. Forgetting that when she called, he had invited her to Sun Valley, he complained about outsiders disrupting his life, asking questions about his work. For several days afterward he worried about what he had said to her, concerned that it might look foolish in print.[3]

When the screen writer Pete Viertel and his attractive wife Jigee (formerly Mrs. Budd Schulberg) arrived at the McDonald Cabins, Hemingway quickly absorbed them into his "mob." The following evening, at Hemingway's invitation, the Viertels joined Ernest and Mary for supper. When they entered the Hemingway cabin, Blackie, an adopted stray dog, was stretched out by the fireplace, books and newspapers were piled on the floor, and Marlene Dietrich was singing sentimental German songs on the phonograph. The group went out to the Sun Valley Lodge, where they were joined by Gary and Rocky Cooper. Later, back at the cabin, Hemingway made some rough comment about Irwin Shaw, a good friend of Pete's and a recent collaborator with him on an unsuccessful play. Mary jumped to her former lover's defense, saying she "adored Shaw." Ernest told Pete of meeting Shaw during the war:

> *"Walking into their unit was a lot like reading Proust," he said,*
> *"the part where he describes all the fairies."*
> *"Shaw's no fairy," Mary replied.*

Not understanding the game in progress, Pete and Jigee watched perplexed at the ball going back and forth across the matrimonial net. Vaguely they realized that they were being tested, but without a clue as to the purpose of the test. Ernest's irritability alarmed Pete,

who thought that Mary's constant corrections of his stories only provoked him further. The man was a contradiction: "his shyness, his
hesitant speech, the apologies that nearly always followed one of his
sarcastic, or even disagreeable, comments." Before the Hemingways
left Ketchum, Pete Viertel "became aware that he [Ernest] was capable of sudden, extreme rages."[4]

At the end of January, Ernest and Mary began tidying up for
the drive back to Key West. Pauline, who was in Havana to speak
with Patrick's doctor, reported that the new tower Mary designed
and contracted to have built was an architectural triumph. Like the
swimming pool with which Pauline once surprised Ernest in Key
West, the tower writing room was Mary's surprise for him at the
Finca. That Pauline knew more about the tower than did Ernest was
further evidence of complicity between former and present wives,
which did not noticeably bother him. In fact, he and Mary intended
to visit with Pauline in Key West before returning to Cuba. On February 1, Pete Viertel helped Ernest pack the Buick, filling the trunk
and the entire backseat with luggage, maps, guns, books, bottles,
fruit, two roasted ducks, and the stray dog, Blackie. Traveling east
across snow-covered Idaho and into Wyoming, Ernest drove while
Mary manned the maps and guidebooks to answer questions about
the passing topography. Four thousand miles and thirteen days on
the road brought them finally to Key West, where Pauline welcomed
them to the familiar house on Whitehead Street.[5]

By February 20, Hemingway was back at the Finca, his weight
down to 216, his mind at ease and ready to return to his writing,
leaving behind a Key West that claimed to have been shocked by
his visit. Earl Wilson, who happened to be passing through the town
on his way to Havana, reported in his gossip column that the town
was "aghast" because Mary and Pauline "have been acting like turtle doves." Visiting Hemingway at the Finca, Wilson, stepping over
the twenty-two cats occupying the ground floor of the new tower,
admired the view from the third-floor writing room. It was here,
Hemingway told Wilson, that he would hide out from unwanted
visitors while completing his novel in progress. "When you're going

good," he said, "when words are falling on your paper like rain, you don't like to be stopped."[6]

Yet he stopped himself often enough, for he was forever inviting friends and chance acquaintances to visit the Finca. On March 7, he was waiting at the Havana airport's arrival gate to welcome Malcolm Cowley and his family. On commission from *Life* magazine, Cowley, who knew Hemingway briefly in the Paris Twenties, was there with Hemingway's consent to write what would be the first important biographical essay on the man and the writer. Already there was a sizable correspondence between them on the project, and more letters would follow their extended interview. It was the sort of in-depth public exposure which Hemingway had long avoided; that he was acceding to it at this point in his life coincided with his own return to places past and to his ongoing revision of his early life.

Housing Cowley, his wife, and son at the Hotel Ambos Mundos assured Hemingway morning writing time to work on the second part of his novel: the cross-country trip taken by the fictional novelist and his newly found love, Helene. Ernest and Cowley's afternoons were spent around the Finca pool or on the *Pilar,* where thirteen-year-old Bob Cowley became seasick, vomiting on the deck. "Hemingway stripped off his jersey," Bob remembered years later, "and wiped it up and threw the jersey into the sea . . . and went on fishing." The working visit was complicated by the arrival, by invitation, of Hemingway's younger sister, Sunny, and her son, Ernest, named for "Uncle Ernie," who despised being called "Uncle Ernie."[7] The usual gin and tonics at pool side, daiquiris at the Floridita, wine with supper, and Scotch afterward may have made Hemingway more than usually talkative about his past, both recent and distant, but what he told Cowley was not noticeably different from stories told to Lillian Ross in Ketchum. As a journalist talking on the record to another journalist for publication, Hemingway revealed details about the wartime patrols of the *Pilar*, his paramilitary engagement at Rambouillet, and the horrors at Hürtgenwald—subjects that heretofore he discussed only off the record.

No sooner was Cowley back on the mainland pursuing Hemingway friends for pithy quotes than Ernest fell into deep remorse for agreeing to the interview, for allowing himself to reveal personal information, and for possibly endangering his residence in Cuba. He asked Cowley not to write anything about the "Caribbean business" because it remained secret information. If the Cuban government found out that not only was he on military patrol while pretending to be fishing but he also operated as a counterintelligence agent for the United States, they would have good reason to suspect him of being a current American agent. Without telling Cowley about his alleged involvement in the Trujillo fiasco, Ernest said he would be in big trouble if his wartime activities were made public. When he was dead, Cowley could tell all; in fact, Ernest gave him the names of those still alive who could confirm and elaborate his stories. The more he pleaded for secrecy, the more he regretted ever agreeing to be part of what now smelled to him like a mortuary. To write a biography of a living writer was tantamount to placing him in the grave.[8] Then, four days later, Hemingway's alter ego was giving Cowley leads to follow up on his early years at Walloon Lake, and telling him the history of the machine gun he carried in the jeep across France and which he used on Germans during the attack on Lanham's command post.[9] In Hemingway's next letter he gave Cowley even more details of the battle in Hürtgenwald, including his temporary impotency throughout the battle. In July, Hemingway told Cowley further details on his life while refusing to read the essay in advance of publication. In fact, he asked Malcolm to state up front that he had not read the piece and would be delighted if the events described were all proved to have never happened.[10]

Cowley must have been perplexed by Hemingway's frequent and contradictory letters, taking away with the left hand what the right hand had given. But this behavior also kept Cowley asking questions, for each of Hemingway's responses would reveal some new piece of biography, some more fabulous than accurate, all provocative and somewhat paranoid. Unsolicited information was given about his father's suicide, not all of it true. About his wounding in Italy, Hemingway asked Cowley to say only that he was severely wounded and received several medals as a result; because he was in "bad trouble" in Italy, too much information might bring it up again. In fact it would be better if Cowley were to leave Italy out completely, for which favor Hemingway would leave Cowley a letter to be opened after he was dead which would explain the "trouble" that had no statute of limitations. Absolutely not to be used in *Life* was the story that there was Indian blood in the Hemingway family, or that one of his sisters was once in love with him. Then, in a rambling, repetitive manner, Hemingway went into great detail about his prowess as a driver of fast automobiles, an activity that he was forced to give up after five wrecks in which people were killed or hurt in all five; in truth, no one was ever killed in a Hemingway auto wreck, but he was a dangerous driver, particularly when drinking.[11]

Why Hemingway was making these revelations is speculative. From letters and other documents, he is clearly worried about his hypertension and his weight, for both of which he records every slight fluctuation. If he went to the war looking for an honorable death, or maybe just not caring whether he lived or died, it was because he did not know if he could ever write a better book than *For Whom the Bell Tolls*. Now, confident in his knowledge that he was working on a novel of such complexity that it would surpass the *Bell*, he felt that he was writing in the shadow of death, but the drugs he was taking to control his blood pressure had side effects which were potentially dangerous for a mind genetically programmed toward depression and paranoia. For the remaining years of his life, his recurring worry was that he would die before finishing the "big book."

But he was also passively seeking the man to play Boswell to his Johnson. Mary, he knew, was keeping a daily journal of their wheres and whens, his ripostes and tantrums, the names of tourist courts and daily mileage. But Mary was not in the same league with Arthur Mizener, for example, who was leading the biographical glorification of Scott Fitzgerald. Perhaps Hemingway thought Cowley was such a man. In his September 5 letter, he gave Cowley permission to do the "book" on him which Scribner's would publish. When "A Portrait of Mister Papa" appeared in *Life* magazine, most of the information Hemingway gave Cowley but asked him not to mention was part of the public piece: the sub patrols right down to armament and objective; the paramilitary activity at Rambouillet; and the battle at Hürtgenwald. By giving Cowley fascinating information, while denying him usage with one hand and directing him to other sources to confirm it with the other, Hemingway had it both ways. He liked having it both ways.

Consciously or not, Hemingway was complicit in the construction of what would be the outline for future biographers: Hemingway the young boxer, the cub reporter, the wounded soldier, the novice writer poor in Paris, Ezra and Gertrude's pet. Turning points were highlighted: the lost manuscripts, the struggle to find a voice, the fight to keep his art uncorrupted, the breakthrough novels, Bimini days, marlin afternoons, African lions, the Spanish war—all culminating in *For Whom the Bell Tolls*. The essay ended with Hemingway's commentary on his art in phrases borrowed from *Green Hills of Africa*:

> *You can do it or not do it in that league I am speaking of. And you only have to do it once to get remembered by some people. But if you can do it year after year after year quite a lot of people remember and they tell their children, and their children and their grandchildren remember, and if it's books they can read them. And if it's good enough it lasts forever.*[12]

Speaking in the prophetic voice, Hemingway gave Cowley the perfect conclusion, and in the process maintained some control of his public life. From his Paris days forward, he read deeply into the lives of the artists—Byron, Yeats, Lawrence the novelist, and Lawrence of Arabia—studying how their fame became them. A man might not control all the variables, but neither could he fail to try. For the next twelve years, with the postwar academic scholars in hot pursuit, Hemingway would continue to manage the revelation of his public and private lives.

No sooner were Cowley and family out the door than Hemingway was inviting Pete Viertel to visit again.[13] Viertel was collaborating with the Hollywood director John Huston on a movie script for *China Valdez*, a movie in which Cuban revolutionists attempt to assassinate President Machado. When the script stalled, Huston decided to go to Havana for possible locations and inspiration. Viertel, knowing something of both Huston and Hemingway, was anxious about their meeting: both were dominant males, both could be provoked to violence, and both were heavy drinkers. Their first meeting was an afternoon outing on the *Pilar* in a heavy sea that quickly took Huston's young wife, Evelyn Keyes, to the verge of nausea.

The following evening, Pete, Jigee, John, and Evelyn were supper guests at the Finca, where introductory martinis and dinner wine were followed by terrace conversation which turned to boxing. When Huston mentioned that he had once boxed professionally as a light heavyweight, Hemingway quickly suggested they put on the gloves and spar a few rounds. Viertel was rightly worried: "I could imagine nothing worse than John and Papa stepping a few fast rounds on the terrace. Mary Hemingway was equally appalled about the prospect of her husband taking on one of his guests. 'Pete . . . do something to stop Papa,' she whispered in my ear." Viertel found Hemingway in the bathroom, stripped to the waist, mumbling, "I'm just going to cool him quick, Pete." Viertel finally persuaded Ernest that both he and John had drunk too much, and the match was avoided.[14]

Huston's two-week stay at the Hotel Nacional ended with a going-away party to which John invited the American consul and the Hemingways, including Pauline, who arrived that afternoon to visit Mary. Meeting in the Huston suite, the gathering was pleasant enough until Huston asked Hemingway about Joris Ivens and the filming of *The Spanish Earth*. Having made documentaries himself during the war, Huston seemed honestly interested, complimenting Ernest on his narration and asking him why he had read it himself.

> *"Orson Welles was supposed to do it," Hemingway said.*
> *"Orson, eh?" Huston said, nodding. "And why didn't he do it?"*
> *Everyone in the room was listening by this time.*
> *"Well, John," Hemingway replied in his gravelly voice . . . "Every time Orson said the word 'infantry' it sounded like a cocksucker swallowing."*

Huston managed to laugh, but to his guests, unaccustomed to sexually explicit language in mixed company, Hemingway's statement "was like a hand grenade going off" in the suite. The U.S. consul and his wife made their excuses and left. The Hemingway party departed soon after for the Finca, pleading that Ernest never ate supper out. The next morning, the Hemingways put to sea on the *Pilar* for a week's fishing trip that lasted to the end of March.[15]

Returning refreshed to his novel, Hemingway wrote ten out of the first fifteen days of April, taking time off only to answer letters. He did have a cash-flow problem, which was resolved when his lawyer, Maurice Speiser, arranged for the film sale of "The Snows of Kilimanjaro" for enough money to repay a $12,000 Scribner loan and to plan an extended European trip in the fall. After two fall seasons in Ketchum, Ernest was ready to find new country. As he told Pete Viertel, when they started putting your picture up in the local real estate office as a reason to buy a house, it was time to move on. He and Mary were booked in September on a small ship bound for Italy, where he asked Viertel to join them if he was interested in working on a joint project. Ernest had imagined a wonderful story to write, but it needed a collaborator: A disabled German submarine is abandoned by its crew, who take over a Cayo Lobos lighthouse where the wartime *Pilar* crew find them. Ernest knew the *Pilar* side of the story; he wanted Viertel to research and write the German side. It would be a short book, which should go well as a movie, but would nonetheless be written as if it were the last book either could write. They could write together in Paris and then, when the snow fell, hole up in the mountains where Pete and Jigee could ski and he could write.[16] It was an uncharacteristic offer for Hemingway to make, one he would never have made on an earlier book. Viertel, uneasy about working with Hemingway, told Ernest he was not the man for the job, pleading that he was not yet sure enough of himself as a writer. He might serve as a research man, but not a collaborator.[17]

Hemingway did not give up on the idea. In a long, rambling, repetitive letter, he renewed the offer, saying if not in the fall then why not late winter. Of course if Pete had commitments, he had commitments, but he needed to see the island setting before he started writing on the project. Ernest assured him, he was not trying to pressure him about the collaboration. Embedded in an already curious letter was an even stranger, unsubstantiated account of Ernest's activity during the Spanish Civil War. Helping others to execute a camp of war prisoners, he claimed he spent the night pulling a trigger that left water blisters on his finger and murder on his conscience. Two months later he told Archie MacLeish that he personally killed twenty-six Germans and extended his World War II combat time from five months to eight. The truth was never enough.[18] In the June letter to Viertel, he admitted to being obsessed by war, but promised to resolve that issue by writing about it.[19]

More and more in his letters, Hemingway was rehearsing his biography, modifying here, exaggerating there, leaving a confusing trail of truths, half-truths, and outright fantasies. At forty-eight, he began saying outrageous things to complete strangers, things he would never have said earlier. What appears at times to be mania can also be read as his response to the canonization of his generation already dead: Tom Wolfe (1938), Scott Fitzgerald (1940), Gertrude Stein (1946), Max Perkins (1947). After reading W. G. Rogers's Gertrude Stein biography—*When This You See Remember Me*—Hemingway wrote an unsolicited letter, telling Rogers how much he enjoyed the book, and how much he loved Gertrude. His only ambition had been to write well. Too bad she had so many ambitions. He "used to listen and learn," and he "always wanted to fuck her and she knew it and it was a good healthy feeling."[20] To Lillian Ross, whom he barely knew, he was writing long letters filled with "fucking" this and "fucking" that, telling an apocryphal story about being a 1920 precinct election judge in Oak Park where he cast the only vote for Eugene Debs, the Socialist presidential candidate serving a prison term for World War I pacifism. It made a good story, but Hemingway was not living in Oak Park at the time, and none of his daily letters to Hadley Richardson during November 1920 mentioned the election.[21] Sometimes these stories were meant to be humorous, but they also had a manic edge to them.

In the June letter to Pete Viertel, which Hemingway knew that Jigee would read, he repeatedly spoke of his sexual prowess. White turtle eggs, he said humorously, were better than testosterone injections or Oreton-M. After eating them plentifully in Bimini, he would walk about with such an erection that natives, passing in the street, would salute it. And he would tell them if they knew someplace better to keep it than in his pants, they should tell him. Both Ernest and Mary sent the letter off with their love to both Viertels.[22] In his next letter to the Viertels, Hemingway sent his love to Jigee, about whom he enjoyed thinking. He said there were at least twenty-two ways he remembered her looking, which was a high score for any woman.[23]

While Viertel was composing his rejection of Ernest's offer, Hemingway's future walked into the Floridita where by appointment he met with the young assistant editor from *Cosmopolitan* magazine. Aaron Edward Hotchner arrived in Havana to persuade the famous writer to participate in a survey on the Future of Literature. After blitzing Hotchner with "Papa Doble" daiquiris and blistering him the next day fishing on the *Pilar*, Hemingway said he was interested in the project if the magazine would also commit to two short stories, as yet unwritten, at a total price of $15,000, and a tacit agreement to serialize the first volume of his long novel, the Bimini story, which was complete in draft.[24] The fee was lower than he might have asked, but contracted pieces written by nonresident citizens while out of the country for six consecutive months were tax-free, an enormous savings given Hemingway's high tax bracket. In order to pay for his European trip, Hemingway needed the *Cosmopolitan* money to pool with the *Holiday* magazine fee for an essay about his life in Cuba. It was writing for hire, which part of him despised, but which he could not pass up. Making $15,000 tax-free from *Cosmopolitan* was for Hemingway the equivalent of making $75,000 taxable dollars. On June 27, just before leaving for a Bahamas fishing trip with his sons, Hemingway returned the signed *Cosmopolitan* contract for stories unwritten and an essay, for which he had no appetite. Fortunately, a change of editors at *Cosmopolitan* scuttled the Future of Literature series, but the magazine honored its contract with Hemingway, asking him to write an essay of his choice. Finally, his choice was not to write an essay, which Hotchner cabled him was fine with the magazine. If he ever had a good idea for one, they were standing by; if not, it was not a problem. The check for $15,000 was being cut anyway for the stories, which Hemingway promised would be the best he could write.[25]

All through July and into August, both Ernest and Mary worked on the Viertels to join them on their European trip so that Pete could collaborate on the book, but to no avail. With his weight down to 210 and his blood pressure at 180 over 100, Hemingway felt he had cheated death once again. The blood pressure was still dangerous, but not as lethal as it had been. Others around him continued to be less fortunate. On August 9, he learned that his longtime lawyer, Maurice Speiser, was dead from prostate cancer. Turning over his tax problems to Speiser's junior partner, Alfred Rice, Ernest refused to be daunted by whatever bad news the mails delivered. Not even his six-month Scribner's royalty report ($7,271 minus $3,000 for Pauline's alimony payments and $1,168 to the Scribner Book Store) could depress him, although he added a sarcastic note to its margin: "Of this Pauline will take $2,000 at 500 per month for Sept–Dec. which is not a bad take for a woman you slept with last in 1937."[26] The afternoon of September 7, Ernest and Mary waved good-bye to friends and retainers as the *Jagiello* pulled away from the Havana pier to take Hemingway back to Italy. Ernest was eager for it; Mary, "the short, happy wife of Ernest Hemingway," as she sometimes called herself, was delighted. Neither could have anticipated how this return to places past would change their lives.

Chapter Twenty-Three

SENTIMENTAL JOURNEY

September 1948 to May 1949

H EMINGWAY WAS ALWAYS going back to places
better left in the past. In 1921, when he married Hadley
Richardson, he took her around Petoskey, Michigan, to
meet his former girlfriends, which only perplexed her and angered
the old flames. Within a year he was telling readers of the *Toronto
Daily Star*:

> *Don't go back to visit the old front. If you have pictures in your
> head of something that happened in the night in the mud at
> Paschendaele or of the first wave working up the slope of Vimy,
> do not try and go back to verify them. It is no good. . . . It is like
> going into the empty gloom of a theater where the charwomen are
> scrubbing.*[1]

That was after taking Hadley back to the Piave River site of his night
wounding; now, twenty-six years later, he was misguidedly taking
Mary back to the same place.

The trip across the Atlantic was leisurely and informal on the Polish
liner. Every night there was champagne at the captain's table, but in

their stateroom, the toilet was as erratic as the ship, sometimes blowing its contents out of the bowl. Once the ship's engines stopped at sea while officers and engine-room stokers argued in different languages about who was to blame. But there was a well-stocked bar that Ernest and Mary enjoyed, as did the ship's officers, one of whom got into a drunken argument with Ernest. When they docked in Genoa, Mary recorded that Ernest was too tight on martinis to deal with bringing their Buick through customs, leaving the chore to her.[2]

Four days later, on September 25, with Richard, their hired driver, at the Buick's wheel, Ernest and Mary drove north to Stresa, where thirty years earlier Ernest on leave hobbled about the village with a cane. At night from the hotel's window one could see across the calm surface of Lago Maggiore to the lights of Palanza, the same lights that the fictional Frederic Henry and the pregnant Catherine Barkley once searched for that stormy night rowing up the lake.[3] But that was in another country of Hemingway's mind, that fictional country where he could control the forces at work. He told Mary he was never able to bring his "girl" to Stresa, never took her to Palanza.[4] That was when he was nineteen and in love with his nurse eight years his senior, the nurse he never forgot or forgave for dismissing their relationship as puppy love.

Swept along by nostalgia, Ernest continued to entertain Mary with stories of his past, stories at least half true. She learned of the Hemingway and Hall family history: Grandfather Hall's Civil War Minié ball that he carried in his hip from fighting Quantrill along the Missouri border; Grandfather Hemingway's inability to sit at the same table with a Democrat. As a young boy in Oak Park, Ernest told Mary that he once caught a robin by salting its tail with one hand and grabbing it with the other, told her that between the ages of nine and fourteen he helped forge horseshoes in Jim Dilworth's blacksmith shop at Horton Bay. "Papa remembers" was how the entries began, as Mary recorded them in her journal for some future use, which may or may not have been spoken between them, but Ernest knew she kept these records. He was laying down the tracks of a future biography, supplementing and enlarging upon themes he established in Malcolm Cowley's essay. At the time he thought Malcolm might do the full treatment, but when Cowley questioned Ernest's high school athletic ability, Mary wrote him a furious letter, insisting that her husband was a star athlete. (It was not true, but she thought it was.) Clearly if Mr. Cowley could not get that simple point right, he had no business doing the biography. Ernest, having it both ways, told Cowley that he was tired of such questions about whether or not he was a high school football star. A man should be allowed to die before such questions were asked.[5]

In one entry it is clear that Mary thought of her journal as a source for a book—whether her own or Ernest's is not clear. After recording several pages of notes on the Hemingway children, Mary's next entry begins, "A better *chapter* than this—when under indictment for killing blue heron & had to leave home & live with Ojibway & later came back to plead guilty at Boyne City in order not to go to reform school [my emphasis]."[6] As with so many of his memories, it was never the same story twice, and each retelling tended to create new details. Before the trip was completed, Mary would have the stories of the bitch mother, the Indian girl, the cowardly father, the adoring sister, the blue heron, the night wounding, and the lost manuscripts memorized.

One area of his shadowy past that he wanted Mary to understand clearly was the situation between his father and mother, and how they destroyed the secure home life of his early years:

> *Papa remembers well how . . . he was an extremely obedient little boy, thought his parents always right & their decisions unquestionable. But as he grew up he was increasingly disturbed by their quarrels when many nights his father revised his will, and they both charged him with family responsibilities beyond his capacity. In the morning they were friends again and looked on him as the only spectator of the quarrel, with hostility. . . . Ernest grew increasingly disillusioned about his parents, chiefly because of their constant quarreling, always calling him in as a witness. He learned that none of the children were made by accident—his parents never made love except to produce children, a restriction laid down by his mother, who was a high*

church Episcopalian. Papa says she was just a "put-off" of other good
fucking ancestors.[7]

Never completely understanding Ernest's storytelling mode of mixing fact and fiction, Mary accepted this account at face value.

Like her predecessors—Hadley, Pauline, Martha—Mary Hemingway listened to story after story of Grace Hemingway's malfeasance
as a mother. She wasted family money on her own extravagances,
buying a $135 hat in 1905 when his father was so poor he had to let
his secretary go. (No one but Ernest remembers such a hat or Dr.
Hemingway ever having had a secretary, and his mother's income,
which was considerable in 1905, was hers to spend.) She listened
to his account of how much he and his siblings enjoyed themselves
when Grace was hospitalized with typhoid fever. "We had no discipline at all by that bitch," he told Mary, and the children never
visited her. "We had complete anarchism in the house," he said.[8] If
Mary was listening closely, she should have gotten a better understanding of Ernest's perplexing temperament: ardent lover before
marriage, turning into argumentative husband. The arguments
between Clarence and Grace Hemingway that were forgotten next
day should have reminded Mary of Ernest's need to provoke similar
arguments, which resulted in long in-house letters of explanation.
His descriptions of Oak Park life might also have provided clues as
to why he was usually more comfortable on the road, in a hotel, or in
rented quarters than he ever was in a place called "home."

From Stresa, the Hemingways drove slowly past the northern
Italian lakes, stopping at Bergamo, where Mary pulled a reluctant
Ernest into the opera house. Late that next morning they continued on through the fall countryside to the fabled lake of Dante and
Pound—Lago Garda—making a pilgrimage stop at Gardone Riviera where Ernest's early hero, Gabriele D'Annunzio, was buried. In
1919, when Ernest returned from his brief but traumatic Italian war,
he gave copies of D'Annunzio's *The Flame* to every young woman
of interest, including his first wife, Hadley Richardson, before their
marriage. Set in Venice, *The Flame* tells of the bright-burning, all-

consuming love of an aging actress for a younger poet, who passionately adores her and with equal passion maintains his independence.
That he can never marry her does not matter to the actress, nor does
his interest in a younger dancer bother her. Theirs is an affair from
the courtly love tradition in which only amorists outside marriage
can achieve love's heights, and, like a flame, the relationship is a
self-consuming artifact.[9]

Three days later they arrived in Cortina d'Ampezzo in the heart
of the Dolomite Mountains. Hemingway's last visit to the mountain
resort was in April 1923, returning from a *Toronto Star* assignment in
the Ruhr to retrieve Hadley, who waited there for him.[10] Untouched
by war, Cortina remained much as Ernest remembered it, sunny,
surrounded by mountain ski slopes, and with good restaurants. So
pleased was he with the resort village that he sent Mary off looking
for winter rentals for the Christmas season. A mile and a half outside
the village, she found Villa Aprile, which she stocked with cut wood,
linens, and other necessities. When Ernest invited Pete and Jigee
Viertel to join them in Cortina for the winter, he said that, as in Ketchum, they could make their own tribal rules.[11] The Viertels, with
enough troubles of their own, were unable to accept the invitation.

With winter quarters secured, the Hemingways moved down to
Venice, a city Ernest had never visited. On October 22, they signed
into the Gritti Palace, the most expensive hotel in town. Ernest once
avoided such elegant surroundings, preferring to get the most for
his money, but after liberating the Ritz in Paris in 1944, he was a
changed traveler. Now, he and Mary were living as if money did not
matter. Bartenders became his old friends and newfound Italians,
like the young Baron Franchetti, provided duck hunts without limits. Shooting newly purchased shotguns, Ernest loved being poled
out by moonlight to sunken duck blinds in the marshes where his
guide would put out the decoys along with two or three live call-
ers. Widgeon early, later mallards and pintails, it was a duck hunter's
dream. None of that four-ducks-and-you're-limited-out stuff as the
hunt had become in Idaho.[12] Venice was his town and Byron's town,
a place where rough writers like the two of them were taken to heart.

At home they were calling him the American Byron, an epithet to which he did not object.

In Venice, Hemingway's stories of his World War I exploits continued to expand until he convinced even himself that while commanding Italian troops he was severely wounded in the marshes defending Venice from the Austrian Army. He took Mary back to Fossalta, almost within view of Venice, where nothing remained that he remembered, the once artillery-broken land now smooth and green. With ceremony, he buried a ten-thousand-lira note ($15) close to the spot where a mortar shell ruined his right knee and his night dreams. That he was, at the time, only a young Red Cross man delivering cigarettes and chocolate to the Italian troops disappeared from the story. There in Venice, he was casting a parable which would, when mature, bear the fruit of his next novel.

On November 1, the Day of the Dead, Ernest and Mary changed their travel plans of going to Portofino. After talking with Giuseppe Cipriani, owner of Harry's Bar, they moved instead into his comfortable inn, Locando Cipriani, on the relatively remote island of Torcello. The tiny community, only a thirty-minute vaporetto ride from Venice, was not a major tourist attraction. Once an important medieval center, it was now lost in time, an almost deserted village of duck hunters, fishermen, and a looming, square-towered basilica. Getting off at the wooden jetty, Ernest and Mary made their way up a grassy path along the canal, leaving their considerable luggage stacked at the dock. A bare, ruined vineyard on their right, ahead what once was the city center, now covered with dead grass crossed by footpaths, and not a sound anywhere except the fading engine of the vaporetto. At Locando they stepped back into the twentieth century: a garden, lovely rooms, porters for the luggage, and a fireplace against the damp chill.

Torcello was Hemingway's sort of place—excellent food and wine at the inn, medieval ruins, few people, and almost no tourists that fall. He would soon count as friends the village priest, Emilio the gardener and duck hunter, and Romeo the waiter.[13] The next day, walking about the small island, he entered the nakedness of Santa Maria Assunta, damp-stoned and musty, dim lit in weak sunlight, its altar unadorned, sanctuary light not burning, the gods departed. Then, having taken in its simplicity, he turned to leave, and there on the west wall, directly behind him, the jewel was embedded: a vast, dimly glittering *Last Judgment* done in Byzantine mosaic. At the fifth and highest level, a solemn, stern Christ pulled one of the saved to glory; layered beneath Him, the community of saints; then bands of angels gathering souls. At eye level were the saved, awaiting passage upward, and the damned being forked down into the floor-level hell, where fires burned and skulls gaped with snakes crawling from empty eye sockets. To leave the church he had to pass beneath the Virgin whose outstretched hands offered him the choice of salvation on his left or the fiery pit on his right.[14] Fallen-away Catholic Hemingway might be, but a peculiar Catholic yet. At the Finca, the Black Priest, Don Andrés, came regularly for food, drink, and conversation, and Ernest never passed up a cathedral. To live in Cuba was to be Catholic or to be nothing, for other religions did not signify. Here in Italy, where he had first encountered the Church, he was, if not a practicing Catholic, at least a passive one.

In mid-November, he sent Mary off in the Buick, with Richard driving, to see the sights of northern Italy. With her insatiable appetite for churches, plazas, and museums, Mary was, to Ernest's sometime chagrin, the typical American tourist. He, meanwhile, remained comfortably set up on Torcello, bonding with locals, looking and listening, absorbing it for future uses. Once a week, there were God's plenty of ducks to hunt, and any afternoon he could shoot the tiny, delicate sparrowlike birds feeding on the local grapes.[15] Mornings were reserved for writing; first letters, then the essay he promised *Holiday* magazine. He reconnected with David Bruce, who was now in Paris heading a special mission to France for the Economic Cooperation Administration, and wrote daily letters to Mary.[16] With no more letters to answer, and his pen point, as it were, resharpened, he sat down there in the late fall on Torcello, now the only inhabitant of the inn, and began writing about Cuba and the Gulf Stream.

Wherever he was, no matter how delightful, he was frequently elsewhere in his head, remembering, comparing, savoring. In his early Paris cold-water flat, he wrote about Nick fishing alone on Big Two-Hearted River. In the heat of Key West, Piggott, and Kansas City, he wrote about the northern Italian spring when Frederic Henry was blown up on the Isonzo River. In the Havana heat, he described snow falling in the Guadarrama Mountains of Spain. Now, in the weak Italian sunlight, he began telling *Holiday* readers why he lived in Cuba. Usually he gave a simple answer such as because "it is too complicated to explain about the early morning in the hills above Havana where every morning is cool and fresh on the hottest day in summer." Then he took his readers with him to the cockfights and the pigeon shoots, reminding us that on those cool mornings at the Finca, he wrote as well as any place he had ever been. It sounded as if he were there, with the morning breeze blowing, palm trees rustling. He had that touch, that ability to project himself into the setting remembered with a clarity and attention to telling details that carried readers with him.

There were, he wrote, many reasons to live in Cuba, reasons he usually did not tell strangers but he would tell us this once,

> *the biggest reason you live in Cuba is the great, deep blue river, three quarters of a mile to a mile deep and sixty to eighty miles across, that . . . has, when the river is right, the finest fishing I have ever known.*

With readers hooked on his bait, he pulled them into the *Pilar* for a detailed lesson on marlin fishing. While taking us out of Havana Harbor past the Cabañas fortress where "most of your friends have been political prisoners at one time or another," he told us about his fishing boat, his faithful mate, Gregorio, and how sometimes flying fish rise in a covey as you enter the stream. With the patience of a dedicated teacher, he described everything we needed to know. With outriggers baited and set, teasers zigzagging in the water, we see the dark purple of a marlin rise to the teaser. Quickly pick up the rod baited with the feather and pork rind just as the marlin hits it. If "he turns his head you hit him, striking hard" to set the hook.

> *Then he feels the hook and jumps clear. He will jump straight up all clear of the water, shaking himself. He will jump straight and stiff as a beaked bar of silver. He will jump high and long, shedding drops of water as he comes out, and making a splash like a shell hitting when he enters the water again.*

By the time Hemingway was finished with the essay, his readers knew what size rods and reels were needed, how much piano wire leader, how heavy a line, and what baits were used to pursue fish two and three times as heavy as the fisherman. He called the essay "The Great Blue River."[17]

At the end of November, when Mary returned from her excursion, filled with impressions of the Uffizi Museum in Florence and her meeting with Bernard Berenson, she found Ernest happy but fuming. She told him about paintings and meals; he told her about overhead shots made in poor light and the material Martha Gellhorn had stolen from him for her war novel, *The Wine of Astonishment*. After four years with Ernest, Mary might have been more concerned about his obsessions that he scratched and scratched until they bled. Martha, he claimed, had used everything he told her about Hürtgenwald, having never been there herself, then ruined the material by having her lover Jim Gavin, the great General, make corrections about which he knew nothing. Marty would always be an ambitious bitch, an amateur without discipline. To hell with her and her books. If she ever died by fire the way Zelda Fitzgerald had recently, he hoped she would take a deep breath and die quickly.[18]

Then there was Ira Wolfert, the journalist much with Hemingway in London before the invasion and later in France. Wolfert's earlier books were reportorial accounts of fighting in the Pacific theater of operations. In 1948, he finished a war novel, *An Act of Love*, which was sent to Hemingway for a supportive blurb. Irrationally, Ernest felt that anyone writing fictively about the European War was invading his domain. The book was so terrible, Ernest said, that he simply could not tell the publisher what he thought. Maybe if he had a really good day with the ducks, he might say that clearly Wolfert did not steal the book because it was so god-awfully written. When he wasn't complaining about Martha or Wolfert, Hemingway was tearing into Mary's onetime lover, Irwin Shaw, and his war novel, *The Young Lions*, which Ernest had not yet read due to the maritime strike preventing books and magazines from reaching him, but about which he had firm opinions. For Shaw's agent to claim the book was better than Tolstoy was absurd: Tolstoy saw real action at Sevastopol while Shaw never killed anyone. If he could only get Shaw in the boxing ring, Ernest would teach him a thing or two about fighting, cut him up slowly until they stopped it bloody in the fifth round, or maybe just take him out quickly in the first. These fantasies were reviewed and revised, again and again—Ernest shadow-boxing in a darkening room.[19]

The cumulative effect of the war novels, which Hemingway said he was sick of reading, was to make him doubt the need for his planned sea-air-land novel beginning in Bimini in 1936 and ending after Hürtgenwald in 1944. Shaw, Wolfert, Martha, and Norman Mailer with his monumental *The Naked and the Dead* were all there ahead of him. Maybe, he told Charles Scribner, the war would only be a noise heard offstage. But when Scribner pointedly asked if that meant the end of the planned trilogy, Ernest quickly replied not to worry about the three-part book. The sea part was taking him longer because it covered two whole years; the air and land parts would go more quickly. He did not say that his attempts to write of Thomas Hudson flying with the RAF were a dead end. Charlie should stop pushing him so hard on this subject. Had he not been taking nauseating medicine daily for his high blood pressure? Was he not still bothered by ringing in his ears? The ruthlessness of war was not yet purged from his system, so Charlie must put up with his author's irritations. Had he not been blown up so badly the last time that he coughed blood for six months after returning to Cuba?[20] (Yes and no: he was coughing blood but not from being blown up.)

Angry about the explosion of war novels, about Scribner's pushing him to finish a book to which he did not yet know the end, Hemingway was furious as well with his new lawyer, Alfred Rice, acquired by default as the assistant taking over the late Maurice Speiser's practice. Apparently the IRS was auditing Hemingway's 1944 tax return, filed on the basis of being a nonresident all of that year. Unfortunately, he did touch down on American soil while en route to England and the war. Technically, those two weeks should have cost him his nonresident taxpayer status. Rice suggested a tax loophole whereby they were due a tax refund, to which Hemingway replied that Rice was never to take unilateral action on any Hemingway business. He, Ernest, not Rice, would "judge whether it is an honorable and ethical action to take, not simply legally, but according to my own personal standards. . . . I need money, badly, but not badly enough to do one dishonorable, shady, borderline, or 'fast' thing to get it. I hope this is quite clear." Then he spelled out in great detail all of his war duties in Cuba—counterespionage, submarine patrols—his war journalism for *Collier's*, the battles he covered, the injuries incurred in the line of duty, and being awarded finally the Bronze Star. "For two bits," he said, "I would quit writeing [sic] if I have to pay dough for what I did in 1944."[21]

The second week in December, the Hemingways closed up operations on Torcello, where Ernest now thought of himself as related somehow to the "tough boys" who once dominated the estuary. After moving back into the Gritti, Mary left him on December 13 to take possession and make ready the Cortina house. That same afternoon Ernest went to lunch with the Duke of Aosta's nephew and a "beautiful, jolly, nice, and ungloomy" girl.[22] He had met eighteen-year-old Adriana Ivancich two days previously while hunting at Baron Nanyuki Franchetti's lodge north of Venice. The Ivancich family, long established and respected in Venetian society, had lately fallen into difficult financial straits. Having sailed, served, fought, and prospered under one hundred and fifty years of Venetian Doges and leaders, the Ivancich family was sadly diminished by the European War. Their country villa near San Michele was destroyed by

Allied bombers and their financial situation greatly reduced. When Adriana's father, Carlo, was murdered in the postwar infighting, family responsibilities fell to Adriana's brother, Gianfranco, and her mother, Dora, neither of whom had sufficient business acumen to restore the family to its previous glory.[23]

With long, lovely black hair, green eyes, and a thin Roman nose, Adriana stepped into Hemingway's fantasy close to the spot that Frederic Henry climbed out of the Tagliamento River on his way to rejoin Catherine Barkley. Wet with rain, she sat by the fire combing and drying her hair, probably not noticing the throaty quality of Ernest's voice as he watched her, but certainly aware she had his full attention. Recently graduated from the protection of nuns, Adriana was a lovely young woman about to discover her power over men. For Ernest, life, fiction, and fantasy were coinciding in ways that he did not stop to question. In *A Farewell to Arms*, he let an older Frederic fall in love with a slightly younger nurse, whose hair the wounded American found incredibly erotic:

> *I loved to take her hair down . . . I would take out the pins and lay them on the sheet and it would be loose and I would . . . take out the last two pins and it would all come down and she would drop her head and we would both be inside of it . . . I would lie sometimes and watch her twisting it up . . . and it shone even in the night as water shines sometimes just before it is really daylight.*[24]

Now, by firelight, watching Adriana's black hair fall in waves, he was the older man, and she the very much younger woman. That he was thirty years older, paunchy, graying, with erratic blood pressure and ringing in his ears, did not matter to him. This was the beginning of a Jamesian novel to be played out in Hemingway's imagination. She was the muse he needed, the muse that Mary, for all her sexual experience, was never able to become.

Dora Ivancich, the watchful mother, could not understand why a man old enough to be a grandfather would be interested in her daughter except for all the wrong reasons. Adriana assured her that

Hemingway's invitations to lunch, to drinks at Harry's Bar, to walks about Venice were harmless. Her friends were always with her; they made him happy. What did they talk about? Adriana was not always sure because Ernest spoke an English that she had not learned in school, but when he laughed, she and her friends laughed. He called her "daughter," and he was the Papa. Dora Ivancich was not reassured. Later, in her memoir, *La Torre Bianca*, Adriana said, "For me he was a much older man, even though there was something of the big child about him. But 30 years [difference] was for me a lifetime. I never thought of being in love with him."[25] But that was not what she wrote at eighteen when she was full of poetry and pictures, forever sketching and dreaming. At eighteen, she was flattered and intrigued by Hemingway's gentleness and the unmistakable if unspoken sexual attraction he felt for her.

Leaving Adriana behind in Venice, Hemingway joined Mary at Cortina before Christmas, where he settled comfortably into Villa Aprile, while continuing to go on duck hunts only a few hours away. On January 16, 1949, the lagoons finally froze up, making the trip into the duck blinds heavy work. There, shooting against the full moon setting, Ernest brought down fifteen ducks, the last of the season. Five days later, Mary was carried down from the slopes by the ski patrol, her right ankle broken from a spill in wet snow. Ernest went with her to the hospital to get the ankle set and plastered, telling Pete Viertel in a letter that the accident would end his writing for at least a month. The letter, with several appendices, continued to refight the Normandy invasion, complain about inaccuracies in Shaw's *The Young Lions*, which he had finally read, and declare he was nauseated by Cowley's *Life* magazine essay.[26] When he finished the Viertel letter, Hemingway cut bottom portions off three pages, his own "black ass," as he called his depressions. What remained was "black ass" enough: Shaw had no right to write about cowardly company commanders. The man should go out and hang himself. What he did not mention to Viertel was the veiled and unflattering presence in Shaw's novel of himself, Mary, and his younger brother Leicester.

Three days after Mary's accident, Hemingway was complaining to Cowley that the *Life* essay was going to cause him serious problems in Cuba, having revealed that the *Pilar* was carrying high explosives during the war and thereby breaching Ernest's elaborate security measures.[27] Apparently no one in Cuba noticed, but the level of Hemingway's chronic paranoia was rising. Later, he told Cowley to forget about writing a book-length biography while he was alive. It was too embarrassing to see himself in his son-of-a-bitch mode, and equally embarrassing to see himself behaving well. He added, darkly, that if the whole truth were told, he would be put in jail. Nor could he let anyone else write about his parents. His mother might be a bitch, but she was family. He cooperated with Malcolm only because, his doctors having convinced him that his raging blood pressure would surely kill him within a year, he wanted to set the record straight on several points, including his efforts during the war. Seeing his life in print was so unnerving and onerous that he would neither cooperate, authorize, nor consent to a full-scale effort. (All the while Ernest was telling Mary detailed stories of his life for her journal, assuming she would use them after his death.) Cowley's counterpunch did not reach Hemingway until he returned to Cuba: a young Princeton professor by the name of Carlos Baker was working on a critical book about Ernest.[28]

All that month of January, Ernest was by turns either gentle and caring, or absolutely miserable and vicious. When a perfectly friendly letter from Pauline told him his sons missed being with him at the Finca for Christmas, and that Greg had seen Bumby in New York, loaning him money for uniforms to return to Army service, Ernest responded in his vitriolic worst: she had sent him a packet of poison, no real information, a couple of letters a year but nothing else, probably due to her laziness or drunkenness. He was sick of hearing about money loaned by her or his sons. Either send him a bill or shut up about it. Then, twisting the knife, he told her that their marriage ended not because of Martha, rather because of coitus interruptus imposed by the Catholic Church when her twice surgically opened womb could not bear another child.[29]

Ernest's surliness was not entirely due to Mary's ankle, Shaw's novel, Cowley's essay, or Pauline's letter. Part of the cause was his own writing, which was not progressing. Having promised *Cosmopolitan* two stories by December 1949, he had nothing yet to send to Ed Hotchner, his go-between on the magazine. In March, he said the one story he'd finished was too "rough" for *Cosmopolitan*, but surely when he returned to the Finca he would have the two stories written on time.[30] The other and more immediate cause for his "black ass" moods was Adriana, with whom he was hopelessly and idealistically in love. For two weeks in January he returned alone to Venice on the excuse of business papers that he needed to sign. In March, he and Mary returned to the Gritti, where they dined one evening with Sinclair Lewis and the mother of Lewis's former mistress. Mary listened, taking mental notes: Lewis's face looked like "a piece of old liver"; when he ate, she could see blobs of food moving inside his mouth; his hands trembled, and his walk was "brittle." During the three-hour meal, Lewis seemed to grow older and more feeble, while Ernest became younger, boyish and shy. Mary was with Ernest at meals and in bed, but she was also much alone. On her mended ankle, she visited museums, went to concerts, seldom mentioning Adriana in her journal although she had to know that Ernest was spending afternoons with her.[31] Mary had seen it all before, from both sides of the scenario: as the younger woman for whom Ernest only had eyes, and as Mrs. Hemingway watching the younger woman being flattered by her husband. This infatuation, Mary was sure, would pass as had the others since their marriage. Nor was she confident enough in being Mrs. Hemingway to take a firm stand.

By the middle of March, Ernest and Mary were back at Cortina, where he was writing every morning about a fifty-year-old infantry colonel duck-hunting on the frozen lagoons with a surly boatman. "I must not let him ruin it," the colonel thinks, "I must keep it entire and not let him do it. Every time you shoot now can be your last shoot and no stupid son of a bitch should be allowed to ruin it."[32] For two weeks the story went beautifully, only to be sabotaged by Hemingway's own physical misfortunes, which followed him everywhere.[33]

On March 28, his eyes became infected, turning into erysipelas that sent him to a hospital in Padua for ten days of penicillin injections and bed rest, his eyes swollen shut and his face covered with oint-ment.[34] By mid-April, when he was mostly recovered, it was time to close down Villa Aprile and return to Cuba. Colonel Cantwell's duck hunt and his three days in Venice were left suspended in Ernest's mind until he could get back to the Finca.

Before leaving Venice for Genoa and home, Ernest invited Adri-ana and her older brother, Gianfranco, to lunch with himself and Mary at the Gritti. Gianfranco was also soon to depart for Cuba, where employment was possible. Ernest told Adriana he would look after her brother's best interests. Mary noted later in her journal that her husband and the far too young Adriana "were busily launching a flirtation." That she thought the "flirtation" was only beginning says how well Ernest had kept Adriana's presence in his life to himself.[35]

Chapter Twenty-Four

VENICE PRESERVED

May to December 1949

O N T H E L A S T D A Y of April, the Hemingways left
Italy carrying a mountain of luggage and Ernest's fledgling
war novel. The duck hunter, Colonel Cantwell, was afoot
on his three-day rendezvous with love and death on the stones and
bridges of Venice.[1] Behind him stood a troop of forebears: Dante's
burning lovers; Byron's gaudy life; Henry James's *Aspern Papers*;
D'Annunzio's inflamed young poet and aging actress; Thomas Mann's
Death in Venice.[2] Ernest knew them all, read and remembered them
all, using them wherever needed. "Sometimes I am Mr. Dante,"
Colonel Cantwell would say, and mean it. By giving his crucial war
memories and a good deal of his recent reading to the dying colonel,
Hemingway was changing the outcome of his proposed sea-air-land
trilogy, which already covered sixteen hundred pages of manuscript.

The slow trip home gave Hemingway leisure to work on the
book, for the Polish ship made frequent overnight stops along the
South American coast.[3] Almost four weeks at sea, he woke early
as always, caught the morning light reflecting on the water before
finding a quiet place to continue the Colonel's memories of wars
long ago and recent, mixing the 1918 defense along the Piava with

the recent debacle in the German woods where Cantwell lost so many good men, poor men, dead men all. Unable ever to dissociate love and war, Hemingway was working toward a different configuration than in his earlier two books, *A Farewell to Arms* and *For Whom the Bell Tolls*. Richard Cantwell's love for the young girl, first called Nicole and then Renata,[4] is hopeless not because of their age difference but because his heart is quite literally failing him. Both the author and his character take Seconal to sleep; both are taking mannitol hexanitrate—Ernest to control his high blood pressure; the Colonel to keep his heart pumping.[5] Old soldiers do eventually die, but they do not go gentle.

After reaching the Finca on May 27,[6] he hired Juanita ("Nita") Jensen as a part-time secretary to whom he dictated afternoon letters, gradually reducing the mountain of unanswered mail. That June at the Finca, correspondence, household chores, and planning a Bahama fishing trip made progress on the unnamed novel slow going. By June 10, Patrick, Gregory, Buck Lanham, and Nanyuki Franchetti from Italy had arrived, ready to board the fishing flotilla— Mayito Menocal's large, well-appointed yacht *Delicias* and Hemingway's *Pilar* with Mary's tiny *Tin Kid* in tow for shallow waters. The trip was well planned, but everything conspired against it: the weather turned rough; Gregorio, his longtime mate, was sick with a cold; Santiago, hired on as engineer, knew nothing of engines; and Gregory's appendix flared up requiring a Navy crash boat to take him into Key West for an emergency operation.[7] When Ernest returned to port, he found a letter from his arthritis-crippled mother, who was turning seventy-seven, telling him how furious she was with the *Life* magazine feature: "They stole the pictures of you and your family when I was not at home and got someone to write it up. We were most disgusted as we know you would be." She also told him to ignore any hospital bills sent to him by her doctors who had accepted her paintings as payment for service. But when they found out how wealthy Ernest was, they came asking for his address, which she refused to give. For her approaching birthday, she wanted nothing from him but his love.[8] Instead, he sent her a book on science and religion, hoping perhaps that it would counterbalance her penchant for supporting mystical religious groups.[9]

At the Finca there was never a shortage of fresh reading material—New York newspapers, current magazines, and stacks of new books, fiction and nonfiction. Before returning from Italy, Hemingway renewed fourteen magazine subscriptions through the Scribner Book Store, ranging from *Field and Stream* to *New Republic*. His order lists were as diverse as his interests: new fiction, military history, books on the Southwest, the American Civil War, and the journals of André Gide in three volumes. In July, he received a twenty-four-volume set of Mark Twain's works, Philip Wylie's new novel, *Opus 21*, Dostoyevsky's *Diary of a Writer*, George Orwell's *1984*, and Eliot Paul's *Life and Death of a Spanish Town*.[10] Some who did not know him thought him an instinctive naif, a raw American product largely uneducated. Those who knew him well were amazed by the breadth and depth of his reading, by the large and growing Finca library and the diversity of his interests. Two to three hundred books a year passed through his hands—books as factual as guides to navigation, as fluffy as murder mysteries. Books arrived as gifts from known authors and complete strangers. He read deeply in biographies and letters of selected writers, including George Gordon, Lord Byron, whose Venetian sojourn echoed in Hemingway's head when creating Colonel Cantwell in the Venice of his imagination. About his own *Don Juan*, Byron had written from Venice:

> *It may be bawdy, but is it not good English? It may be profligate, but is it not life, is it not the thing? Could any man have written it who has not lived in the world? and tooled in a post-chaise? in a hackney coach? in a gondola? against a wall? in a court carriage? in a vis a vis? on a table? and under it?*[11]

Before Hemingway was finished, Byron's fornication in the gondola would reappear in his still unnamed novel.

From mid-July through the end of October, Hemingway worked on the Venice novel five days a week, always leaving himself two days for fishing. Riding what sounded like a manic high, he was amazed at the way the book was writing itself. It was as if he were twenty-five, not fifty, but knowing at twenty-five what he now knew at fifty. While the U.S. Congress spent the summer looking for spies and subversives in government, Hemingway looked for ways to speak of the war without refighting it. Colonel Cantwell's memories, provoked by Renata's continued questioning, are a catalogue of mistakes that killed, orders that maimed, and operational blunders by commanding generals who never saw the front lines. Combining what he knew of Buck Lanham's and Charles Sweeny's careers, Hemingway created the officer who knew too much, was too aware of what had happened and why. Better never to have known, but Cantwell cannot avoid what he has learned at great cost, nor can he erase his memories.[12] Mixing his own observations with his reading of World War II histories and very specific information Lanham supplied from sometimes classified sources, Hemingway buried the war beneath the Colonel's bitterness. The book might be fiction, but its factual details were as accurate as he could make them.

While exhilarated by the flow of the story, living in it, making it up, Hemingway was also making up his own life in ways that are more difficult to understand. All writers, he once said, were liars who, when drinking, would lie to anyone, friends or strangers. He might have also said that fiction carried the connotation of making up events that never took place, in effect, telling lies. Since words can never reproduce reality, all writing, at some level, becomes fiction, making liars of us all. But Hemingway's life and his work were not the same, except for the fact that he was continually inventing both of them. Where once he was loath to speak of himself, the threat of death by aneurysm, hanging over his head since 1947, set loose a torrent of biographical stories, all of them verging at some point on fiction. For example, he told a newly made Italian acquaintance that he held no advance degrees, having barely made it through *military school*.[13] Colonel Cantwell, we learn, graduated in first draft from Virginia Military Academy and in revision from West Point, but Ernest graduated only from high school.

Some of his more wooly inventions were written to Charles Scribner, Sr. In July, with the novel settling down into a daily routine, Hemingway told Scribner that four of his ancestors went on the Crusades, and that he and his son Gregory had inherited genetic traits from his great-great-grandmother, a northern Cheyenne Indian,[14] a fable that amused his sisters. Exaggerations and inventions such as this one may have resulted from Hemingway's use of a newly acquired wire recorder, on which he dictated letters for transcription. Speaking to two audiences, the attractive young woman transcribing the recording and the recipient of the letter, Hemingway was liable to say almost anything. But the deeper he got into the Colonel's character, the more Hemingway began to sound like his invention—rough, brusque, and violence-prone. He gave Scribner a detailed account of killing a "snotty SS kraut" who would not give up the German escape routes. When Ernest threatened to kill him, the German supposedly replied that he would not dare because Americans were "a race of mongrel degenerates," and it violated the Geneva Convention.

What a mistake you made, brother, I told him and shot him three times in the belly, fast and then, when he went down on his knees shot him on the topside so that his brains came out of his mouth or I guess it was his nose.[15]

None of the evidence or the memories of those with him in France support such a story.

A year earlier, Ernest wrote Archie MacLeish that he fought for eight months as an irregular, killing twenty-six armed Germans.[16] To a college professor, Hemingway expanded his war record to include sixteen woundings to himself and one hundred and twenty-two men killed at five different wars.[17] Not even Charles Sweeny, veteran of numerous wars and revolutions, would have claimed to have killed that many men, not in wars where one usually never saw the results of a shot fired. To John Dos Passos, Hemingway said that seven concussions in one year were probably more than a writer should sustain.[18] In a dictated letter to Pete Viertel, after telling him about a new Havana prostitute whom he refrained from bedding, Ernest added, by hand, that he had given in, spent the night with the whore, drank seven bottles of Roederers Brut Champagne '42, and fucked all night, which was the reason he had written only 708 words that day.[19]

The question about these claims is not whether they are true or not, but why Hemingway felt compelled to invent and exaggerate them. That he killed or participated in the killing of at least two German soldiers—at Rambouillet's crossroads and during the attack on Lanham's Hürtgenwald command post—should have been enough. That he suffered two concussions, aggravated by whiskey and more head banging, should have been enough. Always one to tell wild and frequently funny stories, Hemingway was capable of exaggerations but not usually ones like these tales, all of which exposed his underlying need to establish that he was a warrior, an outlaw, a rough character capable of extreme violence. After being wounded in World War I, he immediately began using his ruined knee as visual proof of imaginary deeds. On crutches in Milan, he told a young British officer that he "had been badly wounded leading [Italian] Arditi storm troops on Monte Grappa."[20] By the time he reached Paris in 1921, he had transformed his Red Cross duties into regular Italian Army status. Now he was doing the same thing to his war in France: his status as a war correspondent was disappearing as Hemingway the leader of Free French of the Interior irregulars emerged. Killing increasingly larger numbers of Germans in his imagination until he actually believed it to have happened, he was purging, perhaps, the nightmares of war that haunted his sleep: The German tank at the window, himself with an antitank weapon, he pulls the trigger, but the projectile dribbles out the muzzle and onto the floor. He wakes before it explodes to kill him. Or maybe he could no longer tell the difference between what he imagined and previous reality. Or, more disturbingly, he was, perhaps, *becoming* his fiction.

All of his writing life he was said to create male characters in his own image. While every author is present to some degree in his fictions, Hemingway was more open to this analysis than most because more was known about his active life. However, when one looked closely at his earlier fictions, there were always significant dissimilarities between himself and Jake Barnes, Frederic Henry, or Robert Jordan. Now, at fifty, no longer able to drink with the metabolism of his middle years, and intensely aware that his erratic blood pressure could, at any moment, blow a hole through a major artery, Hemingway was existential to the bone, breakfasting with death as a tablemate.

The more intensely focused he became on his morning fiction, the more the fictive stories he told in letters began to mimic the life of Richard Cantwell, including their shared love for the nineteen-year-old Renata/Adriana. During the Italian journey of the previous year, Ernest had not been in prolonged contact with Adriana, but he was telling Patrick and Gregory that she was one of his "girls" they should visit during their 1949 European tour.[21] While his Colonel pledged his dying love to Renata only in the Finca mornings, Ernest thought of her more often, writing letters that went unanswered. In September, he complained of Adriana's silence to an Italian correspondent, knowing that she would speak to his young muse: "I think she understands plenty, but why not write and take a chance."[22] As if by magic, Adriana's brief letter arrived, saying she had seen his sons in Venice, and that she was going to Paris to study art. Ernest responded immediately. He would be in Paris in November, staying at the Ritz, where he would leave instructions for her calls to be put through to his room. He had "much nostalgia" to see her, particularly in Paris.[23] Having spent spring and summer devoted to her beauty, albeit restricted to the confines of his novel, Ernest was as deeply in love with his half-imaginary Adriana as Cantwell was with Renata.

It was not until August 24 that Ernest, in a note he labeled TOP SECRET, wrote Charles Scribner about the new novel, which he promised by the end of October. Two days later, thanking Scribner for the wire recorder, Hemingway reported that Mary was overwhelmed by the portion of the novel he let her read. So moved was she that she did not care about his whores or his three Italian countesses.[24] More exaggerations and fictions. As with everyone else he wrote that summer, Ernest asked Scribner to say nothing of the novel to anyone, particularly not to Martha. As a result of sowing this admonition on two continents, the word gradually spread through the publishing industry. By July, Hemingway was turning away an inquiry from *Ladies' Home Journal* about his new work, and an attempt by *McCall's* to interview his mother in Oak Park. But he was also writing Lillian Ross of *The New Yorker* about his book, including a list of possible titles: *A New Slain Knight*; *Our One and Only Life*; and *Over the River and into the Trees*.[25] By the end of August an Associated Press man was after Hemingway for an interview, and *Life* magazine was asking for information on the book's content and publication date. In September, Ernest let Ed Hotchner read sixty pages of manuscript as a teaser, asking if *Cosmopolitan* would be interested in it as a serial, an inquiry which Hotchner said delighted his managing editor.[26] A month later, Hemingway announced the book to Al Horwits at Universal Pictures as a property that Al might want to film. Ernest spoke of the book in vague but glowing terms—he wrote it to put Shakespeare on his butt, as if writing were a contact sport.[27]

So sure was Hemingway of this still untitled book that he asked Charles Scribner for a $10,000 loan against it to buy Mary a mink coat. Having been such a bastard while writing the story, he wanted to make it up to her. A gesture, he called it, in the middle of their fight to show her it did not matter how the conflict turned out, he was hers. Without asking about the nature of the family argument, Scribner immediately cabled that the $10,000 was deposited in Hemingway's New York account.[28] Under pressure of his writing, Ernest was irascible and easily pricked. That August, when Martha and Pauline ended up in Venice at the same time, he fumed about what they might be saying of him in *his* town. In September, he sent Charles Scribner an unpleasant letter about Martha's anatomy and her Jewishness, neither of which alleged traits apparently bothered him during their four-year affair. Now he said the reason she was never pregnant by him was that he did not care to father half-Jewish children.[29] Unprovoked by anything Martha was currently doing or saying, these vicious remarks about her continued throughout the year and into the next. All his life he forced his wives to ask for a divorce, which was his way of getting what he wanted without taking the responsibility for it. With Martha, roles were reversed: he was the house husband while she went off on assignments; he was the injured party; and he filed for the divorce on the grounds that she deserted him. It all made him look foolish in his own eyes, and he never forgave himself or her for that embarrassment.

In September, Mary was in Chicago visiting her parents, leaving Ernest to his professed loneliness and the "wild life" he said he enjoyed when no one was there to maintain household discipline. Soon he was bragging to Pete Viertel about his all-night stand with the new whore he called Xenophobia. The very same day he wrote Mary how pleased he was with her purchase of a wild mink coat at Marshall Fields. He mentioned his recently written letters to Marlene Dietrich and Teresa, the Italian countess, explaining he was loving in his letters to these women, but it was Mary he loved, and her alone. He was always true to her and literature and war in his fashion. Simultaneously, he wrote Hotchner that he was out of the "doghouse" with Mary, without saying that it took the most expensive mink coat in Chicago to do it.[30]

While Mary was in Chicago, Ernest, to emphasize his "bad boy" character of which he was so proud, wrote Charles Scribner he was having Xenophobia out to the Finca for lunch. At seventeen, she was lovely, ambitious, and had a talent for her chosen profession. At night she worked her trade, but during the day she liked to hang around "us bad boys."[31] Roberto Herrera, apprentice factotum in Mary's absence, brought Xenophobia out to the Finca, where in the course of the afternoon he photographed her several times. Two days later, Mary returned with her mink, happy to be home with Ernest, but her joy lasted only as long as it took Roberto to get his photographs developed. Noticing that the girl was pictured in three different dresses, indicating that she had been at the Finca at least three times in Mary's absence, Mary exploded, furious with Ernest for allowing a whore into her house. To no avail, Ernest tried to lie his way out of the situation, but lying to Mary, he said, was a quick way to starve to death. He was back in the doghouse again.[32] For the rest of the month he worked to placate Mary, finish the book, negotiate the serial with *Cosmopolitan*, and settle on the title. Mary was the easiest part of the equation to solve, for she always forgave, at least on the surface. It was a curious relationship that puzzled Buck Lanham during his June visit. As he later told biographer Bernice Kert, he "was surprised by . . . Mary's increasing submission to Ernest's exhibitionism. Ernest would sit around the pool or at meals and brag about his sexual conquests (real or imagined), and Mary, covering her embarrassment, would act as though she were proud of his manliness."[33] In private, Mary was not nearly so submissive, or so forgiving. Like all of his wives, she suffered from Ernest's unpredictable mood shifts and his erratic verbal abuse; but when they were alone, she gave as good as she got, sometimes stunning him into silence with language unbecoming to a lady but necessary in her battles with Ernest.

In September, by his own count, Hemingway had written over thirteen thousand words; in October, with publishers' deadlines at his back, he wrote another thirteen thousand. By the end of the month, with Scribner's planning a spring publication and the price set with *Cosmopolitan* for the serial to begin in February 1950, Ernest still had not shown any text to either camp, nor was he committed to a title. On October 12, to quiet rumors that this was Hemingway's "big sea, air, land novel," which had been discussed in gossip columns during the past year, Scribner's issued a press release saying that when told by doctors he had but a short time to live, Ernest put aside his "book of larger proportions" to write a shorter novel he knew he could finish. Hotchner was furious: the blurb in the *New York Times* implied that the new novel was written as something of an afterthought, making the public think they were getting something that was a warm-up for the "big book."[34] By the last day in October, Hemingway wired Scribner's and *Cosmopolitan* the title—*Across the River and into the Trees*—which Charles Scribner did not like. On November 4, Ernest air-mailed the first sixty-two pages and the chapter that introduced the girl, Renata, to *Cosmopolitan*. After "jamming" all summer and early fall, Hemingway's weight hovered around 205 pounds and his blood pressure was dangerously high: 180 over 105.[35]

On November 16, Ernest and Mary flew to New York, checked in without fanfare at the Sherry-Netherland, and spent two days making last-minute additions to their luggage for a return trip to Venice. Two days later, Leonard Lyons's newspaper column reported that Ernest was in town but could not visit with old friends, for he was busy finishing his novel, which was not quite true.[36] By arrangement, Lillian Ross met the Hemingways at the airport and spent the better part of two days with them. Mary in her mink coat was "small, energetic and cheerful." Ernest appeared

> bearish, cordial, and constricted. His hair, which was very long in back, was gray, except at the temples, where it was white; his mustache was white, and he had a ragged, half-inch full white beard. There was a bump about the size of a walnut over his left eye. He was wearing steel-rimmed spectacles, with a piece of paper under the nosepiece.[37]

Ross accompanied Hemingway about New York: buying a coat, supper in the hotel room with Marlene Dietrich one day, lunch there with Charles Scribner the next, and a prowl through the Metropolitan Museum of Art with Patrick, now a sophomore down from Harvard. To read her "Profile" of Hemingway was to read his most recent letters, for he told her the same things he was telling everyone else: a list of writers he had beaten in the literary "ring"; how he wrote *The Sun Also Rises*; advice on boxing; stories of Scott Fitzgerald's ineptitude; and old jokes. Taking it all down in her notes, Ross reproduced as accurately as possible the man in his setting, including three double bourbons at the airport bar, the several bottles of champagne in the suite, and the silver flask that he nipped at in the museum. In the background of the Profile, Mary flits in and out of focus, attending to their fourteen pieces of luggage, unpacking at the hotel, hanging up the coats of visitors, a lady in waiting as it were, almost invisible.

Before boarding the *Ile de France*, recently refurbished from a

troopship to her prewar splendor, Ernest turned over not quite finished typescripts to Scribner's and *Cosmopolitan.* He was leaving
behind a story far stranger than anything he had previously written, a
novel book-ended by the Colonel's last duck hunt and filled with more
allusions and arcane references than anyone expected to come from
him. Mixing and inverting old stories—Dante's *The Divine Comedy*
and D'Annunzio's *Notturno,* among others—Hemingway's account of
his dying Colonel, reduced from his general's rank for some unnamed
fiasco, was a war novel without any war, yet it was largely about the
war. Having "moved through arithmetic, through plane geometry
and algebra," he was now "into calculus." The book was "all done
with three-cushion shots."[38] With a young and beautiful Renata as
the novitiate and the Colonel as her guide, the two unlikely lovers
enter a newly made hell of war, circling down into its levels of mis-
trust, incompetence, butchery, back-stabbing, and losses too terrible
to recount. Their three-day journey, played out against the backdrop
of Venice, is prodded on by Renata's questions. As Cantwell tells her
of malfeasance in high places and muck-ups below, the Colonel fingers her three emeralds in his pocket, given to him to hold in trust,
emeralds similar to the three stones given to D'Annunzio by his muse,
Eleonora Duse. When not engaged in this painful remembering,
Cantwell's impressions of Venice, in light and color, set an aesthetic
backdrop for the story, a sensitivity to place worthy of Pater.[39]

Newer younger writers—Irwin Shaw in particular—might be able
to write convincingly of combat and cohabitation, but could they
write with this kind of complexity where the story reverberated on
several levels? Would readers, fresh from the war and ready to return
to civilian lives, want to be reminded of the remaining bitterness
among professional soldiers? Hemingway was certain that *Across the
River* was the best book he had ever written; certainly it was his most
complex, with little action and much retrospection—not unlike the
retrospective of his own life that he was pursuing. Charles Scribner,
who finally got to read the typescript after Hemingway was at sea,
was concerned that Renata did not appear until the reader was sixty
pages into the story. Couldn't she appear sooner? The book, he said,

was filled with "beauty, restraint and understanding," more so than in Ernest's earlier books. If Ernest wanted to rework any part of it, Scribner's would reset galleys and postpone publication to meet his schedule. In fact, Hemingway asked Scribner to hold off on setting type for the galleys until he was able to rework the last chapters of the novel in Paris.[40]

Ernest, Mary, and the entourage of Don Andrés, Ed Hotchner, and Jigee Viertel boarded the *Ile de France* together—ladies, gentlemen, and private priest off on a spree. Soon after they arrived at the Ritz Hotel in Paris, Ernest came into a windfall of $6,000 in back royalties from his French publisher. He divided the money evenly between himself, Mary, and Jigee to use as mad money on the town. Hotchner—there on *Cosmopolitan*'s expense account to bring back revised copy for the serial—stayed in a less expensive hotel but spent his days with the group. For almost a month, Hemingway worked early mornings revising Cantwell's last day in Venice while revisiting his own old Parisian haunts and keeping his hand in at the race track. No phone calls came from Adriana, who was still in Venice, but Jigee Viertel was close at hand, for Ernest had arranged special rates for her at the Ritz while insisting she use some of the windfall to pay for it. Mary, in public, was comfortable with the arrangement, but when Ernest spent an hour and a half one night in Jigee's room, she was hurt and furious.[41] When Pete Viertel arrived, Ernest was quick to reassure him that "We've looked after your girl." To his chagrin, Pete learned that this included the gift of almost $2,000; "pocket money," Jigee called it. It did not take long for Viertel to realize that Ernest was smitten with his wife, but Jigee assured him there was nothing to their mild flirtation. How could she be anything more than flattered by the attentions of an old gray man with a heavy paunch behaving like a well-mannered schoolboy?[42] Over the next two weeks, Pete was Ernest's new audience for yet another guided tour into the lost days of his Paris youth.

For the first time since the war, Hemingway was writing poetry, but hardly with the same lovelorn sentiments. Jigee at hand and Adriana in Venice, his newfound "girls," produced in Ernest a schoolboy reaction, which Mary neither understood nor tolerated with grace, but she did tolerate it. Whenever an attractive female appeared the least bit vulnerable to her husband's magnetism, Mary became as unimportant as their chambermaid, suffering insults plain and oblique that would have sent a less determined woman to her lawyer. There in Paris, where Mary enjoyed the warmth of her mink coat, Ernest wrote about "the nigger rich . . . wild natural mink is on their backs/Their shoulders, sleeves, and on their flanks." "We leave them all quite easily," he wrote "when dislike overcomes our love." They were poems about Mary without being for Mary.[43]

In another poem, he urged,

> *Now, Mary, you can face it good*
> *And face it in your widow-hood*
>
> . . .
>
> *So sleep well, darling.*
> *Sleep well, please,*
> *And know that I am at my ease.*

"It" was death, his own death, holding heavy sway in a mind not quite right. At Auteuil, he watched the ponies run but thought about the war.

> *Eternity is scarcely found*
> *Until we're underneath the ground*
> *Where thudding hooves will seldom sound.*

The day before Christmas, Ernest and his irregulars left Paris by auto, making their way down the foggy Rhône Valley toward Provence.[44] Traveling in a Packard with trunk and roof rack jammed with a mountain of luggage, Ernest gave intermittent lectures on the passing countryside while the hired driver, Georges, took care of the road. At Nice, the Viertels and Hotchner returned to Paris by train, leaving Ernest, Mary, and their Basque-speaking priest to complete the trip to Venice. In his briefcase Hotchner carried the last three revised chapters of *Across the River*.[45]

THE MIDDLE PARTS
OF FORTUNE

January to October 1950

"NEVER LEAD AGAINST a hitter, and take every-thing he has to get inside. Duck a swing. Block a hook. And counter a jab with everything you own."[1] The advice he gave Lillian Ross, Ernest sometimes forgot, but Mary never did, which stood her in good stead over the next several months. No sooner was Jigee Viertel out of their lives than she was replaced in Venice by Adriana Ivancich, the muse who inspired *Across the River*. Dora Ivancich, mother of the muse, was even more worried than Mary about Hemingway's attentions to her headstrong daughter: "You see this man Hemingway too much," she told Adriana. "It is not normal, a married man, older than you. I don't forbid you to see him, but from time to time, not so many dates. . . . You have to consider what people might think."[2] Adriana was too young to care what people thought, but neither she nor her mother had yet seen the novel in which her iden-tity was so thinly veiled. While Mary visited churches and museums, Ernest waited at the Gritti Palace for Adriana to meet him for lunches at Harry's Bar or slow walks along the narrow waterways.

Count Carlo Kechler, a new-made Italian friend, warned Ernest that his infatuation with Adriana, so apparent to anyone in their near vicinity, was dangerous for both of them. Ernest would not listen. She was his "Black Horse," the code name he gave her. He was Papa; she was "daughter." Mary, trying to ignore the game, maintained as much dignity as the situation would allow. When Adriana came to Cortina with the Hemingways in early February 1950, Mary wrote in her journal that Ernest was "weaving a mesh which might entangle and pain him," but nothing she could say could change that. When Adriana overstayed her second visit to Cortina, her mother summoned her home. Ernest gallantly volunteered to drive her to Venice while Mary remained in Cortina skiing. Before her errant husband returned, Mary was once more in a cast, having broken her left ankle on the slopes.[3]

Revitalized by Adriana's presence, Hemingway made more revisions to the book version of *Across the River* and added two new short stories to the several "black ass" poems written in Paris when his novel was in its death throes.[4] His Italian publisher said that Ernest was a sure bet for the Nobel Prize with his next book, which pleased Hemingway immensely. But with the reality of his Venetian story now hard upon him, Hemingway forbade any translation of *Across the River* into Italian for a period of two years, a gesture which proved no barrier to the scandal soon to break over the Ivancich family.[5] Without even a second cousin as chaperone, Renata and Richard Cantwell drink together at Harry's Bar, eat together at the Gritti Palace, and then ride the elevator up to his room, where they stretch out together on his bed. In Venice, where every act and every gesture carried political nuances at the local level, such blatant behavior in a book spoke volumes about the Ivancich family. Who would care that *Across the River* was a book about the politics of war when the Colonel bundled Renata beneath the gondola blanket and with his "ruined" hand found beneath her clothing "the island in the great river with the high steep banks"? Following her instructions to "hold the high ground," Cantwell brings the young girl to a sexual climax.[6] When the Italian press would link Hemingway's name with Adriana's what else would there be for the gossips of Venice to discuss?

In February, the first of five installments of the novel appeared in *Cosmopolitan*, where Ed Hotchner was no longer on the masthead as an assistant editor. He blamed the new editor, Herb Mayes. Years later Mayes said, "Hotchner's handling of the project for *Cosmopolitan* was so unfortunate that, in February of 1950, the very month we published the first installment . . . it became necessary to ask for Hotchner's resignation."[7] Without specifying the problem, Mayes may have become aware that Hotchner's loyalties were riding mostly with Hemingway in the contractual process, or he may have been upset with the content of the serial. As a young lawyer with a flair for journalism, Hotchner was a survivor who was never looking for a permanent home on the magazine.

As during the previous winter, Ernest and Mary made the Gritti Palace their home base. When he was not correcting galleys for the serialization of *Across the River*, he was shooting ducks, courting Adriana, and enjoying his status at the Gritti. Mary was behaving better than he had any right to expect. On the surface at least, she was friendly with Adriana, despite Ernest's frequent little insults and his public fawning over the young girl. "My god-damned heart," he wrote, "that target of opportunity, sliced straight in half like the judgement of Herod. Only they sliced mine as clean as with a butcher's cleaver and Herod held up the attack."[8] Mary and Dora Ivancich finally met at a lunch arranged by Ernest, who prevailed upon Mary to invite Dora and Adriana to visit them at the Finca. There they could spend time with Gianfranco, who was now working in Havana to restore the family's diminished fortune. Awkward in her walking cast, Mary was embarrassed and angry, but nevertheless did as Ernest asked of her, smiling and tolerant of Dora's hesitant English while mentally classifying the Italian woman as "gray of hair, eyes, manner and wardrobe."[9]

Mary did not speak of the letters from Nita Jensen, whom they left in charge of the Finca. No sooner had the Hemingways left Cuba than Gianfranco moved into their house on a regularly irregular basis, and Nita could not dislodge him, and would not sleep in the same house with him. One night when she arrived, Gianfranco "was here with several women in some fancy station wagon. . . . The following night . . . Sinsky met me and asked me who the man was who was using your room. I just about died. Every time René locked your typewriter away the Italian managed to find it . . . I'm convinced that he's purely a sponger and taking every advantage he can of you."[10] Later, Dora Ivancich responded to Mary's invitation with a cautious note saying she would consider the possibility of a visit. She did not say there was no money to pay for such an extravagance. Nor did she know that Gianfranco, temperamentally unsuited to tedious employment, was enamored with the seemingly carefree life of the writer.

After a self-hosted farewell supper in their Gritti apartment with Adriana's family, the Hemingways departed Venice on March 7 en route to Paris with stops in between at Nervi, Nice, and Aix-en-Provence. In Paris, registering once more at the Ritz, Ernest went to bed with one of his recurring bronchial infections from which he did not recover until Adriana arrived the following week to return to art school. About the same time that Adriana appeared, so did a letter from an almost forgotten person out of the past. Olga Rudge, Ezra Pound's mistress since the mid-Twenties, wrote to remind "Dear Mr. Hemingway" that Ezra continued to molder in St. Elizabeth's Hospital for the Insane in Washington, D.C., incarcerated there by the American government rather than putting him on trial for treason. During the war Pound had made a series of radio broadcasts from Italy urging British and American troops not to fight for their decadent capitalist employers. Olga reminded Ernest that he suggested a year earlier that Ezra might be granted amnesty. Was anything being done about it? The controversial awarding to him of the Bollinger Prize for poetry had only stirred up old arguments and done nothing to rescue him. His wife, Dorothy, she said was "incapable of taking direct action" and "refused to take responsibility of any kind." Hemingway had recently agreed to let his "Homage to Ezra" (1925) be republished in a collection of essays honoring the aging and erratic poet on his sixty-fifth birthday. But adulation would not free the iconoclast who edited Eliot's *Waste Land* into shape, championed James Joyce, and gave Ernest an early boost up the literary ladder. Olga said,

> *Of course the easy way is for E.'s friends to leave him where he is and salve their consciences with tributes to his literary worth—he is simply crawling with literary parasites—none of whom, in the States at least, compromise themselves by touching on the subject of treason . . . it is surely time for his friends, if he has any, to see what can be done.*

She closed the letter asking Hemingway to forgive her bluntness, but other than republish an old essay, "What else have you done for E.?"[11] The unspoken answer was: Nothing. Hemingway realized, however, that were Ezra to be let out of St. Elizabeth's, he would be a man without a passport, vulnerable to a trial for treason, and with no place to go unless Italy would take him back.

During the Hemingways' last week in Paris, Charlie and Vera Scribner, on vacation, rendezvoused with Ernest, who declared the much revised novel now ready for book publication. Earlier in the winter, Adriana at Hemingway's request had submitted drawings to Scribner's for the dust jacket of the novel, which Charlie, apparently not knowing her relationship with Ernest, selected to be used. Ernest was so delighted that he hosted a luncheon for "his partner," as he referred to Adriana, after which he and she walked through St. Germain stopping at a Deux Magots sidewalk table. Watching the young men on the boulevard, Hemingway said that any of them, who were not stupid, would wish to marry a woman as lovely as she. "Since I am not stupid," he continued, "I would feel the same way." When Adriana reminded him he was married, he agreed, but added that two people need not remain married. He might have added that not three blocks away was the apartment on rue Férou where he and Pauline had lived, and that they once sat deeply in love at a Deux Magots table. "I love you in my heart," he told Adriana, "and I cannot do anything about it." The young woman sat there paralyzed, as if waiting for an avalanche to fall. "All I could think of at that moment was that everything was ending, our beautiful friendship was over, finished." Unable to touch her gin and tonic, she waited immobilized. Finally, Ernest said, "I would ask you to marry me if I did not know you would say no." The moment passed. Ernest left a few francs on the table, and they rose to walk through rue Bonaparte, past the Beaux-Arts galleries, to the Seine.[12]

On March 21, the spring equinox, Ernest and Mary left Paris on the boat train to Le Havre, where the next day they boarded the *Ile de France* for New York. Adriana, who helped with the packing, accompanied them as far as the pier. At the Ritz they left behind a trunk, a box of china, and two boxes of books for the concierge to ship to Cuba.[13] Included in their personal baggage they took with them enmity, betrayal, and heartache. No sooner was the ship at sea than Ernest wrote Charles Scribner that his love for Mary and Adriana was like having his heart fed into a meat grinder.[14] To his London publisher, Jonathan Cape, he wrote, asking him to keep references to his war record off the British dust jacket of *Across the River and into the Trees*. Denigrating his most prized moments from the war, Hemingway insisted that he be featured as a writer only, not as a soldier. If the reviewers wanted to prove that he had never run the sub patrols, never flown with the RAF, never fought in the war, never been wounded, never killed anyone, that was fine with him.[15]

By the time the Hemingways reached New York, two installments of *Across the River* had appeared in *Cosmopolitan*, and the third was about to come out. Lillian Ross, who was still working on her *New Yorker* Profile of Ernest, spent more time with him, gathering more details. Marlene Dietrich visited again, saying how much she adored the early chapters of the novel, and Charles Sweeny and Evan Shipman, old friends from the early Paris days, dropped by the Sherry-Netherland to visit. At the Scribner Building, Ernest turned over his final revised draft of *Across the River* for publication in August. On April 5, there was a birthday lunch for Mary with journalist friends, and that night Buddy North, whose Ringling Brothers Circus was in town, invited Ernest, Mary, Hotchner, and Lillian Ross to be his guests at that extravaganza. Ernest fell in love with the big cats, the bears, and the elephants.

The following day, Ernest accidentally ran into Chink Dorman-O'Gowan, an old friend and survivor from the 1918 war not seen for over twenty years. A professional soldier, Chink, now retired from the British Army, had changed his given name of Smith to its original Gaelic form, O'Gowan. Reappearing in Hemingway's life, along with Charles Sweeny and Buck Lanham, Chink made it even more difficult for Ernest to leave the war behind. All three friends, professional military men to the core, felt badly used during the war, but Chink was the most vocal in his complaints. If Hemingway's Colonel was bitter about military politics, Dorman-O'Gowan was absolutely livid to the point of advocating armed rebellion. He was in the States lecturing for the Inter-Party Government of Ireland, preaching the need to remove all British from Northern Ireland. Back in Ireland on his country estate, he was serving as a military adviser to the Irish Republican Army (IRA) while training IRA men in Dartry Woods and giving briefings to battalion-level officers.[16] Over the next several months his correspondence with Hemingway would continue to stoke Ernest's personal bitterness about the war, a bitterness over events whose significance inflated with his every telling of the tale.

On April 6, Ernest and Mary left New York, arriving in Cuba on April 8.[17] For thirteen of the last nineteen months they had lived at sea or on the road—Paris, Venice, Torcello, Cortina—during which time Ernest began, finished, and revised *Across the River and into the Trees* and returned heartsick to the Finca. Mary was returning to the Finca with an impoverished heart, despite her newly acquired Venetian gold trinkets.[18] What once seemed to be another of her husband's romantic but unrequited interludes had churned into a full-blown, embarrassing obsession for which she had no antidote, nor had he. The presence of Gianfranco Ivancich continually reminded Ernest of his now distant muse, Adriana. For Mary, the younger Gianfranco was a comfort as a listener to whom she could tell her woes, and also a potential but probably unrequited lover with whom to needle her husband. But nothing Mary did could distract

Ernest from his deepening fantasies about the fields of love and war. In public, he was usually as charming as ever; but alone with her, he wore his melancholia like a shroud, spewing painful verbal abuse at her while interlarding his real war experiences with new inventions.

Having been an ambulance driver in Italy and a journalist in the Spanish Civil War, Hemingway began seriously rewriting his military service, making it appear as though he had been an armed combatant in both wars. He wrote Buck Lanham that World War I was his kindergarten, at which "If you go crazy from too many times up the same damned hill you can always look at fireing [sic] squad. It could look like two fireing squads if you had double vision from concussion. But you always saw the fireing squad, double vision or not, and sometimes you commanded it."[19] Spurred on by Dorman-O'Gowan's letters inviting him to be part of the IRA revolution, Hemingway's letters to Chink were so ambiguous that one was not sure if he was reporting what he observed or what he participated in. About the Spanish Civil War, he said: "We were beat when they took Irun but we ran it out for two and a half years into the longest holding attack in history. . . . I have it completely and accurate and straight now that have killed 122 (armeds not counting possible or necessary shootings)."[20] For two years during World War II, when submarines were thick in the Gulf, he commanded a Q-ship, the only civilian to do so. Seven of the eleven such ships were lost due to faulty security, which for his boat remained unbreached to this day. "We preyed on everything neutral that was doing any good for Germany and on Miss Submarine." Only four men from his nine-man crew were still alive. None of which was completely true: none of the *Pilar's* crew was killed in action; they never attacked any submarines; the *Pilar* was not a ship of prey, nor were there eleven others like her in Cuba.

Hemingway claimed that he would probably have to fight in the Korean War as well. That's what they had done to him for thirty-two years, tossed him into the fray like a pit bull or a fighting cock with no one willing to take responsibility for him if the action screwed up. He could not remember all the times he had been "pitted." He might not be a professional like Chink, but Ernest implied that he had soldiered for six months in China; two years and three months at sea with his command; a fling with the RAF; and the rest of 1944 into 1945 with Lanham's 22nd Regiment. Three times he was recommended for the Distinguished Service Cross (DSC).[21] He had been in all those places, but not soldiering as he implied. The DSC was not an honor conferred on civilians.

Like many of his war stories, there was a substantial layer of fiction laid down over a foundation of fact until these fabrications devalued his very real and serious work during the war. It was as if he were reliving one of his own short stories. When Krebs of "Soldier's Home" (1925) returned from the war, he found he had to tell lies to be listened to, but "A distaste for everything that had happened to him in the war set in because of the lies he told. All of the times that had been able to make him feel cool and clear inside himself . . . now lost their cool, valuable quality and then were lost themselves."[22] Well Hemingway knew the feeling, having returned to Oak Park after his Italian wounding to spread outrageous stories about his foreign war. He told the *Oak Parker* that he had "received thirty-two 45 caliber bullets in his limbs and hands. Twenty-eight of the slugs, he said, were "extracted without taking an anesthetic."[23]

That was thirty years earlier, understandable exaggerations of a young man eager to prove himself in the world. But here at fifty, half a century old, as he liked to say, the boy was still inventing feats beyond belief for reasons that were not so clear. For those he admired, Ernest tailored the story to the strong suit of his listener. To Charles Scribner, an avid horseman in the British fox hunter mold, Ernest melded his tame experiences at a Wyoming dude ranch with observations of working cowboys to invent Hemingway the wild bronc rider: "I bucked out anything there was in the shoots [chutes] with a bear trap saddle when I need[ed] 100 dollars and did not give a what [you] call it if the back went or not. . . . In a bear trap saddle he can't throw you. You are with him for keeps. But it is 20/1 he breaks your back."[24] To academic Arthur Mizener, Ernest claimed to have been shot "twice through the scrotum" and through both knees, both hands, both feet, and his head.[25] By the end of August, he was telling a fellow writer, Robert Cantwell, that he had been wounded "on twenty-two different occasions . . . due to enemy action."[26] Mary, having no way of knowing where reality left off and fantasy took hold, could not question stories of his life before they met, but she was growing tired, if not concerned, with his constant retelling of them.

Martha Gellhorn, after reading the first installment of *Across the River and into the Trees*, was quick to conclude that her former husband doted only on himself. "I feel sick," she wrote Bill Walton, "shivering sick." She wept for the lost years she spent adoring him. Perhaps those who did not know him would find Colonel Cantwell plausible, but to her the story had "a long sound of madness and a terrible smell as of decay." When she read the second installment, she wrote Walton that this book was "God's vengeance; but Ernest will never know. He will go on . . . always feeling misunderstood . . . always feeling everything is someone else's fault and I think . . . he will end in the nut house."[27]

Mary was troubled and frightened by Ernest's behavior, disturbed by the letters arriving from Adriana, and unsure of the worth of the new novel. When coupled with his increasingly insulting behavior toward her, Mary was being pushed to her limits of tolerance. All his life he bent women to his will, either by romantic intensity in the courtship or by sullen and/or sarcastic treatment in the parting. All his life he fell in love with the emotional impact of a heart attack, undeniable and all-consuming. All his life he wanted a wife to whom he gave the responsibility for the order and discipline of his household. Once a wife, the woman quickly became a mother figure whom he began to resent just as he resented his own mother's control of the Oak Park home. Like his father, when he wished to punish, he demanded a detailed accounting of all expenditures, no matter how small. Unlike his father, he could, with his left hand, spend money as if it had no meaning.

His first three wives knew the game was over when he began purposely embarrassing them in public. In the presence of Adriana, Ernest frequently ignored Mary as if she were hired help; on their return to the Finca, his behavior grew worse. On May 5, barely a month after returning from Italy, Mary and her visiting cousin waited on board the *Pilar* for Ernest to meet them for lunch. When he arrived late, unapologetic, and with the young prostitute Xenophobia on his arm, Mary was hurt to the point of cold fury. The next morning she delivered to him a declaration of independence:

> As soon as it is possible for me to move out . . . I shall move. . . . in 1944 in bed at the Ritz Hotel in Paris . . . I thought you were a straight and honorable and brave man and magnetically endearing to me . . . although I was suspicious of your over-drinking . . . I believed you and in you. . . . I expected to contribute to the marriage . . . absolute loyalty to you and devotion to your projects . . . enterprising service to you and your family and house . . . alertness and tenderness towards you . . . [but] we have both been failures. . . . I have lost your interest in me, your devotion, and also your respect. Your principal failure . . . because of your accumulating ego and your increasing . . . over-drinking . . . you have been . . . undisciplined in your daily living. Both privately and in public you have insulted me and my dignity as a human being and a woman devoted to you and have debased my pride in you in front of friends.[28]

The following day, Mary gave Ernest a detailed listing of how she spent the $1,000 he had deposited in her checking account twenty days earlier. Both an accounting and an indictment, the typed sheet showed that she ate out twice at lunch, bought some cheap costume jewelry, one dress, and some face creams, while spending the rest on household expenses. Only $79.35 went for her personal use. Until the end of June, Mary kept the daily record, including such items as thirty cents for gum and sixty-five cents for a zipper: punch and counterpunch.

While Mary was preparing her May 7 accounting, Ernest was writing Milton Wolf, a onetime friend and commander of the Abraham Lincoln Battalion in the Spanish Civil War. In response to Wolf's asking for a contribution to the Brigade's defense fund, Ernest replied that he helped individuals, not causes. If the Brigade had problems now with congressional investigations of loyalty, had they not brought that upon themselves? Had they not signed on to be tough?[29] He might as well have given Mary a copy of the letter. Had she not also signed on to be tough? The next day he wrote a disjointed letter to Senator Joe McCarthy, the man fomenting the Red scare and making "McCarthyism" a by-word for hysterical government investigations. In his harangue of the senator, Ernest offered to pay for his trip to the Finca where, depending on "Tail Gunner Joe's" weight, he could fight either Ernest or one of his sons. The reasons for the invective are not entirely clear, but the rhetoric was impressive:

> *Senator you certainly bore the bejeesus out of some tax-payers and this is an invitation to get it all out of your system . . . with an old character like me who is fifty years old . . . and thinks you are a shit, Senator, and would knock you on your ass the best day you ever lived.*[30]

There were no interhouse letters to Mary, but neither did she leave as threatened. Somehow a truce was reached, and his short, unhappy wife, for the first time in almost five years, began letters of inquiry to editors to see who was interested in her view of "life with Papa." By May 21, she had a contract with *Flair* magazine and once again there were two writers in the family.

All that summer Hemingway struggled with his wife, his writing, and his public image. First there were book galleys to correct for Scribner's followed by the page proofs. All the while new installments of the serial were appearing in *Cosmopolitan*, sanitized by nameless editors for their American readers. Faced with a much revised and altered typescript, Ernest was hard-pressed to get it right, making yet more changes in chapter endings, which he finished about June 3. Two days later he received the proof for the dust jacket that used Adriana's illustration with new lettering, but the publication date slipped from August to September. Now, with the book out of his hands and no longer emendable, came the reward of anxiety and second-guessing. Supportive words on the serial came in from various friends, whose enthusiasm was not always as strong as Ernest needed. His fishing and shooting friend, Mayito Menocal, Jr., said he was glad that Ernest had cut "the part about Eisenhower being complicated with Kay Summersby" because there would have been a libel suit, even if the general had been sleeping with his jeep driver.[31]

Meanwhile Lillian Ross, having completed her Hemingway Profile for *The New Yorker*, sent Ernest the page proofs for his suggestions or changes.[32] He immediately sent back his comments, which were minimal, saying that he sounded conceited. Ross said no one in the office agreed with him on the conceited part. "Of course," she said, "you talk your special kind of joke language. That's supposed to be . . . one of the points. It would be silly to make you sound like a Henry James character."[33] When the Profile appeared, subtitled "How Do You Like It Now, Gentlemen?" friends of Ernest were quick to respond. Marlene Dietrich was upset by her presence in the piece; Hotchner was cautiously positive, not knowing if Ernest would appreciate it or not. Slim Hayward (Ernest's flirtatious friend and former Mrs. Howard Hawks) thought it "lacked affection."[34] A number of readers took the Profile to be hostile on Ross's part, showing Hemingway as a badly dressed eccentric who liked to lecture to people while drinking champagne early in the morning. Ross later said,

> *People who objected strongly to Hemingway's personality, assumed I did the same . . . they thought . . . I was ridiculing or attacking it. Other people did not like the way Hemingway talked . . . they didn't like his freedom; they didn't like his not taking himself seriously; they didn't like his wasting his time on going to boxing matches, going to the zoo, talking to friends, going fishing, enjoying people . . . they didn't like Hemingway to be Hemingway.*[35]

Ernest himself was ambivalent about his portrait, reassuring when writing to Ross, "shocked" by it when he wrote Carlos Baker, who was working on the first critical book to cover all of Hemingway's fiction. To Dorman-O'Gowan, Hemingway said he was "sorry about that New Yorker thing." Some of the quotes were not actually his, but he thought the article was basically friendly. In another letter, Hemingway said he thought of Lillian Ross as "a good friend although you might not gather it from that Profile."[36]

On July 18, when overdue page proofs on *Across the River* arrived at the Finca, Ernest was in a horrible mood, furious with Jonathan Cape for misspelling Cantwell's name on the dust jacket proofs for the British edition, certain (as always) that Scribner's was not going to push the novel, and his ears still ringing from another concussion suffered on the *Pilar*. Climbing up on the flying bridge to relieve Gregorio at the helm, Ernest slipped on the wet deck as Gregorio turned sharply into the Rincón Channel. Falling into the gaffs, Hemingway's head smashed into a metal clamp, opening a deep, brightly bleeding cut on his skull. It took three stitches to close it, the odor of his own blood now as familiar as the pain—a force five concussion, he called it, measuring it in hurricane terms. His headaches returned, making him irritable as he sunk into a "black-ass" mood, due, he said, to his boredom, pride, and disgust. In August, he wrote Lillian Ross of being tempted, while diving deep into the Gulf Stream, not to come up. True or not, his account was in keeping with his anxiety over the novel and his marriage. "I love A[driana] to die of it," he told Charlie Scribner, "and . . . I love Mary as she should be loved; I hope."[37] It was an old dilemma, one he first experienced when married to Hadley and in love with Pauline; again when married to Pauline and in love with Martha.

With Cowley's biographical essay spread across *Life* magazine, a *Harper's Bazaar* photo essay in an earlier March issue, the Ross *New Yorker* Profile, and a sanitized serial version in *Cosmopolitan*, not to mention sidebars in several national magazines, Hemingway could not have been in a better or worse position vis-à-vis his hostile critics: better in the sense that no matter what the critics said, the reading public was fully alerted to the book; worse because there is nothing like a spotlight for bringing out predators. Released on September 7, *Across the River and into the Trees* was immediately reviewed by every major newspaper and magazine at home and in England, where it had appeared three days earlier. Avid admirers lined up on one side, rabid detractors on the other. John O'Hara prefaced his review by labeling Hemingway "the most important author living today, the outstanding author since the death of Shakespeare." Maxwell Geismar said, "It is not only Hemingway's worst novel; it is a synthesis of everything that is bad in his previous work and it throws a doubtful light on the future."[38] *Newsweek* said it was "his best and most carefully thought out book." *Time* called it a parody of Hemingway's style, giving his "admirers little to cheer about."[39]

East Coast intellectuals, who once put Hemingway at the forefront of American writers, were unusually harsh, as if the bad boy had betrayed them personally. Alfred Kazin felt "embarrassment, even pity, that so important a writer can make such a travesty of himself." Philip Rahv found the novel "so egregiously bad as to render all comment on it positively embarrassing to anyone who esteems Hemingway."[40] In the middle, the lukewarm group, who admired Hemingway but could not admire this novel, spoke of it in terms of texture and scene without passing judgments, hedging their bets. E. B. White paid left-handed homage to the novel with one of his parodies, "Across the Street and into the Grill," which began: "This is my last and best and true and only meal, thought Mr. Pirnie [not Ernie] as he descended at noon and swung east on the beat-up sidewalk of Forty-fifth Street. Just ahead of him was the girl from the reception desk. I am a little fleshed out around the crook of the elbow, thought Pirnie, but I commute good."[41]

Few and far between were those who understood the complexity of Hemingway's structure or his intent of rewriting the descent into the Inferno. Northrop Frye, who did not care for the book, at least saw that it was "intended to be a study in isolation, of how the standards of a decent soldier are betrayed by modern war." Phil Young, already at work on his groundbreaking psychoanalytic study of Hemingway's fiction, argued that while we may not enjoy the violent world of the novel, "we should be hard pressed to prove that it is not the one we inhabit." Old Paris friend and author Eliot

Paul, taking a longer view, called Hemingway's "grasp of contemporary situations . . . profound and a decade ahead of his public's." Ben Redman's analysis of the reviews was quite accurate: "Perhaps we really do know too much about Hemingway, or at least his public poses, to judge his work impartially."[42] These mixed reviews had no apparent impact on sales, as the book quickly sold out the initial printing of 75,000; before the end of September Scribner's ordered a second printing of 25,000, with more printings to come. For twenty-one weeks *Across the River* registered on the *New York Times* best-seller list, running as number one for seven of those weeks. By the first accounting period, 125,000 copies had been sold. Between his forty-five-cent royalties for every copy and the healthy serial fee from *Cosmopolitan*, Hemingway paid off all his borrowings from Scribner's and would enter 1951 debt-free and ahead of the game.

Some good reviews, much public attention, and a best-seller did little to relieve his increasing angst as summer rolled into early fall. Soon Adriana Ivancich and her mother, Dora, were due to visit the Finca, filling him with expectations of the young girl's presence and fears of how Mary might behave. In August, when it looked as if they might not be able to afford the trip, Ernest sent a substantial check to cover the expenses. Adriana was overwhelmed; her mother was frightened, but wanted to make the trip to see her son Gianfranco, her only hope for restoring the family's fallen fortunes. Gianfranco, meanwhile, had managed to lose or be fired from his job (a matter of honor, Ernest called it) and was now, with Ernest's encouragement, writing a novel. By the end of August, a reporter from the European version of *Life* magazine was asking for a photograph of Adriana, for gossip was beginning to spread through Venetian society about the gondola scene in the *Cosmopolitan* serial. Claiming that Hemingway had melded two young women into the character of Renata, the September issue of *Europeo* published photos of Adriana and Afdera Franchetti, the younger sister of Hemingway's Italian friend, Barone Nanyuki Franchetti. Afdera was reported to have said that Ernest was "desperately in love with her . . . twice she had visited him in

Cuba and they had recently spent a month together in Paris, winning millions of francs at Auteuil."[43]

To free his imagination, Dante needed his Beatrice; Petrarch, his Laura. So, too, did Hemingway need his unrequited and impassioned love for Adriana. Regularly, since leaving her behind on the dock at Le Havre, he had written her letters professing his love for her, his admiration of her artwork, and his concern for her future. When the bright blood streamed down his face on the *Pilar*, the heartsick lover professed that his first thought was taking better care of himself for her sake. On August 1, he longed for her looks, her presence, her walk, her talk, the quickness and beauty of her mind. The next day, like some medieval knight at the court of love, he pledged his utter devotion to her. No request of hers would be denied. A week later, she is his "reference point, his direction . . . the northern point on his compass."[44] Hemingway was ever a fond and forceful lover on paper, having wooed Hadley and Pauline at a distance with almost daily protestations of his devotion; but his letters to Adriana were different, filled with love without becoming suicidal in his loneliness. With the object of his affection geographically and decorously out of reach, Hemingway had the perfect romance—his love would ever be unrequited and thus never disappointed, not to mention its lack of consequences.

Unfortunately for Mary, her husband's hopeless love for the Venetian teenager did nothing to enliven their own marital bed. In August, while Mary was away from the Finca arranging housing for her aging and infirm parents, "Louella Parsons, the Hollywood columnist, reported on the radio that the Hemingway marriage was breaking up over an Italian countess with whom Ernest had fallen madly in love and that they were presently living together at the Finca."[45] A phone call from Ernest reassured Mary that the malicious gossip was unfounded, later discovering that in Venice, Afdera Franchetti claimed to be the model for Renata. When Mary returned home, she found Ernest no better for all his apologies. The two of them began a one-cushion billiard version of their conflict, playing shots off Charles Scribner through letters which they did not share

with each other. On October 6, Scribner, disturbed by the correspondence, urged Ernest to be more understanding of Mary, who
probably had good cause for her behavior. He cautioned that "a girl
like A[driana] is really not for us."

The closer the Ivancichs were to arriving in Havana, the worse
Ernest's behavior became. On October 12, Mary wrote a plaintive
letter to Charles Scribner filled with disturbing details:

> *He has been truculent, brutal, abusive, and extremely childish.
> . . . Last night with six at table, I declined to bet with one of our
> guests on a pigeon shooting match. . . . So Ernest denounced me
> several times as "cobarde" (coward). . . . At table his favorite and fre-
> quent means of protesting any word, glance, gesture or food he doesn't
> like is to put his full, freshly served plate on the floor. The other day
> he dumped the entire plate of bread and crackers on top of my plate
> . . . he has called me, and repeated the names . . . whore, bitch, liar,
> moron. On several occasions I have called him a shit . . . it looks like
> the disintegration of a personality to me.*

She closed the letter asking if Charlie knew of any jobs for her in
New York, but cautioned him about answering her letter. Ernest
tended, she said, to open her mail before she saw it.[46]

She might have added that her husband's head was still on fire
from his latest concussion, that old shrapnel in his right leg was on
the move, pressing against a nerve, bloating his leg like a balloon,
that his blood pressure was once again out of control. She might
have said that the New York reviews had hurt him to the quick, and
that she knew how to hurt him more with the young and handsome
Gianfranco. Ernest, of course, knew how to make Mary squirm: at
table telling again and again about some nameless New York woman
holding his penis through lunch and a matinee. In her journal, Mary
continued to record his insults, embarrassments, and outrageous
behavior. He called her "camp follower" and "scavenger." When she
came home with a bruised arm where Gianfranco had gripped her
too hard, Ernest exploded. "Displaying your badge of shame," he said,

shooting out the lamp outside the front door, threatening to shoot off Gianfranco's arm.[47] At sunrise, the day before the Ivancichs arrived, Mary woke him with, "You defend your book publicly, but you don't defend your marriage. You don't write to Lolly Parsons or to anyone who will print it."[48] Ernest did not write the letter. Angry, hurt, and probably scared by her husband's increasingly irrational behavior, Mary did not give up. As complicated as foreign diplomacy, the unwritten rules for their game of love were always changing, never absolute, and difficult for an outsider to follow.

Chapter Twenty-Six

ROADSTEAD OF THE HEART

November 1950 to February 1952

A LL THAT FALL Ernest was despondent, listless, tired, and without joy. His Cuban friends, including his doctors, saw the external signs without understanding that one of the causes was Adriana. After all, how could a man approaching fifty, married to his fourth wife, be lovesick? José Luis Herrera was puzzled enough by his friend's errant behavior that he finally became angry with him. "I have nothing in my head," Ernest complained. "You drink too much," José Luis told him. "I'm fed up with living," Ernest replied. "I can't write. I love only Adriana. I am going to commit suicide." José Luis, who had heard this threat before, was not impressed. "Fine," he told Ernest. "Fine, shoot yourself. Where is the gun? Tell me. I will load it myself and watch you pull the trigger." The next morning José Luis wrote Ernest a letter telling him that "his sickness was intangible and therefore incurable." There was nothing that his friends or doctors could do. He must cure himself. Now he was living in an unreal world, a fantasy world such as a child might construct. José Luis did not doubt that his old friend was indeed in pain, but he was not using it as a resource. Only Ernest could cure Ernest, and the remedy was at hand. He need only begin again to write, pouring his pain into his work. Therein lay the cure. Suicide was selfish when he had so many depending upon him—Mary, his children, his friends in Cuba and elsewhere. When José Luis was certain that Ernest had received his letter, he began to phone the Finca, but René would tell him that Ernest did not wish to speak that day. On the third call, Ernest finally came to the phone, apologetic, saying, "Feo, I am a complete shit."[1] Then the crisis was over, and they did not speak of it again. José Luis then took all of Hemingway's guns from the Finca to his own house, telling Ernest that when he was drunk, he lost his human face. In August, José Luis said that Ernest tried to drown himself in the Gulf Stream "like Martin Eden," but after Adriana appeared at La Finca, Papa was a different man, changed and peaceful. He told José Luis that it was safe to return to him his weapons.

That fall when Adriana and her mother arrived, heads turned wherever the young girl passed, her white, white skin sending out electric signals that men old enough to be her father quite clearly appreciated. Juan Lopez, chauffeur at Finca Vigia, said that Ernest never went driving with the Italian beauty unless a third person were in the car, usually Roberto Herrera. Juan never forgot Adriana's long legs as he held the car door for her to climb in or out. At the Floridita Manuel Perez, the waiter, said that all of the staff were in wonder over this beauty that Papa brought with him like a prize for all to see. Roberto Herrera called her "majestic, elegant, gentle, and tender." Whenever the camera appeared to photograph Adriana and Papa, he always took off his glasses, for they made him look too old, he thought.

Late one night at the Finca, the Ivancichs gathered in the living room where Mary sang along with the music that she would always be true to Ernest, darling, in her fashion, urging him to dance a round with her, his face growing red with embarrassment, heavy as a bear, clumsy, finally throwing his glass of wine in her face. An ugly scene with Ernest's muse, Adriana the impossible, there watching, close enough to smell but never to touch. Shyly he gave her a copy of the book she inspired (albeit dedicated to Mary), eager for her response. "The girl is boring," Adriana told him. "How could your colonel love a girl who is so boring? A girl like that does not exist, if she is lovely and from a good family and goes to Mass every morning. Such a girl would not drink all day like a sponge and be in bed at the hotel." Hurt and saddened, he said he knew such a girl, more than one. Perhaps American girls were like that, she replied, but not a girl from Venice.[2]

For company Mary was polite and cheerful, ignoring Ernest's insults, turning them into jokes, keeping up appearances, ignoring whatever she could. While fishing on the *Pilar*, Adriana cut her finger on a dorsal fin. When Ernest began to suck the blood out of the young girl's wound, Mary turned her back on the spectacle. In private, René, the Finca's major domo, overheard her tell Adriana that she was not afraid of her. Adriana may have helped Ernest recover his ability to write, but nothing serious can happen between them. This little affair shall pass. Adriana and her mother lived in the guest cottage, leaving the Hemingways private time to keep the skirmish going off stage. By early December, Ernest was writing Hotchner that Mary was still giving him hell about visiting Jigee Viertel's hotel room in Paris a year earlier.[3] René remembered Mary telling Ernest that "when people mature they write better. On the other hand, you are writing worse." Ernest became furious, ripped a copy of *Across the River* into shreds, and threw it into the garden.[4]

Gradually, however, Hemingway's emotional life began to even out, following what was now a familiar cycle: a black-ass depression bottoming out in a wallow of irrational behavior that slowly ebbed as he moved back within the range of normal; his emotional temperature would continue to rise, reaching a manic peak, then gradually falling back into the normal range and from there deepen into black-ass behavior. Sometimes the cycle took several years to complete its course; at other times, it was compressed into months or days. At any point there could be a short cycle within a longer one. Frequently when the curve moved upward, he was writing well, followed by depression with a book's publication. Always when a book was completed he was faced with the immediately unanswerable question of what to write next. If the last book was as good as he could create, how then could he now create a better one? Each book used up experience he could not use again, making the answer more difficult to know and longer to find.

He had been cycling this way ever since 1919 when he returned from World War I: when euphoric, nothing could daunt him; when bottomed out, he was increasingly paranoid, moody, and implacable. All of his other wives had been through his entire range of responses, but this postwar trough that almost sucked Mary under was deeper than before and more vicious. He may have been reborn at Hürtgenwald, as he claimed, but it was a bloody rebirthing that embedded horrific images of burned bodies, severed limbs, and blood pumping from unstoppable wounds. That Mary weathered out his postwar depression was due only to her own mental toughness, her refusal to admit defeat, and her memory of their trysting in Paris. She did not yet understand the pattern of his behavior, but she realized that their life seemed to be evening out. Maybe after seeing his wife and Dora Ivancich behaving like chaperons to himself, older than both of them, he began to see how foolish he looked in love with Adriana. Whatever had happened, its effects were obvious: Ernest was writing again. When the *New York Herald Book Review* asked him which recently published books he would recommend to readers, he answered without malice that he enjoyed William Faulkner's *Collected Stories* and Irwin Shaw's *Mixed Company*.[5]

As soon as Adriana and her mother were in residence at the Finca, Ernest returned to what he called the "big book"—the sea, air, land book that was metamorphosing into something quite different than he first imagined. The novelist, Roger, disappeared after the Bimini section to reappear transformed in what would be *The Garden of Eden*.[6] In the sea story that remained, Hemingway took Thomas Hudson through a lonely and depressed period in Cuba while awaiting his next submarine patrol during World War II. His several former wives are all divorced from him or dead, his children killed in accidents, his painting suffering an hiatus. Back at sea, Hudson and his makeshift crew pursue escaping but

well-armed Germans who have abandoned their disabled submarine, killed the natives on a small key in the Old Bahama Channel
for their boats and food, and are fleeing through shallow passages
between small islands. By Christmas Eve, 1950, Hemingway completed the draft of Hudson's dark patrol, ending with the German
ambush that leaves the painter dying on the deck of his boat. The
story's working title—*The Island and the Stream*—would change
much later to *Islands in the Stream*. A week later he wrote Hotchner that Mary read the book in a one-night sitting, and was so
moved by it, her arms prickled with goosebumps, that she forgave
him all his sins. Adriana's response, he said, was the same, putting
him back in the good graces of both women and all was right with
the world.[7]

The period of grace was shortlived. Early in the new year, Dora
received a French newspaper with Adriana's picture captioned:
"Renata, Hemingway's new love." Mary said, "I told you so."
Gianfranco tried to smooth it over. But very quickly Dora moved herself and her daughter into a Havana hotel.[8] Simultaneously, Ernest
began writing what he thought to be the final section of the sea portion of the "big book"—the story of an old Cuban fisherman's losing
battle with a giant marlin. The story, which was meant to counterpoint Hudson's pursuit of the German submariners, was one he had
known since 1936 when he reported in *Esquire* about

> *an old man fishing alone in a skiff . . . hooked a great marlin that . . .
> pulled the skiff far out to sea. . . . The old man had stayed with him
> a day, a night, a day and another night while the fish . . . pulled the
> boat. When he had come up the old man . . . harpooned him. Lashed
> along side the sharks had hit him and the old man had fought them
> out alone in the Gulf Stream in a skiff, clubbing them, stabbing at
> them, lunging at them with an oar until he was exhausted and the
> sharks had eaten all that they could hold.*[9]

Like Hudson, the old fisherman was at the end of his career, fighting a losing battle against huge odds. Like *Across the River* and *For*

Whom the Bell Tolls, it was a three-day story of inevitable loss, a central theme of Hemingway's fiction from his Paris days forward.

The night before Adriana left Cuba, Ernest hosted a formal party in her honor at the Finca for two hundred invited guests. A bar and buffet was set up by the pool, another inside the house; a small orchestra played on the patio. The Finca staff were delighted to see Ernest looking so handsome in his tuxedo.[10] The next morning, February 7, Mary, Dora, and Adriana left by P&O ferry for Key West to pick up the waiting car and drive up the Florida coast to Jacksonville to catch the train to New York. On February 23, the Ivancichs, having been entertained in New York by Hotchner at Ernest's expense, boarded the *Liberté* to return to Italy. The one-sided passion of Ernest for Adriana was cooled by reality. They would remain friends; she would provide more illustrations for some of his work; and there would be continued correspondence; but his obsession was now a memory. Her presence in his life had inspired *Across the River* and inexplicably set him free to write about an old fisherman's epic conflict.

Begun in the new year, the first draft of the old man's battle with the marlin and the sharks was finished in six intense weeks.[11] In the evenings, Mary read each day's production, starting over from the beginning each time: "He was an old man who fished alone in a skiff in the Gulf Stream and he had gone eighty-four days now without taking a fish." Like Ernest, who had gone that many days and more without "taking" a submarine, a "tin fish," this old man's determination did not flag, nor did he ever lose faith in his ability to fish for the marlin. The old man was called Santiago—St. James—patron saint of Spain. By the time the story was finished, Mary told Ernest, "Lamb, I am prepared to pardon you for all the disagreeable things you have done to me."[12] When Hemingway finally put a title on the novella, it was on its surface as simple and direct as the text. He called it *The Old Man and the Sea*.

While Santiago was driving his harpoon into the marlin, whom he loved as his brother, other hunters were following the spore of Ernest Hemingway. For the next ten years, Hemingway would be fighting a rearguard action with biographers, trying to protect his flanks, keep his private life private, and at the same time control his life story to which there were already so many variants. Encouraged by the Cowley essay in *Life*, the Ross portrait in *The New Yorker*, and Sam Boal's two-part take on "Hemingway the man," in *Park East*,[13] academic scholars were beginning their determined pursuit of the writer. Charles Fenton at Yale, Philip Young at Penn State, and Carlos Baker at Princeton, each looking through different-colored glasses, were digging into Hemingway's past. After beginning his research with letters to Hemingway acquaintances, Carlos Baker tried to explain his motives to Hemingway:

> *I would like to destroy the legend, puncture the windbags, clear the air a little, and show your achievement in something like its true dimensions. There has been enough malice and lying and misunderstanding . . . you can trust me. I don't want to invade what is private but only what the public have a right—and indeed a sort of obligation—to know.*[14]

At the same time, Hemingway was writing Baker, objecting vehemently to any invasion of his life, public or otherwise, for it would destroy part of his stockpile of stories to write. If Baker had accepted a publisher's advance to write the book, Hemingway offered to pay the publisher to stop the project. He did not want to read in a stranger's book about his father's suicide, or about his affair with Pauline, or how coitus interruptus ruined his second marriage.[15] It was a strange letter, not unlike the ones he had written Cowley earlier. While seeming to say that there would be no biography, he was simultaneously revealing some of his life's most private parts.

In a long reply, Baker explained his research and his sources, protesting that Hemingway had misread his focus, which was primarily literary, and his motives, which were "entirely honorable."[16] Baker's letter crossed in the mails with Hemingway's reply to his previous letter. From his sickbed, recovering from bronchitis, Hemingway argued that his early life, his journalism, and, in fact, his act of writing were not open to the public. Having already laid down thirty years of inflations, contradictions, and inventions, he now vowed never to tell another person anything about his life, which was to him about as pleasant a subject as a fingertip torn to the quick when its nail was ripped off. A few days later, Ernest told Mary's Time/Life friend, Sam Boal, the same thing: no biography.[17] Yet in his third letter to Baker, Hemingway began feeding the professor harmless and sometimes false information about *Across the River* which Baker should know but could not quote. Thomas Mann's *Death in Venice*, Hemingway said, had little or nothing to do with his novel. Renata's name came from a girl he was once in love with, but the girl in his novel was invented. The Colonel was also invented, using places and situations Ernest knew about.[18]

After that, the gate was open. By April 1, Hemingway was giving Baker fairly detailed information about his early days in Paris, the lost manuscripts, the structure of *For Whom the Bell Tolls*, the writers from whom he learned (Twain, Conrad, Stephen Crane). Henry James and Herman Melville were useful when they were good, but they wrapped everything in miles of rhetoric. Ezra Pound was helpful about half the time. Gertrude Stein told him intelligent things, he said without elaborating. By the end of April, Hemingway was giving Baker details of his writing regime, memories of early days in Oak Park, how he taught himself French in Paris. This epistolary relationship ripened to the point that Hemingway trusted Baker with a typed draft of *The Old Man and the Sea* to read and return.

Viewed from a distance, the Hemingway-Baker correspondence can be read as Ernest's astute cultivation of an admiring college professor who once wrote Hemingway imitations as an undergraduate. That interpretation makes sense retrospectively knowing that Baker became Hemingway's official biographer. But if one reads the letters from the viewpoint of 1951, the story changes. Having lived so long in Cuba cut off from literary friends and with Mary never a particularly astute reader, Hemingway cultivated Baker from the same need that triggered similar letters to Malcolm Cowley and to Arthur Mizener when he was writing his book on Scott Fitzgerald. Baker admired Hemingway's work and told him so in literate analysis, much of which Hemingway confirmed. Having so far been denied the Pulitzer Prize and ignored for the Nobel, having had his last novel sorely misread by the critics, Hemingway, like many writers, needed positive reinforcement from respected sources. As he explained to Baker, he needed intelligent response but was always embarrassed by it, which made him seem surly. He assured Carlos that he did not want to influence the academic book by correcting it in draft. Trust was a self-fulfilling act: Carlos would be trustworthy because Ernest trusted him. Mostly by letter, Baker and others like him would provide the intellectual conversation that Hemingway so badly needed.[19]

At the same time he was encouraging Carlos Baker at Princeton, Ernest was also aiding and abetting Charles Fenton at Yale, who was working furiously on Hemingway's early years when he learned to write, first growing up in Oak Park, then on the *Kansas City Star* before the war, and after the war on the *Toronto Star*. Although Ernest insisted that it did a writer no good to have either his juvenilia or his early journalism reprinted, he was quite cooperative with Fenton, answering questions and directing him to useful sources. As for his later journalism in the 1930s, Ernest said he intended someday to collect and publish it himself.[20] Later that fall, when John Atkins, a British journalist, contacted him from London, Ernest reiterated that there would be no biography of him: too many people would be hurt by it; and he was sick of hearing about it. He would cooperate, however, if Atkins confined himself to Hemingway's published work. In a long, almost effusive letter, Ernest led Atkins through his novels and stories, how and when he wrote them, what he was trying to do in them, all the while getting in some body shots against those critics who refused to judge his work on its own merits.[21]

All that spring and summer, answering few letters and doing little fishing, Hemingway wrote feverishly on the sea book that started in 1936 Bimini and that now included a fourth section—Santiago's battle with the marlin and the sharks. Revising, eliminating, transposing, he worked steadily, trying to ignore letters of inquiry about his life. From Malcolm Cowley, Ernest learned that Philip Young, a professor seeking tenure at New York University, was digging into his past. Hemingway vowed to prevent Young or anyone else from writing about his life while he was still alive.[22] But no matter what threats he put on paper, his life intruded through the weak spots in his defense. From Memphis, Tennessee, his sister Madelaine kept him apprised of his mother's failing health. Having literally forced Grace Hemingway to come to Memphis, Madelaine soon put her into a nursing home, where her condition grew worse. Madelaine, affectionately known as "Sunny," held even less affection for her mother than did her older brother, Ernest. Grace Hall Hemingway was always a difficult woman to love and impossible to command. Approaching her seventy-ninth birthday, she was slipping into a state of hallucinations, no longer able to recognize her family. When the nursing home could no longer deal with her, Grace ended up in a Memphis county hospital mental ward for two weeks, unsure of her own identity. Madelaine wrote Ernest that their mother was "a pitiful old lady, lost, frightened, and at times frantic." It would be a blessing, the doctors assured her, if Grace could die. "They hold no hope for her improvement. This will be her last stop."[23] Eleven days after Sunny wrote that letter, their mother was dead.

Ernest remained at the Finca, but paid the burial expenses; his older sister Marcelline orchestrated the funeral; and Ursula, his younger sister, flew from Hawaii to Oak Park to bury the dominant mother from whom she and Ernest had escaped, both at an early age. Having spent most of his adult life blaming his mother for destroying their Oak Park home life, Ernest was not heartbroken by her death, but the loss reopened old wounds and repressed memories. When Pauline read of Grace's death in the newspaper, she wrote to Ernest, quoting the line from Swinburne: "Life is not sweet in the end." Knowing of Ernest's professed hate for the mother he once called "an all-American bitch," Pauline also understood that the death of a mother is always painful, calling up memories of childhood when she was his love, and he her darling.[24] Pauline's letter arrived on June 30, the day of Grace's burial. Later that day, writing to Carlos

Baker, Ernest said that her death reminded him of how happy their Oak Park home was when he was a child, "before everything went to hell." She did not, he thought, have a happy death.[25]

Three months later, at four in the morning, Pauline lay dying on the emergency operating table of Los Angeles' St. Vincent Hospital. The previous evening, speaking by phone with Ernest about the difficulties of their newly married younger son, Gregory, the two parents and onetime lovers' conversation degenerated into accusations, blame-laying, vituperation, and general misunderstanding. For whatever Gregory had done, including his marriage, Ernest was quick to blame Pauline. She hung up in tears, angry and hurt. During the night she woke with stomach pains; within hours she was dead. The autopsy revealed blocked arteries and hypertension, but the cause of death was

> a rare and unusual tumor of the adrenal medulla, which intermittently secretes abnormal amounts of adrenaline causing extremely high blood pressure. A variety of stimuli could cause the tumor to put out the adrenaline—a sudden stressful incident is often cited . . . her blood pressure skyrocketed . . . [and then] dropped. . . . She died of shock on the operating table.[26]

At the Finca, the October 2 phone call from Pauline's sister, Virginia, devastated Mary, who was quite close with Pauline following Patrick's illness. Ernest tried to cover his loss with an exterior hardness that infuriated Mary, who, stomping out of the living room, said he behaved like a vulture. How could Mary know about the Paris nights and Provence days, mountain flowers in the Wyoming high country, the beach at Hendaye, the hospital room in Billings, or any of the memories that flooded back into his head? Angry, he followed her into the bathroom and, unable to say it all, he spit into her face. "Next day," Mary noted in her journal, "[he] gave me $200 which I gravely accepted."[27] She did not read his letter to Charles Scribner, which said: "The wave of remembering has finally risen so that it has broken over the jetty that I built to protect the open roadstead of my heart and I have the full sorrow of Pauline's death with all the harbor scum of what caused it."[28] More than once that year, Ernest would mutter that people were dying who had never died before.

March through October, despite distractions and deaths, Ernest worked steadily, five days a week, on the "sea book," whose original plan was changing as he progressed on it. His one consistent correspondent on its progress was Charles Scribner, whom Ernest managed to confuse about exactly what it was he was writing. Ernest explained it to him at several points, each consistent if one knew the manuscript well. In March, Hemingway suggested that it could be published in the fall of 1952; meanwhile, he could live on the income produced by a television deal that Hotchner was creating for his short stories. By July, Scribner was worried that Hemingway had three novellas to sell to the magazines, stories which he would then hook together as a novel. On July 20, Ernest tried to explain that he had one very long book (2,000 pages of manuscript), which was broken down into four related sections—each of them a book that could be published separately. The first section (Bimini) he was cutting and revising in a major way; the last two sections (the sea chase and Santiago's marlin) needed nothing else done to them. By October 5, Hemingway was able to report to Scribner that the four subsections were essentially finished, totaling 182,231 words. Parts one and two—Bimini and Cuba—he would further revise after he had some distance from the manuscript. Parts three and four were ready to publish.[29]

Throughout his eight-month correspondence with Scribner, Hemingway belittled and railed against Scribner's newest best-selling author James Jones, whose media image and novel, *From Here to Eternity*, sent Hemingway into paroxysms of anger. Somehow forgetting that his own novel of World War I—*A Farewell to Arms*—was about a soldier who deserted from the Italian Army, Hemingway was furious that a novel about a deserter written by a self-proclaimed deserter overshadowed *Across the River*. Jones, he repeated several times, would eventually kill himself. It was not easy to admit that Mailer, Shaw, and Jones—young writers who grew up reading Hemingway—were passing him by. Nor was it pleasant to know that his early supporters and his own generation were passing from the surface of the earth: Max Perkins, Scott Fitzgerald, Hart Crane, Katy Dos Passos, Robert Benchley, Gertrude Stein, James Joyce, Sherwood Anderson, Josie Russell, Pauline, and his mother were all dead. Evan Shipman who once taught Ernest about the Paris race track was dying from cancer; and with a heart about to fail Charlie Scribner's health was marginal. Archie MacLeish and John Dos Passos, once Ernest's boon companions, he now never saw or heard from. Ezra Pound was in the insane asylum. In October, Hemingway wrote Dorothy Pound, asking questions about Ezra's incarceration.[30] Ernest could not raise the dead, but he might be able to help the old poet who was his literary father in those long-ago Paris years.

As the Cuban season moved through the early fall hurricane months, Hemingway put away the all but finished "sea book" to answer pressing letters. The *New York Herald Book Review* wanted to know the three books that Hemingway recommended from the year's crop. He gave them three fairly obscure choices, adding as a joke that there were several other books he would like to have read if only they were available:

Longevity Pays: The Life of Arthur Mizener, *by F. Scott Fitzgerald*
The Critics: An Harpooner's Story, *by Herman Melville*
He and Lillian: The Story of a Profile, *by Mary Hemingway*
It Went Thataway: The Story of Existentialism, *by Jean-Paul Sartre*[31]

Having gotten wind of another academic critic on his trail, Ernest told his publisher to refuse Philip Young permission to quote from any of his work, for Ernest heard that the work was psychoanalytical. He wanted no one dissecting his psyche in public or anywhere else for that matter. At the same time he gave permission for Carlos Baker, whom he trusted, to quote as necessary. Better for Baker to quote whole passages, he told Charles Scribner, than to mutilate Hemingway's prose with ellipses.[32] He also suggested corrections to Baker's typescript for *Hemingway: The Writer as Artist*. About his participation in World War I, Ernest asked Baker to remove all references to his having been a soldier with the Italian Arditi (which happened only in his imagination), and suggested that instead of using the word "fought," Baker should say that Ernest "served" in that war.[33] For the first time, Hemingway's own fabrications were coming back to haunt him. A good after-dinner story made more interesting with invented details was one thing, but to have it made flesh in a scholarly book was quite another.

The new year began in the same key as the year gone by. In January 1952, Mary's maid, Clara, recently given three months wages and fired by Ernest, was found outside the Finca grounds, comatose, clutching an empty bottle of Seconal tablets. Apparently using Ernest's prescription at a local pharmacy, she purchased two bottles of the barbiturate. Lingering for three days in the hospital, she never recovered consciousness before dying. Ernest, having made several promises to do the same, wrote Charles Scribner that the threat of suicide had been Clara's defense against the world.[34] Charlie probably never got to read Ernest's long letter. In the early afternoon of February 11, Hemingway's publisher, banker, confidant, and friend died suddenly from a heart attack. Now there was no one left, Ernest said, with whom to share a rough joke.[35]

PART THREE

END GAME

1952 TO 1961

Chapter Twenty-Seven

THE ARTIST'S REWARDS

March 1952 to June 1953

A LL THE SIGNS were positive; all the readers agreed. *The Old Man and the Sea* was a stunning book, a story told as simply as a fable, and as tenderly as a love letter. When Broadway and Hollywood producer Leland Hayward read the typescript at the Finca, he insisted that it should be published as soon as possible in a national magazine, *Life* or *Look*. Ernest, chagrined as always with effusive praise, thought Scribner's might not like the idea. Hayward said he would take care of it, taking the typescript with him to New York. For the first time in many years, Ernest was allowing someone else to act as his agent. Simultaneously, he sent a typescript to Wallace Meyer at Scribner's, explaining at some length why what seemed a novella was actually a book that would stand by itself, a book probably better than anything else he had written.[1]

No sooner had Hayward and his attractive wife, Slim, left Havana than the elected government of Carlos Prio was overthrown in an almost bloodless coup led by the kingmaker, General Fulgencio Batista, who quickly resumed business as usual in Havana. "The only blood that will be spilled," he promised, "will be that of those who oppose us." One dictator replaced another, which surprised no one.

From exile, Prio predicted that "the Cuban people will throw Bastista out sooner or later." When accused of having amassed a fortune from his office, Prio said simply, "I think being poor is a sin."[2] On March 11, Ernest and Mary took the *Pilar* out to sea for a fishing vacation while the political dust settled in the capital. Ninety miles down the coast, from the isolated lee side of Paraíso Island, they fished and sunned, ate and slept, counted stars and watched a new moon rising. Safe inside the low island's coral reef, the *Pilar* was home, but the island, with its six palm trees and six pines, was their Eden.

On March 23, a storm rose up, holding them at the island until March 29, when they returned to the Finca to find that another of Ernest's old friends, Dick Cooper, was dead in Africa, Cooper who fished with Ernest in Bimini and fêted him during his 1933–34 safari.[3] There were also excited responses from Scribner's about the book, which they would publish in September and were submitting to the Book-of-the-Month Club. On May 19, the memorandum of agreement between Ernest and his publisher was signed for *The Old Man and the Sea*, with royalties jumping to an unusual 20 percent after the sale of the first 25,000 copies. At the same time *Life*, with Scribner's blessing, agreed to publish the novel in a single issue of the magazine with Ernest on the cover. By the end of May, Adriana Ivancich's dust jacket design, to Ernest's delight, was accepted by Scribner's in lieu of the three covers he rejected.[4] Once to be Mary's book, the dedication was changed, with Mary's approval, to Charles Scribner and Max Perkins—the two men who never lost faith in Ernest and never refused him a loan when he asked.

In all of his correspondence with his publisher, friends, columnists, and critics, Hemingway insisted he had no intention of commenting on the novel, nor would he come to New York for the novel's release. When the *New York Times* and the *Saturday Review of Literature* asked him for written comments to run in their book section, he was so noncommittal in his responses that they were hardly worth printing. Asked if he wished to talk about his writing process, he said: "If I have to talk about a book that I have written, it destroys the pleasure I have from writing it. If the writing is any good everything there is to say has been conveyed to the reader." How long is the big book? they wanted to know. "Very long," he replied. And when would they see it? "As and when it seems best to publish it." After the surfeit of Hemingway interviews and commentaries—Cowley, Ross, Boal—too much had been said about his private life. As he told Charles Scribner, Jr., who had taken over the firm from his late father, Ernest wanted to run only as a writer, not as a controversial public figure. This time out, critics and reviewers would have to deal with his text, for he was giving them no posturing for a target.[5] In *Green Hills of Africa* (1935) he had baited them without mercy—angleworms in a bottle, he called them. If they wanted to read *The Old Man* as allegory or myth, then they could make what they wanted of it. It would be the reviewers who found a resemblance between the shark attack on Santiago's marlin and the critics' attack on Ernest Hemingway.

If he went to New York, some son of a bitch would pick a fight which the columnists would lap up, encouraging everyone to think that Ernest was a bar-room brawler. Which is exactly what happened one Havana night in the Floridita bar. Ernest and Mary were drinking in his favored corner when a woman never seen before begins to tell him what a good time they both had in her bed back in 1944. Getting rid of her, he turns to find a huge man whispering in his ear, singing a dirty song that he has made up about Ernest, who hates to be touched and cannot abide dirty songs. Two left hooks and a right-hand chop as the man goes down ends the session. Fortunately, it happened in Cuba and not in the States, where such a story would confirm what a violent character he was. No one gave literary prizes to a bar fighter. Yet he told the story to Harvey Breit at the *New York Times*, saying it was an example of the person he no longer wanted to be. The new Hemingway would be "a good boy."[6]

Among the several guests in and out of the Finca that May were old friends from Ketchum: Taylor "Beartracks" Williams, Don Anderson, Elaine Perry, and newcomer Forrest "Duke" MacMullen. They put up at the Ambos Mundos, spending their days either at the Finca or out on the *Pilar* fishing. Throughout their visit

Hemingway was his Ketchum self, but kept his mornings free to write. In the evening, Mary would meet their guests for daiquiris and cold stone crab at the Floridita, then take them to the jai alai matches or to a nightclub. One night it was the San Souci; another, the Tropicana. Juan, the Hemingway chauffeur, provided transportation, taking Mary back to the Finca when the evening was over.[7]

Increasingly disengaged from the mainland news—the Korean War, the fall elections—Hemingway, as he turned fifty-three, was intensely aware that he was approaching the end of his writing career. He had plenty of stories left in his head, but he knew the chances of pulling out another one as right as *The Old Man and the Sea* were slim. Ever since William Faulkner received the Nobel Prize for literature in 1949, Hemingway, for whom writing was a competitive sport, wanted the same recognition. In 1947, the prize went to André Gide for his "fearless love of truth and keen psychological insight," wording guaranteed to irritate Hemingway. The next year, T. S. Eliot was the Nobel laureate while Ezra Pound collected dust in the confines of St. Elizabeth's. But Faulkner's award was the one that goaded Ernest the hardest. It may have been only coincidence, but he started to write *The Old Man and the Sea* hard on the heels of Faulkner's much publicized Nobel Prize acceptance speech.[8]

Thus, when Harvey Breit approached Faulkner to review Hemingway's new book, Ernest was fully prepared to misread anything the man from Mississippi had to say. Breit, not understanding the situation, enthusiastically sent Hemingway the statement Faulkner made before he had even read the book:

> . . . *A few years ago . . . Hemingway said that writers should stick together just as doctors and lawyers and wolves do. I think there is more wit in that than truth or necessity either, at least in Hemingway's case, since the sort of writers who need to band together willy nilly, or perish, resemble the wolves who are wolves only in pack, and, singly, are just another dog.*
>
> *Because the man who wrote the* Men Without Women *pieces and* The Sun Also Rises *and* A Farewell to Arms *and* For Whom

the Bell Tolls *and most of the African stuff and most of all the rest of it, is not one of these, and needs no protection.*

So he does not need even this from another writer. Maybe he doesn't even want it. So he gets this for free from one who, regardless of how he rated what remained, has never doubted the integrity of it, and who has always affirmed that no man will be quicker and harsher to judge what remained than [Hemingway] . . . and that if even what remained had not been as honest and true as he could make it, then he himself would have burned the manuscript before the publisher ever saw it.[9]

Hemingway's response to Breit bristled with resentment:

So he writes to you as though I was asking him a favor to protect me. Me, the dog. I'll be a sad son of a bitch. He made a speech, very good. I knew he could never, now, or ever again write up to his speech. I also knew I could write a book better and straighter than his speech and without tricks or rhetoric . . . as long as I am alive he has to drink to feel good about having the Nobel prize. He does not realize that I have no respect for that institution . . . I wish him luck and he needs it because . . . you can't re-read him.[10]

There the story ended. Breit buried Faulkner's statement, and apologized to Ernest for the contretemps.

The closer the publication date for *The Old Man* came, the more anxious Hemingway became. When not writing or fishing, he continued to argue with scholars hot on his trail. Every time Charles Fenton sent him a piece of his doctoral dissertation in progress, Hemingway pointed out mistakes and misunderstandings, complaining that Fenton talked to the wrong people. Survivors never remember right. Each of Hemingway's responses confused Fenton, revealing some new story that usually had little or nothing to do with Ernest's writing apprenticeship and was certainly not printable in the book. Going back, Hemingway insisted (having learned it for himself), was doomed. Everything was changed—the land, the people, the places. Fenton's every reply assured Ernest that his book was not a biography, that Ernest's private life would remain private, and, by the way, here are a few more questions, which Hemingway then would try to answer. Railing against the detective school of literary criticism and laundry-list biographers, Hemingway would, in every other letter, tell Fenton to give up the book. Biographers were the scavengers of literature, the eaters of carrion. He, by God, was going to plant enough booby traps on his corpse to fix them all. Fenton came right back, confident and cocky: this book was going to be written whether Ernest helped or not, and Ernest continued to help, coolly retreating while setting up roadblocks and small ambushes.[11]

However, nothing Phil Young or his publisher Thomas Bledsoe at Rinehart said made Hemingway feel any better about the book that Young was writing. When Ernest received a copy of Young's paper presented at a professional meeting, it confirmed his worst fears. Young and others were practicing psychoanalysis without a license. As Ernest read Young's work, he had suffered a traumatic neurosis in 1918 from being wounded in Italy out of which came all of his writing. To say such a thing was, Ernest felt, as damaging as saying that he suffered from terminal syphilis. Despite his serious misgivings, six pages of them, Hemingway eventually gave in to Young's plea that his tenure and his family's well-being depended on the book. When Ernest learned that Young was a wounded veteran from World War II, he reluctantly told Charles Scribner, Jr., to give him permission to quote. Whatever Bledsoe had to pay Scribner's for the permissions, Ernest instructed his publisher to give his half back to Young.[12]

The three scholars—Baker, Fenton, and Young—were laying down for the postwar generation what would become the academic gospel on Ernest's fiction. Baker's book, *Hemingway: The Writer as Artist*, gave sympathetic, analytic readings of Hemingway's work up to *The Old Man and the Sea*, delineating themes, motifs, and symbolic effects that were frequently just below the surface of the fiction. Fenton's book, *The Apprenticeship of Ernest Hemingway*, gave readers the formative literary experience that Hemingway took to Paris with him in 1921—Oak Park roots, *Kansas City Star* cub reporter before the war, and *Toronto Daily Star* feature writer after the war. Phil Young's book, called simply *Ernest Hemingway*, linked Hemingway to the Twain tradition established with Huck Finn and argued that the wounded man appearing in various guises throughout the fiction was a result of Hemingway's own wounding in World War I. Just as Hemingway's most popular book since *For Whom the Bell Tolls* (1940) was set to sweep the nation, a new generation of academic scholars was about to discover there was more to his fiction than previously imagined. These scholars would teach their findings to college students, many of whom became the high school teachers of the next generation of Hemingway's readers.

While this was happening, Ernest began to write a fiction which fit no one's theory. Had any of the new scholars read the new story about Nick Adams's escape into the Michigan woods pursued by game wardens, they would have been puzzled. Had they seen the beginnings of what would later be called *The Garden of Eden*, they would have torn up their manuscripts and begun again. On May 4, he told Malcolm Cowley that he was beginning a story placed up in Michigan, a story he had put off writing for a long time.[13] Set free by his mother's death, Hemingway was able for the first time since his early Paris fiction to return to the experiences of his youth. The summer of 1915, while transporting two tourists up Walloon Lake in the family motorboat, Ernest impulsively shot and killed a blue heron. When the game warden's son reported Ernest to his father, the warden went to the Hemingway cottage to arrest Ernest. Grace Hemingway faced him down, and later sent Ernest running cross-country to his uncle George's summer place at Ironton. After a few days, Ernest followed the advice of his father, went before the local judge, and paid his fine. The experience—a fugitive on the run from the law—loomed large for a boy barely turned sixteen, and it continued to haunt Hemingway, becoming in his imagination more serious than it was, more threatening. This incident became the first of several encounters with law enforcement that always produced in Hemingway a visceral response more intense than the event might warrant.

As Mary noted in her journal almost four years earlier, the heron story was ready-made for fiction. When Hemingway retrieved the incident, he changed the heron to an out-of-season deer and gave the adventure to his dark double, Nick Adams, about whom he had not written in many years. He found the lake, the woods, and the trout exactly as he had left them, directions still running true. It was like being there once more, only better, because he got to be Nick as a youth, not himself in his fifties. With the help of his younger sister, Littless, Nick escapes into the deep woods to his secret place, another Eden. There he provides fresh trout for supper, and Littless cuts her hair short as a boy's, determined to stay with her brother. Their relationship, bordering on incest, is a different kind of couple in the garden. Littless already has lost her innocence, knowing of good and evil; Nick has already sinned against the local laws. The owner of the lakeside store, Mr. John, likes Nick because "he had original sin."

> *"You're going to have things to repent, boy," Mr. John had told Nick. "That's one of the best things there is. You can always decide whether to repent them or not. But the thing is to have them."*[14]

Surely Hemingway was poaching a bit on Mr. Faulkner's territory, but Ernest didn't see any No Trespassing signs. And the brother-sister relationship also owed something to J. D. Salinger's equally precocious siblings in *The Catcher in the Rye*, a book Ernest read when it came out in 1951.[15] Begun as a short story, "The Last Good Country" began to swell, as had several earlier stories, into what might become a novel, but, like his "Jimmy Breen" story in 1928, Nick and Littless were left in the woods, and their story unfinished. Perhaps Hemingway saw that it was moving from a relatively innocent incident into a tale of murder; perhaps he backed off from the potentially incestuous relationship as being a taboo which no publisher would break. Or it may have been that the story's direction reminded him of a more adult version of a lost Eden that had been on his mind since his 1948 drive through Provence. There on the coast at Grau du Roi where the fishing boat channel came right through the middle of town, he and Pauline once honeymooned while the Gypsy pilgrimage gathered at nearby Les Saintes Maries. Those days too were a bit of Eden remembered. Not that either of them was innocent of either knowledge or deed, but Grau du Roi was their idyllic escape from the small gossips of Paris. It was the new life.

Drawing on several marriages, his own and others, inventing freely out of desire and experience, he began a story that completely changed whatever residual plans he might have had for the "big book" about the sea, air, and land war.[16] The first volume of that vaguely planned trilogy was now a four-part study of the sea before, during, and after the war: the first part told of Thomas Hudson's idyllic life on Bimini and its loss; the second section showed Hudson outcast from Eden, lonely ashore in Cuba between submarine patrols; section three was the sea chase, Hudson's crew pursuing Germans, ending with Hudson bleeding to death on the boat's deck; the fourth section was Santiago's epic conflict with the marlin and the sharks, a different tale of duty, honor, and loss meant to counterpoint Hudson's experience. The air war was long ago abandoned, leaving only a handful of fragments. The ground war in France was related obliquely in *Across the River* as explanation for Cantwell's postwar bitterness. There remained stories to write about the war, but there would be no novel. The sea-air-land trilogy had fallen apart, largely due to the combined effect of Hudson's reminiscences on early life in Paris, the Mizener biography of Scott Fitzgerald, and Hemingway's own memories recharged by the nagging investigations by scholars.

What was developing, without a master plan, was a different sort of trilogy, whose cohesion was not dependent on recurring characters or a coherent chronology. Three separate stories were taking vague form, guided, if guided at all, by Marcel Proust's *Remembrance of Things Past*, a work to which Ernest referred repeatedly in the postwar period. The first story of Hemingway's sequence was completed: Thomas Hudson's painterly life, his fall from grace, and his redemption by duty performed, which Hemingway called *The Island*

and the Stream. The second would become *The Garden of Eden,* the story of young artists whose art and life are compromised by destructive relationships. The third volume would become the partially fictive memoir of Ernest's own early days in Paris, *A Moveable Feast.* Paris in the Twenties was the lynchpin upon which all three stories in some way revolved. Having seen it all, having watched destructive forces interfere with the talents of artists, himself included, Hemingway was writing a complex, multilayered portrait of the artist in the twentieth century. His protagonists—painters and writers—begin their careers in Paris; all find momentary Edens; all, in various ways, largely due to the women in their lives, fall from grace into exile, either dead or dumbfounded.[17] The last voice Thomas Hudson hears tells him, "You never understand anyone who loves you," words that might serve as an epigraph for all three books.

On Labor Day, more than five million copies of *Life* magazine went on sale all across America. From the cover a black and white visage of jowly, mustached Hemingway looked one dead in the eye. His hair thinned and graying, scars visible, mouth set, neither a smile nor a scowl, it was a face familiar if older, staring at the reader not exactly belligerently, but neither was it friendly. Slashed across the upper right-hand corner of the cover against a burnt orange background, it said:

> *AN EXTRA DIVIDEND IN THIS ISSUE*
> ## 'THE OLD MAN
> ### AND THE SEA'
> #### BY *HEMINGWAY*
> *A COMPLETE NEW BOOK*
> *FIRST PUBLICATION*

Inside, beginning on page 35, the novella opened with Santiago preparing for his eighty-fifth day in search of marlin. Twenty pages later, it ended with the old man returned to his shack, sleeping, "dreaming about the lions." It was a precedent for *Life,* publishing a major writer's entire book without interruptive advertisements. It was also the largest run in the magazine's history, a run that quickly sold out. Never before had any author instantaneously reached so large an audience. Six days later, Scribner's published a first edition of 50,000 copies which sold out in ten days; simultaneously, the Book-of-the-Month Club published 153,000 copies, and Jonathan Cape brought out the British edition. Despite the serial and book club versions, for twenty-six weeks *The Old Man* listed on the *New York Times* best-seller list. Before the year was out, translations appeared in nine European languages. Within five years, readers in twenty-six languages as dissimilar as Persian and Latvian had access to translations.[18]

Reviewers' responses to the novella varied in direct proportion to the time lapse between the publication and their review. The first-week reviews were largely positive bordering on adulation. Hemingway was back, had found himself, had recovered his talent. Conrad's and Melville's names were frequently used for comparative purposes. Carlos Baker called Hemingway "one of the few genuine tragic writers of modern times," curiously linking Santiago's struggle with that of King Lear. Harvey Breit gushed over the style, the power, and the beauty of the story. In Nashville, it was called "the old undiluted Hemingway magic." In Chicago, it was billed as "Hemingway at his incomparable best." *Time* magazine thought *The Old Man and the Sea* might be a masterpiece. After the first wave of such statements in prominent places, the New York intellectuals stepped in with counterattacks in all the usual places—*Commonweal*, *Commentary*, the *Partisan Review*. They had to remind their readers how awful *Across the River* was, and how vulgar Hemingway was in his public life: "As a man he has often made an embarrassing spectacle of himself with his posturings, his mooning over adolescent things . . . his antics at the Stork Club." Thus Seymour Krim was able to conclude that this novella was "only more of the same." John Aldridge, the following spring, was "unable to share in the prevailing wild enthusiasm" for *The Old Man and the Sea*, even though it was "a remarkable advance over his last novel."[19]

Hemingway read all the reviews his clipping service sent him, commented to friends on some of them, but generally remained aloof, determined to let the book rise or fall on its own. No whining or complaining. He turned down opportunities to appear on national television, still in its awkward infancy; declined a prestigious speaking opportunity at Princeton; and ignored letters to the editor at *Life*. The only response that apparently thrilled him was a private letter from the art historian Bernard Berenson, who preferred Hemingway's style to Melville's "inflationary magniloquence," and liked his old fisherman "far better than Ahab."[20] As important as the book's reception was the wonderful run of marlin in the Gulf Stream. Not only had Ernest caught his best-selling book, but he had also by September 13 pulled twenty-nine marlin, large and small, across the *Pilar*'s transom.[21] On September 23, Mary flew to New York for a recreational visit, shopping, and a little basking in the afterglow of Ernest's triumph. He preferred to remain close to the Gulf Stream, saying he would only get into trouble in New York. There was also the problem of leaving the Finca when local burglars were raiding it and other homes in the area. Before Mary left, two men broke into the Finca, rifling cabinets and stealing whatever looked valuable while Ernest and Mary slept. Thereafter Ernest began setting perimeter defenses and traps inside the house. Ernest called the intruders the local mau-maus—referring to the quasi-guerrilla war being waged by the East African Mau Mau movement. By October, the Finca was twice robbed without alerting Ernest's "hopeless" night watchman, and Hemingway, with a loaded shotgun beside his bed, slept lightly, waking at the least sound to patrol the house.[22]

Back at Scribner's, Wallace Meyer was planning a *Hemingway Reader* to catch the wave of heightened interest in Ernest's work. In a letter to Charles Poore, editor of the collection, Ernest cautioned that his Italian war experience was largely devoted to convalescing and listening to the talk of those who actually fought in the war. From that secondhand knowledge and what he had acquired on his own, he was able with the help of large-scale maps to invent battles that he had never witnessed. "Then some son of a bitch will come along and prove you were not at that particular fight."[23] Meanwhile, Ernest's own interests were returning to East Africa where his son

Patrick, using part of his inheritance from his mother to buy a farm, was urging his father to visit. Darryl Zanuck's film version of "The Snows of Kilimanjaro" may have added to Ernest's desire to see the Serengeti again, although he noted sardonically the "minor change" Zanuck made by allowing Harry, the gangrenous writer, to live at the end instead of dying.[24] Ernest called it "The Snows of Zanuck." Stung time and again by Hollywood's treatment of his works, Hemingway continued to sell them for the best price he could get. Usually, he avoided the resultant movie. But when Leland Hayward took an option on the film rights to *The Old Man and the Sea*, Ernest, for the first and only time in his career, wanted to be involved in the filming, insisting that the marlin and the sharks be authentic, not backlot Hollywood rubber fish.

At the same time, he and Mary were doing background reading on Africa, planning to spend the summer in Spain, the fall and winter on safari with Patrick. Hemingway was looking forward to an elephant photo hunt, the only large animal he had not seen on his first safari in 1933–34. He had no intention of shooting an elephant, having gotten his fill of killing during the war. Through his reading, moreover, he was already identifying with the elephant. When thanking John Atkins for his straightforward book on Ernest's fiction, he said he would have been more cooperative had not other scholars been hunting him so hard. He felt as "spooked" as any fifty-three-year-old elephant carrying 100 pounds of ivory would feel.[25]

Life at the Finca was quickly becoming a three-ring circus, overrun with visitors, deluged with mail from strangers excited about *The Old Man and the Sea*, and attacked by night prowlers. How the thieves were able to avoid cats, dogs, fighting cocks, and numerous guests bedded in odd corners of the Finca is not clear, but the third break-in on January 17, 1953, ended when Ernest opened fire with his .22 rifle, drawing blood from one of the housebreakers.[26] The thieves were easier to discourage than were the guests. Gianfranco, Adriana's brother, still a permanent lodger upon whom Mary relied for moral support and errands, was returning to Venice, but his replacements arrived in numbers. Christopher La Farge, novelist and hunting companion from 1939, spent six weeks in residence in the guesthouse. Taylor Williams, friend and guide from Sun Valley, came to fish. Don Andrés, the Black Priest, could no longer make the trek up the hill because of his heart condition, but Hemingway's driver brought him back and forth. Evan Shipman, old friend from early Paris days, came to the Finca, as did Jack Hemingway, his wife Puck, and their two-year-old daughter Muffet (Joan), while Jack was on leave from the Army. While one group said hello, another said good-bye. With no prior warning, a lunch for four not uncommonly became a lunch for eight; a carefully planned supper might be abandoned at the last minute to dine out. Through all the chaos, Mary kept the staff organized and functioning, planned meals, paid bills, housed guests, and kept Ernest's life as uncluttered as possible.

Leland and Slim Hayward were in and out as movie plans developed, crashed, and flew again. Accustomed but not inured to Ernest's effect on attractive women and theirs on him, Mary bit her tongue when Slim had the floor, for there was no way she could compete without angering Ernest. After the Hayward visit, Slim sent Ernest a letter, asking him to tell Mary that she, Slim, played a straight game, "being a woman, I know the women's rules and I try always to play from the ladies' tee, as I think you will attest." Decoded, Slim was telling Mary that she was not making a play for Ernest, whose heart all too often was a target of opportunity, as he was the first to admit.[27]

For months the trip to Europe and Africa was put on hold waiting for the movie plans to solidify, which did not happen until early April. In between visitors, Ernest and Mary spent as much time on the *Pilar* as possible, for it was the only place where they could find something like peace. With no ship-to-shore radio, to be out of sight of land was to be out of reach. The last week before Easter, they dropped anchor at their secret place, Mégano de Casigua, an uninhabited islet they called Paraíso Key. There, protected by a barrier reef and with Gregorio, their mate, for cook and company, they were free to swim and beachcomb naked, Ernest to write, Mary to fish for marlin bait in the lagoon. With the radio playing waltzes, the pre-lunch martinis cold and dry, Gregorio cooking fish and rice,

Ernest and Mary sat in the shade of the side canvas, taking in the sea breeze. But no paradise is invulnerable. Roberto Herrera arrived on a sailboat to tell them that the Haywards and Spencer Tracy were arriving to discuss the filming of *The Old Man and the Sea*.[28]

On Good Friday, the Hemingways, the Haywards, assorted friends, and Spencer Tracy, once a drinking man but now a teetotaler, suppered at the Floridita. The week following Easter was spent visiting the fishing village of Cojimar, where Tracy saw prototypes for Santiago at work, hauling nets, carrying masts, more often than not a cigar stub clenched in their teeth. Tracy, who was co-producer on the pending film, initially was going to do the voice-over to the narrative while an authentic Cuban fisherman played the role of Santiago. But soon it was apparent that Tracy wanted to play the role himself, and that his film commitments would not allow him to begin for another two years. After much talk, the actor hosted a going-away supper at the Three Aces in Havana, and Mary recorded in her journal, "it has been the best year in harmony and good friendship between Papa and me." As quickly as possible, she and Ernest were back under the palm fronds of Paraíso Key, where, on May 4, while listening to the evening news, they heard that Ernest had won the Pulitzer Prize for literature. Having been disappointed when the Pulitzer Committee refused the prize to him for *For Whom the Bell Tolls*, Ernest was not particularly thrilled with the announcement, but Mary was delighted. He informed Scribner's that he would not reject the award as Sinclair Lewis once did, but he hoped he did not have to do anything more than say thank you.[29]

Despite island escapes, the tension produced by constant visitors was beginning to erode Ernest and Mary's better selves. The Haywards returned to interrupt once more the isolation on Paraíso, and Ernest was again fuming over Charles Fenton's investigations into his early life. He claimed that he was unable to continue with Nick and Littless in "The Last Good Country" because of Fenton's intrusions. Using registered letters from his lawyer, Alfred Rice, Hemingway was doing everything short of taking the young man to court to stop him. But he could not stop the arguments with Mary, which by

June 1 had once more gotten out of hand. Mary's patience was worn thin with the previous five months of chaos; Ernest was testy from dealing with everything but his writing. For two years since finishing *The Old Man and the Sea*, his writing regime had been continually interrupted by death and business. On May 15, Ernest signed a contract with *Look* magazine for a photo-journalism piece on their African safari for $15,000 in expenses (nontaxable) and $10,000 for the 3,500-word article.[30] When Mary found out, she exploded. Why had she not been told! She had been told. Had not! Her agent was trying to sell the same story based on the journals she would keep. Now that was a dead deal. On into the night the harangue, Mary the scolding wife, Ernest tight-lipped, unwilling to argue.[31] But like all their tiffs, this one, once aired, eventually blew itself out. By June 24, they were packed and on board the *Flandre* as the vessel sailed out of New York bound for Europe.

Chapter Twenty-Eight

THE PHOENIX

June 1953 to March 1954

O N J U N E 2 4 , Ernest and Mary, fortified with 593 pounds of necessities stuffed into twenty-four pieces of luggage, settled down in their double suite on the SS *Flandre* bound for Le Havre, where Gianfranco met them at the customshouse. Awaiting their arrival was a rented Lancia and an Italian undertaker-cum-chauffeur, Adamo, who somehow tied down excess luggage on top of the car. First stop was the Ritz Hotel in Paris to store what they did not need for Spain or Africa; after Paris, they drove through Rambouillet to Chartres, to remember the last time Ernest prayed there in 1944. On down the Loire Valley they drove, Ernest in the front seat; Mary and Gianfranco in the back with the coats, cameras, maps, guidebooks, radio, bottled water, wine, and local papers. Turning south under gray clouds, they eventually arrived at Hotel Eskualduna in Hendaye, bringing back memories of long-ago summers on this same beach with Hadley and then with Pauline, staying in modest oceanfront hotels when a dollar was worth twenty-five francs, which almost paid for the room.[1]

On cold, cloudy July 6, they crossed into Spain, where Ernest had not been since 1939 when Franco's Republican forces finally defeated the Loyalists whom he had supported. All the way down from Paris, Ernest worried about Spanish reprisals, worried that they would not forgive him for *For Whom the Bell Tolls.* In the customshouse, a border guard, framed against a wall bearing the slogan—FRANCO–FRANCO–FRANCO—carefully inspected Hemingway's passport, glancing back and forth from the photograph to his face with an uncertain look. Then a smile of total recognition, a grasping of hands, Hemingway was back in the country where he once felt most at home. As they motored on through the mountains, down into San Sebastián, and over the pass to Pamplona, Ernest sat silently, pleased to see pines and rivers as he had left them, stone houses with brown tiled roofs, oxcarts, women in black dresses bowed down over vegetable gardens, sheep grazing near the pass. Seeing Spain for the first time, Mary was delighted, asking questions, listening to explanations, and making notes.

All that summer in Spain, everywhere that Mary went, she was sure to have her new Hasselblad with its telephoto lens and the Rolleiflex, taking photographs to illustrate potential travel writing. At Sumbilla, she talked her way into a woman's house in order to lean out her window for a shot of a vine-covered bridge. In Pamplona, she photographed bootblacks at the café, a religious procession in the street, Gypsy women cooking stews at the horse fair. At the morning *encierro,* she borrowed a woman's balcony for the best shot of the bulls coming down the cobblestone street, runners barely ahead of the horns. All across Spain, her camera was clicking—storks nesting in a church tower, Basque girls dancing, tavern faces out of Goya, oxcarts, Burgos Cathedral, peasant girls with scythes. At the country home of Dominguín, retired matador and now bull rancher, she photographed the house; at Valencia, the beach and the fish market; at Paterna, the underground homes dug into the hillside. When not photographing, Mary was asking questions, making judgments, and cataloguing discomforts for journalistic use. All the while, she was suffering from a nagging case of colitis which did not respond to treatment.

During the feria of San Fermín, the Hemingway party stayed at Lecumberri outside Pamplona, drove in early some days for the *enci-*

erro in the streets, later on other days to watch the afternoon *corrida* from *barrera* seats. Hemingway could only have been more pleased if in the ring the picadors had not butchered the bulls so badly. Antonio Ordóñez, son of Niño de la Palma (hero of the 1925 San Fermín), was the brilliant attraction, performing beautifully and winning Hemingway's complete admiration. Mary, like Duff Twysden in 1925, was also taken with "the handsome boy, slim, supple, the young smooth face grave but not tense . . . so deft . . . so controlled."[2] The Pamplona gathering that summer was like old home week. After warning those with him to beware of the pickpockets working the crowds, Hemingway immediately had his pocket picked. Peter Viertel, who joined the entourage at St. Jean-de-Luz, was largely bored with bulls and *botas*, but hung in for the entire spectacle. On the Pamplona plaza, they encountered Mary's old co-worker from Time/Life Charles Wertenbaker, and Bob Lowe from *Look* magazine. Bulls were dedicated to Hemingway by matadors not yet born when he saw his first *corrida*. *Botas* were filled and refilled with blood red wine; lobster and codfish stew simmered at breakfast; and always street bands, singing, the *raiu raiu* dancers hopping high, and at night a firework display raining embers down on uncaring roisterers. It was the old Pamplona with new faces, and private ghosts at every corner.[3]

By the end of July, the Hemingways had made the circuit—San Sebastián to Pamplona to Madrid to Valencia back to Madrid, from there to Burgos and back to San Sebastián. They had seen enough *corridas* to start Ernest thinking seriously about an updated version of *Death in the Afternoon*. Mary, who was half sick most of the trip, was weary but pleased. Gianfranco was still talking about running with the bulls in the morning *encierro*, and Adamo, their patient chauffeur, was ready to return home to Udine. Among the luggage were Ernest and Mary's new, handmade safari boots of Spanish leather. Back in Paris, they repacked at the Ritz for the boat trip to Africa. Driving south on August 4, they boarded the *Dunnottar Castle* in Marseilles two days later for the voyage up the Mediterranean, through the Suez Canal, and around the Horn of Africa to Mombasa.

Their safari guide Philip Percival, lured out of retirement, was there at the dock to greet them and their mountain of luggage. Twenty years earlier, Percival led Ernest and Pauline into the East African terrain where as a young man in 1909 he had accompanied the Theodore Roosevelt safari. Now sixty-nine years old and gaunt from tick typhus, Percival agreed to lead the Hemingway safari out of loyalty to Ernest, who had immortalized him as Pop in *Green Hills of Africa* (1935), and out of loyalty to the Kenyan government that was desperate to regenerate the lucrative tourist hunters scared away by the Mau Mau bloodshed in northern Kenya. This native uprising over loss of tribal lands was less threatening to the white Kenyans than the ruling British reaction led the world to believe. By 1956, when the emergency was declared over, only 100 whites but over 13,000 black Africans were dead; 80,000 Kikuyu were penned up in detention camps; and Jomo Kenyatta, future president of independent Kenya, was serving a seven-year jail sentence.

At Percival's comfortable Kitanga Farm, Ernest was delighted to show Mary the changes wrought by twenty years since he had last stood on those grounds. Mayito Menocal, their wealthy Cuban friend, joined the Hemingways, along with Earl Theisen, the photographer hired by *Look* magazine to accompany the safari. Laden with weapons, ammunition, tents, kitchen gear, canned food, whiskey, and water, the caravan moved south, away from Mau Mau territory, to a game reserve opened only to the Hemingway safari, for the government was determined to keep them supplied with abundant animals and ample photo opportunities. After a two-year drought, East Africa was a place of dust, dry leaves, and bleached bones, which was disappointing to Mary. But Ernest knew that anywhere creeks ran or water pooled, they would find game. He also remembered the 1933–34 safari becoming an uneven competition between himself and Key Wester Charles Thompson: Ernest was the better shot, but Thompson got all the best trophies. Now, twenty years older, Ernest found himself in a different situation. His aim was not as steady. At fifty-four, with his genetically weak eyes grown worse, he wore reading glasses and wing-shooting glasses; his wing-shooting abilities were still sharp, but he had never been an accurate shot on standing game.[4] If the animal moved, he was deadly; if it did not, he could be embarrassing to himself.[5] Moreover, he was out of practice with large-bore weapons, having shot nothing larger than an antelope since his last African trip. Menocal, who hunted regularly, was much the better rifle shot, and his kills were often made after a Hemingway miss. That was not the story Theisen had come to photograph.

Close to their Salengai River camp, animal life was rampant: four hundred elephants, twenty rhinos, and at least ten lions lived in the area.[6] Denis Zaphiro, a twenty-seven-year-old game ranger, saw to it that there were ample photo opportunities for Theisen. On the first day into the new country, Zaphiro met them on the dirt road, asking if Ernest was ready to kill a wounded rhino Denis had tracked down. Loading up his heavy .577-caliber weapon used as backup on dangerous game, Ernest walked up to within fifteen paces of the near-sighted rhino before pulling the trigger. Spinning completely about, the rhino raised an enveloping cloud of dust, into which Ernest fired again; the thrice-wounded rhino bolted into the brush. Denis and Ernest followed the blood spoor until light began to fail, but did not find the dead beast until the following morning.[7] A month later, Ernest and Mayito almost simultaneously fired on a leopard made to order for Theisen, who photographed Ernest seated beside the dead cat. Mary argued that Ernest did not know whose bullet killed the animal, but the photo was taken anyway. Privately Ernest promised Mary he would kill another leopard before the *Look* photo-essay ran, which he did, but only after pumping six shots into thick brush where his wounded leopard sought refuge. When Hemingway killed his lion, it was another messy affair. At two hundred yards, he pulled the trigger, heard the slug hit, and saw the lion disappear into the brush without even howling. A half hour later, with the wounded animal cornered, Ernest and Denis both shot twice before the lion died. Two days later, Menocal killed a magnificent black-maned lion with a single shot.

On the hunting part of the safari, Hemingway made few of the clean kills that marked his first safari. Theisen got his pictures, but

Ernest's heart was no longer in the hunt. The Finca's walls were heavy with noble, preserved heads, and he had already begun to identify metaphorically with old trophy animals. Except for the lion, Zaphiro thought that Ernest was not greatly interested in hunting. "He did not, for instance, shoot or even want to shoot an elephant," Zaphiro said later. "He preferred to drive around and look at the animals."[8] In fact, as soon as Menocal and Theisen left the safari at Fig Tree Camp, Ernest and Mary spent more time and effort observing wildlife than killing it. Left for a period of time on their own when Percival returned to Kitanga, they explored the terrain, counted animals, learned their habits, watched the birdlife, and were as free in Eden as it was possible to be in a fallen world. Mary handfed an abandoned newborn Grant's gazelle who attached to her as his mother. At the Kimana Swamp camp, everywhere they looked, something unexpected waited to be seen. A pride of lionesses springing up with their cubs out of the tall grass, moving so smoothly, quickly into deep cover, delighted them. At regular times of day, an elephant herd came to the river, mothers and children, the matriarch standing guard, the yearlings deferential. Each morning was a wonder to see what animals left their traces in the camp at night. Coming back from the toilet tent in the dark, Mary surprised several zebras. One night Denis Zaphiro woke to find a leopard inside the tent with him. Upon discovering a young female, an old lioness, and her cubs close to camp, Ernest and Mary began leaving gifts of wildebeest haunch for them. Although Mary eventually killed a lion who refused to charge, it was the beauty and serenity of Africa, not the hunting, that was most important to both Hemingways.[9]

A year later Denis Zaphiro would fondly recall the craziness that Ernest and Mary brought with them to the safari:

> Papa and I driving at night recklessly through the flowers with the smell of dew on them. . . . The taste of neat gin in my mouth and the young giraffe wheeling away from the headlights as Papa leant out of the car and smacked its rump. The feat when he fell out and I backed into the darkness to find the broken form and there he was sitting up

searching for his glasses, the pistol still clutched in his hand and his
great shoulders shaking with silent laughter.[10]

Intrusions were few and far between, for Roy Marsh's single-engine Cessna brought mail from Nairobi on an irregular basis. In October, when there was talk that Hemingway was due for the Nobel Prize for literature, his hopes rose, only to be deflated when it went to Winston Churchill. A month later the unstoppable Charles Fenton broke through Ernest's defenses with a letter asking for permission for several quotes for the book version of his dissertation, which he promised "leaves completely undamaged all the material and situations you would write about yourself creatively." Ernest, in the middle of his Masai spear training, gave Fenton the necessary permissions, offering to bring him back a blooded spear from what he called his "fucking never-ending apprenticeship."[11] Letters from Hotchner recounted his ongoing negotiations with the television moguls. Ernest's short story, "The Capital of the World," was being performed in two mediums on the Ford Omnibus series. The dramatic adaptation by Hotchner would appear as a stage play, followed by a ballet interpretation of the story, music provided by Ernest's Paris acquaintance, George Antheil. If all went well, Hotchner had rosy plans for more television adaptations of Hemingway. Columbia Broadcasting System was interested in *Across the River and into the Trees*, and several of Ernest's short stories were natural fits for the medium.[12]

Left to their own devices, Ernest and Mary invented games, named the animals, feasted on local bounty, and observed the forbidden fruit of native girls, some already the third or fourth wives of cow-wealthy Masai men. On November 3, Ernest was made an honorary game warden, a title that carried no specific duties but to which Ernest gave the same weight as a battlefield commission.[13] When Mary made a Christmas shopping trip into Nairobi, she returned to find Ernest's head shaved, his clothes dyed the rusty ochre favored by Masai, and armed with a native spear with which he was practicing to kill a lion. With an imagination that operated quite beyond Mary's limits, her husband was creating an elaborate fantasy of becoming a Masai warrior, one with multiple wives, an erotic fantasy that had intrigued him since his first marriage. Shrewder, tougher, more tolerant, and perhaps more foolish than his earlier wives, Mary, realizing that his fantasies added to their sexual adventures, suggested that Debba, his native girl of choice, first might need a bath before joining the family. When Denis Zaphiro returned to the camp before Christmas, he found Debba "hanging around the staff encampment. . . . She was a slovenly-looking brat with a primitive greedy face. She was also none too clean." But he gave little credence to the suggestion that Ernest did more than talk about her as his "fiancée."[14]

On December 20, at the Kimana Swamp camp, Ernest wrote in Mary's journal that he was eager for Mary to turn her hair, as promised, a platinum blonde the way it was in Torcello when they were so happy. He said that

> Mary is an espece [species](sort of) prince of devils . . . and almost any place you touch her it can kill both you and her. She has always wanted to be a boy and thinks as a boy without ever losing any femininity. If you should become confused on this you should retire. She loves me to be her girls, which I love to be, not being absolutely stupid. . . . In return she makes me awards and at night we do every sort of thing which pleases her and which pleases me. . . . Mary has never had one lesbian impulse but has always wanted to be a boy. Since I have never cared for any man and dislike any tactile contact between men . . . I loved feeling the embrace of Mary which came to me as something quite new and outside all tribal law. On the night of December 19th we worked out these things and I have never been happier.[15]

Mary, happy to be complicit in her husband's sexual adventures, reproduced his statement, which he had signed and dated, in her own memoir years later.

From December into January 1954, with the rains having turned the dusty plains billiard table green, Ernest and Mary camped on the north slope of Mount Kilimanjaro. In his new role of honorary game warden, Ernest was quick to recreate an African version of Rambouillet. If elephants grazed through a shamba's cornfield, he was there to make sure they kept moving on. If a lion was killing Masai cattle, Ernest and his rifle were on the case. When natives appeared in the middle of the night with some emergency, it was never too inconvenient for him to attend to it. As honorary game warden and acting game ranger, Hemingway was in command of native game scouts and numerous informers reporting on poachers, a marauding leopard, and potential intrusions of Mau Mau. Here was an experience so rare that it seemed a dream to him, the stuff from which a book might come. Mary kept one set of notes, he another:

> *Old man on the road*
> *Conversation about the house on the hill*
> *We came to kill the lion. Lion ran off.*
> *The old man killed his servants, reporting as a Mau Mau attack*
> *Becomes a local hero*
> *Policeman finally notes all were killed on 29th of the month, pay*
>   *day.*[16]

When he was not on patrol, leaving Mary with their safari natives, he and she were walking their local area, checking on the buffalo herd, on the elephants, on the old lioness—Adam and Eve after the fall returned to an Eden less friendly but no less interesting. Waking early before first light, Ernest would sometimes be out on the trails, armed only with his spear, listening to the morning music of birds and beasts.[17]

Mary, at first dubious about his game rangering, began to reap its rewards when Ernest praised her excessively as "the bravest, loveliest, most understanding and best kitten in and out of bed, and more fun to talk with on any subject and with sounder opinions . . . of anyone . . . the best companion in the field when things are difficult that I have ever known bar none." When Mary told him that Lady Churchill in middle age held many hearts, Ernest asked, "In the palm of her hand?" Mary said, "Yes." Ernest, with a grin, replied, "No better than you holding Mr. Scrooby."[18] With Ernest as her armed backup, Mary photographed furiously—bat-eared foxes, gazelles, kudu, rhino.

During this same period, Roy Marsh, their bush pilot, began taking Ernest and Mary on low-level flights along the river and the plains, the excitement of which thrilled Mary and worried Ernest, who understood the dangers of "flying on the deck." But soon in his letters he was saying the "deck" was his home, while promising Mary a low-level tour of Africa right up to the Congo River basin. On January 21, they took off from Nairobi in Marsh's Cessna, making overnight stops along the string of northern lakes, until on January 23 they were admiring the grandeur of Murchinson Falls at low level when a flight of black and white ibis rose in front of them. To avoid a collision, Marsh went beneath the large birds. Then with a twang and a shudder the single-engine plane ripped through an abandoned telegraph line, ruining the prop and damaging the rudder. Banking sharply to the left, Marsh told his passengers, "Sorry, we're coming down now. Get ready. Get ready." As softly as a light plane can come to rest in heavy brush, Marsh cut the engine, dropping the Cessna into an opening—a successful landing, everyone walking away from it apparently unhurt. But it was soon obvious that Mary, riding in the co-pilot's seat, was in shock—weak pulse, rapid heartbeat—and later a doctor discovered two cracked ribs.[19] Ernest's back, right arm, and shoulder were badly bruised to the point of steady pain, but he and Roy made a camp, gathered firewood, hauled their meager supplies up from the crash site, and avoided the elephant herd into whose home they had descended. It was one o'clock in the afternoon. Roy Marsh's distress calls on the plane's weak radio went unanswered, but a high-flying commercial liner spotted the wreck, reporting that no survivors were visible. By sunset, newspapers around the world were setting banner headlines announcing the death of Papa. That night on the hillside, sleeping on grass bedding, Mary was awakened by Ernest, who asked her not to snore because the noise was making the elephants curious.

The next day a chartered boat, with no knowledge of their cir-cumstance, appeared almost miraculously on the river below them. After negotiating with the elephant herd on the hillside and the boat captain, who overcharged them, Ernest, Mary, and Roy found themselves drinking a cold Tusker beer, watching the riverbank flow past on their way to Butiaba. There they were met by Reggie Cart-right, who had been searching for them in his twin-engine, twelve-seat de Havilland. Assuring the rescued party he could take off from the rough dirt landing strip, Cartright got them aboard and started bouncing down the uneven field. No sooner were they airborne than they nosed down, smashing into the ground. The right engine caught fire, igniting a ruptured fuel tank, quickly turning the plane into a death trap. With the port door jammed, Marsh hurried Mary forward where he and she squeezed through a broken window too small for Ernest to follow. Trapped in a plane that was filling with smoke, Ernest tried to force the jammed door open, but his previ-ously bruised shoulder, leg, and arm made his effort too painful to be effective. Left with no alternative, he butted his bare head against the door, finally wedging it open. By this time the entire plane was in flames, beer bottles exploding like pistol shots. Consumed in the fire were the Hemingways' passports, Mary's expensive cameras, thirty rolls of exposed film, three pairs of Ernest's bifocals, all of their money, and their $15,000 letter of credit.[20]

That evening at Masandi, celebrating their double escape at the bar with pilots and newfound friends, Ernest was groggy and disori-ented. Discounting his exaggerations, this was at least his fourth seri-ous concussion in the last ten years. Alcohol, his sovereign cure for head wounds, was guaranteed to make the concussion worse. Behind his left ear, the scalp was torn and clear fluid was leaking from the wound; one of his kidneys was badly hurt, his overworked liver dam-aged, his shoulder dislocated, his lower intestine collapsed, and he suffered temporary loss of hearing in his left ear and vision in his left eye. In the midnight toilet bowl he could all too clearly see the bloody urine. Later, X-rays would reveal two crushed lumbar vertebrae. In steady pain, he tried as best he could to keep a pleasant face forward;

like a wounded animal, he did not want to let anyone know how serious the damage was.[21] At fifty-four, he was in worse physical shape than when he was blown up at eighteen; his aging body was much slower to heal, never again regaining its full power.

On Monday, January 25, Ernest and Mary, both in considerable pain, were driven to Entebbe where journalists and airline representatives were waiting to interview them. On that same day, international newspapers and radio stations were reporting his probable death on the basis of the earliest news release. On Tuesday, the United Press news service reported and almost every newspaper's front page carried the full story, which began:

HEMINGWAY OUT OF THE JUNGLE;

ARM HURT, HE SAYS LUCK HOLDS

Entebbe, Uganda, Jan. 25—Ernest Hemingway arrived in Entebbe today having survived two plane crashes in the elephant country of Uganda.

His head was swathed in bandages and his arm was injured, but the novelist, who is 55 [sic] years old, quipped: "My luck, she is running very good."

He was carrying a bunch of bananas and a bottle of gin. With him was his wife, the former Mary Welsh. She had two cracked ribs. . . . He waved a swollen arm, wrapped in a torn shirt, and appeared to be in high spirits as he shrugged off the crashes . . . he apparently was not badly hurt.[22]

But Ernest was hurt even worse than he let Mary know. For three days, he rested in the privacy of their hotel room, and on January 28 flew to Nairobi, where the press reported that "he seemed tired and disinclined to talk."[23] At the New Stanley Hotel, Hemingway remained in his room as much as possible, drinking too much, the doctor told him, but paying no attention to the doctor, refusing X-rays, determined to be as invulnerable as his obituaries and their next-day retractions would have him be. To reporters, he insisted he was in good shape, but Mary noted: "The urine samples he keeps in glasses in the bathroom are bright, dark red with an inch of sediment, the wound on the leg not good, hearing bad in the burned ear, eyes bad."[24]

Although Ernest was obviously in poor physical shape, he insisted that they complete the safari with deep-sea fishing just as his first safari had done. Still ailing from her mending ribs and bandaged knee, Mary left him in the Nairobi hotel while she went to Mombasa, where they were renting a fishing boat for a month. With their safari porters, the Percivals, Patrick and his wife Henny all arriving, Mary established their camp at Shimoni. From there she wrote to Ernest:

> It really is a fine place, this—a little like Parajiso, with the big narrow island straight in front and the open sea to the SW and blue high hills against the sunset to the W, Boabab trees . . . NO MOSQUITOES AT ALL. . . .
> I bought a case of gin and some Riesling and Chianti and whiskey. . . .
> The sea is silver now and a dugout with one of those Arab shaped sails floating across it against a golden sky.

Urging him to join them as soon as he felt well enough to travel, Mary signed the letter: "Much love from half a woman or half a boy."[25]

Back in his hotel room, Ernest lived in his pajamas, doctored himself, took meals in the room, and spent part of each day dictating his comic version of the double crash for *Look* magazine, which offered him $20,000 for the exclusive. Illustrated with Earl Theisen photographs, the story ran for twenty magazine pages spread out over two issues. Called "The Christmas Gift," it was a rambling, loosely organized, comic, but remarkably written account of the experience, with asides on Senator Joseph McCarthy, the habits of elephants, the efficacy of Gordon's gin, memories of New York celebrities, strange dreams involving lions, his game ranger adventures, and the night sounds of Africa. In his dreams, he confessed that he was "always between 25 or 30 years old, I am irresistible to women, dogs, and on one recent occasion, to a very beautiful lioness." Nothing in the travel story gave any clue to how badly damaged Hemingway actually was, but he did comment on his obituaries that claimed he had "sought death all his life."

> Can one imagine that if a man sought death all of his life he could not have found her before the age of 54? . . . She is the most easy thing to find that I know of. . . . [I have spent my] life avoiding death as cagily as possible, but on the other hand taking no backchat from her and studying her as you would a beautiful harlot who could put you soundly to sleep forever.[26]

On February 22, Roy Marsh flew Ernest down to Mombasa, where he joined the seagoing safari party on the island. But his jammed vertebrae and other ills kept him largely housebound while the others fished. Then, compounding his problems, he tried to help extinguish a brush fire, but his damaged ear had so affected his balance that he tumbled into the blaze. By the time the natives pulled him out, he was burned on the arms, head, and lips, requiring more bandaging. On March 9, when it was time to call the safari done, Mary dealt with all the details, for Ernest was still recovering from his injuries.[27] Two days later, she supervised the move of forty pieces of luggage, including a leopard skin, several rugs, three hundred books, and African masks, on board the SS *Africa* bound for Venice. Their great escape into the garden of Africa, begun so gaily and finished in pain, was over. As the roofs and palms of Mombasa dropped from sight, Ernest at the railing, his back in serious pain, was a shrunken man. His weight was down to 185; his face puffy with bruises and burns, his eyes unfocused. Plenty of times before he had been badly hurt. Each time he had trained himself back into physical shape. In 1918, when his right kneecap was largely missing, his head concussed, and his legs full of shrapnel, it took him more than a year to recover. In 1930–31, when his right arm was so badly fractured in an auto wreck that it seemed the damaged nerves would never regenerate, he slowly willed them back into action. This time, however, his head was dangerously muddled, and Gordon's gin was no cure. Given enough solitude, most of his injuries would mend, if not perfectly at least to the point that he was not in constant pain; but residual damage to the left side of his brain put him one step closer to that closely studied harlot of whom he spoke.

Chapter Twenty-Nine

FORTUNE AND MEN'S EYES

March 1954 to January 1956

F ROM MOMBASA, the Hemingways returned to Venice on March 23, checking in, once more, at the Gritti Palace, where Ernest finally submitted to X-rays that revealed jammed vertebrae. In steady pain, he went back to bed, his thinking erratic with barbiturates and his vision still fuzzy. One of the first visitors allowed into his room was Adriana Ivancich, who was shocked to see him white-haired and twenty pounds lighter. Without Mary in the room, they had a tear-filled reunion, with Ernest apologizing for the scandal he had caused her with his novel. "Probably it would have been better," he said, "if I had never met you that day in the rain."[1] No longer jealous of the young woman, Mary was ready to hand her husband over to Adriana, to doctors, or to anyone else who would take him, for she had reached her limits as nurse and valet. Ernest, from his side of the court, complained that being trapped in a small room with her was no fun for a wounded man, for she woke surly and never kind.[2] But soon after arriving in Venice, Mary wrote her parents that Ernest was buying her jewels: "the most beautiful, delicate bracelet, very Venetian—a couple of hundred years old . . . and the next day came home with a pin representing part of a gondola and one of the mooring posts."[3] This expensive gesture was, by now, a familiar stage in their complex marriage game: whenever Ernest felt remorse for errant behavior, he usually resorted to gifts of money, clothing, or jewelry to make amends.

Their daily lives in Venice were made increasingly unpleasant by media pressures: reporters, magazines, newsreels, radio interviewers were all at the door. From America came startling offers for exclusives on their African adventures, which were already under contract with *Look*. No private life was left to them as the public fed vicariously on the Hemingway saga. They escaped briefly to the country, but the country could not cure the problem, nor could it mend Ernest's internal ills. He accepted the Award of Merit Medal from the American Academy of Arts and Letters, but begged off attending the New York ceremony, explaining to Archie MacLeish how badly beat up he actually was.[4] In April, his temper frayed from pain, Ernest arranged for Mary to visit London over Easter, pick up old friends of the *corrida*, and motor down to Madrid. Ed Hotchner would drive him down to join her in mid-May. Meanwhile, he checked into a Genoa clinic for further tests, then returned to the Gritti where he occasionally saw Adriana, who was now twenty-four and still unmarried, which for an Italian woman of her station was a cause for more gossip. When he and Hotchner departed Venice on May 6, Ernest's first letters were to Adriana, telling her that leaving her was like an amputation and that he would love her much and always.[5]

Driving along the French Riviera and through Provence with Adamo once more at the Lancia's wheel and Hotchner for travel companion, Ernest tried to be as jolly as possible, given his condition. They stopped at Monte Carlo for a brief evening at the gaming tables, visited the heart of Cézanne and Van Gogh country once more, and stopped long enough in St. Jean-de-Luz to lure Pete Viertel to Madrid, regaling him with fanciful stories of Debba, Ernest's "Wakamba bride." When Ernest arrived in Madrid, his paranoia popped up like an old friend when the newspaper *ABC* ran a brief paragraph about "an enemy of Spain" arriving in the city. After the

San Isidro *corridas* (May 15–17), which Hemingway insisted they all attend, their party joined Viertel and the beautiful film star, Ava Gardner, at the country home of Luis Miguel Domínguín. Mary, keeping a perfect public face, was worried in private about Ernest, who looked as weary and ill as she had left him in Venice.[6]

At the Domínguín bull ring, Ernest watched the now retired matador test the courage and stamina of heifers for breeding purposes. Afterward Ernest and Ava posed for photos with Luis Miguel, but when the Hemingway party returned to Madrid, Domínguín told Viertel that he did not trust Hemingway. Apparently, while evaluating Viertel's ability, Ernest judged that Pete would never write anything significant, which to the Spaniard was no way to speak of a friend. Viertel himself made little of it, but afterward wrote:

> The thing that disturbed me most was Papa's duplicity, a trait I had first become aware of in Paris when Hemingway had denigrated so many of his old friends. In this instance I sensed that his backbiting had been caused by his proprietary attitude toward bullfighting. . . . He was finding it difficult to accept growing old.[7]

Almost everyone who remembered the Hemingway of the previous summer found him incredibly changed by the African plane crashes, his beard whiter, his eyes frequently vacant, his moods mercurial. In Madrid he went to yet another doctor, who advised "continued rest, a careful diet, and a greatly reduced intake of alcohol."[8] On June 6, having driven back to Genoa, Ernest and Mary boarded the *Francesco Morosini* in order to reach Havana without passing through New York City. The Ivancichs, mother and daughter, came to the dock to see them off, a decorous parting and a final one. Ernest and Adriana would never see each other again.

Fifteen days later at sea, Ernest wrote that he had taken only four whiskeys since leaving Italy, which was boring the bejesus out of him and making life for Mary miserable. At lunch in the small ship's dining room, Ernest began harassing Mary about one of his numerous pocketknives she was supposed to have had repaired in Paris. Where was it now? Packed somewhere in the eighty-seven pieces of luggage stowed in the hold, but Mary could not remember in which piece. Ernest became furious, shouting, "You thief!" The other diners were stunned silent as Mary calmly finished her coffee. Returning to their cabin, she wrote Ernest a note: "You used to understand justice and that other people also had feelings and truthfulness. . . . I hope for your sake especially, and for all us friends and lovers of yours that you have not completely lost those qualities."[9]

Finally, thirteen months after leaving Cuba, they returned to the Havana pier, tired, overloaded with luggage, and ready to sit quietly at the Finca to recover from the trip. Instead, Mary almost immediately was forced to go to her father's side in Gulfport, Mississippi, where as a convert to Christian Science he was refusing to take drugs for his uremia and prostate cancer. In the sweltering July heat, Mary tried to bring reason back into her parents' house, while Ernest did his best to put the Finca back in order. On July 20, having gotten both parents into a nursing home, Mary returned to Havana. The next day, Ernest was being honored on his fifty-fifth birthday by the Batista government with Cuba's highest civilian award, the Order of Carlos Manuel de Céspedes. Ernest, who refused to do anything that might indicate he supported the Batista government, insisted the medal be presented at an informal ceremony, not at the presidential palace.[10]

August at the Finca was a continual circus of luncheons with old friends, all wanting to touch the man who had risen from the dead. Bob Lowe, former editor at *Look*, was there for five days, pushing a deal for an African documentary film, for which Ernest agreed to be consultant. Then Hemingway's Havana doctor, José Luis Herrera, was fed and fêted; three days later it was wealthy Lee Samuels, Hemingway's local supporter, who managed the collection of Ernest's manuscripts. Then Ava Gardner arrived, preceded by her much quoted statement that there were only two men she would want with herself on a desert island: Adlai Stevenson, the cerebral Democrat defeated by Eisenhower for the presidency, and Ernest Hemingway. Winston Guest showed up on his way to someplace else, followed by Luis Miguel Dominguín for nine days. In between

Alfred Vanderbilt passed through the Finca wanting Ernest's help with some association of war veterans.[11]

Despite these steady intrusions, Ernest wrote almost every morning, standing at his typewriter to protect his back. He finished one short story and was twenty-one pages into another by mid-August.[12] His concentration was broken temporarily on September 2 when the *New York Times* reported that "Ernest Hemingway is going to write and appear in a motion picture about big-game hunting in Africa," which Darryl Zanuck would produce. That took two days of letters and phone calls to the coast and to Alfred Rice before everyone understood that Ernest Hemingway was never going to be an actor in or a writer of any Hollywood film. That was with his left hand. With his right hand, Ernest was responding to a local journalist's demand for a duel to assuage his honor offended by some remark of Mary's at a cocktail party. No dueling with journalists.[13] No filming with Zanuck. Be polite at Finca lunches, and write every morning on the story that was rapidly becoming "the African book."[14] Then came the annual Nobel Prize lottery to raise distractions to an entirely new level. On October 5, the *New York Times* reported that "Halldør Laxness, 52-year-old Icelandic writer, and Ernest Hemingway are the only candidates seriously considered for this year's Nobel Prize for literature, according to circles close to the Swedish Academy." Three weeks later, the *Times* said the Nobel was a sure thing for Hemingway because after his near-death experience, "some Swedish academicians expressed regret that they had not previously honored him."[15] None of which Hemingway found particularly flattering. If the "academy" that had passed him by so often had to choose only between some Icelandic bard and himself, it was not a field to be proud about, and if they were giving him the medal because he came close to dying, well, to hell with that.

But when the announcement came on October 28 from Sweden, there wasn't any way to say no to the Nobel Prize, not with the world's press corps at your front door and the Swedish ambassador at your dining-room table. So, leaving out his misgivings, Ernest said simply, "I am very pleased and very proud to receive the Nobel

Prize for literature."[16] To the crowd gathered at the front door, he joked about the prize money, saying he would like to share it with his friends, the panhandlers outside the Floridita, but first his own debts must be paid.[17] When Harvey Breit called from New York, Ernest gave him as many pithy quotes as possible, saying he could not "but regret that the award was never given to Mark Twain, nor to Henry James, speaking only of my own countrymen."[18] When *Time* magazine told him they were running his face on their cover whether he helped with the story or not, he invited their reporter, Robert Manning, down for two days of *Pilar* fishing and Hemingway homilies: "Fattening of the body can lead to fattening of the mind. I would be tempted to say that it can lead to fattening of the soul, but I don't know anything about the soul." Hemingway also used the *Time* interview to make a strong public plea for the release of his old friend and mentor, Ezra Pound, from St. Elizabeth's Hospital. "Ezra Pound is a great poet," he said, "and whatever he did he has been punished greatly and I believe he should be freed to go and write poems in Italy where he is loved and understood."[19]

Hemingway excused himself from attending the Nobel award ceremony, saying that he was not yet fully recovered from his African injuries, but he nonetheless needed an acceptance speech for the American ambassador to Sweden to read at the event. Ernest's first impulse was satirical, asking rhetorically what it might profit a man to win such a prize if by doing so he destroyed his present writing through "small politenesses."[20] Finally he prepared a short statement that offended no one, but with barbs beneath its seemingly simple surface:

Writing, at its best, is a lonely life. Organizations for writers palliate the writer's loneliness but I doubt if they improve his writing. He grows in public stature as he sheds his loneliness and often his work deteriorates. For he does his work alone and if he is a good enough writer he must face eternity, or the lack of it, each day.

For a true writer each book should be a new beginning where he tries again for something that is beyond attainment. He should always try for something that has never been done or that others have tried and failed. Then sometimes, with great luck, he will succeed. . . . It is because we have had such great writers in the past that a writer is driven far out past where he can go, out to where no one can help him.[21]

In answer to Faulkner's earlier complaint that Ernest never took chances by attempting the impossible, Hemingway was asking his readers to look again at his work, for its very simplicity did not mean that it was easy to do, or that he did not try to push the limits of his talent. Because they read for immediate gratification, urban reviewers all too often had seen each work as a rerun of earlier themes, and nothing new. What few noticed was that he never repeated himself in the structure of his novels, that he pushed the short story genre beyond its previous limits, and that his style continued to evolve. If his themes were constant, so were those of Picasso.

By December 7, Ernest was in the *Pilar* anchored on the lee side of a small island, riding out a norther and hiding from his pursuers. He complained that he would have to move to Africa or stay permanently at sea in order to get his writing done. The Floridita was now impossible, as was the Finca and Cojimar. It was partially his own fault letting Cowley, Baker, Fenton, Young, Ross, and now Manning get inside his defenses. He worried that the publicity could actually destroy that internal well from which his writing was drawn.[22] He remained at sea through the Nobel award ceremonies, which he and Mary heard fade in and out on their shortwave radio. Returning to the Finca, his desk was covered with inquiries, offers, and announcements of arriving guests—more "brutal" interruptions. Time/Life wanted to give him a $10,000 check for the privilege of having the "first look" at his next book. *Argosy* magazine for men would pay $1,000 if Hemingway would let their photographer into the Finca to take pictures. And Hotchner had a $6,000 commitment from *True* magazine for a feature on Hemingway that required photographs and yet another interview.[23] His life, no longer his own, had become a public sideshow open to anyone. Always the hunter, he was now the hunted, the trophy head to be brought back on film. His broken body was healing more slowly than it ever had before; his mind was full of ants. His black-ass mood was descending like a caul as the year closed out with a National Broadcasting Company hour-long, unauthorized radio documentary, "Meet Ernest Hemingway—the man who lived it up to write it down." Ernest was characterized as "master of the four letter word" and "a two fisted drinker who could down a quart of gin a day if the conversation were good." Max Eastman got to refight his chest-hair battle with Ernest that took place in Max Perkins's office. Leonard Lyons told anecdotes; Al Capp, who never met Hemingway, said that the writer's one and only creation was Ernest Hemingway. Ed Scott, the *Havana Post* journalist who challenged Hemingway to a duel, read from Hemingway's letters to him. Cornelia Otis Skinner read her Hemingway parody, "For Whom the Gong Sounds," and young Marlon Brando read excerpts from *The Old Man and the Sea*.[24]

Into the new year, Ernest, sick of such publicity, kept as much to himself as possible, writing every day and seldom leaving the Finca. The second African story was now moving along nicely as a full-blown novel, unplanned as his novels frequently evolved, with him living in it each day, back at the good camp and the elephants moving, their dung piles smoking in the morning light. The first week in February 1955, he wrote 4,587 words, when previously a good week would have been half that many. His back and kidneys, not yet recovered enough for strenuous exercise, still bothered him, and he avoided anything likely to strain them, turning down invitations to return to Madrid for the San Isidro *corrida*.[25] On February 17, the death of Mary's eighty-five-year-old father took her to Gulfport for his funeral and its aftermath. While she was gone, Ernest did not slide into his customary funk when left alone; rather, he immersed himself in the novel. By the time Mary returned, he had 75,000 words on paper, words which he said were too rough to be printed while he was alive, words, he joked, never to be serialized in the *Sunday Visitor*, the Catholic newspaper for children.[26]

Written in more than one voice but with the character Ernest

Hemingway as its focal point, the manuscript was an ironic, self-deprecating, and humorous account of the contemplative life of the writer juxtaposed against the active life of a temporary game ranger protecting the village of the Wakamba natives, one of whom, Debba, is promised to him as his second wife. Mary, his older wife, is barren, and the writer/hunter yearns for the child Debba will give him. Critics, biographers, and fellow writers all come in for comic kidding, but the Africanization of Ernest Hemingway is serious in the sense that he was looking for some way to escape from his too public life into a simpler world. With Patrick now living in Tanganyika and Gregory there visiting, Ernest was ready to give up his no longer defensible Cuban hilltop in favor of Africa. He had retreated from Key West in 1939 and Ketchum in 1948, for the same reasons that were now making Cuba less the garden spot it once was.[27] Thirty-three years earlier in Paris, he set out to become the best writer of his generation, choosing great writers as his masters and immortality as his goal. He became the writer he set out to be only to find that the cost was high, and rewards sometimes tasted like ashes. In Africa, he explained,

> You do not have to be a literary character. . . . And I can pray to the Mountain, we have an illegal shamba at its foot, and to the trees, the special trees, and keep the customs and laws and break them as the young men do and pay fines and Miss Mary who can't have children can have Debba to help her as a second wife. Debba can have the children.[28]

At the end of his life, Tolstoy tried for religious reasons to dress and live as a peasant; Hemingway, for secular reasons, was moving in the same direction. He clearly understood the pure loneliness of a writer's life, and the burden of being the personage he had become. All his yesterdays with their wonderful stories and novels were just that, yesterdays. A writer is never free from the necessity of writing something better, different, more interesting than his last book, and each book comes with its own anxieties and difficulties. There is no decorous retirement plan except failure for a writer.

Mary, who understood his need to write the African fantasy, remained his supportive wife and faithful reader. She was, after all, a character in the book, with a larger role than Pauline's in *Green Hills of Africa*. If she did not object to sharing Ernest with the fictive version of Debba, perhaps it was more exciting to indulge his fantasy. In a letter to Harvey Breit which Ernest let Mary read, he said, "It doesn't seem so stupid to me to have five wives if you can afford them . . . instead of having one wife at a time and paying them alimony when you need another wife. . . . I am very faithful. But I can be faithful easier to four good wives than to one."[29] Despite a continued parade of Finca guests, despite her father's death in February, and her mother's move back to Minnesota in July, the burdens of which all fell on her shoulders, Mary was always supportive of Ernest's African fantasies until that October. When he announced that he wanted his ears pierced for gold earrings as a sign of his kinship with the Wakamba natives, Mary did her best to convince him that it was a bad idea. Finally she wrote an interhouse note, asking him to reconsider his decision, which would flout "the mores of western civilization," not to speak of the "deleterious effect" earrings would have on his reputation "as a writer and as a man." She continued,

> *The fiction that having your ears pierced will make you a Kamba is an evasion of the reality which is that you are not and never can be anything but an honorary Kamba . . . I know that you are impassioned about Africa and the Africans, writing about them, and allured by the mystery and excitement of becoming one of them. And you know that I love the fun of make-believe as much as you do. But . . . there are other ways of proving brotherhood between you and the Kamba.*[30]

That was the end of the earring crisis.

Despite his best efforts to keep visitors at bay that spring of 1955, Hemingway and the Finca were never without intrusions. First it was an undergraduate from Rutgers bearing a sheaf of short stories which he insisted Ernest must read. Then on the Wednesday of

Easter week, four of Carlos Baker's students from Princeton were knocking at the front door, having first ignored the gate sign telling them no visits without an appointment. Once inside, Ernest was as grandfatherly as possible, soft-spoken, almost shy. The four sophomores, feeling quite adult drinking late morning martinis with the Man himself, listened to his stories about the early days in Paris and how he taught himself to write, stories that by this time were well rehearsed. When asked if he would ever run out of ideas for fiction, he said, "I don't see how I can quit."[31] On the morning of Good Friday, Professor Fraser Drew from Buffalo arrived by appointment to find Hemingway gray-bearded and overweight, dressed in working shorts and an old shirt. "Slow moving and slow speaking," Drew wrote in his notes. "His voice is quiet and low and his laugh . . . is genuine and quiet, also. He is very kind and modest and unassuming." Noting that it was Good Friday, Ernest said, "I like to think I'm a Catholic, as far as I can be. I can still go to Mass, although many things have happened—the divorces, the marriages." He spoke of Father Andrés who lived in the village below the Finca. "He prays for me every day," Hemingway told Drew, "as I do for him. I can't pray for myself any more. Perhaps it's because in some way I have become hardened. Or perhaps it's because the self becomes less important and others become more important."[32] High on Ernest's prayer list were Mary's parents, fallen-away Catholics, Tom Welsh dead, but his soul perhaps still salvageable. Hemingway would send money to his favorite order, the Jesuits, or simply have Don Andrés pray for them at his morning Mass. "The prayers can't hurt them," he said, "and if not entitled to them they will be paid for anyway and the money can't hurt the church."[33]

Ernest might have included himself on his prayer list, for his body was recovering so slowly from the African crashes that now, a year later, he was still in pain. On April 19, with Mary's twenty-foot *Tin Kid* in tow and their locker well stocked with provisions, Ernest, Mary, and Gregorio took the *Pilar* ninety miles down the coast to Paraíso Key for a two-week escape. Each morning Mary fished the reefs, sometimes with Gregorio, but just as often on her own. Having become an excellent sailor as well as fisherwoman, Mary was perfectly capable of taking her open boat out beyond the reefs looking for marlin on her own. For most of the sojourn, Ernest did not fish at all. In the mornings, he would do his exercises and run on the beach, each day feeling stronger, and living part of each day writing in the Africa of his head. Eating well—Gregorio's red snapper in garlic and peppery tomato sauce—drinking little alcohol, reading during the midday heat, sleeping under a sea breeze, Ernest and Mary were at peace with themselves and the world elsewhere. By day, the water turned several shades of blue and green in the bay and along the reefs. At night, the constellations made their steady circle, great and small bear, lion, and dogs, the twins in their slow dance, and if late enough awake, Cassiopeia rising.[34]

On May 3, Ernest and Mary returned to the Finca, which continued to be overrun with guests. Juan Dunabeitia, the Polish sea captain known as "Sinsky," was in drunken residence for a week between sober voyages; Roberto Herrera was there every day working as a private secretary. Alfred Rice, Ernest's New York lawyer, came in to discuss the contract for the filming of *The Old Man and the Sea*, and Taylor Williams from Sun Valley visited on crutches with his foot in a cast. Outside the house, an unusual spring drought continued, turning green growth brown, ruining the flower and vegetable gardens. Then the Finca's aqueduct developed problems, forcing them to haul water in pails from the cistern.[35] Despite intrusions and emergencies, Ernest kept to his morning schedule, writing first and then exercising in the now tepid swimming pool. He was twelve pounds lighter and beginning to feel more like his old self, the old self that ignored doctor's orders, drinking too much too often.

By May 11, he had 404 typed pages of manuscript to which he added each day until June 1, when Pete Viertel and Leland Hayward arrived for the first serious talks about filming *The Old Man and the Sea*.[36] Worried that 98 percent of Hemingway's story took place in an open boat, Viertel suggested that after eighty-four days without a fish, Santiago might look for other work in old Havana before returning to his trade as a fisherman. Ernest listened but killed the idea. Santiago knew only one trade: fishing. It would never enter his mind to seek other employment. Insisting they stick to the story as he wrote it, Hemingway told his guests that this was the only movie of his work he had ever been involved in, and he wanted it right. Trying to joke about it, Viertel suggested that on the eighty-fifth day Santiago might "still not make a catch."

"The Jews have always had a superior attitude toward fishing," Ernest snapped, "probably because fish has never been part of their diet."

"I thought you'd gotten over your anti-Semitism with *The Sun Also Rises*," Pete snapped right back.

Ernest huffed while Pete glared. Hayward calmed both down. Ernest apologized, claiming that the anti-Semitism in *The Sun Also Rises* belonged to his characters, not to him. He was too old now to become anti-Semitic.[37] The evening went on, but it was going to be that kind of a working relationship among the three of them.

When the Cuban location filming began in September, Hayward sent Slim down as his emissary, joining Pete Viertel at the Finca. Putting a woman as attractive as Slim in close proximity to Ernest was a serious mistake. Pete moved into town; Slim moved into the Finca's small guesthouse. That evening before supper, Slim confided to Pete that Mary "had threatened quite calmly to shoot her if she made a play for Papa." When they joined Ernest in the Finca's living room, he was naked to the waist, dressed only in khaki trousers. Sucking in his stomach to prove to Slim how thin he was, Ernest smiled as his trousers dropped to the floor, leaving him stark naked.

"All right for the camera, Pete?" he asked.

"Perfect, Papa," Viertel replied. "Cut and print."

"Please, Papa," Slim pleaded, "put your pants back on!"

He and Pete were laughing, Slim looking away, Ernest pulling up his pants just before Mary walked into the room, curious about the laughter.[38] To her mother, Mary wrote that Slim Hayward was "pretty, quite tall, very slim, and she always has the most wonderful clothes and jewels." Before departing Havana, Slim made Mary a present of her belt and a gold bracelet. On the day of Slim's departure, Pete was shocked when Mary appeared with her once platinum-blond hair now dyed darker to the color of Slim's so admired by Ernest.[39]

Despite Hemingway's organization of the great marlin hunt, complete with hot catered lunches delivered at sea by Mary in the *Tin Kid*, the *Pilar* as camera boat, and native fishermen with hand lines in small, open boats, the film crew was unable to capture Santiago's huge jumping marlin. All of September was spent in this pursuit, which produced 400- and 500-pound marlin, but nothing like the 1,200-pound monster the script required. Already there was talk of moving to a rubber marlin in a Hollywood backlot tank. Hemingway refused, categorically and absolutely. In October and early November, he returned to his African novel, which grew to 694 typed pages by Thanksgiving. That fall Luis Miguel Domínguín came out of retirement to fight a series of South American *corridas* with his now brother-in-law, Antonio Ordóñez. In mid-November, *Sports Illustrated* offered Hemingway $1,000 expenses and a $3,500 fee for his impression of their performances in Caracas, but he and Mary never got to the airport.[40] November 17, after sweating under television lights waiting to receive the Order of San Cristóbal, yet another award from the Batista government, Ernest caught a cold. Then his right foot began to swell, followed by an infection first in his damaged right kidney, then in his left kidney, and finally his liver: acute nephritis and hepatitis was the diagnosis. Put to bed on November 20 under medication, a strict diet, and a limit of one whiskey and water per day, he would not rise again until January in the new year.

Each day the family doctor came to the Finca to check on his patient, making careful notes on his progress. Weak and woozy, Hemingway stuck to the doctor's regimen, fighting off boredom with books, the radio, and his African novel once his head cleared. And of course there were letters to read if not answer. Among them was an envelope bearing the distinctive handwriting of an old Paris friend, Sylvia Beach, who hoped they would meet again soon. "I must ask whether you approve of the way I have handled you in my memoirs," she said, "and whether you authorize my quoting from [your] letters?"[41] Twenty years earlier, when Gertrude Stein published her belittling portrait of Hemingway in *The Autobiography of Alice B. Toklas*, Ernest promised himself that when he had nothing else to write, he would produce his memoirs to even up the score. For several years now, he had been trying out his early Paris days in conversations, letters, and in the unpublished Bimini book. Whether it was Sylvia's letter that pushed him closer to keeping his promise, or the growing legend of Scott Fitzgerald as the madcap writer of the Twenties, is impossible to say, but by the time Ernest was back on his feet in January 1956, he was thinking seriously about the true book of his Paris apprenticeship.

Chapter Thirty

INTIMATIONS
OF   MORTALITY

January 1956 to March 1957

A FTER SIXTY DAYS in bed, reading and writing, taking his medicine, not drinking, gradually recovering strength,
Hemingway rose again at the end of January 1956 only to
be sickened by "Who the Hell Is Hemingway?" in *True* magazine.
Filled with tall tales, half truths, anecdotal stories from friends, and
long quotes from Ernest's own letters and essays (all without permission), it was exactly the sort of story Hemingway now abhorred. Some
critic named Pearson called Hemingway "the bronze god . . . who took
obscene words off the backhouse wall and put them in print . . . here
was the swashbuckling pirate in his own right, living it up to write it
down. . . . He is notorious as master of the four-letter words. He drinks
liquor by the quart . . . absinthe used to be his favorite drink."[1] Having
spent two months without liquor and longer than that without having
published a single four-letter word, Ernest had reason to resent such
statements. Having tried without success to force Scribner's into publishing even longer obscene words, Hemingway's twenty-year total was
exactly one "fucking" in *To Have and Have Not*.

Further into the paste-and-cut story, Hemingway discovered that among his friends were "convicts lately escaped from Devil's Island," and that Jed Kiley, whom he despised, was his "fishing companion." Edward Scott, the *Havana Post* journalist who challenged Hemingway to a duel, recounted the silly incident at great length, quoting Hemingway's last letter on the matter: "For good and sufficient reasons I do not choose to meet Mr. Edward Scott on the so-called field of honor nor anywhere else. I will answer no challenges from him. . . . If any tribunal interprets this as being motivated by cowardice I believe they would be in error. . . . At the present time I am fighting no duels with anyone."[2] Scott forgot to mention that Hemingway was, at that time, freshly back from his disastrous African plane crashes.

On February 6, Earl Wilson's gossip column in the *New York Post* carried an interview with Hemingway saying, among other things, that he was completely cured of hepatitis, that he still had the liver of a twenty-six-year-old, and that his doctors had ordered him to drink six ounces of whiskey a day for his health. "I figure I can do it if I put my mind to it," he was reported to have said with a drink in his hand. Affirming his recuperative powers did not make his liver any better, nor did his doctor's daily notes say anything about drinking that much alcohol. In fact, Hemingway was taking daily doses of several different drugs to keep his rapidly aging body functioning properly: Seconal to sleep; vitamin A for his weakening eyes; vitamin B complex to counteract the effects of alcohol; and methyltestosterone for sexual vigor. Much of this medication was self-prescribed on the basis of Hemingway's wide reading of medical research. When the hepatitis struck, his blood pressure jumped to 178/75; with bed rest and drugs, it gradually came down to 140/68 by the end of February. But by then his red blood cell count was 20 percent below normal. Worried about this anemia, Dr. Herrera immediately ran parasite checks which proved negative on both Ernest and Mary, who also tested anemic.[3]

On January 30, Fred Zinnemann, the director for *The Old Man and the Sea*, flew into Havana to discuss location filming with Ernest, who had scouted out several isolated fishing villages. For the next two months, Hemingway, when not sick, was working in some way on cinematic problems which he found a lot like organizing a safari. It was, in fact, becoming a Hemingway year in Hollywood. Pete Viertel's film script for *The Sun Also Rises* was soon moving into production with the money going to Hadley, as had all earnings from that novel. At the same time, Rock Hudson and Jennifer Jones were starring in a remake of *A Farewell to Arms*, the film rights to which Hemingway had foolishly sold outright before he learned to read the fine print. Having avoided any participation in the several film versions of his work, he was immersing himself completely in the filming of *The Old Man*, determined to have real sharks attacking an actual marlin in an authentic ocean. That was the Hollywood promise written down on paper; but as he was to learn, words written on the West Coast somehow had different meanings from standard English. Moreover, anything scheduled, promised, or planned meant absolutely nothing in the movie business.[4]

On February 10, Hemingway packed up the 856-page typescript of his African novel to devote himself totally to the film project, but he was worried how it would affect him to be away that long from his writing.[5] He might also have wondered how the movie business would affect his marriage. Two weeks later, Mary brought that question to his attention with her in-house state of the union message. Starting slowly, she explained in some detail how women enjoyed going out at night, particularly to the homes of others to see how they lived, decorated, dressed, and ate. Perhaps one night a year, she suggested, they might go out somewhere, anywhere, understanding, of course, that it would be an enormous sacrifice on his part. Pointing out that she had learned to play his games of hunting, sailing, and fishing, was it too much to expect him to humor her a little? Yet when she asked, he became defensive, calling her a liar, and Mary accused him of

> *counter-attacking . . . as though I were your long-time enemy. . . . Has it ever occurred to you how lonely a woman of yours can get. Wake up alone, breakfast alone, garden alone, swim alone, sup*

alone. . . . It may be too much to expect that any of this will cause
you to change your mind in thinking of YOU *versus The Other.*

She signed the note: "M. who feels her life slipping away in a welter
of chaos."[6]

Ernest could not have been more in agreement about the "welter of chaos" that ruled their lives. Trying to coordinate the weather,
film crew, blood bait, and sharks was proving almost impossible.
When the camera crew was ready, the weather was too rough to film.
When twenty gallons of slaughterhouse blood and four tubs of fish
heads were standing by, the film crew was somewhere else. One part
or another never quite got to the right place at the right time. Days
were wasted. Money was spent and spent again. If not the sharks,
then the marlin would not cooperate—too small, too far away, not
jumping enough. When not wasting time at the dock, they wasted
time in conferences or waiting for Spencer Tracy to show up. When
he did arrive, he spent the first evening falling spectacularly off the
wagon at the Floridita. The next day Ernest noted on his calendar:
"Tracy *not* drinking." On the back of the page, he wrote a note to
himself with reference to his conference with Tracy: "You must not
humiliate a man in front of others if you expect to continue to work
with him."[7] In March, a letter from Gary Cooper invited Ernest to go
partners on producing a film of Stewart Edward White's *The Leopard Woman,* set in Africa. Even as much as White was once one of
Hemingway's early literary models, Ernest said if he ever got finished
with filming *The Old Man and the Sea,* he would never again get
involved with movie making. It was not his metier. He joked that
if he helped with *The Leopard Woman,* he could picture "that one
necessary little bit they would want me to do without a double when
I crash the Leopard Woman herself into the snow covered crater of
Mt. Kilimanjaro (Kibo) and then carry her (personally) into Abys-
sinia. . . . Can hear myself being conned, 'Ernie, boy, you owe this to
The Picture.'"[8]

In April, the film crew gave up on large, leaping marlin in the Gulf
Stream, and Leland Hayward agreed to pay for a month's fishing off

the coast of Peru where giant marlin were said to be commonplace. At Capo Blanco—wind blowing sand steadily over barren rocks with oil derricks rising out of the wasteland—they lived at the fishing club's preserve, rising early to spend all day in rough heavy seas trying to find Santiago's fish. Cameras careened, handlers held tight, but no fish floundered. Then Ernest boated a jumping 750-pounder, the largest he had ever taken, but only half the size needed. Larger still, a 950-pounder refused to jump. Other than working Hemingway's weight down to 209 pounds, strengthening his back, and improving his health, the month in Peru was time wasted from the movie's point of view. For backup, Hayward had already purchased film rights to color film of a 1,500-pound world-record marlin splashing in blue seas, and rubber marlins were in the making.[9]

Ernest and Mary were still in Peru when the May issue of *McCall's* magazine ran its "visit" at La Finca Vigia, describing Ernest, not yet recovered from his recent illness, as having "no bounce to his gait, no he-mannish bravado. This is a tired man with a sizable paunch." Handing out his homilies by rote on writing and husbanding, Ernest was on his best behavior, impressing the interviewer with "very dry martinis" and his enormous library piled up throughout the house. When asked his opinion about the Nobel Prize, he could not resist taking another crack at Faulkner whose novel, *A Fable*, Ernest found unreadable. He said, "One shouldn't win the Nobel Prize, then rewrite the Bible and become a bore—I accepted the Bible in its original version."[10] Considering that Ernest was working on his own version of the Garden of Eden, it was an ironic comment.

Upon returning to Finca Vigia in late May, Mary was soon stretched out upon a table with needles in her arm as fresh blood dripped into her veins: an attempt to cure her persistent anemia. Archie and Ada MacLeish were there on a rare visit, seeing Ernest for the first time in many years. Once close friends, they were now but graying shadows of the young men who rambled the Paris boulevards of the Twenties. Archie was there to plot a way to release the incarcerated, irascible Ezra Pound, who never had a good word to say about MacLeish's poetry. Strained as the Hemingway-MacLeish friendship had become during the 1930s, they united in their support for Pound, although it was Archie's persistence that eventually carried the day.[11] On his birthday, Ernest sent Ezra the last of the Nobel money, a $1,000 check, and promised to send him the Nobel medal as well.[12] By the end of the year, Archie was able to report on a workable plan for freeing Ezra. If Attorney General Brownell would agree not to prosecute on the charges of treason, then the question of release could be made on a medical basis, not a political one. Promising there would be no publicity, MacLeish drafted a letter to Brownell for Robert Frost, T. S. Eliot, and Ernest to sign.[13] It would take another year and half before the "midwife" to *The Waste Land* would be set free from his fifteen-year confinement.

After the long and exhausting distraction of movie making, Hemingway did not immediately return to the African novel; instead, to resharpen his blunted pen, he wrote six short stories, mostly about World War II experiences. Based on the ambush at the Rambouillet crossroads ("Black Ass at the Cross Roads") and his judicial hearing ("A Room on the Garden Side"), these stories used material that would have been in the "land" part of the "big book" had Hemingway ever completed that project.[14] With sarcastic references to the war novels of Shaw, Mailer, and James Jones, he insisted that his new stories were about real soldiers speaking in battlefield language about situations in which death was a constant. Scribner's could, he said, publish them after he was dead.[15] After being assured by doctors of his impending death first by high blood pressure and then by internal injuries, his death references, which were becoming more frequent, were understandable. It was the only ending to his story, an ending of which he had been certain since he was eighteen, but now, with friends dying all too regularly, it was not only a certainty but was close enough to smell. This awareness had an adverse impact on his writing, for the only ending that he could now imagine was the death of the protagonist. Even earlier, his novels had ended this way since *To Have and Have Not* (1937). Safe in the bank vault, his Bimini novel ended with Thomas Hudson's life leaking out of his wounds. Only Mary's pleading kept Santiago alive after returning with the shark-stripped skeleton of his marlin. With 200,000 words written on the African novel, Hemingway did not have an ending, although there were plenty of possible death's available—lions, leopards, and Mau Mau revolutionists.

That summer in Cuba, Ernest's red blood cell count rose close to normal; Mary's, however, remained dangerously low. After several blood transfusions, their Cuban doctors suggested a change of climate, which for Ernest was a good excuse to return to Spain where young Ordóñez was fighting brilliantly, and then continue on to Africa for a safari with Patrick. Hemingway booked passage on the *Ile de France* in what Mary referred to as their customary suite, which, with over 100,000 French francs in his Paris bank account, Ernest could well afford. In late August, Ernest took Mary to New York City, where they stayed in the borrowed quarters of Harvey Breit to avoid the press. There they went about last-minute shopping, seeing no one but hearing by phone from Sylvia Beach, who was in the city negotiating with her publisher on her memoirs. She still wanted him to read the "Hemingway passages" for changes he wished, but he assured her to go ahead with publication. It was not until he reached Paris that he read her typescript filled with inaccuracies of too long standing to be corrected.[16]

On September 1, Ernest and Mary boarded the *Ile de France* for a quick five-day trip across the Atlantic. Landing in France, they were met by their new Italian chauffeur with a rented Lancia, which took them first to Paris to reorient and to pick up funds. Pete Viertel found them at the Ritz "petit bar" sitting with Gary Cooper and a young lovely Ernest introduced as "La Comtesse." To Viertel, it was obvious that Hemingway "had once again embarked on one of his imaginary romances." That the relationship was not serious was made obvious by Mary, sitting at the far end of the table, who was massively unconcerned, "having become accustomed to Papa's flirtations." A few days later, Pete arranged a luncheon for Hollywood friends Mel Ferrer, Audrey Hepburn, and Rita Hayworth to meet Hemingway. Seated at a sidewalk café, the group was convivial, Ernest behaving modestly, apparently enjoying the adulation. But when an elderly man approached their table to ask for autographs for his daughter, Ernest turned cold. The movie stars signed, but when it was Ernest's turn, he said, "Sir, you look to me to be a cocksucker." The man departed, hurt; the table went cold. Admitting that he was losing tolerance in his old age, Ernest apologized for what Viertel called his "mercurial changes of mood."[17]

On September 17, the Hemingways traveled by car to St. Jean-de-Luz and crossed into Spain, where they settled into the privacy of the four-star Gran Hotel Felipe II in El Escorial, thirty miles outside Madrid. On the pine-shaded slopes of the Guadarrama Mountains, the hotel was a picturesque refuge perched above the imposing blue-gray granite monastery of San Lorenzo, with its maze of courtyards and rich treasury of Spain's past. In keeping with his idea of updating *Death in the Afternoon*, Hemingway followed the early fall *corridas* that were within easy driving distance. En route to El Escorial, he and Mary enjoyed two days of the Logroño feria where Antonio Ordóñez was brilliant in the ring. Afterward, Ernest made serious plans for the Zaragoza feria in October where Ordóñez promised to dedicate his best bull to Hemingway. The excitement that Ordóñez created in the bull ring was like old times, real and contagious.[18] But the *corridas*, while important to Hemingway, were not as important as the health of himself and Mary. The reason they were staying in El Escorial was its elevation (3,700 feet), which their Cuban doctors hoped would cure their persistent anemia. Their October 22 blood tests showed some improvement: Ernest's red cell count was near normal; Mary's remained 20 percent too low. Their Madrid doctor said that X-rays showed nothing seriously wrong with Ernest's heart, that his cholesterol level was too high, and that Mary was much better. He advised that neither of them was fit for a return to Africa that winter, a trip Ernest was counting on to rekindle his African novel.[19] Ernest refused to accept that decision, saying he was going to Africa with or without the doctor's approval. He did agree to follow the prescribed regimen of diet and exercise, but ignored the doctor's request that he stop drinking all alcohol. As Mary and others noted during the trip, Ernest was once again drinking far too much far too often.[20]

An international crisis, however, conspired to keep the Hemingways out of East Africa. First, Egypt nationalized the Suez Canal; then on October 29, Israel invaded Egypt, trying to keep the canal open, but the Egyptians immediately sank forty ships, blocking the canal to all traffic. Not wanting to take trains through Egypt during the crisis, the Hemingways were faced with a long sea voyage around Africa to reach Mombasa, which neither wanted to make. Calling off the African trip, they returned in November to the Ritz Hotel in Paris, where they underwent another battery of medical tests. Mary was suffering once more from colitis, and nagging anemia was still with both Hemingways, Mary more so than Ernest. Moreover, his cholesterol count was twice normal, indicating possible liver problems. Soon he was referring to his "near fatal" liver condition. None of which stopped them from playing the horses at the Auteuil track, or from having dinner with the Duke and Duchess of Windsor at their country home outside Paris. Ernest found time to spend a day showing Leonard Lyons old Left Bank haunts, explaining fallaciously that he learned the city by driving a taxi after World War I.[21]

When a second test on January 8, 1957, confirmed an elevated cholesterol, Ernest put himself under the care of the *Ile de France* ship's doctor, Jean Monnier, who treated him for liver problems, an enlarged aorta perhaps due to his erratic blood pressure, and facial eczema. Between January 23, when the *Ile de France* sailed for New York, and February 14, when it docked in Cuba, Dr. Monnier injected Ernest with large doses of vitamin B complex, gave him drugs to lower his blood pressure, and treated his eczema with cortisone cream. Nevertheless, on March 2, Hemingway's cholesterol count was 408, driving him into a depressed state, certain that he was fatally ill. Dr. Monnier, responding to Ernest's worried letter, assured him that the laboratory analysis was always inexact, that most of his numbers were within a normal range, and that he should stop worrying and follow the prescribed lifestyle without fail. Then Dr. Monnier repeated what he told his patient on board the ship: "You must *stop drinking alcohol*. . . . I understand that it might be harsh, even painful in the beginning, but you must gradually reduce your drinking to nothing." Simultaneously, his new Havana specialist, Dr. Rafael Ballestero, told him much the same thing: rest, mild exercise, restricted diet, altered medication, and no alcohol.[22]

One of the new drugs, Serpasil, was made recently available to treat psychiatric problems ranging from schizophrenia to depression, anxiety, and nervousness. For Hemingway's anxiety and nervousness during alcohol withdrawal, Dr. Ballestero prescribed the recommended dosage of a .25 mg tablet taken twice a day. Possible side effects included lethargy and sometimes nausea until the patient adapted to the drug, but it could either lower or elevate blood pressure, which should be monitored throughout treatment. Always suspicious of drugs and their side effects, Ernest read and filed away detailed information on this trademarked version of reserpine. Ballestero also prescribed a once-a-month injection of a testosterone drug similar to what Hemingway had been taking orally since 1953. In September, Dr. Herrera continued the Serpasil, renewed Whychol for Hemingway's liver condition, and put him on Oreton, a steroid, to maintain male sex characteristics; Doriden, for a short time, to calm him down; and Ritalin, a mild central nervous system stimulant, to control impulsivity and hyperactivity.[23] He was now taking one drug to sleep, another to control his overactive mind, another to treat his damaged liver, and male hormones to leaven the results. There was no information available on how this pharmacological stew might interact. Some of these drugs, like Seconal, were not to be taken if drinking alcohol—a warning Ernest had ignored for years, but was now forced to obey.[24]

Returning to Finca Vigia with its attendant responsibilities did nothing to lessen Ernest's post-European depression. That his swollen liver which so alarmed Dr. Monnier was a bit less noticeable, and that his blood pressure was much lower did nothing to mitigate the loss of alcohol, upon which he had become dependent without ever admitting it. First he cut back on hard liquor, stopping completely on March 5; then he began limiting himself to "light wines," two glasses at supper. It was a painful and boring experience, facing the day completely sober. When Winston Guest stopped drinking,

Ernest said he grew suspicious of his old friend. Now he could say the same about himself. He thought he had become a boring person to live with, and the only sovereign cure for being around a bore was the alcohol forbidden him. It was similar, he said, to driving a racing car without oil for lubrication.[25]

Along with his enlarged liver, Hemingway brought back from Paris a set of new luggage stuffed full of memories. In the storage room of the Ritz, management found old, forgotten trunks left there when Ernest and Pauline were moving out of the city in 1930. Four days before sailing on the *Ile de France*, Hemingway wrote Lee Samuels of finding his early manuscripts, many of the stories in holograph, some still in the blue copy books he used in the earliest Paris days. Some of it, he said, "was pretty exciting to see."[26] Samuels, a prosperous tobacco broker in Havana, was Ernest's longtime friend and admirer, his sometime banker always good for a loan, and the silent partner in the sale of Hemingway manuscripts when ready cash was needed. These selective sales, which do not appear to have been declared as taxable income by Hemingway, were always a possibility if financial times got really tough. When Ernest told Samuels that the discovery made the trip worth while, he meant financially, but those manuscripts and fragments would soon contribute to the memoirs Hemingway promised to write.[27] Back at the Finca in March, he spent several days sorting his treasure into coherent piles, remembering smells and sounds of a Paris long disappeared, seeing faces of all the old friends, hearing voices now dead. Jim Joyce, Scott and Zelda Fitzgerald, Gertrude Stein, Harry Crosby, Ernest Walsh, Jules Pascin, Ford Madox Ford, and most importantly, Pauline—the dancers all departed, the dancehalls closed down.

Chapter Thirty-One

CUBA LIBRE

April 1957 to December 1958

E RNEST AND MARY remained at the Finca through an extraordinarily hot, humid summer that dulled the appetite, ruined the fishing, and sharpened their tempers. Working steadily on his novel about the loss of Eden, Ernest's attention to his writing was consistently broken by a series of crises and emotional disruptions. His oldest son, Jack, now working as a stockbroker in Havana, became ill, forcing him to bed for two months. In June, Ernest learned that his old Paris days friend, Evan Shipman, was dead.[1] There were continuing problems with rental and upkeep of the Key West property, held jointly by Ernest, Patrick, and Gregory. With Pat in Africa, Greg constantly moving or not answering mail, and Ernest in Cuba, the simplest decision took weeks to reach. Meanwhile in Hollywood, where *A Farewell to Arms* was being remade, David Selznick was rewriting the love story in a more believable fashion which infuriated Hemingway, who had no control over the script.[2]

Hemingway's mail and phone conversations with Alfred Rice were equally frustrating. No matter what directions Ernest gave to Rice, he frequently managed to ignore or misinterpret them, sometimes acting as a literary agent without portfolio and without Ernest's consent.

In August, Rice submitted a distribution of income from the Key West property showing that there was little or no profit, but giving no details on how the income was spent. Ernest was furious.[3] Inexplicably maladroit, Rice, each year, turned the Hemingway income tax return into a marathon event. Because of Ernest's high earnings, he was forced to make quarterly tax payments against expected income. For this purpose, Hemingway set up a special account at the Morgan Guaranty, which for some reason bore no interest even though it usually had $50,000–$70,000 in it. Because Rice arranged for most of the foreign royalties to flow through his office rather than remain in foreign accounts, Ernest's income was always far higher than it might have been, pushing him into the highest tax bracket: for every taxable dollar he earned, eighty-one cents went to the government. Throughout the 1950s, Hemingway's tax bill ranged from $60,000 to $80,000 a year on gross incomes of less than $200,000.

Each morning began early, Ernest standing in front of his typewriter, pecking away at the story of David Bourne and his two women, Catherine and Marita, falling deeper into the abyss of sexual confusion. David wants to write stories about Africa; Catherine wants him to write the story of their marriage. There in the isolated village of Grau du Roi, where the fishing boats were docked literally at the fisherman's door, David was, bit by bit, giving up control of his life to the two women. It was all very exciting at first, and then more complicated and more exciting, with haircuts and blond bleaches, naked romps on far beaches, and nights with no rules. By midmorning, sweat was running down the seams of Ernest's face. On a good day he wrote until late morning, then went to the pool to swim his laps. On a not so good day, he worked on the tax statement for Rice or the list of questions from *The Paris Review*. Against his better judgment, Ernest agreed to participate in the *Review*'s author interview series, not realizing it would be thirty-two pages of questions. On March 4, he spent three and a half prime morning hours answering only three of editor George Plimpton's questions, which he found "profoundly uninteresting."[4]

When it wasn't Plimpton or Rice, it was the problem of how to get

Ezra Pound out of the crazy house. Despite Ezra's difficult, insulting letters to MacLeish, Archie never stopped working the political scene, gathering White House support. Robert Frost, who personally disliked Ezra, supported MacLiesh's effort, albeit with misgivings. Tom Eliot in London added his name to the support group, and Hemingway signed every letter that Archie drafted and pledged $1,500 to be given to Pound to relocate when released. Unfortunately, because Pound was permitted visitors at St. Elizabeth's, he attracted among others, John Kasper, who started an "Ez for Prez" campaign. With Kasper's help, Pound continued to publish tracts on economic reform and political maleficence, which did nothing to help MacLeish's appeal.[5] In June 1957, Archie updated Ernest on the state of their mission, asking him to write one more letter stating his argument

> *that Ezra has been in there for eleven years; that you understand the psychos say he can never be brought to trial; that his continued incarceration under those circumstances has already done us considerable damage abroad . . . that he is a very great poet . . . which raises considerations which . . . should be kept in mind since one of the great pastimes abroad is nailing our asses to the barn door as bloody materialists who care nothing for art or artists.[6]*

Ernest was more than willing to write the letter, but feared that Ezra would not refrain from making political statements, nor from associating with men like Kasper. He could see the media all too easily needling Pound into racist statements.[7] In the letter MacLeish requested be written to Frost, Hemingway emphasized that he could not abide Pound's politics, his support of fascism, or his anti-Semitic and racist views. Nevertheless, Ezra was a great poet, a rare person, for whom a bit of mercy was not out of the question. If he were to die in St. Elizabeth's, the rest of the world would never understand. Citing the political problems of other great poets—Dante, Byron, Verlaine—Hemingway said their poetry outlasted the memory of their offenses. Let it be that way with Ezra.[8] Finally, on April 18, 1958, the indictment of treason against Pound was dismissed because he was and would always be incompetent to stand trial. On May 7 of that year he walked out of St. Elizabeth's free to return to Italy, where he told reporters, "All America is an insane asylum."[9] In his pocket was Hemingway's check for $1,500.

In August 1957, mired in one of his periodic funks about expenditures, Hemingway wrote up a "situation report" for Mary, listing his anticipated expenses that were growing out of control:

Cost of keeping Mary's mother in a rest home	$5,170
Jack Hemingway, various bills	$4,376
Gregory Hemingway	$7,860
Finca Vigia $3,000/month	$36,000
Income Tax (six months)	$40,000

He complained that no one (read, Mary) was making any attempt to hold down expenses. Due to his own unpopularity (read, irritable as hell), he was afraid to make suggestions, but he did note that despite his not drinking, the monthly liquor bill had gone up. His health, he reported, was improving: weight at 203 down from 220; cholesterol reduced from 428 to 208 due to diet and Mary's fine care. He noted that he was in the last half of the sixth month of not drinking, limited to two glasses of wine with dinner. He could not eat out in Havana because it was impossible to do on so little alcohol. He became very "nervous," which made him "unpopular."[10] Whenever Hemingway displayed such concern about money, its lack or its expenditure, he was frequently on the down slope of a depressed period. His detailed and frequent references to the effects of not drinking indicate that the drugs to control his "nervousness" were not working. That he called his condition "nervous" was even more disturbing, for that was the very word Ernest and his sisters once used in Oak Park to describe their father's deteriorating mental state. In 1904, Clarence Hemingway took his first self-prescribed rest cure for his "nerves." He suffered similar despondency and irritability in 1907–09 and 1917–19. Each time he moved further into isolation from his family. By 1928, when he put a pistol to his temple and ended his life, he was suffering from diabetes, angina, hypertension, and severe depression—a condition similar to Ernest's own that summer of 1957.[11]

Despite his physical ills, Hemingway was incredibly productive from late spring all through the summer and into the fall. Visitors came and went, meals were served, fishing provided, but he wrote no matter who arrived. Denis Zaphiro, the game ranger from Kenya, came by invitation and stayed four months, providing Mary the male attention so lacking from Ernest. While Zaphiro was at the Finca, the whole house was awakened at four one morning by a squad of nine Cuban soldiers "looking for a certain oppositionist. No search was carried out and the patrol left. . . . However, the next morning Machakosa [one of the Hemingway dogs] was found dead near the kitchen steps. The dog had been struck on the side of the head with the butt of a rifle or some blunt instrument."[12] Somewhere in the hills of Cuba, two young revolutionaries—Fidel Castro and Che Guevara—were beginning to worry the oppressive Batista government. In the few letters Hemingway wrote that year, he never mentioned anything political, knowing that his American citizenship would be no protection if the night patrol came for him. His lifelong study of revolutions told him that his class would be the first to go. It was not long before bombs were exploding in Havana. By the time one went off in San Francisco de Paula near the Finca, Ernest was already looking for a safe haven to wait out the fall of Batista and its aftermath.

Before Zaphiro returned to Africa, Ernest took a ten-day break to fly with Mary and Denis to New York for the Sugar Ray Robinson–Carmen Basilio boxing match. They put up at the Hotel Westbury on the east side of Central Park, with Ernest paying all the bills.[13] Toots Shor, the restaurateur, picked them up in his Cadillac on fight night. With almost ringside seats, they had a clear view of Sugar Ray's footwork so rare it might have been choreographed and Basilio's battered face puffing up between rounds. Blood and sweat popped off faces with each blow. Other evenings were less visceral, more cultural. One night Ernest dined with Marlene Dietrich while Mary and Denis supped on the in-port *Ile de France* with Dr. Monnier. There were nights at Broadway plays and fall afternoons at the ball park watching the Yankees.[14] Returning to Cuba via a short stop in Washington, D.C., Ernest quickly settled back into his writing routine, alternating between the loss of Eden novel and a new book he started almost accidentally in July when *Atlantic Monthly* asked him to contribute to its hundredth anniversary issue.

His first impulse was to write an essay for the magazine about his relationship with Scott Fitzgerald, but he soon put that sketch away, sending the *Atlantic* two new short stories: "A Man of the World" about a grotesquely blinded bar-room brawler, and "Get a Seeing-Eyed Dog" about a recently blinded writer coming to terms with his condition.[15] Between 1940 and 1957, he had published only two books, but locked away he now had the three-part Bimini book largely completed; in his work room there were 200,000 words written on the African novel; and a large portion of what later was published as *The Garden of Eden* in draft. With two long novels in various stages, he was now starting yet another book, which would become *A Moveable Feast*.

His drafts and revisions of *The Sun Also Rises*, one of the several manuscripts stored at the Ritz, had two unpublished scenes concerning Ford Madox Ford which needed little revision. Soon he was thinking of the memoir as a collection of "short novels"—each chapter a self-contained story. This structure was similar to that of *In Our Time*, his first collection of short stories, which he joined with one-page vignettes that he called "unwritten stories." Quickly he roughed out possibilities for chapters: first meetings with Pound, Stein, and Joyce; Ford Madox Ford and the *transatlantic review*; skiing at Schruns; the Paris apartments; the cafés; meeting Fitzgerald; trips to Pamplona.[16] By Thanksgiving, when Ernest and Mary, both flu-ridden, were bedded down at opposite ends of the Finca, Hemingway was well into his memoirs, averaging a thousand words a day. As he moved back and forth between the Eden novel and early Paris, he was well aware that he was writing about the same period from different perspectives, and that both books tied back to the memories of Thomas Hudson in the Bimini novel. As the year was running out, Leonard Lyons showed up for a Finca lunch, reporting later that Hemingway had put aside his "big novel" to work on an "exciting new project" unlocked by the recovery of his early manuscripts. Lyons said that Hemingway read to him "pieces he's just finished on F. Scott Fitzgerald, Ford Madox Ford and Gertrude Stein."[17]

On New Year's Eve, the phone call from Minnesota told Mary that her mother was dead. She was on a flight out of Havana on the first day of 1958, leaving Ernest with a relatively quiet Finca, which lasted only a few days before a winter storm tore a tree limb off the giant ceiba tree, smashing a hole in the roof above Mary's bed. She returned late that evening to find her bed soaked but the roof repaired. The rest of the winter was one storm after another, bringing unnaturally cold temperatures and effectively ruining the winter fishing. In the village of San Francisco de Paula, Hemingway reported there was unemployment and hunger;[18] in Havana, violence continued—bombs by Castro's rebels and savagery by Batista's national forces. Dead bodies were being dropped off in rural ditches just as they had in the bad old days with Machado. The revolution that Hemingway anticipated was arriving at his doorstep.

Late winter through spring into summer, visitors came to the Finca to be fed and entertained. In January, it was Ernest's old fishing and hunting friend Tommy Shevlin, Hollywood people, and New York columnists; in February, journalists and Hollywood executives; in March, more columnists and sports writers; in May, the Canadian ambassador. When visitors were not interrupting, Alfred Rice and the annual income tax misunderstandings could ruin a morning or sometimes a week. Simply keeping track of his savings accounts, checking accounts, and his seven safety deposit boxes in five different banks in four different towns was a major accounting problem. Having gone almost a year without drinking hard liquor, in March 1958, Hemingway began not only taking his two glasses of Spanish *rioja* with supper but also allowing himself whiskeys.

By that March, "Papa's Liquor" bill for the month was $94 for wine and $45 for whiskey; Mary's was $95.69 for vodka and gin. Throughout the summer, the liquor bill varied, but Hemingway's personal consumption was averaging four to six bottles of whiskey a month and two or three cases of wine. To visitors he claimed he was drinking only light wines and one or two whiskeys, but the numbers say that his need for alcohol was regaining control of his life.[19] Combined with his continued daily intake of tranquilizers, antidepressants, heart medicine, testosterone steroids, and large doses of vitamins, Hemingway's drinking, which was forbidden with several of the drugs, contributed to his steadily deteriorating health. His immune system was noticeably deteriorating: he was sick more often than in previous years, and it took him longer to recover. His condition was also having its effect on Mary. By March, she was taking one pill and Ernest two of Doriden, a sedative to calm the nerves. When used with alcohol, Doriden was potentially addictive and its effects multiplied.[20] It is little wonder that house guests found Ernest nodding off at night in his large living-room chair.

Despite the accumulative effect of drugs and alcohol, Hemingway rose up every morning to write the Paris sketches: Scott worrying about the size of his penis; Cheever Dunning out of his mind on drugs; Zelda Fitzgerald's need to destroy Scott; the pomposity of Ford; Sylvia's bookshop; the loss of his manuscripts. Connecting the pieces was the youthful Hemingway learning his trade: a portrait of the artist as a young man on his way up. In six months the draft was finished, but lacked a conclusion and a title. Titles were always tough, but since finishing *A Farewell to Arms* (1929), he usually had no trouble with conclusions. Yet now, turning fifty-nine in July, he was unable to end either the Paris book or the African novel. He would have the same problem with the Eden novel.

While Ernest was living largely in seclusion during the day, retreating into himself when he was not writing about the Paris days, Mary was assessing her own condition. In notes to herself, she wrote:

You try all your life to merge. Falling in love is building the beautiful deception of two in one. But it is a dream. You are always alone. There are thousands of contented [people] who are never bothered by this. Who knows it and . . . can live with it . . . is strong. . . . "Togetherness" is not a cup of Lipton tea. It is wordless desperation.[21]

It was a good summer for taking stock, for the Cuba around them was crumbling into uncontrolled violence. From their village, young men had been arrested, tortured, and imprisoned on suspicion of aiding the Castro rebels. In April, the police sergeant who led the night sortie on the Finca was killed along with several others. Stories circulated about bodies found in wells, women beaten and tortured, informers on both sides found dead with their tongues cut out. A threat of a general strike hung in the air like a whiff of gas, and those who remembered the general strike bringing down the Machado regime in the 1930s held their collective breath.

At the Finca in July, Ernest and Mary lived cautiously but without any political intrusions. When Ernest stopped work on his Paris memoir, Mary began typing it for his revisions while he turned his full attention to the Eden book, which he did not share with Mary as he had with *The Old Man and the Sea* and the Paris book. In August, Hemingway's concentration was broken when he learned that *Esquire* magazine intended to reprint three of his Spanish Civil War stories in an anthology. Stating emphatically that *Esquire* had purchased only first serial rights to his stories, Hemingway directed Alfred Rice to forbid their republication, for he planned to revise and publish them himself in his next collection of short stories. As a peace offering, he said they could publish one story, "The Butterfly and the Tank."[22] Three days later, the story broke in the *New York Times*:

Ernest Hemingway, stating that the passage of time could affect the public's reaction to a writer's work, instituted court action yesterday to prevent Esquire *magazine from reprinting three short stories he wrote in the Thirties . . . in papers filed in Supreme Court yesterday by Alfred Rice, his attorney, Hemingway charged that to reprint the stories would do more than violate his property rights. Reprinting, he said, would also result in "great injury and irreparable damage" for reasons other than the commercial value of the stories.*[23]

Hemingway was furious with the statements written by Rice and attributed to him. The *Times* story the next day was headlined:

HEMINGWAY SAYS HE WILL DROP SUIT.
"Those statements were made by my lawyer, Alfred Rice, and I have just called him up and given him hell for it," Mr. Hemingway said on the telephone . . . "two of the stories were not as good as I wanted them and I wanted to revise them before letting them go into book form."

In claiming that changing times also changed the way people might read the stories, Rice cited as an example "the writings of men during the time Russia was our ally to the present attitude of people to such men and their writings now that Russia is perhaps our greatest enemy." Ernest said pointedly that Rice may have meant well by such a statement, but that "it does not represent my view." It was not to change the political tone of the stories that he wished to revise them: "I only wanted to remove some of the clichés."[24]

Hemingway might have added that any publicity calling attention to his political position in the Thirties would also raise questions about his present political position in regard to the Batista government. Quickly, Ernest, Mary, and Gregorio took the *Pilar* far out into the Gulf Stream, where the men tore open bunks to take out "heavy rifles, sawed-off shot guns, hand grenades and canisters and belts of ammunition for automatic rifles" and threw the arsenal overboard.[25] Had the government discovered the cache, Hemingway would have been hard-pressed to explain their presence. Immediately after the *Times* stories, Ernest contacted old Ketchum friends, Lloyd and Tillie Arnold, asking them to find a suitable place to rent for the winter. On August 25, they told him the large and well-appointed Heiss house could be rented for $175 a month, to which Hemingway immediately agreed.[26] What may have appeared an overreaction to someone on the mainland, Hemingway's concern for the safety of himself and Mary was well grounded in a lifetime of observing how personal grudges had a way of killing old enemies once revolution set everyone free from the law. He may have been a great friend of the Cuban people, but in the dark of night he was just another rich Americano who was exploiting the Cuban poor. As he explained to Patrick, he was not being unduly frightened, not when one saw the kinds of murder going on all around him. It was not going to get any better soon. Batista would fall, and the new rulers would do some more killing to even things out. He was ready to move out of Cuba, for the rebel government that seemed inevitable would shut down the freedom of the coast to boats like the *Pilar*.[27]

Ernest and Mary spent most of September, when not in bed with bad colds, arranging matters at the Finca so that it would function smoothly while they were in Idaho. First, Mary flew to Chicago to visit friends; then, Ernest picked up Toby Bruce in Key West to be his driver, and on October 6 began the long cross-country drive, meeting Mary and continuing north and westward across the plains to Yellowstone and over to Ketchum by October 15. There they would winter while Ernest hoped to finish both the Paris book and the Eden book, which was already at 160,000 words. Then they would go to Spain in May for the San Isidro *corrida*, remaining there all summer. In the fall they might go on to Africa now that the Suez Canal was reopened. That was the plan as the fall hunting season opened with birds plentiful and flying strong in the dry wind.[28]

In Ketchum, Alfred Rice's latest bad news on income taxes caught up with the Hemingways. With $170,000 income from his published writing and another $15,000 from stock market investments, minus $31,200 for business expenses and personal deductions, Hemingway was left with $153,800 taxable in the 81 percent bracket. The bottom line was a 1958 tax bill of $95,000. After his quarterly installment in January 1959, Ernest would still owe $25,000 on April 15.[29] With almost $90,000 in his New York checking account, Ernest was able to pay his taxes without much pain, and he always insisted that Rice never cut corners when it came to the government. His attitude was partially patriotic, but it was also his residual antipathy for any situation that would take him before the law. But in the Idaho sunshine, Ernest seemed unfazed by his tax bill or anything else. Soon Mary was reporting to Hotchner that Ernest was back into his regular routine, his weight "down to 205, pressure okay, drinking with caution," and back to writing in the mornings and shooting in the afternoons. She urged Hotchner to join them, saying there was plenty of room in the huge house.[30] The Heiss log cabin, located within a stone's throw of Christiania's Bar and Restaurant, became their command post for the fall hunting season.

Those who knew Ernest from his earlier years in Ketchum were disturbed to find him appearing more aged than he actually was, his beard white, his speech slower. "When he came back after [those accidents]," Bud Purdy found him changed. "He was really whacked on the head on that one airplane wreck. I think that's pretty much what did it. He wasn't as sharp after that, I don't think."[31] Locals like Taylor Williams, the Purdys, Don Anderson, Forrest "Duke" MacMullen, Dr. George Saviers, and Don Atkinson formed a Ketchum version of the "summer people" Ernest once gathered around himself at Walloon Lake after the first war, or at Pamplona for the bullfights or skiing at Schruns in the 1920s, or fishing in Key West in the 1930s. Hunters all, they enjoyed the bird season in the pheasant fields around Dietrich and Gooding, along Silver Creek and the irrigation canals where the ducks gathered.

In the Heiss garage, Ernest hung ducks, snipe, and pheasant to age, checking them each day, sniffing for the ripeness he favored. Don Anderson preferred his fresh from the fields, but Hemingway kept his hung by their heads until they were almost ready to pull loose on their own. There he also kept and fed Mr. Owl. Forrest MacMullen explained how the predator came to be there:

> we were hunting, and we'd spooked some birds, and had knocked one down, and the owl went for the bird, and Papa winged it. And he felt bad right after that, he says "I shouldn't have shot that owl." And that's when we picked the owl up, and took it back up to Ket-

chum, put it in the garage you know, with the firewood. And we used to maybe get a road-killed rabbit that was fairly fresh and we'd take them up, and we even on occasions would sit under a tree down in Silver Creek area and shoot blackbirds out of the trees. So it was the case that there were times when we were just out shooting blackbirds for Mr. Owl.[32]

On Fridays the Ketchum "family" would gather in the Hemingways' front room to watch the Friday-night fights on television. There was always food, wine, and plenty of analysis. One evening, Bud Purdy remembered,

We were having a party up at his place for Friday Night Fights— God, he just loved to see those, hear 'em or see 'em on television. And I was, you know, throwing my arms around, he had his granny glasses sitting on the mantle, God I'm knocking 'em on the floor—bam! and broke 'em. Now you'd think that'd make a guy unhappy—"Oh! Never mind, that won't hurt a damn thing," he says. He must have had another pair, I don't know, but anyway I broke his glasses, and that didn't get him excited at all. He was very—I know with us he was always—God he just treated us like royalty.

In public places that winter season, it was not like the old days in Ketchum when Ernest could go about his life unimpeded by strangers seeking his handshake, autograph, or a photo standing beside him. Mary protected him as much as she was able. Ruth Purdy remembered those nights when they would eat lamb shanks together at the Christiania,

Mary would have him in the back, away from the general public, and then she would sit on the edge. They usually put us in that round corner over there in the Christiania, and Bud and I would sit here, and then Papa next to me, and then Mary on the outside so that when people came up, they—she could fend them off. But he was always so generous with his autographs and having pictures taken with him. So if it was possible, Mary would try to protect him, because people, you know, they don't think, and they would take so much of his time when he wanted to be enjoying his lunch or his dinner.[33]

No longer were Ernest and Mary habitués of the Sun Valley Lodge, for now they were more reclusive, sticking with those hunters with whom Ernest felt secure. Mornings he was writing either on his Paris memoir or on David Bourne's fictive life at Grau du Roi. Until the late January snows closed out the bird hunting, there were afternoons in the fields and along the watercourses. With a picnic lunch set out on the tailgate of the station wagon, a fire built to cook and warm, jokes to be told, the air clean, and the sky a brilliant blue, it was the old life recovered. In the field, Ernest seldom took the first shot, preferring to shoot backup, but when he shot, he seldom missed. Before, during, or after shooting, he was always careful, enforcing if necessary the unwritten rules of the shotgun: never approach the car with the breech closed; never point the barrel at anyone; cross a fence with great care, first placing the shotgun against the fence post. And never go into the fields twice with the same fool. As Forrest MacMullen recalled, "One time we were in the stock rack on this pickup at Bud Purdy's place, and this fellow was standing next to Papa, and Papa wasn't looking at him, and the fellow pulled the gun up and fired right next to Papa's ear, and Papa went 'woof,' and I saw the look in Papa's eyes, and that old boy never went out with us again after that incident."

There in Ketchum, where the winter snow did not fall until the new year, Ernest's life became quite simplified: early morning writing, lunches of cold duck or hot soup, bird-hunting afternoons once or twice a week, quiet evenings sometimes with friends, sometimes alone with Mary, and occasional suppers out with his doctor George Saviers and his wife, or with Bud and Ruth Purdy. There was almost no literary talk, for most of his hunting friends were not bent that way, saying right out that they had never read any of Ernest's work.

He liked them the better for it, for it was not his notoriety but his outdoors skills that drew them to him. Only Dr. Saviers admitted to being a Hemingway fan from his college days.

When asked whom Ernest admired, Forrest MacMullen quickly said "the mountain men."

> *He envied those fellas coming down when the traders would come up and trade with the trappers for their furs and for the furs they'd exchange whiskey, lead shot, powder, and a few items, maybe pots or pans or whatever, and they used to have foot races and shooting contests. I guess they used to get drunk and chase the Indian women up there. Papa mentioned that several, several times, as far as envying the mountain men the enjoyment they got out of life.*[34]

A close Cuban friend once said that Ernest was "a man for another era," born either too late or before his time, a man unwilling to conform to midcentury expectations.[35]

Chapter Thirty-Two

EXILES FROM EDEN

January 1959 to January 1960

F ROM KETCHUM, Ernest and Mary stayed up to date on the Cuban revolution's progress. At the very moment that wire services mistakenly reported the Castro rebels' defeat, Batista and his close associates were leaving the country by plane for the safety of the Dominican Republic, taking with them as much of the Cuban treasury as possible. In Havana nightclubs and casinos, tourists celebrating New Year's Eve were hustled back to their cruise ships in the harbor. The next morning in Ketchum, with newspapers hounding Ernest for a statement, he told them: "I believe in the historical necessity for the Cuban revolution, and I believe in its long range aims. I do not wish to discuss personalities or day to day problems." That afternoon, he enlarged his statement for the *New York Times*, adding that he was "delighted" with the revolution's progress. As soon as he hung up, Mary urged him to modify his statement, reminding him that he had no idea what was happening in Havana. Firing squads might be already at bloody work. Reluctantly, he called the *Times* back to change "delighted" to "hopeful." More privately, Ernest admitted that Castro's problem was not the departed Batista regime but the deeply entrenched American interests whose money bought them sweet deals in the past and would be difficult to displace. Castro, he said, was facing enormous problems.[1]

On January 3, snow finally came to Ketchum, piling up two feet over the next four days and marking the end of the long hunting season. Toward the end of January, Bud Purdy invited the seasoned hunters out to his ranch on Silver Creek for the annual magpie shoot, marking the absolute end of field activity until the following autumn. In the Whicher house where they had moved before Christmas, Hemingway settled in to write steadily on *The Garden of Eden*. Cut off from his research library at the Finca, he ordered through the Scribner Book Store an expensive copy of *Records of Big Game Hunting, 1892* to go along with his second copy of *The Wanderings of an Elephant Hunter*. In Hemingway's novel, David Bourne's recollection of his father's elephant hunt was grounded in the accurate details that were Hemingway's trademark.

In February, his semiannual royalty report from Scribner's showed an income of $21,295 on sales of 39,071 copies of his work. The only book apparently out of print was *Across the River and into the Trees*; his best seller continued to be *The Old Man and the Sea*—15,585 copies. Although these figures did not reflect the considerable income from foreign translations and television adaptations, Hemingway's six-month income from Scribner's alone was slightly more than the $20,000 annual median family income of the top 5 percent of the nation. Hemingway usually had more money in his special tax account than 99 percent of the nation made in a year. Had he left his foreign income in the country of origin, paying local taxes on it, his income after all taxes would have exceeded $100,000 a year. In a nation where only 29,000 tax returns listed "author" as profession and probably only 5 percent of those were able to live on their income, Hemingway's financial position was substantial, not even counting his almost $100,000 worth of blue chip stocks, his property in Key West, Cuba, a lot in Bimini, and four newly purchased lots in Ketchum. For the young, experimental writer of those early Paris days who made a fashion statement out of his relative poverty, Ernest Hemingway had come a long way from the cold-water flat above the lumber yard on rue Notre-Dame-des-Champs. Now all but finished was his wry, nostalgic Paris memoir, remembering himself even poorer than he ever was.[2]

That winter in Ketchum, Ernest worked steadily on the complex relationships between artists and women in *The Garden of Eden*. His fictional writer David Bourne was involved in sexual experiments with his wife Catherine and her newfound friend, Marita—a story Ernest did not think publishable in his lifetime. However, on his night table lay a newly minted copy of Vladimir Nabokov's *Lolita,* in which Humbert Humbert's fascination with his prepubescent step-daughter was more sexually outrageous than anything Ernest's triad did in the dark.[3] Working as he did in bursts, the manuscript of *Garden* was now close to ten years in its making. Approaching its final length—over two thousand pages—the draft needed to be revised for consistency just as his African novel did.[4] When younger, it was one book at a time: write, revise, and publish. These later books were being written under far different circumstances. Afterward, many would say that because he left them unfinished, he was no longer able to make the revisions they needed. But to make that judgment one must ignore the talent and diversity at work in *The Old Man and the Sea, Across the River*, and the posthumous *A Moveable Feast*. One must also ignore the massive revisions he made to the Bimini novel, and completely disregard the possibility that these "unfinished" novels were linked in ways that made their endings interdependent. Under no financial pressure to bring any of these books to completion, he always imagined there would be time to finish them. They were to be his legacy, his most complex undertaking. It was like working a crossword puzzle in three dimensions. All he needed was time, which, unfortunately, was no longer on his side. It did not take a medical degree for him to see the truth in the mirror as he carefully combed his hair forward to cover his balding head.

On February 18, when Hemingway thought he had the conclusion of *Garden* in sight, his concentration was shattered by the death of Taylor Williams, his oldest Ketchum friend from the early days of

Sun Valley. Having recuperated from a cerebral hemorrhage suffered the previous spring, the Colonel, as Ernest fondly called Williams, died suddenly when the wall of his stomach opened, flooding his lungs. Taking Taylor's death particularly hard, Ernest was one of the pall bearers at the funeral. Mary, equally distressed, wrote to Charlie Sweeny, himself recovering from a recent stroke, that she was depressed "with this fucking business of growing old." It was so easy when they were young to be courageous, but with age "the exercise of courage narrows down, becomes less fun, and so it's harder . . . what a bloody bore . . . when you begin to wear out. . . . Papa once said to me that he had never given his body any quarter, and I think that's the way to do it."[5] At fifty, with all of Ernest's friends going under, Mary was painfully aware that her husband and his old world were rapidly aging.

By the end of February, Ernest and Mary were packing up to return to Cuba, but with every intention of establishing a place of their own in Ketchum. Despite tourist traffic, there was easy access to diverse bird hunting, and Ernest found it a good place to write. Mary was less enthusiastic about the isolation of Ketchum, where interesting friends were few and cultural activities minimal, but what Ernest wanted she wanted. While she was making floor plans to build a house on their four-lot block, Ernest became interested in Dan Topping's hilltop home, which was on the market for $50,000. On seventeen acres with Big Wood River running below it, the gray, concrete exterior executed in the fashion of the Sun Valley Lodge resembled a fortress. On March 16, without having reached a decision, they left Ketchum with Ed Hotchner, driving south to Las Vegas and the next day to Phoenix. There in a motel room, they watched the second half of Hotchner's television adaptation of *For Whom the Bell Tolls*. It was a short drive the following day to Tucson, Arizona, to visit the seventy-four-year-old painter and old friend, Waldo Peirce. Then east past the O/bar/O ranch in southern New Mexico to follow the Rio Grande down to the Gulf, before bearing east to New Orleans. There Hotchner left them to complete the 4,000-mile drive on their own to Key West. On March 29, they flew into Havana to find the revolution a true socialist uprising, the kind Ernest once hoped for during the Spanish Civil War.[6]

But he also knew that revolutions had a way of turning out badly in the long run. It still might be best to have a safe haven in which to wait things out. Almost as soon as he got back to Cuba, Ernest put a $50,000 check in the mail to buy Topping's Ketchum house outright.[7] Home at the Finca for less than a month, Ernest and Mary labored over unanswered mail, outstanding bills, necessary repairs, and contingency plans for their household while they went to Spain for the summer *corridas*. One of the first new letters to arrive came from Charlie Scribner, Jr., who wanted to tap into the college trade market with a new collection of Hemingway short stories. He was confident that such an anthology would be quite profitable, even more so if Ernest would do short introductions to each story: "a short summary of the circumstances under which it was written . . . [or] a word or two about a character, or how you feel about the story." Ernest responded immediately asking about length and due dates. Scribner suggested 2,500 words minimum, maximum as many words as Ernest cared to write.[8] Feeling that he was in époque mode, Ernest agreed to write the essay. During two manic periods of writing—1947 to 1950, and 1955 to 1958—he published two novels and laid aside four other books all but finished. In his Cuban safety deposit box he had stored the three-part book which would become *Islands in the Stream* and the 200,000 words written on the African novel, *True at First Light*. With him at the Finca he had forty-two chapters of *The Garden of Eden* ready to photostat for safekeeping, and the all but finished Paris memoir, *A Moveable Feast*. The plan was to publish the Paris memoir in 1960; the following year, Scribner would publish a new edition of *Death in the Afternoon* with a lengthy appendix of material Hemingway would gather the coming summer of 1959.[9]

What was less apparent to him and those around him was the emotional pattern of the last twenty years: periods of intensive writing followed by fallow, emotionally depressed periods during which his behavior became erratic and increasingly paranoid. Each trip down his emotional roller coaster took him deeper into his private demons. Each time down, it was more difficult to climb back up. But each time he recovered, his writing exploded. In January 1959, he was peaking from such a productive period. The next thirty months was the dark trip down, this time into newfound depths. The various daily medications that he took for his blood pressure, nerves, liver, insomnia, eyesight, and fatigue were already working against each other, particularly when he was drinking. For ten years he had been taking weekly doses of Oreton-M, a synthetic testosterone that "stimulates the development of male sexual characteristics . . . both the physical and mental status are improved."[10] Usually prescribed for late-developing children, impotence, and aging males during their climacteric, the effects of long-term Oreton usage were not established. Nor was it known what effects Oreton might have when taken with drugs like Serpasil (to relieve anxiety, tension, and insomnia), Doriden (to tranquilize), Ritalin (to stimulate the central nervous system), Eucanil, Seconal (to get to sleep), massive doses of vitamins A and B, and other drugs for an alcohol-damaged liver. Nor was it known what effect alcohol might have on this pharmacological stew, but when Hemingway returned to Spain for the summer his daily wine consumption would be an acid test.

While Ernest kept as invisible as possible at the Finca, the Castro revolution was rapidly transforming the political face of Cuba. Batista officials were under arrest; trials of Batista soldiers ended with public executions, which enflamed the American press, the same press that had largely ignored the violence that characterized the Batista years. In early April, Castro announced that he would visit the United States as a "truth operation," an attempt to quell rumors, answer questions, and refute false claims about his government. As soon as Hemingway heard of Castro's plan, he asked José Luis Herrera, a strong Castro supporter, to set up a meeting between the writer and the revolutionary. As Herrera remembered it,

> Ernest insisted that a meeting with Castro be set up when he learned that Castro was going to New York at the head of the Cuban delegation to the United Nations. He wanted Castro to

be briefed on American politicians and the idiosyncrasies of the American people. Castro assigned Vazquez Candela, assistant editor of the newspaper Revolution, *to go to Hemingway's house. Late at night at Vigia, Ernest opened the door with a pistol in his pocket.*[11]

Unarmed, Vazquez arrived with serious misgivings that the trip was worth making, but after two hours conversation with Ernest, he changed his mind. Sitting in the living room, sipping an Italian white wine, with Bach and Ravel playing softly on the Capehart, Ernest put Vazquez at his ease. The journalist was amazed that Hemingway was concerned that Fidel be warned of the traps he would face with the press and others. Hemingway spoke from his briefing notes, which included information of the biases of various journalists and their publications. He warned that Fidel would be heckled viciously by some organizations, heckled by college students to see how he would react. At all costs, he must not become angry, lose his temper, or make threats. He must expect trick questions from his enemies on *Time* magazine and the *Miami Herald*. He must have direct answers on the influence of communism in the new Cuba. If he could promise to oppose communism, he could have anything he wanted from America. But the ongoing executions must be explained, and the general calmness in Havana and across the country should be emphasized. When Vazquez parted, Hemingway asked that he tell his comrades that Ernest strongly supported the actions of the revolution. In July, when Castro appeared on *This Is Your Life* on TV, he was asked to explain the executions taking place in Cuba. He said, "Let me tell you what Hemingway thinks about that: 'The executions in Cuba are a necessary phenomena. The military criminals who were executed by the revolutionary government received what they deserved.'"[12]

On April 22, Ernest and Mary stowed their considerable luggage on board the *Constitution* bound for Algeciras, Spain, settled into their stateroom, and located the first-class bar. A quick, uneventful passage set them down on the Spanish dock, where their host, Bill Davis, with the practiced eye of a man who collected celebrities, met them. Their luggage was piled on top of a rented pink Ford for the drive to Málaga, just beyond which lay the Davis domain, the doubly gated property called La Consula. Four years later, when the photographer Ben Sonnenberg visited with Bill and Annie Davis, he felt that he was living in a more expensive version of Sara and Gerald Murphy's Villa America at Antibes during the Twenties. At La Consula, the great, the wealthy, the talented, and the famous gathered under its arcades and around its glittering, sixty-foot swimming pool to be entertained, fêted, and flattered by Bill Davis, who "wore blue deck shoes and white duck trousers and that kind of short-sleeved [polo] shirt. . . . He was bald and tall and built like an athlete . . . his mother's family had been the model for the Ambersons in Booth Tarkington's novel. . . . Bill had an obsessive interest in the very rich and their 'arrangements.'"[13] Exactly why the Hemingways were staying as houseguests at Consula was never completely clear to Mary— something about Bill being an old friend with great *afficion* for the *corrida*. Although Ernest would find plenty of ways to spend money that summer, Bill Davis was providing more largesse than either Ernest or Mary had experienced from previous hosts.

As soon as Ernest was moved into his second-floor room, he began working on the introduction to his short stories promised to Scribner's by June 1. As with so much that Hemingway wrote, this essay revealed more about his state of mind than it did about its purported subject: the art of his short story. Written in a voice hardened and condescending, the commentary, whose audience was to be high school and college students, was filled with failed humor, bewildering slang, and gratuitous comments on fellow writers. Belittling the goal of a long life, he advised his reader, "I cannot say fie upon it, since I have never fie-ed on anything yet. Shuck it off, Jack. Don't fie on it. . . . Do I hear a request for ballroom bananas? I do? Gentlemen, we have them for you in bunches." As for the well-made short story in which a gun hung on the wall early in the story must reappear later in some important way, he advised, "With a good enough writer, the chances are some jerk just hung it there to look at it. Gentlemen, you can't be sure. Maybe he was queer for guns, or maybe an interior decorator put it there. Or both."[14] That Hemingway actually thought such offhand comments were appropriate for his audience seems to indicate that either his head or his heart was not in the project. But there is a disturbing tone to his slangy language that harkens back to letters and drafts written in his black-ass period after returning from the European War.

When Mary typed the first draft of the essay, she was "dismayed" by what seemed to her to be "tendentious, truculent and smug . . . [containing] brutal, irrelevant references to a friend of ours." In a note to Ernest, she pointed out passages that needed to be cut, advising him that "This is not like you." Ernest bristled. He cut out the part about their "friend," but left in a long aside on Faulkner's small talent, which was another ominous sign.[15] Whenever he dug up his old grievance with Faulkner, he was usually on the dark side of his emotional curve. Faulkner, he claimed, was always making disparaging remarks about him but maybe that was just the "sauce" talking. That was Faulkner's problem: he drank too much and wrote when he was drunk. That and he talked too much. A writer, said Ernest while doing the same, should never talk too much.

On May 12, Ernest put aside the draft essay to pack up for the trip to Madrid, where Antonio Ordóñez was on the cartel for the San Isidro feria, the beginning of a long and bloody summer. Before leaving Consula, Ernest wrote George Saviers in Ketchum, insisting that he and his wife join Ernest's band of *corrida* gypsies at the Pamplona feria in July.[16] A similar invitation would be sent to Hotchner as a familiar pattern emerged: Ernest assembling a cadre of "summer people" to witness, carouse, and be instructed. The season's focus was the developing competition between Luis Miguel Dominguín, who was returning to the *corrida* from his early retirement, and his brother-in-law, Antonio Ordóñez, reputed to be the best matador in many years and also the son of Cayetano Ordóñez, who in 1925 fought as Niño de la Palma and became the fictional Pedro Romero in *The Sun Also Rises*. Not only was Antonio married to Carmen Dominguín, but both he and Luis were managed by Luis's two brothers. As Hemingway would note, "It looked very hard on family life and very good for bullfighting. It also looked very dangerous."[17] What Ernest did not anticipate was how hard the summer would be on him, his wife, and their marriage.

In the Twenties and early Thirties when Ernest and his wife (first Hadley, then Pauline) followed the *corridas* across Spain, they were not compelled to attend them all. After Pamplona and Valencia there was time to rest up for Madrid. This summer they were beginning on May 30 and continuing to late August, following Antonio back and forth across the wide expanse of Spain. With every *corrida* Hemingway became more involved with Antonio, whom he would watch from front-row seats or down in the narrow *callejon* between the *barrera* and the seats. He had no need for tickets for he came and went as part of Antonio's *cuadrilla*—his picadors, banderillos, personal surgeon, and assorted handlers— "our outfit," Ernest called it, as if he were back in the military. From Cordoba to Seville in time to eat before watching the pics mutilate the bulls, Mary sick with fever, Ernest anxious. The next morning on the road to Madrid for a late lunch and the next afternoon out to Aranjuez.

Sitting with Bill Davis and Ernest, their wives having returned to La Consula, was John Crosby for the *New York Herald Tribune*. On his second bull, Antonio performed at a level seldom seen. Crosby wrote:

> *The lines of the passes became very simple, very slow. Just as a good painter eliminates and eliminates and eliminates, so a classic matador scorns the rococo trimmings. . . . Cape, man and bull blend into a single composition that hangs there in the air and imprints itself on the retina. . . . This was one of the moments that the true aficionado lives for, suffering through countless bad fights.*

Then, suddenly, backing up on rough ground, making a back-to-the-bull pass, Antonio slipped, the cape moved aside, the bull caught him quickly with his horn, deep into his left buttock. Just as quickly the other matadors were in the ring, taking the bull away from the bleeding Ordóñez, now arguing with his handlers who wanted him to leave the ring. Refusing to do so, Antonio picked up his cape and painfully returned to his work.

> *The crowd was hushed, respectful. To square his bull, Ordóñez made a slow pass, agonizingly slow. The bull charged, wheeled, and was still . . . Ordóñez sighted down his sword and with his ebbing strength went in over the horn. It was a marvelously clean and beautiful kill and, as his banderilleros carried him from the ring to the waiting ambulance . . . he was awarded both ears and the tail of the brave bull.*[18]

In the Madrid hospital Antonio was repaired by skilled surgeons, and there he got the only kind of rest he would find that dangerous summer. Ernest and Bill Davis returned to La Consula to restore their own depleted energies.

In his writing room, Ernest finished and mailed his preface for the short stories, finished a short story "Black Ass at the Crossroads," began writing up his notes on the bullfights, and answered mail. Hotchner was working out a four-story deal with CBS and their Buick sponsors, which came together as Hemingway had specified. There would be four live shows bringing the H&H Corporation set up by Hotchner and Hemingway a total of $240,000 for basic rights and Hotchner's adaptations.[19] In New York, Charles Scribner, Jr., was trying his diplomatic best to draft his response to Ernest's preface, which was clearly inappropriate for almost any audience. He agreed with Ernest's list of stories to be included, but wanted to do some judicious editing of the preface. "You did not want to sound pompous," Scribner wrote, "and hit upon a kind of jocular informality. But I am afraid that, insofar as readers will not be expecting this, they may misinterpret it as condescension."[20] After digesting Scribner's response and weighing it in the same basket with Mary's less than enthusiastic critique, Ernest sent

Scribner a brusque telegram to stop not only the preface but the entire short story project. It was, he said, a mistake to try to do three things at once. He would keep his attention totally focused on the *corrida*.[21] It was the first time that anyone at Scribner's had told him a piece of his writing was unpublishable.

On June 27, four weeks after his wounding, Antonio was back in his "suit of lights," entering the bull ring at Zaragoza with Luis Miguel Domínguín beside him, their first meeting in the summerlong, *mano-a-mano* competition, in which the two matadors would each face three bulls apiece in the same afternoon. The pattern would become so ingrained that Ernest could and did follow it in his sleep: drive, eat, dress, watch, eat again if nothing went wrong, sleep briefly to drive on the next morning. Some days there would be no time for sleep, and they would drive through the night: Zaragoza, Alicante, Barcelona, Burgos. By the time they reached Pamplona for the San Fermín feria, the *mano a mano* had caught the attention of American periodicals. *Sports Illustrated* wanted to publish Ernest's take on Antonio and Luis Miguel in the August feria at Málaga. Ernest wired back that he could not because the material would become part of his new edition of *Death in the Afternoon*.[22]

The San Fermín feria brought together in Pamplona Ernest's entire entourage: Mary, Bill and Annie Davis, George and Pat Saviers from Ketchum, Antonio who was not on the feria cartel, and Ed Hotchner. It was the turning point in Mary's summer, which to that moment had been relatively unruffled except for her nagging colds. "Pamplona," Ernest wrote afterward, "is no place to bring your wife."

It is a man's fiesta and women at it make trouble, never intentionally, of course, but they nearly always make or have trouble . . . if she can drink wine all day and all night and dance with any groups of strangers who invite her, if she does not mind things being spilled on her, if she adores continual noise and music and loves fireworks, especially those that fall close to her or burn her clothes . . . if she doesn't catch cold when she is rained on and appreciates dust, likes disorder and irregular meals and never needs to sleep and still keeps neat and clean without running water; then bring her. You'll probably lose her to a better man than you.[23]

He could have added that an inattentive husband might well contribute to his wife's discomfort, for in Pamplona, Ernest's attention was once more distracted by an attractive young woman, Valerie Danby-Smith, who soon was hired on as his secretary. As Mary could not fail to note, her husband and the eighteen-year-old Irish girl with the dark hair and lovely smile became inseparable. In almost any photograph of Ernest taken during Pamplona, Valerie is within reach. She was his ideal student, eager to learn about Spain, *corridas, toreros,* wine, and of course writing. Soon Ernest was dictating his business letters for her to type, while largely ignoring Mary, who was limping about on a painfully broken toe. To Mary this was now familiar behavior, reminding her of Ernest's infatuation with Adriana ten years earlier.

When the Hemingway *cuadrilla* returned to La Consula, Ernest opened Alfred Rice's letter, which began, "I have shockingly bad news for you." Because Rice neglected to report $45,000 on Hemingway's 1957 tax return, he now explained that his mistake, for which he was dreadfully sorry, was going to cost Ernest perhaps as much as $28,000 in back taxes. A month later he recalculated his error to the tune of another $20,000, for a total of $48,000 due on his $45,000 error. "Because it is entirely my neglect," Rice wrote, "I will pay the interest instead of you on the additional tax."[24] Coming as it did when Ernest was emotionally and physically stressed, this new incompetence left him furious. When Rice insisted that he was due 10 percent of all movie and television income because he read the contracts for Hemingway, Ernest redressed him, making it clear to his attorney that he was becoming an unaffordable liability who should not push his luck. Yet, as always to Rice, he signed the letter "Ernie," a form of his name he detested, permitting no one else to use it but his father, dead these thirty years.[25]

For July 21 at La Consula, Mary arranged an elaborate sixtieth birthday party for Ernest, a fête richer than any of his previous birthdays. It began at 10:00 p.m. and continued on through the night, into the following morning, and through part of the day. Invitees included Antonio and Carmen, the Saviers, Hotchner, Valerie, Buck Lanham, David and Evangeline Bruce, Gianfranco Ivancich and his wife, the Maharajah of Cooch-Behar, assorted Spaniards, roving guitars, and a small orchestra. The forty invited guests were supplemented by numerous gate-crashers. Six cases of rosé wine, four cases of champagne, and vast amounts of whiskey and gin washed down the several baked hams, casseroles of codfish and shrimp, and fifty pounds of Chinese sweet-and-sour turkey. The three-tiered cake had ninety candles: sixty for Ernest and thirty for Carmen Ordóñez, whose birthday was also on the twenty-first. After presents and cake came thirty minutes of fireworks, which set a palm tree aflame, bringing out the local fire brigade. At six-thirty the next morning the orchestra was still playing, and guests were drinking Bloody Marys around the pool.[26]

What should have been a triumph for Mary became another intolerable performance by Ernest, who either ignored her completely while keeping arm-in-arm with Valerie, or spoke to her in an abusive, sarcastic manner. He had done this before during depressed periods: treating Mary as if he wished her out of his life. Buck Lanham could not understand why Mary put up with it, or why Ernest did it. Buck took his old friend to task over his cruel behavior, but Hemingway ignored him, later insulting Lanham to the point that their relationship was never the same. Too many late nights, too much wine for too many days, too much adulation and not enough solitude—whatever the cause, Ernest was going down into his depressed persona, a man Mary knew from past experience, but a man very like a stranger.

The summer *corridas* now seemed endless to Mary. After Luis Miguel's goring at Valencia at the end of July, she stayed more and more at La Consula with Annie Davis, leaving the men to their own devices. The two matadors were alternately wounded, hurt, or gored time and again during the bloodiest *corrida* season in many years. No one could remember when there had been so much wind blowing the capes, exposing the bodies of the matadors to the horns. When

Sports Illustrated made Ernest a new offer for a personal essay on the *mano a mano*, he said the price was $30,000 for four to five thousand words, but only if one of the matadors was killed in the ring or permanently disabled, which by August he fully expected to happen.[27] With Luis Miguel and Antonio taking more and more risks, there was excitement and tension every time they entered the ring. Something tragic or magnificent or both might happen that day.

At Málaga on August 14, when the wind calmed and the bulls were each a dream of a bull, the magic became almost unbearable. Eric Sevareid was there, sitting close to Bill Davis and Ernest, who said, "It was the greatest bullfight I have ever seen." It was as if the two matadors were writing a picture-perfect textbook on their art form. Each pass was poetry, each bull was brave, each matador at the height of his powers. Every sword thrust was perfect. Sevareid wrote:

> *Luis Miguel Dominguín is the world's second-greatest bull fighter . . . when he was lifted like a willow wand on the horns of the fifth bull for what seemed an eternity, classic Greek tragedy seemed to have reached its climax. . . . A great bullfighter like Dominguín is in command of the bull because he knows the bull. Ordóñez, the master, is in command of the bull because he is in command of himself. He knows himself. It is the difference between talent and genius, between what a great man can do for himself and [what] the gods can do for him with their touch.*[28]

Leaving Mary behind at La Consula, Ernest, Antonio, and his crew flew the length of Spain in an aging DC-3 for the next day's *corrida* in Bayonne.

They were joined there by Slim Hayward and Lauren Bacall, who complained that Ernest did not understand how great Luis Miguel truly was in the bull ring.[29] By this time it was more than obvious that Hemingway was deeply committed to Antonio in the competition, a commitment that rankled Luis Miguel. Ernest's blatant favoritism toward the younger matador was not an ill-formed judgment.

Time and again, Antonio was outperforming Luis Miguel in ways so obvious that most of the knowledgeable critics would eventually agree with Hemingway that Ordóñez had triumphed in the *mano a mano*. However, Hemingway could have told a different story, a tale of loss, the sort of story that he often wrote when he was young: the aging professional choosing to go out on his feet, selecting his own terrain upon which to lose. But now that he was old enough to have fathered both men, his story was on the side of youth. Once he told Martha Gellhorn that no one he knew had ever recaptured lost youth, but that summer in Spain he forgot his own advice.

Back at La Consula, Mary festered, angry with Ernest's neglect, furious with his belittling the pain of her broken toe, and tired of his bragging and his camp followers. Earlier, when Ernest spent a long supper ignoring her for conversation with Lauren Bacall and Slim, Mary had interrupted the conversation to offer Bacall her two closed hands, asking her to choose one. Bacall pointed to Mary's left hand, which when she opened it revealed a bullet. "That is for anyone who moves in on my man," she said.[30] Throughout August and into September, Mary and Ernest saw little of each other, and when they did he always managed to say the wrong thing, followed by the usual epistolary apologies.

With a younger brother's flair for bad timing, Leicester Hemingway's letter caught up with Ernest in mid-September, announcing that for three years he had been working on a biography of Ernest. Now that he had a publisher, he needed Ernest's permission to reprint several letters used in the text. "You once told me you weren't going to do it [an autobiography]," Leicester wrote, "but that you hoped somebody who really knew you would do a book about you some day and maybe it would be me." Hemingway's response was quick: this book violated the agreement between them that neither would write about the other. Not until he read the entire manuscript would Ernest decide what he thought about its publication. Until then, he refused permission to publish any of his letters.[31]

With his own flair for equally bad timing, Ernest told Mary in mid-September that he had invited Antonio and Carmen to meet them in Cuba on November 1 and drive west with them to Ketchum. Mary was less than thrilled: guests coming into Finca Vigía where they had not been in residence for almost a year. They had no idea what shape the house was in, or to what degree the new Castro government was restricting travel. Ernest seemed unconcerned with whatever problems there might be. Mary, the realist, immediately made plans to return in advance of the royal party, leaving Ernest to his own ill temper, infected kidneys, and smart mouth. On September 20, she flew from Madrid to Paris, stopping briefly at the Ritz. Annie and Bill Davis were worried about her coolness, but Ernest made light of it. Besides each other, no one knew that Mary was once again threatening to leave him, despite the rather large ring Ernest gave her in Madrid, making her "feel like an extortionist." She made it clear to her husband that she was playing the housewife's role in Cuba and Ketchum only long enough to make the two houses presentable. Beyond that she was not certain, but her own welfare would dictate what she did. It was impossible, she told him, to write the letter about their personal relations. "Too clogged up with emotion and loneliness and heartbreak . . . all evidence, as I see it, shows that you have no further use for me in your life. I am therefore beginning to arrange my removal from it, and hope to establish a new life for myself."[32] She signed the letter with "love and devotion," adding a note hoping that there were good pictures in heaven for Bernard Berenson, recently dead.

Hemingway's immediate answer reminded her of his support when she was in trouble, reminded her of the pleasures they had enjoyed. Her letter had broken his heart, but she had written such letters before. Maybe there was some hope. As for himself, the letter could not have come at a worse time. His head was in bad shape. He was trying to write and her "Dear John" had ruined that for him, but he would write somehow because he was a professional. His neck was hurting him, and Rice now needed $51,000 to pay their back taxes. So she could see that she was not the only one in the family with difficulties. He did not want to hold her against her will, but she was going to have to tell him that she was leaving face to face, not in a letter. No middle-of-the-night surprises that she was leaving him.[33] Three days later, he wrote Mary another letter filled with news about Antonio and about problems with his own body, spirit, bankbook, and writing. He was, he said, deep in a "black ass," implying that his condition was a result of her previous letter. On October 27, Ernest received a telegram from Hotchner, to whom Mary had related her decision to leave Ernest. After listening to her side, Hotchner told Ernest not to worry, for Papa was still calling the shots.[34]

From Havana, Mary wrote a long letter detailing the situation in the country and at the Finca. Their friends were surviving in reduced circumstances. Some were optimistic that Americans could still operate in Cuba; others were not. There was very little American currency in circulation, she said, so Ernest should bring enough with him to ensure getting back out of the country. All their Finca staff were fine, but the house itself was in sad shape: almost every machine was either broken or malfunctioning. Their cars needed overhauls; the pool pump was broken (family of dead rats inside); pool filter tanks a mess; record player not working properly; kitchen stove barely cooking; and the *Pilar* needed extensive repairs and cleaning. Mary was replacing windowpanes in the *casita* broken by an explosion during the revolution, and she was attacking the insects eating up the library table. Her bedroom roof and the living-room ceiling were leaking once more. Despite these massive problems, she was not daunted: "I find it lovely being here at home again. . . . Fascinating and happy too, the atmosphere of Cuba . . . everybody so proud of the government's honesty, so proud . . . of their new home-building program, so proud of Fidel's tree-planting which is everywhere visible . . . I hope so very much they will not be disappointed."[35] In the same envelope Mary included a three-and-a-half-page, single-spaced typed letter headed "THIS IS THE PERSONAL LETTER," in which she enumerated with examples the several ways Ernest had mistreated her over the course of the summer, all of which reaffirmed her decision to leave him. She was no longer able to withstand his neglect, "disparagement, cruel and unjust abuse and criticism." When she was sick in Spain, he was never sympathetic; when she broke her toe at Pamplona, he did not take care of her.

> *Most hurtful of all . . . your compliments and attentions and inter-*
> *est and kisses for many girls and women, nothing for me. Noth-*
> *ing spontaneous towards me on your part, not even on the night*
> *of your birthday party . . . if I went to ask you a simple question*
> *. . . your face took on a look of irritation and impatience and you*
> *would say, "I haven't got time. I have to go shit now. I have to go*
> *swim now."*

In Pamplona, he "excoriated" her for days after she was unable to ease a night cramp in his leg. In Valencia, over a minor issue, he called her "the biggest liar I have ever known." No longer did he ask her politely to do anything; he always gave a direct order. "I will not submit," she said, "for the rest of my life to being ordered about." She yearned for "friendship, solidarity, and affection," none of which was he likely again to provide. Therefore, as soon as she repaired the Finca and stocked the new Ketchum house for the visit of Antonio and Carmen, Mary intended to move into a small New York apartment to restart her life as a journalist.[36] Ernest's response was a telegram thanking her for the work she was doing and disagreeing with her complaints and conclusions while respecting her right to hold them.[37] So long accustomed to waiting wives and adoring women, with Martha the one anomaly, Hemingway still did not get the message.

On October 27, Hemingway piled three gun cases, sixteen bags, one suitcase, and six cartridge bags on board the *Liberté* bound for New York. In the pigskin suitcase was packed a small box holding a $4,000 platinum and diamond pin for Mary. On his third day at sea, during which time he remained almost exclusively in his cabin, he wrote Annie Davis a black-ass letter filled with loneliness. He dreaded what awaited him at the Finca, where he would be lectured day and night about his numerous shortcomings, be told by Mary that he could no longer write, that his Paris memoir was worthless, that he was an egotistical, stupid son of a bitch. And he would take it all from her without saying a word, never complaining, trying to make everyone happy while paying the bills. It was as if Mary were trying to drive him to suicide, but her attempts, while well timed, had failed.[38] Whenever he wanted to emphasize his loneliness or trump an irritated wife, Hemingway was apt to threaten suicide, but this letter was different. In the same way that he blamed his mother for driving his father to suicide, he was now blaming Mary. The game was changing rapidly, moving on to dangerous ground. He had invoked the word "suicide" too often, embarrassing friends with detailed directions of how he would do it, taking satisfaction in their discomfort of his scenario. Now that his body was clearly failing, the specter of killing himself loomed larger.

Arriving in New York on November 1, Hemingway avoided most of his friends there, delivered the Paris memoir to Scribner's, and approved of Mary's newfound apartment before boarding the flight south with Antonio and Carmen Ordóñez. They landed at the Havana airport to a twelve-foot Saint's Day banner, music, flags, and photographers welcoming Ernest back to the new Cuba. Surrounded by reporters, Ernest said, "I am very happy to be here again because I consider myself a Cuban. I have not believed any of the reports against Cuba. I sympathize with the Cuban government and with all *our* difficulties [Hemingway's emphasis]." He told reporters, badgering him for a statement about U.S.-Cuban relations, that he considered himself a true Cuban. Then he kissed the hem of the Cuban flag too quickly for the photographers to capture the moment. When asked to repeat it, he refused, saying, "I kissed it with all my heart, not as an actor." Everyone applauded.[39]

In public, Ernest was his jovial self, glad to be home; in private, he and Mary continued their marital and martial games, this time more seriously than ever before. He was sicker than she knew; she was more scared than he knew. On November 8, Mary wrote Annie Davis a lighthearted letter, apparently glad to have Ernest home, but complaining of having to go to Ketchum in advance to prepare the house for visitors. On the same day, Ernest wrote Bill Davis that his relationship with Mary was as difficult as ever. While agreeing to play hostess until Antonio and Carmen left Ketchum, she was still planning to return to her New York apartment in January 1960. She was, Ernest wrote, determined not to let his writing interfere with her own plans to write. He was suffering her demands as cheerfully as possible, hoping to work himself into shape to finish the books in progress. He apologized for the black-ass letter written on board the *Liberté*, but, he claimed, it had been worse than the winter in Hürtgen, his usual absolute zero for black ass. If only Valerie were at the Finca, he might get his life and his letters under control.[40] But Valerie was not there, nor would she ever be the muse he sought. The muse, it seemed, had left no forwarding address.

As soon as she could, Mary with her Jamaican maid, Lola Richards, flew to Chicago en route to Ketchum, leaving Ernest to drive west with their visitors. Ernest, Antonio, Carmen, and Roberto Herrera crossed to Key West, where a new Buick station wagon was waiting for them, courtesy of his television sponsor and in return for a statement they might use in their advertising. The 4,000-mile drive ended at midnight, November 19, when the Buick pulled into Ketchum. The next morning Ernest was on the phone to Bud Purdy, setting up a duck hunt on Purdy's ranch. No sooner had Ernest talked to Bud than a phone call from Antonio's sister in Mexico cut the visit off before it began. Antonio explained that he and Carmen must leave immediately to help his sister.[41] Ernest was despondent. Realizing that he was behaving erratically, slipping in and out of moods too quickly, Lloyd and Tillie Arnold did their best to cheer him up. Don Anderson, Duke MacMullen, Lloyd, and Ernest began a friendly series of trap shoots off the backyard of the Hemingway house. On Thanksgiving Day, the men were throwing clay targets with a handtrap and Ernest was powdering them consistently over the barelimbed cottonwoods. On Friday nights, the same group would gather around Hemingway's television set to watch the boxing matches with Ernest making book on each fight. It was almost like old times.

Had it not been for Mary's intention to leave him, Ernest had much to be happy about. Everyone at Scribner's was excited about his Paris book: Harry Brague said that "the Paris stuff is the Hemingway that no one can ever imitate. It is superb throughout . . . there are some passages I like better than anything Hemingway ever wrote before."[42] Two days after Thanksgiving, Mary's plans were postponed. Crossing frozen terrain while hunting ducks with Ernest and George Saviers, she tripped and fell. Making sure that her loaded shotgun did not accidentally go off, Mary protected it but landed heavily on her left elbow, shattering it on the ice. As soon as they could drive her to the hospital, Saviers and a colleague began the complicated restoration of her seriously damaged elbow. After being released from the hospital, Mary remained in pain to which Ernest was unsympathetic, acting as if she had somehow done this on purpose to interfere with his writing.

By mid-December, Hemingway was moody and depressed, given to emotional outbursts. He objected to doing the grocery shopping even though he was the only one in the house who could drive. As the snow outside the house deepened, arguments and accusations flared up inside. Ernest kept notes; Mary wrote him letters. He said. She said. At two minutes after midnight, December 15, Mary wrote an in-house letter about Ernest's objection to helping her undress, his calling it "maid's work." Mary promised, with an edge to her voice, that she would never ask him to do that again.

> *Then you begged me not to make a fight before going to bed. I begged you please to go to bed. . . . Then you came back from your room and made three accusations. I had done this, you said, "to all your husbands."—It is false and you have No proof. Then you came and said, "You think, now I can get rid of him." False, and wholly false. Then you came and said, "You can only go to bed happy if you have made the fight and made somebody so miserable so they can't sleep all night." . . . Look, Lamb—if you want to get rid of me, please just say so calmly and without all the insinuations and assaults and cruelties. Just say so. But please, let us* NOT

go on with the Nightly false accusations and hurts. I love you. Yes I do.[43]

By the time Christmas had come and gone, Mary was becoming less defensive and more concerned about her husband's increasingly disturbed moods and fantasies, which could surface with the abruptness of turning on a light switch. Driving through Ketchum one cold, snow-blown night, Ernest became upset when he saw lights on in their local bank. "They" were in there checking on his accounts, he said. Tillie Arnold thought it was probably the cleaning women. "They're trying to catch us," Ernest replied. "They want to get something on us." Mary asked who "they" were. "The F.B.I.," he replied.[44]

Chapter Thirty-Three

THE BODY ELECTRIC

January 17, 1960, to July 2, 1961

AT TWO IN THE MORNING in Shoshone, their breaths blowing steam in the subfreezing air, Ernest, Mary, and their maid Lola boarded the Union Pacific's "City of Portland" on the first leg of their return to Cuba. They arrived in Havana by plane from Miami to find Finca Vigia like a refrigerator; without heat, usually unnecessary in Cuba, it was ill fortified against the norther that chilled the island. Ernest immediately returned to his ever-lengthening account of the previous summer's *mano a mano*, and Mary soon agreed that they should bring Val in from New York City to handle his mail and the piles of unfiled paper. By February 8, the young Irish girl was in residence at the Finca, her presence acting as a stimulus to Ernest's writing, which was soon progressing at an almost alarming rate. In less than four weeks he wrote 17,000 words on what was growing inexorably into a book, not the 30,000 essay contracted with *Life*.[1]

In New York, Scribner's was eager to publish the untitled Paris sketches, either in the fall of 1960 or the following spring. Charles Scribner, Jr., said, "The pieces are magically effective and it will make the year for us, whatever year they appear." He also urged Ernest to consider publishing one or more of the chapters in periodicals that were begging for them, sight unseen. Hemingway hedged: the book needed another month's work, which he could not afford to give it until the bullfight story was finished. However, the Ordóñez-Dominguín story, he told Scribner, would either be a long appendix for a new edition of *Death in the Afternoon*, or a separate volume.[2] There were those, Ernest wrote, who probably thought he had no book, that he was borrowing money like Scott Fitzgerald against empty paper, but Charlie knew the Paris book was real and ready to publish should anything happen to him. If Scribner was reading the letter carefully, he must have wondered at the outdated reference to Fitzgerald who surfaced whenever Ernest felt unappreciated. Had he been closer to the Finca, the Scribner owner might also have worried that Ernest was making references to the possibility of overwork killing a man, and that he was not sleeping more than four hours a night. These signs went unheeded at the time, but in retrospect would loom larger.

Money, time, deadlines, endings, movies, television—pressures were building. Functioning as the H&H Corporation, Hemingway and Hotchner were embarked on a lucrative venture that had no immediate end in sight. Although he worried about the deals Hotchner was making for television shows, movies, and the theater, Ernest had to do little but approve them. Hotch was already at work on their next Buick-sponsored production, an hour-long version of "The Snows of Kilimanjaro" with Robert Ryan cast as Harry the dying writer. "Snows" would be followed by "The Gambler, the Nun, and the Radio," fulfilling their four-show contract. Buick was so pleased with the impact of the Hemingway dramas that they immediately gave him another new car and asked for a second series for 1961–62 if Hotchner could guarantee happy endings to adaptations of *A Farewell to Arms*, *The Sun Also Rises*, *To Have and Have Not*, and "The Short Happy Life of Francis Macomber," ludicrous conditions that Hotchner rejected out of hand.[3] The H&H enterprise had an option on Frederick Burnham's *Scouting on Two Continents* as a source for a television series in which Gary Cooper expressed interest. Cooper also wanted to make a movie of Hemingway's short story "After the Storm," with Hotchner doing the film treatment. Ernest warned Hotchner not to get excited about the idea until someone put up hard money. He himself wanted no part in financing any movies or Hotchner's reader's theater collection of Hemingway material entitled *Scenes of Love and Death*. Ernest could easily afford his low-risk profile, for he was literally being swamped with offers of money. German television had recently bought the TV version of "The Killers" for $2,000. In all of these ventures, Ernest risked nothing, and Hotchner did the work: writing the film script adaptations, arguing with the sponsors over their desire to censor productions, and casting the scripts.[4]

With Mary writing an article on Carmen Ordóñez and Valerie tending to tedious correspondence, Ernest buried himself in the story of the two bullfighters, which by the end of February was over 30,000 words. Trapped in a chronological narrative, he found it difficult to leave out any of the *corridas*, many of which began to sound quite similar. He was also faced with the problem of how to end a story over which he had no control. Unless one of the *toreros* was killed or conceded the contest, there was no satisfactory conclusion, particularly when the *mano a mano* was now scheduled to continue into the 1960 season. On February 26, he asked Time/Life for another extension on his deadline, saying he had two thirds of the piece written. The *Life* editor, Ed Thompson, found no problem with the extension, which in turn Ernest could not meet. Thompson wired Hemingway to stop worrying about when the piece was finished, for they wanted it whenever it came. If it ran longer than 30,000 words, there would be extra money for Ernest.[5]

Life was a trade-off. In his early Paris years, Ernest saw clearly, drank hard, lived cheap, stayed up late, worked the next day, but could not sell a story. Then there were no pills to take, no worries about blood pressure, no failing liver or sick kidneys, no doctors poking and prodding. Now with every hand asking for his words, his name, or his presence, the money could not buy him sleep or provide a new liver. He was "in the money," all right, but the money could not save him or his friends. Neither fame nor fortune was going to cure

Gary Cooper's prostate cancer. At Massachusetts General, Ernest's friend was recuperating from radical prostectomy, tubes running into his body at his arm and out of his body below, "looking like some sort of still," Coop wrote, "making a low grade grape juice."[6]

All Ernest could do was write and not think about friends, or about Cuban politics growing steadily more threatening. At his writing platform, standing and typing, he was pounding out a prodigious number of words each day. Blood flowed, bulls died, matadors were rushed to emergency surgeons, wounds healed, the dangerous summer went on and on. Preoccupied in the Ciudad Real bull ring, Luis Miguel was losing the contest, but refused to admit it. What preoccupied Luis Miguel so?

"Death," I said. It was all right to say it in English if you said it low.
"Antonio carries it around for him in his pocket."[7]

That was, he knew, the way all true stories ended, and he had carried that knowledge with him for a long time now.

All that late winter and into the spring of 1960, the Finca was devoid of intrusions, except for a week's visit from George Saviers. By the first week in May the grounds became an explosion of color. Around the pool and house, verbena, bougainvillea, and cola de cameron were in bloom. Jacaranda blossoms floated in the pool, and the air was sweet with the scent of frangipani. In three and a half months Hemingway wrote 84,000 words describing one *corrida* after another.[8] When the weather warmed, he swam a half mile each day in the Finca pool, and fished infrequently. His weight fell to 198, the first time it was below 200 in many years. On Sunday afternoons, he, Val, René, Juan the chauffeur, and Pichilo the gardener attended the cockfights, sometimes fighting Hemingway cocks, sometimes not, but always betting on the bloody fray.[9]

In the Cuban capital and across the country, life was less idyllic. In Oriente province, the Movement of Revolutionary Recovery demanded free elections to turn the country away from communism.

These rebels against the Castro government were being tracked down by Fidel himself. On May Day, Castro stirred a crowd of 250,000 to a frenzy, charging that the United States was fomenting counterplots against him. He warned that Cuba must find a successor for him, for he might be "disappeared" by the northern aggressor. He had good cause for such suspicions. The U.S. Senate was funding a Voice of America radio station to broadcast into Cuba as if it were a nation occupied by the enemy, while the Congress gave President Eisenhower power to withhold $350 million in Cuban technical aid. There was talk of using the U.S. sugar quota money to reimburse displaced Cubans whose property was confiscated by the Castro government. On May 6, former President Harry Truman charged that Castro was a dictator, sowing the seeds for his own destruction. On May 7, Cuba resumed formal relations with Soviet Russia. It did not take a political scientist to see which way the winds were blowing.[10]

At the end of May, Ernest declared that the 100,000-word preliminary draft of the bullfight book was done. However, he was planning to return to Spain for more material on the *mano a mano*, which would extend the story to 150,000 words.[11] With anti-American slogans appearing on familiar walls, Mary urged Ernest to think first of moving as many of their valued possessions as possible off the island, but he refused to consider the idea. This was their home. In her biography, Mary said later, "For seven months I had been considering some manner by which, with the least trauma for each of us, I could retire from what seemed to me his new style of living. But I shelved the idea. He seemed to have so many grave problems confronting him that I could not increase them."[12] Not the least of these problems, which Mary never quite specified, was Hemingway's intake of alcohol, which had once again risen dramatically from the prescribed two glasses with supper. Their January to June liquor bill from Licores Manzarbeitia in Havana was $1,550.49 for eighteen bottles of liquor and fifty-five cases of wine during a period with almost no Finca visitors.[13] Hemingway was fighting with imaginary demons by night and sometimes by day, increasingly worried about money when there was no worry, increasingly questioning the loyalty of old friends. His old concerns about libel suits resurfaced; he warned Hotchner not to call the town Billings in the TV production of "The Gambler, the Nun, and the Radio," for there were people still alive from 1930 who might be offended.[14] He could, when necessary, put on a straight face for the world, keeping whatever was raging inside him under control, but when alone with Mary, he was becoming a stranger. Firmly believing that in his work was his deliverance, he pushed himself harder and harder, adding another 10,000 words to the bullfight book before turning back to the Paris book.[15] His pre-1946 depressions usually followed the completion of a book when he did not know what to write next. His post-1946 depressions were different. Because he was leaving work largely completed but not quite finished, one or more books were always begging for attention. As a result, he would move back and forth among them, even during his depressed periods, and unfinished work was always lurking at the back of his mind. As summer approached in Cuba, Ernest Hemingway was a man pursued, a writer unable to outrun his demons.

At the end of June, Ernest flew Hotchner in from New York to help edit the *mano-a-mano* story for the *Life* essay that was now promised at 40,000 words.[16] But whatever Hotchner suggested to eliminate, Ernest called vital to the narrative. Only with difficult discussion was Hotchner able to reduce the essay version to 70,000 words, or twice the length of *The Old Man and the Sea*. On July 6, after Hotchner left, Ernest reported to Charlie Scribner, Jr., that the book text now reached 120,000 words. Time/Life might not accept the essay, but the book version was a solid piece. First, he said, they should publish the Paris book, then the bullfight book. He had revised and arranged the order of the Paris sketches, but was too stale to add any more. He would try again later, but they already had enough for a book. His weight was down to 194; his eyes were better now with new glasses. The morning news, he said without specifics, was disturbing. Certain that his outgoing mail was being read by postal officials, Hemingway never mentioned Castro or what was happening in the country. But that morning, the Havana news and broadcasts from Florida announced that Castro was threatening to appropriate the property of American foreign nationals in retaliation for Eisenhower cutting off the Cuban sugar quota. Unnamed U.S. officials said they were worried about the safety of Americans in Cuba.[17]

By July 7, Valerie had typed up the bullfight book and Ernest had corrected it; Hotchner had come and gone. Hemingway was making plans to leave for Spain toward the end of the month, but Mary refused to go with him. She was not about to suffer through a summer like the last one. She and Val would wait in New York for Ernest to return. Valerie, on the other hand, wanted to go to Spain with Ernest, but Mary made it clear that was not an option. In fact, Mary was determined to place some limits on her husband's subsidizing the young Irish girl. Her in-house letter began:

> Honey—in the midst of all our other preoccupations, I feel we must think a bit about Valerie and what would be good for her ... I re-suggested to her the idea of taking some courses at Columbia this fall, to augment her education. . . . She was not interested. . . . In consideration of taking Val out to Ketchum this fall, perhaps you should include an estimate of how much use you will make of her as secretary, and the costs of equipping her for life out there and paying her room in town. . . . We must remember that . . . the people of her age are away at college in the fall and she would have little chance of companionship among her own age group.[18]

They certainly could not use Val as a cook and housekeeper, for it "was not at all her cup of tea." Val well understood the conflicted triangle in which she held down one precarious corner. As she wrote to Bill Davis, Mary, who ruled the roost, was intent on keeping her far away from Ernest, who was no longer making the crucial decisions. Resenting Mary's plan, Val wanted to be under no obligation to her, and said she would strike out on her own as soon as life with Mary became too uncomfortable.[19]

On July 25, Hemingway, Mary, and Val took the P&O ferry to Key

West, where the immigration officer remarked that Val's visitor's visa needed to be renewed. Mary said that this information "sent Ernest into a disproportionately large tizzy. He muttered about the dire consequences of law-breaking."[20] Ernest flew on to New York, leaving Mary, Val, and their considerable luggage to follow by train from Miami. After conferences with Alfred Rice, Scribner's, and Hotchner, Hemingway boarded the TWA night flight to Madrid, arriving there the next morning, August 5. Two days after landing, he was cabling and writing Hotchner that the *mano-a-mano* essay should say nothing about the shaving of the bulls' horns, for Dominguín was suing people on that issue. He felt terrible from lack of rest, and had not written Mary because he was dead tired.[21] The next day in New York, Mary received a panicky phone call from Hotchner, telling her that the radio news reported Ernest seriously ill at Málaga. The false report sent Mary scurrying: she booked a flight to Spain, contacted CBS News, sent cables, and sweated the emergency out while feeling helpless to do anything. Finally the news dispatch came through that Ernest was alive, followed by his telegram: REPORTS FALSE ENROUTE MADRID LOVE PAPA.[22] A second reassuring telegram came from Annie Davis: ERNEST OK.[23]

For the second time, he was not dying or dead as reported in the news, but neither was Hemingway "OK." A week later, tired and lonely, he complained that La Consula was full of strangers making him "nervous" and unable to sleep. His head was not right, and he worried that he was having a complete nervous breakdown. It had happened this way before, he assured Mary, and he had recovered to write wonderfully. He asked her to send Val to him if it could be done without creating a scandal, for there was so much mail that he was too tired to answer. The overwork was "deadly"; he could not sleep. Drinking only wine in small amounts was "bad" for him, but without it he became more "nervous." He, who often claimed that he always woke cheerful in the morning, was now waking in terrible shape.[24] In Mary's breezy and detailed letters to Ernest about her life in New York—plays, luncheons, friends to see—she showed little concern about her husband's complaints. But on August 20, Mary sent Val to Europe as Ernest requested, hoping her presence might calm him down.[25] All through September Mary received long, rambling, repetitive letters from Ernest filled with complaints, worries, and other clues that he was deeply mired in the slough of despondency. His weight dropped to 187. Worried that he was overdosing himself with his medicines, he decided to cut them to the bare minimum, despite his "nervousness." When Ernest saw his face on the cover of the September *Life* magazine, he was horrified. He confessed that his mind was in the worst shape ever, and he understood why Mary refused to come with him.[26]

Unnaturally worried about libel suits over the bullfight book, now titled *The Dangerous Summer*, he wired Scribner's to delay setting type until he had a chance to make more revisions.[27] As his several letters to Mary indicate, he was completely disillusioned with the bullfight business and all its components except Antonio. Having worked his head stupid getting the right photos for *Life's* first installment of his essay, Hemingway was mortified by the magazine's final choices, which he felt were terrible. How could he ever apologize to Antonio and Luis Miguel? After his trying so hard to balance the photos so that each man looked his best, *Life* had ruined his reputation for honesty. He could only imagine how awful the Spanish version of *Life* would be, making him not only look stupid but also appear as a betrayer. If shooting himself would make things right with the two matadors, he would do so, but right now he could not afford that "luxury." On September 23, Ernest wrote a plaintive letter to Mary, saying how he wished she were with him to keep him from "cracking up."[28]

On October 8, Ernest landed back in New York, where he did his best to project his confident public persona; but inside he was a shaken, worried man, his self-confidence badly eroded, his memory playing tricks on him, and his nervous system clearly in trouble. Once in Mary's 62nd Street apartment, he refused to go outside, claiming that someone sinister was waiting out there for him. As quickly as possible Mary got him to Ketchum, where they both hoped that rest and quiet would restore his equilibrium. As they arrived at the

Shoshone train station, two men in top coats came out of the Manhattan Cafe across the street. "They're tailing me out here already," Ernest told George Saviers, who met them at the platform. On the short drive to Ketchum, Ernest complained about his kidneys and his blood pressure, which he thought was rising again. When back in his Ketchum writing room, he seemed to be making progress on the Paris book, but his mind would not rest. A call to Morgan Guaranty in New York confirmed bountiful amounts in his various accounts, but the information did not relieve his mind. "He's confusing us," he told Mary. "He's covering up something." When she demanded to know what possible reason the bank might have for doing so, Ernest replied, "I don't know. But I know." He worried that a cottonwood tree blown across the Big Wood River formed a natural bridge across which "anybody" could infiltrate his defenses.[29] On either side of the front door, he had crude glass portals built so that he could see whoever was at the door.

Wherever he looked he found fears. Morose, losing weight rapidly, silent, brooding, and paranoid, Ernest was being sucked into a black hole from which he would not emerge. He worried about his income taxes, his property taxes, and his bills, worried there would not be enough money to pay them. At this time he owned almost $400,000 in Morgan Guaranty bank shares. He worried, quite rightly, that he would not be able to return to Cuba, where his manuscripts and his reference library representing his literary capital was at risk. He worried about the FBI finding out that he brought Valerie into the country illegally, her visa expired. On October 25, he sent Hotchner a $1,500 check to pay Val's tuition at Columbia (a charade) and to apply to her New York living expenses.[30] Thereafter, to keep Mary from finding out how much money he was giving to Val, he arranged to communicate with her through George Saviers, who would be her postal station and banker. Then Hemingway began to worry that he had put Saviers at risk, so he wrote an alibi note for George stating that Saviers never knew what the letters contained or why they were being mailed.[31]

When two college professors from Montana State University

showed up at Hemingway's door, they were shocked to see the ghost of the man standing before them. One of them later wrote, "The only resemblance to the man we had imagined was in the fullness of the face. And even the face was pale and red-veined, not ruddy or weather-beaten. We were particularly struck by the thinness of his arms and legs. . . . He walked with the tentativeness of a man well over sixty-one. The dominant sense we had was of fragility."[32] And when Hotchner came out to Ketchum before Thanksgiving, he too was shocked to find Ernest in such bad shape. Hotchner wrote Bill Davis that the symptoms from the previous summer had grown worse. Mary, he reported, was on the verge of seeking psychiatric help for Ernest, whose grasp of reality was, in some crucial ways, completely missing.[33]

To say that Hemingway was opposed to being treated as mentally ill would be an understatement. Anyone growing up in the first half of this century was loath to be labeled "crazy," for mental illness marked that person as a liability. As Ernest's fictional character, the shell-shocked Nick Adams, said in 1932, "It's a hell of a nuisance once they've certified you as nutty. No one ever has any confidence in you again."[34] George Saviers gently suggested that Ernest should seek help at the Menninger Clinic, but Hemingway refused to go to a solely psychiatric hospital. Then Saviers suggested the Mayo Clinic in Rochester, Minnesota, where Ernest could go to treat his high blood pressure, which had suddenly zoomed to 250 over 125. On the last day of November, Hemingway and Saviers climbed into Larry Johnson's single-engine Piper Comanche to fly across the snow-covered midwest to Rochester, where that night Ernest stood at the check-in desk of St. Mary's Hospital. Fifty-one years earlier, Dr. Clarence Hemingway stood on that same spot, arriving for a clinical visit and refresher course. He wrote a postcard to his eleven-year-old son: "It will be only a few years before you and Papa will be visiting clinics together."[35]

At St. Mary's that night, Ernest was having difficulty answering simple questions: name, address, next of kin, names of parents. When asked the name of his mother, Ernest blanched, mumbled, and became nervously agitated. Saviers stepped in quickly, saying he would finish the form but first it was important to get Ernest into bed and sedated. As a result, Ernest was registered in Saviers's name.[36] By train and plane, Mary followed Ernest to Rochester, checking into the Kahler Hotel as Mrs. George Saviers. On December 4, Ernest in his hospital room wrote "To WHOM IT MAY CONCERN" that his wife Mary never knew of or participated in any of his illegal acts, knew nothing of his finances, used Saviers's name only to avoid the press, and "was never an accomplice nor in any sense a fugitive."[37] For reasons he was never able to articulate fully, Hemingway was certain that state and federal agencies were pursuing him for unnamed crimes.

During his initial physical exam with Dr. Hugh Butt, Hemingway gave his medical history of having hepatitis in 1918 and jaundice in 1956. Dr. Butt's summation said nothing about Hemingway's several serious concussions. The battery of diagnostic tests showed most of Ernest's numbers to be within normal range, except his blood pressure (160/98) and his blood sugar at 130 percent. More tests suggested that he had a mild case of diabetes mellitus. His enlarged liver in conjunction with his diabetes suggested that he might have hemachromatosis, but no follow-up tests were done to confirm that possibility.[38] Hemingway's chronic and severe depression was attributed to his prolonged use of Serpasil, the Ciba company's trade name for their reserpine medication, whose known side effects included depression.[39] Dr. Howard Rome, in charge of Hemingway's psychiatric evaluation, explained to Ernest that his Serpasil depressions "were accelerated by the use of Ritalin which apparently was prescribed to off-set the depression. Thus . . . the situation was compounded."[40] No mention in writing was made of Hemingway's paranoia and delusions, but shortly after his admission to St. Mary's, electroshock therapy began.

With his bowels and bladder completely empty, Ernest was strapped down on the gurney, a white gown his only cover, his muscles slowly relaxing as the injection took effect and the white room began to soften. The nurse applied a greasy jelly to his temples, placed a rubber gag between his teeth to prevent injury, and fixed the electrodes in place. Then the doctor in white pushed a button for electric current to jolt Hemingway's brain into an induced *grand mal* seizure, the equivalent of a concussion. It was some time before he woke from the comalike state, his mouth dry, his head fuzzy, unable to say where he was or why. Ten times Ernest was wheeled into the white room for more electricity to overload his neural connections. Ten times he was convulsed. Ten times he awoke wondering. As one neurologist would later write: "I have no doubt that ECT [electroconvulsive therapy] produces effects identical to those of a head injury. After multiple sessions of ECT, a patient has symptoms identical to those of a retired, punch-drunk boxer. After one session of ECT the symptoms are the same as those of concussion."[41] For a head like Hemingway's, already several times concussed, such a treatment could produce serious brain damage. Short-term memory loss was an expected side effect of ECT, but long-term loss was always a possibility. Later research found one woman's life was ruined after fifteen ECT treatments, at lower voltage than Hemingway sustained, that left her unable to remember the names of close associates, unable to recall if she had money or where it was, and completely erasing three years of her memory.[42]

Late on Christmas Eve, Mary Hemingway sat down on her hotel-room bed and wept as she wrote in her journal that Ernest seemed "almost as disturbed, disjointed mentally as he was when we came here. . . . He no longer insists that an FBI agent is hidden in the bathroom with a tape recorder. . . . He still says . . . that he feels terrible. He still mumbles about breaking the immigration law (he has some unspoken guilt about Val). He is convinced that the Ketchum house will be seized for non-payment of something. . . . Still feels penniless . . . still waits for the FBI to pick him up."[43] Six days later, on New Year's Eve, she wrote out her resolutions:

1. *I will not worry or fret or brood about other women in love with Papa.*
2. *I will try to make each single day, the greatest, the most per-cep-tive, pleasurable, carefree and happy.*
3. *I will not be sad or miserable at night. I will go to bed hopeful.*

4. *I will be disciplined only by my own tastes, not by phony customs.*[44]

Mary Hemingway was standing with her back to the edge of her own limits, emotionally bankrupt, and in her own words, "I feel I too may begin to confuse illusion with reality."[45]

The charade of patient George Saviers was not discovered by the press until January 11, 1961, after which time the hospital was hard-pressed to keep reporters, freelance writers, and the curious away from their celebrity. Finally, Mayo Clinic issued a statement that Hemingway was being treated for hypertension, and "his condition is regarded as satisfactory. . . . It is necessary, however, that his right to privacy be respected and that he have the benefit of rest and quiet." On his hospital-room door, Hemingway placed a hand-lettered sign which should have disturbed his doctors, who were about to send him home cured:

FORMER WRITER *Engaged*
in PREPARATION OF SCHEDULED
FULL SCALE NEWS CONFERENCE
AS PROMISED *in* THE
P-D *by* OUR SPOKESMAN.
PLEASE DO NOT
DISTURB UNLESS *Absolutely*
NECESSARY TO OBTAIN *photographs*
OR CONFIRMATION OF TREATMENT
given EXCLUSIVELY TO THE P-D.[46]

On January 22, Hemingway was discharged from St. Mary's well enough, he was told, to return to Ketchum, where he arrived that evening in Larry Johnson's airplane. There he began keeping a meticulous daily record of his morning weight and bowel movements. January 23, his body, which once weighed as much as 260 pounds, now weighed 171. By March 12, he was down to 166½. On April 5, he scaled out at 164, 36 pounds lighter than a year earlier. When first back in Ketchum, Mary was relieved that Ernest seemed so much better. He remained somewhat silent but not visibly morose. Not ready to deal with visitors, even old friends, Ernest canceled the Friday-night parties watching the televised fights. He and Mary took daily two- to four-mile walks on the iron-hard road running north out of Ketchum, Ernest in front, Mary several paces in the rear. In the evenings, they read from the more than thirty new volumes ordered from the Scribner Book Store, titles diverse as Lawrence Durrell's *The Black Book*, Hershey's *The Child Buyer*, Styron's *Set This House on Fire*, a biography of Ezra Pound, and Shirer's *The Rise and Fall of the Third Reich*.[47] Ernest and Mary had become a country of two with fragile borders, each needy in different ways. Outside their gray, concrete house on the hilltop, the snow piled deep, and in the early mornings when he woke, Ernest could see deer watering on Big Wood River at the foot of the hill.

Each morning Hemingway woke before Mary, made his breakfast, and went to his writing room, where the Paris book with nineteen sketches completed and the bullfight book at 150,000 words were waiting to be finished. But through all of February he apparently wrote nothing but a few letters in which he usually said out of habit that he was "working hard." In New York, Hotchner mounted his reader's theater tour of Hemingway's work, while in Los Angeles, film producer Jerry Wald was bringing together a final contract for *Adventures of a Young Man* based on several of Ernest's short stories. Hemingway's six-month royalty report from Scribner's was for $28,977.33, an increase over the previous six months.[48] None of this information gave Ernest ease of mind, for he was now living in a constricted world that was growing more hopeless each day he could not write. If the problem had been what to write next, he might have been able to face it as he had so many times before. But the problem was how to finish work waiting for an ending, always the most difficult task for him.

Draft after draft was begun on the introduction to the Paris sketches, but each attempt was put aside as inadequate. He told Harry Brague at Scribner's that he had eighteen chapters arranged in their proper order, and was working on the nineteenth chapter, but still had no title. It was, he said, difficult to find a good title with his reference library in Cuba. He asked Brague to send copies of the *Oxford Book of English Verse* and the King James *Bible* with clear print—his old standbys for good titles. In closing, he gave the condition of his health, adding, "You, Max, and Charlie Scribner are accustomed to the lies of Scott—but this is the true gen."[49] Harry Brague must have wondered about that curious sentence, for Scott Fitzgerald was twenty-one years in the grave, Max Perkins and Charles Scribner were both dead, and Charles Scribner, Jr., was a young boy in the 1930s.

By March 1, Hemingway was exhibiting more disturbing symptoms of his returning depression. Deeply worried that he would never return to Finca Vigía, he continued to follow Lee Samuels's directions for funneling money to his Cuban staff through Canadian banks. Samuels assured him by letter that it was both legal and ethical, as far as he knew.[50] The very chance that this ploy was illegal was enough to resurrect Hemingway's paranoia about the FBI. The day he received Samuels's letter, Hemingway warned Hotchner to be careful what he wrote because mail coming into Ketchum might be read by anyone. Nor were the phones safe, for everyone tended to listen in.[51] Around the solstice, March 21, what began as a simple question—had Mary paid Social Security tax on their maid, Mary Williams—evolved into a full-scale emotional explosion. Mary assured Ernest that it was not a problem. He wanted to see her checkbook. She refused to show it to him. He said that when the FBI came in to investigate, they would certainly look at her checkbook. She said, not in America, they could not do that. They were both furious. Ernest wrote two letters to Alfred Rice detailing the three-day war. Mary would not listen to him, he said, and she blamed his concern on his mental illness and his imagination.[52]

On April 15, Hemingway awoke to a newscast claiming that an army of anti-Castro revolutionaries had invaded Cuba. Before the day was done, the Bay of Pigs disaster would be a dark, failed piece of American foreign diplomacy. The Central Intelligence Agency, working with the anti-Castro movement centered in Miami, had armed, trained, and arranged transportation for a small army whose appearance on the Cuban shore they hoped would trigger a general uprising against the communist-leaning Castro government. It was possibly the worst intelligence fiasco of the cold war period. The dissident Cubans were in Miami. Castro was generally popular in Cuba, his reforms approved. A well-armed and well-trained Cuban militia quickly decimated the invaders, for whom there was no escape route. For Hemingway, the Bay of Pigs disaster marked the end of any hope that he might one day return to Cuba. From the darkness into which he was again descending, he was certain he would never again see the Finca, his library, the *Pilar*, or his paintings. The manuscripts for what would become *Islands in the Stream* and *True at First Light*, the African novel, were, he thought, lost to him.[53]

Three days after the Bay of Pigs, Hemingway wrote Charles Scribner, Jr., that the Paris sketches could not be published in their present condition. For a month he had worked on the ending without success. If published, there would be several libel suits, and the book was unfair to Hadley, Pauline, and Scott Fitzgerald. If he had good health, enough time, sources to check, and impeccable taste, he might be able to make the magic work, but worries and his stay at Rochester had broken him down. Since returning from Rochester, everything he had done to the book, he said, made it worse, and there was nothing to do but admit his failure. The only way the book could be published would be to call it fiction, and for Scribner's to bear the burden of all libel suits.[54] The letter was written but not mailed on Tuesday. On Thursday, Mary told Ernest that he was clearly getting worse, and she thought he should return to Rochester for more treatments.

On Friday morning, Mary went downstairs to breakfast and found Ernest

> in the front vestibule of the house with his shotgun, two shells and a note he had written me. For an hour I talked to him—courage, his bravery, faith, love—and managed to delay any decisive action until George [Saviers] arrived, perceived the situation and managed

to take Papa to the Sun Valley hospital where they put him to bed and gave him sedatives.[55]

Poor flying weather kept Hemingway in the local hospital under careful watch. On Monday, April 24, he convinced George Saviers to allow him to return home to complete some unspecified chores. Don Anderson, his boon hunting companion, and nurse Joanie Higgons went along to make sure there were no problems. Ernest was quickly out of the car and into the house. By the time Don reached the living room, Ernest was ramming a shell into his shotgun, but Anderson was able to overpower him, get the gun away, and return Ernest to the hospital. The following day, Larry Johnson, with both Don and George Saviers along, flew Hemingway against his will to Rochester. Mary remained in Ketchum, too emotionally torn apart to go through the clinic routine again.[56] When the plane landed to refuel in Rapid City, South Dakota, Ernest with Don at his heels began going through the hangar and parked cars looking for a gun. At one point he walked toward the whirling prop of an airplane, stopping only when the plane cut its engine.[57]

Hemingway's first Rochester letter to Mary was difficult to read and barely coherent, repeating over and over again that she must keep him informed of her expenditures so that he would know if there was enough money to cover their bills. During his first three days at the clinic, Hemingway went through three sessions in the white room with the electroshock, making his handwriting wobbly and strange. The four-page letter rambled, asking for checks, worrying about taxes, professing loneliness, repeating himself as if he had not said the same thing twice earlier. In closing he said that he was taking the letter to the authorities to get it past censorship, as if it were a wartime situation. His last line apologized for taking three days to write her, and he signed it "Big Kitten."[58] His letters thereafter repeatedly asked about amounts in various bank accounts, never knowing if he could write a check, and all the information that Mary supplied could not put that worry to rest. He was, for example, certain that he had not put aside enough money in his special tax account to cover his 1960 IRS bill. When Morgan Guaranty sent him a letter giving the balance at $136,211.57, he continued to fret, insisting that Mary tell him the worst possible scenario so they could be prepared for it. Nothing she or Rice could say assuaged his fear.[59] On May 5, he reported having a session in the white room the day before which had left him unable to write, and there would be more treatments at the rate of one every two days. Kept in the locked wing of the hospital where a light burned all night long, Ernest was under close surveillance, but was able to leave his room. When he got through by phone to Gary Cooper dying from cancer, Coop told him, "I bet I make it to the barn before you do."[60] On May 13, the actor was dead, and Hemingway, named an honorary pall bearer, was said to be too ill to attend the funeral.

Dr. Howard Rome assessed Hemingway as having the "classical" symptoms of depression: "loss of self-esteem, ideas of worthlessness, a searing sense of guilt, of not having done better by you [Mary], by his family, by his friends." Ernest had reentered the Mayo convinced that he would never be able to write again, which filled him with "humiliation and chagrin" and "all but overwhelmed him with agitation, restlessness, and . . . money matters." As he seemed to improve with the shock treatments, Hemingway and Rome frequently discussed suicide. Ernest pointed out that Rome needed to trust him for there were numerous ways he could kill himself. He did not need a gun when there was glass to break or his belt to form a noose. On his honor he promised Rome he would not kill himself at the clinic. They shook hands, confirming their pact, and thereafter Ernest "went out almost daily for walks, for swims, for target shooting, for meals." The shock treatments continued until Rome was convinced that Ernest was truly better.[61]

But at the end of May, when Mary finally went to Rochester to visit her husband, she was discouraged by what she observed. As she explained to Jack and Patrick,

My first day there [May 23], Papa showed only intense hostility to me—I'd railroaded him there, making them destroy his memory,

would be happy only keeping him as a fixture in a madhouse, would
steal his money, etc. . . . The second day was calm and harmonious.
. . . The third day—7 hours—he made plans for getting out of there,
grew angry because I demurred at the idea of going to the fiesta of
Pamplona.

After three days, Mary was appalled that the doctors thought Ernest
was improving. He told her that he could not go back to Ketchum
because he would be put in jail for nonpayment of state taxes, a situation she had connived. Rice, he said, was lying to them about the
federal tax bill; it had to be more. The Morgan Guaranty bank statements were mistaken.[62]

Deeply worried that the Mayo treatments were not helping Ernest,
Mary could not face another round of suicide attempts in Ketchum.
Their game was no longer a game, and she had exhausted her emotional resources. In New York, she sought advice from a psychiatrist
who recommended the Hartford Institute of Living. On June 7, she
flew to Hartford, Connecticut, where Dr. Gordon Edgren assured
her the Institute, complete with ample grounds, library, swimming
pool, and gymnasium, was ready to help in Ernest's long-term recovery. That night, back in her New York City apartment, Mary wrote
a carefully phrased letter to Dr. Rome at Mayo, asking for his advice
on the Institute of Living. Without saying so directly, she desperately
wanted Rome to recommend that Ernest be transferred to Hartford,
for she knew he would not go voluntarily, particularly if she urged
him. She told Rome, "I would much prefer that Papa does not now
know anything of all this, remembering his convictions about how I
was railroading him into a madhouse."[63]

By phone on June 15, Mary assured Ernest that she had "great
confidence" in Howard Rome's judgment.[64] However, for reasons
Rome must have personally given Mary, he did not recommend
the transfer to Hartford. Having watched Ernest in the presence
of Rome, Mary was certain that her husband had gulled the doctor about the state of his mind. When Rome asked her to come to
his office, she was "dumfounded to see Ernest there, dressed in his

street clothes, grinning like a Cheshire cat." Rome said that Hemingway was ready to go home. In Ernest's presence, Mary could not bring herself to argue with the doctor's decision. Two days later, in a rented Buick with George Brown, Ernest's sometime trainer and old friend, driving, Ernest and Mary began their last cross-country trip west, arriving in Ketchum on June 30. The next day, Ernest seemed happier than he had been in a long time. After a long country walk, he visited George Saviers, and stopped by the Sun Valley Lodge to see Don Anderson, who was out of his office. That night Mary, George Brown, and Ernest were sitting at a corner table of the Christiania Restaurant. When Ernest asked their waitress about two men at another table, he was told they were salesmen. Salesmen would not be out on a Saturday night. "They're FBI," Ernest said. Mary redirected his attention to the bottle of wine on the table, and the meal ended pleasantly enough. Later that evening, Ernest and Mary harmonized on a favorite Italian tune as they went to their separate bedrooms.[65]

Sunday morning, July 2, Ernest was awake before the sun rising over the mountains east of Ketchum lit his bedroom window. There would be no more white rooms with electrodes stuck to his head. He could not go back to Cuba, but neither could he go back to a locked ward. If he could not write, then he could not write, but there was one thing left he could do well, a thing for which he had practiced all his adult life. In bathrobe and slippers, he padded softly past Mary's room where she was sleeping soundly. Down the stairs and into the kitchen, he found the ring of keys on the windowsill, and moved toward the basement stairs. In the locked storeroom where Mary had his shotguns for safekeeping, the odor of gun oil and leather was an old friend. From the box of 12-gauge shells, he pulled out two and dropped them in his pocket. Picking up his favorite Boss shotgun, he turned out the light and climbed slowly back up the stairs to the first floor.

Born in July, blown up in Italy in July, Pamplona in July, it was, of all the months, his most memorable. On the first of July each summer of his youth, the family boarded the steamer that carried them up Lake Michigan for their two months at Windemere. July was the cottage, the lake, and the woods. It was trout fishing and camaraderie with the summer people, baseball games in the village, campfires in the night. July was faces and places no longer within reach. July was the big wound in Italy when he died for the first time only to come back out of the explosion to find his kneecap somewhere in his boot and his head ringing like a bell. Now, so many Julys later, he stood in the foyer beside the empty gun rack, broke open the breech of his shotgun, slipped in two shells, and snapped the breech shut. The taste of gun oil and powder solvent filled his mouth as cold steel made contact against his hard palate. The clock on Mary's bedside table clicked as the minute hand moved to 7:30. Then two, almost simultaneous explosions woke her to her widowhood, her world, changed, utterly changed.

CODA

ERNEST HEMINGWAY WAS the embodiment of
America's promise: the young boy from Oak Park who set
out to become the best writer of his time. With pluck and
luck, talent and wit, hard work and hard living, he did just that. In
the process he told us that pursuit was happiness, that man alone
was no fucking good, and that any story followed far enough would
end badly. Before he burned out, he lived constantly out on the edge
of the American experience. In the process he fathered sons, wrote
books, influenced friends, and won every prize available to a writer.
He remodeled American short fiction, changed the way characters
speak, confronted the moral strictures confining the writer, and left
behind a shelf of books telling us how we were in the first half of this
century. His is a classic American story: the young man who transforms himself following his ambition, succeeds beyond his dreams,
and finally burns out trying to be true to the person he has become.
His imagination, which created "Big Two-Hearted River," also created his paranoia. His ambition, intensity, creative drive, sense of

duty, belief in hard work, and faith in the strenuous life carried him to the pinnacle of his profession, provided him wide recognition and considerable wealth, before destroying him when he could no longer meet their demands. It is an old story, older than written words, a story the ancient Greeks would have recognized.

CHRONOLOGY

1929

May 5 Hemingways have returned to Europe.

July 6 Ernest, Uncle Gus, and Jinny Pfeiffer at Pamplona; Pauline in Paris.

July Ernest and Pauline in Valencia and Santiago de Compostela.

Sept. 27 *A Farewell to Arms* published in New York.

Oct. 24 Stock market crash in New York.

Dec. 20 Hemingways, Fitzgeralds, Dos Passos join Murphys in Switzerland.

Dec. 31 Hemingways return to Paris.

1930

Jan. 9 Hemingways sail for United States. Arrive in Key West on February 2.

March 15 Max Perkins visits in Key West. Hemingway begins *Death in the Afternoon*.

April John and Katy Dos Passos, Archie and Ada MacLeish visit in Key West.

July 13 Hemingways and children arrive at L-Bar-T ranch in Wyoming.

Nov. 1 In auto wreck near Billings, Montana, Hemingway's right arm severely fractured.

Dec. 21 Hemingway released from Billings hospital. He and Pauline go to Piggott for Christmas.

1931

Jan. 3 Hemingways return to Key West.

April 29 Hemingways buy Key West house; Pauline two months pregnant.

May Pauline and Patrick go to Paris; Ernest to Spain.

June 26 Ernest and Pauline are in Madrid.

July 6 Ernest, Bumby, and Sidney Franklin in Pamplona.

July–Aug. Hemingways are in Valencia, Santiago de Compostela, Madrid.

Sept. 23 Hemingways sail for New York.

Oct. 14 Hemingways are in Kansas City.

Nov. 12 Gregory Hemingway delivered by cesarean section.

Dec. 19 Hemingways and two children are back in Key West.

1932

Jan. Hemingway finishes *Death in the Afternoon*.

March Hemingway writes "After the Storm."

April 20 Hemingway in Havana for two months of fishing.

July 12 Ernest and Pauline arrive at Nordquist L-Bar-T ranch.

August Ernest writes "The Light of the World."

Sept. 23 *Death in the Afternoon* published in New York.

Oct. 16 Pauline leaves for Piggott; Ernest for Key West.

Nov. 15 "Fathers and Sons" begun.

Dec. Hemingways in Piggott from Thanksgiving through Christmas. Hemingway finishes "A Clean Well-Lighted Place."

1933

Jan. 8–20 Hemingway in New York. Meets Tom Wolfe and Arnold Gingrich.

Feb–April Hemingway in Key West, finishes four stories.

April 13 Hemingway is back in Havana for two months of marlin fishing.

May 24 Jane Mason wrecks car with Hemingway children inside.

July 3 Hemingway's first wife, Hadley Richardson, marries Paul Mowrer in London.

August First issue of *Esquire* features Hemingway's "Marlin Off the Morro: A Cuban Letter."

Aug. 7 Hemingways sail from Havana for Spain. Arrive Santander, August 17. Ernest remains in Spain until October 20.

Oct. 27 Hemingway in Paris when *Winner Take Nothing* is published in New York. He finishes "One Trip Across."

Nov. 22 Ernest, Pauline, and Charles Thompson sail from Marseilles to go on their African safari.

Dec. 20 Hemingway party departs Nairobi on two-month safari.

1934

Jan. 16 Ill with amebic dysentery, Hemingway is flown to Nairobi for treatment; rejoins safari January 21.

Feb. 28 Hemingways depart Africa, stop at Haifa, then return to Paris.

March 27 Hemingways sail for New York. Arrive April 3.

April 12 Hemingways back in Key West.

May 11 Hemingway brings his new fishing boat, *Pilar*, to Key West. Begins *Green Hills of Africa*.

July 18 Hemingway takes the *Pilar* to Havana. Returns October 26.

Nov. 16 Draft of *Green Hills of Africa* finished.

Dec. 19 Hemingways leave Key West for Christmas in Piggott.

1935

Jan.–March Hemingway writes in Key West.

April 7 Hemingway accidentally shoots himself in the leg.

April 14 Hemingway takes *Pilar* to Bimini for tuna fishing.

May First serial installment of *Green Hills* printed in *Scribner's Magazine*.

Aug. 15 Hemingway returns to Key West.

Sept. 2 Hurricane drowns hundreds of veterans on Matecumbe Key.

Sept. 17 *New Masses* prints Hemingway's "Who Murdered the Vets?"

Sept. 24 Hemingway is in New York for the Joe Louis–Max Baer heavyweight championship fight; remains in the East for the next month.

Oct. 25 *Green Hills* is published in New York. Hemingways return to Key West.

1936

Feb. Hemingway in a fist fight with Wallace Stevens.

April Hemingway finishes drafts of "The Snows of Kilimanjaro" and "The Short Happy Life of Francis Macomber."

April 27 Hemingway on the *Pilar* arrives in Havana.

May 27 Hemingway returns to Key West.

June 4 Hemingways leave for Bimini.

July 16 Hemingway leaves Bimini for Key West. Spanish Civil War begins.

July 27 Hemingways leave Key West for Piggott and Nordquist ranch in Wyoming.

Oct. 27 Hemingways leave for Key West with Hemingway having written 352 pages of *To Have and Have Not*.

Dec. Hemingway meets Martha Gellhorn in Key West.

1937

Jan. 10   Hemingway leaves Key West for New York.

Jan. 25   Hemingway returns to Key West.

Feb. 17   Hemingway is back in New York.

Feb. 27   Hemingway sails for France as war correspondent for North American News Alliance.

March 10   Hemingway is in Paris.

March 16   Hemingway flies to Valencia, Spain, then on to Madrid by car; soon joined there by Martha Gellhorn.

April   While reporting on the war, Hemingway works with Joris Ivens filming *The Spanish Earth*.

April 26   Guernica destroyed by Nationalist bombs.

May 9   Hemingway returns to Paris.

May 12   Hemingway reads from *To Have and Have Not* manuscript at Sylvia Beach's bookshop. Next day sails for New York.

May 26   Hemingways leave for Bimini.

June 4   Hemingway flies to New York to address the American Writers Conference. Returns to Bimini two days later.

June 20   Hemingway does a quick round trip to New York to complete *The Spanish Earth. To Have and Have Not* is finished.

July 6   Hemingway leaves Bimini for New York.

July 8   Hemingway, Gellhorn, and Ivens are dinner guests at the White House for Roosevelt's viewing of *The Spanish Earth*.

July 10   Ernest, Pauline, and Ivens leave for Hollywood to raise funds for Loyalist cause in Spain.

July 21   Hemingway back in Bimini reading proof on *To Have and Have Not*.

Aug. 3   Hemingway leaves Bimini for Key West.

Aug. 10   Hemingway is in New York.

Aug. 11   Max Eastman scuffle in Perkins's office.

Aug. 14 Hemingway sails from New York for France.

Sept. 6 Hemingway departs Paris with Gellhorn for Madrid.

Oct. 15 *To Have and Have Not* published in New York. Hemingway working on *The Fifth Column*.

Dec. 28 Ernest joins Pauline in Paris.

1938

Jan. 12 Hemingways sail for Nassau, Havana, and Key West.

Jan. 29 Hemingways are in Key West.

March 19 Hemingway leaves from New York for France.

March 31 Ernest and Martha leave Paris for Spain.

May 16 Ernest and Martha return to Paris.

May 30 Hemingway arrives in New York and on to Key West.

June 22 Hemingway flies to New York for the Louis–Schmeling heavyweight fight.

Aug. 4 Hemingways leave Key West for L-Bar-T ranch.

Aug. 31 Hemingway sails for France where he meets Martha. They remain there all of September and October.

Oct. 22 *The Fifth Column and the First 49 Stories* is published in New York.

Nov. 24 Pauline is in New York when Ernest returns from France.

Dec. 5 Hemingways return to Key West.

1939

Jan. Early in January Hemingway returns to New York and Martha. His play, *The Fifth Column*, is in production.

Jan. 24 Hemingway flies back to Key West.

Feb. 8 Hemingway's mother visits for six days.

Feb. 15 Hemingway takes ferry to Havana. Begins *For Whom the Bell Tolls*.

March 14 Hemingway returns to Key West with two chapters written.

April 5   Hemingway takes *Pilar* back to Havana. Meets Martha.
May   Martha rents Finca Vigia outside Havana. Ernest moves in with her.

1940

Mar. 7   *The Fifth Column* opens in New York.
c. July 25   Hemingway delivers *For Whom the Bell Tolls* type-script to Scribner's.
Sept.   Martha Gellhorn, Hemingway, and his three sons are at Sun Valley Lodge.
Oct. 21   *For Whom the Bell Tolls* is published.
Nov. 21   Ernest and Martha are married in Cheyenne, Wyoming.
Dec. 21   Scott Fitzgerald dies.

1941

Jan. 31   Hemingways depart San Francisco en route to China war zone.
Feb.–April   Hawaii, Hong Kong, Namyung, Canton Front, Chung-king, Rangoon.
April 29   Ernest is back in Hong Kong.
May 6–17   Ernest flies to Manila, Guam, Wake Island, Hawaii, San Francisco.
June 1–15   Ernest and Martha are in New York City and return to Cuba.
mid-Sept.   Hemingways are at the Sun Valley Lodge.
Oct. 27   Martha's book, *The Heart of Another*, is published.
Dec. 3   Leave Sun Valley to return to Cuba.
Dec. 7   Japanese attack Pearl Harbor.

1942

Mar.–Aug.   Ernest edits *Men at War*, writes preface.
May   German submarines begin raiding in the Gulf of Mex-

ico. Hemingway proposes using the *Pilar* for armed patrols. He also initiates a counterintelligence operation in Cuba.

July 16   Martha leaves for two-month Caribbean assignment for *Collier's*.

July 28   *Pilar's* first short patrol in Cuban waters.

Aug.   More short patrols along northwest coast.

Nov.   Counterintelligence operation taken over by Gustavo Durán.

Nov. 20   *Pilar* begins first fully armed cruise.

1943

Jan.–Mar.   *Pilar* on short patrols along northwest coast of Cuba.
May 20–

July 20   *Pilar* on first extended patrol in Old Bahama Channel.

June 27   Martha finishes *Liana*.

Aug.–Sept.   *Pilar* in port awaiting next assignment and having repairs.

Sept. 20   Martha leaves for England on *Collier's* assignment.

Oct.–Dec.   Hemingway alone at the Finca. No sub patrols assigned.

1944

Feb. 1   Hemingway closes down *Pilar* patrols.

Mar. 13   Martha returns to Cuba from England.

April 23   Ernest and Martha fly to New York, where he becomes *Collier's* front-line correspondent.

May 13   Martha leaves by freighter in convoy for England.

May 17   Ernest lands in England by military aircraft. Soon meets Mary Welsh.

May 23   Ernest is in car wreck, severe scalp lacerations and concussion.

May 31   Martha arrives in London.

June 6   D-Day: Normandy invasion. Ernest at Omaha Beach.

June 15–30   Hemingway flies missions with the RAF.

July 18   With Patton's army at Néhou, France.

July 28   He joins the 22nd Infantry Regiment.

Aug. 18–24   Hemingway at Rambouillet with David Bruce of OSS.

Aug. 25   Liberation of Paris. Hemingway at the Ritz Hotel.

Sept. 7   Hemingway leaves Paris to rejoin 22nd Regiment.

Sept. 26   Hemingway returns to Paris and Mary Welsh.

Oct. 6   Hemingway cleared of charges of being armed correspondent. Stays in Paris.

Nov. 9–

Dec. 3   Hemingway returns to 22nd Regiment for the Battle of Hürtgen Forest.

1945

Mar. 6   Hemingway departs Paris for return to Cuba.

April 12   President Franklin D. Roosevelt dies in office.

May 8   Mary arrives to live at the Finca. Germany surrenders.

June 20   Auto accident with Ernest driving. Mary hospitalized.

Oct.–Dec.   Hemingway works on Bimini novel begun before the war.

1946

Feb.–June   Ernest in "black-ass" depressed mood, but writes Bimini novel steadily.

Mar. 13   Ernest and Mary are married. Mary becomes pregnant.

July 21   Ernest has 1,000 pages written on Bimini novel.

July 28   Gertrude Stein dies in Paris.

Aug. 19   En route to Ketchum, Idaho, Mary's fallopian tube bursts. Emergency surgery; she almost dies. No baby.

Sept. 12   Ernest and Mary arrive at Ketchum.

Nov. 18   Hemingways depart Ketchum for New Orleans.

Dec. 1   Hemingways in New York City.

1947

June 13   Hemingway awarded Bronze Star for World War II service.

June 17   Max Perkins dies.

July–Aug.   Hemingway's blood pressure becomes dangerously high.

Aug.–Sept.   Hemingway is involved in Dominican Republic coup attempt.

Oct. 3   Hemingway in Ketchum to avoid possible Cuban arrest.

Nov.–Dec.   Hemingway works on the Bimini novel in Ketchum.

Dec. 24   Hemingway meets Lillian Ross.

1948

Feb. 1–20   Ernest and Mary leave Ketchum and return to Cuba.

Mar. 7   Malcolm Cowley arrives in Havana to write Hemingway essay for *Life*.

Mar.   Peter Viertel and John Huston arrive in Havana.

June   Aaron Hotchner arrives in Havana.

Sept. 7   Hemingways sail from Havana for Italy.

Sept. 25   Hemingways leave Genoa to drive through northern Italy.

Oct. 22   Hemingways arrive at Gritti Palace in Venice.

Nov. 1   Hemingways move to Locando Cipriani on Torcello.

Nov.   Ernest writes "The Great Blue River" for *Holiday* magazine.

mid-Dec.   Back in Venice, Ernest meets Adriana Ivancich. He and Mary move to Cortina.

1949

Jan. 21   Mary breaks her right ankle skiing.

early Mar.   Hemingways return to Venice. Meet Sinclair Lewis.

mid-Mar. They return to Cortina. Ernest begins a short story that will grow into *Across the River and into the Trees.*

Mar. 28 Ernest's eyes become infected with erysipelas. He spends ten days in a Padua hospital.

April 30 Hemingways sail from Genoa to return to Cuba.

May 27 Arrive at Finca Vigia.

July–Oct. Hemingway writes steadily on *Across the River.*

Sept. Hemingway contracts with *Cosmopolitan* to serialize *Across the River.*

Nov. 16 Ernest and Mary fly to New York en route to Europe on *Ile de France.*

Nov.–Dec. Hemingways, Viertels, and Hotchner in Paris together.

Dec. 24 Hemingway and entourage leave Paris by car for Provence.

1950

Jan. Hemingways back in Venice at the Gritti Palace.

Feb. Ernest alternates between Venice and Cortina, where Mary breaks her left ankle skiing. First installments of *Across the River* run in *Cosmopolitan.*

Mar. 7 Hemingways depart Venice by car for Paris.

Mar. 21 Hemingways leave Ritz Hotel to meet *Ile de France* for trip home.

Mar. 27–

April 6 Hemingways in New York City.

April 8 Hemingways arrive in Cuba.

May 13 Lillian Ross "Profile" of Hemingway appears in *The New Yorker.*

June 3 Hemingway finishes revisions to book galleys for *Across the River.*

July Ernest suffers another concussion on board the *Pilar.*

Sept. 7 *Across the River and into the Trees* is published in New York.

Oct. 28   Adriana and her mother, Dora Ivancich, arrive at the Finca.

Nov.–Dec. Hemingway completes his Bimini novel, calling it *The Island and the Stream*.

1951

Jan.   Hemingway begins writing *The Old Man and the Sea*.

Feb. 7   Mary, Adriana, and her mother leave Cuba for trip to New York.

Feb. 17   Hemingway finishes first draft of *The Old Man and the Sea*.

April–Oct. Hemingway works on revising and cutting the Bimini novel.

July 28   Grace Hemingway dies. Ernest does not attend the funeral.

Oct. 2   Pauline Pfeiffer Hemingway dies in Los Angeles.

1952

Feb. 11   Charles Scribner, Sr., dies in New York.

May 4   Hemingway begins "The Last Good Country."

Sept. 1   *Life* magazine prints *The Old Man and the Sea* in one issue.

Sept. 8   Scribner's publishes the novel in hardback.

1953

May 4   Hemingway wins the Pulitzer Prize for *The Old Man and the Sea*.

June 24   Ernest and Mary sail from New York bound for Europe on the *Flandre*.

June 30   They dock at Le Havre and drive to Paris.

July 3   Leave by car for Spain.

July 6–14 In Pamplona for feria, first time since 1931.

Aug. 6   Hemingways board the *Dunnottar Castle* in Marseilles for Mombasa.

Sept.–Dec.   Hemingways on safari in Kenya.

1954

Jan. 21   Safari ends.

Jan. 23–24   Ernest and Mary survive two plane crashes at Murchinson Falls.

Feb.   Recovering in Nairobi, Ernest writes "The Christmas Gift."

Feb. 22   Ernest joins Mary at Mombasa for fishing.

Mar. 11   Hemingways board the SS *Africa* at Mombasa bound for Venice.

Mar. 23   Hemingways arrive in Venice.

Mar.   Hemingway accepts the American Academy of Arts and Letters Award of Merit Medal.

May 6   Hotchner and Hemingway depart Venice by car for Spain.

May 15–17   Ernest attends the San Isidro feria in Madrid.

June 6   Hemingways board the *Francesco Morosini* at Genoa bound for Havana.

July 21   Ernest is awarded Cuba's highest civilian award, the Order of Carlos Manuel de Céspedes.

Oct. 28   Hemingway is awarded Nobel Prize for literature. He is working on the African novel, *True at First Light* (1999).

1955

Jan.–June   Hemingway works on the African novel.

July–Sept.   Hemingway assists with the script and filming of *The Old Man and the Sea*.

Oct.–Nov.   Hemingway returns to the African novel.

Nov. 20   Ernest sick with nephritis and hepatitis. Remains in bed into January.

1956

Feb. 10 Hemingway abandons the African novel to work on *The Old Man and the Sea* filming.

April–May Ernest and Mary in Peru, fishing for a giant marlin for the film.

c. May 23 Hemingways return to the Finca. Ernest writes several World War II short stories.

Sept. 1 Hemingways board the *Ile de France* bound for Europe.

Sept. 17 Leave Paris for Spain by car.

Sept.–Oct. Attending *corridas* in Spain.

Nov. 17 Leave Spain, return to Paris.

1957

Jan. 23 Ernest and Mary on board *Ile de France* returning to New York. They take with them two trunks full of Hemingway's 1920s writing found stored at the Ritz.

Feb.–June Hemingway is at work at the Finca on what will become *The Garden of Eden* (1986).

c. July Hemingway begins his memoir, published posthumously as *A Moveable Feast* (1964).

Sept. 22–28 Ernest, Mary, and Denis Zaphiro in New York City.

Oct.–Dec. Hemingway alternates between the African novel and memoir.

Dec. The Castro revolution to overthrow the Batista government in Cuba gathers head.

1958

Jan.–July Hemingway writes steadily on his Paris memoir and *The Garden of Eden*.

May 7 Ezra Pound is released from St. Elizabeth's Hospital.

Aug. Ernest rents a house in Ketchum for the winter.

Oct. 6–15   Ernest drives from Key West to Ketchum. Mary joins him there.

Nov.–Dec.   Ernest writes mornings, hunts in the afternoons.

Dec. 31   Batista flees Cuba. Castro revolution succeeds.

1959

Jan.–Feb.   Hemingway works on *The Garden of Eden* at Ketchum, reaching forty-five chapters.

Feb. 18   Taylor Williams dies.

Mar. 16–29   Ernest and Mary leave Ketchum and travel to Havana.

April   Hemingway buys the Topping house in Ketchum.

April 22   Hemingways board the *Constitution* bound for Algeciras, Spain.

May   Hemingway writes "The Art of the Short Story" at La Consula.

June–Sept.   Ernest follows the Ordóñez–Dominguín *corridas*.

July 7–14   At the Pamplona feria, Valerie Danby-Smith joins the Hemingway party.

July 21   Ernest's sixtieth birthday party at La Consula.

Sept. 20   Mary flies from Madrid to Paris and back to Havana. Threatens to leave Ernest.

Oct. 27   Hemingway boards the *Liberté* bound for New York.

Nov. 1   Arrives in New York. Leaves copy of Paris memoir with Scribner's.

c. Nov. 4   Ernest, Antonio, and Carmen Ordóñez arrive at Havana airport.

Nov. 19   Ernest and the Ordóñezes arrive at Ketchum.

Nov. 27   Mary shatters her elbow in a hunting accident.

Dec.   In Ketchum, Ernest becomes more paranoid and withdrawn.

1960

Jan.–May   Hemingway writes steadily on *The Dangerous Summer*.

Jan. 17   Ernest and Mary take train to Miami and fly to Havana.

Feb. 8   Valerie arrives to act as Ernest's secretary.

July 25   Ernest, Mary, and Val leave Havana by ferry for Key West.

Aug. 4   Ernest flies to Madrid. Mary and Val remain in New York.

Aug. 20   Mary sends Val to join Ernest in Spain.

Oct. 8   Ernest returns to New York. Soon after, he and Mary go to Ketchum.

Oct.–Nov.   Hemingway's erratic moods, paranoia, and despondency become worse.

Nov. 30   Dr. George Saviers flies with Ernest to the Mayo Clinic, where he undergoes electroshock treatments.

1961

Jan. 22   Ernest is released from Mayo Clinic and returns to Ketchum.

Feb.–Mar.   Ernest loses weight, cannot write. Becomes more morose.

April 15   Bay of Pigs fiasco in Cuba.

April 21   Ernest prevented from shooting himself. Sedated and hospitalized in Ketchum.

April 24   Second attempt to kill himself is thwarted.

April 25   Ernest is flown back to Mayo Clinic.

May 23   Mary visits Ernest at Mayo, finds him no better. Doctors disagree.

June 26–30   Ernest is released from Mayo and driven to Ketchum.

July 2   Ernest Hemingway commits suicide with his favorite shotgun.

ACKNOWLEDGMENTS

FOR BOOK I

FOR PERMISSION to quote from texts, letters, and unpublished materials, I am grateful to Charles Scribner's Sons, now part of Simon & Schuster; *The Hemingway Review*; the Hemingway literary estate; and the Hemingway Foundation.

For reasons too numerous to count, I acknowledge and wish to thank Maurie and Marcia Neville, Megan Desnoyers, Steve Plotkin, John and Marsha Goin, Dave Meeker, Sarah Means Smith and Verna Chester, Dick Davison, Turner's Revenge, David LeDuc, Robert Trogdon, Amy Vondrak, Jeff Stoner, Lisa Ann Acosta, ENG-491 honors class, Anthony Mason, Patrick and Gregory Hemingway, Carlos Baker, the true scholars who gather in the back room of the Monroe County Library, Wright Langley, Louise at Hürtgenwald, Stoney and Sparrow in the high country, Jerry in Paris, reporters at the *Billings Gazette*, old friends from the Supper Club, Marty Peterson, continuous support from the members of the Hemingway Society, Tom Riker, Amy Cherry, Miriam Altshuler, Ted Johnson, Bill Henderson, North Carolina State University, its D. H. Hill Library and Interlibrary Loan staff, Princeton University Library, John F. Kennedy Library, University of Tulsa Library, the Library of Congress, University of Delaware Library. And to remember Paul Smith, who died before he could correct all the mistakes in this book. And to thank my wife, who in thirty years of questing has never questioned the goal. To thank my mother, Teresa Donnici Reynolds (1910–1995), who took us home to Kansas City and who died as this book was borning. To thank my father, Raymond Douglas Reynolds (1909–1991), who taught me to read maps and rocks. To thank them both for bearing a child in the 1930s. To thank all others from that Great Depression whom I found remembered in odd angles of this hutment we call our culture, waiting for me when I needed them.

FOR BOOK II

STANDING ON THE BACKS of scholars before me, I have, with help from many friends, brought this last volume of my Hemingway biography to term. Had it not been for Carlos Baker's work, his example and his encouragement, none of these volumes would have been written. Twenty-six years ago, Carlos called Charles Scribner, and said, "Charlie, there's a young man in my office who needs to see the Hemingway-Perkins correspondence." For several beats of my heart, I could not breathe. The same thing happened when Jo August first handed me the blue *cahiers* containing the first draft of *The Sun Also Rises* in which the ink seemed scarcely dry.

This last volume owes much to many. Quite literally it depended upon the help of Al DeFazio and Rose Marie Burwell. Al loaned me his files on the Hemingway-Hotchner relationship; Rose Marie loaned me all of her files and notes on Hemingway's posthumously published manuscripts and on the Scribner Archive materials at

Princeton. Their combined help reduced by three years the research time I spent on this book. At the John F. Kennedy Library in Boston, curator Stephen Plotkin was vital to my research, always keeping me informed when new materials were opened. Interlibrary loan at North Carolina State University and at the Santa Fe Public Library brought me what I needed. Maurice and Marcia Neville provided generous access to crucial materials not available to the public. Dave Meeker gave the same sort of help with Martha Gellhorn materials. John and Marsha Goin opened to me their Hemingway collection before it was sold. Ann Adelman's copyediting eliminated enough errors to make an author blush. Bob Lewis's keen eye read proof to prevent my usual mistakes.

I am equally grateful to Bernice Kert for her book, *The Hemingway Women*, to Larry Martin for keeping me in mind, to John Unrue for interviewing Forrest MacMullen, to Ken Kinnamon for loaning me the Paporov book, and to Marty Peterson who opened doors, always remembered, set a great table, and put to rest the question of which onion sandwich was the better. At North Carolina State University, I depended on Amy Vondrak and Ed Hoffman for their research skills, and on Sarah Smith for keeping me focused. In Idaho, I was given assistance by Marsha Bellavance, Buck Levy, Pierre Saviers, Don Anderson, Duke MacMullen, Bud and Ruth Purdy, Clara Spiegel, and the historical section of the Ketchum Library. In New York, it was Miriam Altshuler, my agent, and Amy Cherry, my editor, whose great faith in this project was vital. In Santa Fe, I relied on my son-in-law, Ed Shipman, for moving us, lifting, hauling, wiring, and advising. Calico-Hickey was here for me when my back would not work. David Salazar provided creature comforts at El Farol's bar and restaurant. Samuel Adelo translated, on short notice, crucial sections of the Paporov book. Tom Riker's conversation and sense of humor kept my head straight. Shauna got us into the house, Tor and Murph fixed the roof, Ed built the drain, Dierdre and Elijah kept the house warm. Finally, I must thank the Hemingway Society, my friends here and abroad, and the numerous strangers who have written me over the years, urging me to finish this work.

NOTES

The following abbreviations are used throughout the notes.

NEWSPAPERS

Citizen	*Key West Citizen*
Gazette	*Billings Gazette*
NYT	*New York Times*
NYTBR	*New York Times Book Review*
Post	*Havana Post*
SRL	*Saturday Review of Literature*
Tribune	Paris edition of the *New York Herald Tribune*

PEOPLE

AI	Adriana Ivancich
Berenson	Bernard Berenson
Cowley	Malcolm Cowley
CS	Charles Scribner
CSjr	Charles Scribner, Jr.
Dos Passos	John Dos Passos
EH	Ernest Hemingway
Fenton	Charles Fenton

FSF	F. Scott Fitzgerald
Gingrich	Arnold Gingrich
GHH	Grace Hall Hemingway
Hickok	Guy Hickok
Hotchner	A. E. Hotchner
Lanham	Charles "Buck" Lanham
MacLeish	Archibald MacLeish
MG	Martha Gellhorn
MP	Max Perkins
MW	Mary Welsh
MWH	Mary Welsh Hemingway
PH	Pauline (Pfeiffer) Hemingway
Pound	Ezra Pound
VDS	Valerie Danby-Smith

LIBRARIES

FDR	Franklin D. Roosevelt Library, Hyde Park
JFK	John F. Kennedy Library, Boston
LILLY	Lilly Library, University of Indiana
LOC	Library of Congress
MCL	Monroe County Library, Key West
PUL	Princeton University Library
Stanford	Stanford University Library
Tulsa	University of Tulsa Library
UCal	Bancroft Library, University of California, Berkeley
UDel	University of Delaware
UTex	Humanities Research Center, University of Texas
UVa	University of Virginia Library (Alderman Library)

HEMINGWAY BOOKS

AFTA	*A Farewell to Arms* (Scribner's, 1929)
AMF	*A Moveable Feast* (Scribner's, 1964) **
ARIT	*Across the River and into the Trees* (Scribner's, 1950)

By-Line	*By-Line: Ernest Hemingway*, ed. William White (Scribner's, 1967) **
CSS	*The Complete Short Stories of Ernest Hemingway* (Scribner's, 1987)**
DIA	*Death in the Afternoon* (Scribner's 1967)
DS	*The Dangerous Summer* (Scribner's, 1985)**
FWBT	*For Whom the Bell Tolls* (Scribner's, 1940)
GHOA	*Green Hills of Africa* (Scribner's, 1936)
GOE	*The Garden of Eden* (Scribner's, 1986) **
Islands	*Islands in the Stream* (Scribner's, 1970)**
	Men at War (Crown Publishers, 1942)
OMAS	*The Old Man and the Sea* (Scribner's, 1952)
SAR	*The Sun Also Rises* (Scribner's, 1926)
SL	*Ernest Hemingway: Selected Letters*, ed. Carlos Baker (Scribner's, 1981)**
	True at First Light (Scribner's, 1999) **
THHN	*To Have and Have Not* (Scribner's, 1937)
WTN	*Winner Take Nothing* (Scribner's, 1933)

**Works published posthumously

OTHER BOOKS

Baker	Carlos Baker, *Ernest Hemingway: A Life Story* (Scribner's, 1969)
Berg	Scott Berg, *Max Perkins* (E. P. Dutton, 1978)
Bruccoli	*The Only Thing That Counts*, ed. Matthew Bruccoli (Scribner's, 1996)
Burwell	Rose Marie Burwell, *Hemingway: The Postwar Years and the Posthumous Novels* (Cambridge University Press, 1996)
Carr	Virginia Spencer Carr, *Dos Passos: A Life* (Doubleday, 1984)
Conversations	*Conversations with Ernest Hemingway*, ed. Matthew Bruccoli (University Press of Mississippi, 1986)

Donaldson   Scott Donaldson, *Archibald MacLeish: An American Life* (Houghton Mifflin, 1992)

Donnelly   Honoria Murphy Donnelly, *Sara & Gerald: Villa America and After* (Times Books, 1982)

First War   Michael Reynolds, *Hemingway's First War* (Princeton University Press, 1976)

Fuentes   Noberto Fuentes, *Hemingway in Cuba* (Lyle Stuart, 1984)

Hanneman   *Ernest Hemingway, A Comprehensive Bibliography*, Vol. 1, ed. Audre Hanneman (Princeton University Press, 1967)

High on the Wild   Lloyd Arnold, *High on the Wild* (Grosset & Dunlap, 1968)

HIW   Mary Hemingway, *How It Was* (Knopf, 1976)

HL   James Brasch and Joséph Sigmund, *Hemingway's Library* (Garland Publishing, 1981)

Homecoming   Michael Reynolds, *Hemingway: The American Homecoming* (Blackwell, 1992)

HR   *The Hemingway Review* (University of Idaho Press)

Kert   Bernice Kert, *The Hemingway Women* (Norton, 1983)

LG   Linda Miller, *Letters from the Lost Generation* (Rutgers University Press, 1991)

Ludington   Townsend Ludington, *John Dos Passos* (E. P. Dutton, 1980)

McLendon   James McLendon, *Papa: Hemingway in Key West*, rev. Ed. (Key West: Langley Press, 1990)

Mellow   James Mellow, *A Life Without Consequences* (Houghton Mifflin, 1992)

Meyers   Jeffrey Meyers, *Hemingway* (Harper & Row, 1985)

Papa   Gregory Hemingway, *Papa* (Houghton Mifflin, 1976)

Paparov   Uri Paparov, *Hemingway en Cuba* (Moscow, 1979; siglo XXI editors: Mexico City, 1993), Spanish trans. Partida T. Armando

Paris Years   Michael Reynolds, *Hemingway: The Paris Years* (Blackwell, 1989; Norton, 1999)

Paul Smith   Paul Smith, *A Reader's Guide to the Short Stories of Ernest Hemingway* (G. K. Hall, 1989)

Reading   Michael Reynolds, *Hemingway's Reading* (Princeton University Press, 1981)

Reception   *Ernest Hemingway: The Critical Reception*, ed. Robert O. Stephens (Burt Franklin & Co., 1977)

Rollyson   Carl Rollyson, *Nothing Ever Happens to the Brave* (St. Martin's Press, 1990)

Ross   Lillian Ross, *Portrait of Ernest Hemingway* (Simon & Schuster, 1961)

Samuelson   Arnold Samuelson, *With Hemingway: A Year in Key West and Cuba* (Random House, 1984)

Slim   Slim Keith with Annette Tapert, *Slim* (Simon & Schuster, 1990)

Thomas   Hugh Thomas, *The Spanish Civil War* (Harper, 1961)

True Gen   Denis Brian, *The True Gen* (Grove Press, 1988)

TWMAA   Martha Gellhorn, *Travels with Myself and Another* (Allen Lane, 1978)

Viertel   Peter Viertel, *Dangerous Friends* (Doubleday, 1992)

YH   *Young Hemingway* (Blackwell, 1986; Norton, 1998)

BOOK I

PROLOGUE

1. O. O. McIntyre, "Drop In Again, Ernest," *Kansas City Times*, March 9, 1929.

CHAPTER 1: 1929

1. PH–EH, May 1 and 3, 1929, JFK.
2. MP–EH, telegram, April 4, 1929, JFK.
3. EH–MP, undated, c. April 1929, PUL. A characteristic exaggeration: Ernest and Pauline were never evicted from an apartment because of FSF.

4. See *First War*, pp. 20–66, and *Homecoming*, pp. 167–217.

5. See Alan Price, "I'm Not an Old Fogey and You're Not a Young Ass: Owen Wister and Ernest Hemingway," *Hemingway Review*, 9 (Fall 1989), 82–90, for a detailed analysis of this relationship.

6. Owen Wister–MP, May 6, 1929, PUL.

7. MP–Owen Wister, May 17, 1929, PUL.

8. FSF–EH, May 17, 1929, JFK.

9. EH–Robert Bridges, May 18, 1929, PUL.

10. MP–EH, May 24, 1929, PUL.

11. FSF–Zelda Fitzgerald, Summer (?) 1930, *Correspondence of FSF*, ed. M. J. Bruccoli and M. M. Duggan (Random House, 1980), pp. 240–1.

12. Zelda Fitzgerald–FSF, early fall 1930, *Correspondence of FSF*, p. 248.

13. FSF–EH, June 1929, JFK.

14. Typescript of *A Farewell to Arms*, JFK.

15. EH–MP, June 23, 1929, JFK. This letter is dated in *Selected Letters* as June 24; internal evidence (Mass and the steeplechase at Auteuil) says otherwise.

16. Item 845, Hemingway Collection, JFK.

17. Janet Flanner–EH, [June 18, 1929], JFK.

18. Nino Frank–EH, June 19, 1929, JFK.

19. H. G. Leech–EH, June 28, 1929, JFK.

20. George Antheil–EH, July 1, 1929, JFK.

21. Victor Llona–EH, Aug. 6 and 10, 1929, JFK.

22. Paul Johnson–EH, Aug. 31, 1929, JFK.

23. Paul Reynolds–MP, August 12, 1929, JFK.

24. Paul Reynolds–EH, Aug. 30, 1929, JFK.

25. MacLeish–EH, mailed June 24, 1929, JFK.

26. Scribner's clipping file, once in the Scribner's offices, now probably at PUL.

27. *Tribune*, Monday, June 24, 1929. Mary Hickok was not in Pamplona. Pat Morgan was.

28. *Tribune*, June 25, 1929; reprinted "Proclamation," *In transition: A Paris Anthology* (London: Phillips & Company Books, 1990), p. 19.

29. "Hemingway Gives Up Old Life with Literary Success," *New York Evening Post*, Nov. 18, 1929, p. 6.

30. *Tribune*, June 28 and 29, 1929. Total government receipts for fiscal 1928–29 were $3,998,694,187. In 1995 dollars, this figure would be roughly $28 billion.

31. "What with Drinking Wine and Dancing for 11 Days, Spain's Fiestas Tire One," *Brooklyn Daily Eagle*, July 29, 1929.

32. *El Pensamiento Navarro*, July 7–10, 1929; *100 Años de Carteles de las Fiestas y Ferias de San Fermin* (1882–1981) (Pamplona: Caja de Ahorros de Navarra, 1982), [np], 1929 feria.

33. "Crowds Revel in Fire, Wine and Chaos," *Brooklyn Daily Eagle*, July 22, 1929.

34. Ben Ray Redmond, "Spokesman for a Generation," *Spur*, 44 (Dec. 1, 1929), 77.

35. "Young Matador Risks His Life," *Brooklyn Daily Eagle*, July 25, 1929.

36. Hickok–EH, July 23, 1929, first read in a private collection, copy now at JFK.

37. EH–Louis Cohn, July 29, [1930], Cohn Collection, UDel.

38. See *Imaxe de Compostela*, ed. José Luis Cabo Villaverde and Pablo Coasta Bujan (Santiago: Publicacions do Coag, [nd]).

39. EH–Waldo Peirce, Aug. 29, 1929, copy at JFK.

40. PH–EH, c. July 7, 1929, JFK: "Do you want me to bring any of these stories you started."

41. EH–MP, June 7, 1929, *SL*, p. 297.

42. EH Journal, Aug. 12, [no year], internal evidence dates it 1929; JFK.

43. *Tribune*, Aug. 5, 1929, "2 Die, 20 Hurt in Nuremberg Hitlerite Riot."

44. *Tribune*, Aug. 10, 1929, "Flossie, Who Barred No Bars, Has Gone." See Hemingway's MS statement about her in *Paris Years*, p. 229.

45. *Tribune*, Aug. 11, 1929.

46. EH–Waldo Peirce, Aug. 29, 1929, copy at JFK.

47. See *H:PY*, 230–1, 252, and Hemingway's "The Summer People," published posthumously in *The Nick Adams Stories* (Scribner's 1972).

48. "Or the morning we had come in the gates of Paris and seen Salcede torn apart by the horses at the Place de Greves." *GHOA*, p. 108. I am indebted to my thesis advisee Robert Trogdon for this connection.

49. Hemingway Journal, Aug. 13, [no year], letters mentioned from Victor Llona and Owen Wister date it as 1929, JFK. Sixty-five centavos was worth roughly ten cents at the exchange rate of 6.75 pesetas to the dollar.

50. EH–Dos Passos, Sept. 4, 1929, *SL*, p. 303; EH–MP, Oct. 31, 1929, *SL*, p. 311.

51. EH–MP, April 15, 1925, *SL*, p. 156.

52. EH–MP, [c. Aug. 1929], from Santiago de Compostela, PUL.

53. For any reading reference that does not appear in a footnote, see *Reading*.

54. During the previous spring, Fitzgerald and Hemingway discussed the possibilities of using a medieval setting for their fiction. Soon afterward, at Sylvia Beach's lending library, Ernest borrowed Coulton's *Life in the Middle Ages* and Villehardouin's *Chronicles of Crusaders*, and he apparently bought a copy of Haye's *Ancient and Medieval History* published that year. See *Reading*. He also owned a copy of Lecky's *History of European Morals Augustus to Charlemagne* (1869), which he took to Cuba with him in 1940.

55. "Neo-Thomist Poem," first published in Ezra Pound's journal, *The Exile*, Spring 1927. Hemingway's footnote explains: "The title Neo-Thomist refers to temporary embracing of church by literary gents."

56. See *First War* and *YH*.

57. "The Earnest Liberal's Lament," *Der Querschnitt*, Autumn 1924, reprinted in *88 Poems*, p. 52.

58. EH–Mary Pfeiffer, Aug. 12, 1929, Carlos Baker Collection, PUL.

59. "Market Still on Its Upward Move," *Tribune*, Aug. 26, 1929.

60. *Tribune*, Sept. 2, 1929. Hemingway may well have read this story in a Madrid paper which would have been available in Palencia.

61. W. K. Klingaman, *1929: The Year of the Great Crash* (New York: Harper & Row, 1989), pp. 234–5.

62. "Swan Song of the Little Review," *Tribune*, Sept. 1, 1929.

63. Paul Nelson–EH, Dec. 30, 1929, JFK.

64. EH–MP, Sept. 7 and 9, 1929, first read in Scribner's offices, now at PUL.

65. FSF–EH, Aug. 23, 1929, JFK; EH–FSF, Sept. 4, 1929, *SL*, p. 305.

66. EH–FSF, Sept. 13, 1929, *SL*, p. 306.

67. Harry Crosby–EH, Oct. 3, 1929; *Tribune*, Oct. 6 and 7, 1929.

68. EH–MP, Oct. 4, 1929, JFK. The novel was priced at $2.50.

69. MP–EH, Oct. 15, 1929, first read at Scribner's offices, now at PUL.

70. MP–EH, Oct. 15, 1929, JFK.

71. Fanny Butcher, "Here Is Genius," Oct. 20, 1929, reprinted from *Chicago Tribune*, Sept. 28, 1929.

72. Henry Hazlitt, "Take Hemingway."

73. "Not Yet Demobilized," *New York Herald Tribune Books*, Oct. 6, 1929.

74. Agnes Smith, "Mr. Hemingway Does It Again," *New Yorker*, Oct. 12, 1929, p. 120; Henry Seidel Canby, "Story of the Brave," *Saturday*

Review of Literature, Oct. 12, 1929, pp. 231–2; Clifton P. Fadiman, "A Fine American Novel," *Nation*, Oct. 30, 1929, pp. 497–8.

75. Fanny Butcher, "Here Is Genius," *Tribune*, Oct. 20, 1929.

76. Linda Simon, *The Biography of Alice B. Toklas* (Garden City: Doubleday, 1977), p. 122.

77. EH–FSF, c. Oct. 22 or 29, 1929, *SL*, pp. 308–9; other evidence establishes the date as Oct. 22.

78. Allen Tate–Carlos Baker, April 19, 1963, Baker Collection, PUL.

79. Seward Collins–EH, Oct. 3, 1929, JFK. By this time eight to ten days usually moved a letter from New York to Paris.

80. See *Gertrude Stein: A Composite Portrait*, ed. Linda Simon (New York: Avon, 1974); *The Biography of Alice B. Toklas*; *Perpetual Motif: The Art of Man Ray* (Washington: National Museum of American Art, 1988); James Mellow, *Charmed Circle* (Praeger, 1974), photos.

81. Allen Tate–Carlos Baker, April 19, 1963, Baker Collection, PUL; and Allen Tate, "Random Thoughts on the 1920s," *Minnesota Review*, Fall 1960, pp. 46–56.

82. Ibid.

83. EH–FSF, Oct. 24, 1929, *SL*, pp. 309–11.

84. *Tribune*, Oct. 25, 1929.

85. *Tribune*, Oct. 26, 1929.

86. *Tribune*, Oct. 27–30, 1929; Klingaman, *1929: The Year of the Great Crash*, pp. 270–86; *SL*, p. 311.

87. Flechtheim was the publisher of *Der Querschnitt*, which promoted modernist painters at his several galleries. There are two bills for *Monument in Arbeit* at the JFK: one dated Nov. 15, 1929, and signed by Flechtheim is for 1,600 marks; the second, dated Nov. 18, from Galerie Simon for 30,000 francs. The total of the two is approximately $1,500, or the average annual income for the American workingman in 1929. Thanks to Jenny Agner, Klee specialist presently at Brown University, for helping with the provenance. In Mary Hemingway's will this picture was left to Gregory Hemingway.

88. EH–MP, Nov. 10, 1929, JFK.

89. Reprinted edition, *The Education of a French Model* (New York: Boar's Head Books, 1950), pp. 10–11.

90. See Paul Smith, pp. 223–4. In fact, on any points about the short fiction, see Paul Smith.

91. Dorothy Parker–Robert Benchley, [Nov. 7, 1929], in *LG*, pp. 47–53. Donnelly, pp. 48–54.
92. Sara Murphy–FSF, April 3, 1936, *LG*, p. 161.
93. MacLeish–Henrietta Crosby, Dec. 12, 1929, *Letters of Archibald MacLeish*, pp. 231–2.

CHAPTER 2: 1930

1. *New York Times*: *La Bourdannais*, with stops at Vigo and Halifax, arrived several days late in New York at noon on Jan. 25.
2. Scribner's Hemingway author file #9, first read at Scribner's offices, now at PUL.
3. *Post*, Feb. 1, 1930: *La Bourdannais* arrived yesterday. EH–Waldo Peirce, Feb. 7, 1930, copy at JFK.
4. Grace Hemingway–EH, Feb. 6 and 24, March 9, 1930, JFK; Hadley Hemingway–EH, March 10, 1930, JFK.
5. Waldo Peirce–EH, March 17, 28, and 29, 1930, JFK; EH–Waldo Peirce, May 9, 1930, JFK.
6. "The Fishing Life of Ernest Hemingway," *The Fisherman*, Jan. 1958, p. 85.
7. MacLeish–EH, [April 1930], JFK.
8. EH–Waldo Peirce, May 9, 1930, JFK; *Historical Statistics of the United States*, Bicentennial Edition (1975), p. 164.
9. Royalty statement attached to MP–EH, March 4, 1930, JFK. In 1995 dollars, his 1929 income translates to almost $160,000. In 1929, a one-way transatlantic liner ticket might cost $85–135, a new automobile $600–1,000. In 1930 a five-bedroom furnished house in Havana during the winter season rented for $350 a month.
10. *WTN*, p. 121. See *Homecoming*, pp. 197–8, and Paul Smith, pp. 217–22.
11. EH–Waldo Peirce, [c. April 6, 1930], copy at JFK.
12. EH–Henry Strater, May 20, 1930, *SL*, p. 322.
13. A. G. Pfeiffer–A. M. Teixidor, June 3 and 4, 1930, JFK; "Must have" books were *Tauromachia Completa* (1836), *Gran Diccionario Tauromaco* (1896 edition), *La Tauromachia de Rafael Guerra*, and *Doctrinal Tauromaco de Antonio Fernandez de Heredia* (1904). "Needed

if found" books were *Los Novillos* (1892) and *Los Toros en Madrid* (1892). The one-year subscriptions were to: *El Clarin, Toreros y Toros, El Eco Taurino,* and *La Fiesta Brava.* The bound back issues were of *Sol y Sombra* or *La Lidia* (1917–29), *El Clarin* (1925–29), and *Zig-Zag* (1923–25).

14. *Citizen,* June 14, 1930.
15. EH–Louis Henry Cohn, April 23, [1930], Cohn Collection, UDel.
16. EH–Louis Henry Cohn, June 24, [1930], Cohn Collection, UDel.
17. EH–MacLeish, June 30, 1930, *SL,* pp. 325–6; EH–Louis Cohn, c. Sept. 3, 1930, Cohn Collection, UDel.
18. "Visit by Ernest Hemingway," *Kansas City Star,* July 6, 1930, p. 3.
19. Onsite research and Ralph Glidden, *Exploring the Yellowstone High Country* (Cooke City, 1982). Much of what others have written of this area will not match a 1:60,000 terrain map.
20. Hemingway Fishing Log, 1930–34, JFK; Eaton film, DPS 28:c, JFK.
21. EH Hunting Log, 1930–34, JFK. Kills dated Aug. 23 and 30; Baker, 212–3; Absaroka-Beartooth Mountains 15×30 minute quadrangle map (Rock Mountain Surveys: Billings, Mont., 1987) 1:67,000. EH–Louis Cohn, c. Sept. 3, 1930, Cohn Collection, UDel. See EH–Henry Strater, c. June 20, 1930, *SL,* p. 324, for information on the rifle. See also Eaton film, JFK.
22. "The Clark's Fork Valley, Wyoming" first published in *Vogue,* Feb. 1939, reprinted in *By-Line,* pp. 298–300.
23. Eaton film, JFK.
24. EH–Louis Cohn, July 29, 1930, Cohn Collection, UDel.
25. EH–MP, Aug. 12, 1930, *SL,* pp. 326–8; EH–Henry Strater, c. Sept. 10, 1930, *SL,* pp. 328–9.
26. EH–MP, July 24, 1930, PUL.
27. EH–MP, Aug. 12, 1930; EH–Louis Cohn, [Sept. 3, 1930], Cohn Collection, UDel. See also Paul Smith.
28. EH–Louis Cohn, [Sept. 2, 1930], Cohn Collection, UDel; Paul Smith, "The Bloody Typewriter and the Burning Snakes," in *Hemingway: Essays of Reassessment,* ed. Frank Scafella (New York: Oxford U.P., 1991), pp.81–3.
29. *DIA,* typescript, p. 1, JFK.
30. EH–MP, Sept. 3, 1930, PUL. One attempt to revise "Mr. and Mrs. Elliot" became the verso of MS p. 189 of *DIA,* UTex.

31. Edward Stanley, *A Familiar History of Birds* (London: Longmans, Green, 1881), pp. 1–2; Ernest Hemingway, "A Natural History of the Dead," *WTN*, pp. 97–8.
32. "A Natural History of the Dead," pp. 97–106.
33. Patrick Hemingway Collection, PUL.
34. EH–William Horne, Sept. 12, 1930, Baker Collection, PUL.
35. EH–MP, Oct. 28, 1930, PUL.
36. Assignments of Copyrights, vol. 786, pp. 97–110, LOC. Contract is dated Sept. 17, 1930, and signed for Hemingway by Matthew G. Herold, attorney in fact. Hemingway's share was $24,000.
37. "Noted Novelist Is Injured in Auto Accident," *Gazette*, Nov. 2, 1930. Carlos Baker interview with Floyd Allington, July 20, 1964, PUL.
38. Mary Pickett, "Hemingway in St. Vincent: The Booze Also Rises," *Gazette*, April 8, 1983, 2-D/6, interview with Dorothy Buller and Bernadette Martin; "Noted Novelist Is Injured in Auto Accident," *Gazette*, Nov. 2, 1930.
39. Baker, p. 217; *Gazette*, November 5, 1930.
40. "Hemingway in St. Vincent;" Baker, p. 217. Kangaroo tendon, which was packaged in hermetically sealed glass tubes, was one of several binding materials in medical use in 1930. *New York Times*, Nov. 6, 1930.
41. EH–MacLeish, c. Nov. 22, 1930, *SL*, p. 330.
42. "Hemingway in St. Vincent." See also Pauline's appended note to the Hemingway letter she typed to Waldo Peirce, c. Nov. 28, 1930, copy at JFK and in Baker, p. 217.
43. "Two Wounded in Mystery Shooting," *Gazette*, Nov. 10, 1930, pp. 1, 2; "Sunday Fracas Still a Mystery," Nov. 13, 1930. Billings was and remains a center for processing sugar beets.
44. EH–MacLeish, Nov. 22, 1930, Baker, p. 218; EH–MP, Nov. 24, 1930, PUL.
45. "Hemingway at St. Vincent." In 1943, Florence Cloonan died in Denver from a heart attack.
46. See *Reading*.
47. *New York Times*, Nov.–Dec. 1930.
48. Among the most popular songs of 1930, according to Roger Lax and Frederick Smith, *The Great Song Thesaurus* (New York: Oxford U.P., 1984), pp. 55–6.
49. EH–Henry Strater, c. Dec. 15, 1930, *SL*, p. 335.

50. MacLeish–MP, Jan. 4, 1931, *MacLeish Letters*, p. 31; Donaldson, *An American Life*, p. 207.

51. A letter from a Mr. Snooks quoted in MP–Henry Strater, [c. Dec. 1930], Baker Collection, PUL.

52. EH–Henry Strater, c. Dec. 15, 1930, *SL*, p. 335; EH–MacLeish, c. Dec. 15, 1930, LOC.

53. EH–Owen Wister, December 26, 1930, UVa. In his next book, *Green Hills of Africa*, he attempts what he says here cannot be done.

CHAPTER 3: 1931

1. *Citizen* and *Post*, Jan.–May 1931.

2. EH–Mary Pfeiffer, Jan. 28, 1931, PUL.

3. *Citizen*, Jan.–Feb. 1931; EH–Waldo Peirce, Jan. 17, 1931, MeW/ JFK.

4. *Citizen*, Jan. 2 and 5, 1931.

5. *Citizen*, Feb. 3 and 10, 1931.

6. *Citizen*, Jan.–Feb. 1931.

7. *Citizen*, Feb. 3, 1931.

8. *Citizen*, April 28, 1931.

9. *Citizen*, Feb. 25, 1931.

10. *Citizen*, March 9, 1931.

11. *Citizen*, Jan. 9, 1931.

12. *Citizen*, Feb. 27, 1931.

13. *Citizen*, Jan. 27, 1931.

14. Baker, pp. 219–21; Hemingway Fishing Log, 1931, JFK.

15. EH Fishing Log, 1930–34, JFK; *Citizen*, February 4, 1931.

16. *Citizen*, Feb. 4, 1931.

17. Elinor Langer, *Josephine Herbst* (Boston: Little, Brown, 1983), pp. 106–12.

18. Isidor Schneider, "The Fetish of Simplicity," *Nation,* Feb. 18, 1931, 184–6.

19. *Citizen*, March 14, 1931. The Sidleys owned a large cabin at the L-Bar-T.

20. Item 624, Hemingway Collection, JFK.

21. EH–FSF, April 12, 1931, *SL*, p. 339.

22. EH–MP, April 12 and 27, 1931, Scribner Collection, PUL. See *Reading*.

23. Uncorrected typed carbon, MCL; EH–MacLeish, April 19, [1931], LOC.

24. Item 754, JFK.

25. *Citizen*, April 30, 1931.

26. Monroe County Deed Book, D-3, p. 153; Toby Bruce interview, Aug. 1, 1965, MCL; PH–EH, May 11, 16, 1931, JFK.

27. *Tribune*, May 11, 1931.

28. EH–Waldo Peirce, May 14, 1931, JFK.

29. *Tribune*, May 15–18, 1931.

30. Quintana–EH, May 23 and June 26, 1931, JFK.

31. *DIA*, pp. 276–7.

32. *Tribune*, May 28, 1931.

33. *DIA*, pp. 218–9.

34. *Tribune*, May 31, 1931.

35. *Tribune*, June 17, 1931.

36. *Tribune*, June 26–27, 1931.

37. EH–Dos Passos, June 26, 1931, *SL*, p. 341.

38. *Tribune*, June 29–July 1, 1931.

39. EH–MP, Aug. 1, 1931, PUL.

40. Quintana–EH, June 25, 1931, JFK.

41. *DIA*, pp. 87–90.

42. Paul Mowrer–EH, June 27, 1931, JFK; Winifred Mowrer note, undated, JFK.

43. EH–Guy Hickok, July 15, [1931], private collection; EH–MacLeish, July 28, [1931], LOC.

44. *Tribune*, July 1931.

45. EH–MP, Aug. 1 and Dec. 9, 1931, PUL.

46. EH Notebook, inventory, JFK; bills, 1931, Galerie Simon, JFK.

47. Beach Collection, PUL; *Reading*.

48. Don Brown, "Hemingway Back in Paris; Sails for New York in Week," *Tribune*, September 20, 1931.

49. "The Ghost of a Writer," *Kansas City Star*, Oct. 21, 1931.

50. Wambly Bald, "La Vie de Bohème," *Tribune*, Sept. 23, 1931.

51. EH–L.H. Cohn, [Nov. 16, 1931], UDel.

52. EH–Waldo Peirce, c. Nov. 1, 1931, *SL*, p. 343.

53. Hickok–EH, Dec. 30, 1931, JFK.

54. EH–Hickok, Dec. 12, 1931, private collection.
55. EH–MacLeish, Dec. 9, 1931, LOC.
56. *DIA*, p. 232.
57. *DIA*, p. 91.
58. *DIA*, p. 222.
59. *DIA*, pp. 273–5.
60. EH–MP, Dec. 9, 1931, PUL.
61. EH–MacLeish, Dec. 9, 1931, LOC.
62. *DIA*, galley 79, UDel.
63. *New York Times*, Dec. 10, 1931.
64. EH–MP, Dec. 26, 1932, *SL*, 346–8; EH–MacLeish, Dec. 23, 1931, LOC; *Citizen*, Dec. 23, 1931.

CHAPTER 4: 1932

1. EH–George Albee, Jan. 31, 1932, UCal.
2. EH–Mary Pfeiffer, Jan. 5, 1932, *SL*, pp. 348–50.
3. "Death in the Afternoon," holograph notes in a private collection.
4. MP–EH, Jan. 5, 1932, JFK.
5. EH–MP, Jan. 5–6, 1932, *SL*, pp. 351–2.
6. *DIA*, p. 95.
7. Parish baptismal index, Key West; baptismal certificate, JFK; EH–MacLeish, Jan. 14, [1932], LOC; EH–MacLeish, Jan. 28, [1932], LOC; EH–MP, Feb. 7, 1932, PUL.
8. EH–MP, Feb. 7, 1932, PUL.
9. *New York Times*, Feb. 4, 1932.
10. EH–MacLeish, Feb. 9, [1932], LOC.
11. MacLeish–EH, [Feb. 29, 1932], *Letters of Archibald MacLeish* (Boston: Houghton Mifflin, 1983), p. 246.
12. Dos Passos–EH, [Feb. 1932], *Fourteenth Chronicle*, pp. 402–3.
13. EH–MacLeish, Dec. 9, 1931, LOC.
14. Item 22, JFK; corrected galleys, UDel.
15. [Feb. 1932], JFK, fragment unmailed.
16. A. G. Pfeiffer–EH, Feb. 24, 1932, JFK.
17. *Miami Daily News*, [no date], clipping in MCL. Passenger and crew number was reported variously between 400 and 488. The ship apparently sank on September 12, 1919.

18. Items 226a and 226b, JFK; MS Am 1199, Houghton, Harvard; *WTN*, p. 9. See Susan Beegel, *Hemingway's Craft of Omission* (UMI Press, 1988), Chap.4, for full account. See also Paul Smith.
19. *WTN*, p. 67.
20. *WTN*, pp. 75–88.
21. *True Gen*, p. 91.
22. MacLeish–EH, [April 7, 1932], *Letters*, p. 247.
23. See Scott Donaldson's *MacLeish: An American Life* for the most complete analysis of this relationship.
24. EH–MP, April 5, 1932, JFK.
25. EH–MP, April 5, 1932, JFK.
26. MP–EH, April 19, 1932, PUL, Amory Blaine is the hero of Fitzgerald's novel *This Side of Paradise*.
27. Grace Hemingway–EH, April 5, 1932, JFK.
28. Grace Hemingway–EH, March 13, 1932, JFK.
29. EH–Grace Hemingway, April 8, 1932, Lilly.
30. See *YH* and *Homecoming*. EH–Robert Coates, Oct. 5, 1932, in *New Yorker*, Nov. 5, 1932, pp. 86–7.
31. Item 355, JFK. Use of "niggers" is not meant to be inflammatory, rather to remind the reader that white Americans in the 1930s used this term as casually as salt.
32. "Log of the HMS *Anita*," JFK; *New York Times*, April 27, 1932.
33. "Incoming, Outgoing Ships," *Post*, April 27, 1932; John Unterecker, *Voyager: A Life of Hart Crane* (1969), pp. 754–9.
34. EH–Waldo Peirce, June 6, 1932, JFK.
35. EH–MP, May 14, 1932, JFK; EH–Strater, c. May 22 and June 10, 1932, PUL.
36. "Log of the HMS *Anita*" and typescript, JFK.
37. *Anita* log, JFK.
38. *Post*, April 28, 1932.
39. *New York Times*, May, 1932.
40. *Post*, May 16, 1932.
41. *Post*, May 3, 1932.
42. EH–MP, May 14, 1932, PUL.
43. EH–MP, June 2, 1932, PUL; EH–Bud White, June 2, 1932, JFK.
44. EH–MacLeish, June 2, 1932, LOC.
45. EH–Henry Strater, June 10, 1932, PUL.
46. *Post*, June 8–10, 1932.

47. EH–MacLeish, June 2, 1932, LOC; First Union Trust of Chicago–EH, June 13, 17, and 18, 1932, Tulsa.
48. PH–EH, four letters, May 1932, JFK.
49. PH–EH, letters May and June, 1932, JFK.
50. Memoir of Josephine Wall Merck, undated, JFK.
51. Item 548, 549, JFK; Scott Donaldson, "The Case of the Vanishing American," *Hemingway Notes*, Spring 1981, pp. 16–19; *YH*, 104–5.
52. Hemingway Hunting Log, 1930–34, JFK.
53. EH–Bill Lengel, misdated as c. Aug. 15, 1932, *SL*, p. 367. More likely first week in July.
54. EH–MP, Aug. 9, 1932, PUL.
55. EH–Paul Romaine, July 6, 1932; Aug. 9, 1932, *SL*, pp. 363–5.
56. "An Autopsy and a Prescription," *Hound & Horn*, July–Sept. 1932, pp. 520–39.
57. EH–MacLeish, [Aug. 27, 1932], LOC.
58. "Correspondence," *Hound & Horn*, Oct.–Dec. 1932, p. 135.
59. *DIA*, pp. 70–72.
60. Hemingway Fishing Log, 1930–34, JFK.
61. EH–MacLeish, July 31, 1932, LOC.
62. Murphy–MacLeish, Sept. 8, 1932, *LG*, pp. 63–5; Donnelly, pp. 66–8.
63. Murphy–MacLeish, Sept. 8, 1932, *LG*, p. 65.
64. "Dissertation on Pride," *New York Sun*, Sept. 23, 1932, p. 34.
65. Herschel Brickell, "What Bullfighting Means to the Spaniards," *New York Herald Tribune*, Sept. 25, 1932, p. 12.
66. R. L. Duffus, "Hemingway Now Writes of Bull-fighting As an Art," *New York Times*, Sept. 25, 1932, pp. 5, 17.
67. Robert M. Coates, "Bullfighters," *New Yorker*, Oct. 1, 1932, pp. 61–3; Granville Hicks, "Bulls and Bottles," *Nation*, Nov. 9, 1932, p. 461; Malcolm Cowley, "A Farewell to Spain," *New Republic*, Nov. 30, 1932, pp. 76–7.
68. Hemingway Hunting Log, JFK; EH–MacLeish, Oct. 13, 1932, LOC; EH–Henry Strater, Oct. 14, 1932, *SL*, p. 370.
69. Nordquist bill dated Oct. 15, 1932, Tulsa.
70. Mario Sanchez's painted bas-reliefs, Martello Tower, Key West Historical Society.
71. *Citizen*, Nov. 8–10, 1932; PH–EH, Nov. 8, 1932, JFK; Hemingway family papers, UTex; *New York Times*, Nov. 12, 1932.
72. Ralph Stitt–EH, c. Dec. 2, 1932, JFK.

73. *New York Times*, Dec. 6, 1932, p. 27.
74. Stitt–EH, Dec. 6, 1932, JFK.
75. Gus Pfeiffer–EH, Dec. 8 and 10, 1932, JFK.
76. EH–MP, Dec. 7, 1932, *SL*, p. 379. This blurb appeared as quoted in *Washington Post* early in 1933, JFK.
77. EH–MacLeish, Dec. 22, 1932, LOC; Hemingway Hunting Log, 1930–34, JFK.
78. EH–MacLeish, Dec. 22, 1932, LOC; Hemingway Hunting Log, 1930–34, JFK; various newspapers.
79. *WTN*, pp. 13–17.

CHAPTER 5: 1933

1. EH–MP, Jan. 4 and 7, 1933, PUL.
2. Berg, p. 215–25.
3. EH notebook, Jan. 1933, private collection; EH–Eric Knight, Jan. 31, 1933, PUL.
4. Josephine Merck, "Stray Comments About Ernest Hemingway," unpublished, JFK.
5. *Nation*, Jan. 18, 1933, pp. 63–4.
6. *True Gen*, pp. 89–90; EH notebook; Kert, pp. 245–6.
7. Gingrich, *Nothing but People* (Crown, 1971), pp. 85ff. Memoir less than accurate in the details.
8. EH notebook; *Citizen*, Jan. 23, 1933.
9. *New York Times*, Feb. 16, 1933; *Citizen*, March 10, 1933.
10. EH–Dos Passos, c. March 10, 1933, PUL.
11. EH–Albee, Feb. 16, 1933, UCal.
12. Shevlin–EH, Feb. 7, 1933, JFK; *Citizen*, Jan. 31, 1933.
13. *WTN*, p. 147.
14. Items 648a, 648b, and 529a, JFK. See Donald Junkins, "Philip Haines Was a Writer" and "Hemingway's Paris Short Story," *Hemingway Review*, Spring 1990, pp. 2–48.
15. EH–MP, Feb. 23, 1933, PUL. This novel has been misidentified elsewhere as the beginning of *THHN*.
16. Gingrich–EH, Feb. 24, 1933, private collection; Gingrich–EH, April 24 and May 26, 1933, JFK.

17. EH–Gingrich, March 13, 1933, *SL*, pp. 383–4. For a more romantic version of the negotiations, read Gingrich's *Nothing but People*, which is right in everything but the accuracy of chronology, dialogue, and places.
18. EH–Gingrich, March 17, 1933, private collection.
19. EH–Gingrich, April 3, 1933, *SL*, p. 384.
20. Mary Post–EH, Feb. 24, 1933, private collection.
21. Item 813, JFK.
22. The three villages mentioned, Fornaci, San Dona, and Zenzon, are all roughly eight kilometers from Fossalta, enclosing it in a triangle, one leg of which is the Piave River.
23. For a detailed analysis of the story's structure, see Paul Smith, pp. 268–75.
24. Gaby Delys and Harry Pilcer had a nightclub act in Paris before the war, but Hemingway never saw her dance. See *Paris Years*, p. 82.
25. Item 815, JFK; *WTN*, p. 53.
26. See *Homecoming*, pp. 103–4.
27. *Citizen*, April 1, 1933.
28. Author interview with Anthony Mason.
29. PH–EH, May 21 and 25, 1933, JFK.
30. In undated clipping from Daniel Lord's column in *The Sign*, [c. 1930s], JFK; Hemingway notebook in private collection.
31. *Citizen*, March 29, April 5, 1933.
32. EH–Dos Passos, c. March 10, 1933, PUL.
33. EH–MP, March 13, 1933, PUL.
34. Charles Scribner–EH, March 31, 1933, JFK.
35. *Citizen*, April 12, 1933; EH Fishing Log, 1930–34, JFK.
36. *Citizen*, April 14, 1933; EH Fishing Log, 1930–34, *New York Times*, April 14–15, 1933.
37. *New York Times*, April 15, 1933.
38. EH calendar log, 1933, JFK.
39. Jane Armstrong, "Ernest Hemingway Returns in Quest of Giant Marlin," *Post*, April 14, 1933.
40. *New York Times*, April 21, 1933.
41. See Carleton Beals, *The Crime of Cuba* (Lippincott, 1933), photo #28.
42. Anthony Mason interview.
43. *Post*, May 25, 1933.

44. Anthony Mason interview.
45. Grace Hemingway–EH, JFK.
46. PH–EH, May 27, 1933, JFK.
47. *Post*, May 27, 1933. The *Anita* log puts marlin 30, 31, and 32 on May 25.
48. Anthony Mason interview; *Post*, June 4, 1933.
49. *Post*, July 5, 1933.
50. *Post*, "Waterfront Gossip," June 9, 1933.
51. EH–MacLeish, July 27, 1933, LOC.
52. Jane Mason–EH/PH, Sept. 2, 1933, JFK; Dr. K.P.A. Taylor–EH, July 19, 1933, JFK.
53. See *Anita* log, 1933, JFK, pp. 62–4.
54. EH notebook on *WTN* in Baker Collection, Box 17, Folder 6, PUL; *Anita* log, 1933, JFK, p. 62; EH–Gingrich, June 7, 1933, *SL*, p.393. Another copy of this letter in a private collection adds, "Have come down the coast for a while at Cabanas," not in *SL*.
55. MP–EH, June 19, 1933, JFK.
56. See *YH*, pp. 77–87; *Homecoming*, pp. 100–201, 206–7.
57. Item 384, JFK.
58. MSS are simplifed here: see Items 222, 382, 383, 384, 385, 513, 522, and 816, JFK, and *WTN*, pp. 151–62; see Paul Smith, pp. 307–17, for best entry to the MSS.
59. EH–MP, July 13, 1933, PUL and Maryland.
60. Gertrude Stein, *The Autobiography of Alice B. Toklas* (Harcourt Brace, 1933).
61. EH–Janet Flanner, April 8, 1933, *SL*, p. 388.
62. "Bull in the Afternoon," *New Republic*, June 7, 1933, pp. 94–7.
63. Scribner-1, Box 2, Folder 12, PUL.
64. MP–EH, wire, June 12, 1933, JFK; EH–MP, June 13, 1933, *SL*, p. 394.
65. Letter attached to EH–MacLeish, June 12, 1933, LOC.
66. EH–MacLeish, June 28, 1933, LOC.
67. EH Fishing Log, 1933, JFK.
68. "Town Tales Told in Tabloid," *Post*, July 8, 1933.
69. *Post*, July 19, 1933.
70. John Raeburn, *Fame Became of Him* (Indiana U. Press, 1984), pp. 45–50.

CHAPTER 6: 1933–34

1. *Post*, Aug. 3 and 4, 1933; *New York Times*, Aug. 4–13, 1933.
2. EH–MP, Aug. 10, 1933 (mailed in Bermuda on August 11), Scribner-1, PUL.
3. Anthony Mason interview and *Post*, Aug. 13, 1933.
4. See *Homecoming*, pp. 145–57, and *Hemingway: Up in Michigan Perspectives*, eds. F. J. Svoboda and J. J. Waldmeir (Michigan State U. Press, 1995), pp. 105–26. This MS has never been published. Also Item 617, JFK.
5. *GHOA*, MS-309-10, UVa.
6. Hadley Mowrer–EH, Aug. 23, 1933, formerly in the private John and Marsha Goin Collection.
7. Waring Jones Collection, Xerox copy in Baker Collection, PUL; Goin Collection: dinner bill at Hotel Roma (La Coruña), Aug. 17, 1933; letters received at Hotel Avenida (San Sebastián), Aug. 22, 1933; Kert, pp. 250–1.
8. Hanneman, Vol. 1, p. 36.
9. Items 222-1 and 222a, JFK; EH–MP, Aug. 31, 1933, Scribner-1, PUL. Alternate titles were "Long Time Ago Good," "Tomb of a Grandfather," and "Indian Summer."
10. Cass Canfield–EH, Oct. 19, 1933, Goin Collection.
11. EH–MP, Sept. 18, 1933, Scribner-1, PUL.
12. EH–Gingrich, Sept. 26, 1933, private collection.
13. "The Friend of Spain: A Spanish Letter," *Esquire*, Jan. 1934.
14. Pound–EH, Aug. 13 and Sept. 29, 1933, copies in JFK.
15. Story published in *Cosmopolitan*, April 1934, pp. 20–3, 108–22. EH–Mrs. Mary Pfeiffer, Oct. 16, 1933, *SL*, pp. 396–9.
16. EH–PH, Oct. 16, 1933, JFK.
17. EH–PH, [Oct. 24, 1933], JFK.
18. *Tribune*, Oct. 9, 1933.
19. EH–Gingrich, Sept. 26, 1933, private collection.
20. Item 265a, JFK, unpublished; this overheard incident will reappear years later in *A Moveable Feast*. In EH–PH, Oct. 17, 1933, JFK, he says the sketch was written to submit to *The New Yorker*.
21. Jonathan Cape–EH, Oct. 2, 1933, JFK, refers to sending Hemingway four books, *While the Billy Boils*, Sean O'Faolain's *Midsummer Night*

Madness, Brazilian Adventure, and William Plomer's *The Child of Queen Victoria.* The hunt was canceled because of rain.

22. EH–Mr. Hall, Oct. 16, 1933, JFK, enclosed in a letter to PH on Oct. 19.

23. EH–Mrs. Paul Pfeiffer, Oct. 16, 1933, *SL,* pp. 396–9.

24. EH–PH, Oct. 16, 1933, JFK.

25. EH–Clifton Fadiman, Nov. 26, 1933, PUL.

26. This Protestant conundrum affects more than one American writer, including, at times, Hawthorne, Melville, and Twain.

27. EH–Mr. Hall, Oct. 16, 1933, JFK.

28. EH–PH, Oct. 19, 1933, JFK.

29. PH–EH, Oct. 22, 1933, JFK.

30. *Tribune,* Oct. 16, 1933.

31. In 1995 dollars, the safari cost close to $200,000.

32. Hotel bill, October 1933, JFK.

33. To-do list, Tulsa; Pauline's safari notebook, Stanford.

34. EH–Gingrich, Nov. 21, 1933, private collection.

35. Morrill Cody–Carlos Baker, Sept. 18, 1962, PUL.

36. Wambly Bald, "A Farewell to Montparnasse," *Tribune,* July 25, 1933.

37. *Esquire,* Feb. 1934, p. 156.

38. Gingrich–EH, Oct. 13, 1933, JFK.

39. MP–EH, telegram, Oct. 26, 1933, JFK.

40. MacLeish–EH, telegram, Oct. 31, 1933, JFK.

41. MP–EH, telegram, Nov. 11, 1933, JFK.

42. MP–EH, Nov. 6, 1933, JFK.

43. See *Reception,* pp. 135–47.

44. Louis Kronenberger, "Hemingway's New Stories," *New York Times Book Review,* Nov. 5, 1933.

45. EH–MP, Nov. 16, 1933, *SL,* pp. 399–401.

46. EH Passport, JFK.

47. EH Notes, CO-365, Box 17, Folder 6, PUL; hotel bill, Dec. 9–10, 1933, JFK; Daniel Streeter, *Denatured Africa* (Garden City Pub., 1926); McLendon, p. 99.

48. Elspeth Huxley, *Out in the Midday Sun* (Viking, 1985).

49. *YH,* pp. 228–9.

50. Jane Mason–EH, Nov. 1, 1933, JFK.

51. Paid bill for 550 pounds, Dec. 14, 1933, Tulsa; EH–J. F. Manley, Nov. 6, 1933, JFK; *YH,* pp. 228–33.

52. *YH*, pp. 29–30; *SAR*, p. 10.
53. EH–Gingrich, Dec. 19, 1933, private collection.
54. "Ernest Hemingway's Introduction," Jimmy Charters and Morrill Cody, *This Must Be the Place* (Herbert Joseph, 1934), pp. 1–3.
55. Bill Lengel–EH, Jan. 26, 1934, JFK.
56. *East African Weekly Times*, Dec. 15, 1933.
57. *East African Weekly Times*, Dec. 1, 1933–Jan. 19, 1934.
58. *Esquire*, April 1934, p. 19.
59. Hemingway hotel bill, Jan. 16–22, 1933, Goin Collection.
60. EH–MP, Jan. 17, 1933, PUL.
61. H. Kortischoner–EH, Dec. 22, 1938, JFK.
62. Pauline Hemingway's safari journal, Stanford. The total kill was probably larger, but these are all she recorded. The details of the safari, unless otherwise noted, all come from this journal.

CHAPTER 7: 1934

1. *Citizen*, April 12, 1934.
2. EH–Gerald Murphy, April 27, 1934, *LG*, p. 83.
3. Brentano's book bill, March 23, 1934, JFK. See also *Reading* and *Library*.
4. EH–Gingrich, April 12, 1934, private collection.
5. Contract dated April 18, 1934, *Pilar* papers, JFK. A black boat at sea is difficult to see during the day and impossible at night.
6. EH–MP, April 30, 1934, Scribner-1, PUL.
7. EH–Gingrich, March 24, 1934, private collection.
8. EH–Gingrich, April 12, 1934, private collection.
9. *Green Hills of Africa* holograph MS, UVa; M.A. theses of David LeDuc and Robert Trogdon, N.C. State University; Barbara Lounsberry, "The Holograph Manuscript of *Green Hills of Africa*," *Hemingway Review*, Spring 1933, p. 36.
10. *Vanity Fair*, March 1934, p. 29.
11. Charles Cadwalader–EH, March 6, 1934, and EH–Cadwalader, April 2, 1934, Baker Collection, PUL.
12. Several telegrams in early April 1934, JFK.
13. "Out in the Stream: A Cuban Letter," *Esquire*, Aug. 1934, pp. 19, 156, 158.

14. "The Law of the Jungle," *New Yorker*, April 14, 1934, p. 31.

15. EH–Sara Murphy, April 27, 1934, *LG*, p. 84.

16. *Citizen*, April and May, 1934.

17. Lawrence Conrad, "Ernest Hemingway, " *The Landmark*, Aug. 1934, p. 397.

18. EH–MP, April 30, 1934, Scribner-1, PUL.

19. *Post*, May 2–5, 1934.

20. Ibid., May 4, 1934.

21. *Pilar* papers, May 5, 1934, JFK.

22. *Citizen*, May 1934.

23. FSF–EH, May 10, 1934, JFK.

24. EH–FSF, May 28, 1934, *SL*, pp. 407–9.

25. *Citizen*, May 10, 21, and 23, 1934.

26. *Citizen*, July 5, 1934.

27. *Citizen*, July 6–18, 1934.

28. *Pilar* papers, JFK.

29. "To Get for Cuba" shopping list, Goin Collection; EH–Gingrich, July 14, 1934, private collection; EH–MacLeish, c. July 11, 1934, LOC.

30. Samuelson, pp. 64–68. Samuelson's book, edited posthumously, is filled with small errors (names, dates, places); where we differ my sources may be checked against his text.

31. *Post*, July 21, 1934.

32. *Post*, July 25, 1934.

33. "Genio After Josie: A Havana Letter," *Esquire*, Oct. 1934, p. 21.

34. *Post*, August 1–15, 1934.

35. Photograph, JFK.

36. *Post*, Aug. 7, 1934.

37. *Post*, Aug. 28, 1934.

38. *Post*, Aug. 14 and 17, 1934.

39. EH–Mary Pfeiffer, Aug. 20, 1934, PUL.

40. *Post*, Sept. 4 and 5, 1934; EH–Cadwalader, Sept. 6, 1934, PUL.

41. See PH–EH letters of September, 1934, JFK.

42. EH–Gingrich, Sept. 13, 1934, private collection.

43. Tourist Identification Card, Sept. 14, 1934, JFK. PH–EH, Sept. 15, 1934, JFK.

44. EH–MP, Oct. 3, 1934, PUL.

45. MP–EH, Oct. 6, 1934, PUL.

46. EH–Lester Ziffin, Nov. 23, 1934, Baker Collection, PUL.

47. *Post*, Oct. 4 and 5, 1934.

48. EH–Cadwalader, Oct. 18, 1934, Baker Collection, PUL. In the May 1936 *Esquire* letter, Hemingway used the experience for "There She Breaches! Or Moby Dick off the Morro," pp. 35, 203–05.

49. Ludington, pp. 329–30.

50. *Post*, Oct. 21, 1934.

51. *Post*, Oct. 26, 1934; EH–Gingrich, Oct. 25, 1934, private collection; Oct. 16, 1934, *Post* in the Hemingway Collection, Tulsa; EH–Murphys, Nov. 7, 1934, *LG*, p. 96.

52. PH–EH, Oct. 5, 1934, JFK; "She Was Papa's Washerwoman," *Miami Herald*, Aug. 30, 1964.

53. *Miami Herald*, Dec. 12, 1976.

54. EH–Gingrich, July 15, 1934, *SL*, p. 410.

55. Robert Frost to friends, Dec. 1934, *Selected Letters of Robert Frost*, ed. Lawrence Thompson (Holt, Rinehart & Winston, 1964), pp. 413–15.

56. *Citizen*, Oct.–Nov. 1934; Garry Boulard, "State of Emergency: Key West in the Great Depression," *Florida Historical Quarterly*, Oct. 1988, pp. 166–83.

57. *GHOA*, MS-308, UVa.

58. Kert, p. 269, based on interviews with all three sons. Ada's possibly lesbian nature became apparent to the boys only years later.

59. Gregory Hemingway interview with MSR.

60. Katy Dos Passos–Murphys, Dec. 2, 1934, *LG*, p. 100.

61. MP–EH, Nov. 10, 1934, PUL.

62. EH–Murphys, Nov. 16, 1934, *LG*, p. 97; EH–Gingrich, Nov. 16, 1934, *SL*, p. 410; EH–MP, Nov. 16, 1934, PUL.

63. MP–Owen Wister, Nov. 21, 1934, PUL.

64. *Time*, Nov. 1934, reprinted in *Citizen*, Dec. 4, 1934.

65. "Notes on Life and Letters," *Esquire*, Jan. 1935, p. 21; EH–Gingrich, Nov. 19, 1934, private collection.

66. *GHOA*, p. 21.

67. EH–MP, Nov. 20, 1934, PUL.

68. MP–EH, Nov. 22, 1934, PUL.

69. MP–EH, Nov. 28, 1934, PUL.

70. *Citizen*, Dec. 5, 7, and 8, 1934.

71. EH–MP, Dec. 14, 1934, PUL.

72. *Citizen*, Dec. 19, 1934; Hotel Peabody bill for EH, wife, and one son, Dec. 22, 1934, PUL.

CHAPTER 8: *1935*

1. *Citizen*, Jan.–March 1935.
2. *Citizen*, Dec. 20, 1934, Jan. 11, 1935.
3. *Citizen*, March 1, 1935.
4. *Citizen*, March 4, 1935.
5. *Citizen*, April 11, 1935.
6. Katy Dos Passos–Sara Murphy, Jan. 1935, *LG*, pp. 109–10.
7. PH–Sara Murphy, Jan. 1935, *LG*, p. 102.
8. *Papa*, p. 19.
9. EH–MP, Jan. 16, 1935, PUL; Burt MacBride–EH, Jan. 21, 1935, JFK; MP–Lawrence Kubie, Jan. 22, 1935, PUL.
10. Burt MacBride–EH, Jan. 23 and 25, 1935, JFK; *Citizen*, Jan. 24, 1935.
11. *Citizen*, Feb. 2, 1935; Berg, photographs.
12. MP–EH, Feb. 4, 1935, PUL.
13. EH–Gingrich, Feb. 4, 1935, private collection.
14. EH–MP, telegram, Feb. 18, 1935, PUL; MP–EH and EH–MP telegrams, Feb. 19, 1935, PUL.
15. Several telegrams and letters back and forth between Hemingway and MP, Feb. 19–22, 1935, PUL.
16. EH–MP, Feb. 22, 1935, PUL; Sara Murphy–Hemingways, Sept. 12, 1935, *LG*, p. 142.
17. Murphys–Hemingway and Dos Passos, March 14, 1935, Waring Jones Collection, copies in PUL.
18. Donnelly, pp. 88–90; telegrams in Waring Jones Collection, copies in PUL.
19. EH–Gerald and Sara Murphy, March 19, 1935, *LG*, p. 118.
20. Ernest Hemingway, "The Sights of Whitehead Street: A Key West Letter," *Esquire*, April 1935, p. 25.
21. EH–Patrick Murphy, April 5, 1935, *LG*, pp. 126–9; to-do list, Hemingway notebook previously in Goin Collection.
22. "On Being Shot Again: A Gulf Stream Letter," *Esquire*, June 1935, pp. 23, 156–7.

23. Numerous Hemingway letters, JFK; Algernon Aspinall, *The Pocket Guide to the West Indies*, rev. ed. (London: Sifton, Praed, 1935), p. 71; "The Wet Way from Bimini to Florida," *Literary Digest*, Feb. 15, 1930, p. 17; EH–MP, June 3, 1935, PUL; EH–MacLeish, June 2, 1935, LOC.

24. John Dos Passos, *The Best of Times*, pp. 208–14.

25. Katy Dos Passos–Gerald Murphy, June 20, 1935, *LG*, pp. 131–2.

26. Mary Hemingway–Carlos Baker, Baker Collection, PUL.

27. EH–MP, May 1, 1935, PUL.

28. EH–MacLeish, June 2, 1935, LOC.

29. EH–Gingrich, June 4, 1935, *SL*, pp. 414–5; Mary Hemingway–Carlos Baker, March 12, 1962, Baker Collection, PUL.

30. *Papa*, pp. 35–37.

31. Meyers, p. 285; Mellow, pp. 469–70.

32. EH–MP, July 4, 1935, PUL.

33. EH–MP, April 14, 1935, PUL.

34. EH–MP, July 2, 1935, PUL.

35. MP–EH, July 9, 1935, PUL.

36. *GHOA*, p. 150.

37. EH–MP, June 19, 1935, PUL.

38. MP–EH, June 28, 1935, PUL.

39. EH–MP, July 30, 1935, PUL. "Pursuit and Failure" was added later.

40. EH–MP, July 30, 1935, PUL; various notes in Goin Collection; "The President Vanquishes: A Bimini Letter," *Esquire*, July 1935, p. 167.

41. *Citizen*, Aug. 5, 1935.

42. EH–MP, c. Aug. 15, 1935, PUL; EH–Gingrich, Aug. 23, 1935, PUL.

43. *Citizen*, Aug. 20 and 31, 1935.

44. "The 1935 Labor Day Hurricane," *Coral Tribune*, week of September 11, 1954, MCL.

45. EH–MP, Sept. 7, 1935, PUL.

46. *Citizen*, Sept. 5, 1935.

47. *Coral Tribune*, week of Sept. 11, 1954.

48. *Coral Tribune*, week of Sept. 4, 1954.

49. *Coral Tribune*, week of Sept. 18, 1954; *Citizen*, Sept. 5–7, 1935.

50. *Citizen*, Sept. 5–8, 1935; EH–MP, Sept. 7, 1935, PUL.

51. Maurine Williams, "Weep Twice for Them," *Citizen*, Sept. 6, 1935.

52. EH–MP, Sept. 7 and 12, 1935, PUL; EH–Sara Murphy, Sept. 12, 1935, *LG*, pp. 142–3.

53. Ernest Hemingway, "Who Murdered the Vets?" *New Masses*, Sept. 17, 1935, pp. 9–10.

54. EH–MP, Sept. 7, 1935, PUL.

55. "Million Dollar Fright: A New York Letter," *Esquire*, Dec. 1935, pp. 35, 190B. A year later Max Schmeling defeated Louis.

56. Subtitled "A Serious Topical Letter," *Esquire*, Sept. 1935, pp. 19, 136.

57. Sara Murphy–PH, Oct. 18, 1935, *LG*, p. 148. Hemingways at the Westbury Hotel, East 69th.

58. See Hanneman, Vol. 1, Item A-39.

59. *Newsweek*, Oct. 26, 1935, pp. 39–40; DeVoto, "Hemingway in the Valley," *Saturday Review of Literature*, Oct. 26, 1935, p. 5; Charles Poore, "Ernest Hemingway's Story of His African Safari," *New York Times Book Review*, Oct. 27, 1935, pp. 3, 27; Carl Van Doren, "Ernest Hemingway, Singing in Africa," *New York Herald Tribune Books*, Oct. 27, 1935, p. 3; "Hunter's Credo," *Time*, Nov. 4, 1935, p. 81.

60. Reader's letter, May 9, 1935, JFK.

61. Qualified voters list, *Citizen*, Nov. 1, 1935; Election results, *Citizen*, Nov. 13, 1935.

62. EH–Ivan Kashkin, Aug. 19, 1935, *SL*, p. 419.

63. EH–Dos Passos, Dec. 17, 1935; EH–Mr. Green, Dec. 21, 1935, private collection.

64. EH–FSF, Dec. 16, 1935, *SL*, pp. 424–5.

65. EH–Dos Passos, Dec. 17, 1935, *SL*, pp. 425–7.

66. EH–MP, Dec. 17, 1935, PUL.

67. MP–EH, Dec. 20, 1935, PUL.

68. EH–Mr. Harris, Dec. 12, 1935, private collection.

69. 1934–35 Hemingway notebook, internal dating, Goin Collection.

70. See Paul Smith, pp. 321–6. EH–Sara Murphy, March 19, 1935, *LG*, p. 118. The question, older than literature, was most clearly stated in Housman's poem "To an Athlete on Dying Young."

71. EH–Gingrich, Dec. 9, 1935, private collection.

72. Published, with several words blanked out, in the Feb. 1936 *Esquire* as "The Tradesman's Return," pp. 27, 193–6.

73. EH–Mr. Green, Dec. 24, 1935, private collection.

74. EH–Mr. Hopkins, Dec. 31, 1935, private collection.

CHAPTER 9: 1936

1. *Citizen*, Jan.–March and Jan. 11, 1936.
2. EH–Ivan Kashkin, Jan. 12, 1936, *SL*, p. 432.
3. EH–Mary Pfeiffer, Jan. 26, 1936, *SL*, p. 436.
4. Feb. 11, 1936, *LG*, p. 156.
5. See "The Short Happy Life of Francis Macomber" and "The Snows of Kilimanjaro." Many argue for an affair with Jane Mason, but corroborative evidence is less than convincing. For every affair he did have—with Pauline, Martha Gellhorn, Mary Welsh—evidence is plentiful.
6. F. Scott Fitzgerald, *The Crack-up*, reprint, ed. Edmund Wilson (New York: New Directions, 1945), pp. 69–74.
7. EH–Dos Passos, Jan. 13, 1936, *SL*, p.433.
8. *Citizen*, Jan.–Feb. 1936; EH–Mary Pfeiffer, Jan. 26, 1936, *SL*, pp. 433–7.
9. Baker, p. 617.
10. EH–Sara Murphy, Feb. 27, 1936, *SL*, pp. 438–40; EH–Dos Passos, April 12, 1936, *SL*, pp. 446–7.
11. EH–FSF, Nov. 24, 1936, *SL*, p. 232.
12. *The Crack-up*, pp. 75–80.
13. EH–MP, Feb. 7, 1936, *SL*, p. 438.
14. *Esquire*, Aug. 1936, pp. 27, 194–201.
15. FSF–EH, July 16, 1936, JFK; EH changed the name to Julian.
16. Item 692, JFK.
17. *Citizen*, March 11, 1936.
18. *Ladies' Home Journal*, June 1933, p. 35. Hemingway Collection, MCL.
19. *Citizen*, March 16, 19, and 20, 1936; EH–MP, April 9, 1936, *SL*, p. 443.
20. O. O. McIntyre, "New Eyes on Key West," *Kansas City Star*, June 2, 1936.
21. EH–John Weaver, April 12, 1936, PUL; EH–Gingrich, April 19, 1936, private collection.
22. EH–MP, April 19, 1936, PUL.
23. *Citizen*, April 22–26, 1936.
24. Arturo Suarez, "Waves from the Waterfront," *Post*, April 28, 1936.
25. *Post*, May 13, 1936; PH–Gerald Murphy, July 17, 1936, *LG*, p. 171; EH–Sara Murphy, June 13, 1939, *LG*, p. 227.

26. *Post*, May 10, 1936; Sara Murphy–EH, May 20, 1936, *LG*, p. 165.

27. *Post*, May 5, 1936; Sara Murphy–PH, May 11, 1936, *LG*, pp. 164–5; *True Gen*, p. 98, friend unidentified.

28. PH–EH, May 22, 1936, JFK.

29. *Citizen*, May 23–28, 1936; EH–Dos Passos, June 10, 1936, PUL; EH–MacLeish, May 31, 1936, LOC. Baker, who may not have seen the MacLeish letter, misread the Dos Passos letter, placing the experience between Miami and Bimini with Patrick Hemingway on board.

30. Granville Hicks, "Small Game Hunting," *New Masses*, Nov. 19, 1936, p. 23.

31. Baker Collection, Box 24, Folder 2, PUL.

32. Pound–EH, June 12, 1936, JFK.

33. EH–Abner Green, June 18, 1936, private collection. Green worked for the American Committee for the Protection of the Foreign Born. In EH–Green, July 2, 1936, private collection: "You can sign my name to any protest telegrams when there is an emergency to help anybody in a jam."

34. Baker Collection, Box 24, Folder 1, PUL.

35. Marjorie K. Rawlings–MP, June 18, 1936, PUL.

36. Arnold Gingrich, *Nothing but People* (Crown, 1971), p. 276.

37. PH–Gerald Murphy, July 17, 1935, *LG*, pp. 170–1.

38. Marjorie K. Rawlings–MP, June 18, 1936, Baker Collection, PUL.

39. "The Revolutionist" first appeared as vignette 11, *In Our Time*; Item 239a, paragraph beginning "In Paris there was a revolution being plotted . . ."; so-called Jimmy Breen MS, Item 529b, JFK, working title "A New Slain Knight." See *Homecoming*, pp. 145–57, and *Hemingway: Up in Michigan Perspectives* (MSU Press, 1995), pp. 105–28.

40. EH–MP, July 11, 1936; EH–Abner Green, June 18, 1936, private collection.

41. EH–MP, July 11, 1936 (Cat Cay), *SL*, pp. 447–8.

42. Item 211, JFK.

43. EH–Grace Hemingway, July 18, 1936, private collection; Thomas, pp. 131–8.

44. EH–Gingrich, July 21, 1936, private collection; EH–Nordquist, July 25, 1936, Baker Collection, PUL; *Citizen*, July 27, 1936; Harry Burns–Carlos Baker, April 29, 1963, PUL.

45. "Literary Felonies," *Saturday Review of Literature*, Oct. 3, 1936, p. 3.
46. EH checks, Waring Jones Collection, copies at PUL, Aug. 10–Oct. 29, 1936; Hadley H. Mowrer–Jack Hemingway, Aug. 24, 1936, Baker Collection, Box 17, Folder 11, PUL.
47. *True Gen*, pp. 98–100.
48. EH–Gingrich, Sept. 16, 1936, *SL*, p. 451.
49. EH–Gingrich, Aug. 25, 1936, Baker Collection, PUL; EH–Gingrich, Sept. 16, 1936, *SL*, p. 451; EH–MP, Sept. 26, 1936, *SL*. p. 454.
50. Item 204, *THHN* MS, JFK, p. 178–9, 190.
51. See Item 212-3, *THHN* typescript, JFK, p. 61.
52. Item 204-8, pp. 230–32, JFK, quoted in Robert Fleming, "The Libel of Dos Passos in *To Have and Have Not*," *Journal of Modern Literature*, Spring 1989, pp. 588–601.
53. See Carr, pp. 350ff.
54. Item 212-3, typescript, JFK.
55. M. K. Rawlings–EH, Aug. 1, 1936 (arrived Aug. 16), JFK.
56. EH–Rawlings, Aug. 16, 1936, *SL*, pp. 449–50.
57. EH–Mary Pfeiffer, Aug. 11, 1936, Baker Collection, PUL.
58. *True Gen*, p. 98.
59. EH–MacLeish, Sept. 26, 1936, *SL*, p. 453.
60. EH–MP, Sept. 26, 1936, *SL*, p. 454; MP–EH, Oct.1, 1936, Scribner-1, PUL.
61. Checkbook, copies of Waring Jones Collection, PUL; EH–Harry Burns, Oct. 24, 1936, and (taxidermists) Jonas Brothers–EH, Nov. 9, 1936, Baker Collection, PUL.
62. *Citizen*, Nov. 12, 1936. Toby Bruce claims to have driven Ernest, Pauline, and both sons to Key West, but all evidence says otherwise. Two undated letters, PH–EH, [Nov. 1936], JFK; *Citizen*, Nov. 21 and 30, 1936. Later EH said the pool was Pauline's folly, but he was planning it before she returned to Key West.
63. John Peale Bishop, "Homage to Hemingway," *New Republic*, Nov. 11, 1936, p. 40.
64. EH–Richard Armstrong, July 25, 1936, Christie's East auction catalog, Feb. 21, 1996, item 137.
65. Richard Armstrong–EH, Aug. 27, 1936, JFK; Richard Armstrong–EH, Sept. 2, 1936, Baker Collection, PUL; Christie's East catalog.
66. EH–Gingrich, Oct. 3, 1936, private collection.

67. Deleted "Interlude in Cuba," *THHN* MS, p. 460, renumbered p. 416, JFK.

68. *Post*, Dec. 6, 1936; EH–MP, Dec. 14, 1936, Scribner-1, Box 3, Folder 15, PUL; check stubs, Waring Jones Collection, copies PUL.

69. Harry Sylvester, "Ernest Hemingway: A Note," *Commonweal*, Oct. 30, 1936, p. 11. The tall tale must have come from Hemingway.

70. EH–Sylvester, Dec. 15, 1936, Baker Collection, PUL.

71. *The Diaries of Dawn Powell*, ed. Tim Page (Steerforth Press, 1995), p. 203.

72. *Citizen*, Dec. 28 and 31, 1936. See McClendon and other biographies.

CHAPTER 10: 1937–38

1. Kert, 282–92; Rollyson, pp. 1–62; *Saturday Review of Literature*, Sept. 26, 1936; Eleanor Roosevelt, syndicated column, "My Day," Sept. 16, 1936.

2. Martha Gellhorn, *The Face of War* (Atlantic Monthly Press, 1988), "1959 Introduction," p. 1.

3. MG–Eleanor Roosevelt, Jan. 5, 1937, cited in Kert, p. 291.

4. MG–Eleanor Roosevelt, Jan. 13, 1937, FDR.

5. *Citizen*, Jan. 8 and 11, 1937; MG–Pauline Hemingway, Jan. 14, 1937, PUL. All references to Martha Gellhorn letters are from notes made before she closed her correspondence and from citations in earlier biographies.

6. PH–EH, Jan. 13 and 17, 1937; *New York Times*, "Writer to Aid Loyalists," Jan. 12, 1937; Baker, p. 299.

7. PH–EH, Jan. 12, 13, 16, and 17, 1937, JFK.

8. MG–Eleanor Roosevelt, Jan. 13, 1937, FDR.

9. Quoted in *Citizen*, Jan. 20, 1937.

10. *True Gen*, pp. 101–2.

11. *Citizen*, Jan. 25, 1937.

12. The Hemingway letter has been lost. Patrick died on Jan. 30, 1937. Journal entry, Jan. 16, 1937, in Donnelly, pp. 114–20.

13. See Baker, p. 300, and MacLeish–EH telegrams, Feb. 11, 15, and 16, 1937, JFK.

14. EH–Pfeiffers, Feb. 9, 1937, *SL*, pp. 457–8. Addressed "Dear Family,"

this letter is one of the few he did not address only to Mary Pfeiffer. Also EH–Harry Sylvester, Feb. 5, 1937, *SL*, pp. 456–7.

15. MG–EH, Feb. 8, 1937, quoted in Kert, p. 294.

16. PH–MP, March 6, 1937, Scribner-1, Box 3, Folder 17, PUL; MG–Eleanor Roosevelt, Feb. 9, 1937, FDR; *New York Times*, Feb. 28, 1937. Hemingway sailed on the *Paris* on Feb. 27. PH–EH, three letters early March 1937, JFK; EH checkbook, March–May 1937, Baker Collection, PUL.

17. Samuelson, pp. 16, 22.

18. MG–EH, Feb. 15, 1937, quoted in Kert, p. 294.

19. Joris Ivens, *The Camera and I* (International Publishers, 1969 [written in 1943–44]), p. 111. For complete Ivens–Hemingway relationship see William Brasch Watson, "Joris Ivens and the Communists: Bringing Hemingway into the Spanish Civil War," in *Blowing the Bridge*, ed. Rena Sanderson (Greenwood Press, 1992).

20. Louis Fisher–Geikas, Feb. 25, 1937, formerly in the Goin Collection.

21. Watson 1982 interview with Ivens, "Joris Ivens and the Communists," p. 49.

22. Kert, pp. 294–6.

23. See Hugh Thomas, *The Spanish Civil War*; Robert Rosenstone, *Crusade on the Left*; Herbert Matthews, *Half of Spain Died*; Ronald Fraser, *The Blood of Spain*; Alvah Bessie, *The Heart of Spain*.

24. Gellhorn, *The Face of War*, p. 11.

25. Josephine Herbst, *The Starched Blue Sky of Spain* (Harper Collins, 1991), p. 132.

26. *True Gen*, pp. 111, 116. Josephine Herbst, more accurately, puts Hemingway's rooms at the three hundred level, which would have been the fourth floor in Europe.

27. Hemingway checkbook, March–May 1937, Goin Collection, shows the following payments in francs: 1500, Evan Shipman: canned goods for Madrid; 4000 Sidney Franklin: Sidney and Evan; 400 Sidney: cash loan; 750 Shipman: cash loan. Exchange rate: 29 francs to the dollar.

28. Shipman information due to Sean O'Rourke's research into Shipman's 1954 testimony before the Subversive Activities Control Board.

29. Herbert Matthews, *The Education of a Correspondent* (Harcourt, Brace, 1946), p. 68, hereafter Matthews.

30. "Hemingway Sees Dead Strewing Battlefield," March 22, 1937, in William Brasch Watson's meticulously edited "Hemingway's Spanish Civil War Dispatches," *Hemingway Review*, Spring 1988, p. 19, hereafter cited as Watson, "Dispatches."

31. Watson, "Ivens and the Communists," pp. 48–9.

32. Hemingway NANA dispatch #10, Watson, "Dispatches," p. 38. As in all news stories written from Hemingway cables, the original was more terse.

33. Martha Gellhorn, "Only the Shells Whine," *Collier's* (July 17, 1937), pp.12–13, 64–65.

34. *Tribune*, May 11, 1937.

35. Francis Smith, "Hemingway Curses, Kisses, Reads at Sylvia Beach Literary Session," *Tribune*, May 14, 1937. Several secondary sources have mistakenly said he read "Fathers and Sons."

36. *Tribune*, May 13, 1937.

37. Martha Gellhorn, "A Reporter at Large: Madrid to Morata," *New Yorker*, July 24, 1937, p. 31.

38. These letters, which are closed to quotation, are in the JFK and the PUL.

39. See EH dispatches in Watson, "Dispatches," pp. 24–42.

40. *Citizen*, May 26, 1937.

41. See MG–Roosevelt correspondence, June 1937, FDR.

42. An insert crossed out on *THHN* MS, p. 356, JFK.

43. Item 208, JFK. Emphasis added later.

44. "Fascism Is a Lie," *New Masses*, June 22, 1937, p. 4. The *New York Times* buried the story on p. 9, covering it in three column inches, less than it gave to a local meeting of the Notre Dame alumni association. *Time*, June 21, 1937, pp. 79–81, gave it five full columns with five photographs, including one of Hemingway.

45. Dawn Powell–John Dos Passos, undated, UVa, quoted in Ludington, pp. 376–7.

46. Paul Romaine–Carlos Baker, Feb. 4, 1963, PUL; Prudencio De Pereda–Carlos Baker, June 2, 1967, PUL.

47. EH–MP, Thursday, [June 10, 1937], Scribner-1, PUL; Berg, pp. 324–5.

48. PH–EH, [June 21 and 22, 1937], JFK; Prudencio de Pereda–Carlos Baker, June 2, 1967, PUL.

49. EH–Mary Pfeiffer, Aug. 2, 1937, *SL*, p. 460.

50. PH–Sara Murphy. July 8, 1937, *LG*, pp. 194–5.

51. EH–Mary Pfeiffer, Aug. 2, 1937; dinner clothes: EH–PH wire, July 6, 1937, Tulsa; MG–Eleanor Roosevelt, Sunday, [July 11, 1937], FDR. Finally Hemingway read the narrative himself for the film.

52. Ernest Hemingway, "The Heat and the Cold," reprinted in *The Spanish Earth*, limited edition published by Jasper Wood (Cleveland, 1938), from *Verve*, Spring 1938, p. 46.

53. Herbst, *Starched Blue Sky of Spain*, pp. 154–57; Carr, pp. 365–75; Ludington, pp. 366–72; MacLeish interview with Carlos Baker, PUL.

54. EH–Dos Passos, c. March 26, 1938, *SL*, pp. 463–5.

55. EH–Mary Pfeiffer, Aug. 2, 1937, *SL*, pp. 459–61.

56. *New York Times*, Aug. 14, 16, and 17, 1937; *Newsweek*, Aug. 21, 1937, p. 4; *Time*, Aug. 23, 1937, p. 66; and many columnists.

57. "Talk of the Town," *New Yorker*, Nov. 27, 1937.

58. Cape–EH, Aug. 10, 27, and 30, 1937, JFK and Goin Collection.

59. Bank accounts: Guaranty Trust–EH, Aug. 26 and Sept. 2, 1937, and Guaranty account statement, Sept. 1, 1937, Goin Collection. Wallach: doctor's prescription for Mr. Hemmingway [sic], Aug. 26, 1937, Tulsa.

60. John Sommerfield, *A Volunteer in Spain* (Knopf, 1937), p. 104.

61. Watson, "Dispatches," p. 49.

62. Martha Gellhorn, "Men Without Medals," *Collier's*, Jan. 15, 1938, p. 10. Poet Edwin Rolfe's account of Belchite, where he fought with the Lincoln Battalion, curiously does not mention Merriman in the final assault, where Rolfe was present. Merriman appears throughout Rolfe's book, *The Lincoln Battalion* (Veterans of the A. Lincoln Brigade, 1939). See Baker, p. 623.

63. Rooms 113/114 at a special group price of thirty pesetas (about $5) a day: Hotel Florida bills, PUL and JFK.

64. Basics: Grocer's bill delivered to Hemingway at the Foyot, Waring Jones Collection; extraordinaries: Sara Murphy–EH, Sept. 20, 1937, JFK.

65. Watson, "Dispatches," p. 54; Hanneman, p. 155.

66. See Copyright, General Index 1938–45, Entry No. D unpub 54650, LOC. Subtitled "But Not for Love."

67. With Morris Musselman, EH wrote youthful farces "Hokum" and "Jomeo and Ruliet." His sister, Marcelline Sanford, copyrighted a one-

act farce, "Be Seated," in 1938, D unpub 39510, LOC. Fitzgerald, Faulkner, Dos Passos, and Wilder all wrote plays, with varying success.

68. The longest attempt at theater was "The Dictator—A Play," 30 pages, Item 365, JFK, probably done in the late 1920s. A substantial amount of his known reading was focused on theater. See *Reading* and *Library*.

69. See *Reading* and *Library*.

70. Item 80, JFK.

71. Ernest Hemingway, "Preface," *The Fifth Column and the First Forty-nine Stories* (Scribner's, 1938).

72. Ernest Hemingway, *The Fifth Column and Four Stories* (Scribner's, 1969), p. 44.

73. EH–FSF, July 1, 1925, *SL*, pp. 165–6.

74. *The Fifth Column and Four Stories*, pp. 80–3.

75. *Time*, Oct. 18, 1937, pp. 80–1, 83–5; portrait by Waldo Peirce; fifteen captioned photos documenting EH's life from Oak Park to the war in Spain.

76. Lewis: *Newsweek*, Oct. 18, 1937, p. 34; *Nation*, Oct. 23, 1937, pp. 439–40; Cowley: *New Republic*, Oct. 20, 1937, pp. 305–6; *New Masses*, Oct. 26, 1937, pp. 22–3. Sales: Hanneman, p. 41.

77. *Tribune*, Dec. 25, 1937.

78. The *Normandie* departed Dec. 18, arriving New York Dec. 23. Martha writes EH on board, thus could not have been at Teruel as most biographers have her. The *Europa*, from which PH writes Sara Murphy, left New York Dec. 16, arriving Cherbourg Dec. 21. *Tribune*, Dec. 22, 1937.

79. Watson, "Dispatches," pp. 67–8.

80. *LG*, p. 203.

81. Baker, pp. 323–4; Baker Collection, Box 18, Folder 8, PUL. The Hotel Elysée marks the first time Hemingway moves from the Left to the Right Bank. Sara Murphy–EH, Sept. 20, 1937, *LG*, p. 201: three of Hemingway's trunks were stored at this hotel by Sara.

82. Books: Waring Jones Collection, Brentano's book bill for 3,168.50 francs paid in January 1938 (approximately $110), PUL. Wallach: Baker Collection, Box 18, Folder 8, has prescription for Drainochol (extract of jaborandi and artichoke), Chophytol, and Belladinol. Translation: pneumatic, Jean Gardner(?)–EH, Jan. 12, 1938, JFK.

83. Pauline's passport shows Southampton date, Baker Collection, PUL; *Gripsholm* did not stop in a French port, *Tribune*. Reporters: PH–EH [Aug. 17, 1937], JFK. *New York Times*, Jan. 26–9, 1938.

84. *Citizen*, Jan. 29, 1938.

85. "Hemingway Tells of War, New Play, in Interview," *Citizen*, Feb. 1, 1938.

86. EH–Hadley Hemingway Mowrer, Jan. 31, 1938, *SL*, pp. 462–3. I and others have said EH took the *Pilar* to Havana around Feb. 1. The *Gripsholm*, en route from New York, docked in Havana about Feb. 2; he may have gone over to pick up freight from France.

87. "Spain and Her Lesson of War," *Oak Leaves* (Oak Park, Ill.), Feb. 3, 1938, on meeting of Jan. 31.

88. Grace Hemingway–EH, [Feb. 3, 1938], JFK, included another clipping of the marriage of his sister Madelaine (Sunny) to Kenneth Mainland.

CHAPTER 11: 1938–1939

1. Gregory Hemingway interview; *Homecoming*, pp. 124–6.

2. Bowers urged the implementation of this plan in a March 30 cable and in an April 3 confidential letter to the U.S. Secretary of State, cited in Jeffrey Shulman, "Hemingway's Observations on the Spanish Civil War," *Hemingway Review*, Spring 1988, pp. 147–9. Edgar Mowrer is the brother of Paul Mowrer, second husband of Hadley Hemingway Mowrer.

3. Vincent Sheean, *Not Peace but a Sword* (Doubleday, 1939), pp. 235ff. EH and Pauline were still married when book appeared. *New York Times*, April 25, 1938, says raid came five minutes into film; also EH got a five-minute ovation when introduced.

4. Matthews, *Education of a Correspondent*, pp. 132–3; Watson, "Dispatches," pp. 73–5; MG–Eleanor Roosevelt, "Barcelona, April 24 or 25" [1938], FDR.

5. Martha Gellhorn, "On Apocryphism," *Paris Review*, Spring 1981, p. 284.

6. Kert, pp. 315–6.

7. See Watson, "Dispatches," pp. 75–82.

8. EH–John Wheeler, June 2, 1938, in Watson, "In Defense of His Reporting from Spain," *Hemingway Review*, Spring 1988, p. 120.

9. See John Raeburn, *Fame Became of Him* (Indiana U. Press, 1984), pp.

87–91. Will Watson, "The Pravda Article," *Hemingway Review*, Spring 1988, p. 115.

10. Ernest Hemingway, in Watson, "Dispatches," p. 86.
11. See Claude Bowers–Secretary of State, May 17, 1938, in Schulman, *Hemingway Review*, Spring 1988, pp. 149–50. "Hemingway Returns, Tired of War in Spain," *New York Times*, May 31, 1938.
12. *Citizen*, May 31, June 2 and 3, 1938.
13. Florida Auto Registration card, Waring Jones Collection, CO365, Box 17, PUL.
14. Paul Smith, pp. 369–74.
15. See Jay Allen–EH, July 8, 1938, JFK.
16. EH–MP, July 12, 1938 [two letters same date], *SL*, pp. 467–71.
17. EH–MacLeish, c. mid-July 1938, JFK, quite possibly not mailed, but does reflect his state of mind. See MacLeish's measured response, MacLeish–EH, Aug. 6, 1938, *MacLeish Letters*, pp. 294–5; EH–Ralph Ingersoll, July 18 and 27, 1938, JFK.
18. *Citizen*, June 18 and July 13, 1938.
19. McLendon, pp. 182–7.
20. [MG]–EH, JFK.
21. CO365, Box 24, Folder 1, PUL.
22. EH–Mary Pfeiffer, Aug. 18, 1938, Baker Collection, PUL; hotel bill, JFK.
23. Kert, p. 317, interview with Patrick.
24. EH–Mary Pfeiffer, Aug. 18, 1938, Baker Collection, PUL.
25. Baker, p. 333. The book was published without a dedication.
26. MG–Eleanor Roosevelt, Aug. 14, 1938, FDR. Address on stationery: 18 Square du Bois de Boulogne, XVI.
27. PH–EH, [Sept. 1–5], 10, and 28, 1938, JFK. Sept. 10 letter misdated at JFK as 1936.
28. Hanneman, pp. 46–7; *Saturday Review of Literature*, Oct. 15, 1938, p. 5; *New York Times Book Review*, Oct. 23, 1938, p. 4; *Nation*, Dec. 10, 1938, pp. 628, 630; *Time*, Oct. 17, 1938, p. 75; *New Masses*, Nov. 22, 1938, pp. 21–2; *New Republic*, Nov. 21, 1938, pp. 367–8.
29. EH–MP, Oct. 28, 1938, *SL*, pp. 473–5.
30. Hadley Richardson–EH, Jan. 8, 1921, JFK.
31. Grace Hemingway–EH, Dec. 25, 1938, JFK.
32. *New York Daily Mirror*, Jan. 15, 1939, p. 3.
33. *New York Daily Mirror*, Jan. 17, 1939.

34. Kert, pp. 322–3.

35. PH–Sara Murphy [Jan. 1939], *LG*, pp. 219–20, misdated as Dec. 1938.

36. EH–Mrs. Paul Pfeiffer, Feb. 5, 1939, *SL*, pp. 475–7, misdated Feb. 6; MG–Mrs. Roosevelt, Feb. 3, 1939, FDR.

37. The *Pilar* remains temporarily in Key West: see PH–EH, [Feb. 28, 1939], JFK.

38. EH–MP, Feb. 7, 1939, *SL*, p. 479. Twelve years later the story became *The Old Man and the Sea*.

39. Pauline's letters are being sent to the Ambos Mundos, but the *For Whom the Bell Tolls* manuscript says it was written first in the Hotel Sevilla-Biltmore. Waring Jones Collection, PUL, CO365, Box 17 confirms the Biltmore. EH–Tommy Shevlin, April 4, 1939, *SL*, p. 484.

40. PH–EH, [Feb. 28, 1939], JFK; PH–Sara Muprhy, [March 10, 1939], *LG*, p. 222.

41. Bill from Sevilla-Biltmore Hotel, March 18, 1939, Waring Jones Collection, PUL.

42. Item 83, JFK.

43. EH–MP, March 25, 1939, *SL*, pp. 482–3.

44. Kert, pp. 325–6.

45. MG–Eleanor Roosevelt, May 17, 1939, FDR.

46. Martha Gellhorn, *A Stricken Field* (Duell, Sloan & Pearce, 1940), p. 87.

47. Lionel Trilling, "Hemingway and His Critics," *Partisan Review*, Winter 1939, p. 53.

48. EH–Grace Hemingway, May 28, 1939, private collection; EH–Patrick Hemingway, June 30, 1939, *SL*, pp. 486–8; PH–EH, July 12, 1939, JFK; EH–Mrs. Paul Pfeiffer, July 21, 1939, *SL*, pp. 491–2.

BOOK II

PART ONE

CHAPTER 12. RINGING THE CHANGES

1. *FWBT*, p. 471.

2. *Havana Post*, March 15, April 25, 1940.

3. "Notes on the Next War," *Esquire* (Sept. 1935).

4. EH–MP, July 13, 1940, Scribner Collection, PUL.

5. Rollyson, pp. 153–4. Martha's story was not published.

6. "Ernest Hemingway Talks of Work and War," *NYT* (Aug. 11, 1940), reprinted in *Conversations*, pp. 17–20. *NYT*, July 26–Aug. 3, 1940.

7. EH–Gustavo Durán, March 5, 1940, Baker Collection, PUL.

8. "Post-war Writers and Pre-war Readers," speech before American Association of Adult Education printed in *New Republic* (June 10, 1940), 789–90. See Donaldson, pp. 334–6.

9. "War Writers on Democracy," *Life*, June 24, 1940, 8.

10. Gerald and Sara Murphy–EH, [fall 1926] and Sept. 6, 1926, *LG*, pp. 21–4.

11. [July 29, 1940], *LG*, p. 252.

12. [c. late December 1940], *LG*, pp. 260–1.

13. *NYT*, July 31, 1940.

14. MP–EH, July 31, Aug. 1, 1940, PUL; I am indebted to the meticulous research of Robert Trogdon's unpublished essay, "Making the Blockbuster."

15. Quoted in Kert, p. 343. See Kert throughout for the clearest view of the Hemingway-Gellhorn relationship. Edna Gellhorn's framed portrait remained in Finca Vigía long after Martha's disappeared. It is now at the JFK.

16. Harry M. Hagen, *This Is Our . . . St. Louis* (St. Louis: Knight Publ., c. 1970), p. 540.

17. Rollyson, p. 4. "Mrs. Gellhorn Still on the Firing Line," *St. Louis Post Dispatch,* Dec. 15, 1963.

18. Martha Gellhorn, "Cuba Revisited," *Time Out* (Jan. 7–14, 1987).

19. Quoted in Kert, p. 343; Kert was the last biographer to have access to the Gellhorn papers at Boston University before Gellhorn closed them into the next century.

20. c. Aug. 8, 1940, Bruccoli, p. 285.

21. See *Hemingway's First War* (Princeton U. Press, 1976) for revisions to *SAR* and *AFTA*. See Thomas Gould's "Authorial Revision and Editorial Emasculation in . . . *For Whom the Bell Tolls*," in *Blowing the Bridge*, ed. Rena Sanderson (New York: Greenwood Press, 1992), pp. 67–82.

22. Scribner's, many years later and without fanfare, restored the bulls' appendages in the text.

23. MP–EH, Aug. 26, 1940; EH–MP, Aug. 26, 1940, Bruccoli, pp. 289–94.

24. EH–MG, [nd], two notes, JFK.

25. Paporov, pp. 42–4.

26. See *Reading;* it has been suggested that Toby Bruce selected the library shipped to Cuba in December 1940. A letter from Pauline to EH, November 1940, in Fuentes, p. 328, makes it clear that Bruce inventoried and packed books EH selected.

27. Kert, p. 344.

28. EH–Hadley, Dec. 26, 1940, *SL*, p. 520.

29. J. Donald Adams, "The New Novel by Hemingway," *NYTBR* (Oct. 20, 1940), 1; Margaret Marshall, "Notes by the Way," *The Nation* (Oct. 26, 1940), 395. Howard Mumford Jones, "The Soul of Spain," *SRL* (Oct. 26, 1940), 5; Clifton Fadiman, "Hemingway Crosses the Bridge," *New Yorker* (Oct. 26, 1940), 66; Edmund Wilson, "Return of Ernest Hemingway," *New Republic* (Oct. 28, 1940), 591–2.

30. Hanneman, Vol 1, pp. 51–2; the six previous Hemingway books' combined first printings totaled only 57,804 copies.

31. EH–Durán, [fall 1940], Baker Collection, PUL. Neither claim was even close to the truth.

32. Author interview with Bud and Ruth Purdy, 1995.

33. EH–MP, c. Oct. 12, 1940, *SL*, pp. 517–8.

34. Author interview with Purdys.

35. EH–CS, c. Oct. 21, 1940, *SL*, p. 519.

36. *NYT*, Nov. 21, 1940. Certificate of Marriage, JFK. Witnesses: Jean Wilson and William E. Mullen.

37. PH–EH, [Nov. 22, 1940], in Fuentes, pp. 327–8.

38. "Back to His First Field," *Kansas City Times* (Nov. 26, 1940), in *Conversations*, pp. 21–4.

39. Matthew J. Bruccoli, *Fitzgerald and Hemingway: A Dangerous Friendship* (New York: Carroll & Graf, 1994), pp. 204–6, 229.

CHAPTER 13. TO MANDALAY AND BACK

1. *TWMAA*, pp. 19–33.

2. *Ta-Kung-Pao*, Chungking (Feb. 23, 1941), quoted in Warren K. J. Sung's M.A. thesis, Tamkang College of Arts and Sciences, June 1979. For Sung's thesis I am indebted to Marsha Goin and her late husband John.

3. Hollington K. Tong, *China and the World Press* (Nanking, 1948), p. 159.
4. *TWMAA*, pp. 40–1.
5. Ibid., pp. 49–53.
6. Augustus Pfeiffer letter (July 21, 1941) relaying information from an EH letter of July 14, 1941. H. H. Kung was married to Madame Chiang Kai-shek's sister.
7. *TWMAA*, p. 55.
8. "ERNEST HEMINGWAY Tells How 100,000 Chinese Labored Night and Day to Build Huge Landing Field for Bombers," *PM* (June 18, 1941), pp. 16–17.
9. *Chungking Central Daily News* (April 15, 1941) in Warren K. J. Sung's M.A. thesis.
10. EH–MG, May 2, 1941, JFK.
11. EH–MG, May 12, 15, 17, and 19, 1941, JFK.
12. *NYT*, April 20, 1941: Gallup Poll reports 79% opposed to sending troops; 69% opposed to sending planes; 67% opposed to sending ships.
13. *NYT*, April 24, 1941, p. 6.
14. "ERNEST HEMINGWAY Says We Can't Let Japan Grab Our Rubber Supplies . . . ," *PM*, June 11, 1941, p. 6.
15. "After Four Years of War in China Japs Have Conquered Only Flat Lands," *PM*, June 16, 1941, p. 6; "ERNEST HEMINGWAY Says China Needs Pilots as Well as Planes to Beat Japanese in the Air," *PM*, June 17, 1941, p. 5.
16. Russell Whelan, *The Flying Tigers* (New York: Viking Press, 1942), pp. 34–5, 211.
17. "ERNEST HEMINGWAY Says Aid to China Gives U.S. Two-Ocean Navy Security," *PM*, June 15, 1941, p. 6.
18. EH–Henry Morgenthau, July 20, 1941, JFK.
19. "Ernest Hemingway, Noted Author, Visits Key West," *Key West Citizen*, June 7, 1941.
20. "Joe Russell, Local Saloon Operator, Dies in Havana," *Key West Citizen*, June 21, 1941.
21. EH–PH (c. Aug. 1, 1941), misdated in *SL* as June 9, 1941, p. 524.
22. Registration certificate, Aug. 23, 1941, JFK.
23. MP–EH, April 4, 1941, PUL; EH–MP, April 29, 1941, PUL, in Bruccoli, pp. 307–8.

24. EH–PH, July 19, 1941, *SL*, p. 525.
25. "Snoopers Find Ideal Nazi Base Off Mexico," *Baltimore Sun*, Aug. 22, 1940.
26. "Miskito Keys: Ideal Hideouts for Nazis," *Baltimore Sun*, Aug. 23, 1940.
27. "Nazi Found in Costa Rica, Too," *Baltimore Sun*, Aug. 27, 1940.
28. EH–Leicester Hemingway, June 28, 1941, in *My Brother, Ernest Hemingway* (1961; reissued 1996, Sarasota, FL: Pineapple Press) pp. 300–1.
29. MG–Jane Armstrong [July 25, 1941, and Aug. 22, 1941], private collection.
30. EH–MP, Aug. 26, 1941, in Bruccoli, pp. 309–10.
31. EH–Janet Flanner, April 8, 1933, *SL*, pp. 386–9.
32. MG–Jane Armstrong [Aug. 22, 1941], private collection.
33. EH–MG [nd], internal evidence places it in 1941, JFK.
34. Jonathan Utley, *Going to War with Japan* (U. of Tennessee Press, 1985), pp. 151–6.
35. EH interview in *St. Louis Star-Times* (May 23, 1941), p. 1, in Bruccoli, pp. 29–30. A *Saturday Review of Literature* poll of thirty-nine literary critics gave twenty-one votes to *FWBT* as the best novel of 1940—*NYT*, April 26, 1941.
36. EH–MP, Sept. 1, 1941, Bruccoli, pp. 312–3.

CHAPTER 14. VOYAGERS

1. EH–MP, Nov. 15, 1941, *SL*, pp. 528–9.
2. *Slim*, pp. 43–4.
3. *High on the Wild*, p. 67.
4. LOC, Copyright Division, renewed in 1968 as Martha Gellhorn.
5. *SRL* (Dec. 6, 1941), p. 10, in Berg, p. 405.
6. EH–MP, Nov. 15, 1941, Bruccoli, pp, 313–4.
7. Glenway Wescott, "The Moral of Scott Fitzgerald," *New Republic* (Feb. 17, 1941), pp. 213–4.
8. Hanneman, Vol. 1, pp. 217–9; EH–MP, Nov. 15, 1941, *SL*, p. 527.
9. EH–Sinclair Lewis, Nov. 15, 1941, Yale.
10. EH–MP, Dec. 11, 1941; EH–CS, Dec. 12, 1941, *SL*, pp. 531–3.

11. On earnings of $137,357, Hemingway paid $104,000 in 1941 taxes, $4,000 of which he was forced to borrow from Scribner's to meet the bill.

12. MG–Evan Shipman, April 7 [1942], private collection.

13. EH–MP, May 30, 1942, Bruccoli, pp. 318–20; MP–EH, June 8, 1942, Bruccoli, pp. 320–2; MP–EH, July 8, 1942, *SL*, pp. 533–5.

14. See chap. 6 of my early book, *Hemingway's First War* (Princeton U. Press, 1976).

15. *Men at War*, p. xi.

16. Ibid., pp. xiv–xv.

17. EH–Mr. G., May 3, 1942, JFK.

18. Cdr. C. Alphonso Smith, USNR, "Battle of the Caribbean," *United States Naval Institute Proceedings* (Sept. 1954), 976–82.

19. *U-Boat War*, pp. 567–78. War Diary, Commander, Gulf Sea Frontier on microfilm, National Archives.

20. War Diary, May 1, 1942.

21. War Diary, May 18, 1942, OPNAV update.

22. See *NYT*, Jan. 4, 1942, p. 4; Jan. 11, 1942, p. V, 7:1; Jan. 25, 1942, p. 20; April 19, 1942, p. iii, 7.

23. *NYT*, June 28, 1942, p. 21.

24. *NYT*, July 26, 1942, p. 22.

25. See *Reading*, Item 1357, Felix Luckner, *The Last Privateer*, misidentified in *SL*.

26. Office of Naval Intelligence publications ONI 220-M and ONI 220-G. EH's copy of 220-M at JFK.

27. *Havana Post*, May 2, 1942.

28. Spruille Braden, *Diplomats and Demagogues* (New York: Arlington House, 1971), pp. 282–4.

29. National Archives, Confidential Letter File, American Embassy, Havana, 1942–3.

30. "The United States and Cuban-Spanish Relations," Oct. 28, 1942, copy in the Hemingway Papers at the JFK.

31. *NYT*, Jan. 4, 1942, p. 1; Jan. 2, 1942, p. 11; Feb. 1, 1942, p. 6.

32. "The Invaders," *Newsweek* (July 6, 1942), p. 304; *Newsweek* (Aug. 17, 1942), pp. 29–31.

33. *NYT*, July 2, 1942, pp. 1, 8.

34. *Newsweek* (July 13, 1942), pp. 27–8.

35. *Havana Post*, April 14, 1942.
36. National Archives, RG-84: Foreign Service Posts, Havana Embassy Confidential File 1Comejen: a 942-43 Part 2: 711-815.6.
37. Martha Gellhorn, "Cuba Revisited," *Time Out* (Jan. 7–14, 1987).
38. Olive G. Gibson, *Isle of a Hundred Harbors* (Boston: Bruce Humphries, 1940), pp. 55–60.
39. Jack Hemingway, *Misadventures of a Fly Fisherman* (Dallas: Taylor Publishing, 1986), p. 39; *Papa*, p. 47.
40. *TWMAA*, p. 64.
41. Rollyson, pp. 172–4.
42. Kert, p. 371.
43. For a full account, see Martha Gellhorn, "Messing About in Boats," *TWMAA*, pp. 64–106. Her itinerary included Haiti, Puerto Rico, St. Thomas, Tortola, Virgin Gorda, Anguilla, St. Martin, St. Barthélemy, Saba, St. Kitts, Surinam, French and Dutch Guiana.
44. "A Little Worse Than Peace," *Collier's* (Nov. 14, 1942), pp. 18–9, 84–6; "Holland's Last Stand," *Collier's* (Dec. 26, 1942), 25–9.
45. EH–MG, July 31 [1942], JFK. For a very different version see Gregory's *Papa*, p. 80.
46. EH–MG, Aug. 10/16, 25, Sept. 1, 8, 19, 31, Oct. 14, 15, 1942, JFK.
47. *Havana Post*, Sept. 9, 1942. EH–Col. Hayne D. Boyden, Nov. 2, 1942, JFK.
48. Braden, *Diplomats*, pp. 284–5.
49. FBI File, Oct. 8, 1942. Hemingway's FBI File was obtained for the author under the Freedom of Information Act by Russell Judd Boone in 1982.
50. EH–Shipman, Aug. 25, 1942, *SL*, p. 538.
51. FBI File, Oct. 9, 1942.
52. Item 527, JFK.
53. FBI File, Oct. 9, 10, 1942.
54. War Diary, June–October 1942.
55. See http://www.uboat.net/boats.htm.
56. *Havana Post*, Sept. 9–20, 1942.
57. Item 273, JFK; Consuelo Hermer and Marjorie May, *Havana Manana* (New York: Random House, 1942); *Clipper Guide to Cuba* (Havana, 1947); Fuentes, pp. 9, 10, 229–30.
58. EH–Hayne D. Boyden, Nov. 2, 1942, JFK. It has been commonly held

that the *Pilar* patrols began in June 1942. Letters and documents at the JFK make it clear that the first armed cruise did not take place until mid-November.

59. *Pilar* papers, JFK; Typed report of the incident dated Dec. 10, 1942, Havana, also at JFK.

60. War Diary, Dec. 9, 1942.

61. C. H. Carson, "Memorandum for Mr. Ladd," June 13, 1943, FBI File.

62. D. M. Ladd, "Memorandum for the Director Re: Ernest Hemingway," Dec. 17, 1942, FBI File.

63. John Edgar Hoover–Agent Leddy, "Re: Ernest Hemingway," Dec. 17, 1942, FBI File. Hoover has mistaken Leicester Hemingway's news stories for those of Ernest.

64. Hoover memorandum, Dec. 19, 1942, FBI File. Several references to EH prior to 1942 suggest that the FBI followed his activities through-out the 1930s, particularly his pronouncements on avoiding the next war and his indictment of the government in *New Masses* for the death of veterans in the 1935 Matecumbe hurricane.

65. Kert, pp. 375–6.

CHAPTER 15. AMERICAN PATROL

1. Quoted in Kert, p. 376.

2. EH–MG, Jan. 7, 1943, JFK.

3. "Communication with Pilar" (March 7–14, 1943) in *Pilar* Papers, JFK, listing code words and directive to track the *Comillas* from the time she rounded Cape San Antonio.

4. Nov. 9, 1942, letter to EH without signature, JFK.

5. *Pilar* Log (1942–3), JFK.

6. War Diary, Jan. 23, 1943.

7. "Confidential to the Ambassador," Feb. 10, 1943, JFK.

8. Hemingway FBI File, "Memorandum for Mr. Ladd," June 13, 1943.

9. War Diary, April 1–10, 1943. *Torpedoes in the Gulf*, pp. 235–8; Jurgen Rohwer, *Axis Submarine Successes: 1939–45* (Naval Institute Press, 1983).

10. Quoted in Donaldson, p. 358.

11. EH–MacLeish, April 4, 1943, *SL*, p. 544.

12. EH–MacLeish, c. May 5, 1943, *SL*, p. 544.

13. EH–Allen Tate, Aug. 31, 1943, *SL*, pp. 549–51.

14. War Diary, April 1–May 20, 1943.

15. War Diary, May 22, 1943.

16. *Pilar* Log, JFK. Although the 1941 calendar on which the log was kept would seem to indicate that these events took place in 1942 (see Baker), Hemingway letters from 1942 place him elsewhere, and the War Diary indicates 1943. See George Miller memorandum to "Master, Yacht Pilar," June 2, 1943, from Liaison Office in *Pilar* Papers, JFK. EH–MG, June 3, 1943, JFK, and following confirms this point.

17. In Fuentes, Gregorio remembers Confites as a supply base, but as the *Pilar* Log makes clear, the supply base was Nuevitas.

18. *True Gen*, p. 144. See also EH–MG, Thursday, June 1943, JFK, response to her chap. 16.

19. *Pilar* Log, June 8–10, 1943, JFK.

20. *Pilar* Log, June 11–14, 1943, JFK; War Diary, June 6–14, 1943. Postwar accounts of U-boat losses do not mention a sub lost at this date in these waters, but at the time, the kill was taken to be true.

21. EH–MG, June 16 and 30, 1943, JFK.

22. *Liana* (Scribner's, 1944), p. 279.

23. EH–MG, undated in-house letter, clearly 1943, JFK.

24. EH–MG, June 22, 1943, JFK.

25. *Pilar* Papers, JFK. *Papa*, p. 78. EH–MG, June 17, and Wednesday, June, undated 1943, JFK. Martha did not have all the male cats castrated as has been suggested elsewhere.

26. EH–MG, June 7, 1943, JFK; six pages are typed, single-spaced, one is holograph.

27. *Pilar* Papers, along with July 9, 1943, letter from Miller at Nuevitas, JFK.

28. EH–Mr. [Roy] Hawkins, July 20, 1943, JFK.

29. War Diary, July 19, 1943.

30. Philip Wylie and Laurence Schwab, "The Battle of Florida," *Saturday Evening Post* (March 11, 1944), 14–5, 52–8. If Hemingway's patrols were as foolish and childish as some critics have expressed, then the same must be said of the efforts of hundreds of other private yachtsmen.

31. EH–Mr. [Roy] Hawkins, July 20, 1943, JFK.

32. Ellis O. Briggs, *Shots Heard Round the World* (New York: Viking Press,

1957), p. 68. Briggs has Winston Guest present at the shoot, but EH letters clearly put him in Colorado.

33. Briggs, *Shots Heard*, p. 73.

CHAPTER 16. INTERMEZZO

1. MG–EH, June 28, 1943, quoted in Kert, pp. 379–80.
2. Author interview with Gregory Hemingway.
3. EH–MP, May 30, 1942, PUL, in Bruccoli, p. 318.
4. EH–Mr. G[rover], c. May 5, 1942, JFK.
5. EH–MacLeish, c. May 5, 1943, LOC, in *SL*, p. 545.
6. EH–MacLeish, Aug. 10, 1943, LOC, in *SL*, pp. 548–9.
7. EH–Allen May, Aug. 31, 1943, Fuentes, p. 340.
8. Lilian Beath–EH, Sept. 1 and 3, 1943, JFK; Marcelline Hemingway Sanford–EH, Sept. 9, 1943, JFK.
9. MG–EH, Oct. 21, 1943, Kert, p. 384.
10. War Diary, October 1943.
11. EH–Hadley Mowrer, Nov. 25, 1943, *SL*, p. 555; EH–MacLeish, Dec. 26, 1943, copy in Baker files, PUL.
12. Kert, pp. 388–90.
13. EH–MG, Jan.13, 1944, JFK.
14. EH–MG, Jan. 31, 1944, JFK.
15. EH–Ramon LaValle, Feb. 2, 1944, Baker Collection, PUL.
16. Charles Colebaugh–EH, March 10, 1944, JFK.
17. *Collier's* (March 4, 1944), quoted in Kert, p. 391.
18. EH–MP, March 12, 1944, PUL and JFK, in Bruccoli, p. 327.
19. Quoted in Kert, pp. 391–2.
20. Spruille Braden–EH, March 7, 1944, JFK. EH–Charles Colebaugh, March 30, 1944, JFK. In London he showed the letter, which he carried in his shirt pocket, to more than one person.
21. Earl Wilson, "It Happened Last Night," *NY Post*, May 2, 1944.
22. OSS, Shepherdson–Robert Joyce, May 1, 1944, JFK.
23. Quoted in Kert, p. 392.
24. Julia Edwards, *Women of the World: The Great Foreign Correspondents* (Boston: Houghton Mifflin, 1988), pp. 130, 149–57. Iris Carpenter, *No Woman's World* (Boston: Houghton Mifflin, 1946), pp. 32–5, 44–55.
25. EH–MP, March 12, 1944, Bruccoli, p. 332.

26. *The Diaries of Dawn Powell*, ed. Tim Page (South Royalton, VT: Steerforth Press, 1995), p. 231.

27. A signed one-dollar bill, a "short snorter," signed by Hemingway and other passengers, including John Ringling North, on May 17, 1944, JFK.

28. Kert, p. 392.

29. *TWMAA*, p. 280. Martha remembered the voyage lasting eighteen days; she apparently arrived on May 31.

30. *HIW*, pp. 93–4.

31. *The Times* (London), "U.S. War Correspondent Injured," May 25, 1944, p. 2. Kert, p. 398.

CHAPTER 17. PUTTING ON THE RITZ

1. "Voyage to Victory," *By-Line*, p. 340.

2. "OMAHA BEACHHEAD (6 June–13 June 1944)," *American Forces in Action Series*, CMH Pub 100-11, Center of Military History (Washington, D.C., facsimile reprint, 1984), p. 41.

3. *By-Line,* pp. 344–55.

4. Group Capt. G. W. Houghton, RAF, to F/Lt. R. G. Teakle, July 28, 1944, JFK.

5. "London Fights the Robots," *Collier's* (Aug. 19, 1944), in *By-Line*, p. 361; Baker, pp. 395–7.

6. Quoted in Baker, p. 399.

7. *88 Poems*, "First Poem to Mary in London," p. 104.

8. *HIW*, pp. 102–6.

9. H. R. Stoneback, "Hemingway's Happiest Summer," *North Dakota Quarterly*, Vol. 64, no. 3, 1997, pp. 190–3. For more details than possible here, see the entire essay.

10. *ARIT,* p. 224.

11. Duke Shoop, "Dine on Chili and Wine," *Kansas City Star*, July 31, 1944, pp. 1–2.

12. EH–Mary Welsh, July 31, Aug. 1, 1944, *SL*, pp. 558–61.

13. "Hemingway 'Captures' Six," *NYT*, Aug. 4, 1944, p. 3.

14. Hemingway–Lanham Chronology, 1944–5, Baker Collection, PUL. Hereafter cited as Lanham.

15. Henry T. Gorrell, "A Close Hemingway Call," *Kansas City Star*, Aug. 6, 1944, p. 6.

16. Robert Capa, *Slightly Out of Focus* (New York: Henry Holt, 1947), pp. 166–8.

17. Ibid. Ten years later Capa would step on a Viet Minh landmine in Vietnam and die.

18. Stoneback, "Hemingway's Happiest Summer," p. 197. Hemingway signed in: "August 6, 1944 Ernest Hemingway Finca Vigia–San Francisco de Paula-Cuba Avec 4[iem] Division USA."

19. Quoted in Meyers, p. 404.

20. *True Gen*, pp. 150–9.

21. See Stoneback's "Hemingway's Happiest Summer," pp. 199–201, for the original research on this previously dark period of Hemingway's war.

22. Maj. R. L. Norling (G-4), Aug. 20, 1944, handwritten note, JFK.

23. World War II diary of Col. David K. E. Bruce, *OSS against the Reich*, ed. N. D. Lankford (Kent State U. Press, 1991), pp. 160–1. Hereafter cited as Bruce.

24. Robert Aron, *France Reborn*, trans. Humphrey Hare (New York: Scribner's, 1964), p. 287.

25. Bruce, pp. 165–6.

26. David Bruce–EH, June 12, 1955; attached to the note is a 1947/48 account of the four days at Rambouillet given to a reporter, JFK. Russians taken prisoner on the eastern front were often put into German uniforms to fight on the western front.

27. Bruce, pp. 168–9. For a more colorful description of this scene and those preceding, see Hemingway's "Battle for Paris," and "How We Came to Paris," reprinted in *By-Line*, pp. 364–83.

28. Bruce, p. 170.

29. Bruce–EH, Aug. 23, 1944, JFK.

30. Bruce, pp. 171–8.

31. *The Very Rich Hours of Adrienne Monnier*, trans. Richard McDougall (New York: Scribner's, 1976), pp. 416–7; Noel Riley Fitch, *Sylvia Beach and the Lost Generation* (New York: Norton, 1983), pp. 402–7.

32. Malcolm Cowley, "Hemingway at Midnight," *New Republic* (Aug. 14, 1944), pp. 190–5.

33. EH–MW, Aug. 27, 1944, unfinished and unmailed, *SL*, pp. 564–5. Mary says it was misdated, for she arrived at the Ritz on August 26, *HIW*, p. 113.

34. *HIW*, p. 114.

CHAPTER 18. DOWN AMONG THE DEAD MEN

1. War Diary, JFK; EH–MW, Sept. 8, 1944, *SL*, pp. 565–6.
2. Lanham, pp. 9–11; Hemingway's ETO Chronology, p. 13; War Diary, pp. 11–12. Today, near the postwar bridge, a bronze plaque quotes Lanham in French: "Avant l'arrivée des ingénieurs vos adroits artisans ont construit ici un pont en 45 minutes." [Before the arrival of engineers, your adroit artisans built a bridge here in 45 minutes.] Beneath the name Lanham is the date: 10.9.44.
3. EH notes on endpaper of *A Few Facts About France: Part I*, JFK.
4. *Collier's* (Nov. 18, 1944), reprinted in *By-Line*, pp. 392–400.
5. Lanham, pp. 15–16.
6. 88 *Poems*, "Poem for Mary (Second Poem)," p. 107.
7. Lanham, p. 17.
8. EH–MW, Sept. 23–24, 1944, JFK.
9. Hemingway Collection, JFK.
10. MW–EH, Oct. 1, 1944, JFK.
11. Cdr. Harry C. Butcher (PRD, SHAEF)–EH, Oct. 2, 1944, JFK. It was the Third Army because Hemingway had never gone through formal channels for transferring to the 22nd Infantry.
12. Transcript of EH testimony on Oct. 6, 1944, Nancy, France, JFK.
13. EH–Paul Leahy, June 26, 1952, JFK.
14. EH–*Collier's*, Press Wireless, attention Lacossitt, undated, but postmarked Oct. 25, 1944, JFK.
15. *HIW*, pp. 127–36; AG 201–EH, Nov. 9, 1944, SHAEF orders to report to the First Army.
16. The details of the 22nd Infantry's battle in Hürtgenwald is largely based on Robert Rush's detailed history—"Paschendale [sic] with Treebursts"—which he posted on the Web and which is "the complete account of the 22d Infantry Regiment in the Hürtgen Forest, with the day by day Regimental Journal Files and After Action Reviews of the surviving soldiers." Also the Lanham-Hemingway Papers at PUL; Rose Marie Burwell's interview with Bill Walton at the JFK; Charles Whiting, *The Battle of Hürtgen Forest* (New York: Orion Books, 1989).
17. War Diary, Sept. 1944, and his "War in the Siegfried Line," *Collier's* (Nov. 18, 1944), reprinted in *By-Line*, pp. 392–400.
18. EH–Henry La Corsitt, Nov. 16, 1944, in Fuentes, p. 351.

19. Robert Rush, "Paschendale [sic] with Treebursts."
20. EH–MW, Nov. 16–18–19–20, 1944, in Fuentes, pp. 351–6. MW–
    EH, two letters both dated Nov. 14, 1944, JFK.
21. MW–EH, Nov. 15, 1944, JFK.
22. Lanham, p. 27.
23. EH–MW, Nov. 23, 1944, Fuentes, p. 361.
24. EH–MW, Nov. 25, 1944, Fuentes, p. 364.
25. EH–MW, Nov. 29, 1944, in Fuentes, p. 369.
26. Walton reading from unpublished memoir in Burwell interview, JFK.
27. Whiting, pp. 133–4; Rush; Garcia was the only Medal of Honor winner
    at Hürtgenwald to live to receive his award.
28. EH–MG, Dec. 5, 1944, JFK.
29. Burwell interview with William Walton, JFK.

PART TWO

CHAPTER 19. STARTING OVER

1. EH–MW, March 6, 7, 13, 16, 1945, JFK.
2. PH–EH, March 17, 1945, JFK.
3. EH–MW, March 20, 1945, JFK. See also EH–Lanham, April 2, 1945,
   SL, p. 578; EH–MP, April 14, 1945, PUL.
4. See Hemingway: The 1930s; EH–Lanham, April 14, 1945, SL, p. 586.
5. EH–MW, April 9, 1945, SL, p. 581; EH–Lanham, April 14, 1945, SL,
   p. 585. Lanham book: Infantry in Battle.
6. EH–MW, April 14, 1945, SL, p. 584; Baker, p. 447.
7. EH–Carol Gardner, c. December 1945, Fuentes, pp. 386ff. See also
   EH–Lanham, April 14 and 20, 1945, SL, pp. 585–8.
8. EH–Lanham, June 9, 1945, Fuentes, p. 383.
9. Papa, pp. 95–6; Meyers, pp. 418–20; Baker, pp. 448–9.
10. MW–EH, October or November 1945, Mary Hemingway Papers, JFK.
11. Mary Welsh Journal, June–July 1945, JFK.
12. Kert, p. 421.
13. EH–MP, July 23, 1945, SL, p. 593; Mary's Journal, 1945, JFK.
14. MW–Pamela Churchill, July 4, 1945, JFK.
15. MW–EH, undated [1945], JFK.

16. Kert, p. 421.
17. Mary's Journal, Oct. 7, 1945, JFK.
18. MW–Eleanor Welch, undated answer to Oct. 1, 1945, telegram, JFK.
19. Mary's Journal, Oct. 13, 1945, JFK.
20. MW–Welch, Oct. 13, 1945, JFK.
21. Mary's Journal, Dec. 19, 1945, JFK.
22. See "Martha Gellhorn Hurt in Crash," *NYT*, Dec. 14, 1944, p. 6.
23. Martha Gellhorn, *Love Goes to Press,* ed. Sandra Spanier (U. of Nebraska Press, 1995).
24. MG–EH, May 28, 1945, and EH–MG, undated and perhaps unsent, Fuentes, pp. 376–81.
25. MSS Items 310, 310a, 525a, and 564c, Hemingway Collection, JFK.
26. EH–Childnies, Oct. 19, 1945; EH–Mouse, Oct. 24, 1945 (both letters to his sons), JFK; EH–MP, Oct. 31, 1945, Bruccoli, p. 336.
27. MWH–Parthy Vanderwicken, Dec. 20, 1945, JFK.

CHAPTER 20. RULES OF THE GAME

1. The best study of this period is Rose Marie Burwell's *Hemingway: The Postwar Years and the Posthumous Novels* (Cambridge U. Press, 1996). See also Robert E. Fleming's equally perceptive *The Face in the Mirror: Hemingway's Writers* (U. of Alabama Press, 1994). Because different editors, including Mary Hemingway, apparently did not realize Hemingway's objective, they removed significant material from the posthumous publications. To speak of the published *Islands in the Stream, The Garden of Eden,* or *A Moveable Feast* as Hemingway's work is, therefore, only partially true.
2. MW–EH, October or November 1945, Mary Hemingway Papers, JFK.
3. MW–EH, Jan. 27, 1946, Sunday (misdated Jan. 28), Mary Hemingway Papers, JFK.
4. "Dearest Kittener" letters in Mary Hemingway Papers, JFK.
5. EH–Lanham, Feb. 21, 1946, PUL.
6. EH–MW, Jan. 24, 1946, JFK.
7. MW–EH, Jan. 27, 1946 (misdated Jan. 28), JFK.
8. Mary's Journal, March 13, 1945, Mary Hemingway Papers, JFK. March 14 is usually thought to be the date of the wedding.
9. MWH–Connie Bessie, March 27, 1946, JFK.

10. MG–MWH, misdated April 29, [1946], by Mary as 1945 in her papers, JFK.

11. MG–MWH, July 25, [1946], also misdated as 1945.

12. *Slim*, pp. 74–5.

13. Hadley Richardson–EH, Jan. 8, 1921, JFK.

14. Dr. James Gough–MWH, May 6, 1946, Mary Hemingway Papers, JFK.

15. EH–Mouse [Patrick Hemingway], June 21/30, 1946, JFK. Grace Hemingway–EH, June 30, 1946, JFK.

16. Mary's Journal, June 23, 1946; Mary Hemingway Papers, JFK.

17. EH–Lanham, June 30, 1946, PUL.

18. Ibid.

19. Grace Hemingway–EH, July 21, 1946, UTex.

20. EH–Lanham, June 30, 1946, PUL.

21. EH–MG, Aug. 5, 1946, JFK, marked "unsent" in Hemingway's hand.

22. EH–Lanham, Aug. 25, 1946, JFK; *HIW*, p. 189.

23. EH–Lanham, Aug. 28, 1946, JFK. EH checks written to hospital and to RNs Hazel Miller and Edith Vance; paid bill from Casper Typewriter Exchange, Aug. 27, 1946; Nonresident Wyoming fishing license, Aug. 30, 1946; East Gate entry permit, Yellowstone, Sept. 12, 1946: all at the JFK and in private collections.

24. EH–Slim Hawks, Oct. 9, 1946, photo facsimile on wall at Ketchum Korral.

25. Baker, pp. 458-9.

26. Mary Harington, "They Call Him Papa," *New York Post Weekend Magazine* (Dec. 28, 1946), 3; Roger Linscott, "On the Books," *New York Herald Tribune Book Review* (Dec. 29, 1946), 13; *New Yorker* (Jan. 22, 1947), all three reprinted in *Conversations*, pp. 42–9.

27. Connie Bessie–MWH, Nov. 18, 1946, JFK.

CHAPTER 21. YEAR OF THE DOG

1. EH–MWH, May 5, 1947, JFK.

2. EH–MP, March 5, 1947, *SL*, pp. 615–8.

3. *True Gen*, p. 187.

4. EH–MWH, May 2, 3, 4, 1947, JFK; EH–Lillian Ross, July 2, 1948, *SL*, p. 645.

5. EH–MWH, May 2, 1947, JFK.

6. EH–MWH, May 5, 1947, JFK.

7. EH–MWH, May 14, 1947, JFK.

8. EH–Lanham, May 24, 1947, PUL.

9. EH–Lanham, June 5, 1947, PUL.

10. Mary Hemingway File, misc. personal notes, dated June 4, [1947], but more likely June 14, JFK.

11. EH–MWH, June 26 and July 8, 1947, JFK.

12. Faulkner–EH, June 28, 1947, JFK.

13. Faulkner–EH, "Dear Brother H," July 19, 1947, JFK.

14. EH–Faulkner, July 23, 1947, *SL*, pp. 623–5.

15. EH–CS, Sept. 18, 1947, *SL*, p. 628. Townsend Ludington, *John Dos Passos: A Twentieth Century Odyssey* (New York: Dutton, 1980), pp. 432–3.

16. *NYT*, Aug. 7, 1947.

17. *NYT*, Aug. 21, 1947.

18. Paporov, pp. 93–6.

19. *NYT*, Sept. 30, 1947.

20. Paporov, pp. 100–4.

21. Thomas Leonard, *Day by Day: The 1940s* (New York: Facts on File, 1977), pp. 716–28. Dated license to operate a motor vehicle in the park, JFK. EH–MWH, October 2, 1947, JFK.

22. EH–MWH, October 1947, JFK. Mary sent the newspaper clippings to him.

23. *Diario de la Marina* (Oct. 17, 1947), in Fuentes, p. 252.

24. Fuentes, pp. 253–4; EH–MWH, Oct. 3, 1947, JFK. Herrera also said Hemingway returned a week later to dispose of his "arsenal," which could not have happened with Ernest in Sun Valley.

25. EH–Lanham, Oct. 24, 1947, PUL.

26. EH–Lanham, Oct. 24, Nov. 27, Dec. 28, 1947, PUL.

27. *High on the Wild*, p. 85; Baker, p. 463. *NYT* obituary, Dec. 22, 1947.

28. EH introduction to 1948 edition of *AFTA*.

CHAPTER 22. ENTER BIOGRAPHERS, STAGE LEFT

1. Constance Montgomery, *Hemingway in Michigan* (Vermont Cross-roads Press, 1977), p. 199.

2. Ross, p. 12.
3. Viertel, pp. 14, 16.
4. Ibid., pp. 10–14.
5. Mary's typed travel log, JFK, says they left on Feb. 15, but numerous letters and other dateable events (the Santa Fe snowstorm) insist they left Feb. 1. EH–Gregory, Feb. 21, 1948, JFK.
6. Earl Wilson, "It Happened Last Night," *NY Post*, Feb. 26, 1948.
7. Robert Joyce quoted in *True Gen*, pp. 195–8.
8. EH–Malcolm Cowley, April 9, 1948, private collection.
9. EH–Cowley, April 13, 1948, private collection.
10. EH–Cowley, June 9, 25, 28, July 5, 15, 1948; Cowley–EH, June 22, 1948, all in a private collection.
11. EH–Cowley, July 15, Aug. 19, 25, Sept. 3, 5, Nov. 15, 16, 29, Dec. 31, 1948, all in a private collection.
12. Malcolm Cowley, "A Portrait of Mister Papa," *Life* (Jan. 10, 1949), 86–101.
13. EH–Peter Viertel, March 10, 1948, private collection.
14. Viertel, pp. 30–41; the movie, staring John Garfield and Jennifer Jones, became *We Were Strangers*.
15. Viertel, p. 46.
16. EH–Viertel, June 10, 1948, private collection.
17. Viertel–EH, June 16, 1948, JFK.
18. EH–MacLeish, Aug. 27, 1948, LOC.
19. EH & MWH–Viertels, June 28, 1948, six pages, typed and handwritten, single-spaced, in private collection.
20. EH–W. G. Rogers, July 29, 1948, *SL*, pp. 649–50.
21. EH–Lillian Ross, July 28, 1948, *SL*, pp. 646–9. See *YH*.
22. EH & MWH–Viertels, June 28, 1948, private collection.
23. EH–Viertels, July 9, 1948, UVa.
24. *Papa*, pp. 3–12; Hotchner–EH, June 11, 1948, JFK; contract between *Cosmopolitan* and Hemingway, June 11, 1948, JFK. The novel has been mistakenly identified as *Across the River and into the Trees*.
25. EH–Hotchner, June 27, 1948, UVa; Hotchner–EH, July 7, 1948, JFK; Hotchner–EH, July 21, 1948, JFK; EH–Hotchner, Sept. 7, 1948, UVa.
26. EH–Viertel, Aug. 8, 9, 1948, private collection; Royalty report, Aug. 30, 1948, JFK.

CHAPTER 23. SENTIMENTAL JOURNEY

1. "A Veteran Visits the Old Front," *Toronto Daily Star*, July 22, 1922.
2. Mary Hemingway's Italian Journal, unpublished, Mary Hemingway Collection, JFK; hereafter cited as Italian Journal. See Baker and Meyers.
3. *AFTA*, p. 270.
4. Italian Journal, Sept. 26, 1948.
5. EH–Cowley, April 25, 1949, private collection.
6. Italian Journal, Nov. 14, 1948.
7. Italian Journal, Sept. 17, Nov. 12–14, 1948.
8. Italian Journal, Nov. 14, 1948.
9. See *YH* index for D'Annunzio.
10. See *Paris Years*.
11. EH–Viertel, Nov. 12, 1948, private collection.
12. Ibid.
13. EH–Patrick and Gregory Hemingway, July 17, 1949, PUL.
14. See any of the picture guidebooks to Venice, and Sean O'Faolain, *A Summer in Italy* (New York: Devin-Adair, 1950), pp. 199–213.
15. Italian Journal; EH–David Bruce, Nov. 27, 1948, JFK.
16. Baker, p. 648.
17. "The Great Blue River," *Holiday* (July 1949), in *By-Line*, pp. 403–16.
18. EH–CS, November 1948, PUL.
19. EH–Viertel, Nov. 12, Dec. 13, 1948, private collection.
20. EH–CS, Dec. 9 and 31, 1948, PUL.
21. EH–Alfred Rice, Dec. 15, 1948, *SL*, pp. 654–7.
22. EH–Viertel, Dec. 13, 1948, private collection.
23. Baker, pp. 469–70; Kert, pp. 435–41.
24. *AFTA*, p. 118.
25. Quote in Kert, pp. 435–43.
26. EH–Viertel, Jan. 19, 1949, private collection. Letter begun on Jan. 19 and finished Feb. 9.
27. EH–Cowley, Jan. 24, 1949, private collection.
28. EH–Cowley, March 9, April 25, 1949; Cowley–EH, May 3, 1949, all in a private collection.
29. PH–EH, undated [Christmas 1948], JFK; EH–PH, Jan. 26, 1948 [sic], misdated. Should be 1949, JFK.

30. Hotchner–EH, Feb. 17, 1949, UVa; EH–Hotchner, March 9, 1949, UVa.
31. Italian Journal, March 1949, JFK.
32. *ARIT*, p. 7.
33. EH–Lanham, March 11, 1949, PUL.
34. Italian Journal, March 1949; Baker, p. 471; EH–Jack [?] April 11, 1949, from Cortina, JFK.
35. Kert, pp. 442–3.

CHAPTER 24. VENICE PRESERVED

1. Typescript *ARIT*, opening page, "Cortina d'Ampezzo, March, 1949," JFK.
2. See *Reading* and *HL*.
3. EH–Patrick Hemingway, May 29, 1949, PUL; *NYT*, May 23, 1949, reports EH in Cristobál, Canal Zone, on May 22.
4. The name Renata probably comes from the character in D'Annunzio's novel *Notturno*, a novel Cantwell likes (p. 52).
5. For explanations of hexanitrate and numerous other obscure references in *ARIT*, Miriam Mandell's superb *Reading Hemingway: The Facts in the Fiction* (Metuchen, NJ: Scarecrow Press, 1995) is indispensable.
6. EH–Kip Farrington, May 29, 1949, JFK.
7. Baker, p. 473.
8. GHH–EH, June 3, 1949, JFK.
9. EH's Scribner book bill for April–July 1949: *Human Destiny* by Pierre Lecomte du Noüy "to G. Hemingway," JFK. The "G." could have been Gregory, but Grace is more likely.
10. EH's Scribner book bill for April–July 1949, JFK.
11. Letter, Oct. 26, 1819, written from Venice (published in *Byron's Letters and Journals*, Vol. 6, ed. Leslie A. Marchand).
12. The World War II experience of Hemingway's friend and professional soldier from the 1918–24 period—E. E. Dorman-O'Gowan—has been suggested as a model for Cantwell. But Hemingway's accidental reacquaintance with Dorman-O'Gowan in March 1950 took place well after the typescript for *ARIT* was completed and book galleys corrected.
13. EH–Carlo Kechler, Aug. 11, 1949, JFK.

14. EH–CS, July 22, 1949, PUL.

15. EH–CS, Aug. 27, 1949, *SL*, p. 672.

16. EH–MacLeish, Aug. 27, 1948, LOC.

17. EH–William Seward, Aug. 11, 1949, JFK.

18. EH–Dos Passos, Sept. 17, 1949.

19. EH–Viertel, Sept. 29, 1949, private collection.

20. Eric Dorman–O'Gowan memoir, Carlos Baker files, PUL.

21. EH–Mouse and Gigi, July 17, 1949, PUL.

22. EH–Teresa, Sept. 24, 1949, JFK.

23. EH–AI, Oct. 3, 1949, JFK.

24. EH–CS, Aug. 24 and 25–26, 1949, PUL.

25. EH–Ross, Oct. 3, 1949, JFK.

26. EH–CS, Sept. 8, 1949, PUL; Hotchner–EH, Sept. 3, 1949, JFK.

27. EH–Al Horwits, Oct. 3, 1949, JFK.

28. EH–CS, Sept. 21, 1949, PUL; CS–EH, Sept. 21, 1949, JFK. $5,000 was for the coat; $5,000 for other expenses.

29. EH–CS, Sept. 14, 1949, PUL.

30. EH–Viertel, Sept. 29, 1949, private collection; EH–MWH, Sept. 29, 1949, JFK; EH–Hotchner, Sept. 29, 1949, UVa.

31. EH–CS, Oct. 1, 1949, PUL.

32. EH–CS, Oct. 4, 1949, PUL; EH–Hotchner, Oct. 11, 1949, UVa.

33. Kert, p. 444.

34. CS–EH, Oct. 13, 1949, PUL; Hotchner–EH, Oct. 24, 1949, and numerous other earlier letters, JFK.

35. Lanham–EH, Oct. 30, 1949, PUL.

36. *NY Post*, Nov. 18, 1949, p. 38.

37. Lillian Ross, "Profiles: How Do You Like It Now, Gentlemen?" *The New Yorker* (May 13, 1950), p. 36.

38. EH–Harvey Breit in a letter appearing in *NYTBR* (Sept. 17, 1950), 14. In *Conversations*, p. 62.

39. See Adeline Tintner, "The Significance of D'Annunzio in *ARIT*," *HR* (Fall 1985), 9–13; George Montiero, "Hemingway's Colonel," *HR* (Fall 1985), 40–45; Peter Lisca, "The Structure of Hemingway's *ARIT*," *Modern Fiction Studies* (1966), 232–50; Major James Meredith, "The Rapido River and Hurtgen Forest in *ARIT*," *HR* (Fall 1994), 60–6.

40. CS–EH, undated [Nov. 1949], JFK. Hotchner–EH, undated [Dec. 1949], JFK.

41. *HIW*, p. 249.
42. Viertel, pp. 80–6.
43. 88 *Poems*: "The Road to Avallon," p. 122; "Poem to Miss Mary," p. 119; "Across the Board," p. 120; "Black-Ass Poem after Talking to Pamela Churchill," p. 121.
44. Mary's Journal, December 1949, JFK.
45. Viertel, p. 98.

CHAPTER 25. THE MIDDLE PARTS OF FORTUNE

1. "Profile," *The New Yorker* (May 13, 1950), pp. 42–3.
2. Kert, pp. 447–8.
3. Cited in *ibid.*, pp. 448–9.
4. EH–Cowley, Jan. 27, 1950, Gritti Palace, private collection.
5. Baker, p. 482.
6. *ARIT*, pp. 151–7.
7. *SRL* (July 9, 1966), p. 9.
8. EH–Hotchner, [late Jan. 1950], UVa.
9. Kert, p. 449.
10. Juanita Jensen–Papa and Mary, Nov. 29, 1949, JFK.
11. Olga Rudge–EH, March 13, 1950, JFK, marked "Rec. Mar. 16, 50."
12. Kert, pp. 450–1, citing *La Torre Bianca*, pp. 96–101, and correspondence from Adriana, October 1980.
13. R. Mourelet–EH, April 5, 1950, JFK.
14. EH–CS, March 22, 1950, PUL, cited in Baker, p. 482.
15. EH–Jonathan Cape, March 21, 1950, Cape Archives.
16. Interview with private source. See www//cavan.local.ie/history/people/soldiers
17. Turista Card #1095, stamped April 8, 1950, Havana, JFK.
18. See Mary Hemingway's last will and testament, dated Oct. 26, 1979, JFK.
19. EH–Lanham, April 15, 1950, PUL, *SL*, p. 687.
20. EH–Dorman-O'Gowan, May 2, 1950, *SL*, p. 691.
21. EH–Dorman-O'Gowan, May 21, July 10, July 15, Aug. 8, 1950, PUL.
22. *Collected Short Stories*, p. 111.
23. *YH*, p. 57.
24. EH–CS, July 19, 1950, PUL, *SL*, p. 706.

25. EH–Arthur Mizener, May 12, 1950, *SL* pp. 694–5.

26. EH–Robert Cantwell, Aug. 25, 1950, *SL*, p. 709.

27. MG–William Walton, Feb. 3, March 9, 1950, courtesy of Rose Marie Burwell.

28. MWH–EH, May 6, 1950, JFK.

29. EH–Milt[on Wolf], May 7, 1950, private collection.

30. EH–Joséph McCarthy, May 8, 1950, JFK, *SL*, p. 693; the letter may not have been sent.

31. Mayito Menocal, Jr.–EH, April 28, 1950, JFK.

32. Ross–EH, April 26, 1950, JFK.

33. Ross–EH, May 5, 1950, JFK.

34. Hotchner–EH, May 17, 1950, JFK; Nancy (Slim) Hayward–EH, May 21, 1950, JFK. "Profile" appeared in *The New Yorker* (May 13, 1950), pp. 36–62, at that time the longest profile the magazine had printed.

35. Preface, *Portrait of Hemingway* (New York: Simon & Schuster, 1961), pp. 14–15.

36. EH–Dorman-O'Gowan, May 21, 1950, JFK; EH–Harvey Breit, July 9, 1950, *SL*, pp. 701.

37. EH–CS, July 19, 1950, *SL*, pp. 706–7; EH–Dorman-O'Gowan, c. July 27, 1950, *SL*, pp. 707–8; Baker, pp. 484–5; EH–CS, July 9–10, 1950, *SL*, p. 704.

38. John O'Hara, "The Author's Name Is Hemingway," *NYTBR* (Sept. 10, 1950), pp. 1, 30; Maxwell Geismar, "Across the River and into the Trees," SRL (Sept. 9, 1950), pp. 18, 19.

39. "The New Hemingway," *Newsweek* (Sept. 11, 1950), pp. 90–95; "On the Ropes," *Time* (Sept. 11, 1950), pp. 110, 113.

40. Alfred Kazin, "The Indignant Flesh," *The New Yorker* (Sept. 19, 1950), pp. 113–18; Philip Avrh, *Commentary* (Oct. 1950), pp. 400–2.

41. *The New Yorker* (Oct. 14, 1950), p. 28.

42. Northrop Frye, *Hudson Review* (Winter 1951), pp. 611–12; Philip Young, *Tomorrow* (Nov. 1950), pp. 55–6; Eliot Paul, *Providence Sunday Journal* (Sept. 10, 1950), p. VI-8; Ben Ray Redman, "The Champ and the Referees," SRL (Oct. 28, 1950), pp. 15, 16, 38.

43. AI–EH, Aug. 25, Sept. 4, 1950, JFK; Baker, p. 486.

44. EH–AI, July 3, Aug. 1, Aug. 2, Aug. 9, 1950, UTex. See N. Ann Doyle and Neal B. Houston, "Letters to Adriana Ivancich, *HR* (Fall 1985), pp. 14–29.

45. Kert, p. 455.

46. MWH–CS, Oct. 12, 1950, PUL.

47. Mary's Journal, misdated 1951, typed draft from rough notes, JFK. EH–Dorman-O'Gowan, Oct. 15, 1950, private collection.

48. EH holograph note dated "0600 27/10/50" in Box 6, Other Material, Folder: Notes Miscellaneous, JFK. EH–Harvey Breit, Oct. 26, 1950, PUL.

CHAPTER 26. ROADSTEAD OF THE HEART

1. Paporov, pp. 177–9. Feo was Ernest's nickname for his friend.

2. Kert, pp. 456–7, based on *La Torre Bianca*, pp. 136–40, 162–6.

3. EH–Hotchner, [Dec. 7, 1950], UVa.

4. Quoted in Paporov, p. 196.

5. *New York Herald Book Review* (Dec. 3, 1950), p. 6.

6. The diligent reader will follow my oversimplification of this narrative's various drafts with Rose Marie Burwell's book-length study of Hemingway's postwar writing.

7. EH–Hotchner, Jan. 5, 1951, private collection.

8. Kert, pp. 459–60.

9. "On the Blue Water: A Gulf Stream Letter," *Esquire* (April 1936), reprinted in *By-Line*, pp. 239–40.

10. Anna Stark in Paporov, p. 193.

11. Item 190, *The Old Man and the Sea* typescript with holograph corrections, JFK. Because only a typescript remains, there has been speculation that the novella was written years earlier, but EH's daily word count seems to indicate that this typescript is the first draft.

12. Paporov, p. 197.

13. "I Tell You True," *Park East* (Dec. 1950), 18–9, 46–7; (Jan. 1951) 36, 48–9.

14. Carlos Baker–EH, Feb. 15, 1951, JFK.

15. EH–Baker, Feb. 17, 1951, Stanford.

16. Baker–EH, Feb. 21, 1951, JFK.

17. EH–Baker, Feb. 24, 1951, Stanford; Sam Boal–EH, Feb. 27, 1951, JFK; EH–Sam Boal, March 10, 1951, JFK.

18. EH–Baker, March 10, 1951, Stanford.

19. EH–Baker, April–Aug. 1951, Stanford. Baker held up his end of the trust, but was disappointed with Hemingway's evasiveness. "He lied to

me," Baker said. "Why would a grown man tell lies?" See Bill Walton's comment in *True Gen*, p. 304.

20. Fenton–EH, Aug. 20, Sept. 9, Sept. 18, 1951, JFK; EH–Fenton, Aug. 31, Sept. 13, Sept. 23, 1951, private collection. Fenton's book, *The Apprenticeship of Ernest Hemingway*, was serialized in *Atlantic Monthly* (March–May 1954) and published that year by Farrar, Straus.

21. EH–John Atkins, Oct. 24, 1951, private collection. Atkins's book was *The Art of Ernest Hemingway* (London: P. Nevill, 1952).

22. EH–Cowley, May 13, 1951, private collection.

23. Madeline Hemingway–EH, June 17, 1951, JFK.

24. PH–EH, undated, marked "Rec. June 30, 1951," JFK.

25. EH–Baker, June 30, 1951, Stanford.

26. Kert, pp. 463–4. Certificate of Death, attached to Alfred Rice–EH, Oct. 22, 1951, JFK.

27. Mary's Journal, October 1951, JFK.

28. EH–CS, Oct. 2, 1951, PUL, in *SL*, p. 737.

29. EH–CS, March 5, April 11–12, May 18–19, July 20, Oct. 5, 1951, *SL*, pp. 720–39. CS–EH, March 20, July 6, July 30, 1951, Scribner Archives, PUL.

30. EH–Dorothy Pound, Oct. 22, 1951, PUL, in *SL*, pp. 741–2; EH–D. D. Paige, Oct. 22, 1951, PUL, in *SL*, pp. 739–41.

31. "On the Books," *New York Herald Book Review* (Dec. 9, 1951), p. 3.

32. EH–CS, Oct. 12, 1951, PUL.

33. EH–Baker, Oct. 7, 1951, PUL.

34. EH–CS, Feb. 1, 1952, Scribner Archives, PUL; *HIW*, pp. 291–2.

35. Wallace Meyer–EH, telegram, Feb. 11, 1952, JFK; EH–Vera Scribner, Feb. 18, 1952, PUL, in *SL*, pp. 748–9.

PART THREE

CHAPTER 27. THE ARTIST'S REWARDS

1. *HIW*, pp. 295–6. EH–Wallace Meyer, March 4, 7, 1952, *SL*, pp. 757–60.

2. *Newsweek* (March 24, 1952), pp. 60–1; *Time* (March 24, 1952), p. 38.

3. *HIW*, pp. 296–7. Marjorie Cooper–EH, March 23, 1952, JFK.

4. Signed copy, Hemingway Collection, JFK. EH–Adriana Ivancich, May 31, 1952, UTex, in *SL*, pp. 762–3.

5. *NYTBR* (Sept. 7, 1952) and *SRL* (Sept. 6, 1952), reprinted in *Conversations*, pp. 66–9. EH–CSjr, May 12, 1952, PUL. Also letters to Harvey Breit and others too numerous to cite.

6. EH–Breit, Aug. 4, 1951, JFK. Breit did not publish anything about the incident.

7. James Plath interview with Forrest MacMullen, 1998. MacMullen did not fish.

8. EH–Breit, June 23, 1952, JFK.

9. Faulkner quoted in Breit–EH, June 25, 1952, JFK.

10. EH–Breit, June 27, 1952, *SL*, pp. 768–70.

11. EH–Charles Fenton, June 12, 1952, private collection; EH–Fenton, June 22, 1952, PUL; EH–Fenton, June 18, July 29, 1952, *SL*, pp. 764–5, 774–8; Fenton–EH, June 7, June 14, July 24, July 31, 1952, JFK.

12. EH–Philip Young, March 6, May 27, 1952, *SL*, pp. 760–2; EH–Baker, June 4, 1952, Stanford.

13. EH–Cowley, May 4, 1952, private collection.

14. "The Last Good Country," *CSS*, p. 523. The published version has been sanitized. The manuscript is at the JFK.

15. *HL*, p. 323. Hemingway met Salinger during the liberation of Paris, and enjoyed reading the young soldier's copies of *The New Yorker*.

16. When *The Garden of Eden* began is difficult to pinpoint. Carlos Baker said 1946; Rose Marie Burwell thinks 1948. Because I do not think he could have begun the story before his mother and Pauline were both dead, I suggest 1952.

17. My analysis remains speculative because we have yet to read Hemingway's texts as he left them to us. See Burwell and those who follow for other views.

18. Hanneman, Vol. 1, pp. 63–4, 87, 175–205. In America, the book sold retail for $3.00.

19. See *Hemingway the Critical Reception*, ed. Robert O. Stephens ([n.p.]: Burt Franklin Co., 1977), pp. 339–71.

20. Berenson–EH, Sept. 6, 1952, quoted in Baker, p. 656.

21. Daniel Longwell–EH, Aug. 8, 1952, JFK; EH–Berenson, Sept. 13, 1952, *SL*, pp. 780–1; Baker–EH, Oct. 23 and Nov. 7, 1952, JFK.

22. EH–Patrick Hemingway, Sept. 22, 1952, PUL and JFK; EH–Alfred Rice, Oct. 8, 1952, JFK.

23. EH–Charles Poore, Jan. 23, 1953, *SL*, p. 800. See *Hemingway's First War* for the "son of a bitch" who fulfilled this prophecy.

24. EH–Hotchner, July 21, 1952, UVa.

25. EH–John Atkins, Dec. 28, 1952, private collection.

26. EH–Berenson, Jan. 24, 1953, *SL*, p. 802; Baker, p. 508.

27. Nancy (Slim) Hayward–EH, July 12, 1953, JFK.

28. Mary's Journal, March 1952, JFK.

29. EH–Wallace Meyer, May 6, 1953, *SL*, pp. 821–2.

30. EH–William Lowe, May 15, 1953, JFK.

31. EH–MWH, in-house letter, June 1, 1953, Fuentes, pp. 396–9.

CHAPTER 28. THE PHOENIX

1. MWH's Spanish Journal, private collection; *HIW*, pp. 322–5; Baker, p. 511.

2. MWH's Spanish Journal. Niño de la Palma was immortalized as Pedro Romero in *The Sun Also Rises*.

3. MWH's Spanish Journal; Viertel, pp. 182–9.

4. When wing-shooting with a shotgun, the hunter keeps both eyes open, tracking the bird. Hemingway apparently did the same with a rifle when the animal was moving.

5. See MWH's African Journal, 1953–54, JFK.

6. Baker, pp. 514–15.

7. *HIW*, p. 345. See this text for the most detailed account of the safari.

8. Quoted in Meyers, p. 502.

9. MWH's African Journal, JFK; *HIW*, pp. 342–66; Philip Percival–MWH, Dec. 3, 13, 1953, JFK. They did, however, fill their licensed quotas, taking back a number of heads: two lions, one leopard, nine antelope, one buffalo, warthog, and several leaping hares. EH–Percival, Feb. 27, 1954, JFK.

10. Denis Zaphiro–MWH, Jan, 6, 1955, JFK.

11. Fenton–EH, Nov. 26, 1953, JFK; EH–Fenton, Dec. 5, 1953, private collection.

12. Hotchner–EH, Dec. 1 and 14, 1953, JFK.

13. Honorary Game Warden form #128, dated Nov. 3, 1953, JFK.

14. Zaphiro is quoted in Baker, p. 659.

15. *HIW*, pp. 370–1.

16. Notes are similar to but not the same as document in JFK.
17. EH–Harvey Breit, Jan. 3, 1954, *SL*, pp. 825–7. EH–Alfred Rice, Jan. 11, 1954, EH–John Hemingway, Jan. 12, 1954 [misdated 1953], both at JFK.
18. MWH's African Journal, Jan. 3 and 4, 1954, JFK.
19. *HIW*, pp. 376–7; Hemingway, "The Christmas Gift," *Look* (April 20, May 4, 1954), reprinted in *By-Line*, pp. 432–3.
20. MWH's African Journal, JFK; EH–James Kidder, American Consulate, Feb. 10, 1954, listing losses for insurance purposes. The airline insurance reimbursed 15,500 shillings. The plane was not overloaded because the bulk of the Hemingway luggage was left behind at Entebbe and Nairobi.
21. Numerous Hemingway letters from the period at the JFK. MWH's African Journal, JFK; Baker, pp. 520–3.
22. *NYT*, Jan. 26, 1954, pp. 1:6. This story became the basis for a popular song "The Heming Way," lyrics by Ogden Nash, beginning, "A bunch a bananas and a bottle of gin."
23. *NYT*, Jan. 29, 1954.
24. MWH's African Journal, Feb. 7, 1954, JFK.
25. MWH–EH, Shimoni, Tuesday [1954], probably Feb. 9, JFK.
26. "The Christmas Gift," *Look* (April 20, May 4, 1954), reprinted in *By-Line*, p. 460. Dictated to Mrs. Kitty Figgis.
27. MWH–her parents, March 9, 1954, Nyali Beach Hotel, JFK.

CHAPTER 29. FORTUNE AND MEN'S EYES

1. Kert, pp. 478–9.
2. EH–Hotchner, March 14, 1954, private collection.
3. MWH–parents, April 4, 1954, JFK.
4. MacLeish–EH, May 5, 1954, JFK.
5. EH–Adriana Ivancich, May 9, 1954, *SL*, pp. 830–1.
6. Viertel, pp. 222–9; Kert, p. 480.
7. Viertel, pp. 228–9.
8. Baker, p. 525.
9. *HIW*, pp. 400–1.
10. Ibid., pp. 402–5.
11. MWH, Aug.–Nov. 1954 account book; EH–Hotchner, Sept. 9, 1954, private collection; MWH–parents, Oct. 5, 1954, JFK.

12. EH–Jack Hemingway, Aug. 17, 1954, private collection.
13. See Pedro Sánchez Pessino–EH, Aug. 24, 1954, JFK.
14. Published as *True at First Light* (Scribner's, 1999).
15. *NYT*, Oct. 26, 1954.
16. *NYT*, Oct. 29, 1954.
17. *HIW*, p. 411.
18. "The Sun Also Rises in Stockholm," *NYTBR* (Nov. 7, 1954), p. 1.
19. "An American Storyteller," *Time* (Dec. 13, 1954), pp. 70–7. See also Robert Manning, "Hemingway in Cuba," *Atlantic Monthly* (Aug. 1965), pp. 101–8, reprinted in *Conversations*, pp. 172–89.
20. Item 713, JFK, paraphrased here for lack of permission to quote.
21. Reprinted in *Conversations*, p. 196.
22. EH–Hotchner, Dec. 7, 1954, private collection.
23. E. K. Thompson (*Time*)–EH, Dec. 20, 1954, JFK; EH–Hotchner, Dec. 31, 1954, private collection.
24. As described in Jack Gould's "Radio in Review," *NYT*, Dec. 22, 1954, p. 34.
25. EH–Bill Davis, Feb. 25, 1954, private collection.
26. EH–R. M. Brown, Sept. 14, 1954, UTex, in Burwell, p. 138.
27. The manuscript to what is now called *True at First Light* has been closed to most scholars. I am relying on Rose Marie Burwell's account of that MS, which she read at Princeton. See Burwell, chap. 5.
28. Letter to R. M. Brown, UTex, quoted in Burwell, p. 143.
29. Quoted in *HIW*, p. 422.
30. MWH–EH, Oct. 4, 1955, JFK. Given male decorum in 1999, EH was only forty-four years ahead of the curve.
31. "Hemingway Tells of Early Career," *Daily Princetonian* (April 14, 1955), reprinted in *Conversations*, pp. 99–102.
32. Fraser Drew, "April 8, 1955 with Hemingway," *Fitzgerald/Hemingway Annual*, 1970, pp. 108–16, reprinted in *Conversations*, pp. 89–98.
33. EH–Dorman-O'Gowan, March 14, 1955, private collection.
34. MWH Notebook, April 19–May 3, 1955, JFK.
35. *HIW*, pp. 422–3.
36. EH–Baker, May 2, 1955, Stanford; EH–Jack Hemingway, May 11, 1955, private collection.
37. Viertel, pp. 251–4.
38. Ibid., pp. 267–8. For a slightly different account, see *Slim*, pp. 144–5. Mary in *HIW* does not mention the scene.

39. MWH–Mrs. Welsh, Sept. 25, 1955, JFK. Viertel, p. 269. *Slim*, pp. 146–7.

40. Richard Johnston (*Sports Illustrated*)–EH, Nov. 14, 1955, JFK; Sid James–EH, telegram, Nov. 22, 1955, JFK.

41. Sylvia Beach–EH, Nov. 6, 1955, JFK.

CHAPTER 30. INTIMATIONS OF MORTALITY

1. *True* (Feb. 1956), p. 18. EH read the February issue by Jan. 22, 1956.

2. *True*, p. 30.

3. Hemingway medical files, JFK. EH–Alfred Rice, Jan, 24, 1956, JFK and *SL*, pp. 853–5.

4. EH–Jack Hemingway, Jan. 22, 1956, private collection.

5. EH–CSjr, Feb. 10, 1956, PUL.

6. MWH–EH, Feb. 27, 1956, JFK.

7. 1956 Calendar, Jan.–March, JFK.

8. Cooper–EH, March 5, 1956, JFK; EH–Cooper, March 9, 1956, JFK and *SL*, pp. 855–6.

9. MWH–parents, April 22, 29, May 7, 1956, JFK; EH–Wallace Meyer, April 2, 1956, *SL*, pp. 857–8; EH–Percival, May 25, 1956, *SL*, pp. 860–1.

10. Kurt Bernheim, "*McCall's* Visits Ernest Hemingway," *McCall's* (May 1956), reprinted in *Conversations*, pp. 105–8.

11. MacLeish–EH, June 23, 1956, JFK. Donaldson, pp. 441–2.

12. EH–Ezra Pound, July 19, 1956, *SL*, pp. 864–5. The medal was apparently given to a Catholic shrine in Cuba instead.

13. MacLeish–EH, Dec. 15, 1956, JFK.

14. MWH–Baker, Sept. 19, 1961, JFK: "About the novel, *Land, Sea and Air*, would you help me . . . to let fade away the idea that any such book existed in writing."

15. EH–CSjr., Aug. 14, 1956, in *SL*, pp. 868–9. Other stories were: "Get Yourself a Seeing-Eyed Dog," "Indian Country and the White Army," "The Monument," and "The Bubble Reputation."

16. Sylvia Beach–EH, Sept. 8, 1956, JFK; Margaret Marshall (Harcourt, Brace)–EH, Sept. 7, 1956.

17. Viertel, pp. 308–10.

18. EH–Hotchner, Sept. 30, 1956, UVa.
19. EH medical files, Oct. 22, 1956, JFK.
20. EH–Breit, Nov. 5, 1956, *SL*, pp. 872–73; Baker, p. 535.
21. Wally Windsor–MWH, Nov. 25, 1956, JFK. "The Lyons Den," *NY Post*, Jan. 21, 1957.
22. Jean Monnier–EH, March 18, 1957, and Rafael Ballestero–EH, March 20, 1957, EH medical files, JFK.
23. EH medical files, JFK.
24. His 1957 tax statement to his tax lawyer (JFK) lists the following drugs for Hemingway: Whychol (10/day all year); Ecuanil (1/day, 300 days); Seconal (80 tabs); B-complex (8/day, all year); Vi-Syneral (4/day all year); Oreton M (3 weekly, all year); Serpasil (3/day for 8 months); Ritalin (1.5/day for nine months); Doriden (1/day for 2 months).
25. EH–Hotchner, May 20, 1957, UVa. See Tom Dardis, *The Thirsty Muse* (Boston: Ticknor & Fields, 1989), pp. 157–209, for the best analysis of Hemingway's alcoholism.
26. EH–Lee Samuels, Jan. 19, 1957, UTex. For a complete list of these MSS, see Lee Samuels–EH, Sept. 6, 1957, JFK.
27. Burwell, pp. 150–3.

CHAPTER 31. CUBA LIBRE

1. Ellen Shipman Angell–EH, June 25, 1957, Fuentes, pp, 413–14.
2. EH–Wallace Meyer, May 24, 1957, *SL*, p. 875.
3. EH–Rice, Aug. 28, 1957, JFK.
4. EH–George Plimpton, March 4, 1957, *SL*, p. 874.
5. C. David Heymann, *Ezra Pound: The Last Rower* (New York: Viking Press, 1976), pp. 210–37.
6. MacLeish–EH, June 19, 1957, JFK.
7. EH–MacLeish, June 28, 1957, *SL*, pp. 876–8.
8. EH–Robert Frost, June 28, 1957, enclosed in letter to MacLeish, *SL*, pp. 878–80.
9. Heymann, *Ezra Pound*, pp. 250–7.
10. "Situation Report," dated Aug. 18, 1957, JFK.
11. *YH*, pp. 64, 70–1, 77–87, 100–2.
12. *NYT*, Aug. 22, 1957, p. 8.

13. Hotel Westbury bill for Sept. 22–28, 1957, for all three, $582.47, JFK.
14. *HIW*, pp. 446–7.
15. EH–Breit, June 16, 1957, PUL. See Item 486 at JFK for likely draft of Fitzgerald story. *Atlantic Monthly* (Nov. 1957), pp. 64–8.
16. A synopsis of Item 692.5 at JFK.
17. "The Lyons Den," *NY Post*, Dec. 12, 1957.
18. EH–Gianfranco Ivancich, Jan. 31, 1958, *SL*, pp. 881–3.
19. Mary Hemingway account pages appended to tax information for 1958, JFK.
20. EH 1958 tax information, JFK; Duke Medical School library, medical historian, and current warnings on labels.
21. Recently opened Mary Hemingway Collection, Notes, Miscellaneous, JFK.
22. EH–Rice, Aug. 3, 1958, JFK. Draft and revisions.
23. Layhmond Robinson, "Hemingway Brings Suit to Stop Reprint of Spanish War Stories," *NYT*, Aug. 6, 1958, p. 1.
24. *NYT*, Aug. 7, 1958, p. 27.
25. *HIW*, pp. 449–50.
26. Arnolds–EH, Aug. 19 and 25, 1958, JFK.
27. EH–Patrick Hemingway, Nov. 24, 1958, *SL*, pp. 887–9.
28. Ibid.
29. Rice–EH, Oct. 8, 1958, JFK.
30. MWH–Hotchner, Nov. 5, 1958, JFK.
31. Author interview with Bud and Ruth Purdy, 1996.
32. John Unrue interview with Forrest MacMullen, 1995.
33. Author interview with Purdys, 1996.
34. John Unrue interview with Forrest MacMullen, 1995.
35. Paporov, p. 43.

CHAPTER 32. EXILES FROM EDEN

1. EH–Gianfranco Ivancich, Jan. 7, 1959, *SL*, pp. 890–1. Note drafting statement undated in Hemingway Collection, JFK. *HIW*, pp. 457–8. EH–Harry Brague, Jan. 24, 1959, *SL*, pp. 891–2.
2. *Historical Statistics of the United States*, Vols. 1 and 2 (Washington, D.C.: U.S. Government Printing Office, 1975).

3. Scribner Book Store bill, Jan. 1959, JFK. Mailed *Lolita* to Ketchum on Oct. 24, 1958.

4. Again, see Rose Marie Burwell for the detailed examination of these manuscripts.

5. EH–Harry Brague, Feb. 22, 1959, *SL*, pp. 893–4: he was on chap. 45 of *Garden*. MWH–Charles Sweeny, March 3, 1959, JFK.

6. Waldo Peirce–EH, March 23, 1959, JFK; EH–Jack Hemingway, March 30, 1959, private collection.

7. *High on the Wild*, p. 128.

8. CSjr–EH, April 7 and 16, 1959, PUL; EH–CSjr, April 12, 1959, PUL.

9. EH–CSjr, April 12, 1959, PUL; EH–Alfred Rice, April 10, 1959, JFK.

10. See *Physician's Desk Reference to Pharmaceutical Specialties and Biologicals* (1947 edition) and *Professional Products Information*, (1947 and 1953 edns.).

11. Paporov, pp. 397–8.

12. Ibid., pp. 398–9. Hemingway briefing notes, filed under Cuba, undated, JFK.

13. Ben Sonnenberg, "La Consula," *Paris Review* (Summer 1991), pp. 277–9.

14. "The Art of the Short Story," *Paris Review* (1981, 25th anniv. issue), 85–103.

15. *HIW*, p. 469.

16. EH–George Saviers, May 11, 1959, private collection.

17. *DS*, p. 65.

18. John Crosby, "Afternoon with the Bulls," *New York Herald Tribune* (June 1959).

19. Hotchner–EH, May 13, 1959, JFK; Hotchner–EH, telegram, May 26, 1959, JFK. After paying Hotchner's expenses plus 50% of the money, Rice's 1%, and taxes on the remainder, Hemingway took home less than $25,000 on the deal.

20. CSjr–EH, June 24, 1959, JFK.

21. EH–CSjr, undated draft in blue spiral notebook once part of the Bill Davis Collection and now in a private collection.

22. Two wires dated July 7, 1959. *Sports Illustrated*–EH and EH–Syd James, JFK.

23. *DS*, pp. 135–6.

24. Rice–EH, June 29 and July 27, 1959, JFK.

25. EH–Rice, Aug. 8, 1959, JFK. Dictated to VDS.
26. Baker, p. 547. MWH, July 22, 1959, addressee unknown, JFK.
27. EH–Thompson Time/Life, telegram, Aug. 8, 1959, JFK.
28. Eric Sevareid, "Mano a Mano," *Esquire* (Nov. 1959), pp. 40–4.
29. EH–MWH, Aug. 20, 1959, written from Bilbao, private collection, copy in JFK.
30. *Slim*, p. 187.
31. Leicester Hemingway–EH, Aug. 31, 1959, JFK; EH–Leicester, Sept. 14, 1959, copy in Fuentes, p. 307, and in private collection.
32. EH–MWH, Aug. 31, 1959, JFK; MWH–EH, Oct. 8, 1959, JFK.
33. EH–MWH, Oct. 13, 1959, JFK.
34. EH–MWH, Oct. 15, 1959, JFK; Hotchner–EH, Oct. 27, 1959, JFK.
35. MWH–EH, Oct. 19, 1959, private collection, copy in JFK.
36. MWH–EH, undated but appended to letter of Oct. 19, 1959, read in a private collection, possibly a copy in JFK.
37. EH–MWH, Oct. 26, 1959, private collection and JFK.
38. EH–Annie Davis, Oct. [sic] 3, 1959, "a bord Liberte" misdated, actually November, private collection.
39. Paporov, p. 400.
40. MWH–Annie Davis, Nov. 8. 1959; EH–Bill Davis, Nov. 8, 1959, both in a private collection.
41. Baker, p. 551. *HIW*, pp. 477–9.
42. Brague–EH, Nov. 5, 1959, JFK.
43. Hemingway notes in a private collection; MWH–EH, Dec. 15, 1959, JFK.
44. *HIW*, p. 481.

CHAPTER 33. THE BODY ELECTRIC

1. EH–Bill Lang (Time/Life), Jan. 11, 1960, JFK; Hotchner–EH, Jan. 31, Feb. 10, 1960, JFK; EH–Hotchner, Feb. 8 and 18, 1960, UVa.
2. CSjr–EH, March 23, 1960, JFK; EH–CSjr, March 31, 1960, JFK.
3. Hotchner–EH, April 5, 1960, JFK.
4. Hotchner–EH, Jan. 31, Feb. 10, 13, March 5, 1960, JFK; EH–Hotchner, Feb. 8, March 12, 1960, UVa.
5. Ed Thompson–EH, telegrams, April 6 and 14, 1960, JFK.

6. Hotchner–EH, April 20, 1960, JFK; Gary Cooper–EH, May 2, 1960, JFK, in response to EH telegram.

7. *DS*, p. 187.

8. EH–Hotchner, May 9, 1960, UVa.

9. EH–Gianfranco Ivancich, May 30, 1960, *SL*, p. 903; MWH–Annie Davis, May 13, 1960, private collection.

10. *NYT*, April and early May 1960.

11. EH–Rice, May 31, 1960, JFK.

12. *HIW*, p. 485.

13. Newly opened material (1998) in Hemingway Collection, JFK.

14. EH–Hotchner, June 27, 1960, JFK.

15. EH–George Saviers, June 20, 1960, *SL*, p. 904.

16. Hotchner–Bill and Annie Davis, June 29, 1960, private collection.

17. EH–CSjr. July 6, 1960, *SL*, pp. 905–6. *NYT*, July 6 and 7, 1960.

18. MWH–EH, July 13, 1960, in-house letter, JFK.

19. VDS–Bill Davis, July 7, 1960, private collection.

20. *HIW*, p. 485.

21. EH–Hotchner, Aug. 7, 1960, UVa.

22. *HIW*, p. 488.

23. Hotchner–Bill Davis, July 26, 1960, and telegram to Bill Davis undated, both in private collection. Annie Davis–MWH, telegram, Aug. 11, 1960, JFK.

24. EH–MWH, Aug. 15, 1960, JFK.

25. MWH–EH, Aug. 19, 1960, JFK; VDS–MWH, Aug. 27, 1960, JFK.

26. EH–MWH, Sept. 3, 1960, JFK. EH–MWH, Sept. 7, 1960, JFK. Similar statement to Hotchner in EH–Hotchner, Sept. 8, 1960, UVa.

27. CSjr–EH, telegram [Aug. 15, 1960], and letter, Aug. 15, 1960, JFK.

28. EH–Hotchner, Sept. 17, 1960, UVa; EH–MWH, Sept. 23, 1960, JFK.

29. *HIW*, pp. 492–3.

30. EH–Hotchner, Oct. 25, 1960, UVa.

31. EH–George Saviers, Nov. 12, 1960, private collection.

32. Seymour Betsky, "A Last Visit," *Saturday Review* (July 26, 1961), p. 22, quoted in Baker, p. 555.

33. Hotchner–Bill Davis, Nov. 19, 1960, on Christiania Motor Lodge letterhead, private collection.

34. "A Way You'll Never Be," *CSS*, p. 310.

35. Clarence Hemingway–EH, Oct. 1910, read in the Carlos Baker files at Princeton.

36. Baker, p. 556. Saviers interview on documentary film not yet made public.

37. Letter dated Dec. 4, 1960, *SL*, p. 909.

38. Dr. Howard Butt–EH, Jan. 19, 1961, in Hemingway's own medical files, JFK.

39. "Reserpine in the Treatment of Neuropsychiatric Disorders," *Annals of Internal Medicine* (Sept. 3, 1952).

40. Dr. Howard Rome–EH, Jan. 21, 1961, in Hemingway's own medical files, JFK.

41. S. Sament, "Letter," *Clinical Psychiatry News* (1983), 11.

42. L. Andre, "ECT: The Politics of Experience," given at Quality of Care Conference, Albany, New York, May 13, 1988.

43. Mary Hemingway note, Christmas Eve, 1960, JFK.

44. Note written on Kahler Hotel letterhead and dated 01:45 hrs, 1961, JFK.

45. Christmas Eve note cited above.

46. Hemingway's own medical files, JFK.

47. Scribner Book Store order sheet July 1960–Jan 1961, JFK.

48. Jerry Wald–EH, Jan. 30, 1961, JFK; EH–Hotchner, Feb. 18, 1961, UVa; Harry Brague–EH, Feb. 13, 1961, JFK.

49. EH–Brague, Feb. 6, 1961, *SL*, pp. 916–18.

50. Lee W. Samuels–EH, March 3, 1961, JFK.

51. EH–Hotchner, March 6, 1961, UVa.

52. EH–Rice, March 22 and 23, 1961, JFK.

53. Susan Beegel, scholar and editor of the *Hemingway Review*, first saw the relationship between the Bay of Pigs and Hemingway's attempts at suicide.

54. EH–CSjr, April 18, 1961, PUL. This letter was not mailed. MWH sent it to Harry Brague on July 18, 1963.

55. MWH–Ursula Hemingway Jepson, April 25, 1961, JFK.

56. Ibid.

57. Baker, pp. 560–1.

58. EH–MWH, April 28, 1961, JFK.

59. Joséph Lord–EH, May 15, 1961, JFK. Telephone notes EH kept at St. Mary's, JFK.

60. Quoted in Meyers, p. 559. Hadley Mowrer–EH, May 20, 1961, JFK.
61. Dr. Howard Rome–MWH, Nov. 1, 1961. Hemingway's own medical files, JFK.
62. MWH–Jack and Patrick Hemingway, June 2, 1961, JFK.
63. MWH–Dr. Howard Rome, June 7, 1961, JFK.
64. EH notes from phone conversation dated June 15, 1961, JFK.
65. *HIW*, pp. 500–2.

INDEX